Y0-AEV-969

Andrew Portoraro
P.O. Box 681, Stn. P
Toronto, Ont.
M5G 2Y4

# Professional Linux Deployment

Mike Banahan, Michael Boerner,
Ian Dickson, Jonathan Kelly,
Nikhilesh Kumar Mandalay,
Richard Ollerenshaw, Jonathan Pinnock,
Ganesh Prasad, Joel Rowbottom,
Geoff Sherlock and Mark Wilcox

Wrox Press Ltd. ®

# Professional Linux Deployment

© 2000 Wrox Press

All rights reserved. No part of this book may be reproduced, stored in a retrieval system or transmitted in any form or by any means, without the prior written permission of the publisher, except in the case of brief quotations embodied in critical articles or reviews.

The author and publisher have made every effort in the preparation of this book to ensure the accuracy of the information. However, the information contained in this book is sold without warranty, either express or implied. Neither the authors, Wrox Press nor its dealers or distributors will be held liable for any damages caused or alleged to be caused either directly or indirectly by this book.

wrox

Published by Wrox Press Ltd. Arden House, 1102 Warwick Rd, Acocks Green, Birmingham, B27 6BH
Printed in Canada
ISBN 1-861002-8-74

# Trademark Acknowledgements

Wrox has endeavored to provide trademark information about all the companies and products mentioned in this book by the appropriate use of capitals. However, Wrox cannot guarantee the accuracy of this information.

Linux is a trademark of Linus Torvalds.

# Credits

**Authors**
Mike Banahan
Michael Boerner
Ian Dickson
Jonathan Kelly
Nikhilesh K. Mandalay
Richard Ollerenshaw
Jonathan Pinnock
Ganesh Prasad
Joel Rowbottom
Geoff Sherlock
Mark Wilcox

**Additional Material**
Neil Matthew
Rick Stones
Gavin Smyth

**Managing Editor**
James Hart

**Editors**
Jon Hill
Andrew Polshaw
Adrian Young

**Development Editor**
Richard Collins

**Technical Reviewers**
Robert Baskerville
Mike Boerner
Mark Grieshaber
Chris Harshman
Jerry Heyman
Dave Hudson
Jonathan Kelly
Giles Lean
Marty Lesner
Neil Matthew
Bill Moss
Gavin Smyth
Rick Stones
Bruce Varney
Chris Whitworth
James Youngman

**Design/Layout**
Mark Burdett
William Fallon
Jonathan Jones
John McNulty

**Cover**
Chris Morris

**Index**
Martin Brooks
Andrew Criddle

Thanks to Larry Ewing (lewing@isc.tamu.edu) and the GIMP for the chapter divider.

# About the Authors

### Mike Banahan

Mike Banahan is Managing Director of GBDirect Ltd, specialists in e-commerce consultancy and the UK's leading providers of Linux training. He has been a significant figure in the UNIX world since 1978; co-authoring *The UNIX Book*, writing technical standards that defined the platform, and building the UK's largest UNIX consultancy – The Instruction Set.

### Michael Boerner

Michael is a consultant working out of the St. Louis area. He has 18 years experience as a IT professional with stints in several national laboratories, government and private institutions, as well as in commercial companies. His formal education is in Physics with a significant amount of experience in scientific and business software development. His present passion is Linux, and in particular, Beowulf. He can be contacted via email at michael@boernerconsulting.com or through his company web site at www.BoernerConsulting.com.

*I would like to thank my family and friends who supported and assisted me during this project. I would like to thank Mark Grieshaber for his assistance and extensive experience in the distributed computing world. I would also like to give special thanks to:*

AOpen America Inc. (www.aopenusa.com), who provided the Intel Celeron PPGA systems and outstanding support.

Advanced Micro Devices (AMD) (www.amd.com), who provided their K6-2 400 with 3dNow.

Seagate Inc. (www.seagate.com), who provided a batch of hard drives that made my project substantially cheaper and more successful than would otherwise have been.

*Finally, I would like to thank my wife, Dr. Lisa Weaver, whose consistent support and encouragement enabled me to complete all the work.*

### Ian Dickson

Ian Dickson has set up and maintained networks running Novell NetWare, Windows NT, MacOS, SCO, Solaris, HP-UX, FreeBSD and Linux – in bad times, like his present job, all at once!

### Jonathan Kelly

Jonathan Kelly is a Systems Analyst for Julien Inc., a stainless steel products manufacturer in Quebec City. He has a BS in Computer Science from Université Laval. A Linux user since 1994, his job permits him to apply Open-Source solutions to his employer's problems. It has been known for him not to spend all of his waking hours in front of computers – among other things, he enjoys reading, and trains to add degrees to his Tae Kwon Do black belt.

## Nikhilesh Kumar Mandalay

Nikhilesh Kumar Mandalay is a freelance programmer working in Bangalore, India, though he lived in Myanmar (Burma) for much of his earlier life. He enjoys programming with Linux, though he mostly earns his living as a database administrator.

## Richard Ollerenshaw

Richard Ollerenshaw is a student of electronic engineering at York University, England. He consults on Internet strategy for small businesses and business start-ups in a wide range of traditional industries. In addition he maintains several large websites as well as sitting on the web support team of a major voluntary body.

In his spare time he performs and coaches trampolining. Other interests include sport simulation using Java and C.

## Jonathan Pinnock

Jonathan Pinnock started programming in Pal III assembler on his school's PDP 8/e, with a massive 4K of memory, back in the days before Moore's Law reached the statute books. After turning his back on computers for three years in order to study Mathematics at Cambridge University, he was forced back into programming in order to make a living, something that he still does from time to time. These days, he works as an independent developer and consultant, mainly in the City of London. He is the author of *Professional DCOM Application Development*, but hopes that this will not be held against him.

Jonathan lives in Hertfordshire, England, with his wife, two children and 1961 Ami Continental jukebox. His moderately interesting web site is located at www.jpassoc.co.uk, and he can be contacted on jon@jpassoc.co.uk.

## Ganesh Prasad

After a varied career first as a civil engineer, and then in marketing and finance, Ganesh Prasad took up IT, and over the last 13 years has not looked back, working first in India, then Dubai and now in Australia. He now works in the Internet Development Services group of a large multinational systems integration company. His professional experience has always been in commercial applications software development, and among his achievements, was on the team that developed the first Java-based Internet Home Banking product in the Middle East (NBD's "HomeBank"). He was also involved in the development of the first Java-based Corporate Banking product in Australia (the Commonwealth Bank's "ecommCorporate").

He is a fervent enthusiast of the Linux OS and Open Source software, believing that we will all enjoy high-quality, efficient, friendly, trustworthy and inexpensive software in the years to come. However, he has two wishes for the future; first, for Java to join the ranks of truly free software, and second, for there to be a truly free database system that matches Oracle. If, in the next few years, his two wishes come true, then, as he puts it, he will be in software Utopia.

## Joel Rowbottom

Joel Rowbottom is well-known among the UK ISP system administration community, holding Cisco, Microsoft and Novell professional qualifications along with a degree, and participating in several major contract projects in both a technical and management role. He is currently Managing Director of Mailbox Internet Ltd.

## Geoff Sherlock

Geoff Sherlock has worked for some years in Systems Support, Administration and Applications Development for a specialist Natinal Health Service Trust Unit in Liverpool, England and has recently taken a post for Applications Development Engineer in the telecommunications industry in Hertfordshire, England.

## Mark Wilcox

Mark is the Web Administrator for the University of North Texas. He's also the author of *Implementing LDAP*, also published by Wrox Press, and is a regular columnist for Netscape's *ViewSource* magazine.

*To my wife Jessica and to Dr. Kevin McKinney and Dr. Mitchel Kruger who made sure I was around to finish my chapter.*

# Table of Contents

## Chapter 6: Building a Data-Driven Web Site: E-commerce with Linux     137

# Chapter 7: Using Database Applications with Linux   163

## Chapter 8: Using Directory Services and LDAP        201

# Chapter 9: Linux as an Internet Gateway     233

# Chapter 10: Configuring Linux as a Firewall and Proxy    273

# Chapter 11: Cryptography and the Linux Connection 299

# Chapter 13: Implementing Distributed Systems    403

## Chapter 14: EntireX — DCOM on Linux     **443**

# Chapter 15: Case Study: Migrating to Linux              473

# Appendix A: Linux 101                                    491

# Introduction

Over the past few years we have seen the Linux operating system grow from a hobbyist's toy to a secure, stable, and feature rich multi-user alternative to commercial systems for PC networks. With the explosion of the Internet, network managers familiar with the UNIX operating system have been using Linux to power their mail servers, web servers, Domain Name Servers, gateways, and routers. Until recently these deployments only really occurred in academic institutions. However with major software companies porting their databases and other applications, and the growing dissatisfaction with the cost of purchasing and maintaining NT or commercial UNIX systems, Linux has been adopted in many enterprises. This book will teach the professional systems administrator what steps need to be taken to replace their existing network systems with Linux and so have a platform in place that is not only cheaper and more stable than the alternatives, but is a great development environment for programmers.

## What Does this Book Cover?

This book starts with a description of and argument for Linux. It will list many of the arguments for and against Linux and discuss how accurate they are, and will contain numerous web references to get more information. It should enable you to construct a detailed argument for or against adopting Linux within your company's enterprise. If you decide to adopt Linux, we then progress by teaching how you can replace your NT file and print servers using the popular Samba package, without your Windows client machines ever noticing the difference, except with a possible increase in performance.

After a discussion of free software, we then move on to setting up a web server using the extremely popular Apache, which currently makes up over half of the world's web servers. It will show you how to get and install Apache, as well as provide some basic tips on configuration. In the same chapter we will also show you how to set up an FTP server. This chapter is followed by a case study that explains how to set up an e-commerce site on Linux using Apache.

In chapter seven, you will learn how to install and configure two database packages – the free, but very fast and stable, MySQL, and the free and more advanced object relational database PostgreSQL. Advice is also given on installing Oracle. Following this we show how to install and set up an LDAP server, which, as you may know, can provide address book or name server facilities to your enterprise.

The next two chapters give details on how to replace or upgrade your network and Internet workhorses with Linux servers. It instructs on setting up routers, gateways, mail servers, DNS servers, and also proxies and firewalls to help keep your intranets secure, whether your connection to the Internet is via a leased line or a dial-up connection. In chapter 11, you can learn how to legally set up 128 bit encryption for your virtual private networks and web servers – whether replacing an existing system or creating a new one. You also learn how to use the GnuPG package to implement mail or file encryption.

The next two chapters introduce to you clustering which has enabled IBM to create a system comparable with a Cray supercomputer for 3% of the cost. You will learn what to consider before deciding whether or not to set one up, such as the hardware that should be employed. You will learn how to set up such a cluster and use it to power your Apache web server and Sybase database using PCs, but gaining performance normally far beyond that capable of such hardware. We then discuss how it is possible to use DCOM on Linux. This enables you to access and enhance existing applications on your NT servers so that you can get the most potential from your existing network. We end with a case study, which details a large system changeover from an HP-UX based system, to PCs running Linux. This chapter should help your developers when they are porting existing applications over to Linux.

In the appendices, there are three tutorials that we included in case you have never seen a UNIX command line before. They should give you enough information to get started and become a systems administrator for a Linux server.

# Why Is This Book Different

There are countless books available that tell you how to use a specific package or how to install and use Linux, this book is geared towards a specific purpose, that of using Linux for your intranet and Internet servers, thereby replacing your equivalent NT servers. It does have instruction on using Linux, but that isn't the main focus.

This book assumes that you are already a successful IT manager and instructs you enough on how to install and implement the relevant packages. This book will sit at the root of a tree of Linux programming knowledge, and we hope we can convince you to use Linux by showing you how to use it for your usual intranet and Internet tasks, while tantalizing you with more information. If you want more details then you can read the relevant online documentation or purchase the required book, which we will point you towards. This should be the first book you turn to if you are thinking of deploying Linux across your enterprise.

For those of you impatient for more information, you can turn to one of our other books.

# Who is this Book For?

This book is for network managers. It should allow you to install the underlying structure of a Linux network, integrating with whatever Windows systems that you wish to keep. Our other books go into great detail about the programming of both platforms, and developers can still refer to these as necessary.

# Required Knowledge

In this book, it is assumed that you are experienced in network administration. This book is geared towards changing from NT to Linux so it is assumed that you have experience in NT administration. It is assumed that you know about networking, the language and tools needed to set up NT shares, and general system administration duties, such as those to do with security. Where knowledge of certain protocols, e.g. TCP/IP, is required, we have gone into more detail in the relevant chapters.

# Conventions

We have used a number of different styles of text and layout in the book to help differentiate between the different kinds of information. Here are examples of the styles we use and an explanation of what they mean:

> *Advice, hints, and background information comes indented and italicized, like this.*

---
**Important information comes in boxes like this.**

---

Bullets are also indented, and appear with a little box marking each new bullet point, like this:

❑ **Important Words** are in a bold type font

❑ Words that appear on the screen in menus like File are in a similar font to the one that you see on screen

❑ URLs will be printed as so: http://www.wrox.com/; whereas e-mail addresses will shown as support@wrox.com.

❑ Code and details of configuration options have several fonts. If it's a word that we're talking about in the text, for example when discussing the ipchains command, it is printed as so. If it's a block of code or a command line that you can type in as a program and run, or part of a configuration file, then it's in a gray box:

```
[global]
netbios name = office
workgroup = MY_WORKGROUP
server string = Linux file/print Server
```

❑ Sometimes you'll see code in a mixture of styles, like this:

```
[global]
netbios name = office
workgroup = MY_WORKGROUP
server string = Linux file/print Server
hosts allow = 10.0.0.
security = user
encrypt passwords = yes
guest account = nobody
```

The code with a white background is code we've already looked at and that we don't wish to examine further. Output from a command, or command line commands will look like the code with the white background above; the command you type to get the output is displayed in a bold font. Note that we use $ as the *prompt* when you enter the command as an ordinary user, and # when you need to enter it as the root user.

```
$ cat /usr/local/samba/lib/my_users.map
# This is my Samba user name map
marc = marc Admin
jonathan = jonathan
bernard = bernard
mireille = mireille
mariejo = marie1d Mary dba
```

These formats are designed to make sure that you know what it is you're looking at. We hope they make life easier.

# Tell Us What You Think

We've worked hard on this book to make it useful. We've tried to understand what you're willing to exchange your hard-earned money for, and we've tried to make the book live up to your expectations.

Please let us know what you think about this book. Tell us what we did wrong, and what we did right. We'll answer, and we'll take whatever you say on board for future editions. The easiest way is to use e-mail:

feedback@wrox.com

You can also find more details about Wrox Press on our web site. There, you'll find the code from our latest books, sneak previews of forthcoming titles, and information about the authors and editors. You can order Wrox titles directly from the site, or find out where your nearest local bookstore with Wrox titles is located.

## Customer Support

If you find a mistake, please have a look at the errata page for this book on our web site first. If you can't find an answer there, tell us about the problem and we'll do everything we can to answer promptly! Appendix D outlines how you can submit errata in much greater detail. Just send us an email:

support@wrox.com

# 1

# Linux in the Enterprise

*This chapter is based upon the a web article* – The Practical Manager's Guide to Linux – *that can be found at* http://www.osopinion.com.

In 1998, the Mexican government embarked on an ambitious project to equip 140,000 schools with computers. They found the license costs of Microsoft Windows so high, even with volume discounts, that they opted to use Linux instead, saving an estimated $124 million.

When Digital Domain rendered the visual effects for the movie *Titanic*, they needed a large server farm to handle the processing load. Ultimately, they settled on 105 servers based on the Compaq/Digital Alpha chip, running Linux.

Linux is the world's fastest-growing operating system. A report from the International Data Corporation stated that during 1998, it grew at a rate of 212%. Another report estimated that Linux would grow faster than all other operating systems *combined* between 1998 and 2003. In 1999, another IDC survey found that Linux was already in use in 17% of large corporations. It has real advantages in its low price, stability, growing set of applications, and total vendor and architecture neutrality. Sooner or later, your customers, your boss, your development team will ask you to evaluate Linux; it has become too important to ignore. In this chapter, you will read how good a network operating system Linux can be, and why it would be worth investing some time to investigate it.

# The History of Linux

From a purely technical standpoint, Linux is just another variant of UNIX: it is POSIX and X/Open compliant. What makes it unique is something other than its technology. To really understand the reasons for its amazing popularity, it's worth delving into just a little bit of history. In the following section we'll examine where the motivation for Linux came from, how it got to where it is today, and a little of what I think the future may hold.

# The GNU Project and the Free Software Foundation

In 1984, Richard Stallman, a researcher at MIT's Artificial Intelligence labs, started the **GNU project** as a reaction to the (then) relatively new practice of keeping source code secret and enforcing software licensing. He saw the withdrawal of source code as a curtailment of programmers' freedom to modify and improve software. He also saw the license restrictions on copying as being at odds with his philosophy of being a good neighbor and sharing ideas.

Stallman set out to do nothing less than rewrite all the software then commonly in use – single-handed if need be – and make it free for everyone to use, modify and redistribute. His goal was to recreate a complete operating environment that was free of such restrictions, with all the tools and utilities that a computer user would ever need. At the time, UNIX was the most modern operating environment, and so he chose to model his system after it. But because he was against the restrictive licensing of UNIX by AT&T, he called his project by a recursive acronym: **GNU**, for *G*NU's *N*ot *U*NIX.

> *Richard Stallman proved to be a formidable programmer. He single-handedly wrote free versions of many popular UNIX utilities. Among his lasting software contributions are the GNU C compiler* gcc*, and the* emacs *text editor.*

The GNU project is now in the hands of the **Free Software Foundation** (**FSF**), which was established to raise funds to produce free software. However, as Stallman is fond of saying, "*When you say 'Free', think free speech, not free beer.*" The FSF is not against software being sold for money, as long as the source code is available and other programmers have full rights to modify and redistribute the software. You can find the GNU project's homepage on the Web at http://www.gnu.org.

## *The Importance of the GNU General Public License*

Richard Stallman wrote some amazing software, but the contribution for which he will probably be remembered is not a piece of software but a legal document. He quickly realized that even if he wrote great software and gave it away, someone else could come along, make a few changes to the code, and then copyright the whole lot by claiming it to be a different product. Thus, the aim of sharing would be defeated and he would be foolishly giving away something that others could simply exploit.

He came to the conclusion that he had to design a special license to ensure that the software he wrote *remained* public, and that all modifications and improvements, no matter who made them, were made available to everyone. Ironically, as the legal system has no mechanism to protect publicly owned intellectual work, Stallman had to rely on copyright law itself to design a license that was opposed to it in spirit! The way it works is very interesting, demonstrating that even Law can be a malleable medium to a creative mind.

Under the terms of the license, software is first copyrighted, thereby preventing someone else from seizing control of it at a later date. Rights are then granted to the public to use, copy, modify and distribute it, subject to certain carefully defined conditions. The conditions are that anyone modifying the code for later redistribution has to make their source code public on the same terms. No proprietary modifications are allowed, except for private use. The license is known as the **GNU General Public License** or **GPL**. It's also called **copyleft**, because in a sense it is the opposite of copyright. It grants freedom instead of restricting it. The GPL is a painstakingly drafted legal document that runs to more than eight printed pages, and its preamble starts like this:

```
The licenses for most software are designed to take away your freedom to share
and change it. By contrast, the GNU General Public License is intended to
guarantee your freedom to share and change free software - to make sure the
software is free for all its users.
```

Ideology aside, the GPL is a very *pro-user* license, unlike commercial licenses that are biased towards the vendor.

## Free or Open-source?

The GPL is all about free software, but as soon as you start researching the subject, you'll come across open-source software as well, in contexts that imply the two terms are interchangeable. In fact, the latter term was coined more recently, and implies a different philosophy: the open-source movement seeks to disassociate itself from what it sees as the ideological baggage in the GPL, while the GNU Project objects to parts of the Open Source Definition on the grounds that software released under it is less than free.

In this book, we will use the terms interchangeably, as the difference between the two will not affect the arguments we make. The GNU project's web site sums up the situation like this: "...*the Free Software movement and the Open Source movement...disagree on the basic principles, but agree on most practical recommendations. We work together on many specific projects.*" If you wish, you can read the contents of the web sites given below, and decide on which side your allegiance lies.

## Degrees of Freedom

Many people think that free software, public domain software, and shareware are the same thing; but this is not so. Shareware is commercial software. Authors of shareware programs expect to be paid, just like authors of any commercial software, but they are willing to allow free distribution of their software in order to popularize it. Upgrades and bug fixes are available to those who pay for the copies they receive; the source code is typically not available. Shareware is more a marketing technique than a form of software freedom.

Public domain software, while free, is not under copyright at all; which means that someone making modifications to it can claim copyright on the modified version and take it out of circulation. GPL-ed software, on the other hand, is copyrighted by the original author and licensed to the public, albeit under very generous terms. It ensures that the software remains perpetually free – in fact, it's *G*uaranteed *P*ublic for *L*ife.

*There are other free licenses as well, such as the BSD and X11 licenses that have been dubbed 'copy-neutral' because they enforce no restrictions at all on copying and redistribution – not even the GPL's condition that changes should be made available to the public.*

*Troll Tech, which developed the Qt GUI library on which the Linux KDE desktop is based, received strong criticism from the open source community for releasing its library under a license that was not seen as truly 'free'. After much persuasion by developers, Troll Tech revised the license to conform to open source principles. Sun's Community Source License also attempts to tap into the open source developer pool, but its terms are viewed as too restrictive and response has been poor.*

The GPL and other free software licenses may seem very quaint concepts in the commercial world of copyrights, patents, and non-disclosure agreements. However, increasing numbers of high-quality software products are given away every year under such licenses, and increasing numbers of computer users are using them: they form a credible threat to established vendors of commercial software. Even if you don't agree with the philosophy, you need to understand how they work.

### References

The GNU GPL:
http://www.gnu.org/copyleft/gpl.txt

Open Source Definition:
http://www.opensource.org/osd.html

The BSD License:
http://www.dislessici.org/opensource/bsd-license.html

The Artistic License:
http://www.weblint.org/artistic.html

# The Last Piece in the Puzzle

Richard Stallman wrote an amazing amount of software, but despite all his efforts, he did not succeed in creating a complete, working system. The core (or **kernel**) of the system did not yet exist, though almost everything else was done. All that software is now famous as 'the GNU utilities', and there's even a Windows version that's distributed with Microsoft's NT Resource Kit. (Bound by the terms of the GPL, Microsoft includes the source code as well.)

In 1991, a Finnish computer science student named Linus Torvalds wrote the first version of a UNIX-like kernel for his own use, and posted the code on the Internet with a request to other programmers to help him build it up into a working system. The response was overwhelming, and what began as a student's pet project rapidly developed into a serious operating system kernel. Looking around, Torvalds found that virtually everything else he needed was already there in the form of the GNU utilities and other free software. He put them all together and named the complete operating system after himself: Linux, for *Linus*' UNI*X*. And in perhaps the most momentous decision of all, Torvalds released the source code for the Linux kernel under the GNU General Public License.

*The entire system is also sometimes called GNU/Linux, to reflect the large proportion of GNU software bundled with the Linux kernel.*

Today, the entire GNU/Linux system (hereafter referred to as 'Linux' for simplicity), kernel and utilities are freely available with source code for anyone to use, modify, and redistribute. Judging from the frenetic activity on the developer web sites, thousands of qualified programmers from around the world are accepting the GPL's invitation to modify and improve the system in all the ways they think fit.

# UNIX is Back

With apologies to Mark Twain, reports of UNIX's demise have been greatly exaggerated. Yes, many of us remember how UNIX, the great cross-platform hope of the last decade, betrayed our faith and fragmented into a zillion not-so-compatible versions. UNIX has always been a great network operating system, possibly the greatest in terms of features and security, but the truth is that most people's experience of computing begins and ends with Windows. Microsoft's ubiquitous OS has dominated the desktop market, and its NT product has been taking over the low-end server market too.

The creation and subsequent development of Linux, however, have given UNIX a new lease of life. As you'll soon see, Linux is an extremely competent, secure, stable server operating system – but it's a very unusual animal. All of the software that comprises Linux is free to download and use, with no restrictions. You can buy it from commercial vendors, but when you do so you're paying for the distribution, the manuals, the media, the packaging and the support – not the software.

For all those connected with IT in the enterprise, the advent of Linux is a crisis in the Chinese sense: it represents both danger and opportunity. Budget managers have a responsibility to spend their organization's money wisely, and to avoid vendor lock-in where possible. Provided that adequate arrangements are made for support and maintenance, Linux could prove a very cost-effective platform for many organizations, a fact that will not long escape the notice of senior management with an eye on the bottom line.

If you have some control over your company's purse strings, you should prepare early for the day when you're asked to evaluate and report on the feasibility of using Linux. You must have sufficient knowledge of Linux to argue convincingly either way: how much of the enthusiasm has foundation and how much of the criticism holds water. There are real costs associated with learning a new environment and new skills, and Linux does require more knowledge of your computer systems and network than Windows. Before you make a large-scale commitment to that investment, you need to know that it will be worthwhile.

# What Does Linux Hold For Me?

In this chapter, we will attempt to argue that the return of UNIX in the form of Linux is a good thing for all computer users. The severe downward price pressure it exerts on every competitor is an absolute delight. A credible alternative to existing operating systems also means greater choice and a buyer's market, which makes arm-twisting by vendors less feasible. And as a consolation for the technically aspiring, the initial pain of a rigorous UNIX boot camp will soon pay off in the form of a far deeper knowledge of computers and of computer science.

Linux also provides a unique career opportunity for dynamic managers who are willing to take considered risks to pull ahead of the pack in the eyes of senior management. If you manage to realize Linux's promise of high-performance computing with high uptime and radically reduced cost of ownership, then you can deliver impressive value to your organization.

If you're responsible for staffing, watch out for a skills shortage. Even with a GUI, Linux is quite different from Windows, and the people in the trenches who need to work with it will need to be trained on a different set of skills. UNIX has re-emerged thanks to Linux and the Internet, and UNIX skills are once again at a premium. Budget for UNIX-related training, and look for UNIX skills when hiring. It's not a one-horse race anymore.

# An Analysis of Linux

It may be that you have no plans to use Linux for serious work in your business. It may even be that you never do use it for this purpose, but you can count on it being around for at least the next few years, and you should certainly consider familiarizing yourself with what it can do – call it insurance, if you like. In this section, we'll examine the most commonly cited strengths and weaknesses of Linux, to see where it stands today.

## The Arguments for Linux

You have probably already heard the most commonly cited strengths of Linux – an eye cast over the popular computing press reveals comment and debate from all points of view. Let us examine ten of these issues more carefully, and try to separate hyperbole from reality. In no particular order, the things we'll look at are:

1. Zero price point
2. Do-it-yourself flexibility
3. Freedom from licensing headaches
4. Stability
5. Performance
6. Standards compliance
7. Diverse hardware support
8. Interoperability with existing systems
9. Virus-proof design
10. Strong cryptography worldwide

### *Zero Price Point*

Linux is often touted as being free, though in practice no organization will install software without a support agreement in place. Given that support for Linux by reputed vendors is mushrooming, it is very likely that Linux will be used by many organizations with this kind of third-party support arrangement. So hype notwithstanding, Linux will never be a zero-cost solution. However, when an organization looks at *licensing* costs, especially over multiple users and multiple computers, it may find that Linux *does* deliver a significant cost advantage after all.

Computer Currents magazine estimated that a fully configured Windows NT server with a web server, e-mail, development tools and database would cost more than $4500 to set up. Hardware costs being the same, an equivalent Linux setup would cost only $50 for a Red Hat CD with all this software bundled. What's more, the Windows license fees need to be multiplied by the number of such installations, whereas the Linux solution incurs only a one-time cost, as the software can be freely installed on an unlimited number of machines.

> *The cost of Red Hat CD packages has changed since that survey, but the price difference is still large. At the time of writing, their most expensive package cost $150 and contained extensive support options; their cheapest (which still contains all software packages) cost $40.*

In early 1999, Hewlett-Packard began to offer unlimited, 24x7 worldwide telephone and e-mail support for Linux, with a guaranteed response time of less than two hours, for a fee of $130 per month per server. The support agreement even covers Linux systems from other vendors. Taking this as a ballpark figure for the cost of support from other third-party vendors as well, the argument in favor of Linux appears to be justified, and of the order of $3000 per server in the year of purchase (assuming zero support costs for Windows NT). Microsoft and its partners also offer a variety of support options with different pricing terms, so the Linux cost advantage should be even greater if NT support costs are factored in.

Another, less obvious, cost advantage of Linux is its ability to run on older machines with less memory and disk capacity, which translates into savings on hardware. Each subsequent release of Windows, on the other hand, seems to require upgrades to hardware as well. Faster chips constantly appear, but are saddled with increasingly bulky software, neutralizing their speed advances. Microsoft says the *minimum* hardware requirement for Windows 2000 is a Pentium 166 with 32MB of RAM; for a "Windows 2000 ready PC", both of those specifications are doubled.

Given that the benefits of Windows 2000 are best obtained when it runs on both servers and workstations, an organization may find that committing to Windows 2000 entails costly hardware upgrades across the board, and would be wise to work out the costs in advance. IT managers should conduct a serious comparative analysis of Linux and Windows 2000 at the time of the latter's release, taking into account features, license fees, support charges *and* hardware upgrade requirements. Linux can still run on a 386 with 4MB of RAM, and the more power you give your PC, the better Linux performs.

In the past, it has been pointed out that, *Linux is free only if your time is worthless*, a valid reference to the difficulty for a relative novice of finding and editing various the configuration files that are necessary in order to administrate Linux. However, new administration and configuration tools such as Red Hat's `linuxconf`, SuSE's `YaST` and Caldera's `lizard` provide centralized, graphical administration, largely eliminating the need to edit configuration files by hand. As such tools improve, the effort and steep learning curve associated with effective Linux system administration should reduce to acceptable levels.

### References

The Computer Currents article:
http://www.currents.net/magazine/national/1524/inet1524.html

Hewlett-Packard's 24x7 worldwide support package for Linux:
http://www.news.com/News/Item/0,4,35392,00.html

The Mexican school computerization project (Scholar Net):
http://www.wired.com/news/news/technology/story/16107.html

Linux and the Titanic:
http://www.linuxjournal.com/issue46/2494.html

## Do-it-yourself Flexibility

One of the advantages of Linux that's voiced most frequently is that users can easily modify the software to suit their requirements, and in fact there are two aspects to this. First, unlike most commercial software (which is distributed only in binary form), the Linux source code is readily available, making it *physically* possible to modify and recompile it. Second, the GNU General Public License expressly permits anyone to modify and redistribute the software, making this *legally* possible as well.

So, should you make changes to Linux code, just because you can? Unless your needs are very specialized and you know exactly what you're doing, don't do it. Apart from anything else, you risk making your version incompatible with future Linux upgrades. The availability of Linux source code is important in the same way that the availability of spare parts for your car is important. It doesn't usually mean that you intend to fix or replace parts yourself, but it should give you greater confidence that when it needs to be done, it can be done relatively easily.

To give an example of such a case, a 1998 report provided evidence that Microsoft had decided against developing an Icelandic version of Windows 95 because the limited size of the Icelandic market couldn't justify the cost. When approached by volunteers from Iceland who offered to perform the task, Microsoft refused on the grounds that the Windows source code was secret. There is no similar problem with Linux, because there are no cost considerations and no permission is required in order to modify the software. It will come as no surprise, then, that an Icelandic version of Linux's K desktop environment *does* exist.

### References

Microsoft vs. Iceland:
http://kyle.seattletimes.com/news/technology/html98/alticel_063098.html

## *Freedom From Licensing Headaches*

Using commercially licensed software carries with it the responsibility of ensuring that you comply with the license at all times. Exceeding the licensed number of installations, even inadvertently, is a crime. In many countries, the CEO of a company that's found to be in breach of software license contracts is personally accountable and, in theory, can even go to jail for it. This means that organizations must keep track of the number of purchased licenses and the actual number of installations of every piece of software that they use – a significant administrative overhead. Organizations that purchase large numbers of licenses of many different software products find that they need the help of special license management software, a product that seems like a solution to an artificial problem.

Sometimes, production systems fail to scale under unexpectedly heavy loads because a piece of software enforces limits on the number of concurrent connections or transactions, based on the number of purchased licenses. Some products do permit utilization slightly above the licensed limits, but it is nevertheless irritating when services are affected for reasons that are not technical but legal/commercial, and which could easily be resolved without the need for such drastic enforcement.

Linux and other free software products do away with such considerations. You can install the software on any number of machines without breaking the law. In effect, Linux gives you an unlimited user, unlimited installation license – an indisputable plus for those who are currently held accountable for even inadvertent license violations. Scalability is restricted only by the technical limitations of a system.

> **Note that commercial products running on top of Linux may still be subject to license restrictions.**

Linux's free license also means that you don't need to worry about *changes* in vendors' licensing terms. The elimination of Microsoft's concurrent licensing for Office and BackOffice was an unpleasant surprise for many organizations that saw their licensing costs go up sharply. Linux and other free software could be an enormous boon to managers who are exposed to such volatile license regimes.

### References

The Business Software Alliance on penalties for licensing violations:
http://www.bsa.org/uk/penalties

Fines paid by companies that breached software license agreements:
http://www.elronsw.com/metering.html

Microsoft eliminates concurrent licensing:
http://www.infoworld.com/cgi-bin/displayArchive.pl?/97/45/t07-45.6.htm

Forbes reports on Microsoft's license fee hikes:
http://www.forbes.com/forbes/98/0907/6205050a.htm

## Stability

As even IBM says on its web site, Linux is stable, functional and offers value. However, it is sometimes remarked that the reason *why* Linux rarely crashes is that it isn't required to do as much as other operating systems. If Linux is loaded to comparative levels, the argument goes, it will crash as often. However, there is a vast amount of evidence that Linux-based servers, even heavily loaded ones, rarely go down. An indirect indication of Linux's stability is the curious fact that organizations that provide support for Linux generally don't offer per-incident support schemes – they aren't profitable!

Ultimately, stability is more important than price, because in production environments, the costs of downtime can easily wipe out purely monetary savings. Indeed, many users claim that to them, stability is the single most attractive feature of Linux. In the end, stability is largely an architectural issue, because bugs in implementation can (in theory) be squeezed out over time. To accept Linux as a truly stable operating system, we need to look beneath the hood and satisfy ourselves that its architecture is sound and its implementation is largely bug-free. The following analysis is therefore necessarily more technical than the rest of this chapter. We will use the familiar Windows architecture as a basis for comparison, wherever relevant.

The impression that operating systems become less stable as more applications run on them probably owes its origin to pre-2000 versions of Windows, where installed applications overwrite system DLLs (dynamic-link libraries) with impunity. Such errant applications also fail to uninstall cleanly, and often leave behind mutually inconsistent versions of crucial system libraries. Thus, a Windows machine that has had many applications installed and uninstalled over time gradually becomes less stable due to the large number of incompatible system DLLs, and the only solution is a complete reinstallation of the OS itself.

When the Windows registry first appeared, it must have seemed a good idea, because it offered a flexible and standard way for all configuration information to be stored in a single location. However, it became a much-abused repository that lost its initial clean and compact structure. Moreover, since it is shared by the operating system and user applications, an application that corrupts the registry can render the entire system unusable. The registry is a *single point of failure* with no protection from poorly written user applications – a matter of grave concern in an operating system that is increasingly being used for mission-critical tasks.

> It must be noted that NT has improved on the design by having a different registry for each user; however each registry can still get bloated and corrupted, and installation of software can be more awkward than it needs to be.

By contrast, the UNIX/Linux approach has always strictly separated system objects from user objects. The directory structures and file permissions of a UNIX system are expressly designed to protect the operating system from the actions of ordinary users and their applications. UNIX was designed for multiple users right from the start, and it has mechanisms to protect users from each other.

In the standard UNIX tradition, Linux stores files as shown in the table below. Even if the directory names are unfamiliar, the consistency and logic in this structure should be readily apparent:

| Type of application | Shared libraries (DLL equivalents) are stored in | Binaries (executable files) are stored in |
| --- | --- | --- |
| Programs required at boot-up time | /lib | /bin |
| Applications bundled with the OS but not required at boot-up time (compilers, editors, etc.) | /usr/lib | /usr/bin |
| General applications installed by users and not bundled with the OS | /usr/local/lib or /usr/local/app/lib | /usr/local/bin or /usr/local/app/bin |
| Superuser programs required at boot-up time | /lib | /sbin |
| Superuser programs not required at boot-up time | /usr/lib | /usr/sbin |

The programs in /sbin and /usr/sbin are commands that are normally only run by the system administrator, and the permissions of some of these commands are set so that only the superuser can run them. The PATH environment variable ties together all the bin directories, and each application knows which dynamic libraries it needs (with the help of a program called ldconfig), so any required file can be found at runtime. User applications can therefore run without interfering with the operating system itself.

> *For more information about the layout of the Linux file system and typical locations of the files stored within it, take a look at Appendix A, Linux 101.*

With Windows 2000, Microsoft has approached the problem of stability by making the operating system protect itself: there is a core set of about 300 DLLs that are prevented from being overwritten by applications. Even so, UNIX's from-the-ground-up separation of system and user applications is more elegant and easier to enforce. As stated in Appendix A, there are differences between UNIX versions (and even between Linux distributions) with regard to the exact directories that are used to store system and user applications, but the philosophy and general framework are the same.

### Installing, Upgrading and Uninstalling

The install/upgrade/uninstall procedure, with its potential library version problems, is also handled cleanly in the Linux environment. If a piece of software (say, Acme 3.2) is to be installed, the shared library files are copied to /usr/local/acme_3.2/lib, and the executables to /usr/local/acme_3.2/bin. System and other application directories are untouched by the installation, and the system's stability is therefore unaffected. In addition, it's possible to create a symbolic link called /usr/local/acme that acts as a shortcut to /usr/local/acme_3.2. The PATH environment variable and ldconfig then use the symbolic link and refer to /usr/local/acme/bin and /usr/local/acme/lib respectively, rather then the actual directory names. Such a setup can run Acme 3.2, with the ability to upgrade 'tentatively'.

If the organization later upgrades to Acme 3.3, the files for the new version can be copied into new directories `/usr/local/acme_3.3/lib` and `/usr/local/acme_3.3/bin`, and the symbolic link `/usr/local/acme` is merely modified to point to `/usr/local/acme_3.3` instead. The PATH environment variable remains unchanged, but the symbolic link now points to the new version, enabling it to be used without a reboot or even a re-login. Most importantly, the older libraries, which could potentially cause version incompatibility problems, *no longer appear in the path*. Their presence in the system cannot affect the application. If there are any problems with the new version, the organization can roll back just by switching over the symbolic link. Later, once the new version has been pronounced stable, the system administrator can delete the old version.

Uninstalling an application just involves deleting its directories and the symbolic link, which again does not affect the libraries of other applications or system libraries. Special utilities like the Red Hat Package Manager `rpm` and its graphical derivative `glint` make all these operations transparent to the user – although you should be aware that because they're oriented towards end users, they allow only a one-step upgrade, not a tentative upgrade option. The `rpm` command takes care of package dependencies and version requirements as well.

Linux symbolizes both continuity and change. It has a modern user interface and comes with many innovative applications, but its fundamental UNIX-based design is time-tested. Linux, it must be remembered, has the advantage of a *quarter century* of UNIX experience to draw on, and the right lessons appear to have been learned.

### References

IBM's endorsement of Linux's quality and stability:
http://www.software.ibm.com/data/db2/linux

Windows NT's "blue screen of death" – reasons:
http://www.webshopper.com/jhtml/templates/display_content.jhtml?id=129634

Also, *NC World* magazine at http://www.ncworldmag.com keeps an archive of excellent articles that analyze the fundamental design differences between Windows and UNIX, and their consequences for networked users.

## Performance

At present, Linux delivers impressive performance in the workstation and low to midrange server arena, where it competes head to head with Windows NT. In the realm of high-performance, multiprocessor servers, it has a little way to go, although there is a significant development effort underway to improve matters. In this section we'll examine the nature of the current position and how it came to pass, and find out what plans exist to move forward from this base.

Linux was designed to be highly efficient in its use of system resources. Version 2.0 of the Linux kernel could run in text mode on a 386 with just 4MB of RAM. Version 2.2 is bigger, but it still only requires 8MB of RAM. (In graphical mode, the recommended requirement is about 32MB.) Linux grew up on resource-poor PC hardware, earning its parsimonious, no-bloat reputation. It has been extensively tested and optimized to run on single-processor Intel machines, and shows impressive performance against other operating systems, as evidenced by benchmarks conducted by ZDNet and others. It generally beats Windows NT and even Solaris on single-processor hardware. Only one another free operating system (FreeBSD) is as fast.

The UNIX approach of separating graphics and windowing capabilities from the kernel and placing them in user space allows servers to run in text mode, vastly reducing the burden on the underlying hardware. Linux allows users to bring up the graphical environment for administration, if so desired, and to disable it at all other times, helping to squeeze the maximum performance from the hardware. In contrast, Windows NT servers must always run in the more resource-hungry graphical mode, even when they're not being administrated, because windowing and graphics are built into the Windows kernel and cannot be disabled. This is an acceptable design for a desktop operating system, where these features are constantly in use, but it's less than optimal for a server.

UNIX is excellently positioned as a server operating system to serve *thin clients*. The X Window System is expressly designed to be network-transparent, which means that applications can be neatly partitioned such that number crunching and database access occur on the server, and the presentation (display) logic alone runs on the client. As the thin-client architecture gains popularity on account of its reduced cost of ownership, X's unique windowing model should prove increasingly popular as well. To give a practical example, an office's desktop needs could be catered for by 486 PCs with decent graphics cards. For the processing power, a server could perform the number crunching and send the results to the X server. There are few equivalents to this aspect of X in the MS Windows world; Windows Terminal Server is a candidate, but at present the WTS license terms make it uncompetitive with true thin-client architectures.

## Multiprocessor Machines

There is also considerable experience with Linux on dual-processor Intel machines, and this translates into acceptable performance on such hardware as well. Older kernels could not use more than one CPU effectively, but the 2.2 kernel released in January 1999 *can* utilize two CPUs with at least 185% performance compared to a single-CPU machine.

The 2.2 and later kernels also enable Linux to scale up to 4 CPUs and beyond, but the performance gain is not linear. Web server and file server benchmarks with the 2.2 kernel indicate that Linux lags its commercial rivals on 4 CPU Intel servers with 2GB of RAM at high loads. It is nevertheless remarkable that an operating system developed by volunteers is even comparable in performance to commercial alternatives that have had millions of dollars invested in their development.

*8-CPU servers running Linux are already available, and commercial vendors such as Penguin Computing, VA Linux Systems, and even Intel are keen to improve Linux performance on such systems.*

Linux runs in *native 64-bit mode* on 64-bit processors such as the Alpha, UltraSPARC and MIPS chips. Linux performance on 64-bit systems is reportedly much better than on high-end, 32-bit Intel-based systems – which is not surprising when you consider that all data channels are twice as wide. Linux-based Alpha servers from Compaq/Digital are now available from $3500 and up; this is low-end Intel server territory, but it's certainly not low-end from a performance viewpoint. With a zero license fee for Linux, this arguably represents the best value in the server market today.

Finally, at the very high end, Linux-based Beowulf clusters can yield supercomputer-class performance for many types of applications. An IBM Netfinity cluster costing $150,000 posted performance figures rivaling those of a Cray supercomputer costing $5,000,000 – equivalent performance at 3% of the cost!

### References

Linux beats Solaris on single-processor SPARC hardware:
http://www.cs.uml.edu/~acahalan/linux/benchmark.html

ZDNet's benchmark of Linux vs. NT on single-processor systems:
http://www5.zdnet.com/products/stories/reviews/0,4161,387506,00.html

ZDNet's price/benefit comparison of Linux and Windows NT:
http://www.zdnet.com/sr/stories/news/0,4538,2196127,00.html

ZDNet's benchmarks on 4-processor systems:
http://www.zdnet.com/pcweek/stories/news/0,4153,401970,00.html?chkpt=zdnnp1ms
http://www.zdnet.com/pcweek/stories/jumps/0,4270,401961,00.html

Compaq's DS10 Webbrick Alpha-based server for $3500:
http://www.news.com/News/Item/0,4,36340,00.html

IBM's Linux-based supercomputer:
http://www.infoworld.com/cgi-bin/displayStory.pl?99039.ecsuperlinux.htm

## Standards Compliance

Linux cannot have proprietary features. Under the terms of the GNU General Public License, it is illegal for any entity to make modifications to Linux for public distribution without making the corresponding source code publicly available. With one stroke, this removes the incentive to produce a proprietary variant. The license therefore ensures that the only changes to the system that will last are those accepted by the Linux community. The community has no vested interest in creating proprietary standards and protocols, and so the OS coalesces around industry standards. This is not mere theory; Linux today is a POSIX-compliant operating system, and its constituent subsystems support all relevant ANSI, ISO, IETF and W3C standards.

> **Certification, however, is a different issue, and the Linux community is against having to pay standards bodies for something that doesn't really benefit it. Currently, therefore, Linux is in the position of being compliant with some standards without actually being certified as such.**

Ironically, while Linux does a good job of supporting industry standards, there is still a lack of standardization between different Linux distributions. Although most of these differences are minor – they usually involve variations in the applications bundled with Linux, the versions of those packages, the installation utilities, and the locations they use for various system files – they are an irritation that does not improve the general perception of the operating system. In response, the **Linux Standard Base project** has sprung up that aims to unify all distributions in a number of respects. It is in the interests of users for this effort to succeed, since it will make for a more predictable and uniform user experience.

### References

UNIX 98:
http://www.xopen.org

POSIX and UNIX 98:
http://lwn.net/lwn/980611/standardseditorial.html

Linux Standard Base home page:
http://www.linuxbase.org

## Diverse Hardware Support

Linux runs on an enormous range of processors – RISC and CISC, 32-bit and 64-bit. Linux's native architecture is of course the Intel x86 family (and all compatible processors), but it also runs on Motorola's 68k, the IBM/Apple/Motorola PowerPC, Compaq/Digital's Alpha, MIPS chips, Sun's SPARC and UltraSPARC, and Intel's StrongARM. At the time of writing (December 1999), Hewlett-Packard's PA-RISC chip is perhaps the only major one on which Linux does not yet run, but HP is assisting the Puffin Group to port Linux to PA-RISC. Intel is also *supporting* Linux, and its stated objective is to make Linux run fastest on its chips. Intel is providing technical information about its 8-processor motherboards to the Linux community, so that high-end Xeon servers running Linux can be a cost-effective alternative to customers. Intel has also been sharing information about its IA-64 architecture, on which Linux already runs.

This breadth of chip support is a tremendous achievement that no other operating system (except the FreeBSD variants) can boast. Linux has fulfilled the UNIX promise of hardware independence that was belied when UNIX split into incompatible proprietary versions. Users of Linux thus gain an extra degree of independence from hardware vendors.

Before we leave this subject behind, you should be aware that not everything in the garden is rosy. Linux support for diverse CPUs is excellent, but it does not deal with as many peripherals and cards as, say, Windows does. It is always sensible to consult a hardware compatibility list before choosing a new piece of hardware to add to a Linux machine. As it gains wider acceptance, it is likely that hardware manufacturers will release Linux drivers for their products, but at present a degree of care is necessary.

### References

HP, the Linux PA-RISC port and the Puffin Group:
http://www.hp.com/pressrel/mar99/01mar99e.htm

Linux and Intel's Merced:
http://www.crn.com/dailies/weekending030599/mar02dig09.asp

Cygnus GNUPro toolkit for Merced enables Linux to be compiled for that platform:
http://linuxtoday.com/stories/5434.html

Linux-USB Project:
http://www.linux-usb.org

Linux Plug-and-Play project home page:
http://www-jcr.lmh.ox.ac.uk/~pnp

Intel's UDI and the Linux community:
http://www.zdnet.co.uk/news/1998/37/ns-5501.html

Linux runs an MP3 music player for cars:
http://www.wired.com/news/news/technology/story/18236.html

Linux hardware compatibility list:
http://metalab.unc.edu/LDP/HOWTO/Hardware-HOWTO.html

## Interoperability With Existing Systems

Linux is widely claimed to be able to coexist with other operating systems, and even to talk some proprietary protocols. Linux can talk SPX/IPX in a Netware environment, AppleTalk in a Macintosh network, and even SNA to IBM mainframes. But for most organizations, the most important and relevant aspect of Linux's claimed interoperability is its ability to coexist with Windows machines in heterogeneous networks.

We'll be examining a number of ways in which a Linux machine can complement or even replace Windows machines in the enterprise, and you'll see that there are a number of means by which this can occur. The first way, and the simplest technologically, is down to the fact that Windows and Linux can both talk the UNIX-native TCP/IP protocol. Windows machines use TCP/IP when they act as web servers, proxies and gateways, so provided that it follows the same rules, Linux can be used for the same purpose. You'll find more information about this aspect of using Linux in the middle chapters of the book.

Another way that Linux can be used as a replacement for Windows is by providing file and print services through **Samba**, a product that, like Linux, is released under the GNU General Public License. A Linux server running Samba (which we'll begin to investigate in the next chapter) can emulate a Windows NT server so well that Windows clients are unaware of the difference. Windows workstation users can use their favorite Explorer file manager to manipulate files on the Linux server, and even use drag-and-drop. Microsoft had the Samba developers foxed for a while with their NT Domain Security encryption system, but the resourceful team worked around that. At the time of writing, Samba can let Linux do anything an NT server can do *except* emulate a Backup Domain Controller, and that capability is reportedly not far away.

Given Linux's ability to scale up to multiprocessor, 64-bit machines, Samba gives users a serious way to obtain NT-like file servers at levels of power and stability that NT itself cannot currently reach; and to operate a complete Windows network without using any NT servers at all. As a side-benefit, this also eliminates the need for Windows client-access licenses. Samba is such a popular piece of software that SGI (formerly Silicon Graphics) has announced that it is bundling it with its high-end UNIX servers. It has also announced that Linux (not IRIX) will now become its lead operating system.

Finally, for those who wish to *run* Windows applications on a Linux platform, there are a couple of options. In one corner is the commercial product VMware, which lets users run Windows as a guest operating system hosted by Linux. It has won favorable reviews, but it is not a cheap option, weighing in at $300 a copy for commercial users. Furthermore, it doesn't eliminate the need for a Windows license, and it requires a beefy hardware configuration in order to run these two operating systems one on top of the other. In the other corner is the Windows Emulation Project (WINE), which aims for nothing less than the ability to run Win32 binaries on Linux. It's currently in a very early phase of development, but if WINE succeeds, Linux will one day be usable just like a Windows workstation.

### References

Linux and AppleTalk:
http://www.linuxworld.com/linuxworld/lw-1999-04/lw-04-uptime.html

Samba home page:
http://www.samba.org

Samba on SGI:
http://www.zdnet.com/products/stories/reviews/0,4161,394079,00.html

WINE project home page:
http://www.winehq.com

VMware home page:
http://www.vmware.com

## Virus-proof Design

It should not have gone unnoticed that recent virus attacks have left Linux machines pretty much unaffected.

On UNIX-like systems, there are two, clearly demarcated levels of privilege – let's call them user and administrator. A normal user (or a program run by a normal user) is not able to delete system files or files belonging to other users, because such actions require system privileges; the administrator of a UNIX system is the only one with system privileges. Therefore, normal users of UNIX have limited ability to cause damage to their systems by importing suspect files from elsewhere – the scope of virus activity is extremely restricted.

Like UNIX, Linux can be considered as relatively virus-proof compared to operating systems such as MS-DOS, Windows 3.1, Windows 95, Windows 98 and the Macintosh OS.

> *You may have heard of UNIX 'worms'; these are programs that choke systems by replicating themselves endlessly and filling up storage, even if they have no privilege to actually delete or corrupt files. Worms are not as destructive as viruses, and can also be blocked with a little diligence.*

Windows NT also has separate user and administrator privilege levels, so in theory it's as virus-proof as any version of UNIX. However, Windows *applications*, even on NT, are vulnerable to a new kind of virus: **macro viruses** spread through e-mail attachments and infect Word and Excel documents. There is no security sandbox (of the kind used to control Java applets) in the Microsoft Office products, and so macros attached to Word and Excel documents that arrive through e-mail are capable of doing considerable harm. As long as Windows lacks a sandbox to restrict imported macros, this will remain a security risk.

Security administrators would do well to imbibe what agriculturists have known for years: a diverse crop is more resistant to blight than a homogeneous one. A mixed environment consisting of Linux and Windows machines is likely to prove fairly resistant to virus infestations – not only because some of the machines in the network will remain unaffected, but also because heterogeneity acts as a natural barrier to the propagation of viruses, which are usually written to exploit the weaknesses of a specific operating system. A Windows PC could escape attack by merely being behind a Linux machine. Thus, the presence of Linux machines in a Windows network could reduce the damage area of a potentially deadly virus, at the minor cost of increased administrative overheads.

### Proceed With Caution

We cannot afford to be complacent. Although Linux enjoys a virus-proof reputation at present, it has largely escaped the attention of virus writers because of its limited market presence compared to the ubiquity of Windows computers. As Linux gets more popular, viruses (or more precisely, Trojan horses) targeting it will surely appear. A Linux virus could certainly result in careless users losing their own files, even if system files and the files of other users are unaffected. Personal computer owners should be particularly careful not to log into their systems as the superuser for anything other than administrative tasks. Inadvertently downloading viruses while logged in as the superuser can result in wholesale damage, just as it can on a Windows PC. However, it is highly unlikely that a single virus could ever attack both Windows and Linux, so the advantages of a heterogeneous network will remain.

### References

Report on the Chernobyl virus:
http://news.bbc.co.uk/hi/english/sci/tech/newsid_329000/329688.stm

Report on the Melissa virus:
http://news.bbc.co.uk/hi/english/sci/tech/newsid_307000/307162.stm

## Strong Cryptography Worldwide

If you wanted to set up a web site for secure electronic commerce, you would need to encrypt the communication channel between your customers and your site so that no prying eyes could tell what business is taking place. The standard technology for doing this is called SSL (Secure Sockets Layer), pioneered by Netscape. However, if your company is not based in the US or Canada, and it's not a bank or other financial institution, you cannot (at the time of writing) get a US-developed hardware or software product with strong cryptographic capabilities. Even if you're a North American company, you cannot implement a truly secure transnational network (a **virtual private network**) linking your various international branches and business partners together. The problem is not technical, but legal/political.

Most popular commercial software (operating systems, web servers and communication software) comes from US companies and is subject to US laws that currently forbid the export of encryption software that exceeds 56-bit strength. The policy is aimed at preventing international terrorists from being able to communicate through a channel so secure that even US law enforcement agencies cannot tap it. But when you know that the Electronic Frontier Foundation has demonstrated the cracking of a secret message (encrypted using a 56-bit algorithm) in just 56 hours, using a computer costing just $210,000 to build, you could be excused for being unenthusiastic about the security of products that US companies are allowed to sell you. For reasons like this, the Indian government has warned against the use of US security software, and may even ban its use altogether.

For a few years now, companies like Germany's Brokat have made a comfortable living selling independently developed, strong cryptographic products to customers outside the US and Canada. A large number of German and other European banks have used Brokat's proprietary solutions to acquire strong cryptography legally. (This was before the US Commerce Department made an exception for banks and financial institutions.) However, these products are not cheap – the artificial scarcity of what are ultimately just (well-known) mathematical algorithms has raised the price of legally available cryptographic software. The Wassenaar agreement between 33 advanced countries to restrict the export of products with strong cryptography is unlikely to improve this situation.

The solution to this seemingly intractable problem is delicious in its irony. You cannot *buy* any such product, but you *can* get one free. As we'll investigate in Chapter 11, you can download the source code for the free Apache web server from anywhere, including the US. Then, you can legally download the popular and free SSLeay SSL package (independently developed by an Australian, Eric A. Young), and the Apache `mod_ssl` package, from any site *outside* the US. What's more, you can have the SSLeay source code independently audited to satisfy yourself that the cryptographic algorithms have been faithfully implemented with no hidden trapdoors or dilution in strength, something you cannot do with any commercial (binary-only) software.

> *Interestingly, Netscape always uses 128 bits for SSL, even in 40-bit strong products – they merely send the remaining 88 bits in clear text. Without the ability to check the source code and compile it afresh, there is no way to ensure that such surreptitious dilution of strength is not taking place in the 'strong' cryptographic products that are available commercially.*

Of course, this entire issue has only an indirect bearing on Linux (although the Apache-Linux combination is a very common one). Apache runs on all versions of UNIX as well as on Windows NT, though at present, the NT version is not as stable. If you fall outside of the boundaries the US government has laid down for the legal use of strong cryptography, Apache-on-UNIX may be the only way to implement (verifiably) secure e-commerce, with Apache-Linux being a very natural solution.

Other free, strong cryptography products include PGP (Pretty Good Privacy), a public-key cryptography package; its GNU equivalent GPG (GNU Privacy Guard), which uses no patented algorithms; and the Cryptix Java classes for free use in Java applications. Also recently announced is the comprehensive FreeS/WAN strong cryptography package to provide secure communications over TCP/IP networks like the Internet. Unlike SSL, which can only encrypt the Hypertext Transfer Protocol (HTTP) traffic between browsers and web servers, FreeS/WAN can encrypt *any* TCP/IP traffic. All of these free products work with Linux, and the source code can be audited to your satisfaction.

### References

The Electronic Frontier Foundation web site:
http://eff.org

Apache home page:
http://www.apache.org

SSLeay home page:
http://www.ssleay.org

Netscape's 40-bit SSL hack:
http://www.cs.bris.ac.uk/~bradley/publish/SSLP/chapter4.html#4.4.3

PGP download page:
http://meryl.csd.uu.se/~d95mno/PGP.html

GPG home page:
http://www.d.shuttle.de/isil/gnupg/gnupg.html

Cryptix home page:
http://www.cryptix.org

FreeS/WAN home page:
http://www.xs4all.nl/~freeswan

# The Arguments Against Linux

Linux is certainly *not* a perfect operating system, and its weaknesses are paraded regularly by friend and foe alike. As before, we've assembled ten of the most frequently voiced arguments against the operating system. In this section we'll re-examine them, see how many hold true today, and consider how serious are those that remain. Our subjects are:

1. User-unfriendliness
2. Installation problems
3. Scarcity of applications
4. Poor documentation
5. Lack of high-end features
6. Security concerns
7. Lack of support
8. Absence of legal recourse
9. Lack of ownership
10. Uncertain roadmap

## *User-unfriendliness*

It is impossible to read an article on Linux written for a non-UNIX audience without coming across phrases like *primitive command line*, *cryptic commands*, and *arcane syntax*. Undoubtedly, users accustomed to the friendly graphical interfaces of Windows and the Macintosh *can* balk at having to type apparently mysterious incantations at a prompt, but things are changing fast.

There are two popular graphical desktop environments for Linux. KDE ('K' Desktop Environment) is slightly more mature, and the main criticism heard about it these days is that it's rather too clean. GNOME (GNU Network Object Model Environment) is at an earlier stage of development, but it allows users to customize it *ad infinitum*. Neither interface is yet as polished and complete as the Windows or Macintosh desktops, but they have developed to their current states in an amazingly short time. Recall that it was only with version 3.1 that Windows became tolerable, and that it took another three years for Windows to achieve its current levels of usability in the form of Windows 95.

> *These interfaces have already pulled ahead of Windows in some respects. For example, if you delete a program manually, a reference to it still appears on the* Start *menu. GNOME and KDE automatically detect the (manual) removal of a program, and stop displaying references to it.*

A couple of screenshots of these interfaces follow; this one shows the K Desktop Environment running a Macintosh theme:

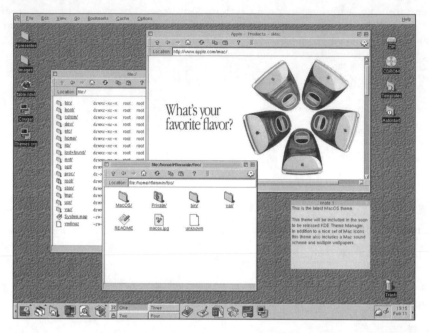

While this one demonstrates GNOME, customized to the hilt. Notice the strangely shaped button in the top center of the figure:

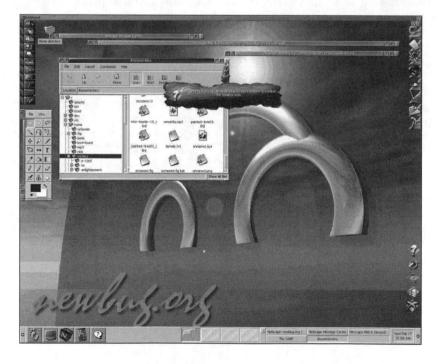

Besides, to turn the user-friendliness argument around, a command line is an excellent complement to a GUI in many situations. Even with an extremely friendly GUI, a user may find certain operations difficult to express with a graphical metaphor – piping the output of one program to the input of another comes to mind. Also, a point-and-click interface does not allow users to specify operations on objects that are not currently visible or do not yet exist, a limitation from which typed commands do not suffer.

With a graphical environment similar to that of Windows or the Macintosh now established, Linux's command line and scripting interface may emerge as a major selling point for advanced users. Windows and Macintosh treat all users alike, irrespective of skill level, and do not allow users to acquire more control over their machines with increasing experience. UNIX and UNIX-like systems, on the other hand, scale extremely well with experience, rewarding advanced users with dramatically greater productivity.

### References

Gnome home page:
http://www.gnome.org

KDE home page:
http://www.kde.org

Simple UNIX Bourne shell script tutorial:
http://www.ocean.odu.edu/ug/shell_help.html

A Macintosh user's perspective on Linux:
http://www.applelinks.com/warpcore/apr99/wc-8.shtml

## Installation Problems

There have been many articles in the popular computing press that recount in painful detail the travails associated with installing Linux, and these are invariably contested by Linux supporters who claim that it's really easy. In truth, though, it *is* somewhat problematic for lay users to install Linux. Even though Linux does a reasonably good job of detecting the hardware components of a PC, it does require some enlightened input from the installer. Disk partitioning and mounting file systems are relatively advanced concepts, especially for users who are used to the simple drive letters of Windows.

With some Linux distributions, the user has to know the details of the graphics adapter card and monitor in order to provide all the information the installation program requires. Installing Linux on an existing Windows machine to gain dual-boot capability (the ability to run either operating system) has its own traps to watch out for. Windows assumes that it owns the whole disk, and can grasp control of the master boot record away from lilo, the boot loader that enables you to select your operating system at boot up. In a related problem, system administration tools quite often assume all partitions to be Windows partitions, and might try to perform operations that are not legal on a Linux file system.

Having said this, you must remember that most users don't normally install operating systems on their computers. Rather, they arrive pre-installed by the hardware manufacturer, whether the machine is a PC workstation or server running Windows, a SPARC machine running Solaris, an RS/6000 running AIX, or something else. It may be that the toughest OS to install is (say) HP/UX, but the user doesn't know and shouldn't care. With the availability of Linux computers off-the-shelf from manufacturers like VA Linux Systems, Compaq and Dell, OS installation is less of an issue, although those who want to try out Linux by installing it on an old machine would benefit by enlisting the help of an experienced person.

## References

Fortune magazine's *The Dreyfuss Report*, on the difficulties of installing Linux:
http://cgi.pathfinder.com/fortune/technology/dreyfuss/1999/04/26/index.html

Caldera OpenLinux home page:
http://www.calderasystems.com

Review of Caldera OpenLinux:
http://www.linuxworld.com/linuxworld/lw-1999-04/lw-04-penguin3.html

Dell selling PCs with Linux:
http://www.dell.com/us/en/bsd/topics/linux_linuxhome.htm

Dell supplying Linux on entire server line:
http://biz.yahoo.com/bw/991206/nc_red_hat_1.html

Compaq expects Linux to popularize 64-bit Alpha chips:
http://www.news.com/News/Item/0,4,34119,00.html?tag=st.cn.sr1.dir

# Scarcity of Applications

Nobody chooses operating systems for their own sake. It's the applications that run on them that matter, and for some time now critics of Linux have justifiably asked, "Where are the applications?" To try and answer this question satisfactorily, we need to look at two different environments: the server side and the client side.

## The Server Side

Internet and web applications have never been a problem. Sendmail, a free mail transport program that is estimated to handle 70-80% of the world's e-mail, runs on Linux. Linux also has a natural fit with the free web server Apache, which according to the Netcraft survey has 54% of the Internet web server market, with Microsoft's IIS (Internet Information Server) at 25%, and Netscape's Enterprise Server a poor third at 8%. Furthermore, the *Squid* caching proxy is very popular with Internet ISPs; Java is available for Linux (though it typically lags a little behind Solaris and Windows – the Java 2 port had been completed and was undergoing testing at the time of writing); and Lutris Technologies has made its Enhydra Java Application Server open source.

Despite the success and widespread acceptance of these packages, however, the major software vendors have been slow to release their server-side products for Linux. As you'll see in Chapter 7, for example, Linux sports a number of good-quality, 'free' databases, of which MySQL and PostgreSQL are perhaps the best known, but brands like Oracle, Sybase and Informix haven't been available. Enterprise customers can be reluctant to trust their most valuable information to an unknown quantity, and the absence of the big names makes them suspicious of the platform as a whole.

Since late 1998, however, the database vendors have been jumping on board the Linux bandwagon. Now, all the major databases, with the exception of Microsoft SQL Server, are available on Linux with varying support and fee options. Happily, this has been the spur for other manufacturers to follow suit, and there are now very few categories of server application that have no Linux implementation. SAP has announced a port of its Enterprise Resource Planning (ERP) software, making Linux a viable contender in the enterprise server market. On the middleware front, BEA has a Linux port of its Tuxedo TP monitor client, and Computer Associates has ported its Unicenter TNG systems management environment to Linux.

### The Client Side

The desktop is a slightly different proposition. For all its strength on the server side, Linux remains in its infancy as a client-side platform, although the pool of available applications is certainly growing. Perhaps the best showcase example of a free, commercial-quality Linux desktop application is the GIMP (GNU Image Manipulation Program), a worthy competitor to Adobe's Photoshop. GIMP packs about 80% of Photoshop's features into 0% of the price, and even has a scriptable interface that Photoshop lacks. Organizations designing web page graphics may find the GIMP to be a serious alternative to Photoshop; there's even a Windows version:

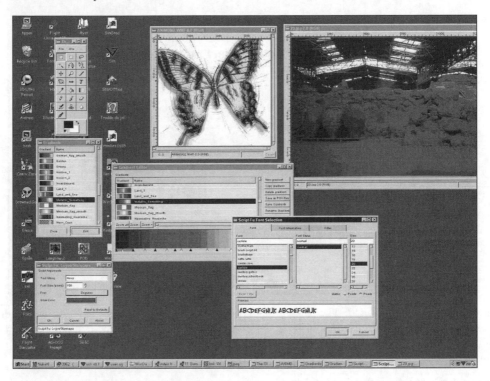

To highlight such applications as evidence that Linux is completely ready to replace Windows on the corporate desktop, though, would be to ignore the fact that there is one application above all others that's familiar to and relied upon by an enormous number of businesses: Microsoft Office. More than Windows itself, this is the killer application that gives Microsoft its large share of the corporate desktop. If moving to Linux entails losing compatibility with MS Office, most organizations would choose to remain with Windows.

Compatibility here takes two forms. First, many corporate desktop users have been trained on the interface and features of the Microsoft products, and there is understandable reluctance about moving to new products and having to relearn those skills. Second is the issue of file formats, which Microsoft is known to change with every new release of Office. Just because your 'alternative' is compatible now doesn't mean it will remain so in the future, and trying to standardize on a particular version of Office won't work because you run the risk of being unable to handle documents produced by other organizations using later versions. Some try to use HTML, RTF (Rich Text Format), and PDF (Portable Document Format) to gain a certain amount of vendor independence, but the Office products are clearly in a higher league.

This is not to say that office (with a small 'o') suites aren't available for Linux – in fact there are quite a few, both free and commercial, and they all show some compatibility (in both the above senses) with MS Office. The GNOME and KDE desktops both ship with free applications of this type; here, for example, is a screenshot of the KSpread package from the KOffice suite:

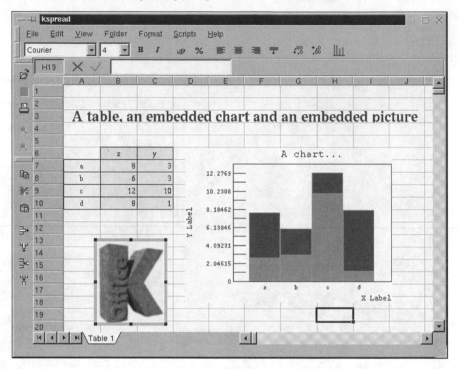

On the commercial side, Corel's WordPerfect Office Suite and Sun's StarOffice both have very similar interfaces to Microsoft Office, minimizing the training effort involved in switching to them. They also claim complete compatibility with MS Office file formats. StarOffice for Linux is now free for download, and CDs can be ordered from Sun for a nominal fee.

To conclude, Linux on the desktop has a long way to go. Numerous applications are there, but for many users the most important one is not. Perhaps the best hope for Linux would be if the commercial vendors were to switch from proprietary formats and embrace XML for their files – such standardization would be a boon to all users, and give considerable assistance to the cause of cross-compatibility. We will dwell no longer on client-side Linux applications in this book; our business is with the server side.

### References

MySQL web site:
http://www.mysql.com

PostgreSQL web site:
http://www.postgresql.org

Sendmail home page:
http://www.sendmail.org

Netcraft's web server market share survey:
http://www.netcraft.com/Survey

Squid home page:
http://squid.nlanr.net/Squid

Java-Linux project home page:
http://www.blackdown.org

Enhydra application server home page:
http://www.enhydra.com

Tuxedo on Linux:
http://www.fi.infn.it/DFS/news-comp.dce/msg00463.html

The KOffice home page:
http://koffice.kde.org

The GIMP home page:
http://www.gimp.org

Corel WordPerfect for Linux:
http://linux.corel.com/linux8/index.htm

StarOffice web page:
http://www.sun.com/dot-com/staroffice.html

HP OpenMail (a replacement for MS Exchange and Outlook):
http://www.ice.hp.com/cyc/om/00/index.html

## Poor Documentation

It is a rare software package indeed that is sufficiently intuitive to be used without documentation. At the very least, good documentation includes installation, user and administration manuals, and on-line help for all software products. Development tools must, in addition, have reference manuals and sample code. One of the downsides of Linux starting out as a programmer's operating system is that programmers tend to require minimal (but highly technical) documentation in order to understand and improve upon the work of others. Corporate users, on the other hand, are not interested in the software for its own sake, but as a tool to get their work done. The documentation required by them is of a very different kind.

The current problem with Linux documentation is not scarcity but an overabundance of largely mediocre material that's difficult to search. The Linux community has long recognized this weakness, and there are efforts (notably the **Linux Documentation Project**, whose purpose is to provide a centralized access point) to bring it in line with that enjoyed by commercial systems.

In some ways, a web-based document collection is better than a set of physical manuals, because that's the most dynamic and flexible way to document an ever-evolving piece of software. However, the need for physical documents cannot be dismissed. There is an impressive selection of commercial books and manuals for GNU/Linux software, and new editions are released fairly frequently. Fortunately, Linux *is* UNIX for most practical purposes, so most UNIX documentation applies to Linux as well – and there is plenty of that around.

Looking at another aspect, it's noticeable that most Linux documentation is in English, a situation the GNU project is seeking to address through a mailing list of voluntary proofreaders (proofreaders@gnu.org). They hope to maintain, on an ongoing basis, a collection of high-quality documents for all free software. Speakers of other languages organize themselves on a voluntary basis to translate documentation from English. Linux documentation in German, Japanese, French and Korean, for example, is reasonably extensive.

There is hope on both fronts: the new Linux desktop environments, Gnome and KDE, have good online documentation as one of their explicit objectives. Both environments support internationalization, making it possible to provide help in several languages. It is significant that Windows $9x$ comes with only a slim user manual for the operating system – it is so consistent and intuitive that some initial training and a little practice are sufficient for most users, with online help filling in the gaps. GNOME and KDE follow the same model.

### References

The Linux Documentation Project:
http://www.linuxdoc.org

The Linux System Administrator's Guide:
http://www.linuxdoc.org/LDP/sag/index.html

The Linux Network Administrator's Guide:
http://www.linuxdoc.org/LDP/nag/nag.html

The Linux Programmer's Guide:
http://www.linuxdoc.org/LDP/lpg/index.html

The Linux HOWTOs:
http://www.linuxdoc.org/HOWTO/HOWTO-INDEX.html

The Linux man (manual) pages for download:
ftp://ftp.win.tue.nl/pub/linux/docs/manpages

Linux FAQs (Frequently Asked Questions):
http://www.linuxdoc.org/FAQ/Linux-FAQ.html

## Lack of High-end Features

Linux is a relatively new operating system, developed largely by volunteer programmers. Until recently, these developers have not had access to high-end, expensive hardware (with the possible exception of Linux on Sun (UltraPenguin) and the port to Alpha with the help of Digital). At the moment, therefore, it's not surprising that Linux is treated as a low- to mid-range operating system – a category in which it performs quite well. However, many vendors are now making large systems available for independent developers to work on, and Linux is gradually logging more hours on high-end hardware.

Many users worry about the scalability of Linux. They fear that if their workload increases, it may not be possible to upgrade their hardware and continue to use Linux. The newer kernels, however, run on multiprocessor machines with better scalability, and this is being improved all the time. On 32-bit chips, Linux can use the full theoretical maximum of 4GB of virtual memory ($2^{32}$ bytes) – *except* on Intel chips. According to a senior kernel developer, it is not possible to run over 2GB of memory efficiently on a PC, so Linux kernel 2.2 currently enforces this limit. Linux can use 64GB on the UltraSPARC.

However, Linux scalability is still not fully optimized, its support for large files is very new, and it has no support for ccNUMA (Cache-Coherent Non-Uniform Memory Access) architectures. You cannot host multiple independent OS domains on the same box, the Linux journaling file system (of which there are three alternatives) is new and largely untested, and a logical volume manager is "next on the agenda". That's a sizable list, but there are projects underway to address all these limitations, and the results should begin trickling in over the year 2000. In spite of these current deficiencies, Linux is likely to be adequate for quite a range of application requirements, although it cannot yet match high-end operating systems such as AIX, Solaris, Tru64UNIX, or HP-UX.

The established UNIX vendors seem to have adopted a defensive marketing strategy. They offer Linux on their low-end proprietary hardware, and their own in-house OS for their high-end hardware. Thus, temporarily at least, they project a 'complete' product line. It will be interesting to see how long this strategy works. It is an oft-repeated market maxim that "90% of the market is at the low-end" – that's what enabled a PC maker like Compaq to grow large enough within a decade to take over makers of larger systems like Digital and Tandem. It has also contributed to the market share gains of Windows NT against these more powerful operating systems.

These UNIX vendors may soon find Linux to be a curate's egg. It could help them sell so many (low-end) machines that they have to make the decision whether to continue pushing their own OS at all. Linux could make them realize that hardware is what gives them their margins. In a bid to maintain relative market share, each of them may be persuaded to donate the high-end features of their own operating systems to Linux, moving it up the scale and ultimately replacing those proprietary systems altogether.

### References

Linux Beowulf cluster-based supercomputers:
http://cesdis.gsfc.nasa.gov/linux/beowulf/beowulf.html

IBM's Linux-based supercomputer:
http://www.infoworld.com/cgi-bin/displayStory.pl?99039.ecsuperlinux.htm

SGI to release technologies:
http://www.it.fairfax.com.au/990309/openline1.html

Cygnus GNUPro toolkit for Merced enables Linux to be compiled for that platform:
http://linuxtoday.com/stories/5434.html

## Security Concerns

The fact of Linux's source code being common knowledge is enough to make many companies' security advisors recommend against its use. Many organizations subscribe to the "security through secrecy" doctrine, even though that has been discredited in professional security circles. In fact, a truly secure system is one that does *not* rely on the secrecy of its internals. Encryption algorithms, for instance, are generally publicly known. The DES (Data Encryption Standard) algorithm (and its derivative, the Triple-DES algorithm) has been studied intensively over the past two decades, but no fatal weaknesses have been found. Triple-DES is now regarded as one of the most secure encryption algorithms, precisely because it has stood up to close scrutiny.

There is great advantage in having a system hardened through exposure, analysis, review and attack. A closed, secret system cannot be hardened so quickly, and can have bugs and loopholes that go undetected for a long time. If anything, the open-source nature of Linux lets security problems be found and fixed quickly. There are many stories of security fixes for Linux being made available within *hours* of an attack being known about. So from a security angle, Linux, FreeBSD, and other open-source systems can be preferable to the closed source operating systems available from commercial vendors. The bugs and security deficiencies in commercial systems will continue to remain undetected until the day a cracker exploits them.

To illustrate this argument, it's worth mentioning the example of a TCP wrapper Trojan horse attack that took place in 1998. The TCP wrapper software is an open-source program for secure network connections on UNIX/Linux, and it's distributed in both source and compiled forms. Given its sensitive nature, it was no wonder that someone downloaded the source code, added a trapdoor to it, recompiled it and loaded the compromised executable back to the web site.

Now, open-source software may be open, but the systems that its authors use are anything but naïve. Every piece of software has a checksum (called a **message digest**) that's digitally signed by its author and placed on the same web site as the software. Since the author's public key is accessible from many independent sources, the message digest can be deciphered. When compared with the freshly calculated message digest from the downloaded software, the user must see no difference. If there *is* a difference, it means the software has been tampered with.

And so the TCP wrapper Trojan horse was detected after no more than 52 downloads had taken place. (Those 52 people had not bothered to cross-check the message digest, or had not reported the discrepancy.) There was no way the attacker could have digitally signed the doctored executable without the author's private key, so it was only a matter of time before the deception was uncovered. The security of the web site in question was also immediately tightened through better configuration to prevent such uploading of compromised software in future. The lesson is, then, that open-source software has perfectly sound security systems, but users must use them properly to obtain their benefits.

### References

Open source and security:
http://www.linuxworld.com/linuxworld/lw-1998-11/lw-11-ramparts.html

TCP wrapper Trojan horse attack:
http://www.linuxworld.com/linuxworld/lw-1999-03/lw-03-ramparts.html

Download page for TCP wrapper and other tools:
ftp://ftp.porcupine.org/pub/security/index.html

The Secure Shell administration program `ssh`:
http://www.ssh.fi

Firewall-building tool *Mason* licensed under GNU GPL:
http://users.dhp.com/~whisper/mason

## Lack of Support

By commercial standards, the argument that Linux is not well supported still holds some water. Till late 1998, the only support one could get for Linux was in-house (if a company had a resident UNIX guru) or through Internet mailing lists. The latter might seem a particularly poor way of obtaining support, were it not for the fact that people have actually received quality suggestions and solutions quickly through this medium. No wonder Infoworld awarded its 1997 badge for *Best Technical Support* to the Linux community as a whole.

The kinds of formal support structure more familiar to IT management were thin on the ground, but they are beginning to arrive. Hardware vendors are prepared to stand behind the versions of Linux that they supply with their boxes. Furthermore, and as well as Hewlett-Packard's support package mentioned earlier, IBM has announced a more comprehensive, if more expensive, support service: an organization called LinuxCare has been formed purely for Linux support. Other third-party support can also be hired. Many common free software packages have counterparts for commercial support. Cygnus supports the GNU compilers and other tools; Scriptics supports Tcl/Tk; Cyclic Software supports CVS; Sendmail Inc. supports Sendmail, and there are a number of others.

In short, given that a user is not dependent upon a single supplier for support and fixes, it may soon be possible to arrive at a nicely tailored support arrangement addressing the specific requirements of a site, which could include quality of service, price, and any other relevant factors. Linux has made the differences in concept between software license fees and support fees explicit in the minds of users. With luck, the availability and the demand for third-party support will feed off each other, propelling Linux's acceptance.

### References

Linux community gets best technical support award 1997:
http://www.infoworld.com/cgi-bin/displayArchive.pl?/98/05/poy6a.dat.htm

IBM's ServerProven Program:
http://www.techweb.com/wire/story/TWB19990323S0016

LinuxCare home page:
http://www.linuxcare.com

## Absence of Legal Recourse

When organizations choose a software package, they need assurance that there is someone who can be held legally accountable if things go wrong. However, Linux, like all other free software, comes with absolutely no warranty. You cannot sue Linus Torvalds or Red Hat or Compaq if your Linux server goes berserk and trashes your precious data. (No such case has been reported, of course, but we are talking about a hypothetical possibility.) How can an organization be expected to expose itself to risk without legal recourse?

First of all, it must be clarified that when you pay for commercial software, you are not *purchasing* the product; you are paying for a license to *use* the product. Ownership of the software remains with the vendor. The legal framework governing software use is not Consumer Protection Law but Contract Law – and the latter is much less consumer-friendly than the former. Once you agree to the terms of the software license agreement, you are bound by it – but how many people read the license terms before installing a piece of software?

In 1998, a bug was discovered in Microsoft's Access 97 database product. Under a specific but rare set of circumstances, details entered by a user could end up being attached to the wrong record – you can imagine the consequences if a hospital's medical records or police records were to be so affected! Of course, the bug was soon fixed, but it shed an interesting light on Microsoft's legal liability. It turned out there was a clause in the license agreement that said, in effect, Microsoft was not responsible for any data corruption caused by the software. It sounds ridiculous that a database product should not be responsible for data, but Microsoft's terms are by no means exceptional. *No* software vendor takes responsibility for the integrity of your data. 'No liability' clauses exist in *all* commercial software license agreements, and yet we all cheerfully click the I Agree buttons when we install new pieces of software.

If the situation you're complaining about is explicitly covered by the contract, and you have signed it, you may have no case because consent is a powerful principle in law. Organizations need to consult expert legal opinion to assess the extent of legal protection they really have when the chips are down, as opposed to the protection they think they have. If commercial software doesn't give you any more legal protection than free software, using Linux instead of a commercial alternative will not increase your risk after all.

### References

The Microsoft Access bug:
http://www.zdnet.com/zdnn/stories/zdnn_smgraph_display/0,4436,2131609,00.html

## Lack of Ownership

Corporate users are understandably reluctant to use software that emerged from the woodwork without a respected commercial organization behind it. The lack of reputed ownership is one of Linux's major perceived drawbacks, and one of the places where it raises its head is in the issue of standards. A single owner can enforce much-needed standards, and while the various distributions of Linux are drawn from the same code base, they are different enough to cause confusion and some real incompatibilities, eerily reminiscent of the UNIX wars. Such a bleak scenario might not come to pass this time around, but in the meantime, the Linux Standard Base project is worth watching and deserves all the encouragement it can get.

This concern aside, however, more and more users are beginning to consider lack of ownership as a blessing, because it is almost impossible for a vendor to control Linux. Users and packaged software vendors alike have seen for themselves the control that large software companies have over their popular products, and the leverage it gives the companies against their partners and customers. Hence, many in the industry today are relieved that Linux can never be similarly controlled to suit any vendor's agenda. The GNU General Public License removes all incentive for proprietary code versions, because it forces all software changes (that are not for in-house use) to be released to the public. Only features most useful to the community find their way into the product.

Linux will continue to be used and improved as long as there are people interested in it, without being affected by the economic and business pressures to which commercial products are vulnerable. Netware's future, for example, is crucially tied to Novell's profitability, but Linux will continue even if Red Hat (for example) goes under. As users' awareness of free software's nature and longevity becomes more sophisticated, their confidence in Linux should increase. In the main, Linux's lack of ownership is a mere issue of perception, not an actual weakness.

### Uncertain Roadmap

Where is Linux going? What features will it sport next year? And what about the year after that? Alas, there is no roadmap for the system. Linux developed in the anarchic medium of the Internet, and there is no strong visionary company that can provide reassuring plans of the features that Linux will support in the years to come. How is an organization to commit to an operating system that has no planned development path?

Again, a close examination of Linux's development process reveals this is actually *desirable*. Linux acquires those features that its users find useful. Anyone is free to write code and extend Linux to support the features that they need. If those requirements are common enough, they form part of a mainstream distribution. It is akin to a market economy that responds sensitively to demand, unlike a planned economy where a few people make decisions based on their limited projections, and often end up guessing wrong. Linux development is in ferment, and new ideas appear all the time. Contributions to Linux increase with its user base, in turn driving its acceptance. The best of these contributions are determined by the market, improved by proportionately as many users as are interested in it, and are gradually absorbed into the mainstream.

# The Shape of Things to Come

We hope that the arguments presented here will have gone some way to convincing you of Linux's increasing maturity as an enterprise-class operating system, but the only way to know for sure is to try it out. Perhaps you're still unsure about compatibility or stability; maybe you're skeptical of its suitability for mission-critical data – it is only with exposure to the inner workings of the system that you will decide whether or not you are willing to use this operating system. Later in the book, we'll have demonstrations that test all these features, but in the next chapter we'll begin with an example that represents one of the simplest and most transparent ways of using Linux in your enterprise, at minimal risk to your business's security. We're going to investigate just how completely a machine running Samba can replace NT file servers in your network.

# Summary

We have looked at most of the commonly cited strengths and weaknesses of Linux, and seen that Linux does have some very impressive strengths, while its weaknesses are being addressed at pace. Looking at where Linux was couple of years ago and where it is today, we can see that if it keeps up its current rate of improvement, Linux will play a very important role in the IT industry in the very near future. There is hardly a market niche where it will not be a strong contender.

History is not a very good guide to tell us what heights Linux will scale in the years to come, because the Internet phenomenon that spawned Linux is a recent one. The massive, worldwide development of open source software is unprecedented. As the wheels of the Linux juggernaut churn on, we can only watch and wait. This is nothing short of a windfall for users and consumers, and if you read the rest of this book, you will learn how best to steer this vehicle in the right direction for your enterprise.

# 2

# Integrating Windows and Linux using Samba

Samba is a software package that makes it possible to provide Windows file and print services on a Linux system. It is a well-known fact that MS Windows is the dominant force in the desktop market. However, in the past, organizations that wanted to provide file and print services to Windows machines had few options as to what went into the server room. They could go with NT servers, Novell NetWare or proprietary UNIX solutions like SCO VisionFS or Digital PATHWORKS. In all cases, these were expensive undertakings. Samba has become an additional option that a great many people find extremely attractive. This attraction is threefold. First, for many companies, their Windows NT server's license feeding frenzy is getting unbearably expensive. Samba is *free* with no licensing costs. Second, Samba runs on Linux and other free UNIX clones. Besides paying nothing for the operating system, organizations can benefit from UNIX's legendary stability and its wealth of scripting possibilities for automating tasks. Of course, proprietary UNIX systems such as Solaris, AIX, SCO UNIX or HP-UX can also benefit from Samba. Companies like SGI even offer commercial Samba support on their IRIX operating system. Third, but not least, Samba is *fast*. Earlier this year, a benchmark published by ZDNet revealed that Samba outperformed Windows NT by an impressive margin. In another benchmark, a Linux/Samba combination went head to head with NetWare 5.0 and showed that it "either matched or surpassed Netware's ability to serve files in each test".

So as that U2 song goes, it is arguable that Samba is "even better than the real thing". This chapter will show you how to set up a functional Samba server. As it has evolved into a rather versatile piece of software, a chapter such as this cannot cover all of its possibilities. However, enough information is presented here to suit your needs; a resources section is provided at the end of this chapter should you need more information.

This chapter will cover:

- ❏ Samba concepts
- ❏ Installing and troubleshooting Samba
- ❏ Server configuration issues
- ❏ Client configuration issues

*A quick note: All of the open-source software described in this chapter compile and work on most versions of UNIX, but this is a book about Linux. So while this chapter refers to Linux, the majority of the information contained therein is applicable most other versions of UNIX.*

# Samba Concepts

So besides that Brazilian dance, what is Samba?

Technically, Samba is a software suite for Linux and UNIX, providing file and print services through the Server Message Block (SMB) protocol. Originally designed by IBM for PC networks, this protocol's destiny is now largely ruled by Microsoft. The name Samba follows the hallowed UNIX tradition of straightforward (some would even say uninspired) names for software. It comes from a dictionary search by its creator, Andrew Tridgell, who was looking for a word resembling the acronym SMB.

Samba is open source software under the GNU General Public License. Apart from Linux and many mainstream UNIX variants, it has also been ported to a number of other operating systems, such as AmigaOS and VMS. The SMB protocol allows Windows, DOS, and OS/2 machines to share file systems and printers with each other. As Windows' native protocol is SMB, no third-party software is required for it to talk to a Samba server. This way, a Linux box can be seamlessly integrated to a Microsoft network without being any the wiser.

## SMB / CIFS

Note that in a true fashion-conscious way, the SMB protocol was recently re-dubbed the Common Internet File System (CIFS). For the purposes of this chapter, we'll stick to the traditional SMB notation.

Windows machines natively communicate through the NetBEUI protocol. Instead, Samba uses TCP/IP, the networking *lingua franca* of UNIX, and by extension, the Internet. If your network talks to the Internet, then you probably have set this up already.

# System Requirements

The first requirement for a successful Samba installation is to use a test machine. If things go wrong at some point, this will give you the peace of mind that you would not have, if you used a production server. The software you will need are the GNU utilities tar and gzip. These will allow you to uncompress the Samba source package. To compile, you will need to have the GNU C compiler gcc installed on your machine. You will also need the gawk package, the GNU version of the awk text pattern scanning and processing language. All of these are usually installed along with a Linux distribution. To make sure all of these are present on your system, you can try using the which command. For example, to find the location of the tar command, you would use which tar.

If one of these is missing, you can install it from your Linux distribution CD or get the latest version from http://www.gnu.org.

# Getting and Installing Samba

There are three ways of obtaining Samba. The first one is through a distribution. If you bought or downloaded a Linux distribution, you probably already have Samba. Again, to make sure, use the following commands:

```
# find / -name smbd -print

# find / -name nmbd -print
```

I'll explain what smbd and nmbd stand for shortly. The difference between the command find and the command which is that in this case the former searches through your entire hard drive (by using the /) whereas the latter only searches through your system PATH. This distinction is important because in order to run Samba, the required binaries do not need to be in the path; however, gcc and gawk do need to be or the compilation of Samba will fail.

Given open source software's frenzied development pace, the version you have might be less than fresh. If you don't mind not having all of the latest features and bug fixes, you can go right ahead and jump to the section titled *A Test Configuration*. If not, read on.

# A Note about Upgrades

For each new release, the Samba README file states, "This is the latest stable release of Samba. This is the version that all production Samba servers should be running to apply all current bug-fixes." It's usually advantageous to believe this and upgrade regularly. One caveat, though, is to upgrade your test server first. This server should run the same Linux version as your production server or servers. Furthermore, you would be well advised to wait a week or two after the patches come out before installing the new release on your servers. The Samba mailing list or the comp.protocols.smb Usenet newsgroup (see the *Resources* section at the end of this chapter) are perfect places to find out about the glitches associated with new versions.

Let us look at the two other methods of installation, from a source archive or from a binary package.

# Locating the Source

Point your web browser at http://www.samba.org. This site lists all of the Samba website mirrors. Pick the one that most closely matches your needs. On the site's download page, you'll be offered to download the source or binary package. The following section deals with installing from the source package.

## Compiling and Installing

Once you have the source on your Linux machine's hard drive, it's time to uncompress it:

```
$ tar xvfz samba-latest.tar.gz
```

Now change directory to the samba-x/source directory (at the time of this writing, Samba is at version 2.0.6, so I would type cd samba-2.0.6/source). You now need to use the command su, to give you root permissions in order to compile and install. You then run the script which will configure Samba to compile and install on your system. You may want to run ./configure -help before proceeding, to see the different switches you can use. For convenience, I've included an abbreviated output of that command here:

```
--with-smbwrapper       Include SMB wrapper support
--with-afs              Include AFS support
--with-dfs              Include DFS support
--with-krb4=base-dir    Include Kerberos IV support
--with-krb5=base-dir    Include Kerberos 5 support
--with-automount        Include AUTOMOUNT support
--with-smbmount         Include SMBMOUNT (Linux only) support
--with-pam              Include PAM password database support
--with-ldap             Include LDAP support
--with-nisplus          Include NISPLUS password database support
--with-nisplus-home     Include NISPLUS_HOME support
--with-ssl              Include SSL support
--with-sslinc=DIR       Where the SSL includes are (defaults to /usr/local/ssl)
--with-mmap             Include experimental MMAP support
--with-syslog           Include experimental SYSLOG support
--with-netatalk         Include experimental Netatalk support
--with-quotas           Include experimental disk-quota support
--with-privatedir=DIR   Where to put smbpasswd (/usr/local/samba/private)
--with-lockdir=DIR      Where to put lock files (/usr/local/samba/var/locks)
--with-swatdir=DIR      Where to put SWAT files (/usr/local/samba/swat)
```

Since I wanted to mount SMB shares from Windows machines on my Linux server, here's how I ran configure:

```
# ./configure --with-smbmount
```

And this is an excerpt of the output:

```
creating cache ./config.cache
checking for gcc... gcc
checking whether the C compiler (gcc -O ) works... yes
checking whether the C compiler (gcc -O ) is a cross-compiler... no
checking whether we are using GNU C... yes
checking whether gcc accepts -g... yes
checking for a BSD compatible install... /usr/bin/install -c
checking for gawk... gawk
checking whether gcc and cc understand -c and -o together... yes
checking that the C compiler understands volatile... yes
checking host system type... i686-unknown-linux
...
checking configure summary
configure OK
creating ./config.status
creating include/stamp-h
creating Makefile
creating include/config.h
```

This will create Samba's `Makefile` that tells the compiler how to build the various binaries and where to put them along with various files. Let us now compile with:

```
# make
```

The output you get should resemble this:

```
Using FLAGS =  -O -Iinclude -I./include -I./ubiqx -I./smbwrapper -D_LARGEFILE64_
SOURCE -D_GNU_SOURCE  -DSMBLOGFILE="/usr/local/samba/var/log.smb" -DNMBLOGFILE="
/usr/local/samba/var/log.nmb" -DCONFIGFILE="/usr/local/samba/lib/smb.conf" -DLMH
OSTSFILE="/usr/local/samba/lib/lmhosts"  -DSWATDIR="/usr/local/samba/swat" -DSB
INDIR="/usr/local/samba/bin" -DLOCKDIR="/usr/local/samba/var/locks" -DSMBRUN="/u
sr/local/samba/bin/smbrun" -DCODEPAGEDIR="/usr/local/samba/lib/codepages" -DDRIV
ERFILE="/usr/local/samba/lib/printers.def" -DBINDIR="/usr/local/samba/bin" -DHAV
E_INCLUDES_H -DPASSWD_PROGRAM="/bin/passwd" -DSMB_PASSWD_FILE="/usr/local/samba/
private/smbpasswd"
...
Compiling rpc_server/srv_lsa.c
Compiling rpc_server/srv_lsa_hnd.c
Compiling rpc_server/srv_netlog.c
Compiling rpc_server/srv_pipe_hnd.c
...
Linking bin/nmblookup
Compiling utils/make_printerdef.c
Linking bin/make_printerdef
```

Once that's taken care of, type:

```
# make install
```

The reason for these last two steps is that some people prefer to install applications by hand. The make install command puts the various Samba files in default emplacements that not everybody agrees on. Experts may skip this and copy the binaries and assorted configuration files by hand to where it suits them. Here is an abbreviated output of the command:

```
Using FLAGS =  -O -Iinclude -I./include -I./ubiqx -I./smbwrapper -D_LARGEFILE64_
SOURCE -D_GNU_SOURCE  -DSMBLOGFILE="/usr/local/samba/var/log.smb" -DNMBLOGFILE="
/usr/local/samba/var/log.nmb" -DCONFIGFILE="/usr/local/samba/lib/smb.conf" -DLMH
OSTSFILE="/usr/local/samba/lib/lmhosts"   -DSWATDIR="/usr/local/samba/swat" -DSB
INDIR="/usr/local/samba/bin" -DLOCKDIR="/usr/local/samba/var/locks" -DSMBRUN="/u
sr/local/samba/bin/smbrun" -DCODEPAGEDIR="/usr/local/samba/lib/codepages" -DDRIV
ERFILE="/usr/local/samba/lib/printers.def" -DBINDIR="/usr/local/samba/bin" -DHAV
E_INCLUDES_H -DPASSWD_PROGRAM="/bin/passwd" -DSMB_PASSWD_FILE="/usr/local/samba/
private/smbpasswd"
...
/usr/local/samba/swat/include/header.html
=====================================================================
The SWAT files have been installed. Remember to read the swat/README
for information on enabling and using SWAT
=====================================================================
```

This will install Samba's various components in the right places. This completes the installation from source. You are now almost ready to start Samba for the first time.

## Doing a Binary Installation

On Red Hat, or any Linux distribution supporting the RPM system, a Samba binary install is very easy. You simply download the RPM file and type rpm -i *samba-package*.rpm. Edit smb.conf, and start the daemons by one of the two methods outlined in the next section. That is it. You will find that the main disadvantage of installing at RPM in his way (and installing from your Linux distribution CD) is that the version may be less recent than that of the source download. However, the difference is only days (and sometimes hours) between the release of a new version of Samba and the corresponding RPM. If you listened to my advice and waited before upgrading, you should have no problems getting the most recent release on RPM. The other more important inconvenience of this method is that Samba was compiled on somebody else's machine. As such it is a version of the software that may have options you don't want or need and lack others you *do* need. If we wanted to be paranoid, we could also warn that a pre-compiled version obtained from someone else *could* contain deliberate security holes or a virus.

## A Test Configuration

You need to test whether or not the installation works. To do so, create a configuration file for Samba called smb.conf. If you did a source installation, Samba expects to find this file in /usr/local/samba/lib. In the case of a binary installation, this file is usually located in /etc. This somewhat conforms to the Filesystem Hierarchy Standard (FHS) recommendation for local system configuration files. It is rather convenient as the system configuration files for modern Linux systems are all located in that directory. Note that it is possible to do a source installation that mimics a binary installation. This might be useful if you want to upgrade a binary install with code from the source package. This is done through the configure script I mentioned earlier. For example, to compile Samba while specifying that smb.conf is in /etc, you would type this:

```
# ./configure --with-privatedir=/etc
```

Here is a minimal `smb.conf` file that can be used to test a system:

```
; My Samba test configuration

[global]
netbios name = OFFICE                    ; The Windows network name for the server
workgroup = mynetwork                    ; The name of your Windows workgroup
server string = Linux file/print Server ; The server's network description
```

### Validation

A very good habit to pick up is to use `testparm` and use it often. Part of the Samba suite, `testparm` is a diagnostic tool that makes sure no mistakes are present in `smb.conf`. You should run this before enabling any changes to Samba's configuration. This fine tool is described with more detail in the *Samba's Components* section below.

# Running Samba

Running Samba involves starting two daemons on your server. The `nmbd` daemon's task is to perform machine name lookup and service announcement (Hi! my name is office and these are my shares) on the network. The `smbd` daemon takes care of user authentication and of granting access to shares and services. Note that while there are as many `smbd` daemons as there are client connections on the server, there should only be one active `nmbd` daemon per Samba server.

# Starting Samba with inetd

There are two mutually exclusive ways to start these daemons. The first one involves `inetd` where a new `smbd` daemon is started automatically each time a client requests SMB shares. As such, it tends to be less hungry for memory than using a script. A disadvantage is that it has a slower response time than starting the daemons through scripts. Another big disadvantage, in my view, is that the `smbd` and `nmbd` daemons don't show up in `ps` or `top` outputs. Others may disagree with me on this, as it is assumed that `inetd` will start daemons as needed. However, since Samba can be such a critical service on a network, you may always need to know whether it is running as it should. Using `inetd` would not allow you to install system-monitoring scripts that use `ps` to monitor the Samba daemons. However, should you wish to use this method, or just experiment with it, here's what you need to do:

Add these two services to the file `/etc/services`:

```
netbios-ns 137/udp
netbios-ssn 139/tcp
```

Modify the file `/etc/inetd.conf` as well:

```
netbios-ns dgram udp wait root /usr/local/samba/bin/nmdb
netbios-ssn stream tcp nowait root /usr/local/samba/bin/smdb
```

Then, do `killall -HUP inetd` to restart these services. This should start Samba on your server.

# Starting Samba through a Script

The simplest way to start Samba with standalone daemons is to input the following commands:

```
# /usr/local/samba/bin/nmbd -D
# /usr/local/samba/bin/smbd -D
```

Then, if one needs to restart the daemons after modifying `smb.conf`, he would need to type:

```
# killall -HUP nmbd
# killall -HUP smbd
```

Typing four commands each time one wishes to restart Samba could get tiresome very quickly. Fortunately, a convenient little script named `smb.init` is located in the `packaging/RedHat` directory of the Samba source archive. If you did a binary installation, this script is probably already installed. In any case, I've reproduced it here:

```
#!/bin/sh
#
# chkconfig: 345 91 35
# description: Starts and stops the Samba smbd and nmbd daemons \
#              used to provide SMB network services.

# Source function library.
. /etc/rc.d/init.d/functions

# Source networking configuration.
. /etc/sysconfig/network

# Check that networking is up.
[ ${NETWORKING} = "no" ] && exit 0

# Check that smb.conf exists.
[ -f /etc/smb.conf ] || exit 0

# See how we were called.
case "$1" in
  start)
    echo -n "Starting SMB services: "
      daemon smbd -D
      daemon nmbd -D
      echo
      touch /var/lock/subsys/smb
      ;;
  stop)
    echo -n "Shutting down SMB services: "
      killproc smbd
      killproc nmbd
```

```
        rm -f /var/lock/subsys/smb
        echo ""
        ;;
   status)
        status smbd
        status nmbd
        ;;
   restart)
      echo -n "Restarting SMB services: "
        $0 stop
        $0 start
        echo "done."
        ;;
   *)
      echo "Usage: smb {start|stop|restart|status}"
      exit 1
esac
```

Though the script is for the Red Hat distribution, it can be rather easily adapted to other Linux flavors. You need to place this script (usually renamed as smb) in the /etc/rc.d/init.d directory. You then must issue the command: ln -s /etc/rc.d/init.d/smb /etc/rc.d/rc3.d/S91smb, this will create a link to the script if you start in run level 3. Just replace the number with the correct run level for your system. You would use run level 5, if you have a graphical login screen on Red Hat. Linux will then be able to automatically start Samba at reboot. Incidentally, you do not need to set this up if you used rpm to install Samba.

The smb script allows you to do four things:

❑   ./smb start – starts the nmbd and smbd daemons.

❑   ./smb stop – stops the daemons.

❑   ./smb restart – stops and then restarts the daemons.

❑   ./smb status – display the status of the daemons in the format

```
smbd (pid 8722 30840 27482 21005 18077 7229) is running...
nmbd (pid 625) is running...
```

On some distributions such as SuSE, you may get instead:

```
Checking for service smb: OK OK
```

# Did Everything Work?

If Samba started without errors, type the following command:

   # **nmblookup OFFICE**

This will give the following output:

```
Sending queries to 10.255.255.255
10.0.0.2 OFFICE<00>
```

Though your IP address will vary, getting a similar response means that your server is functional. If you did not get such a response, it's possible your `smbd` and `nmbd` daemons did not start properly, so try to start them again. It is also possible that the `smb.conf` file is incorrect or that Samba could not find it. Make sure it's in the right directory for the type of installation you performed. For instance, if you did a source installation, Samba will not work if `smb.conf` is in `/etc`, unless your forced the `configure` script to read it from there during the installation, as shown earlier.

# Getting Answers to Problems

It is possible that Samba still doesn't work. In that case, here is my own troubleshooting procedure, which has solved most of my problems. The philosophy of this method is *speed*. Reading manuals and books is the obvious, ideal way to really understand a problem and how to solve it. However, this takes time and requires a focused mind. Personal experience has shown that both these resources may be scarce when the main production server goes down and a solution has to be found *now*.

To use this method successfully, you will need three things: paper, a pen, and access to the Internet.

- ❏ If you get an error message from the console, jot it down or redirect it to a text file, which could be printed or attached to an e-mail.

- ❏ If you don't get an error message, you need to have a look at your system logs.

- ❏ The file `/var/log/messages` is the standard log file for your system. You can use `tail /var/log/messages` to display the ten most recent log entries. Jot down anything suspicious.

- ❏ Samba also has log files. The file `log.nmb` relates to `nmbd` and `log.smb` contains the entries concerning the `smbd` daemons. If you did a binary install, they are located in `/var/log/samba/`. For a source installation, they are located in `/usr/local/samba/var`. Again, use `tail` to display the recent entries. Advanced users may also want to exploit open source software's greatest asset: access to the source code. Programmers usually comment their code and an explanation of just what the error message means may be found this way. A search of the Samba source code with the error message as search key may yield useful results.

- ❏ Fire-up your favorite web browser and point it at http://www.deja.com. Among other things, this site contains a searchable archive of all the lore of Usenet newsgroups. Use the suspicious error messages as search keys. This is an extremely useful site to troubleshoot computer-related problems.

- ❏ If you did not find an answer to your query, do not despair. Go to http://www.samba.org and pick a mirror site close to your location. Go to the archives section of the site. This section contains an archive of the different Samba mailing lists. Perform a search with your error message as search key.

- ❏ If you still cannot find a satisfactory solution, I suggest you subscribe to the Samba mailing list (instructions for that are provided in the Resources section of this chapter). In my experience, well-formulated questions posted to that forum get prompt, well-formulated answers. Here is a (fictitious) example:

```
Hello,

I'm a new user and I've just installed Samba 2.0.6 on Red Hat Linux 6.1 with
kernel 2.2.13 on a P3-500Mhz. The machine has a 12 Gig hard drive and 128 megs of
RAM. For some reason, Samba won't start. I did a source install. It compiled and
installed without complaints. But when I try to do ./smb start from
/etc/rc.d/init.d, nothing happens. I've checked my logs and here are what I think
are relevant messages:
From /var/messages:
...
From /usr/local/samba/var/log.nmb:
...
From /usr/local/samba/var/log.smb:
...
My smb.conf file looks like this:
...

I've browsed the documentation on the Samba website and did a search on deja.com,
but didn't find any information about this. Does anyone have any words of wisdom
to share?

Thanks in advance!
```

Notice the amount of information I've given at the beginning of the message. I give out the server's Samba version, the operating system name and version and the specifications to my machine. This kind of information will enable the reader to help me more efficiently. Note that you can also post your message to a Usenet newsgroup such as `comp.protocols.smb`. This may indeed double your chances of getting an answer.

# Samba Security

A security level determines how users will access shares and services on the server. There are in fact four of these levels (share, user, server, domain), I'll focus on the two more common (and useful) security levels for Samba. Note that just like starting Samba, you cannot mix and match. You will need to decide which of the security levels you will use for your entire server.

An important fact to keep in mind about Samba security is that it does *not* replace Linux's own file system security. For instance, even if a user has been granted permission by Samba to delete a file, if Linux's own permissions don't grant this privilege, he will not be able to delete it. So the Linux security settings take precedence over Samba security settings.

## Share Level

In this level, security is on a per-share basis. That is, each share has an associated password. The advantage of share-level is that it's not necessary to create accounts for each user on the network. The disadvantage is that a user only needs to know a share's password to access it. Using this mode also leads to potential confusion as a share could have several passwords corresponding to different access schemes. For example, the share `bigdrive` could have the password `mackenzie` for read-only access, but to gain read-write access, a user would need to use the password `calhoun`.

## User Level

This is the default and most commonly used security level for Samba. To access a share, a user must supply a username/password combination that is present in the file smbpasswd and the user must have access to the share specified in the smb.conf file. As in the case of the /etc/passwd file, smbpasswd contains a list of all the users of the Samba server along with their passwords.

User names on Windows network can be up to 255 characters in length, which is seldom the case in Linux. This can get confusing as a user known as Richard-Alexander33120 on the NT server might be able to log in with richa on the Linux server. As a solution, Samba offers the possibility of using a user map. The map is a simple text file looking like this:

```
# This is my Samba user name map
marc = marc Admin
jonathan = jonathan
bernard = bernard
pe = pierre-etienne boss
systems = @systems-group
```

On the left is the Linux user name and on the right there are the corresponding Windows user names. Notice that a user can have several aliases. The last line shows that it is possible to map a Windows NT group to a Linux username.

This is activated by adding the following line to smb.conf:

```
username map = /usr/local/samba/lib/my_users.map
```

The user name map can be placed anywhere on the server; I suggest keeping it in the same directory as smb.conf.

## Server Level

With this level of security, the Samba server does not validate the passwords against its own smbpasswd file. Instead, it asks another server to validate them. Such a server can be another Linux Samba server, a Windows NT Primary Domain Controller (PDC) or a Windows 2000 PDC on the network. In large networks with many servers, this is a very useful feature, which allows for all passwords to be kept in a central location for all servers. It can be activated by adding the following lines in the [global] section of the smb.conf file:

```
security = server
password server = MYPDC
```

In the second line, you can specify the location of the password server. Using server-level security still requires creating Linux user accounts on the Samba server, as they are needed for file manipulations. It is worth mentioning that a drawback of this method does exist; if your PDC goes down, the shares on your Samba server will be inaccessible.

## *Domain Level*

At first glance, this is almost identical to server-level security. The difference is that Samba is now a fully fledged member of the Windows domain. This means that the network's PDC does the validation of the username and password. Since version 2.0.6 you don't even need to specify the PDC as Samba will try to find it.

# Configuring Samba: a Tour of smb.conf

The file smb.conf is the configuration file for Samba. Its syntax intentionally resembles that of Windows .ini files. Below is a sample configuration for a small network. I will explain what these key/value pairs mean afterwards.

```
[global]
netbios name = office
workgroup = WORKGROUP
server string = Linux file/print Server
hosts allow = 10.0.0.
security = user
encrypt passwords = yes
guest account = nobody
local master = no
domain master = no
preferred master = no
os level = 0
# Performance
socket options = TCP_NODELAY SO_KEEPALIVE SO_SNDBUF=4096 SO_RCVBUF=4096
printing = lpr
print command = /usr/local/bin/lpr -P%p %s -r
lpq command   = /usr/local/bin/lpq -P%p
lprm command  = /usr/local/bin/lprm -P%p %j
load printers = yes

[homes]
comment = Users' home folders
hide dot files = yes
browseable = no
writable = yes

[printers]
comment = All Printers
browseable = yes
printable = yes
guest ok = no
writable = no
create mode = 0700

[software]
comment = Software
path = /home/software
read only = yes
guest ok = yes
```

```
[design]
comment = Design group's folder
path = /home/design
read only = no
public = no
valid users = @design yves simon
read list = yves simon
write list = @design
create mask = 0770
directory mask = 0770
force group = design
```

First I will divide up this file into its relevant sections.

# [global]

Settings placed in this section are the global settings used throughout the server. You can override many of these by specifying a different value under the individual share.

| | |
|---|---|
| netbios name = office | The NetBIOS name of the server. Setting something different than the Linux host name can get confusing very quickly, so I advise against it. This is obviously essential. |
| workgroup = WORKGROUP | The name of your Windows workgroup or NT Domain. |
| server string = Print/file Server | The NetBIOS server string that appears in the Network Neighborhood. |
| hosts allow = 10.0.0. | A security measure that limits which IP addresses can access the server. You can specify a range like this, or give a comma-separated number of addresses. This key/value pair works like a bit mask, so that in this instance, all computers having IP addresses in the 10.0.0.1 to 10.0.0.255 would be allowed to access Samba. If the Samba server is not in this range of addresses, add localhost after the subnet address to prevent problems. |
| security = user | The security level for this server. This is the most important setting for Samba and the valid settings are: user, share, server, and domain, which have been explained earlier. |
| encrypt passwords = yes | Turn password encryption on. Windows 98 and Windows NT 4 SP3 use encrypted passwords by default. |

| | |
|---|---|
| `guest account = nobody` | The guest account is for users who don't have an account of their own on the server. Nobody is quite a good account to use, or you could create another dummy account. |
| `local master = no` | Prevents Samba from participating in local master browser elections on a subnet. If this is set to `yes`, it doesn't mean that the server will become the master browser, just that it will take part in the elections. |
| `domain master = no` | Prevents Samba from attempting to become a master browser for the domain. If you set this to `yes` and if you have an NT PDC, then they will both claim to be the master browser for the domain and you will get some strange behavior. The default setting is `auto`, which means it only attempts to become the domain master if the server is set to be the PDC. |
| `preferred master = no` | Prevents Samba from initiating an election when starting. If set to `yes`, then Samba will attempt to become the domain master on startup. If the `domain master` key is set to `yes`, then this will guarantee that the server becomes the master browser, unless other servers are set up in the same way. If `preferred master` is set to `auto`, then it only tries to initiate an election, if `domain master` is set to `yes`. |
| `os level = 0` | This sets the chance Samba has of becoming a local master browser. Setting it as zero means that it will always lose, setting it to 65 will ensure it wins against any NT server. |
| `socket options = TCP_NODELAY SO_KEEPALIVE SO_SNDBUF=4096 SO_RCVBUF=4096` | This option should increase your performance. It transmits packets immediately even if the data unit is smaller than the minimum payload size. This should not be used when accessing a Samba server across the Internet, and should be used with care when accessed over different network segments, as it increases network load. Increasing the send and receive buffer (`SO_SNDBUF` and `SO_RCVBUF`) values can yield a small but appreciable speed increase. Since this is dependent on a great many things such as network topology, equipment and operating systems, the effectiveness of this option is relative. More information on this can be found in the `setsocketopt` and `smb.conf` man pages. |

| | |
|---|---|
| `Printing = lpr` | Specifies the printing system used. Samba does not have its own printing system and so you can use any system you like – in this case the `lpr` system that comes with Linux |
| `print command =`<br>`/usr/local/bin/lpr -P%p %s -r` | This is the actual command used to print a document. This is using the `lpr` system and the `%` characters are escape characters. These are detailed later. |
| `lpq command =`<br>`/usr/local/bin/lpq -P%p` | Specifies what print queue control command Samba sends to Linux. This is the command used to display the print queue so it can be viewed from a Windows client. |
| `lprm command =`<br>`/usr/local/bin/lprm -P%p %j` | This is the command Samba sends to Linux in order to delete jobs from the print queue. |
| `load printers = yes` | Loads the printers list from `/etc/printcap`. If you set this as `no`, you can specify each printer you wish to share individually, which is useful if you have printers that you want to give different share permissions to. |

# [homes]

This share is used to provide a different share for each authenticated user, a home directory in effect. As each user is required to have an account on the server, then each person accessing the share will have a home directory on the server. This is where the share points to when accessed, which provides some privacy and security to the files saved there by the user.

| | |
|---|---|
| `hide dot files = yes` | This hides any file starting with a dot, as these are usually UNIX configuration commands and not something a Windows users needs to see. |
| `browsable = no` | This hides the share from all but its owner. If you want the share to appear to all when the server is clicked on in Network Neighborhood, then set this to `yes`. |
| `writable = yes` | This allows write access to the share. If you are setting up a public share, you would most probably set this as `no`. |

# [printers]

This is a share used when you want to provide access to all of the printers provided in the /etc/printcap file. They will each be available from this share.

| | |
|---|---|
| printable = yes | The default value for this is no, if it is set to yes then you are declaring that this service is a printer. |
| guest ok = no | This is synonymous with public = no. This means that guest access is disallowed, or a valid user name and password has to be entered to use this printer. |
| create mode = 0700 | This sets what the Linux file permissions will be of any file created on or copied to this drive. The example means that only the owner of the file or print job can amend it. |

# [software]

This example share could be used to store installable software images.

| | |
|---|---|
| read only = yes | This means what it says. The share cannot be written to or altered in any way by the client accessing it. This is useful for shares such as this where software is available to install on the client's local drive. |
| path = /home/software | The location on the file system that this share allows access to. |

# [design]

This is the share of a department in an organization. Members of the department (in this example, the design department) have full read and write access to the share. Two users from another department have been granted read-only access to the share.

| | |
|---|---|
| valid users = @design user1 user2 | This option allows you to specify which users can access this share. Using the @ symbol means that you can specify an entire Linux group of users. In this case, members of the group design and two other users will be able to access this share. |
| read list = user1 user2 | These two users can read files from the share, but they cannot write to it. |
| write list = @design | The members of the group design can read and write files in this share. |
| force group = design | This ensures that files created in this share are accessible to members of the design group. |

Note that for this to work, I needed to set a directory mask that modifies the Linux file system permissions to allow group read in this directory.

# Using Samba as a Primary Domain Controller

For some applications, such as simple file-and-print sharing, it is possible to have a Windows network without Windows servers. You can set Linux up with Samba so that it acts as a Primary Domain Controller (PDC). However, this feature is still quite new and at the time of writing, there is no provision for a Samba Backup Domain Controller. It is also important to mention that Windows NT clients can benefit from rudimentary PDC support in the 2.0.x versions of Samba. This last functionality is improving with each new release of Samba and is supposed to reach maturity in the forthcoming 2.1 release of Samba.

An excellent resource to keep close at hand is the Samba PDC FAQ available at: http://us1.samba.org/samba/docs/ntdom_faq/samba_ntdom_faq.html or at another Samba mirror.

To make a Samba server a PDC, we need to make some modifications to the smb.conf file outlined earlier. These changes are outlined below:

```
# This goes into the [global] section of smb.conf
# A Samba PDC must use the following settings:
security = user
encrypt passwords = yes

# This machine will be used to validate logons from Windows clients
domain logons = yes

# I want this server to rule the NT domain. These keys will make sure it will.
os level = 255
preferred master = yes
domain master = yes
local master = yes

# We need to create this new share
[netlogon]
comment = Netlogon share
path = /usr/local/samba/netlogon
public = no
create mask = 0644
directory mask = 0755
```

Note that I'm not using roaming user profiles here. A roaming user profile allows an NT user to use any machine on the network. The user data (preferences, application data, wallpaper, and so on) are stored on the server. We use Microsoft Outlook at our company and many users' mailboxes and personal folders can be over a hundred megabytes in size. I quickly found out that even on a 100-megabit network, the performance became unacceptable. For those of you in a different situation, the FAQ listed above can show you how to set up roaming profiles.

A client machine using Windows 9x can now log in on this server. Windows NT machines however need a bit more work. In addition to user accounts, NT functions with the concept of *workstation* accounts. On an NT server, the client would use the **Create a Computer Account in the Domain** feature in the Windows NT networking setup. Samba handles this differently through the creation of a Linux user account corresponding to the machine in question. Here is what I did on my Linux server to add my NT workstation to the domain:

```
# useradd PC02$
```

PC02 is the name of my NT machine. I needed to add a $ at the end. Note that the machine name must be all capitals. You must also use a blank password for this account.

```
# smbpasswd-a -m PC02
```

This adds my machine to the smbpasswd file. The −m switch tells the program that it is a machine account we're adding. The $ postfix is not needed.

The NT workstation now has an account on the domain.

# Samba Components

In the true spirit of UNIX, Samba is not a big executable file but rather a group of programs each doing a specific task. I have already talked about the two most important components, smbd and nmbd. Now let me introduce to you some other programs that are part of the suite. Exhaustive man pages have been written for each of these and you can type man samba to get an overview of many of these commands.

## smbstatus

This prints out the status of connections to the Samba server. It tells which user is using what service and so on.

```
Samba version 2.0.6
Service      uid       gid      pid      machine
------------------------------------------------
jonathan     jonathan  syst     2609     pc01   (192.168.0.14) Mon Aug 23 09:04:36
1999
software     marc      design   11821    pc02   (192.168.0.21) Sat Aug 14 21:00:49
1999
intranet     bernard   syst     31915    pc03   (192.168.0.30) Thu Aug 19 07:45:53
1999
Locked files:
Pid     DenyMode    R/W      Oplock          Name
--------------------------------------------------------
2609    DENY_WRITE  RDONLY   EXCLUSIVE+BATCH  /home/jonathan/report2.pdf  Wed Aug
25 15:14:02 1999
11821   DENY_NONE   RDWR     NONE            /home/software/vi.zip    Fri Aug 27
10:30:54 1999
31915   DENY_DOS    RDONLY   EXCLUSIVE+BATCH /usr/local/html/faq.html  Sat Aug 28
11:52:21 1999

Share mode memory usage (bytes):
    1043864(99%) free + 4056(0%) used + 656(0%) overhead = 1048576(100%) total
```

This output is divided into three sections. The first section tells us which user on which machine uses which service. For example, the user marc from machine pc02 is using the share software. The machine pc02 has an IP address of 192.168.0.21. The share was last accessed by the client on Saturday, August 14 at 21:00:49 1999 EST. The second section lists the files in use by these users. Notice that the users permissions on these shares (the DenyMode and R/W columns) are displayed. If we come back to our marc user, he is working on the file vi.zip and has read/write (RDWR) permissions. The last section displays the amount of system resources used by Samba.

### About Oplocks

Notice in the output of smbstatus, the Oplock column. An opportunistic lock or oplock is a file caching mechanism that increases read/write performance. Unfortunately, some Windows 9x clients may experience problems with oplocks. To diagnose whether this is the case, you will need to monitor your log.smb file. If some entries resemble this:

```
[1999/11/04 11:15:, 0] smbd/oplock.c:oplock_break(734)
oplock_break: receive_smb timed out after 30 seconds.
```

You are experiencing problems with oplocks. While the Samba team is working on solving this problem once and for all, you can turn off oplocks for that share by using oplocks = false. This will give a performance hit of about 30%. However, not doing this could lead to file corruption for the affected machines.

Another possibility is that your problem has the form of a faulty network hub or switch. If you connect a Windows machine experiencing oplock problems and the Samba server *alone* on the same hub and the problems disappeared then all you need to do is replace the faulty equipment.

# smbadduser

If you decide to skip using a user map, a useful script is available in the Samba source package, smbadduser, which allows you to add a user to the smbpasswd file. The syntax is:

```
smbadduser UNIXusername:sambausername
```

You will then be prompted for a password for the new user. This password will be the one used to log on to the Windows NT network, if your Samba server is not the network's PDC. It is very important that you make sure the password on the Samba machine and the NT server are one and the same or logging on the network will fail.

# smbmount and smbumount

Available if you compiled Samba with the --with-smbmount option. The smbmount command will allow you to mount SMB shares on the network in a manner similar to NFS, whereas the smbumount (spelt correctly) command will enable you to unmount SMB shares. For more information see the *Clients – Linux* section.

# smbtar

This is a backup tool that dumps SMB shares directly to a tape, and restores shares from a tape. This is the syntax:

```
smbtar [<options>] [<include/exclude files>]
```

And these are the various options:

```
Option:              (Description)              (Default)
  -r                 Restore from tape file to PC  Save from PC to tapefile
  -i                 Incremental mode             Full backup mode
  -a                 Reset archive bit mode       Don't reset archive bit
  -v                 Verbose mode: echo command   Don't echo anything
  -s <server>        Specify PC Server
  -p <password>      Specify PC Password
  -x <share>         Specify PC Share             backup
  -X                 Exclude mode                 Include
  -N <newer>         File for date comparison
  -b <blocksize>     Specify tape's blocksize
  -d <dir>           Specify a directory in share \
  -l <log>           Specify a Samba Log Level    2
  -u <user>          Specify User Name            jonathan
  -t <tape>          Specify Tape device          tar.out
```

# smbclient

This component is very useful for general testing. Its syntax is as follows:

```
smbclient service <password> [options]
```

And these are the options:

```
  -s smb.conf            pathname to smb.conf file
  -O socket_options      socket options to use
  -R name resolve order  use these name resolution services only
  -M host                send a winpopup message to the host
  -i scope               use this NetBIOS scope
  -N                     don't ask for a password
  -n netbios name.       Use this name as my netbios name
  -d debuglevel          set the debuglevel
  -P                     connect to service as a printer
  -p port                connect to the specified port
  -l log basename.       Basename for log/debug files
  -h                     Print this help message.
  -I dest IP             use this IP address to connect to
  -E                     write messages to stderr instead of stdout
  -U username            set the network username
  -L host                get a list of shares available on a host
```

```
-t terminal code        terminal i/o code {sjis|euc|jis7|jis8|junet|hex}
-m max protocol         set the max protocol level
-W workgroup            set the workgroup name
-T <c|x> IXFqgbNan      command line tar
-D directory            start from directory
-c command string       execute semicolon separated commands
-b xmit/send buffer     changes the transmit/send buffer (default: 65520)
```

Among other things, this program allows access to SMB shares through a UNIX console, print files on shared printers and send messages to Windows clients if they have Windows Messaging installed. However, smbclient really shines when used as an installing or troubleshooting tool. For instance, if you want to find out what shares the server called office has, you would type:

```
# smbclient -L office -N
Added interface ip=10.0.0.2 bcast=10.255.255.255 nmask=255.0.0.0
Domain=[MY_DOMAIN] OS=[Unix] Server=[Samba 2.0.6]

        Sharename      Type        Comment
        ---------      ----        -------
        hp5si          Printer     HP Laserjet 5si printer
        hp4000n        Printer     HP Laserjet 4000n printer
        fax            Printer     Network Fax
        company        Disk        Public folder
        applications   Disk        Software files
        intranet       Disk        Intranet files

        Server                     Comment
        ---------                  -------
        GROUPWR                    NT Exchange server
        OFFICE                     Linux file and print server
        ATTIC                      Linux backup server

        Workgroup                  Master
        ---------                  -------
        Workgroup                  Administrator
```

smbclient gives the network configuration for the machine, followed by its software configuration, then the description of each share. The last two categories respectively display the names and description of the servers on the Windows network and the identity of the Primary Domain Controller for the network.

# testparm

As we have seen before, this diagnostic tool makes sure no mistakes are present in Samba's configuration. You should run this before any changes to the smb.conf file are enabled.

```
Load smb config files from /etc/smb.conf
Processing section "[homes]"
Processing section "[laserjet]"
Processing section "[fax]"
Processing section "[shared]"
Processing section "[software]"
Processing section "[design]"
Processing section "[contracts]"
Loaded services file OK.
WARNING: You have some share names that are longer than 8 chars
These may give errors while browsing or may not be accessible
to some older clients
Press enter to see a dump of your service definitions…
```

If a mistake is made, such as entering the text "This is a comment" without commenting it out with a #, testparm would display:

```
Load smb config files from /usr/local/samba/lib/smb.conf
params.c:Parameter() - Ignoring badly formed line in configuration file: This is
 a comment
```

Typing errors are also caught by testparm. If the writable = yes key/value pair in the [homes] share has an erroneous extra t, testparm would give the following message:

```
Processing section "[homes]"
Unknown parameter encountered: "writtable"
Ignoring unknown parameter "writtable"
```

You can then go and correct the mistakes in the smb.conf file.

# swat

As these lines are being written, the web is in great fashion. Many software companies are releasing products that can be accessed through a web browser; even word processors can be made accessible over the Internet. However, there is, as yet, no official effort to make SMB shares available through web browsers. However, two different but identically named projects called smb2www have achieved some measure of success in this endeavor. You can look up the details of these projects at http://us3.samba.org/samba/smb2www/ and www.scintilla.utwente.nl/users/frank/smb2www/.

The Samba team has so far concentrated their efforts on the system administration side. A tool named the **Samba Web Administration Toolkit** or **swat** allows Samba to be configured through a web browser. In short, it is a graphical front end to smb.conf. Purists may balk at this, but there are at least three very good reasons for such a tool to exist:

❏ While remote configuration through telnet is one of Linux's greatest assets, this is extremely secure. Since some organizations severely restrict or even ban telnet, swat still makes it possible to configure and administer Samba remotely.

❏ swat makes it possible for someone to administer Samba without learning the Linux command-line. One important benefit is that the local Linux expert can at last call in sick as the system is now relatively easy to configure.

❏ The Samba team is integrating more and more documentation into swat.

This is the swat home page:

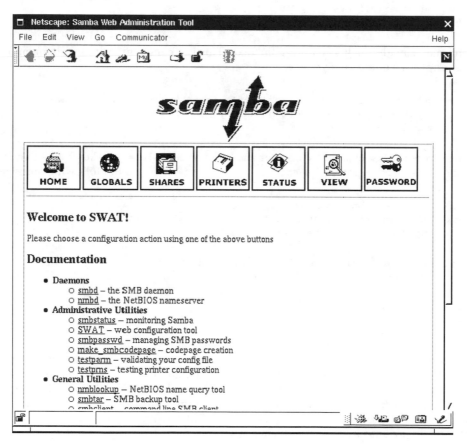

Since it is part of the suite, installing Samba installs swat. To use it, you will need to enable it on your system. Before proceeding any further though, you may want to test-drive it first. The site http://anu.samba.org/cgi-bin/swat/ contains a demo of swat you may experiment with. If you decide you like swat and want to enable it, you can do so by adding the following line to the file /etc/services.

```
swat 901/TCP
```

The actual number port number can be anything under 1024. The Samba documentation suggests using 901 because it is not officially used by any other application. Note that using a port number above 1024 can be a potential security risk on some systems. If you decide to use something other than 901 (for security reasons, for example), browse through /etc/services to make sure this port number is not already taken.

Once the new service is created, you need to add the following line to /etc/inetd.conf:

```
swat stream tcp nowait 400 root /usr/local/samba/bin/swat swat
```

As we have seen earlier, the inetd daemon would then start swat each time a client requests the service. Note that the directory specified in this line is for the installation of Samba from the source code. If you performed a binary installation, swat can usually be found in /usr/sbin or sometimes /usr/share. The last step is to restart inetd with killall –HUP inetd.

Now swat should be accessible from your web browser. You can fire it up and point it to (say) http://yourservername:901 and the application main window should appear. It is very simple to use, you navigate it like a web site – it is, after all, just that. It also has an exhaustive help system, which gives it a low learning curve.

# Clients for a Samba Server

This section describes how to configure the three operating systems most likely to connect to a Samba server.

## The Windows Operating Systems

> **The one important condition to use Samba for these operating systems is to have TCP/IP installed and configured. Furthermore, Many versions of Windows come with the NetBIOS and IPX/SPX protocols installed by default. Not removing them may lead to communication problems with the Samba server.**

A new feature was introduced by Samba 2.0.4. It allows Windows NT clients to modify the Unix file permissions on a share as if it were an NT server. While interesting, this is still in development and evolving with each new release of Samba. A document describing this in more detail is available here: http://us1.samba.org/samba/ftp/docs/textdocs/NT_Security.txt. Otherwise, these clients can talk to a Samba share with no further configuration.

# Linux

Most Linux distributions do not support the SMB protocol natively. While this trend is changing with distributions such as Red Hat 6.1 supporting SMB "out of the box", it is not yet widespread. To enable such support, you'll need to customize your server's kernel. The procedure is not that difficult but varies from server to server. The reason for this is quite simple – people customize kernels to get the best performance out of Linux. So they will only add in support for their server's hardware and the features they require. This may have been done for you when you installed your Linux distribution, as most installation tools will compile the kernel to your specific requirements. If not, then the procedure I give below is a quick-and-dirty one that has worked for me on several machines. While it will give you a good idea on how to proceed, it may not work for you. Before we go forward, I suggest you have a look at your distribution documentation. It usually contains a section on compiling kernels. Furthermore, the Kernel HOWTO located at http://www.linuxdoc.org/HOWTO/Kernel-HOWTO.html can be an invaluable resource.

First, you need to obtain a copy of the Linux kernel source and install it on your system. You may get it from your distribution CD or if you wish to get a newer version http://www.kernel.org should provide what you need.

Though it can be done from the system console, I find the graphical kernel configuration utility much easier to use. Start the X Window System and then in an xterm, go to the /usr/src directory and cd to the kernel source subdirectory (for example, it's linux on my server).

Now type:

```
# make xconfig
```

This will start the GUI kernel configuration tool. Now click on Network File Systems.

| Linux Kernel Configuration | | |
|---|---|---|
| Code maturity level options | IrDA subsystem support | Partition Types |
| Processor type and features | Infrared-port device drivers | Native Language Support |
| Loadable module support | ISDN subsystem | Console drivers |
| General setup | Old CD-ROM drivers (not SCSI, not IDE) | Sound |
| Plug and Play support | Character devices | Additional low level sound drivers |
| Block devices | Mice | Kernel hacking |
| Networking options | Watchdog Cards | |
| QoS and/or fair queueing | Video For Linux | |
| SCSI support | Joystick support | Save and Exit |
| SCSI low-level drivers | Ftape, the floppy tape device driver | Quit Without Saving |
| Network device support | Filesystems | Load Configuration from File |
| Amateur Radio support | Network File Systems | Store Configuration to File |

This will bring up the following window:

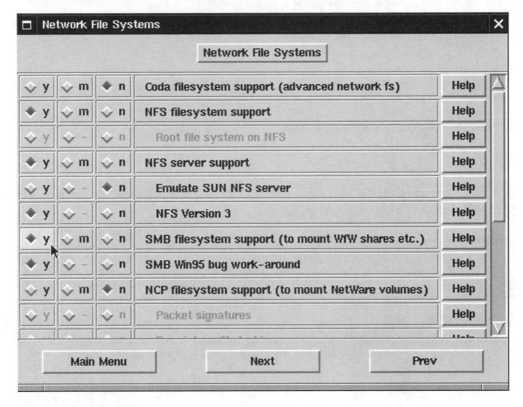

Set the two SMB options to y. Click on Main Menu. Once there, click on Save and Exit. Now in your xterm window, type:

```
# make dep
```

This will prepare the kernel for compilation. After that, type:

```
# make bzImage
```

This will compile the kernel itself. Once that's done, you will need to install the new kernel with

```
# make install
```

This will prepare your system for the new kernel. In my case, I like to keep a copy of the previous kernel, just in case the kernel compilation and installation fails. Go to the /usr/src/linux/arch/i386/boot directory. Among other things, there should be a file named bzImage there. Copy it to /boot with the name bzImage-2, like so:

```
# cp bzImage /boot/bzImage-2
```

Now go to the /etc directory. You will need to edit a file called `lilo.conf`. This file tells Linux which kernel to use when booting. Change the following line:

```
image=/boot/bzImage
```

To this one:

```
image=/boot/bzImage-2
```

Save and close the file. Then, run the command:

```
# /sbin/lilo
```

This will enable the changes you've made and load the new kernel on reboot. You can now reboot with a command such as this:

```
# shutdown -r now
```

This is one of the few times where you will have to reboot your machine. Just about every other part of the operating system can be restarted without rebooting using the `kill -HUP` command.

## Connect to a Share

Once support for SMB is part of the kernel, connecting to shares is very simple. You need to use `smbmount`, which we briefly met earlier on in the chapter. It has the following syntax:

```
smbmount //server/share mountpoint [options ...]
```

And the various options are:

```
-d debuglevel            Set the debuglevel
-n netbios name.         Use this name as my netbios name
-N                       Don't ask for a password
-I dest IP               Use this IP to connect to
-E                       Write messages to stderr instead of stdout
-U username              Set the network username
-W workgroup             Set the workgroup name
-t terminal code         Terminal i/o code {sjis|euc|jis7|jis8|junet|hex}
```

For example, I have a Windows NT server named NT01 that has a share named `bigdrive`. I possess a user account on the NT server and my username is `john`, my password is `flakel`. To connect to this share from Linux, I would need to type:

```
# smbmount //NT01/bigdrive/ /myshare john%flakel
```

Note that the /myshare directory must exist on the Linux machine before mounting the share. By default, only root may use this command. Since smbmount makes sure that the user has the necessary rights to mount the directory on the mount-point, it would be reasonably safe to make it available to all users. To disconnect the share, the process is very similar:

```
# smbumount //NT01/bigdrive/ /myshare
```

Please note that since the 2.0.6 release of Samba, smbmount has been changed to be used together with the standard mount command:

```
mount service mountpoint [-o options,...]
```

The options are as follows:

```
username=<arg>                  SMB username
password=<arg>                  SMB password
netbiosname=<arg>               source NetBIOS name
uid=<arg>                       mount uid or username
gid=<arg>                       mount gid or groupname
port=<arg>                      remote SMB port number
fmask=<arg>                     file umask
dmask=<arg>                     directory umask
debug=<arg>                     debug level
ip=<arg>                        destination host or IP address
workgroup=<arg>                 workgroup on destination
sockopt=<arg>                   TCP socket options
scope=<arg>                     NetBIOS scope
guest                           don't prompt for a password
ro                              mount read-only
rw                              mount read-write
```

This command is designed to be run from within /bin/mount by giving the option '-t smbfs', for example:

```
mount -t smbfs -o username=chuck,password=motdella //qonos/test /data/test
```

The example command above would mount the remote share test on the machine named qonos on the local mount point /data/test. The username used to mount the share is chuck, with the password motdella. This method allows the unmounting of SMB shares just like any other mounted partition. So to unmount /data/test, you would now use

```
# umount /data/test
```

Samba version 2.0.6 also allows Linux to mount SMB shares at startup. This is done by editing the /etc/fstab file which contains the definition of all the mounted filesystems on the machine. For instance, adding this line to /etc/fstab:

```
//qonos/test /data/test smbfs username=chuck,password=motdella 0 0
```

Would mount /data/test at startup. If I wish to mount a share from a Windows 98 machine, I could add this to fstab:

```
//win98pc/share-drive /var/win98-share smbfs defaults 0 0
```

This would mount the remote share share-drive from the machine win98pc to /var/win98-share on the local machine. It is assumed that the share doesn't have any password associated with it, as is often the case with shares from Windows clients.

# Summary

In this chapter, we have seen how to set up Samba as an alternative to Windows NT for file and print services on a network. We have also seen how to troubleshoot a Samba installation, and below are listed various web sites and texts from which you can get more help. We have seen how to use Samba together with NT, and shown how it may be possible to substitute NT completely with a Samba Primary Domain Controller. A user-friendly front end to Samba named swat has also been discussed. Finally, we covered the issues relating to configuring Windows and Linux as clients to access a Samba server.

# Resources

Here is a non-exhaustive list of resources relevant to the different software packages described in this chapter. Most of them have been invaluable during my installation of Samba and the writing of this chapter. I do believe you will find them useful yourself.

### Books

Eckstein, Robert, David Collier-Brown, and Peter Kelly. *Using Samba.* O'Reilly, 1999. ISBN 1-56592-449-5.

Carter, Gerald, and Richard Sharpe. *Teach Yourself Samba in 24 Hours.* Sams, 1999. ISBN 0-672-37609-9.

Garms, Jason et at. *Windows NT Server 4 Unleashed.* Sams, 1997. ISBN 0-672-31002-3

Welsh, Matt, Matthias Kalle Dalheimer, and Lar Kaufman. *Running Linux, 3rd Edition.* O'Reilly, 1999. ISBN 1-56592-469-X.

Toth, Viktor T. *Linux: A Network Solution for Your Office.* Sams, 1999. ISBN 0-672-31628-5.

### Web Sites

The list of mirrors for the official Samba website. Unsurprisingly, it is the most important online resource on the topic.
www.samba.org/

This is the website for official Samba mailing lists.
lists.samba.org/

A ZDNet article showing that Samba outperformed Windows NT in a benchmark test.
www.zdnet.com/sr/stories/issue/0,4537,396321,00.html

Another ZDNet benchmark where Linux/Samba are favorably compared to NetWare 5.0.
www.zdnet.com/sr/stories/issue/0,4537,398022,00.html

An excellent guide to Samba by Benoit Gerrienne.
www.ping.be/linux-and-samba

### Mailing List

This is the address to use if you wish to subscribe to one of the Samba mailing lists. The most useful for the new user is the samba list. You can subscribe by sending an e-mail to this address containing *subscribe samba <Your Full Name>*. listproc@samba.org

### Usenet

This is the main Samba newsgroup on Usenet. Along with the mailing list, you should subscribe to this.
comp.protocols.smb

This is a smaller newsgroup on the topic.
Mailing.unix.samba

And another one centered on Linux.
linux.samba

# 3

# Case Study: a Linux Workgroup Server

## Introduction

Picture a company growing at a very fast pace, which means that it needs to acquire new computers and update its software. If that company wishes to remain on the right side of the law, it will need to purchase the software along with server licenses to keep pace with the new equipment's software requirements. Now like many others, the company has unilaterally cast its lot with proprietary software. This means mounting license costs on both the client and server ends. Let us pretend that the management in this company is wondering if open-source software could fulfil some of its needs, while reducing licensing costs.

For many small to medium-sized companies or departments within large organizations, Linux can be both an inexpensive and effective workgroup server. As we have seen in the previous chapter, the Samba suite allows it to provide robust file and print services to Windows clients. In this case study, you will see a more fully-fledged Samba installation. We will then go one step further and provide two additional services to a company's Windows users: fax serving and backup serving. These applications are available thanks to Linux's building block approach that makes it easy to find new ways to use existing software or to interface it with other applications and produce powerful solutions for the enterprise. An introduction to a software package called VNC will round off this chapter. VNC allows remote, cross-platform access to Linux, UNIX, Macintosh and Windows computers.

This chapter will cover:

- ❑ A real-world Samba installation
- ❑ Integrating fax serving software and Samba
- ❑ A Linux "live backup server"
- ❑ Virtual Network Computing (VNC)

# File and Print Serving

Let us consider that our company has around eighty workstations running either Windows NT or Windows 95. In addition to these, there are a couple of UNIX boxes and a Windows NT server providing groupware services through Microsoft Exchange. The IT department of this company undertakes a project to provide transparent file and print services to the Windows clients through a Linux/Samba combination.

The new system could consist of three Samba servers:

- ❑ The first is the main production server, called `office`. This is the machine where Windows users store their files and through which they use the networked laser printers. Though unrelated to this chapter, the server also provides DNS services using BIND (see Chapter 9), an intranet server using Apache (see Chapter 5), and an e-mail server using qmail (http://www.qmail.org). This server also serves as a fax server from which users could send faxes as easily as they use a standard printer. This system uses Samba and its installation is described in detail below.

- ❑ A second server, called `attic`, is the backup server. It stores two days of backed up files from the production server and copies them to a tape drive each day. The installation of the `attic` server is described in more detail in the *Live Backup Server* section later in the chapter.

- ❑ The last server, imaginatively dubbed `test`, is a test platform. Every new Linux kernel and application is installed here first. This allows one to play with the latest toys without jeopardizing the production servers. This server can also be used to try to reproduce bugs that might have been generated on the two other servers. Doing this can help determine whether the problem is software related, (and if so, where – the kernel or the application) or hardware-related.

# Setting up the Shares

This is the `smb.conf` file for the server `office`.

The User-Level security authentication was used for this server. This permits certain independence between the NT and Samba servers, which can come in handy during a new installation. This means that any user authentication problem lies with a configuration problem in Samba. The drawback is that user accounts/passwords need to be manually replicated across both servers.

```
[global]
netbios name = office
workgroup = MY_WORKGROUP
server string = Linux file/print Server
hosts allow = 10.0.0.
security = user
encrypt passwords = yes
guest account = nobody
nt acl support = no
local master = no
domain master = no
preferred master = no
os level = 0
# Performance
socket options = TCP_NODELAY SO_KEEPALIVE SO_SNDBUF=4096 SO_RCVBUF=4096
printing = lpr
print command = /usr/local/bin/lpr -P%p %s -r
lpq command   = /usr/local/bin/lpq -P%p
lprm command  = /usr/local/bin/lprm -P%p %j
load printers = no

[homes]
comment = Users' home folders
hide dot files = yes
browseable = no
writable = yes

[laserjet1]
comment = Laserjet printer, room 026
postscript = yes
path=/tmp
printable = yes
writable = yes
create mode = 0700
browseable = yes
guest ok = no

[laserjet2]
comment = Laserjet printer, room 103
postscript = yes
path=/tmp
printable = yes
writable = yes
create mode = 0700
browseable = yes
guest ok = no
valid users = ceo, cfo, vp1

[shared]
comment = Shared folder
path = /home/shared
read only = no
public = yes
create mask = 0777
```

```
[software]
comment = Software
path = /home/software
read only = yes
public = yes

[design]
comment = Design group's folder
path = /home/design
read only = no
public = no
valid users = @design yves simon
read list = yves simon
write list = @design
create mask = 0770
directory mask = 0770
force group = design
```

Notice that it is a modified version of the smb.conf file provided in the preceding chapter, different lines are shown in bold. Let's look at the new shares in more detail:

# [laserjet1] and [laserjet2]

Our example company has two laser printers. One, called laserjet1, is accessible by any employee in the building. The second printer, laserjet2, is restricted to only three users. Such a situation requires Samba to handle printers differently from the previous chapter. Instead of using the [printers] share, which automatically loads every printer with the same configuration, each printer here has its own share definition.

The [laserjet2] share has a valid users key that regulates who can access it (in this case, the users ceo, cfo and vp1). Notice that the last line of the [global] section was changed from:

```
load printers = yes
```

to:

```
load printers = no
```

This is mandatory in order to use this method. Restricting access to a printer works just like a disk share: you use the valid users key to tell Samba which users or groups can print to it.

Before moving on, it might be relevant to explain a bit more about how Samba enables access to printers. We saw in the previous chapter that Samba does not have a printing system of its own and instead calls whatever system is installed on Linux that allows it to print. In the case of the standard lp system, Samba calls it and sends the relevant information as command line arguments:

```
/usr/local/bin/lpr -P%p %s -r
```

The $-P$ switch indicates which printer to use. So the printer chosen by the Windows user replaces the %p variable. %s is the actual file to be printed and $-r$ tells Linux to delete the file from the spool directory after it has been printed.

Other very good printing systems exist, such as LPRng (http://www.astart.com/lprng/LPRng.html) or the Common UNIX Printing System, or CUPS (http://www.cups.org/). If you decide to use one of them instead of lp, you need to tell Samba through the printing key in the [global] section of smb.conf. The syntax of the following lines:

```
print command = /usr/local/bin/lpr -P%p %s -r
lpq command   = /usr/local/bin/lpq -P%p
lprm command  = /usr/local/bin/lprm -P%p %j
```

may also need to be modified.

Of the two systems mentioned, only LPRng is currently supported this way. However, this does not mean that CUPS is unusable with Samba. It means you need to consult that system's documentation to find out how to interface it with Samba.

# [design]

This share is used by some of our engineers. They create new CAD models that are sometimes consulted by people in the drafting department. This is a good example of a complex share; here are the details:

| | |
|---|---|
| valid users = @design yves simon | Members of the UNIX group design and two other users will be able to access this share. |
| read list = yves simon | These two users in the drafting can read files from the share, but they cannot write. |
| write list = @design | The members of the group design can read and write files in this share. |
| force group = design | This ensures that files created in this share are accessible to members of the design group. Notice that for this to work, I needed to set a directory mask that modifies the Linux file system permissions to allow group read in this directory. |

This concludes our treatment of the shares definitions for the office server. As you can see, Samba offers a great deal of flexibility in how it makes resources available on a network. You are encouraged to peruse the smb.conf man page to see how Samba could be further customized to meet your organization's own needs. The shares for attic are described in the *Live Backup Server* section later in this chapter.

# Fax Serving

In addition to printers and files, modems can be useful resources to share across a network. In concert with fax management software, Samba can be configured to provide this as well. There are several open source fax software applications available. We will focus on mgetty+sendfax, a popular application that allows the sending and receiving of faxes on Linux machines.

> *Another popular faxing package not covered here is HylaFAX (available at http://www.vix.com/hylafax). You are of course invited to experiment with both to find out which is best for you.*

You can obtain the source package for mgetty+sendfax at http://www.leo.org/~doering/mgetty/ .

You will also need to have the ghostscript package (available at http://www.cs.wisc.edu/~ghost/) with fonts on your server along with the NetPBM package (available at ftp://wuarchive.wustl.edu/graphics/graphics/packages/NetPBM/). These utilities will allow mgetty+sendfax to perform different graphic file manipulations on the faxes. These are usually present on any Linux distribution CD-ROM. For my own installation (Red Hat 6.0), I proceeded as such:

I mounted my Red Hat CD-ROM with:

```
# mount /dev/cdrom /cdrom
```

The directory /cdrom is an arbitrary decision on my part. You can mount your CD-ROM anywhere you like. Remember though that the mount command will not create the mount directory. It needs to be created beforehand or the mount procedure will fail. Then, cd to the /cdrom/i386/RedHat/RPMS directory (this may vary from version to version). This contains the optional binary packages included with Red Hat Linux.

```
# rpm -i ghostscript-5.10-10.i386.rpm
# rpm -i ghostscript-fonts-5.10-3.noarch.rpm
```

As for NetPBM, it is probable it was installed on your Linux server by default, and to make sure type which pbmtext. If it isn't installed, you may need to get the source code from the FTP site mentioned above.

Once you have downloaded the mgetty+sendfax archive on your server's hard drive, decompress it. Change directory to mgetty-1.0.0 and copy the file policy.h-dist to policy.h. This sets your init strings of the modem (the string of characters sent to a modem to initialize it), the fax number, the communication ports on which your modems are installed, and so on.

I left the file as it was. I found it more useful to use the runtime configuration files mgetty.config and sendfax.config which we will come to in a moment.

You can now compile the software with:

```
# make
```

And install it with:

```
# make install
```

You now need to add an entry in your server's /etc/inittab file for mgetty+sendfax. On my server, I added this:

```
S0:23:respawn:/usr/local/sbin/mgetty -C auto -x 4 /dev/ttyS0
S1:23:respawn:/usr/local/sbin/mgetty -C auto -x 4 /dev/ttyS1
S2:23:respawn:/usr/local/sbin/faxrunqd
```

The first two lines correspond to the modems connected, respectively to COM ports 1 and 2, which, in the Linux world, are known as ttyS0 and ttyS1. The third line is for a daemon that scans the fax queue and sends the new additions.

A little configuration still needs to be done. You'll need to edit the following six files:

| | |
|---|---|
| /usr/local/etc/mgetty+sendfax/mgetty.config | This is mgetty's configuration file. |
| /usr/local/etc/mgetty+sendfax/faxrunq.config | The fax daemon's configuration file. |
| /usr/local/etc/mgetty+sendfax/sendfax.config | The configuration file for sending faxes. |
| /usr/local/etc/mgetty+sendfax/fax.allow | The list of users allowed to use the fax service. |
| /usr/local/etc/mgetty+sendfax/faxheader | This is the header added to each fax you send. |
| /usr/local/lib/mgetty+sendfax/new_fax | When a fax comes in, call this script. |

I've included my own files. They should be self-explanatory.

### /usr/local/etc/mgetty+sendfax/mgetty.config

```
# mgetty+sendfax's configuration file

speed 115200
rings 1
login-time 60
answer-chat "" ata CONNECT \c \r

# This is the debug level, i.e. how verbose the logs will be.
debug 4
```

```
# This sets the local fax's phone number.
fax-id 418 555-5555

# This sets under which ID the fax programs will operate.
fax-owner root
fax-group uucp
fax-mode 0640

# This is where I set the init string for each modem
# I use ordinary 3Com/US Robotics Courier modems.

# In the Linux world, ttyS0 corresponds to COM port 1
port ttyS0
init-chat "" atz0&f1&k1s27.5=1s56=128

# ttyS1 corresponds to COM port 2
port ttyS1
  init-chat "" atz0&f1&k1s27.5=1s56=128
```

### /usr/local/etc/mgetty+sendfax/faxrunq.config

```
# This file configures the fax daemon

# No need for good news.
success-send-mail n

# Bad news, though, are relevant.
failure-send-mail y

#  I abhor clutter. This deletes the successfully sent faxes.
delete-sent-jobs y

#  This is where the log file is located.
acct-log /var/log/acct.log

# This indicates that two modems are available to send faxes.
fax-devices ttyS0:ttyS1

#  This is the log file for the fax daemon.
faxrunqd-log /var/log/faxrunqd.log

#  This tells the system how many log files to keep.
faxrunqd-keep-logs 5
```

### /usr/local/etc/mgetty+sendfax/sendfax.config

```
# This is sendfax's configuration file

# I crave information. You should too.
verbose y

# I have a modem on my server's two COM ports.
fax-devices ttyS0:ttyS1
```

```
# This is my outgoing fax number.
fax-id 418-555-5555

# This is the dial-out prefix I use.
dial-prefix ATD

# If the transmission of the page fails, try three times
max-tries 3

# If the third try fails (moan!) continue with the next page.
# For some situations, this may not be a good idea to put 'Y
# the recipient will get an incomplete transmission (or nothing at all).
# Putting 'N'will abort after three tries (in this case) and report an error.
max-tries-continue y
```

**/usr/local/etc/mgetty+sendfax/fax.allow**

```
# The list of Linux user accounts who can send faxes.
bernard
jonathan
marc
```

**/usr/local/etc/mgetty+sendfax/faxheader:**

```
# This puts a standard fax header at the top of each transmitted page
# @T@ will be replaced by the fax recipient's name at runtime, @P@ will be
# replaced by the current page number and @M@ by the total number of pages for
# the transmission.

Fax  from:  MY COMPANY INC. 418 555-5555    To: @T@    Page: @P@ of @M@
```

The script new_fax is available in the samples/new_fax.all sub-directory of the mgetty+sendfax archive. Here is what it looks like on my system:

**/usr/local/lib/mgetty+sendfax/new_fax:**

I only had to customize one line in this script. The | lpr -h -Php5000n is the command to print a new fax (using lpr), without a header page (-h) using the printer called hp5000n in the /etc/printcap file.

For some, it may be necessary to modify other lines (such as the print resolution). Note that this script was written with Hewlett-Packard's Laserjet series of printers in mind. Using it with laser printers from other vendors could require some tweaking.

```
#!/bin/sh

# make sure $PATH includes the pbm tools!
PATH=/usr/bin:/bin:/usr/local/bin

HUP="$1"
SENDER="$2"
PAGES="$3"
```

```
G3TOPBM=g32pbm
shift 3
P=1

while [ $P -le $PAGES ]
do
        FAX=$1
        RES=`basename $FAX | sed 's/.\(.\).*/\1/'`

        if [ "$RES" = "n" ]
        then
                STRETCH="-s"
        else
                STRETCH=""
        fi

        $G3TOPBM $STRETCH $FAX \
        | pnmscale -xysize 2479 3508 \
        | pgmtopbm -fs \
        | pbmtolj -resolution 300 \
        | lpr -h -Php5000n

        shift
        P=`expr $P + 1`
        rm -f $FAX
done
exit 0
#--
#\ klaus@snarc.greenie.muc.de--kweidner@physik.tu-muenchen.de--2:246/55.4
```

Once everything is configured, you can restart inittab with:

```
# kill -HUP 1
```

Your server is now ready to receive faxes. They will be sent to /var/spool/fax/incoming.

You now need to add the following to your /etc/printcap file:

```
fax:\
        :lp=/dev/null:\
        :sd=/var/spool/lpd/fax:\
        :if=/usr/local/etc/mgetty+sendfax/faxfilter:\
        :sh:\
        :sf:\
        :mx#0:\
        :lf=/var/spool/lpd/fax/fax-log:
```

The printcap file is the printer configuration file for Linux. Every printer your Linux server uses, whether it is directly connected to it or available on the network, is usually detailed in that file.

# Fax Serving — Integration with Samba

You can send and receive faxes from the server. Now it's time for the useful part: allowing users to send some from their computers. To do so, I use a very useful piece of software called Respond. It's written by Gert Doering and available at http://www.boerde.de/~horstf/ in a Windows zip file named Respond.zip. It is composed of two parts:

❑ On the Linux server-side, there is a Perl script called printfax.pl.

❑ On the Windows client side, there are two programs, CONFIG.EXE and RESPOND.EXE.

When a print job is sent to the fax, Samba calls printfax.pl that communicates with RESPOND.EXE on the client's PC. The user is prompted for a fax number to send the file to and then the fax is sent on its way. Respond has several features like delaying the sending of faxes, a phonebook, and a sending history.

## Installing — Server Side

You will need to download printfax.pl and copy it to /usr/local/bin. Make the file executable using the command:

```
# chmod +x printfax.pl
```

You will need to add the following share to your smb.conf file:

```
[fax]
comment = Fax (Samba)
postscript = yes
path = /tmp
printable = yes
print command = (/usr/local/bin/printfax.pl %I %s %U %m; rm %s) &
public = yes
writable = yes
create mode = 0700
browseable = yes
guest ok = no
```

Let's look some of this share's key-value pairs:

❑ The line postscript = yes tells Samba to send the print job as a Postscript file. This is the format mgetty+sendfax uses to send the fax.

❑ The key-value pair printable = yes means that this share is a printer (or printer-like device in this case).

❑ The print command line is in fact a two-line script. The breakdown is as follows:

| | |
|---|---|
| /usr/bin/local/printfax.pl | This calls a Perl script that sends faxes. |
| %I | This is the IP address of the client machine. |
| %s | This variable is the print job to be faxed. |

| | |
|---|---|
| `%U` | This is the username of the current user. |
| `%m` | This is the NetBIOS name of the server machine. |
| `rm %s` | This will delete the spooled print job after it is faxed. |

## Installing — Client Side

Download the latest Respond zip file from the website. Unzip its contents to a directory. If you add `RESPOND.EXE` to the StartUp folder of the Start Menu, you will see the following icon in the system tray:

It's now time to add the fax printer to your Windows client. Follow the normal procedure by using the Add Printer Wizard in Control Panel:

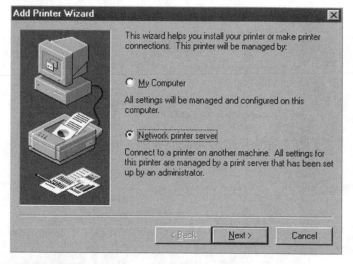

Select the fax printer on your Samba server. You will then get the following message:

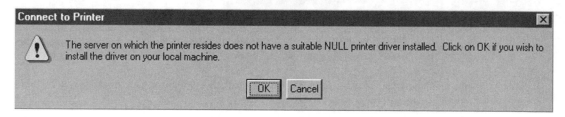

Click on OK. The Add Printer
Wizard will now ask which printer
driver to use. Select any
Postscript-capable driver you like.
In my experience, the HP Laserjet
4/4M Plus PS works fine, others
also recommend the Apple
Laserwriter Plus driver.

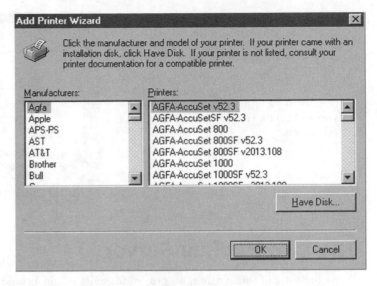

You should now have the fax printer installed:

fax on OFFICE

It's now possible to send a fax from
any Windows application that's able to
print. Say you want to send a letter
from Word to your friend Robert
McPerson. Type your letter and then
print it using the fax printer. The
following window will appear:

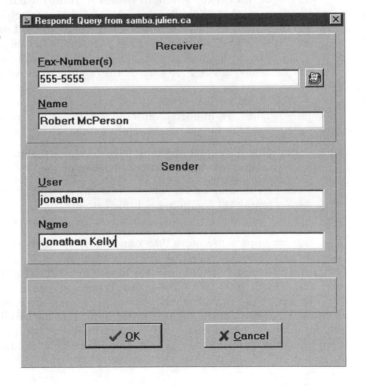

Input the necessary information and click OK. This will tell the server to send the fax. If you believe you'll send faxes to Mr. McPerson regularly, click on the Rolodex-like icon at the right of the Fax-Number(s) box and bring up the history/phonebook list. This allows you to build a simple contact list of fax recipients.

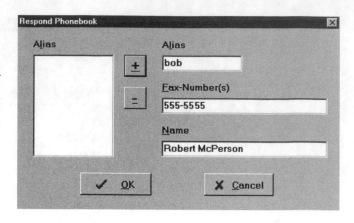

# The Live Backup Server

At the time of this writing, no provisions exist within Windows servers, or indeed Samba, for a server-side recycle bin or trashcan. When a file on the server is deleted, it is gone forever. Some undelete software packages do exist, but they rarely have a hundred percent recovery rate. But what about the good old backup tape? It has its place and a very important one indeed in any organization's backup solution. However, restoring data from the tape can take hours and in this day and age, that is just too slow. A quicker way to achieve efficient backups, however, does exist. We are fortunate to live in a time of inexpensive hard drives with huge storage capacities, and as such, it is now possible to assemble a cheap, dedicated backup server that would keep live copies of the previous day's data. If Samba were used, it can be arranged for users to securely restore their files themselves. The hardware that is required is as follows:

❑ A small computer or an old server. CPU horsepower is not important in this application. This is an important difference with NT, where you would need a moderately powerful machine for such lightweight a task.

❑ One or several big hard drives. You need enough for the operating system and one or several multiples of a day's backed-up data.

❑ Depending on the amount of data you wish to backup, a fast network card may be an important component of this system.

You may opt to use more than one server. This may be safer if security between departments is important. Please note that this system should *not* be used in place of a tape backup solution. It is rather a complement to such a system. One of the reasons such a server was set up was this: taking a backup directly from production servers took far too much time and in some cases had some impact on performance and availability. For example, our main database server had to be down for a good portion of the night in order to for it to back itself up. The backup server solves this problem as a hard drive dump on a fast network takes relatively little time. It can then copy the data to tape during the day without bothering the production servers.

Technically, such a server is relatively easy to set up. You will need to do a new Linux and Samba installation on a dedicated machine. Remember to ensure SMB support in the kernel. Here is the `smb.conf` file for the `attic` server:

```
[global]
workgroup = MY_WORKGROUP
server string = Live backup server
hosts allow = 10.0.
security = user
encrypt passwords = yes
tc/smbpasswd
local master = no
local master = no
domain master = no
preferred master = no
wins support = no
wins proxy = no
os level = 0
socket options = TCP_NODELAY IPTOS_LOWDELAY SO_KEEPALIVE SO_SNDBUF=4096
SO_RCVBUF=4096
load printers = no

[homes]
comment = Backup user share
hide dot files = yes
path = /var/backup/office/home
browseable = no
read-only = yes
```

What we aim to accomplish here is to allow users to access a read-only version of their home share, as it was the day before. To do so, the users need to be created on the attic server as well. This can be done quickly by copying the `/etc/passwd` file from the production server to this machine.

Then, change the users' home directories from `/home/user` to `/var/backup/office/home/user`.

Then to back-up the server, we use the push method: mount the shares you want to backup with `smbmount` and copy their contents on the backup server (so the client "pushes" its data on the server). You can automate this process with a `cron` script.

So on the production server we can use use a script such as `backup_script` (included below), which can be copied to the `/etc/cron.daily` directory. On Red Hat systems, this directory may contain scripts that will be run once per day by the operating system. If you decide to use this script, remember to render it executable by using `chmod +x filename` or it will not run.

Another option is to use `crontab -e`. This allows you to directly edit the `cron` configuration and provides much finer control on when you want your scripts to be run. You could then add:

```
00 19 * * * /usr/local/sbin/backup_script 2>/var/log/backup-error-
log
```

This would run `backup_script` located in `/usr/local/sbin` each day at 19:00 and pipe the error messages from that script to the `backup-error-log` file located in `/var/log`.

Here is the script in question:

```
#!/bin/csh

# Script to back up the / and /home directories to attic
# Written by Marc Gauthier, Modified by Jonathan Kelly
# Last Modified: December 20, 1999

echo "Starting backup `date`">/var/log/backup-log

cd /
tar clf - .|(cd /var/backup/office;tar xf -)

cd /home
tar clf - .|(cd /var/backup/office/home;tar xf -)

echo "End of backup `date`">>/var/backup/log_backup
```

In this script, we are taking a backup of two of the server's partitions (the `/` and the `/home`). These partitions are slices of a hard drive or complete hard drives (just like C: or D: drives in the Windows world). For instance, if we use the `df` command on the `office` server, we would get:

```
Filesystem          1k-blocks       Used Available Use% Mounted on
/dev/hda1             995115      116557    827152  12% /
/dev/hda5            5242407      608133   4362872  12% /usr
/dev/hda6             995115      126338    817371  13% /var
/dev/sda1            8566007     5759672   2362140  71% /home
attic:/var/backup1/ 10069923     5887052   3660299  62% /var/backup
```

So the script above would not take a backup of `/usr` or `/var` even though they are below `/` in the file system hierarchy.

Then, if users want to access yesterday's files, they just need to access their home share on this server! This simple application is an example of the flexibility combined with the power of Linux scripts.

Would we wish to store two days of backups on the `attic` server, all that's needed it to install an additional drive and add the following script called `transfer-day2` to `attic`'s `crontab`:

```
#!/bin/csh

# Script that clears the 2nd day backup on the third day and transfers the
# data from the first day to the 2nd day
# Written by Marc Gauthier, Modified by Jonathan Kelly
# Last Modified: December 16, 1999
```

```
echo "Deleting / on backup2 `date`">/var/log/log-transfer-day2
rm -rf /var/backup2/office/slash/*
echo "Deleting home on backup2 `date`">>/var/log/log-transfer-day2
rm -rf /var/backup2/office/home/*

echo "Transfering Day 1 of / to Day 2 `date`">>/var/log/log-transfer-day2
mv -f /var/backup1/office/slash/* /var/backup2/office/slash
echo "Transfering Day 1 of /home to Day 2 `date`">>/var/log/log-transfer-day2
mv -f /var/backup1/office/home/* /var/backup2/office/home

echo "Transfer Completed `date`">>/var/log/log-transfer-day2
```

So with `crontab -e`, add the following line:

```
0 18 * * * /usr/local/sbin/transfer-day2
```

So this would make Linux fire up the script at 18h00 every day.

# Deployment

The final part of deploying a new system is of course to make it available to users. This entails configuring client machines and work colleagues shown how the system works. A useful tool to help achieve this is called Virtual Network Computing (VNC). It has been developed by AT&T Laboratories at Cambridge. You can download it from http://www.uk.research.att.com/vnc/. It is available for many platforms including Linux and Windows.

Here is an excerpt for the VNC webpage:

*It is, in essence, a remote display system which allows you to view a computing 'desktop' environment not only on the machine where it is running, but from anywhere on the Internet and from a wide variety of machine architectures. (...) For this simple mode of operation, you could achieve a similar effect by installing an X server on your PC. The important factors which distinguish VNC from other remote display systems such as X are as follows: No state is stored at the viewer. This means you can leave your desk, go to another machine, whether next door or several hundred miles away, reconnect to your desktop from there and finish the sentence you were typing.(...) It is small and simple. (...)It is truly platform-independent. A desktop running on a Linux machine may be displayed on a PC. Or a Solaris machine. (...) It is sharable. One desktop can be displayed and used by several viewers at once, allowing CSCW-style applications.(...)It is free! You can download it, use it, and redistribute it under the terms of the GNU Public Licence.*

The best way to understand VNC is through an example.

A support technician in an organization receives a call from a colleague. He has recently received a Linux workstation and claims his web browser is unable to access the Internet. Having installed VNC on all machines on the network, our technician decides to use that system to help his colleague.

The first step is to start a VNC server on the Linux workstation. From his Windows machine, the technician telnets to the Linux box:

```
[tech@bigstation]$ vncserver

You will require a password to access your desktops.

Password: ********
Verify: ********
xauth:  creating new authority file /home/tech/.Xauthority

New 'X' desktop is office.mynetwork.com:1

Creating default startup script /home/tech/.vnc/xstartup
Starting applications specified in /home/tech/.vnc/xstartup
Log file is /home/tech/.vnc/office.mycompany.com:1.log
```

This creates a VNC session on the Linux machine. The technician can now start a VNC viewer on his own workstation:

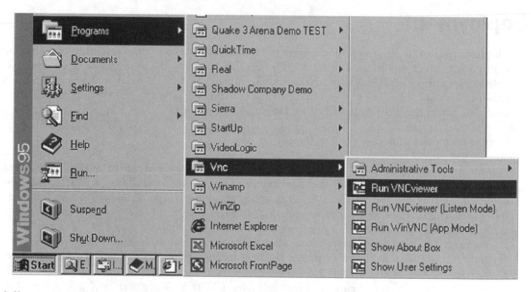

The following window appears:

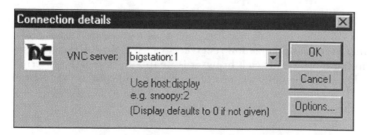

Since there is an active VNC session on `bigstation`, the technician gets a password prompt:

Entering the correct password brings up a VNC window containing a remote desktop:

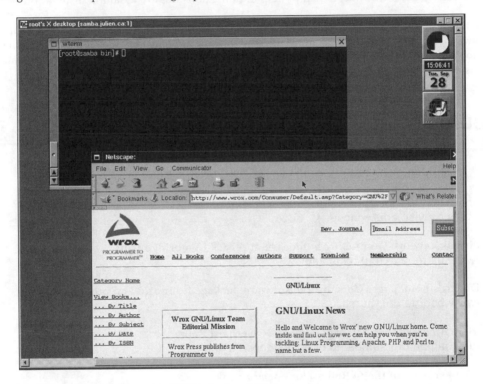

Once the technician is done using VNC, he can kill the server using:

```
$ vncserver -kill :1
```

on the Linux workstation. Note that the VNC website contains a lot more documentation and FAQs on the topic. Hopefully, this example demonstrates VNC's potential as a support tool. If we apply this to a Samba server deployment, VNC could be used to remotely show users how to access their shares and send faxes.

# Summary

This chapter has demonstrated the setup of a real-world Samba server. We have seen that resource sharing through Samba is extremely flexible and can be fine-tuned to meet most organization's requirements. The chapter then has shown how Samba can be extended with other open source software and offer new features to users. Fax serving functionality was added to Samba, allowing Windows users on a network to send faxes from their computer. The concept of live backup servers was introduced, where an inexpensive Linux machine can reduce the server downtime of a backup solution. As a value-added feature, integrating Samba to such a system allows users to access yesterday's versions of their files in case of accidental deletion. To conclude the chapter, a software package called VNC was introduced to help organizations deploy a Samba installation.

While the system introduced in this chapter offers features that are competitive with proprietary software, all of its software components are open source. This means that software and licences costs for this system are zero. It is also able to run on much lower end machines than similar systems on Windows or Solaris machines.

# Resources

Here are a some Internet resources that were helpful in writing this chapter.

### Web

The Ghostscript PostScript homepage.
http://www.cs.wisc.edu/~ghost/

The Virtual Network Computing homepage at AT&T Cambridge Labs.
http://www.uk.research.att.com/vnc/

Gert Döring's homepage. Contains the software package Respond and other useful files.
http://www.boerde.de/~horstf/

The original *Faxing with Samba* document by Gerhard Zuber.
http://us2.samba.org/samba/ftp/docs/textdocs/Faxing.txt

The online version of the O'Reilly *Using Samba* book.
http://us2.samba.org/samba/oreilly/using_samba/

This is the mgetty+sendfax homepage. It contains a FAQ, a lot of useful documentation and a link to a newsgroup archive on the subject.
http://alpha.greenie.net/mgetty/

### Mailing List

You can use this address to subscribe to the mgetty+sendfax mailing list. Send it an empty e-mail. It will answer with instructions on how to subscribe:
mgetty-request@muc.de

# 4

# Linux, The Internet, and Free Software

The last two chapters should have gone some way to making the case for Linux in your server room. You've witnessed at first hand how a free operating system and a piece of free software are able to synthesize one part of Windows NT's functionality almost perfectly, and in the remainder of the book you'll see many other examples of this type. We'll be introducing a few of them in this chapter.

Even presented with this compelling evidence, though, people accustomed only to commercial software products tend to come up with some very reasonable questions. "Where exactly does free software come from?" "Can I be sure that free software is reliable and secure enough for my needs?" "How can I be sure that any free software I adopt will continue to be supported and developed in the future?" For the answers, we need to examine the relationship between free software and the Internet, and how the two have developed together.

The Internet blurs geography: contacting and exchanging information with other people has become incredibly easy. It is also a natural agent of *disintermediation* – the elimination of the middleman. As such, it has enabled the formation and cooperation of technical communities, whose output has in turn gone to enrich the Internet that spawned them. It's a virtuous circle, and one of its chief products is a variety of reliable free software.

# "iFreeSoft"

Long disdained (perhaps rightly so) as the output of hobbyists and college students, as unpolished, unsupported, and unworthy of serious consideration, free software was rarely mentioned in serious conversation except with derision. With a few exceptions (notably the high-quality GNU family of products from the Free Software Foundation), most free software was the work of one or two individuals. Much of it was unpolished with sparse documentation, and user-unfriendly in the extreme. Crucially, it was usually free only in terms of price – source code was typically not available – so it was impossible to see what was going on under the covers. From a business perspective, it was trustworthy for no more than the most trivial tasks.

If truth be told, these criticisms can still be applied to a considerable quantity of free software – PC-based freeware (for Windows and DOS), in particular, is frequently 'closed-source', and retains the problems mentioned above. However, the Internet is a wind of change blowing through the world of *truly* free software, allowing software developers to cooperate easily regardless of their geographical location. Where support for free software existed before, opportunity has arisen and been taken to improve the quality of programs and broaden the scope of projects being attempted. The free software applications we'll examine in this book have seen steady improvement in all of the areas highlighted above; the mistake many people make is to think that the UNIX-based free software of today is the same unreliable stuff they came across some years ago.

What we see today is, to coin a term, "iFreeSoft": free software in the age of the Internet. Perhaps the closest analogy is with airplanes before and after the invention of the jet engine. It would be a mistake to dismiss a modern jet fighter as nothing more than a World War I biplane, just because we have failed to understand how the jet engine has revolutionized aviation. The Internet has acted as an enabling technology for developers: Internet-based tools have evolved to let them communicate, control the versions of their software, review each other's work, and so on.

## Why Do They Do It?

Just stating that developers *can* do this, however, does not adequately explain *why* they should choose to do such a thing. One of the powerful motivating factors for programmers to participate in the development of free software has been the extremely innovative set of software licenses that have been drawn up to accompany it, typified by the prescient GNU General Public License we discussed in Chapter 1.

> *As you've seen, the term 'open source' is also used to describe free software, and its introduction has had the effect its creators desired: it removes the opportunity for confusion with old-style freeware, and thereby rids itself of any stigma attached to it. People who sniffed at the mention of free software now pay to attend conferences on open source.*

It is the free software licenses that have 'closed the circuit' and unleashed creative energy. In general, software developers do not mind giving their work away (for one thing, it allows them to demonstrate their skills to their peers), but they *do* mind being exploited. If there was a chance that someone else could use their work, make money from it, and in the process prevent them from using or extending their own software, most programmers would not even bother working. But the terms of the free software licenses we see are such that the software written by a developer is more or less guaranteed to remain publicly available to all, including the developer himself. It is the license that provides the final incentive for sharing.

In a sense, the wheel has come full circle. Early Internet-related software, such as Sendmail, (the most dominant e-mail software even today) and BIND (the most widespread domain name service), has always been open source, although the term didn't exist when they were developed. Now once again, we see high-quality free software available for Internet applications. Without the Internet, open source would have been just a good idea. The Internet has made open source practical and workable.

## How Can It Pay?

The Internet's capacity for changing things has extended to the software market. In economists' terms, the marginal cost of software is zero: it costs nothing to create the second copy of a piece of software, though the cost of producing the first copy is significant. Commercial software vendors need a way to recoup the initial costs of software development, and have found it in the form of software licenses and legislative backing against 'piracy'. What the Internet has done with free software is to spread the initial cost of software development over many part-time, volunteer programmers.

The model being adopted by many of the companies producing open source software is to *give away* their products, charging instead for the support they provide. The rationale for this is that greater volume and a larger user base will generate sufficient support income to (at least) compensate for the sacrificed margins. This argument is expanded eloquently by Eric Raymond in his article *The Magic Cauldron*, which can be found in many places on the Internet, including http://www.tuxedo.org/~esr/writings/magic-cauldron/magic-cauldron.html.

## The Web as a Platform

If there is one other thing the Internet has done for software, it is the elevation of protocols over products. The Internet is truly vendor- and operating system-neutral. Anyone can play, as long as they agree to play by the rules. On the Internet, connectivity and interoperability are more important than differentiating features. Just as software platforms have been defined in the past through APIs (Application Programming Interfaces), the Web is being defined as a platform for applications through a similar set of APIs: the Internet protocols. Thankfully, for customers and IT users, Internet protocols are open and non-proprietary.

This is a very powerful force that militates against the natural urge of commercial organizations to differentiate their products in order to gain competitive advantage. Products that do not interoperate through the standard Internet protocols do not survive, however wonderful their features may be. Open standards are the great leveler, and free and commercial software can interoperate by adhering to them properly. Linux itself was born of the Internet, and its UNIX pedigree virtually guarantees that it will support all the standard Internet protocols. Web server software, e-mail, file transfer, and network news are available out of the box with any Linux distribution.

# The Importance of Open Standards

Before the Internet became such an important part of our lives, it was possible to have islands of proprietary technology. At first, computers were stand-alone. Interoperability was rarely a concern. So computer vendors had no need to pay any attention at all to standards – they could just define their own. Proprietary standards were attractive to vendors because they allowed them to 'lock in' customers. Once a customer began to rely on a certain platform, he was locked into its proprietary API, and could not readily switch to another vendor.

In the following era of LANs (Local Area Networks), it became necessary for computers to talk to each other. However, vendors still found it possible to establish proprietary networking standards to tie their machines together, forming slightly larger islands than before. SNA, DECNet, NetBIOS, NetBEUI, WINS and Novell's SPX/IPX are some examples. But all the while, the Internet was incubating and growing, and TCP/IP, the backbone protocol suite of the Internet became more refined.

With the arrival of the Internet, the proprietary networking protocols have withered and are dying. NetWare now supports TCP/IP as its 'native' protocol. IBM mainframes have begun to understand TCP/IP in addition to SNA, and DECNet is nowhere in sight. Open standards have triumphed over proprietary ones in networking; today, the Internet is the world's most open and standard platform, because there is a single standard definition for each of its basic APIs (protocols).

*This is not to say that* all *proprietary technologies are on the way out. To take an obvious example, Microsoft technology, in the form of the Windows OS, the* .doc *and* .xls *document formats, the Exchange/Outlook extensions to e-mail, and the COM component architecture, is established in most organizations and households. In perception, if not in fact, the Microsoft way has become the 'standard' way to do many things on the desktop, and there is little evidence to suggest any change in this situation in the near future.*

The Internet protocols, however, are already pretty well entrenched, and it will not be easy for any company, no matter how powerful, to 'de-commoditize' them (as the euphemism goes). A company that attempts to do so will isolate itself from the Internet, rather than co-opt it – it would be akin to sawing off the branch on which it sits. A company needs to control both the client and the server in order to control the protocol between them, and the server market is not dominated by Windows. With the Linux option (and its native support for open standards) now viable, future dominance of the server market by Microsoft – or indeed any other single vendor – appears an increasingly slim possibility.

# The Internet Protocols

For evidence of how open standards and open source complement one another, and how free software has been in use and development for critical tasks over long periods, one need look no further than the products that implement and utilize the various Internet protocols. Many of the Internet's earliest and hardiest applications were open source, and that tradition has been continued: as new protocols like DAV (Distributed Authoring and Versioning) come along, free software products are developed that use them.

In this section, we're going to examine some Internet protocols old and new, and give details of free software implementations of them. Where appropriate, we'll also suggest where to look for further information.

# TCP/IP: The Backbone of the Internet

The Internet uses the TCP/IP protocol suite, which is a family of protocols layered one on top of the other. The most important members of this family are, of course, TCP and IP. IP (Internet Protocol) is a network-level protocol that deals with the route through several intermediate machines and networks that messages must take to reach an ultimate destination. TCP (Transmission Control Protocol) is a connection-oriented protocol layered on top of IP, responsible for guaranteeing that messages reach their destination.

Essentially, each progressively lower layer of the TCP/IP protocol suite places its own 'header' in front of a message packet from the next layer up. A TCP/IP message would have an IP header in front of a TCP header, which in turn would prefix any other headers from protocols at higher layers.

The remarkable thing about the TCP/IP suite is the foresight of its designers. Any protocol can be layered over another, and it is not necessary that TCP should be directly over IP. Each protocol's header has a 'next protocol' field pointing to the next, and IP's header normally says the following information is a TCP header, but it need not do so! This is the feature that allows secure IP today – when security is required, a new protocol called IPSec is routinely layered between TCP and IP. The IP header then refers to IPSec as the 'next' protocol, and the IPSec header (when decrypted) points to TCP as the 'next' protocol. Such forethought in a technology a quarter of a century old!

## Routers and Routing

Routing, or forwarding, is the process by which messages get passed across from a computer in one network to one in another network. The IP protocol is intimately tied to routing, which is why it is called the "inter-net" protocol. Any UNIX computer can function as a router, because routing is a basic networking feature in UNIX. As you might expect, Linux comes with all the software required to function as a highly capable router, and many companies are now selling extremely inexpensive routers that are no more than stripped-down PCs running Linux, whose support for Telnet (remote login) makes it possible to configure these routers remotely.

Linux routers are every bit as capable as dedicated commercial routers, some of which are much more highly priced. For examples, you could take a look at the sites listed below.

### References

Imagestream IS:
http://www.imagestream-is.com/News_5-24-99.html

Nbase-Xyplex:
http://www.nbase-xyplex.com

## The Linux Router Project

As if Linux routers were not simple enough, the Linux Router Project aims to make it trivial for users to set up a router using plain PC hardware. They have produced a 'mini-distribution' of Linux that is small enough to fit on a single floppy, and it's easy to set up a router using it. The system boots off the floppy and resides in memory. It is also extremely fast, and more advanced routing functions can be added through extra packages. The project is currently working on web-based configuration utilities, which should make it even simpler to set up any kind of router for no more than the cost of a basic PC. Check out the Linux Router Project at http://www.linuxrouter.org.

## Domain Name Servers

A Domain Name Server (DNS) translates addresses like www.somehost.com into IP addresses like 10.1.1.1. The venerable BIND (Berkeley Internet Naming Daemon) is still the best-known and most widespread DNS software, and also one of the Internet's oldest open source products. BIND is one of the products adopted by the Internet Software Consortium (http://www.isc.org) as a UNIX reference implementation of a standard protocol. We'll be examining the niceties of routing and domain name servers on Linux platforms in Chapter 9.

# HTTP and the Web

Arguably, the most important Internet protocol today is HTTP (Hypertext Transfer Protocol), because it underlies the World Wide Web that finally made the venerable Internet an everyday medium. This protocol has led to the spectacular rise of two kinds of software that were unheard of just a few years ago: browsers and web servers. In the following sections, we take a look at the state and future prospects of free web software, and at how its story offers encouragement to those considering the adoption of free software today.

## Apache: The World's Most Popular Web Server

Apache is one of the poster children of the free software movement, and we'll be giving it more detailed coverage in the next chapter, when we examine how to configure a Linux machine as a web server for your network. However, the story of its success is also appropriate to this discussion, so some elaboration is sensible here too.

Next to Linux, Apache is the best-known free software success story. Indeed, it is more successful in the web server market than Linux is in the operating system market, with a market share greater than all of its rivals put together. As well as market share, the http://www.netcraft.com web site can determine what server any other site is using, and it reveals some interesting facts. Apache is such a capable high-end web server that, as of December 1999, it runs Microsoft's Hotmail site (with over 40 million users), and its homepage site at http://homepages.msn.com.

The free availability and reliability of Apache are not its only attractions. In another display of foresight, Apache has a standard mechanism to add external modules that build on its functionality. In this way, the web server can be customized and modernized exactly as its administrator requires: if there's a feature you don't want, don't install it; when new modules become available, they can be added at will.

> *Among the external modules available for Apache are* mod_perl *(which allows Perl CGI scripts to be interpreted and run within Apache's memory space, rather than starting up the Perl interpreter each time in a separate process),* mod_jserv *(which allows Apache to use Java servlets), and* mod_php *(which allows Apache to run HTML-embedded scripts in a Perl-like language called PHP).*

Apache is not a toy, but a production-quality web server that's consolidating its lead over its rivals, not only in market share but also in core features. IBM has made Apache the centerpiece of its WebSphere e-commerce server, though they refer to it as the "IBM HTTP server powered by Apache". IBM is also contributing code to the Apache project to ensure that it remains the world's pre-eminent web server. In May 1998, no doubt impressed with Apache's popularity, VeriSign reversed its initial decision not to provide site certificates to open source web servers. After that, the share of Apache in SSL-enabled web sites jumped from nothing to 25%.

Apache runs on virtually every brand of UNIX, and also on the IBM AS/400. It has recently been ported to the Windows NT platform, though the NT version is not yet claimed to be as stable as the UNIX version. When it stabilizes, and when its graphical interface (still under development) becomes more refined, Apache should give IIS a run for its money on its home turf as well.

### References

The Apache Project:
http://www.apache.org

`mod_perl`:
http://perl.apache.org

`mod_php`:
http://www.php.net

`mod_jserv`:
http://java.apache.org

The Netcraft web server survey:
http://www.netcraft.com/survey

## The Mozilla Project: The Web's Battle of the Bulge

Netscape Communications saw the writing on the wall when Microsoft began to give away its Internet Explorer software free of charge. The move was designed to cut off Netscape's air supply and chase it out of business. It was an inescapable conclusion that Netscape would have to do likewise and stop charging for Navigator/Communicator altogether. But the big surprise when Netscape finally succumbed to the inevitable was the counterpunch in the announcement. Netscape went one better than Microsoft: it announced that it was giving away the source code as well.

Netscape's management reasoned that opening up the source code was the only way to reinvigorate Communicator and keep Explorer from dominating the browser market. They set up an independent organization called Mozilla.org to oversee development of the next version of Communicator. Barely seven hours after the code was released, an Australian group applied a cryptographic patch (called "Cryptozilla") to make Mozilla 128-bit SSL-capable.

Admittedly, progress thereafter has been slower. The Mozilla project took six months to decide what to do about the layout (rendering) engine, the heart of the browser, but the result was worth it. Rather than fixing the irretrievably broken layout engine already in Communicator, they wrote a fresh one from scratch. The new engine, called Gecko, is a revolution in many ways. It is the smallest, fastest and most standards-compliant rendering engine of all. What's more, it is designed to be embeddable. Already, Neoplanet.com has released a browser that incorporates Gecko. We may soon see mobile phones (with Gecko embedded) that allow users to browse the Net. Gecko is also available as an ActiveX control, which will allow it to be plugged into Internet Explorer and used to replace Microsoft's layout engine!

Mozilla has made plodding progress so far, but appears to be on track. Even the resignation of one of its top developers, Jamie Zawinski, hasn't really hurt the project. External contributions are increasing, and it seems that the world will have a completely free, standards-compliant browser very soon.

Open source development is driving acceptance of open standards, and the outcome here should be that developers will no longer need to use the least common denominator of web features to get pages to render the same way on all browsers. The Mozilla project can be found at http://www.mozilla.org, and while we'll be giving it no further coverage in this book, it stands as an excellent example of how the open-source community can improve and innovate.

### WebDAV: Moving The Web from Read-Only to Read/Write

WebDAV (DAV stands for Distributed Authoring and Versioning) is the next logical step for the Web. It is an open standard being developed by the IETF (Internet Engineering Task Force) that defines the HTTP extensions required to allow users to edit and manage files collaboratively on remote web servers. WebDAV aims to convert the Web from a read-only medium to a writable one – but depending on who you listen to, it could do much more than that. Some consider it to be the Internet's own file system; others see it as a document management protocol for the Web.

HTTP has already become an open and standard way to access many types of data stores, but only in read mode. DAV provides a similarly open and standard way to write to such stores as well. It supports locking to prevent authors from overwriting each other's work, and copy and move operations. Versioning support and access control list management are under development. Apache supports WebDAV (through the addition of a module), and so too do Microsoft IIS 5.0 and Internet Explorer 5 – facts that gives good cause for optimism that Microsoft is increasingly prepared to adopt open standards.

> *The WebDAV site at* http://www.webdav.org *hosts the Apache module* mod_dav *that will DAV-enable the Apache web server. Red Hat bundles* mod_dav *with its e-commerce server; you can find the IETF web site at* http://www.ietf.org.

# Electronic Mail

E-mail was one of the very earliest Internet applications, and Sendmail is the oldest and most widespread server-side mail software. Sendmail is estimated to handle 70-80% of the world's e-mail, which works out to billions of messages a day!

Sendmail is one of the most complex pieces of software on the UNIX platform, and it has had to be modified repeatedly throughout its history because it was not designed with security in mind – every newly discovered exploit had to be countered by a patch. It is testimony to the free software community that these fixes are performed diligently and made available quickly as problems arise.

Partly as a reaction to Sendmail's monolithic complexity and lack of integrated security features, newer mail software has emerged. The most famous of these is Qmail, which was designed from the start to be modular and secure; other notable free mail packages include Zmailer, Exim and Postfix. In this book, however, we will stick with Sendmail when we describe how to set up your Linux machine as a mail server for your enterprise in Chapter 9.

*References*

Sendmail homepage:
http://www.sendmail.org

Qmail homepage:
http://www.qmail.org/top.html

Zmailer homepage:
http://www.zmailer.org

Exim homepage:
http://www.exim.org

Postfix homepage:
http://www.postfix.org

## Web-based E-mail

The success of Hotmail has resulted in a demand for web sites offering browser-accessible e-mail. Perhaps the best free software product is IMP, which lets any web site host mailboxes for its users, accessible through a standard web interface. IMP is fully featured and customizable, and should prove extremely useful to web portals and others wishing to offer a range of services under a single roof. You can find its homepage at http://web.horde.org/imp.

## Mailing List Managers

Mailing list managers (MLMs) have been around for a while, with names like LISTSERV and Majordomo. A recent addition is Mailman, written in Python, the increasingly popular object-oriented scripting language. Mailman is easy to install and configure, and lets various groups create and manage their own mailing lists through a standard web interface – which is of course customizable. Like web-based e-mail, this can be a very useful service for a portal to offer. Its homepage may be found at http://www.list.org.

# Firewalls and Proxies

The Internet brings with it many dangers. Connecting an organization's network to the Internet opens up the possibility that malicious elements from anywhere in the world can gain access to its computers and the data they hold. Viruses and crackers are a genuine threat to your enterprise, and that's one of the reasons why firewalls and proxies have become popular. We'll be covering these topics in depth in Chapter 10, but here's a quick taster.

A **firewall** is a computer that physically sits between the Internet and an organization's network. Since all network traffic is then forced to flow through the firewall, it can examine every packet to see where it comes from, where it's trying to go, and what protocol it is speaking. A firewall can be configured to allow only specific types of traffic to go through. It can prevent access from some areas entirely. It can be made to allow only certain protocols and not others. Very complex rules can be set up in this manner, and the firewall can also keep records of access and attempted access in log files to help administrators.

A **proxy server** (or just "proxy") is a piece of software that often works in conjunction with a firewall to enforce certain restrictions. It can also provide caching to speed up access to frequently requested files. Basically, if an organization sets up a proxy on its network, its internal users connect to it whenever they want to connect to a machine outside. The proxy then connects to the external machine on their behalf, and relays information back and forth.

The reasons to set up a system like this are many. First, the firewall can now be set up to permit external access to the proxy alone. All internal machines are automatically protected because they cannot be directly accessed from outside under any circumstances. (In the absence of a proxy, direct access would have to be provided, which always runs the risk of misuse.)

Second, a proxy set up in this way performs 'network address translation' or 'IP masquerading', allowing an organization to run an independently administered internal network with unlimited private IP addresses, without the need to register for an equivalent pool of real IP addresses. The proxy can "map" internal IP addresses to those in the available pool, and reuse them over and over for those internal client machines that happen to be connected at a particular time. External parties are kept ignorant of the number of hosts, their addresses and the topology of the organization's network – a major security plus.

Recent Linux kernels (2.2.0 and later) have sophisticated firewall capabilities built in. There is a utility called ipchains that manages the rules to be set up for the firewall. (The name "ipchains" refers to the input, output and forwarding rules for all IP traffic.) The latest Linux kernel also allows for built-in proxy capability, although there's also a separate caching proxy called Squid that is used in conjunction with web servers to speed up access to frequently accessed web pages.

### References

Linux firewall tool:
http://linux-firewall-tools.com/linux/firewall

Squid caching proxy homepage:
http://squid-cache.org

# Database Servers

It may not be immediately clear how database servers fit into this discussion, but when you start to consider how to access data on a remote machine, it makes perfect sense to use one of the standard protocols for the task. As we shall see when we investigate further in Chapter 7, connections to Linux's two principal free database servers are made using TCP/IP.

Databases are perhaps the area in which there is most resistance to free software – data security is a very sensitive subject, and corporations are inclined to choose names that they trust. For the next couple of years, therefore, large production sites are likely to continue to rely on commercial RDBMS software, and from that perspective it's easy to see the motivation for vendors like Oracle, Sybase and Informix to release their products for the Linux platform.

But this advantage of commercial databases could erode quickly. The free software database market is naturally segmenting into two, and its reputation is improving apace. The small, lightweight database segment is increasingly gravitating towards MySQL, a simple and fast (though not full-featured) SQL database that has recently been released under the GNU GPL (though the GPL does not apply to the very latest version). A graphical front end for MySQL is also available, and maturing quickly.

The higher-end database segment is moving towards PostgreSQL, which is object-relational and a natural universal server for multimedia databases. The commercial Illustra database (which was later incorporated into Informix) was originally based on PostgreSQL! With the recent addition of fine-grained concurrency control into PostgreSQL, it is gradually acquiring higher-end features. In a couple of years, it could well give the commercial databases a run for their money.

### References

MySQL homepage:
http://www.mysql.org

PostgreSQL homepage:
http://www.postgresql.org

# LDAP and Directory Servers

In Chapter 8, we'll take a look at directory servers, a hitherto neglected (but potentially very useful) tool. They differ from relational databases in that they are oriented towards situations where data is looked up far more frequently than it is updated – they could be thought of as "write seldom, read mostly" databases. Directory servers are also flexible in the kind of data they store.

One possible application for directory servers is as repositories for digital certificates. In future, as e-commerce picks up, it will be necessary for web sites to store large numbers of digital certificates to authenticate business counterparts, such as customers and suppliers. Directory servers are the ideal storage technology because they can store arbitrary data and look things up extremely quickly. Digital certificates are likely to be checked far more often than they are updated.

Until recently, the only game in town was Netscape's Certificate Server. However, the free OpenLDAP (http://www.openldap.org) is fast approaching its feature set. As of version 1.2.7, OpenLDAP does not support LDAP v.3 features, but it is slated to do so in version 2.0. With a version 3-compliant LDAP server available, another gap in the free software server-side line-up will be plugged. It will be possible to build a complete, production-quality site using only free software; the success of Red Hat's e-commerce server is an exciting indicator of what could happen.

# Web Application Servers

An interesting category of servers has appeared in very recent times: web application servers. These are servers that run application business logic, and which provide a web interface either by themselves, or by piggybacking onto web servers. The distinguishing feature of all of them is that they are servers for application logic that happen to have an HTTP front end and are accessible through browsers.

For UNIX-based systems, the market leading web application servers today are the commercial Weblogic from BEA, and NetDynamics from Sun. However, competition from free software equivalents is increasing. The server that appears farthest along the development curve is Enhydra, version 2.2 of which has been demonstrated running with Bull's free implementation of Enterprise Java Beans (EJB).

At the lower end of the market, a quick way to knock together web sites is emerging in the form of Zope. It is not a static web site builder, however – Zope is written in Python, and can be extended using Python scripts.

Both Zope and Enhydra were initially developed by commercial organizations that later gave away the source code. Because the consultancy business built upon a popular product is very lucrative, it can make more sense to part with the source and popularize the product than to attempt to charge money for it.

We won't be examining application servers any further in this book; if you're interested in learning more, there are a number of web application servers available as free software, and some of them are listed below.

### References

Enhydra homepage:
http://www.enhydra.org

EJBoss homepage:
http://www.ejboss.org

Hamilton homepage:
http://microstate.com/hamilton/index.htm

Locomotive homepage:
http://www.locomotive.org/locolink/disp?home

Zope homepage:
http://www.zope.org

Midgard homepage:
http://midgard.greywolves.org

Flashpoint homepage:
http://www.bouldersoftware.com

# Summary

Free software is affordable and readily accessible to all. Common free software applications are likely to be bundled with most Linux distributions, so users do not have to purchase them as extras. Even if a distribution does not include a particular free software product, it can usually be downloaded and installed with minimal effort, since most free software products work with Linux, and distribution formats like RPM (*R*ed Hat *P*ackage *M*anager) make installation extremely simple.

Free software has demonstrated an uncanny ability to attract contributions from the best minds on the Internet, and the best free software can match or beat commercial software on features and code quality. Applications benefit from fast and furious bug fixing, and of course they will always remain unbeatable on price. As user suspicion, the last impediment to their adoption, slips away, their position in the market and in the enterprise seems assured.

Linux and other free software were born of the Internet, and they are helping to enrich the Internet in a hundred different ways. Through it all, they remain open and non-proprietary, and never stop improving. For the foreseeable future, it seems that free software and the Internet will continue to enrich each other. In the chapters to come, we'll take up the stories of many of the technologies discussed here one by one, examine their implementations on Linux, and investigate how to put them to use in your enterprise.

# 5

# Deploying Web and FTP Servers

The success of the Internet lies in its ability to provide information, quickly and cheaply to anyone at any time, and to facilitate fast communication on a global scale. As a result, computers have now been installed in homes and in workplaces that are able to connect to the Internet and draw from an almost unlimited supply of information. Indeed, every business that wants to succeed well into the twenty-first century needs to make use of and contribute to this technology. At the center of this communication network are the **web servers** that supply information back to the client. However, web servers should supply not just static information, that is unchangeable text and graphics on a standard HTML page, but are able to respond to the needs of the user. This requires a web server to resolve the request of the user and respond accordingly. Technologies now exist that enable the web server itself to fetch and process data before sending it to the client.

Telnet was originally used to run programs on remote computers, e-mail was used to communicate and FTP or Gopher was used to transfer large files. Telnet and e-mail are still used, and FTP has become the preferred way to make files available across the Internet, but the real revolution in Internet use over the past few years has been the introduction of a new method of searching and viewing information, the World Wide Web (WWW).

The WWW was originally developed in the European Center for Particle Research (CERN). CERN developed a program to serve information in HTML format across HTTP – a web server, and another program to receive and view it – a web browser. These programs were subsequently developed by the National Center for Supercomputing Applications at the University of Illinois and renamed NCSA and Mosaic respectively. Mosaic went on to become the commercial Netscape Navigator product, which from version 5 onwards has been decommercialized and is now open source again. On the other hand, the NCSA server has been open source all along. The server has been improved by successive patches, and has been renamed Apache. In over ten years of dedicated development, Apache has been extended to implement numerous technologies and is considered to be the most stable web server available, when run on its native Unix or Linux operating systems.

Apache's scalability, zero cost and its customizability, make it the most popular web servers available – running over 4.3 million web sites, over half of the WWW, as of October 1999 (figures from Netcraft at www.netcraft.com).

The development of FTP servers has not followed the same pattern as that of web servers. However, the ability to resume broken downloads, by starting the download process part way through a file, is a major recent advance. There are numerous FTP servers available for Linux, but the most fully featured and well-tested server is the one developed at Washington University. WU-FTP provides a complete FTP server solution, as well as having a large user base which ensures continued development, and updates, where necessary.

As I have said at the very beginning of this section, web servers now require the ability to respond to the user by server-side processing. The CGI (Common Gateway Interface) allows you to execute scripts such as Perl on your server, providing particularly powerful text handling capabilities. More recently, the Java servlet has providing the ability to execute more complex routines on the server. Either technology allows you to provide different content and perform different actions depending on the user's actions. JavaServer Pages (JSP) are the latest addition to the Java family, which do the same task as Microsoft's Active Server Pages (ASP) – processing user requests using server-side code and returning the information to the user as plain HTML.

Apache has excellent implementations of each of these technologies with the release of the `mod_cgi`/`mod_perl` modules (for fast CGI script execution) and ApacheJServ (a servlet), with JSP support through Jakarta becoming available at the time of writing. There is another advantage to these technologies; if you decide to change operating system or web server, you will be able to transfer these scripts with very little editing – the same cannot be said of ASP!

This chapter will not only demonstrate how to install both the Apache web server and the WU-FTP server, but will show you how to configure the installations to meet your requirements, including providing basic security to your servers. It will also show you how to perform essential administration tasks, such as analysing log data and will suggest potential options to replace proprietary technologies, such as ASP, and will cover technologies such as ApacheJServ, CGI and SSI. Finally you will be given tips on how to get the server working as quickly as possible following a crash.

# Deploying the Apache Web Server

In this section you will learn how to set up Apache on a Linux machine. You will be shown the system requirements for setting up the server and the modifications you will need to make to the Linux operation system configuration files to prepare it for installation. In addition to stepping through the installation process itself, you will find out how to configure Apache to meet your own requirements. Then, you will learn how to add a virtual host to the server, review some technologies to provide interactivity to your web site and how to provide useful reports on web site usage by examining the contents of access log files.

# System Requirements

The following list gives the requirements that need to be met when setting up an effective production web server. For a test web server, it is possible to install to any machine with as little as 30 MB of free disk space, any processor speed, and a static IP address if you want to test it on line.

❑ **Permanent Internet connection** – as an experienced system administrator, you will probably already know exactly the requirements for your site. If not, a good rule of thumb is to allow a minimum of 10 kilobytes per second per simultaneous user. So if you expect a maximum of twelve users on your site at any one time, a 128K leased line would be the minimum requirement. Obviously the content of your pages will make a big difference, and experience is the best teacher as far as choosing a connection is concerned. If your site is purely for intranet use, this will not concern you.

❑ **URL and IP address** – You will need to purchase at least one domain name and IP address. Entering your primary IP address and host name when originally installing Linux is the quickest way to gaining a bulletproof basic network configuration – if you didn't set them during the installation, they can be edited later. You will need a further IP address and hostname for each additional virtual host you wish to run – although these hostnames can be subdomains of a single registered domain name (e.g. `apache.wrox.co.uk` is a subdomain of `wrox.co.uk`). An FTP server and a web server may share a host name but they will use a different port.

❑ **DNS server** – You will need access to a DNS server to allow Internet users to resolve your domain names. For many companies, this access will be provided through a corporate account with a major network provider – although Linux is itself capable of running fully featured name servers if you will make sufficient use of it to justify the maintenance effort. Adding entries will be as simple as contacting that provider.

❑ **Linux machine** – The ideal requirements here are plenty of memory and a fast, ultra-wide SCSI hard disk, since these are what will see the most work – IDE hard disks may prove to be a bottleneck if server demand increases. The entire software (including the operating system) will unlikely take more than 1GB, so a typical 10GB hard disk available today will be more than ideal and allow plenty of space for growth. 64MB of RAM should prove enough for up to 10 000 hits per day; if you find memory swapping is taking place, it is a simple matter to add more RAM (and you should do this because swapping causes serious performance degradation). If using server-side Java technologies, add at least another 32MB for the Java Virtual Machine (JVM). Where significant server-side processing is used, the speed of the processor is also important – the faster the better. If connected to the Internet, the Linux machine should not be used for any non-Internet purposes. If you are using the server as part of an intranet, then the installation of a firewall will be necessary; this way the effect of any security breach will be minimized.

# Preparing Linux for Installation

The installation should always be performed in a clean environment – this involves formatting the hard disk and installing Linux from scratch. Make sure your version of Linux is up-to-date – stack and TCP/IP bugs are occasionally found in the Linux kernel, and an up-to-date distribution will keep you one step ahead of the hackers. The latest security bulletins are available from CERT (http://www.cert.org) and it is useful to subscribe to their security mailing lists. This chapter assumes you are using Red Hat Linux 6.1, but the steps are very similar for all Linux distributions.

It is crucial that only essential services are running; Linux is capable of running everything from `ping` to fully featured name servers, and by default, it will. When not fully configured, these represent a security loophole – so it is best to unselect all the obvious communication services during the Linux installation (anything with `ftp`, `mail` or `web` in the title). Make sure that `make` (an install utility) and `gcc` (the C compiler) are selected – we will use them later.

Once the install is completed, edit the `/etc/inetd.conf` file, or equivalent, which contains a listing of all the network services started on the machine. Insert a # symbol at the start of the line containing the name of the services which are not needed; particular services to disable include `finger`, `cfinger` and `portmap` which provide useful information for hackers, and if you don't require it, `telnet`. Telnet allows easy remote management, but if you don't intend to use it, removing it closes one more possible security loophole. Finally, after a reboot, we can type netstat –a | `more` for a listing of remaining services:

```
tcp    0    0 *:printer        *:*              LISTEN
tcp    0    0 *:linuxconf      *:*              LISTEN
tcp    0    0 *:auth           *:*              LISTEN
tcp    0    0 *:login          *:*              LISTEN
```

The first 20 or so lines contain the useful listing of services – the lines to look for have the word `LISTEN` at the end, signifying that they are ready to accept connections. As long as you don't see `portmap`, `finger`, `sendmail` or `ftpd` (unless deliberately installed and configured), we have a relatively safe environment to continue with.

# Installing Apache Web Server

Traditionally, Apache required recompiling every time you wanted to add a new feature, or 'module', as all modules were compiled into the Apache executable. More recently, the Apache group have incorporated support for DSO linking, which, like DLLs in Windows, allow new modules to be added later without recompiling the whole program. We will install Apache using DSO linking, which will make installation of ApacheJServ and other modules easier. Static linking is very slightly faster in operation than DSO linking, and some older distributions of Linux will not allow DSO. If you have to do a static installation, just leave out the `--enable-module=most` and `--enable-shared=max` parameters in step 4.

1.  If you are using Red Hat 6.0, you first need to correct an error in the distribution, by making a C header file available from its correct location. Type:

    ```
    # ln -s /usr/include/db1/ndbm.h /usr/include/ndbm.h
    ```

2.  Download the latest version of Apache (http://www.apache.org) to `/usr/local/src`, unzip and extract it:

    ```
    # tar -xvfz apache_x_x_x.tar.gz
    ```

3.  Enter the created directory:

    ```
    # cd /usr/local/src/apache_x_x_x
    ```

The next three steps configure, build and install Apache. The first parameters supplied to the configure script specify the path for the apache installation.

**4.** `# ./configure --prefix=/usr/local/apache --enable-module=most --enable-shared=max`

**5.** `# make`

**6.** `# make install`

That's it - Apache is installed! We will cover the configuration fully later in the chapter, so for now we will just configure enough to test it:

**1.** Open `/usr/local/apache/conf/httpd.conf` for editing. This contains every configuration command for the entire server, so it may look quite intimidating. However, don't be put off as it is simpler than it looks!

**2.** Search for the `ServerName` directive (about a third of the way through). Replace it with `ServerName http://localhost` — we will use a real network identity later, but using localhost for now provides us a simple check of our Apache installation. Save and close `httpd.conf`.

**3.** Start the apache server with the command `/usr/local/apache/bin/apachectl start`.

**4.** If Netscape, or some other web browser, is installed, type `http://localhost` into the location bar. If not, type `lynx localhost` at the command line. Either way, you should be presented with a congratulations page:

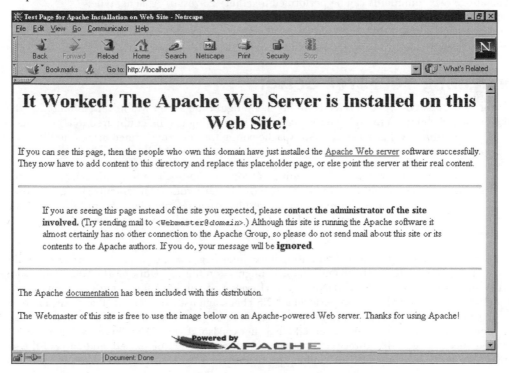

# Getting to Know the Web Server

Your working web server installation should be self-contained within /usr/local/apache. If you installed Apache differently (e.g. using a Red Hat RPM), and find your configuration changes aren't having any effect, try searching for stray files: type find / -name httpd.conf − print. Some proprietary distributions place the active httpd.conf in other folders.

Inside /usr/local/apache will be a set of further directories, the ones we will use are:

- ❑   bin - contains all the program executables
- ❑   cgi-bin - which is the default location for CGI files
- ❑   conf - contains all the Apache configuration files
- ❑   htdocs - the default root directory for your web site. A sample index.html file is already in this directory to produce the 'It Worked' page you saw in the last section
- ❑   logs - contains all the server logs by default. We will deal with these in more depth later.

We will change the locations of the default web site root directory and CGI location later when we cover Apache configuration, and develop a consistent placement of all web site content within the /home directory where it is well separated from the application. Separating content from application is a useful technique if your fellow system administrators make the occasional mistake when updating web site content.

To start Apache, type: /usr/local/apache/bin/apachectl start.

To stop Apache, type: /usr/local/apache/bin/apachectl stop.

The above two commands can be performed together. To restart Apache, type: /usr/local/apache/bin/apachectl restart. The alternative command /usr/local/apache/bin/apachectl graceful does the same but finishes serving any current requests first.

# Configuring Your Web Server

The greatest asset of Apache is its flexibility in configuration − you will never be limited to the settings the original developers thought you would want! Everything can be configured to a per-directory level, or even a per-file level if necessary. All Apache configuration is performed using one file: httpd.conf. There are many configuration commands, but all follow a similar format.

Apache will work fine with its default settings, as long as the ServerName directive is set, so you can begin with the original settings and gradually move toward your requirements changing a few settings at a time, restarting Apache each time to see the results. Apache only reads the httpd.conf file when starting. In fact, the chances are most of the default settings will never need changing, and that you will use a few useful commands repeatedly. We will cover all these essential commands.

An important general rule is to avoid using hostnames (e.g. www.trampolining.net) unless the command requires them. Hostnames in the configuration file will work most of the time, so long as you have told Linux where to find a DNS server. However, if you have filtered any content using hostnames, Apache will need to perform a DNS check against every client IP address, increasing server load. On the other hand, if you filter against IP addresses, Apache already has the information in order to function without forcing an unwanted DNS check. Also, if your DNS server is down when Apache is started, any configuration directives containing hostnames won't be parsed, and parts of the server will not be started. This can cause intermittent problems when the DNS server is down or contains bad data.

The effect of a command depends on where it is placed. The first section of `httpd.conf` contains global environment directives, which affect the entire server and all virtual hosts running on it. The next section configures the main, or primary server. Settings here also provide the default settings for all virtual hosts. The third and final section configures the virtual hosts themselves.

Within section two or three you might want to apply settings to a single directory only. This is achieved using a directory container; the settings are placed within a pair of HTML-like tags, which define which directory to apply the settings to. (We will meet other containers when configuring virtual hosts.) Note there is no trailing slash on the directory.

```
<Directory /any/directory>
   Settings here
</Directory>
```

## Section 1: Global Environment

The first directive that you will come across is this one:

```
ServerType standalone
```

`ServerType` may be either `standalone` or `inetd`. For all but the lowest-use servers, use `standalone` as Apache will be permanently ready and waiting for any requests itself. The `inetd` option caters for users who wish to start Apache when requests are received on a specified port; this introduces start-up delays which will only be acceptable if the server rarely functions as a web server.

The following directives tell Apache to maintain a pool of between 5 and 10 spare server processes, ready for new requests:

```
MinSpareServers 5
MaxSpareServers 10
```

Adaptive spawning implemented in Apache versions 1.3 and upwards means there should be no reason to change these except on very high load servers. However, be wary of over-trusting benchmarking utilities, as these generate a step change in request volume over a few seconds, which do not occur in reality. The directive below prevents more than 150 clients connecting simultaneously, to prevent the server locking during periods of high usage:

```
MaxClients 150
```

If you find that clients are being refused a connection during periods of high usage, try increasing this number. If you find the server is locking up or becoming very slow during periods of high usage, you may consider lowering this number as a temporary measure to keep the server running until you can provide higher capacity. More information on optimizing for high loads can be found in *Professional Apache* by Peter Wainwright, published by Wrox Press (ISBN 1861003021).

## Section 2: Primary Server Configuration

To reduce the chance of malicious damage to your system, we give Apache processes the minimum possible security privileges on your machine:

```
User nobody
Group nobody
```

Any CGI scripts run by Apache will inherit these settings. CGI scripts will be discussed later in the chapter.

The following e-mail address will be suffixed to any error messages Apache sends to the client. Setting it to your address ensures visitors have a way to inform you of problems with your site. You may of course feel this is not a good thing!

```
ServerAdmin richard@trampolining.net
```

Obviously you would put your address in here, not mine.

The `ServerName` directive tells Apache the hostname of the primary host. It is essential, and proves a common cause of headaches if it is set wrongly:

```
ServerName www.trampolining.net
```

Suppose a client requests `http://www.trampolining.net/news`, where `news` is a directory. This is not a valid HTTP request as the trailing slash is missing. Apache will ask the browser to visit the correct URL, `http://www.trampolining.net/news/` using `ServerName` to reconstruct the URL. If `ServerName` is not correctly set, the redirect URL returned will be invalid (e.g. `http://not-set/news/`) and a 404 'File not found' error, or a DNS resolution failure will be returned. If you do not yet have a valid hostname, you can use the machine IP address here instead.

This directive specifies where to look for the contents of the web site; this directory will appear as the root directory of your web site, and is where all the HTML files will be placed.

```
DocumentRoot "/home/www/trampolining.net/"
```

The following container contains directives that apply to the entire system:

```
<Directory />
  Options FollowSymLinks
  AllowOverride None
</Directory>
```

These permissions prevent anyone browsing around private system files. Because of this default denial of access, we will need to explicitly allow access to any directories we intend to use using another directory container. Subdirectories inherit the same Apache permissions as their parent unless refined by later directory containers. The following tag specifies the beginning of the main directory container.

```
<Directory /home/www/trampolining.net>
```

This is used to allow access to the main server root directory. Later directory containers may refine the permissions we have set here for the whole of `/home/www/trampolining.net`.

The `Options` directive tells Apache what it is allowed to serve to the user.

```
Options Indexes FollowSymLinks Includes ExecCGI
```

An index allows Apache to produce a listing of most of the files in a directory if there is no `index.html` or other file specified in `DirectoryIndex`. If `Indexes` is not included here, a 'forbidden' HTTP response will be returned. `FollowSymLinks` will allow users to follow any symbolic links you create to other directories.

`Includes` and `ExecCGI` are the remaining valid operators, and will be covered in more detail in the section called *Technologies for Effective Sites* later in this chapter. Briefly, `Includes` tells Apache to allow Server Side Includes (SSI) in this directory to be parsed (`IncludesNoExec` is the same except it will not honor SSI `exec` commands). In the same way, `ExecCGI` allows CGI files in this directory to be executed, which is not the most secure way to provide CGI support, but the most convenient.

Now take a look at this directive:

```
AllowOverride None
```

If `AllowOverride` is set to `All`, then wherever a file called `.htaccess` exists in a directory, the `httpd.conf` settings for that directory will be overridden by the settings in that file. This allows you to keep `httpd.conf` to a reasonable length by defining per-directory settings in individual `.htaccess` files. However, this is a poor method of configuration as making changes can become a chore – any number of `.htaccess` files may require editing, even for a simple update. Setting `AllowOverride` to `All` will also mean that every time a request is received for a directory, whether or not an `.htaccess` file is present, Apache will search for one, thereby increasing server load.

A better alternative, if you are concerned about the length of `httpd.conf`, is to group extra settings in another file, (e.g. `/usr/local/apache/conf/football-websites.conf`), and then force Apache to read this by placing `'Include /usr/local/apache/conf/football-websites.conf'` at the end of `httpd.conf`. We will this principle later in this chapter when we configure ApacheJServ.

This section defines who is allowed to view your web site. Setting `'Allow from all'` will allow anyone to visit your web site – there is more about restricting access in the *Logs and Analysis* section.

```
Order allow,deny
Allow from all
```

This is the end of the directory container – we have finished setting the default permissions!

```
</Directory>
```

When a client requests a directory, Apache first checks to see whether there is a `DirectoryIndex` directive defined there which it can serve instead. So when requesting http://www.trampolining.net, the actual file returned is http://www.trampolining.net/index.html. Apache will check for each of the named files in order; in this example we have chosen to serve `index.html` in preference to `index.htm`. If neither `index.html` nor `index.htm` is present, either a 403 'forbidden' response, or a directory index will be returned, depending whether `Indexes` is set in the `Options` command as above. If you use SSI or JSPs, you might want to add `index.shtml` or `index.jsp` to this list.

```
DirectoryIndex index.html index.htm
```

This is an example of a `Files` container; it will apply to any matching file, anywhere on this host or any of the virtual hosts. It prevents clients viewing any `.htaccess` configuration file which provides useful information to a hacker.

```
AccessFileName .htaccess
<Files .htaccess>
    Order allow,deny
    Deny from all
</Files>
```

The next directive of note is:

```
HostnameLookups Off
```

When set to `On`, Apache will attempt to resolve the IP address of every client before writing to the logs, so that the logs contains 'machine.isp.net' instead of '123.123.123.123'. It heavily increases server load, and load upon your Internet connection. In the *Logs and Analysis* section we will configure Analog to do this much more efficiently.

This directive tells Apache where to log errors:

```
ErrorLog /usr/local/apache/logs/error_log
```

This log collects most error messages, including CGI errors and errors occurring on virtual hosts (unless your virtual host has its own `ErrorLog` command). A useful trick when troubleshooting is to type `tail -f /usr/local/apache/logs/error_log`, which will show the end of the log in real time. Then browse around the site, seeing exactly what is causing errors and when the errors occurred.

The following directive tells Apache where to log accesses.

```
CustomLog /usr/local/apache/logs/access_log common
```

It takes an added parameter that tells it which of the predefined log formats to use. This may be `common`, the NCSA standard log, `combined`, the most useful log format (which provides nearly all information in one log), `referer` (which records only referrer details) or `agent` (which records only user agent details). It is even possible to create several different logs concurrently using separate `CustomLog` commands, and much more – see *Professional Apache* for more details.

`ErrorDocument` commands allow you to return a pre-selected page in place of standard Apache error pages. This preserves the corporate image of a site and minimizes any unprofessional impression which would inevitably be created in this situation. `ErrorDocuments` can be created for any or all HTTP error responses, but the important ones to cover are 404 ('File not found') and 500 ('Server error', usually caused by script or servlet failure).

```
ErrorDocument 404 /missing.html
```

# Adding Virtual Hosts

Virtual hosts allow you to provide another web site from the same server. To the user, the virtual host looks and feels identical to how it would if it was the primary host. For example, in addition to providing www.trampolining.net on my server, I might want to run a completely different web site called www.sport-science.net.

Since HTTP 1.1, virtual hosts can be accessed by each one listening to a different IP address (the traditional approach), or to one IP address, with an HTTP header telling the server which virtual host to serve. While the second approach is well supported by Apache, the small number of browsers still in use which are not compliant with HTTP 1.1 forces us to adopt the traditional approach.

Linux allows up to 256 IP-based virtual hosts per network card, although the number of file descriptors available will probably limit us to a mere 200 or so. There are two parts to adding a virtual host. First, you must set up the network configuration to force Linux to 'listen' to the other IP addresses. Second, you will also need to configure Apache to listen.

## Network Configuration

The primary host listens to the machine's IP address as specified during Linux setup (or subsequently through Linuxconf, for example). We will need another IP address for each virtual host, and also need to register the URL and IP address with a Domain Name Server.

By default, network connections only listen to information sent to them. After all, why waste time listening to information meant for other machines? To provide virtual hosts, we need to listen to requests sent to our virtual hosts' IP addresses. Luckily, Linux provides direct support for this IP masquerading. (IP masquerading is one reason why network transmissions, like e-mail and telnet, are so easy to intercept.)

Typing ifconfig will produce a listing of network services, along with technical information about each of them. We are interested in the device eth0, which is the first to be listed (eth0 represents your first network card). If there are masquerades already defined, these will be listed underneath as eth0:0, eth0:1, and so on. If you have multiple network cards, you may reference them as eth1, eth1:1 and so on.

```
eth0      Link encap:Ethernet  HWaddr 00:50:04:86:89:61
          inet addr:123.123.123.122  Bcast:123.255.255.95  Mask:255.255.255.0
          UP BROADCAST RUNNING MULTICAST  MTU:1500  Metric:1
          RX packets:184263 errors:4 dropped:0 overruns:0 frame:5
          TX packets:104402 errors:0 dropped:0 overruns:0 carrier:0
          collisions:762 txqueuelen:100
          Interrupt:11 Base address:0x1000

lo        Link encap:Local Loopback
          inet addr:127.0.0.1  Mask:255.0.0.0
          UP LOOPBACK RUNNING  MTU:3924  Metric:1
          RX packets:7858 errors:0 dropped:0 overruns:0 frame:0
          TX packets:7858 errors:0 dropped:0 overruns:0 carrier:0
          collisions:0 txqueuelen:0
```

We will set up a virtual host for www.trampolining.net with an IP address of 123.123.123.123. Type: `ifconfig eth0:0 123.123.123.123`, where 0 is the first available masquerade (set to 0 here since none have been defined yet) and `123.123.123.123` is the IP address of your virtual host. Next we need to set up routing: type `route add -host 123.123.123.123 dev eth0:0`. If all goes well, typing `ifconfig` should now produce this:

```
eth0       Link encap:Ethernet  HWaddr 00:50:04:86:89:61
           inet addr:123.123.123.122  Bcast:123.255.255.95  Mask:255.255.255.0
           UP BROADCAST RUNNING MULTICAST  MTU:1500  Metric:1
           RX packets:184263 errors:4 dropped:0 overruns:0 frame:5
           TX packets:104402 errors:0 dropped:0 overruns:0 carrier:0
           collisions:762 txqueuelen:100
           Interrupt:11 Base address:0x1000

eth0:0     Link encap:Ethernet  HWaddr 00:50:04:86:89:61
           inet addr:123.123.123.123  Bcast:123.123.123.255  Mask:255.255.255.0
           UP BROADCAST RUNNING MULTICAST  MTU:1500  Metric:1
           Interrupt:11 Base address:0x1000

lo         Link encap:Local Loopback
           inet addr:127.0.0.1  Mask:255.0.0.0
           UP LOOPBACK RUNNING  MTU:3924  Metric:1
           RX packets:7858 errors:0 dropped:0 overruns:0 frame:0
           TX packets:7858 errors:0 dropped:0 overruns:0 carrier:0
           collisions:0 txqueuelen:0
```

That's it – our network configuration is ready for virtual hosting.

## Apache Configuration

Apache configuration consists of adding a few lines to `httpd.conf` and restarting the server:

```
<VirtualHost 123.123.123.123>
```

Just as `<Directory>` containers contained directives applying to that directory, `<VirtualHost>` containers contain all the directives related to that virtual host. Any directives not included take as default the settings assigned in the primary server section. A notable exception is the directive `Options +Includes` (explained in the later section entitled *Server-Side Includes*), which must be placed in the `Directory` container of each virtual host where it is used – it is not inherited.

These directives are required, and have the same effect as when used before for the primary host.

```
DocumentRoot /home/www/sport-science.net
ServerName www.sport-science.net
```

These two directives create logs specifically for this virtual host. If no logging command is given, log messages will be redirected to the primary host logs.

```
CustomLog /usr/local/apache/logs/sports_science_access_log combined
ErrorLog /usr/local/apache/logs/sports_science_error_log
```

This `Directory` container gives the client permission to access the `DocumentRoot`. Without it, a forbidden HTTP response is returned.

```
<Directory "/home/www/sport-science.net">
  allow from All
</Directory>
```

This tag ends the `VirtualHost` container. Restart the server, and assuming your DNS entry has had 12-24 hours or so to propagate across the web, your virtual host should be up and working.

```
</VirtualHost>
```

# Technologies for Effective Sites

Undoubtedly the biggest cost in deploying any web site is the design and maintenance. If you have used ASP in the past, you will be aware of the focus on reducing maintenance costs. If every time you want to make a content or design change, you need to edit every page on the server by hand, maintenance becomes prohibitively expensive and error-prone. Server Side Includes (SSI) allow text which is common to every page, to be specified in one file. The other pages can then include it before the document is sent to the client, using an SSI command. Furthermore, if the site is to be able to present more than purely static content, it needs some way of adapting the content it serves to the actions of the client. It needs the intelligence provided by programming languages, such as the ability to perform calculations, handle information and provide feedback to the user.

CGI (Common Gateway Interface) allows scripts to run on the server. The main language used is Perl which is a scripting language providing excellent text processing power as well as standard programming tools. These scripts can handle user input and process it, store it and return customized pages. Apache implements standard script support, and can also provide super-fast script support using `mod_perl`.

Alternatives to CGI for providing fast server-side processing come with Java servlets and JavaServer Pages. Java servlets are complete programs which run on your server, providing a complete portable development environment for your applications. Apache implements full servlet support with the help of ApacheJServ, which we will install later on in this section.

Java Server Pages are from the same family as servlets, but instead of being separate programs, they are HTML files with Java code inserted in-line, and executed before the document leaves the server, combining incredible programming power with the simplicity of in-line code. Support for JSP is provided by project Jakarta, which we will briefly discuss later on.

## Server-Side Includes

The real `trampolining.net` web site contains over 100 separate HTML pages, and that may be small compared to the web sites you plan to deploy. Nearly every page follows exactly the same format in terms of design and layout, including a copyright statement at the end of every page. At the end of the year, all 100 pages needed the copyright statement updated to read © 1999, 2000.

To attempt to update all these manually would be tedious and error-prone. Instead, Server-Side Includes (SSI) are used to include one HTML file within the others. Any commonly repeated text could be inserted using SSI:

```
<!--#include virtual="stylesheet.shtml" -->    Includes a standard stylesheet
<!--#include virtual="navbar.shtml" -->        Starts the page table and include
                                                a standard navigation bar

Main content here

<!--#include virtual="copyright.shtml" -->     Closes table, adds copyright
statement
```

The include commands insert the contents of the named files at that point. The named file is relative to the directory of the main file; subdirectories can be accessed (e.g. `<!--#include virtual="subdir1/included.html" -->`) as can files in parent directories (e.g. `<!--#include virtual="../fromparent.html" -->`) and the included files can themselves contain SSI commands if they end in .shtml. These inclusions are all performed before the document leaves the server – the client will only ever see a normal HTML page. At the end of the year, I only need to change copyright.shtml, for all the pages on my site to be updated – a huge saving in maintenance time.

SSI includes other useful commands: CGI scripts can be called using the `<!--#exec cgi="/cgi-bin/script.pl" -->` command, with the output written directly into the page sent to the client. This prevents the client knowing the script even exists, so is a useful security aid.

You can insert text which automatically updates using the `<!--#echo var="LAST_MODIFIED" -->` command, which allows an extended set of standard variables to be inserted automatically each time the page is called, to show the date for example. Listings of the available commands are available online in the Apache mod_include documentation.

Apache provides excellent support for SSI with just a few commands. Because SSI increases server load, it is traditional to suffix any file containing SSI with .shtml. Setting up Apache to parse *.shtml means it won't waste time attempting to parse normal HTML (*.html) files. This part of the configuration takes place in the primary server section of httpd.conf, outside of any <Directory> containers. In fact, the directives are already there – about three quarters of the way through the file and just need uncommenting. These two lines tell Apache what content type .shtml should be allocated, and tells the internal SSI handler to parse .shtml files before serving them to the client.

```
AddType text/html .shtml
AddHandler server-parsed .shtml
```

Adding index.shtml to this directive allows .shtml files to be served as directory indexes by preference; or in other words if index.shtml exists in the root directory of my server, it will be served to someone requesting http://www.trampolining.net.

```
DirectoryIndex index.shtml index.html index.htm
```

It is then necessary to turn on SSI support in every directory container in which you wish to use it. If SSI is not working on a virtual host, check this command is present in that virtual host's directory container:

```
<Directory /home/www/trampolining.net>
Options Indexes FollowSymLinks Includes ExecCGI MultiViews
Options +Includes
AllowOverride None
Order allow,deny
Allow from all
</Directory>
```

For more information on Apache SSI look up http://www.apache.org/docs/mod/mod_include.html

## Common Gateway Interface

Better known as CGI, this technology is the simplest way to deploy interactive content on your web site. Scripts are freely available to perform everything from form handling to maintaining complete discussion forums. Scripts are usually written in Perl and interpreted as they are used. However as with any program running on your server, they represent a potential security risk. It is possible to configure Apache to interpret scripts from anywhere on the system, but this means anyone with access to directories containing web pages can create potentially harmful scripts.

To minimize this, CGI scripts are run from a special directory, usually called cgi-bin, and have file permissions set that allow remote users to execute them, but only allowing write access to root. The first line of the Perl script must also be changed to read the location of the Perl interpreter on your system – type which perl to find it.

The httpd.conf file already contains the necessary directives in the primary server section, so we just need to uncomment them and change any locations if necessary – note the trailing slashes:

```
ScriptAlias /cgi-bin/ "/home/www/cgi/"
```

The above directive tells Apache to treat any request to /cgi-bin/ as a request for a script, and to look for that script in the server directory /home/www/cgi/. This is inherited by any virtual hosts, unless we define a different ScriptAlias in the corresponding VirtualHost container, so in this example, http://www.trampolining.net/cgi-bin/script.pl and http://www.sport-science.net/cgi-bin/script.pl will each point to /home/www/cgi/script.pl.

Now look at this Directory container:

```
<Directory /home/www/cgi/>
    AllowOverride None
    Options None
    Order allow,deny
    Allow from all
</Directory>
```

This sets the permissions for your CGI directory to the absolute minimum necessary to run scripts. No-one will actually be able to read the scripts as any request will instead run them. These minimum permissions will also make life more difficult for hackers trying to access your scripts.

## mod_perl

The mod_perl program allows Perl scripts to be run very fast by a dedicated Perl interpreter within Apache, which will not need starting separately for each request. Perl scripts are reported to run between two and twenty times faster than mod_cgi, depending on the script itself. However the increased speed of script processing comes at a price.

The mod_perl module is a complex module that is complicated to install and configure, and the actual steps needed depend on the versions of mod_perl and Apache being used; it also has three user modes, and thirty configuration options during build. Therefore, detailed installation instructions are beyond the scope of this book, though you can get more help from the INSTALL text file that comes with the mod_perl download or from the Apache web site (www.apache.org). Furthermore, the installation of mod_perl *will* break your existing Apache configuration. It has to be installed first and Apache reinstalled on top, which mean that you will have to customize Apache again from scratch. You have to decide, right from the onset, whether to include mod_perl in your server system, as it is currently very difficult to incorporate it later on.

The discussion on mod_perl has been left until now, because its benefits would only become apparent under conditions of very heavy server usage. For moderate or low usage, then CGI is only marginally slower and there is little advantage in having the increased script processing power that mod_perl offers. The mod_perl program is an advanced application that should be considered for use, only if very high server usage is anticipated.

### An Example Installation

Below is a very standard installation procedure for mod_perl. Download the module from www.apache.org and uncompress it to /usr/local. Then carry out the following steps.

> The installation steps reproduced below are highly simplified and can only be said to work on *most* systems. You should look up the Apache documentation for more detailed instructions.

```
# cd /usr/local/mod_perl
# perl Makefile.PL APACHE_SRC=../apache_version/src\
> DO_HTTPD=1 USE_DSO=1 USE_APACI=1 EVERYTHING=1
# make && make test && make install
# cd ../apache_x.x.x
# make install
```

After the installation is complete, and mod_perl and Apache are working as they should, then Apache will need to be configured for mod_perl. This consists of adding a few directives to httpd.conf. The first tells Apache to look for /home/www/fast-perl/anyscript.cgi given a request for www.trampolining.net/fast-perl/anyscript.cgi.

```
Alias /fast-perl/ /home/www/fast-perl
```

The next lines tell Apache to allow scripts to be executed in this directory, and to execute them by passing them to `mod_perl`:

```
<Location /cgi-perl>
   AllowOverride None
   SetHandler perl-script PerlHandler
   Apache::PerlRun
   Options ExecCGI
   allow from all
   PerlSendHeader On
</Location>
```

`mod_perl` is a powerful and configurable module. Much more information on configuration is available from the Apache on-line documentation.

## Java Servlets

Java is a programming language developed by Sun Microsystems. It is unique in that once compiled, Java programs will run on *any* machine, architecture or operating system with the help of a Java Virtual Machine (JVM). The compiled program, called a servlet, is not designed to run on any specific machine but instead on a JVM, a piece of software which provides a standard set of commands like that of a chipset. JVMs can and have been developed for nearly all the important operating systems, guaranteeing that well-written code should work on any platform without recompilation. This cross-platform portability is an important feature of the Java development environment which ensures that your development resources will never be made obsolete by new hardware – investment will survive a change of platform.

Java servlets are called by the browser, but are run on the server with the results being sent to the browser. This eliminates any need to worry about the browser type as no code is sent. It is possible to implement infinitely complex algorithms using Java servlets, but if the servlet is designed to return output as pure HTML, the results will be viewable by even the simplest text based browsers.

Servlet support in Apache is performed using ApacheJServ, a fully featured Java servlet runtime container supporting all commands up to JSDK 2.0. While the ApacheJServ modules are not particularly big, the Java Development Kit which is required to compile servlets and provide the JVM, is a huge 45 MB in size (the zipped archive is just over 19MB in size), and using servlets will also cause a step increase in memory requirement of around 32MB due to the JVM. However, the benefits of servlet technology far outweigh the cost of set up, so read on!

Servlets are relatively more difficult to configure than CGI, and Java may take some getting used to – it is a very powerful language with many similarities to C++. However, Java offers the increased security of its in-built security model which makes it much more difficult for hackers to cause damage by passing harmful system commands to the servlet. Complex tasks like chat-rooms or server-side parts of games are also ideally suited to Java, because you can create servlets which will stay alive right from their initial instantiation. While Perl is ideally suited to text processing applications, Java can be used to develop code of infinite complexity with extensions available to make multi-tier distributed applications possible. With the help of MySQL, details of which you will find at www.mysql.org, it is possible to use SQL databases. You will find a more complete discussion of these topics in the Wrox publication *Professional Java Server Programming* (ISBN 1-861002-77-7).

To run ApacheJServ requires the Java Development Kit 1.2 for glibc 2.1 from
http://www.blackdown.org. (Note that older Linux distributions may require the glibc 2.0 version.) The
JDK is currently only available as a `bzip2` archive, so you will need to install the `bzip2` utility as well
(http://sourceware.cygnus.com/bzip2/). You will also need the Java Servlet Development Kit (JSDK)
version 2.0 from http://java.sun.com/products/Servlet. Download JServ from http://java.apache.org
and extract into the `/usr/local/ApacheJServ-1.0` directory and type the following commands:

```
# mkdir /usr/local/apache/src/modules/jserv
# cd /usr/local/ApacheJServ-1.0
# ./configure --prefix=/usr/local/ApacheJServ-1.0 --with-apache-\
> install=/usr/local/apache --with-jsdk=/usr/local/JSDK2.0/lib/jsdk.jar
# make
# make install
```

ApacheJServ should now be installed and configured. Open `httpd.conf` for editing and add this
directive to the very end of the file:

```
Include /usr/local/ApacheJServ-1.0/example/jserv.conf
```

Appending this command forces Apache to read `jserv.conf` from its installed location. Future
versions of ApacheJServ may instead install this file in the same directory as `httpd.conf`. The
`jserv.conf` file contains all the commands to configure the Apache side of ApacheJServ.

Restart Apache, give it a moment to two for JServ to begin accepting requests, and if everything works,
visiting http://localhost/example/Hello should produce a success page!

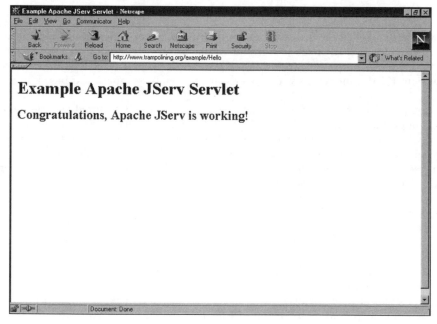

If this does not work, then your version of ApacheJServ configures `/servlet` as the test zone, which
means that you would have to type http://localhost/servlet/Hello.

## *Java Server Pages*

While Java servlets offer boundless possibilities for powerful server-side processing, for simple applications they can be quite unwieldy. Perhaps you want to insert the time and date at one point on your page, and perform a calculation at another; using JavaScript or a Java Applet prevents older browsers viewing your page correctly. You could use a single servlet to create the whole page. However, the page content itself is now mixed up within Java code, making maintenance difficult – particularly if the programmers and web designers are different groups of people. Alternatively, you could keep the page content in an HTML file which uses Server-Side Includes to call successive CGI scripts to insert the correct text at each point. This way the web designers can maintain the HTML without worrying about the code. However, this simple page now has one HTML file and several CGI scripts associated with it, which again makes maintenance complicated.

For simple applications, the ideal solution would be to have the Java code and HTML contained in a single file. It will have the look and 'feel' of HTML, so the web designers can understand it, but would contain additional code which would be run on the server before delivering the page back to the client. Sun's new member of the Java family, JavaServer Pages (JSP), provides this solution. Code can be inserted in line within the HTML, which is executed on the server and the results merged with the HTML in the output. This parallels how Microsoft's ASP works, and JSP is emerging as the cross-platform challenger to ASP in this field.

The file which leaves the server is pure HTML, so unlike JavaScript and Java Applets, which have to be run on the client, you can have the interactivity and programming flexibility of Java while ensuring that all existing HTML browsers can display the output. Furthermore, you maintain all the advantages of Java's portability should you later decide to change operating system or web server. There are already many web sites that use JSP instead of ASP.

Up until recently, the main open source JSP implementations were GNU Server Pages (GSP) and GNU Java Server Pages (GNUJSP), which are independent development efforts despite their similar names. Both are written as regular Java servlets, and although they are difficult to install and configure, they can be used to create JSPs and develop web sites. Information on GSP and GNUJSP can be found at www.bitmechanic.com and www.klomp.org/gnujsp respectively.

However, JSP support in Apache now is in the form of a module called Jakarta. At time of going to press, Jakarta is in final pre-release form, so by the time you read this Jakarta will almost certainly be in production release. The latest version of Jakarta and its installation instructions are available online at http://jakarta.apache.org.

# Logs and Analysis

To develop a web site effectively, you will need to regularly analyze the web site's log files, which contain data on everyone who accesses the site. From it you can determine, the number of requests made, the identities (IP addresses) of the clients and the pattern of hyperlinks that are followed across the web site. While small scale information can be gained by manually viewing the log files, this technique is not appropriate for finding large-scale trends. Each request for a page creates 60 bytes or so of data that is added to the log file – more if images are requested along with the pages, which is usually the case. Multiplying this number by, say, 200 daily page requests means that roughly 50-60 kilobytes of data added to the log each day. Therefore, manual viewing is in reality restricted to small samples of the logs.

To automatically analyze the complete logs, we will be using Analog, a small yet powerful program which is configurable, scalable and free. It is currently the most popular log file analysis program on the web (a 25% market share according to a GVU report at http://www.gvu.gatech.edu). It will be configured to produce separate reports for each virtual host, and update them each morning, and the reports will only be read by authorized people.

## Manual Logfile Analysis

While manual analysis will not be suitable for viewing overall trends, it allows you to interpret the logs with human intelligence. For example, if you notice lots of visitors are requesting one page then leaving, you may want to investigate ways of encouraging them to stay on your site. Do you provide links to other relevant pages? Are they arriving directly into a frame and being trapped with no links out? Are your pages so large, or your connection so slow, they are giving up waiting and leaving the site?

You will have chosen where to place your logs when editing `httpd.conf`. Simply open one in an editor and concentrate on a small section. Below is an extract from `access_log` on my machine (with the IP addresses replaced by dummy ones):

```
231.231.231.231 - - [02/Oct/1999:19:47:35 +0000] "GET / HTTP/1.1" 200 9621 "-"
"Mozilla/4.0 (compatible; MSIE 4.01; Windows 95)"
231.231.231.231 - - [02/Oct/1999:19:47:41 +0000] "GET /trampnetmini.gif HTTP/1.1" 304 -
"http://www.trampolining.net/" "Mozilla/4.0 (compatible; MSIE 4.01; Windows 95)"
231.231.231.231 - - [02/Oct/1999:19:47:58 +0000] "GET /trampnetmini.gif HTTP/1.1" 304 -
"http://www.trampolining.net/" "Mozilla/4.0 (compatible; MSIE 4.01; Windows 95)"
231.231.231.231 - - [02/Oct/1999:19:47:58 +0000] "GET /coach.gif HTTP/1.1" 304 -
"http://www.trampolining.net/" "Mozilla/4.0 (compatible; MSIE 4.01; Windows 95)"
231.231.231.231 - - [02/Oct/1999:19:47:59 +0000] "GET /news.gif HTTP/1.1" 304 -
"http://www.trampolining.net/" "Mozilla/4.0 (compatible; MSIE 4.01; Windows 95)"
231.231.231.231 - - [02/Oct/1999:19:47:59 +0000] "GET /improve.gif HTTP/1.1" 304 -
"http://www.trampolining.net/" "Mozilla/4.0 (compatible; MSIE 4.01; Windows 95)"
231.231.231.231 - - [02/Oct/1999:19:47:59 +0000] "GET /merger.gif HTTP/1.1" 304 -
"http://www.trampolining.net/" "Mozilla/4.0 (compatible; MSIE 4.01; Windows 95)"
231.231.231.231 - - [02/Oct/1999:19:47:59 +0000] "GET /chat.gif HTTP/1.1" 304 -
"http://www.trampolining.net/" "Mozilla/4.0 (compatible; MSIE 4.01; Windows 95)"
132.132.132.132 - - [03/Oct/1999:16:30:45 +0000] "POST /cgi-bin/poll.pl?voted HTTP/1.1"
302 291 "http://www.trampolining.net/" "Mozilla/4.0 (compatible; MSIE 4.01; Windows
95)"
132.132.132.132 - - [03/Oct/1999:16:30:46 +0000] "GET / HTTP/1.1" 200 10137
"http://www.trampolining.net/" "Mozilla/4.0 (compatible; MSIE 4.01; Windows 95)"
132.132.132.132 - - [03/Oct/1999:16:30:47 +0000] "GET /trampnetmini.gif HTTP/1.1" 200
6971 "http://www.trampolining.net/" "Mozilla/4.0 (compatible; MSIE 4.01; Windows 95)"
132.132.132.132 - - [03/Oct/1999:16:30:47 +0000] "GET /improve.gif HTTP/1.1" 200 4727
"http://www.trampolining.net/" "Mozilla/4.0 (compatible; MSIE 4.01; Windows 95)"
132.132.132.132 - - [03/Oct/1999:16:30:49 +0000] "GET /merger.gif HTTP/1.1" 200 4526
"http://www.trampolining.net/" "Mozilla/4.0 (compatible; MSIE 4.01; Windows 95)"
```

The first number in each line is the IP address of the client. By following an IP address through the log, you can find the path an individual visitor took through your site. (Office networks and ISPs such as AOL employing proxies represent around 25% of web traffic, and can cause a single user to appear to come from multiple IP addresses, or allow users to receive some pages without them appearing in your logs. This technique remains accurate the remainder of the time, and is normally accurate even during access via a proxy server, assuming there are not multiple caches. However there is no way round this growing problem).

There follows the date and time, followed by the requested filename and the version of HTTP in double quotes. A single slash (/) here represents a directory request, which usually returns `index.html`. The number immediately following the request is the HTTP success code which is either 200 or 304 as shown above. Any unsuccessful requests, i.e. producing 403 (Access forbidden) or 404 (File not found) codes go into the `error_log` file.

The next field is the referrer, which in all of the above log entries is http://www.trampolining.net/. The identity of the referrer depends on what file is being logged at the time. In the case of images, the referrer is simply the page that contains the image, but in the case of pages, it is the page the browser was previously viewing – this gives a good idea where your visitors are coming from. The final pieces of information are the browser and the version of operating system.

As you can see, each page can generate many lines of log so to make this kind of following easier, we can cut out some of the unwanted information. To follow the path of just one client, type:

```
$ grep 231.231.231.231 /usr/local/apache/logs/trampolining_access_log | more
```

This will display only log entries created by the client with IP address 231.231.231.231.

There are many log file entries corresponding to images, which are often of little interest. To view only page entries, type:

```
$ grep 'html HTTP' /usr/local/apache/logs/trampolining_access_log | more
```

You can even view page requests from a single client:

```
$ grep 'html HTTP' /usr/local/apache/logs/trampolining_access_log | grep
231.231.231.231
```

A final technique allows you to watch current requests in real time. This command is:

```
$ tail -f /usr/local/apache/logs/trampolining_access_log
```

You can make this easier to read by removing the image requests and displaying only page requests:

```
$ tail -f /usr/local/apache/logs/trampolining_access_log | grep 'html HTTP'
```

## Automatic Analysis

This is the vehicle by which we will obtain an overview of our system's usage. Installation of analog is quite simple:

❑ Download Analog from http://www.statslab.cam.ac.uk/~sret1/analog/ to `/usr/local/analog/`.

❑ Change to the `/usr/local/analog` directory.

❑ Open the `analhead.h` file for editing and change ANALOGDIR to `/usr/local/analog/`.

❑ Type `make`.

We also need to prepare a directory for the reports and populate it with the necessary images:

- ❑ Type `mkdir /home/www/trampolining.net/analog`.
- ❑ Copy `/usr/local/analog/images/*` to `/home/www/trampolining.net/analog`.

That's it - Analog is ready for use.

Analog is set up using configuration files; the default is `analog.cfg` which we will edit now, and later on we will create an additional configuration file for each virtual host.

`LOGFORMAT` specifies the format of log used. Analog natively supports the Apache formats `COMBINED` and `COMMON`. `LOGFILE` tells Analog where to look for the access log.

```
LOGFORMAT COMBINED
LOGFILE /usr/local/apache/logs/access_log
```

`HOSTNAME` specifies the name to put at the top of the report.

```
HOSTNAME "www.trampolining.net"
```

Remember we told Apache not to resolve IP addresses? This little section tells Analog to resolve them, but is much more efficient because addresses are only resolved once, and then written to the cache file specified in `DNSFILE`. `DNSGOODHOURS` is the number of hours to trust an entry in the cache file, `DNSBADHOURS` is the number of hours to wait before attempting to resolve a bad IP address again. `DNS WRITE` tells Analog to try to resolve unknown IP addresses, then write them to the `dnsfile.txt` file. The alternative command `DNS READ` would tell Analog to skip IP addresses which didn't exist in the `dnsfile.txt` file, thus saving time. On the first run, Analog will complain about `dnsfile.txt` not existing – ignore it, Analog will create it.

```
DNSFILE /usr/local/analog/dnsfile.txt
DNSGOODHOURS 1250
DNSBADHOURS 350
DNS WRITE
```

This directive tells Analog where to create the report.

```
OUTFILE /home/www/trampolining.net/analog/trampolining_net_report.html
```

`HOSTEXCLUDE` directives tell Analog to ignore accesses from a certain IP address or hostname. This allows you to report what your visitors do, without being influenced by your own visits! In this example I exclude all page accesses from Cambridge University using Cambridge's IP allocation, and exclude all accesses from York University using the resolved hostnames.

```
HOSTEXCLUDE 131.111.*.*
HOSTEXCLUDE *.york.ac.uk
```

If your web site contains pages with other extensions than `.htm` or `.html`, for example JSPs or `.shtml`, you will need to add them here to include them in the page counts, otherwise Analog will assume them to be images.

```
PAGEINCLUDE *.htm,*.html,*.shtml
```

Save your completed file as `analog.cfg` then type `./analog` (or `./analog +g/other-config-file.cfg` if you have an additional config file). If all goes well, you should get a report like this:

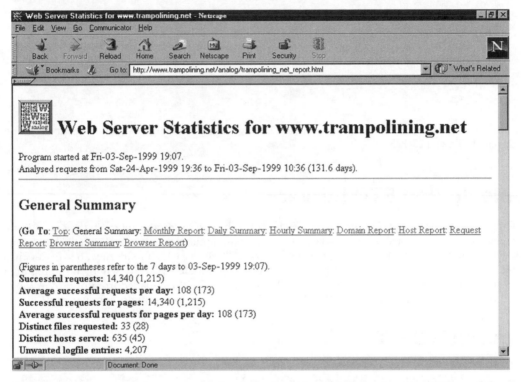

You will need to create a configuration file for each virtual host, and save it with a different filename, e.g. `trampolining_net.cfg`. Finally we are ready to schedule Analog to run each morning. We do this using a *cronjob*, a Linux feature that allows tasks to be run at regular times. We will need to create a separate task for each report, and run them at different times to prevent multiple simultaneous Analog processes clashing.

The set up of cronjobs requires you to use the `vi` editor, which is explained in Appendix B. This is what you type at the `vi` command prompt;

```
55 0 * * * /usr/local/analog/analog
55 1 * * * /usr/local/analog/analog +g/trampolining_net.cfg
```

The cronjob is now set up to run Analog at 0:55 a.m. each morning, which will write to the default configuration file, `analog.cfg`, and again at 1.55 a.m. to run Analog with the configuration file `trampolining_net.cfg`.

Our final task is to protect the reports from unwelcome visitors. To do this, we will create a directory container for the `/home/www/trampolining.net/analog/` directory in the primary server section of `httpd.conf`:

```
<Directory "/home/www/trampolining.net">
  Options Indexes FollowSymLinks
  Options +Includes
  AllowOverride None
  Order allow,deny
  Allow from all
</Directory>
```

```
<Directory "/home/www/trampolining.net/analog">
  Order allow,deny
  Allow from 123.123.123.123
</Directory>
```

This will deny the contents of `www.trampolining.net/analog` to anyone except the owner of IP address 123.123.123.123.

# Deploying an FTP Server

While FTP servers are less prevalent in the current web browser driven Internet, they are still the primary method of distributing very large files and maintaining large stores of files. This section will demonstrate how to deploy an effective anonymous FTP server which modern web browsers will be able to access directly. As we said right at the beginning of the chapter, we will be installing the server developed by Washington University, WU-FTP, which can be downloaded from http://www.wu-ftpd.org. For more information on WU-FTP, look up http://www.landfield.com/wu-ftpd/.

## Installing WU-FTP

To install WU_FTP, you will need to carry out the following procedure:

1. Download WU-FTP and extract to `/usr/local`

2. Type `./build CC=gcc lnx` – Note that to build the `ftpd` daemon, you might have to install the `byacc` utility first, which contains the `yacc` parser.

3. Type `./build install`

4. We need tell Linux to use WU-FTP for FTP requests by editing `/etc/inetd.conf`. Look for a line beginning `ftp`, and make sure it is uncommented. Then edit it to look like this:

   ```
   ftp stream tcp nowait root /usr/local/wu-ftpd ftpd -laio
   ```

**5.** Type `ps -uax | grep inetd`, which will produce a listing of system processes with the word `inetd` in the title. You should get output like this:

```
root        354  0.0  0.4  1252  528 ?        S    Oct21   0:00 inetd
root      19048  0.0  0.3  1152  440 pts/2    S    19:31   0:00 grep inetd
```

The first of the two is of importance to us (the second merely being the search just carried out). What the listing does is provide us with the process ID (PID) which is 528 in the above case.

**6.** Restart `inetd` by typing `kill -HUP PID`, where PID is the process ID listed from step 5.

The latest download of WU-FTP comes with a `configure` script. It can be installed, from the `wu-ftp-version` directory, using the `./configure`, `make`, `make install` sequence of commands as in the other installations in this chapter.

There we have it! The Washington University File Transfer Protocol daemon is installed and ready for action! We can check the installation by typing `ftp www.trampolining.net`, or whatever your hostname/IP address is. You should be presented with a login screen, and you will be able to log in using a standard Linux user account and password set up on your system.

```
connected to www.trampolining.net.
220 www.trampolining.net FTP server (Version wu-2.6.0(1) Fri Nov 12 11:43:54 GMT
1999) ready.
Name (www.trampolining.net:none):
```

# Configuring WU-FTP

To provide access to the general public we need to allow anonymous access. Before doing this, we need to create a safe directory for anonymous users, which will appear to them as the root of the FTP server. This prevents anonymous users browsing around your machine to obtain private information! We also need to create a user account for anonymous FTP users to use.

## Creating an FTP directory

We will create our FTP directory in `/home/` and adopt a traditional directory structure:

```
mkdir /home/ftp
mkdir /home/ftp/bin
mkdir /home/ftp/etc
mkdir /home/ftp/pub
```

The first, `/home/ftp`, will be the root directory of our anonymous FTP server. `/home/ftp/bin` will contain links to commands we want to allow FTP users to use, in particular `ls` (to list the contents of a directory) and `cd` (to change directory). `/home/ftp/etc` is present to hold a password file if necessary and `/home/ftp/pub/` is the public directory which contains the files we are making available.

All directories and files within this structure should be owned by root, and none of them should have Group or All write permissions. This will prevent the user editing any of the files – by editing the contents of /home/ftp/bin/, a user could execute any code on your machine. All the directories should have All read and execute permissions, to allow users to enter the directory (execute permission) and read the contents (read permission). Finally, all the files contained should have All and Group read permissions only – this will allow users to download files, but not change or execute them on your server.

You may require the creating of yet another directory, as follows:

```
mkdir /home/ftp/incoming
```

This directory is special in that it is available for users to upload files to. For this reason, it must have Group and All write permissions and but *not* Group and All read permissions which will prevent users viewing the contents of this directory. While this is the standard way to implement two-way FTP access, it does pose a security risk – users could potentially upload illegal files and use your server to store them. It is a serious policy decision whether or not to provide this service – if you do, be sure to set a umask to prevent uploaded scripts being executed. A slightly more secure system involves removing All write permissions from this directory too, then creating subdirectories with full read, write and execute permissions – these can then be accessed by 'trusted users'. Anyone you have not told the location of these folders to should be unable to find them, since /home/ftp/incoming cannot be listed – there are no read permissions for All.

To summarize, this is how I suggest that you set the access permissions for your FTP site:

```
drwxr-xr-x root    root  bin/
drwxr-xr-x root    root  etc/
drwx--x--x root    root  incoming/
drwxrwxrwx root    root  incoming/secret
drwxr-xr-x root    root  pub/
-rwxr--r-- root    root  pub/any.file
drwxr-xr-x root    root  etc/
```

## Configuring Linux for WU-FTP

The most important change is to modify the main Linux /etc/passwd file to ensure the anonymous FTP user is limited to /home/ftp/pub. Open the file for editing, you should see a listing like this:

```
ftp:x:14:50:FTP User:/home/ftp:
nobody:x:99:99:Nobody:/:
gdm:x:42:42::/home/gdm:/bin/bash
xfs:x:100:233:X Font Server:/etc/X11/fs:/bin/false
username:x:500:500::/home/username:/bin/bash
```

If no FTP user exists, use the root command adduser to add ftp. The important line begins with ftp, which contains the user settings for FTP User. Note there is no entry after the final colon. This ensures no command shell is made available to the FTP User. To force /home/ftp/ to be treated as root directory, we edit this line slightly, adding a decimal point where we want the user to be rooted. The final /pub ensures they are initially placed in that directory:

```
ftp:x:14:50:FTP User:/home/ftp/./pub:
nobody:x:99:99:Nobody:/:
gdm:x:42:42::/home/gdm:/bin/bash
xfs:x:100:233:X Font Server:/etc/X11/fs:/bin/false
username:x:500:500::/home/username:/bin/bash
```

Finally, we need to create a set of configuration files for WU-FTP in /etc. Luckily there is no need to create them by hand, as WU-FTP distribute a default set with the program, which will prove fine for our anonymous server. We will copy these default files to /etc:

```
# cd /usr/local/wu-ftpd
# cp ftpaccess ftpusers ftpconversions ftpgroups ftphosts ftpusers /etc
```

We can implement an extra security touch. In /home/ftp/ type:

```
# touch .rhosts .forward
# chown root .rhosts .forward
# chmod 400 .rhosts .forward
```

There are some final modifications which are not strictly necessary but make anonymous access that little bit easier. Hard linking /home/ftp/bin/ls to point to /bin/ls will allow clients to list the directory through FTP. Make sure that the owner is root and it has group, owner and all execute permissions only. Copying /etc/passwd and /etc/netconfig into /home/ftp/etc/ will provide the replace the user and group IDs for each file and folder with their corresponding names. However these files contain far too much sensitive information and need editing. Only groups and users owning files within the FTP directory should be left in, and password information should be left out – there should just be an x after the user name, not a random string of characters. Anonymous access should now be available.

# Making your Servers Persistent

In the event that your Linux machine crashes or loses power, the priority is to get the machine serving requests as quickly as possible. This can be eased greatly if the system has been designed to recover from a crash - if the services start themselves on boot up, it can save a great deal of time trying to remember what needs to be started!

There are two main services that need special attention in order to enable autostart. First, we need to make sure the network is ready for requests. The ifconfig utility must be configured for each virtual host. We can make this automatic by editing /etc/rc.d/rc.local, or the equivalent file for your Linux distribution. At the end of this file we append all the commands we used originally when we set up the virtual hosts:

```
# setting up IP masquerading for virtual hosts
echo "setting up IP masquerading for virtual hosts"
ifconfig eth0:0 123.123.123.123
route add -host 123.123.123.123
```

The other service we need to start is the Apache web server. Again we will start this by appending the setup command to a boot file. Editing the boot script of the machine is a simple way to do this. You could create a startup script in init.d (called apache) and link to it from S20apache in rc2.d. A sample file follows:

```
#!/bin/bash
#(@) A startup and shutdown script for Apache

case "$1" in
      start)
            # Starts Apache Server
            echo -n "Starting Apache Web Server"
            /usr/local/apache/bin/apachectl start
            ;;
      stop)
            # Stops Apache Server
            echo -n "Stopping Apache Web Server"
            /usr/local/apache/bin/apachectl stop
            ;;
      restart)
            # Restarts Apache gracefully
            echo -n "Restarting Apache after serving current web requests"
            /usr/local/apache/bin/apachectl graceful
            ;;
      *)
            # Incorrect parameter
            echo "Usage: $0 start | stop | restart"
            exit 1
esac
exit 0
```

You can create the symbolic link by changing directory to rc<n>.d (where <n> is your runlevel - usually 3, but you might also want to create one in rc5.d if you use a graphical login.) Create the link by entering ln -s /etc/rc.d/init.d/apache /etc/rc.d/rc3.d/S20apache.

# Summary

In this chapter you have learned how to install the highly popular Apache web server and configure it to meet your requirements and set up virtual hosts. You were shown how to install and configure the ApacheJServ servlet as well as how to modify your Apache configuration to make use of SSI and CGI. Other newer powerful technologies such as mod_perl and JSP were also briefly discussed. You were also instructed in the setting up and configuration of one of the main open source FTP applications WU-FTP.

In addition to setting up the servers, this chapter also covered an important administrative task, namely the analysis of the server logs files, with some discussion on manual analysis using command line tools and automatic analysis using the free Analog tool. Finally you learnt some tips on server persistence – by making minor alterations to system files you can restart Apache on reboot and have it ready to receive requests.

For a discussion on the advanced configuration of Apache, and for other information on Apache itself, ApacheJServ and JSP, see *Professional Apache*.

# References

## *Web*

The Apache home page:
http://www.apache.org/

Security bulletins for Internet services:
http://www.cert.org

Java Servlets Page:
http://java.apache.org

WU-FTP's web site:
http://www.wu-ftpd.org

More information on WU-FTP:
http://www.landfield.com/wu-ftpd/

Analog logfile analyzer site:
http://www.statslab.cam.ac.uk/~sret1/analog/

Jakarta Development site:
http://jakarta.apache.org

## *HOWTOs*

Details on how to set up web servers and clients:
```
WWW-HOWTO
```

How to set up a multi-purpose web server:
```
Apache SSL PHP/FI frontpage mini-HOWTO
```

## *Books*

Peter Wainwright, *Professional Apache*, Wrox Press, ISBN 1861003021
Danny Ayers et al, *Professional Java Server Programming*, Wrox Press, ISBN 1861002777

# 6

# Building a Data-Driven Web Site: E-commerce with Linux

Training Pages (http://www.trainingpages.co.uk), the UK's leading web directory of training products and services, proves that leading-edge web sites are well within the grasp of competent programmers armed with open-source tools like Linux, Apache, the GNU compilers, Perl, and the other odds and ends supplied with a typical Linux distribution. Even though it's only two years old, Training Pages performs session-tracking, statistics collection and data mining, sports a shopping cart, and has numerous features that take it well beyond what most commercial sites offer.

The initial idea for the site popped up over a few beers one night, when the technical department set off to wash away the dust and sweat of a hard day pounding the keyboard. A lot of conflicting requirements got thrown into the mixing bowl, and what emerged surprised us all. The most astonishing thing was that the 'brilliant' ideas of the night before (and we're never short of those) still made sense the morning after. That was a rare thing indeed, considering the madcap notions that usually get aired on one of those nights.

This chapter is about the ideas, the plans, the way we set about building a dynamic, data-driven web site – and the pitfalls and some of the dead ends that we found on route. We think – hope – that there will be something useful in here for anyone wanting to do something similar, and we've included information that should be interesting for coders, administrators, managers and marketers. The result for us is a framework that is already proving its value in e-commerce applications and proof, if any more were needed, that Linux and free software is a great choice for this kind of job. Since we built the framework it has been applied with only minor changes to a number of other projects, and has proved itself to be stable, reliable and robust.

# The Cunning Plan

Our Friday night celebrations have never lacked imagination; they simply tend to lack judgment and alignment with a recognizable version of reality after the first hour or so. This has, naturally, never dampened the spirits at the time. On one such Friday, we found ourselves sitting around and pondering the philosophical issues of the moment, when the topic came around to why most web sites were so dull and boring. Our gang was convinced that it could do much better, and we started listing how. A plan began to emerge.

Once the 'what' was dealt with, the commercial case was exhaustively analyzed, even continuing all the way to the curry house. The conversation would normally have been reduced to grunt-level by then, so it did seem that there was the germ of a good idea in it all. After chewing the basics over for a while, we couldn't see much wrong with the plan, so we set about refining the ideas.

There wasn't – and isn't – one single, compelling argument in favor of the plan; it's more a combination of things that add up to make sense as a whole, so they're listed below in no specific order, just outlining each facet as it occurred to us.

At the time we were thinking about it, the industry was having a love affair with 'portal' web sites. These are supposed to bring lots of things together and encourage high levels of traffic, thereby selling advertising and generally being A Good Thing. We were a little skeptical, but it shaded our view. The thing that really caused (and still causes) frustration was scouring dozens of web sites to find information about a particular product or service. Each commercial operator has its own web site, with different layouts, different levels of information and usually no decent searching or navigational tools.

If you're looking to buy something – a holiday, a flight, a used car or whatever – what you actually want is a single point where all the information is in one place in a common, easily navigable format. We really couldn't find many examples of this done well. At the time, the airlines all had their own sites, selling their own fares, but it was near impossible to find it all consolidated so that you could search for lowest fare/most convenient connections, etc. We wanted to show that there was a better way: something like an online directory, rather than a heap of different catalogs from single suppliers. With the wave of venture capital that has since hit the 'e-industry', this eventually changed – but our ideas were being formulated in early 1998.

We were also frustrated by the low-tech crud that passes for the average web site. Most sites are *still* pretty dire, typically full of pretty pictures but seriously lacking in information. We reckon this is mainly because they're still built by design companies used to working with paper who neither know nor will thank you for telling them that these things can be live, dynamic and filled with valuable facts. Considering how easy it is to create tailored web sites where the pages are aimed at helping the viewer rather than easing life for the designer or maintainer, it's a disgrace that the world still tolerates anything else, but it clearly does. We were certain we could do much better.

A fair amount of our business is training. We enjoy it; our team contains talented educators and we have excellent training materials for our core subjects. We wanted to expand our market there, because when it's done well it's great for the company. It is financially rewarding, gives us the chance to meet lots of people face to face and broaden our own experience, and gets us out of the office – sometimes even to interesting places. Our problem is that it's a constant battle to find new customers, and we're specialized to the point where you don't get a lot of repeat business. Finding an easy way to market ourselves would be extremely welcome. Our plan seemed to have a lot to offer along these lines too.

So, the Cunning Plan was to bring all of these ideas together: a training-oriented database, organized totally around live data, presented in the form of a web search engine with shades of Yahoo and borrowing the better ideas that we could pick up or think up for ourselves. With luck, it would prove to be a highly useful resource, and might one day become a revenue generator in its own right. In any case, we could point to it as a demonstrator of our capabilities, and we could get the "Why does nobody do it right?" frustration out of our system.

# How the Site Should Work

Having worked in professional training for many years, we knew quite a lot about how that market operates. Most training companies send out mountains of brochures with which they bombard likely purchasers. They have to advertise (but bemoan the expense) to try to find new customers, even though they realize that in the main it's not hugely effective. Despite their best efforts to do otherwise, the companies get the majority of their business from existing customers for the simple reason that the customers prefer to work that way. For most purchasers of training, it's more effort to locate a new source and try it out than to go with the tried-and-trusted supplier you've worked with for years.

At the periphery, it's difficult, though established companies have established customers and well-understood training curricula, technology changes (partly through need and partly through fashion). Odd niches spring up, and specialist areas have always existed where the volume isn't interesting to the large players. So how do the suppliers and the customers meet up in these cases?

The Internet could be one way that customers can search for suppliers, but the search engines are too general, and it's particularly hard to focus the search to one area. In the UK, it's not very interesting to find Perl training suppliers in New Zealand. Our idea of a UK-only database makes a lot of sense in this case. We have a lot of experience of the training market in both the UK and the US, and they are worlds apart – not just geographically, but in business terms too. We felt that if we built it 'right' for the UK, variants of it could be built for other areas or regions.

We didn't want to spend our lives maintaining and updating the data, so we concluded that the best thing to do was to provide sign-up and maintenance forms so that anyone could 'join' the database, and then post and edit details of their own products. The most visible examples of this style of web site are the classified advertising pages (for example, http://www.classifieds2000.com) and sites in the general mould of HotMail, GeoCities and their ilk. Traditional directories are always out of date and take an army of administrators to maintain. Using the Web to build what are essentially user-maintained databases is just one example of how the technology allows you to build business models that can dramatically alter the cost structure of an existing industry.

However, we wanted to go a stage further than this. It's strange but true that there is a dearth of market research data available for the professional training market in the UK. Training companies may well know to the last fraction how well their own courses are selling, and what the sales trends are over time, but they usually have no clue at all about their competitors. So, a highly successful company might completely miss the fact that a brand new market is springing up around them, unless they listen very carefully to their customers' more unusual requests. Even if those requests do get noted, it's very hard to substantiate the size of the market and the overall level of interest.

We felt that a valuable feature of an intelligent web site would be the ability to track market trends based on click patterns, and then to present that information analytically for those who are interested. Frankly, we thought we'd be able to charge good money for that information once word got around, so we designed the database with that in mind. We are convinced that this will be a common feature of all major sites before long, but we don't know of many that do it yet.

We chatted, plotted, schemed and hatched various ways of implementing our thoughts. It wasn't all that difficult. The components and most of the approach seemed simple and obvious, so long before paralysis by analysis set in, we simply rolled up our sleeves and started hacking away, using what might be dignified by the term 'RAD' (Rapid Application Development) if we wanted to be pompous. In reality, it was a lot more like "code it, try it, if it doesn't work, throw it away and start again". It helps to have a pretty strong mental image of what the architecture should be, but that probably only comes after building a lot of software in the past.

# Software Choices

The basic components of the system were obvious. There was no budget, so the software had to be free. We needed to prove that *we* could do it; so off-the-shelf packages weren't much of a choice. It had to fulfill our unstated belief that open-source software is not just a match for commercial alternatives, but in many cases it's a hands-down winner. There was no contest. It was going to be Linux for the operating system, Apache, as the web server and then a suitable database, and finally a mixture of whatever seemed best to write the database queries and presentation logic in.

Linux was easy. We'd been using it for long enough, it never crashes, takes next to no maintenance, and runs on low-specification hardware as well as commercial systems do on high-end servers – there was hardly any serious alternative.

Very similar arguments can be applied to Apache. Its flexibility of configuration and use goes way beyond anything we would ask it to do, and while its performance isn't at the 'screaming' end of the scale, raw performance was the last thing on our minds anyway. We were thinking in terms of tens of hits per minute, not thousands of hits per second.

> *That said, the British Royal Family's web site uses Linux/Apache on fairly run-of-the-mill hardware, and copes with some million or so hits a day, according to its manager in an interview on SlashDot (*http://www.slashdot.org*) in October 1999. We've found that Apache/Linux running on an ancient 486 DX/66 can flood a 10Mbps Ethernet with ease – and that's a* lot *of pages being served. Unless you're doing some pretty hairy processing in the database, you're unlikely to find that system performance is the issue; for many web sites, getting hold of enough bandwidth at a sensible price is likely to be the bigger concern.*

The database called for at least two seconds' worth of thought, because there were two strong contenders: MySQL and PostgreSQL. A straw poll around the table demonstrated that we had in-house knowledge of the former and none of the latter, and we believed that MySQL was more than adequate for the job. The MySQL web site (http://www.mysql.org) lists an impressive array of users, which helped to bolster our confidence, and we already knew that it powered SlashDot, which is an extremely heavily loaded site.

> *The database options available for the Linux platform, both free and commercial, are covered in detail in the next chapter.*

The choice of scripting and coding languages was trickier. The 'obvious' contender for data-oriented Linux-based web sites is the Hypertext Preprocessor, PHP. Now, in all honesty, we weren't PHP experts, but our reading of the situation was that it works well for pages where HTML has the greater part of the job and the data management component is modest. There will certainly be people who disagree, but that was our understanding at the time.

PHP embeds the script into HTML pages, which are interpreted by the web server as they are processed for delivery to the user's browser. PHP is available as an optional plug-in for Apache, which is very useful for high-performance sites. There are thousands of web sites built using it, and it clearly works extremely well. The scripting language resembles Perl, and there is a rich set of excellent ideas embodied in the language and the implementation.

For good or ill, we chose *not* to use PHP, but to go down a different route. This decision can be laid partly at the door of ignorance, partly because we started with small plans that grew and we were too lazy to learn PHP before starting to code, and partly because our instincts leaned away from it. Overall, though, we think we got it right for the needs of this project.

> *Since we made the decision, we've come to know PHP better and acknowledge it as a quality product; our own usage of it has been standalone rather than through the Apache module, which is probably a simpler alternative for modest-volume servers. For more information about it, check out* http://www.php.net.

Our instinct drove us to build a framework that was applicable to more than just the training web site. We felt this site would be mostly logic (programming), not presentation (HTML). We also wanted to be able to offer it in various languages, so we didn't think that embedding the code in the pages was the right way to go about things. Instead, we turned it on its head and decided to separate the code and the HTML as rigorously as we could.

When the project was mooted, the consensus was that Perl would be a fine tool to use. The crude prototype was given no time allocation, and was going to be done as a spare time (that is, the hours when normal people would be sleeping or having a life) project. It's embarrassing to have to reveal the truth, but in the very early stages we had a problem getting the Perl/MySQL interface going, so as a short-term expedient we started off with C++, intending to make a break later. Later on, when we had upgraded to a slightly later version of Red Hat Linux, the Perl DBI interface to MySQL just worked – we never did fathom the original cause of the problem.

Anyone with experience of typical software projects will know exactly what happened next – by the time we fixed the Perl problem, the C++ part was twitching happily on the slab and grew rapidly. Before we knew it, there was no turning back. The upshot is that we now have 11,000 lines of C++ in the delivered code, and 350 of Perl. Quite a lot of the C++ code comprises our own reusable libraries for string and object handling, but the effect of the early decision remains with us to this day. We're happy with the result, but it's hard to answer when people ask what fundamental principle made us opt for C++. The answer is mostly, "We just did.". Separating the layout and the code was a good idea. We are extremely pleased with the result – it's not perfect, but it works very well for us. Similar ideas exist in some commercial products, and they do it better, but the total cost to us was about half a day of coding. We can alter it if we later decide that we don't like it, but right now we have no plans for change. We can tweak the logic without having to change the places that layout and styling are done; equally, we can make substantial changes to the layout without having to recompile the C++. One of the disadvantages of the PHP approach is that when you change one, you can never be sure you haven't broken the other.

# Operational Details

Most of the pages that typical visitors will see are generated entirely by CGI programs. There are some 'static' information pages (and a whole section of the site designed for the use of search engines) that work differently, but it's the CGI that is the centerpiece.

If you're not familiar with CGI programs, a quick outline will help. We've configured our Apache web server so that requests for pages with names ending in `.html` or `.htm` are delivered as normal web pages – their contents are copied straight out to the user's browser with no changes. Naturally, they will have to contain HTML just like any other standard web page.

If the page name ends with `.cgi`, something different happens: the corresponding file on our server is treated not as data but as a program. The server runs the program, collects its output, and passes *that* back to the user's browser. Making this work is well documented in the Apache literature, and involves nothing more than a few small changes to the `httpd.conf` and `srm.conf` configuration files. We had to add `index.cgi` to the `DirectoryIndex` directive:

```
DirectoryIndex index.cgi index.shtml index.html
```

And also an `AddType` directive:

```
AddType application/x-httpd-cgi .cgi
```

And finally, in the root directory configuration (`ExecCGI` is the bit that matters):

```
Options Includes Indexes FollowSymLinks ExecCGI
```

CGI sounds forbidding if you don't know what it's about, but it's really no more than a simple way of passing data into those `.cgi` programs. When the 'submit' button on a web page is pressed, any data in the form is encoded and sent back to the server, along with the URL of the program that must handle the form. The server finds the program, sets it running, and passes in the encoded form data.

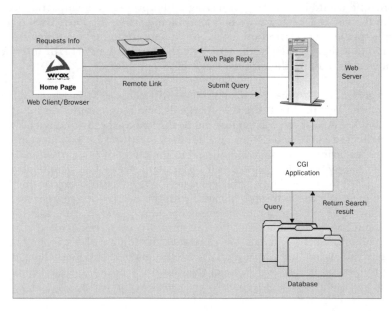

CGI is basic, reasonably flexible, and adequate for many web-based interactions. However, it isn't particularly fast – a new process has to be started to execute the CGI program – and it's particularly poor if you need to maintain a persistent state. We've worked on systems where just connecting to the database can take two or three seconds; if each CGI program has to open its own connection, then every page will suffer that delay.

FastCGI and Apache with `mod_perl` both allow the program to run permanently, so the delay can be incurred just once; these are solutions we have had to adopt with other projects. Fortunately, MySQL connects in milliseconds, so we could take the more basic approach. If we ever run into load problems where the new-process-per-program overheads begin to rise, we could move over to FastCGI and probably gain a lot of speed (though we would probably just use a meatier processor – perhaps a multiprocessor system – instead).

# Client-side Validation

We thought it would be nice if more intelligence could be given to the browser, so that incorrectly completed forms were detected earlier and we wouldn't have to spend so much time putting in the error-handling and reporting – the web-form/CGI model of working is clunky at best. To this end, we put some effort into adding JavaScript to some of the pages to improve error checking, but not every browser supports JavaScript. As a result, we still have to provide all of the error handling at the server end too.

Ultimately, adding JavaScript proved not to be a great plan. The site had been working well before we added it, but afterwards we started to see evidence of weird errors and failures with the forms that were being sent back. Taking the JavaScript out again stopped it immediately, and we concluded that for the small benefit it brought, the problems were a poor payoff.

*This was clearly a client-side problem caused by faulty browsers, and there was nothing we could do about it at the server end, other than spend hours tuning the JavaScript trying to track down and eliminate the client-side failures. The payback just wasn't worth it. JavaScript has worked well for us when we've been building intranets and had some control over the browser population, but we took the problems to be further evidence of the general non-portability of JavaScript in the world at large.*

# Server-side Code Selection

We started off by having a separate program for each interaction, with names like `index.cgi`, `get_cats.cgi`, `show_course_details.cgi`, and numerous others. By about the third one, however, we realized that this wasn't very efficient – the programs contained a lot of code that was common to all of them, and there was very little code specific to the actual queries. As a result, we put all the code into a single executable, and used the program name (which is available through its argument list) to select the action.

We avoided having multiple copies of the executable by creating symbolic links with different names that all pointed to the same copy of the program, so apparently different CGI programs with names like `lost_login.cgi`, `do_maint.cgi` and `get_cats.cgi` all simply reference the single executable called `cgiprog`.

The symbolic link tactic worked for a while, but as the numbers of different names increased, they became a nuisance to manage. The development code was running on one system and the production version on another, and we used a very simple mechanism to copy things from one to the other – so simple, in fact, that it didn't handle the links well. That's what comes of sending stuff around as e-mailed archives.

The most popular solution that emerged was to add a hidden 'action' field to each form, and to have that select the code to be executed in the monster combined program. You can see this by looking either at the HTML source of pages that contain forms, or at the corresponding URL when the pages are retrieved using a GET instead of a POST. To save you the trouble, here's a sample URL: http://www.trainingpages.co.uk/lost_login.cgi?action=show&sessionkey=xxxxxxxx

None of this was particularly difficult to do, and the final tactic evolved over time. We never did get around to picking a single standard, so the live site still shows the mixture of approaches.

# HTML Generation

Quite early on, we had to come up with a way of generating the HTML to send back to the user's browser. We decided to use 'template' files that contained the framework of the HTML, but with tags inserted to show where content needed to be replaced by the results of the database lookup. There are lots of commercial tools that use a similar approach, but we didn't think an investment like that was worthwhile when we could write it ourselves in a few hours, with the bonus of being able to make it do exactly what we wanted. Extra features were added as and when we perceived a need for them, but it's still only a small piece of code that does the template tag replacement.

The tag replacement language in the template files has proved to be a great success. By far the greatest part of the HTML lives in the templates, allowing the C++ code to concentrate on the application logic. The templates can easily be modified by anyone who knows HTML and spends a few minutes learning what the other tags do. The whole look and feel of the site can be changed without needing to change the C++. Our separation of layout from content isn't perfect, but it has helped a lot. The C++ still has to produce a limited amount of HTML – especially for tabular output – and if we could stir ourselves to make the effort, changing that would be the next stage in enhancing the tag language.

As the language stands, most tags start with '%'. A tag consisting simply of <%anything> is replaced by the text associated with 'anything'. It's possible to assign values to these tags either in the template files or in the C++ code. Setting them in the template files is very helpful in controlling the overall look and styling. We can start with a line like this:

```
<%tfont=<font face="arial, helvetica" size="+1" color="#006666">>
```

And then later we can do this:

```
<%tfont>Here is some text in the special font</font>
```

If we ever want to change the appearance of the 'tfont' style, we just change the assignment to tfont in a single place. This really *can* be a single place, since the tag language supports file inclusion, with <%include stdddefs.tpl> being found at the head of most template files. The stddefs.tpl file contains the standard definitions of fonts and colors for all of the pages. Change them there, and the entire site changes immediately. We chose this in preference to style sheets because at the time we started there were plenty of browsers that wouldn't understand them – and if you use this approach, style sheets are redundant.

The tag language is not very clever, but it does what we need. Adding conditional sections to the template files helped us to control another problem: the proliferation of template pages. We can get by with a relatively small number of template files because all of the pages in a similar family are written along the lines of:

```
<%include stddefs.tpl>
... standard header section ...
... preamble to standard body section ...
<%?pagetype_1>
... stuff for page type 1 ...
<%/pagetype_1>
<%?pagetype_2>
... stuff for page type 2 ...
<%/pagetype_2>
... standard end of page stuff ...
```

The entire tag replacement language is implemented in fewer than 250 lines of ugly C++ code. There's a single (global) instance of an object whose job is to provide an interface to the tag language. It's implemented by a class that we called htpl (from HTML template), and its name is Mytemplate, which may well help to confuse anyone who knows about C++ templates (it has nothing to do with them). When the program starts running, and after figuring out what it's going to do, the appropriate template filename is plugged into the Mytemplate object.

Execution of the program usually involves a number of database queries that get packaged up into textual results. These are pieced together as strings in the C++ code, and eventually inserted into the template object using an array-like syntax; the index of the array is another string that matches a template tag name. The C++ code has lots of lines that look like these:

```
Mytemplate["cat_name"] = cat_name;
Mytemplate["title"] = "Training Pages : <%cat_name> Category";
```

When the program exits, the Mytemplate object is destroyed. In its destructor, which C++ calls just before it finally gets destroyed, the code to process the template file is called. The lines are parsed looking for tags to replace, and each time a tag like <%title> is found, the corresponding string in Mytemplate is used to replace it. Each time a tag is replaced, the line is rescanned for more replacements, so we can even use tags that reference other tags.

# Checking our Homework

We have a fetish about producing correct HTML, but once you take into account the various nested files and conditional sections that we use, it's hard to guarantee that we manage it, so we apply a belt-and-braces check. The code that does the tag replacement opens a pipe to a shell script called doweblint. This script acts as a wrapper for the popular weblint program that checks HTML for validity. If the weblint tool reports an error, the offending page is e-mailed together with the error message to our development team. This causes a rapid response to fix the error, because no one likes to have their mailbox filled up with whining messages from weblint.

weblint is not the fastest program in the world, but it takes less than a second for it to check pages of the size we generate. If we started to get high levels of traffic through the site, we'd probably have to use a different strategy, but it's nowhere near being a significant bottleneck yet. The Perl script that calls weblint looks like this (though the e-mail is now sent to someone different):

```
#!/usr/bin/perl5 -w

# Catch write-on-broken-pipe signals to clean up temporary files
$SIG{'PIPE'} = \&terminate;

$tmpfile="/tmp/tp.$$";
$tmpfile2="/tmp/tp2.$$";

# Open a pipe into weblint, taking a copy into tmpfile2 in case of error
if(open(W,
   "| tee $tmpfile2 | weblint -x netscape -d here-anchor - 2>&1 >$tmpfile")) {
   while(defined($input=<STDIN>)) {
      print W $input;
   }
   close W;

   # If weblint reports errors (through return status) e-mail the problem back
   # - all the original page, numbered please
   if($? != 0) {
      system("cat -n $tmpfile2 >> $tmpfile");
      system("mail -s \"bad weblint, $ARGV[0]\"".
             " weblint\@trainingpages.co.uk< $tmpfile");
   }

   # And clean up behind
   &terminate;
}
exit;

sub terminate
{
   unlink($tmpfile);
   unlink($tmpfile2);
}
```

# The Database

MySQL is free for use so long as you install it yourself (an interesting license condition). It costs $100 in one-off quantities if you sell it pre-installed. It's fast, it's simple, and it works. The version we used (3.21.33) provides a reasonable implementation of standard SQL with one rather irritating restriction: it doesn't support nested SELECT statements. If you need high-level database support like transactions with commit and rollback, or the ability to checkpoint the database and then replay a transaction log, it's going to disappoint you. Apart from that, we haven't had the slightest problem with it.

MySQL works in client-server mode. Applications make a network connection to the server, and all of the queries and results are communicated through the connection. As you'll see in the next chapter, there are numerous drivers available for this interface, including ODBC, JDBC, Perl DBI and a C-language library.

We decided to cook up an object-like interface to the C library in C++. The CGI program creates a single Connection object, and then uses that to run Query objects repeatedly. Here's a sample of the code from one of the many test and debugging programs:

```
// Connect to database 'training' on system 'landlord' with user 'fred'
// and password 'fredpass'
Connection c("training", "landlord", "fred", "fredpass");
if(!c)
{
    cout << "Failed to open database: reason " << c.error() << endl;
    return 0;
}

Query cq(c, "select * from company");
if(cq)
{
    array_of_String aos;
    cq.fetch_row(aos);
    cout << "First column value is " << aos[0] << endl;
}
```

If a query succeeds, we retrieve a row of the result set into an array_of_String object (one of our own classes), and then access each field by indexing into the array. This may not be smartest or most efficient way of using the C interface, but it works well for us, and we have got no plans to change. MySQL now comes with an 'official' C++ binding that was released after we had rolled our own – needless to say, we created ours in the very first stages of coming to grips with the MySQL C language bindings.

All of the management, maintenance and daily use of the database is done through the web interface that we have written using the CGI programs. Initially, we didn't have all of the management pages done, and we needed to get the first few hundred courses inserted into the database while the development was continuing in parallel. By far the quickest way to whistle up a few data-entry forms was to use one of the Windows-based tools (we chose MS Access) and to talk to MySQL through its ODBC driver. Those tools are nice, and Linux really needs something as simple and easy to use. At the time of writing we're still not aware of anything as good in the free software domain. There are several projects underway to get there, so we are hopeful. However just as we put this chapter to bed, StarOffice seems to have promise, but we haven't had the time to look into it in detail.

As a consequence of using Access, we had to insert some fake 'primary key' columns into tables that didn't really need them, but they were stripped out once the job was done; we've finished with Access now. Here's the current set of tables in the database, as reported by MySQL:

```
authlist         category         category_links   company
config           course           course_category  course_date
deleted_courses  deliveries       difficulty       duration
enquiries        hotlist          keyword_banners  link_images
link_info        location         random_banners   see_also
sessionkeys      stat_category    stat_course      stat_hotlist
stat_keyword     virtualcats
```

And a description of the columns in the company table:

| Field | Type | Null | Key | Default | Extra |
|-------|------|------|-----|---------|-------|
| company_name | char(150) | Yes | | NULL | |
| contact_address_1 | char(150) | Yes | | NULL | |
| contact_address_2 | char(150) | Yes | | NULL | |
| contact_address_3 | char(150) | Yes | | NULL | |
| contact_postcode | char(12) | Yes | | NULL | |
| contact_web | char(200) | Yes | | NULL | |
| contact_telephone | char(40) | Yes | | NULL | |
| contact_fax | char(40) | Yes | | NULL | |
| info | char(255) | Yes | | NULL | |
| password | char(10) | Yes | | NULL | |
| unique_id | bigint(21) | | Pri | 0 | auto_increment |
| contact_email | char(200) | Yes | | NULL | |
| logo | char(40) | Yes | | NULL | |
| contact_name | char(150) | Yes | | NULL | |

Rather than spend time agonising over what *should* be the primary key for each table, we make a lot of use of auto_increment columns to provide us with guaranteed unique primary keys instead. None of us could remember enough relational database theory to decide whether this was an approved thing to do, but once again it seemed to be the pragmatic way forward.

# Session Management and Tracking

With the template idea proven to work, and the database giving no problems, we had to get stuck into nitty-gritty design. We wanted to add a 'hotlist' to the site, so that anyone browsing could make a note of courses that looked interesting, and later review them at leisure without having to repeat the search. Though we call it the hotlist, it's exactly the same as a 'shopping cart' on a retail site.

If you don't know how the Web works, this would seem to be a simple feature to add. Most computer systems wouldn't have the slightest problem in relating one mouse click to another, allowing us to track the items added to the hotlist, and then displaying it when it was needed. Unfortunately, when you move to the Web, it's not simple at all.

The way that web servers work – a feature of the HTTP protocol used – makes it *very hard* to relate one page request to another. Each one comes in anonymously and independently of any other. If you request one page and then click on a link in that page, the new request is unrelated to the first. It's not at all easy to 'track' a user of a web site. You might anticipate being able to use Internet addresses (IP addresses, not e-mail addresses) to identify people, but they can change with time, and if you're using a proxy, the address could be the same as thousands of others who visit. This is a well-known and tricky problem for web site designers. The way that it's handled more-or-less transparently by some commercial web servers in their interface to server-side programming is one of the strong ease-of-use arguments that their vendors will make.

We weren't prepared to trust commercial software. Some time ago, we were using a large, well-known book retailer in the UK to order some books, when a problem arose in the middle of filling in the allegedly 'secure' order form. When a colleague used a different PC to look at the site in order to see what might be wrong, using a different web browser, the 'secure' details page popped up onto the screen, including the credit card number! Our guess is that they were using the IP address of the requester to distinguish between sessions – but since we go through a firewall, all of our web browsers appear to have the same address. We decided to create our solution by hand, then we would be able to fix it ourselves if anything went wrong. Our approach involved session keys, cookies and modified links on all the pages.

Each visitor to our site is tracked using a 'session key'. Our session keys are just numbers, and as long as they are different for each visitor, their values are not important. (We ensure uniqueness by doing things like encoding the time of day and the process ID of the specific CGI program.) Every time a new visitor arrives, a session key is generated for them and used as an index into the database where the session-tracking information is kept. Once we have associated a session key with a session, we ensure it's linked with each subsequent page request by attempting to hand it out in a cookie and *also* embed the session key in every form and page-to-page link that is generated. This is another example of our trying to cover all the bases, and it's necessary here for a very good reason.

## Cookies

Cookies are supported by all the common web browsers. They work a bit like a cloakroom ticket; when you hand in your coat or bag, you are given a ticket. The cloakroom staff don't know who you are; they just know that when you hand back the ticket, they give back your property. Similarly, cookies are handed out by web sites, and when you request the next page from the site, your browser hands back the appropriate cookie. The web site doesn't know who you are, but it sees the cookie it gave out a while ago, so it can figure out from that (if it's smart enough) how to track your session.

When we generate a new session key, we encode it into a cookie and hand it over to the visitor. If their browser supports cookies, we will see that same key coming back in with each subsequent request, and we can use it to retrieve their session details. It's easy, it's simple, but (through gritted teeth) it's not reliable. If *every* browser supported cookies, that would be all we would need to do. Unfortunately, not all of them do, and the popular ones allow you to turn them off if you are paranoid about remaining secret. Because of this, we can't rely on cookies being available to us. We see about ten percent of visitors using cookie-free browsers.

## Embedded Links

Our second method of session tracking is to embed the session key in every link and form we generate when the server delivers pages to the user's browser. That means that every time a link is followed or a form submitted, we get handed the session key back as part of the URL, and we can extract it. Since every page (apart from the home page) is always the result of clicking a link or submitting a form, we can reliably track sessions in that way.

> *If the embedded-link approach is guaranteed to work, why should we bother with cookies? The answer is that we* want *visitors to be able to leave, come back days later, and still find that their hotlist is preserved. That won't work if we only use the links/forms method. Of course, if they don't have cookies, then we can't do it, but most visitors* do *have cookies working.*

The combined approach gives the widest coverage and works well in practice. One important piece of housekeeping is to discard sessions that are dead and gone, which requires a small amount of care. If someone visits with cookies turned off (or they're a new visitor) we have to create a new session key. If they leave our site and then come back, we can only identify them if they present us with a cookie. Each (apparently) new visit requires a new session key, but many session keys will eventually be lost and become moribund. At present, we retain them for about three months, and then delete them from the session key table in the database. If someone comes back from the dead, we have to ignore their session key and treat them as new, which may mean telling them to delete their previous cookie. It took a day or so of trying the various combinations before we were happy with this, but now it works fine.

A side issue of this aspect of the project is "maintenance sessions". These occur when one of the vendors logs in to the 'editing and updating' area of the site. We can't possibly require every page request to be accompanied by a username and password, so these are requested only at initial sign-in. Maintenance sessions are identified in the database by associating a particular company with the session. Each time activity happens on the session – a page is requested or a change is made – a timer is reset. If the timer reaches a fixed limit (which is kept short), the link to the company is broken and we revert to an ordinary session. This helps to avoid the situation where someone logs in to do maintenance on a shared PC and then leaves, but someone coming along later can find the maintenance stuff in the history list and click back into the session. Again, this is working well, and doesn't require brand new sessions for maintenance.

## A Drop of the Hard Stuff

The session-retrieval and cookie-checking code is reproduced below; it should give the general drift as well as showing a serious chunk of the real live stuff. It is also about as complicated as things get. Much of the application logic consists of large amounts of very straightforward string handling, giving rise to hundreds of lines of very simple C++ – but this isn't one of those bits!

```cpp
#include "cgiprog.h"

bool getsesskey()
{
   // Set this while testing the code
   const bool testing = true;

   if(testing)
      Log::debug("Enter getsesskey");

   String cookiesession;
   Mysession.lasttimeon = 0;

   // Go looking for a cookie-based session, expiring old ones if necessary
   Cookielist cl(getenv("HTTP_COOKIE"));
   for(int cookies = 0; cookies < cl.element_count(); cookies++)
   {
      Cookie &thiscookie = cl[cookies];
      String cookiename = thiscookie.Getname();
      if(testing)
         Log::debug("Retrieved cookie: " + cookiename);
      if(cl.element_count() > 1)
         Log::debug("saw list-cookie " + cookiename);

      // Force all to expire - reset the lucky one later
      thiscookie.Setexpired();

      // If we haven't yet got a cookie-based session, try for one
      if(cookiesession.is_null())
      {
         Mysession.retrieve(Con, cookiename);
         if(!Mysession.isvalid())
         {
            Log::debug("Failed to retrieve cookie-based sessionkey " +
                    "for previous user, sql error is \"" +
                    Mysession.error() +
                    "\", cookie seen was: \"" + cookiename + "\"");

            // And don't leave the valid flag stuffed
            Mysession.revalidate();
         }
         else
         {
            cookiesession = cookiename;
            Mysession.lasttimeon = Mysession["timelastused"].ulongval();
            if(testing)
```

```
                    Log::debug("Retrieved session from cookie " + cookiename +
                           " timelastused " + Mysession["timelastused"]);
        }
     }
}


// End of cookie retrieval
// cookiesession is non-null if a successful session was retrieved. If that
//  is the case, the Mysession object is also valid and contains real data

// The 'global' form - picks up the session etc. Missing bits (such as
//  session key) are inserted below. It IS a global now
// Form Myform;

// Fairly tricky logic to get session management correct
bool valid_form_session = false;

String& formsesskey = Myform["sessionkey"];
Log::debug("Have form session key \"" + formsesskey + "\"");

// Retrieve this from the form if there is an incoming session key
Session formsession;
if(!formsesskey.is_null())
{
   formsession.retrieve(Con, formsesskey);
   if(formsession.isvalid())
   {
      valid_form_session = true;

      // Always prefer this - may be the wrong thing to do, but...
      Mysession = formsession;
      Mysession.lasttimeon = Mysession["timelastused"].ulongval();
      if(testing)
         Log::debug("Retrieved valid session from " +
                    " incoming session key " + " timelastused " +
                    Mysession["timelastused"]);
      Mytemplate["sessionkey"] = formsesskey;

      // Check that this matches the cookie (if any)
      if(!cookiesession.is_null() && formsesskey != cookiesession)
      {
         // The user's cookie will get reset later
         // String ncookie = mkcookie(formsesskey);
         // Mytemplate.htmlhdrs["Set-Cookie"] = ncookie;
         Log::debug("session key mismatch with punter's cookie! : session " +
                    formsesskey + " cookie " + cookiesession);
      }
   }
   else
   {
      Log::debug("Invalid form session key presented: " + formsesskey);
   }
}
```

```
    if(!valid_form_session)
    {
        if(cookiesession.is_null())
        {
            // Form no good and no cookie to go by...
            sessionkey skey;
            Mytemplate["sessionkey"] = skey;
            formsesskey = skey;

            if(testing)
                Log::debug("Generate new session: " + formsesskey);
            Mysession["sesskey"] = skey;

            // Mytemplate.htmlhdrs["Set-Cookie"] = mkcookie(skey);
            if(!Mysession.insertinto(Con))
            {
                error("Failed to create sessionkey for new user, reason is " +
                      Mysession.error(), "internal", Mytemplate);
                return false;
            }
        }
        else
        {
            // Invalid form session but valid cookie - all is ok
            formsesskey = cookiesession;
            Mytemplate["sessionkey"] = formsesskey;
            if(testing)
                Log::debug("Use cookie not invalid form "+
                           "session, cookiesession= " + formsesskey);

            // This is badly named!
            Mytemplate["retrieved_cookie_session"] = ctime(&Mysession.lasttimeon);
        }
    }

    // Update the timestamp and put back into the session table
    Mysession.update(Con);

    // Set an expiry date in the future, then add all the cookies
    // to the template ready to be sent out
    cl.byname(formsesskey).Setexpires(time(0) + 60L * 60 * 24 * cookiedays);
    Mytemplate.mycookies = cl;

    if(testing)
        Log::debug("Last time on gives " +
                   String(ctime(&Mysession.lasttimeon)).substr(1, 24));

    return true;
}
```

You can probably see from the code that we make a lot of use of Log::debug() — a static function that writes messages into a file called dblog in the same directory as the web server's access logs. There are also Log::error() and Log::fatal() functions that write recognizable strings into the log. The fatal error log code is supposed to e-mail us, but in its current form it doesn't. Usually, one of us has a window open onto the dblog while we sit in the office, keeping an eye on the state of activity and watching for error symptoms. Some days, nobody is watching, but it's useful to get a feel for the state of play and level of activity.

In general, the code has been structured so that most of the general housekeeping is independent of the particular application logic — although we do keep finding ways of improving the generic parts and reducing their dependence on the application-specific components. This process will probably continue forever.

Probably the least successful tactic was to be skeptical of the GNU C++ compiler's exception handling. We worked hard to check every possible error condition and to log it to a debug file. We have probably missed some, but here's a typical chunk of the C++ code:

```
if(category_id == String::NULLSTRING)
{
    error("Failed to find non-null category id in current session" +
          indexsession + " in get_cats()", "internal", Mytemplate);
    return 0;
}

if(!Myform.contains("sitemap"))
{
    String s(time(0));
    Query mq(Con, "insert into stat_category(time, category_id) values(" +
             quote(s.cstring()) + ", " + quote(category_id) + ")");
    if(!mq)
    {
        Log::fail("Failed to update stat_category table " +
                  "in get_cats(), reason is: " + mq.error());

        // can continue, this is not fatal, we just miss a click
    }
}
```

The important points to note from the code above are that we have to provide a reasonable error handler for every conceivable problem, and that about 50-60% of the total code volume is for dealing with error conditions. This is a fact of life in serious software development; that's how it works.

### Exception Handling

If there is support for it in your development language, a much better tactic is to make use of exception handling. You can write most of the code on the presumption that things *do* work, and provided you have written the lower layers to throw appropriate exceptions (rather than testing every function call), you can surround large chunks of logic with their own try-catch sequences. In retrospect, this would have saved us a lot of coding, shrunk the size of the programs by at least a quarter, and probably sped up the development by more than that.

The reason we didn't this technique was sheer prejudice. C++ compilers have not traditionally been very good at implementing exception handling, and it introduced yet another unknown at a time when we didn't want one. In the latest version of the framework, we *are* starting to use C++ exceptions for error handling – a *very* big benefit that we couldn't get easily if we'd used Perl. We'll check that it's reliable, and then spread it throughout the code. It's a shame that C++ doesn't use Java's compile-time facility to tell you about uncaught exceptions, because that would make the migration process much more simple. We'll have to do it by eye when we come to do this.

# Site Tricks and Tactics

Building a site isn't much good if nobody uses it. A database is useless if it's empty. We had to get around these problems to make the site of any use to anyone, so the first tactic was to pre-populate it from the brochures of some major training companies. We weren't stealing their copyright, and if any had objected, we would have removed them from the site, but in fact none did. Seeding the database took a while, but it meant that when the database went live, it had useful information in it. Once live, the entries in the database are maintained by the training providers themselves, and we do very limited maintenance on it. We just insist on controlling the way that the categories are organized, and sometimes rearrange them through a handful of maintenance screens that are only usable from inside our Linux-based Internet firewall.

> *You can read more about setting up a Linux machine as a firewall in Chapter 10.*

We decided that, like most other commercial directories, a basic listing should be free, with options to pay for enhanced features. This has certainly proved to be popular. We seeded the database with about 20 companies and 500 or so course listings; at the time of writing it has just rolled over 4,500 courses and 350 training providers. The 'enhanced features' are the ability to be sorted to the top of listings, to associate a company logo with course details, to buy banner space, and to buy keywords in category searches. So far, we're not pushing those commercial opportunities – we prefer to build traffic through the site and then charge a realistic figure, rather than starting low and then racking the rates up later.

To be fair to all of the providers listed, we randomize the presentation of courses within the listings. Each session has its own random number generator. The effect is that you see the same ordering within a single session, but other users with other sessions see a different order. Courses with the list-to-top flag set have a large positive bias added to them, so that they will always come above courses without the flag. If two providers both have list-to-top set, their courses are arranged at the top in a similar randomized fashion.

Here's a (slightly edited) extract from the course selection logic:

```
String CourseQuery = "select c.course_title, c.course_detail, c.unique_id, \
                c.location, c.duration, c.difficulty, c.company_id, \
                c.priority + rand() as priority, cc.course_id FROM \
                course c, course_category cc WHERE \
                cc.category_id = " + quote(category_id) + " AND \
                cc.course_id = c.unique_id order by priority desc";

// Log::debug("In pick_courses, query so far is " + CourseQuery);
```

```
// Initialise random seed
Query mq(Con, "select rand(" + Mysession["seed"] + ")");
if(!mq.query(CourseQuery))
{
    error("SELECT Query failed:" + mq.error(), "internal", Mytemplate);
    return 0;
}

// List of courses now ready to show...
```

## Dealing with Search Engines

Getting a database like this listed with the search engines *sounds* like a good idea, but it's problematic. You want them to point to you so that the public can find you, but you *don't* want them sending their robot link-followers to crawl all over your site. The robots are programmed to follow every link on a site, which would mean that they would endlessly be causing sessions to be generated, adding courses to their (huge) hotlists and so on. As a consequence, there would be some very strange listings showing as search results. This is decidedly unwelcome.

Instead, we created a `robots.txt` file (the standard thing to do) that bars them from using any of the dynamic parts of the site. We set up a nightly task that queries the categories and the courses in the database and generates a whole sheaf of static HTML pages – a catalog of the database contents – each of which links into the live part of the site. We point the search engines at those pages instead, and have a secret hidden link from the home page that also points to them, further encouraging webcrawlers to find them. This approach has proved to be very successful at getting the site indexed by the major robotic search engines, and we'd certainly use it again for a similar site. The static pages can be found at http://www.trainingpages.co.uk/static, if you want to look.

> *You can find a full specification of the* `robots.txt` *format at*
> http://info.webcrawler.com/mak/projects/robots/norobots.html

## External Links

The next tactic for driving up the traffic was to look at our own categories and then go hunting for specialist web sites that contain pointers to useful resources. Our goal was to get them to point to us, saying, "If you want training in poodle grooming, click here." We didn't want those links just to point to the home page, so we created a special entry-point direct to the appropriate category.

A wrinkle that gives us more flexibility is that rather than pointing directly to our category for poodle grooming (we don't *actually* have that one yet), we have 'virtual categories' that can be set to point to whichever of the current categories is most appropriate. The virtual category means that requests for "poodle grooming" can point to "pet care" in the early days, to "show dogs" when that category is worth setting up as a separate entity, and finally to "poodle grooming", if we get that far. The other site (the one that links to us) will never have to change.

We keep an eye on our referrer-log, and it's clear that this is an important way of building up traffic to the categories. For an example of a virtual link, try http://www.trainingpages.co.uk/get_vcats.cgi?vcat=Linux.

## *Gathering Statistics*

Something we haven't seen much of yet, but which we are sure will become a necessity, is our statistics collecting capability. Every click to the site is logged along with the time and date it was made, what category and course were involved, etc. Even keyword searches are captured; you name it, we probably capture it.

This means that the statistics tables in the database are not small, but they allow us to do *lots* of data mining. We can rank the most popular courses against others in their category; we can rank the categories; we can see preferences moving over time; we can dump the data to spreadsheets for graphical analysis; we can even generate graphs to show the public (free) and the course providers (not free) where the market is going and what is proving to be popular. A basic example is shown below; you can always see the live ones by browsing to http://www.trainingpages.co.uk/info.cgi?page=graph.

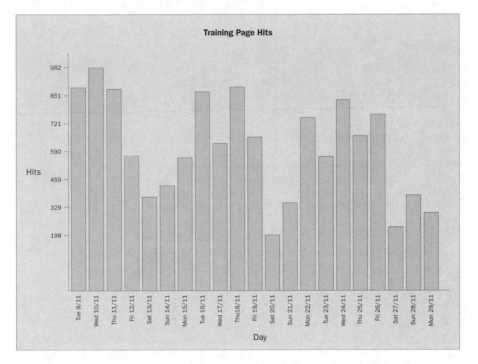

At the moment, we don't know of anyone else who can offer live, consolidated market research of this nature. That doesn't mean it's not available, but it's not currently a feature of most web sites. The truth, however, is that it's incredibly easy to add – the statistics-gathering code is a tiny fraction of what we had to do. The graphing may not be beautiful, but we simply picked the Perl modules to do it, and off we went. This is the only part of the site that we created using Perl.

The code for graphing daily access figures is not too complicated, though the arithmetic went badly wrong when we moved to Daylight Saving Time – we lost a day from the graph. That's why, if you read this fragment, the date calculation isn't as transparent as it might be:

```perl
#!/usr/bin/perl
use DBI;
use Time::Local;
use Graph;

# The Database Information
my $database = "training";
my $hostname = "landlord.gbdirect.co.uk";
my $data_source = "DBI:mysql:$database:$hostname";
#my $alt_data_source = "DBI:mysql:$database:localhost";
my $username = "xxx";
my $password = "xxx";

@days = ("Sun","Mon","Tue","Wed","Thu","Fri","Sat");

my $dbh = DBI->connect($data_source, $username, $password)
or $dbh = DBI->connect($alt_data_source, $username, $password)
or die "Can't connect to $data_source: $DBI::errstr \n";

my $days = shift @ARGV;
$days = "21" if $days eq "";
$now = time;
my $freq;

if($days =~ /m/i) {
   ($sec,$min,$hour,$mday,$mon,$year,$foo,$bar,$foobar) = localtime($now);
   if($mon == 0) {
      $mon = 11;
      $year--;
   } else {
      $mon--;
   }
   $lastmonth = timelocal($sec,$min,$hour,$mday,$mon,$year,$foo,$bar,$foobar);
   $gap = $now - $lastmonth;
   $days = $gap / 86400;
}

$from = $now - (($days - 1) * 86400);
($sec, $min, $hour, $mday, $mon, $year, $foo, $bar, $foobar) = localtime($from);

# MB - count from 5 AM since that's just after log rotation - plus it helps
# avoid oddities caused by 25-hour days when the clocks change!
$hour = 5;
$min = 0;
$sec = 0;
$from = timelocal($sec, $min, $hour, $mday, $mon, $year, $foo, $bar, $foobar);
$to = $now;
```

```perl
$sth = $dbh->prepare("SELECT time FROM stat_course".
                     " WHERE list_type <> 'L' AND time > $from AND time < $to");
$rv = $sth->execute or die "Can't Execute Query : $sth->{errstr}";
while($row_ref = $sth->fetchrow_arrayref) {
    $day = $from + (86400 * int(($row_ref->[0] - $from) / 86400));
    $freq{$day} = 0 if !defined ($freq{$day});
    $freq{$day}++;
}

$sth->finish;
$sth = $dbh->prepare("SELECT time FROM stat_category".
                     " WHERE time > $from AND time < $to");
$rv = $sth->execute or die "Can't Execute Query : $sth->{errstr}";
while($row_ref = $sth->fetchrow_arrayref) {
    $day = $from + (86400 * int(($row_ref->[0] - $from) / 86400));
    $freq{$day} = 0 if !defined ($freq{$day});
    $freq{$day}++;
}

$sth->finish;
$sth = $dbh->prepare("SELECT time FROM stat_keyword".
                     " WHERE time > $from AND time < $to");
$rv = $sth->execute or die "Can't Execute Query : $sth->{errstr}";
while($row_ref = $sth->fetchrow_arrayref) {
    $day = $from + (86400 * int(($row_ref->[0] - $from) / 86400));
    $freq{$day} = 0 if !defined ($freq{$day});
    $freq{$day}++;
}

$sth->finish;
$dbh->disconnect;

$graph = new Graph;
$max = 0;

foreach(sort keys %freq) {
    ($sec,$min,$hour,$mday,$month,$year,$dow,$bar,$foobar) = localtime($_);
    $month++; #Doh! localtime returns values 0-11 for the months :)
    $graph->data("$freq{$_}", "$days[$dow] $mday/$month");
    $max = $freq{$_} if $freq{$_} > $max;
}

print "Content-Type: image/gif\n\n";
$graph->title("Training Pages Hits");
$graph->keys_label("Day");
$graph->values_label("Hits");
$graph->value_min(0);
$graph->value_max($max+20);
#$graph->value_labels("0, $max");
$graph->value_format(".0");
$graph->tick_number(5);
$graph->height(380);
$graph->width(530);
$graph->output
```

# Overall Experience

After about three months of effort, the bulk of the site was up and running. There are fewer than six staff months of work in the whole thing, but we think it stacks up better than 99% of all the web sites we have ever seen. It's generating increasing levels of traffic, regular training leads for us and the other providers who are listed, and on a day-to-day basis we can just leave it running – it looks after itself.

Our site is built completely from free software, and it's extremely reliable. At this moment, the server (which hosts a dozen other commercial web sites) is showing an uptime of 220 days; its most recent restart was due to a fault at our leased-line provider's end that meant we had to swap a card over to prove the fault wasn't ours. Prior to that, it had never crashed or needed to be rebooted since we installed it nine months ago. Rough tests show that with no optimization at all in our code, it can service 2-3 requests per second – more than our bandwidth could ever support. It's running on an AMD K266 processor with 64MB of RAM. It says it has a load average of 0.01 – that is, it's 99% idle.

If we were to begin again from scratch, we would switch to C++ exception handling and replace our tag language with PHP, which is more powerful, more widely used, and better supported. What we have works perfectly well, but when it comes to building software that works, we think of ourselves as perfectionists. The process of development may sound odd and arbitrary in places, but the delivered code was produced with a lot of care and attention to detail. We have to say that we think it's a success!

# 7

# Using Database Applications with Linux

The history of databases has closely followed the evolution of enterprise computing. Database systems have been the workhorses of the enterprise, the *de facto* choice for deploying strategic and mission critical applications. Today, fault-tolerant, distributed, highly parallel, highly scalable and high performance databases have proliferated the enterprise. Any operating system making a serious foray into the enterprise arena has to reckon with the need for production class databases running on it. Linux is fast emerging as a serious contender in the enterprise segment, and it comes as no surprise that the Linux needs all the power of the enterprise database if it is to compete with proprietary operating systems in this area. In this chapter, we'll try to evaluate the significance and capabilities of Linux as a platform for enterprise database deployment.

## The Case for Linux as your Database Server

Here, we shall examine the various premises for Linux as the platform of choice for running enterprise databases. We shall also see how Linux and some of the various enterprise databases are integrated together as well as highlighting some of the shortcomings of Linux in this area.

### Robustness and Availability

The term **robustness** means that the information contained in a database persists even after a system failure and that the database itself is not prone to failure. When someone talks about how often the database is available for actual data processing, they are talking about **availability**. For example, a database application has to make itself available twenty-four hours a day, seven days a week, a front on which Linux scores highly.

When we consider robustness, we also need to look at **recovery** – the ability to resurrect the database after a crash and salvage data. This is directly influenced by the file system. Windows NT has NTFS, and Solaris has UFS, both of which support journaling, which is the process of maintaining information about file system transactions so that in the event of an abrupt shutdown of the operating system, the file ystem can quickly be brought back to a state of consistency. However, the `ext2` file system which is the current file system on Linux, does not support journaling, hence there is the real possibility of the file system becoming inconsistent after a crash.

In a file system that supports journaling, information about reads or writes made to the file system, or **transactions** (as they are called), are recorded in such a way that they can be used later to repair the file system after a crash or a failure to shut down properly. Resierfs is a new file system for Linux that supports journaling; more information on Reiserfs can be found at http://devlinux.com/projects/reiserfs/.

Support for journaling comes at the cost of performance, i.e. there is extra overhead incurred in logging file system transactionsthat would be required to resurrect the file system after a crash. The `ext2` file system does not have this overhead, and hence performs better than most other file systems with journaling enabled. But if we plan to use a database that has recovery features built into it (and most commercial RDBMSs do), we may never experience data loss, since the database itself takes care of data consistency and recovery. However, recovery of the file system will take longer under Linux as diagnostic programs like `fsck` will still need to examine the file system comprehensively.

Clustering is another issue that affects availability. In a clustered system, the participating machines are connected together to provide fault tolerance and load balancing. Whereas there are several approaches to clustering we also need to understand whether our deployment scenario really needs it. We need to start thinking of clustering if we are looking for a high-availability environment with load balancing between servers. The Beowulf project attempts to provide a clustering solution on Linux. Currently clustering on Windows NT is enabled by interconnecting participating machines using fiber channel controllers. On the other hand Beowulf uses fast Ethernet to interconnect participating hosts, which is slower. Clustering is further discussed in Chapters 12 and 13.

The biggest obstacle to using Beowulf for database deployment on Linux is that none of the database vendors yet support it in their offerings. However, see Chapter 13 which presents a simple (non-Beowulf) Linux clustering example using Sybase. Clustering on Windows NT is used by database vendors to provide fail-over implementations, e.g. the Failsafe product by Oracle.

## Performance

Performance is one of the primary considerations for most enterprises when deploying databases. Often large enterprises are not held back by high hardware costs, and they're willing to throw expensive hardware at the operating system for that extra performance boost. Database vendors often use TPC (Transaction Processing Performance Council) benchmarks (see www.tpc.org) to calibrate database performance on different platforms. Again performance is an issue closely tied with the type of application that being deployed. For example, if the application is a back-end database for web clients to do searches on, then there is often no need for database transactions, foreign keys, row-level locking and other advanced features which are supported by commercial databases. A simpler database might thus fit the bill, for example MySQL (www.mysql.org) which does not have the features just described but is about four times faster than most commercial databases. Commercial databases are usually compared using TPC benchmarks (see http://sizing.com/html/tpc-core.htm). Unfortunately, at the time of writing, Linux has no TPC results published for it.

Also, the Linux threading model is not mature enough to be utilized by most database vendors, and compared to Windows NT, which has a mature threading model, there are some shortcomings in system performance. Having said that, Linux processes, which are equivalent to threads on Windows NT, largely preclude data corruption, because one process cannot affect the data of another process, unlike threads which share data, which is therefore corruptible.

The conclusion here is that, if the implementation does not call for using the advanced database features mentioned above, or if threading is not an issue, an open source database such as MySQL on Linux is often the best solution.

## Price

Linux scores very well in this department, simply because it is cheap (or free if you want) to acquire and you do not have to pay for any upgrades. Of course, the price is not *just* the financial cost of the Linux distribution CD. Usually, the hidden costs for most software solutions take the form of the total cost of maintenance, in other words expensive support contracts. Linux has traditionally been supported by the GNU/GPL community that fostered and nurtures the Linux movement. Thus support cost is practically zero.

For the same hardware configuration, Linux offers a better price proposition than its competitors. But the fact remains that large, performance-focused enterprises may not really see a price advantage for server installations; in the average enterprise, there are not a lot of database servers in comparison with the number of personal productivity workstations.

## Support

With its open software ideals, Linux redefines the issue of support. In the traditional sense of management information services (MIS) personnel dialing a hotline for immediate answers to their problems, support for Linux is not as extensive. In a nutshell - unlike the proprietary companies, Linux doesn't have a centralised point where people can come to have their programming problems solved. But this is fast changing with many industry heavyweights offering full-fledged support for Linux. An example is HP which offers round-the-clock support for Linux at US$130 per server per month. Traditionally, support for Linux has always come from online forums and is community-driven; developers regularly post bug fixes on the web – in many cases, within hours of a problem being reported, e.g. the Pentium *f00f* bug; for more information on the *f00f* bug see http://x86.ddj.com/errata/dec97/f00fbug.htm.

Analysts predict a slew of companies that will emerge with Linux support as their mainstay – IBM, HP and Compaq seem to have caught on. As for commercial databases are concerned, the vendors are as committed to support their software on Linux as on any other platform.

## Migration and Coexistence

Considering that the decision has been made to adopt a new platform for application deployment, the immediate tasks are to migrate existing applications to the new system, if required, while at the same time get currently installed applications to coexist with your new system.

If you bought into the idea of running your database on a Linux server, what would this entail in terms of migrating your existing enterprise applications? Since most database applications are written in fourth generation languages like SQL, which are independent of the operating system, this should not be an issue. As for interoperability, most serious database vendors offer interconnectivity options. For example Oracle on Linux comes with JDBC and ODBC support. It must however be noted that you can't access an ODBC-enabled source from MySQL, whereas the reverse is possible.

## Administration

Administration is another issue that determines the choice of which database to deploy. The manpower costs associated with database administration are quite significant especially in the case of traditional commercial databases such as Oracle, which are complex applications. As for open source databases like MySQL, which are much simpler by comparison, the level of expertise required for database maintenance is nowhere near as large.

Now, most databases available on mainstream operating systems are available on Linux (with the exception of Microsoft's databases) and so any administrative issues are actually those that are specific to a particular database. This means that the system administrator will have to become somewhat expert in administering the database as well as the operating system.

## Tuning Flexibility

Operating systems offer little flexibility in terms of tuning it to suit the database deployed on it. In the best scenario you could tweak performance variables in start-up files. However, Linux has an upper hand here since the source code is freely available; the kernel source code is at hand, so it can be modified to squeeze that last ounce out of the hardware/database combination. I know most users don't indulge in kernel coding as a pastime, but nevertheless the option exists, which is a definite advantage over those vendors who don't offer the ability to fine-tune the operating system to this level. An example of this is the description of how to tune the Linux kernel to increase the share memory resources for Oracle, so that it performs better. For more information refer to the *Oracle Administrator's Reference for Oracle 8.0.5 on Linux.* This is available for free download from the Oracle Technical Network website (http://technet.oracle.com) – you might require prior registration however.

## Determining the Size of the Application

Finally, before we deliver a verdict as to whether Linux can be efficiently used for deploying an enterprise database or not, we need to look at what we want out of it. If the goal is a highly scalable environment, Linux suffers due to the fact that many of the scalability features supported by databases are not available on Linux because of the lack of tools to support these. Linux falls short when it comes to SMP (symmetric multiprocessor) configurations, support for very large files (greater than 2 GB), kernel multithreading, asynchronous I/O etc, which are often required by database solutions to offer advanced functionality and performance. Many of these come in handy when you need a scalable, high-volume database setup.

On the other hand, Linux measures up quite handsomely when it comes to small and medium-sized deployments. In fact, when run on small to medium-sized single-CPU architectures, Linux outdoes Windows NT on several counts. More importantly, open source databases like MySQL on Linux outperforms commercial databases in certain scenarios that do not require transactions, row-level locking, stored procedures and foreign keys.

## In Conclusion

The choice of Linux as a database deployment platform can be reduced to determining the size and scope of the application to be deployed and weighing up what additional features the database offers with what Linux is able to cope with.

Having taken a look at the various considerations in deploying a database application on Linux, we shall explore some of the actual choices of database available to us. In particular, we shall take a look at two open source databases. The first is MySQL, a lightweight solution that outperforms some of the high-end enterprise databases in certain areas. The second is PostgreSQL which is also an open source solution but is armed with many of the functionality that is not available in MySQL. Finally we shall also take a look at Oracle on Linux, a powerful commercial database from the Oracle Corporation.

To conclude this section, I can say that Linux is a good operating system on which to deploy a database. As we shall see, MySQL turns out to be a compelling solution to certain deployment scenarios which calls for its lightweight features, and PostgreSQL proves to be a more complete and general-purpose database solution in the open source domain, and Oracle, a traditional database solution with many in-built features.

# A Non-Commercial Database on Linux: MySQL

MySQL is a compact, easy-to-use database server, ideal for small and medium-sized database applications. It is a client/server implementation that consists of a server daemon called `mysqld` and many different client programs. It supports client APIs for a set of programming languages including C and Perl. It is available on a variety of UNIX platforms as well as Windows NT, and Windows 95/98. On Linux, it uses threading, which makes it a high performance and highly scalable database server. It supports standard SQL syntax.

## Features of MySQL

### Standards Supported

MySQL supports entry-level ANSI SQL92 and ODBC level 0-2 SQL standard. So any database application conforming to these standards will work on MySQL.

### Language Support

The database server `mysqld` can issue error messages in many languages including English, French, German, Italian and Spanish. By default, MySQL uses the ISO-8859-1 (Latin1) character set for data and sorting, but recompiling the sources can change this. Instructions for changing the default character set for data and sorting are given in the `INSTALL-SOURCE` file of the source distribution.

### Programming Language APIs for Clients to Access the Database

Language APIs provide library functions to connect/access information from the database. Database applications can be written in different programming languages by using the client API of the language in question. A client API for C is included with the MySQL distribution, but other language APIs are also available:

| Language | Location |
|---|---|
| MySQL Eiffel wrapper | http://www.mysql.com/Contrib |
| MySQL Java Connectivity (JDBC) | http://www.mysql.com/Contrib |
| MySQL PHP API | http://www.php.net |
| MySQL C++ API | http://www.mysql.com/Contrib |
| MySQL Python API | http://www.mysql.com/Contrib |
| MySQL TCL API | http://www.binevolve.com/~tdarugar/tcl-sql |
| MySQL Perl API | http://www.mysql.com/Contrib |

### Large Tables

As we described earlier, MySQL stores each table in the database as a separate file in the database directory. The maximum size of a table in MySQL is restricted by the operating system file size limit which is 2 GB in the case of Linux, though on other operating systems file size can be a maximum of 4 GB. If a big table is going to be read-only, the `pack_isam` utility can be used to merge and compress the table; `pack_isam` packs the data files by 40%-70%.

### Speed, Robustness and Ease of Use

MySQL is about two to three times faster than other relational databases. You can look at the benchmark site of MySQL (www.mysql.com/benchmark.html) to get the results of the benchmark done on MySQL and other databases using the generic DBI/DBD Perl Interface.

> *The Database Independent Interface (DBI) is a database interface module for Perl that defines a set of methods, variables and conventions that provide a consistent database interface, independent of the actual database being used.*

MySQL is also very easy to manage – you don't need a trained database administrator to administer a MySQL installation.

### Cost Advantage

MySQL is an open source relational database, and is distributed free of charge for UNIX and OS/2 platforms.

# Installing MySQL on Linux

The binary and source distribution of MySQL for Linux are available on the MySQL web site (www.mysql.com); the current (at the time of writing) stable version of MySQL is 3.22.27.

## *Software and Hardware Requirements*

MySQL is a *very* scalable database server. It can run on very small hardware configurations, but it works equally well on large configurations. All of the executables are statically linked, so it does not require any libraries to be installed on the machine it runs on. If you want to write client applications in Perl, then you need to install Perl version 5.004 or later. You can install MySQL either using RPMs or a binary distribution.

## *Installation from RPMs*

The MySQL distribution for Linux consists of four RPMs:

❑   `MySQL-3.22.27-1.i386.rpm` – the server for `i386` systems

❑   `MySQL-client-3.22.27-1.i386.rpm` – client programs for `i386` systems

❑   `MySQL-bench-3.22.27-1.i386.rpm` – Perl DBI benchmarks/tests for `i386` systems

❑   `MySQL-devel-3.22.27-1.i386.rpm` – include files and libraries for `i386` systems

To install a minimal distribution of MySQL, only the first two of the above RPMs need to be installed. If you're interested in developing database applications the last in the list should be installed. To install an RPM package, use the following command:

```
# rpm -i MySQL-3.22.27-1.i386.rpm
```

This will be the file layout of MySQL after installation:

| Directory | Contents |
| --- | --- |
| `/etc` | Startup scripts |
| `/usr/bin` | Utilities, client programs and scripts |
| `/usr/doc` | Documentation |
| `/usr/info` | Information file |
| `/usr/sbin` | `mysqld` server |
| `/usr/share` | Error messages for different languages |
| `/usr/man` | `man` pages |
| `/usr/include` | Include files |
| `/usr/lib` | Libraries |
| `/var/lib/mysql` | Root directory of MySQL databases |

The RPM installation creates the root directory for MySQL databases in /var/lib/mysql. All the databases in MySQL will be created under this directory. For example, if you create a database called shop_cart, then MySQL will create a directory called /var/lib/mysql/shop_cart. All the tables of the database are stored as files inside the database directory, so if a table named music_shop is created in shop_cart database, music_shop.frm, music_shop.ISD and music_shop.ISM files are created in the /var/lib/mysql/shop_cart directory. The definition of the music_shop table is stored in the music_shop.frm file, all the records (the actual data) of the music_shop table are stored in music_shop.ISD, and all the indexes on the music_shop table are stored in the music_shop.ISM file. It also creates an operating system user by name mysql. All the files in the /var/lib/mysql directory are owned by the mysql user, which is the default user ID for the mysqld server. The RPM installation also creates appropriate files in /etc/rc.d directories, so that the mysqld server is started every time the machine boots up. The RPM installation also creates two databases: mysql and test.

## Installing from a Binary Distribution

Steps involved in installing MySQL from binary distribution:

❑ Download the binary files from the MySQL web site.

❑ Unpack the distribution in the install directory.

```
# cd /usr/local
# tar xvzf mysql-3_22_27-pc-linux-gnu-i686_tar.gz
# mv mysql-3.22.27-pc-linux-gnu-i686/ mysql
```

❑ Change the PATH variable.

```
# PATH=$PATH: /usr/local/mysql/bin:/usr/local/mysql/sbin
```

❑ Create privilege tables of MySQL by executing the mysql_install_db script.

```
# cd mysql
# scripts/mysql_install_db
```

The mysql_db_install script creates data directory under the install directory, all the MySQL databases are stored under this directory.

❑ Copy support-files/mysql.server to /etc/rc.d/init.d and make appropriate links, with this mysqld will get started automatically when the machine boots.

```
# cp support-files/mysql.server /etc/rc.d/init.d
# chmod +x /etc/rc.d/init.d/mysql.server

# ln -s /etc/rc.d/init.d/mysql.server /etc/rc.d/rc0.d/K90mysql
# ln -s /etc/rc.d/init.d/mysql.server /etc/rc.d/rc1.d/K90mysql
# ln -s /etc/rc.d/init.d/mysql.server /etc/rc.d/rc2.d/S90mysql
# ln -s /etc/rc.d/init.d/mysql.server /etc/rc.d/rc3.d/S90mysql
# ln -s /etc/rc.d/init.d/mysql.server /etc/rc.d/rc4.d/S90mysql
# ln -s /etc/rc.d/init.d/mysql.server /etc/rc.d/rc5.d/S90mysql
# ln -s /etc/rc.d/init.d/mysql.server /etc/rc.d/rc6.d/K90mysql
```

The MySQL installation creates a database user root with no password and having all privileges. After installing MySQL the administrator should change the password of root. The utility mysqladmin can be used to change the password.

❏ The following command changes the password of user root to root123

```
# mysqladmin -u root password root123
```

# Administering MySQL on Linux

In this part of the chapter we will look at how typical database administration tasks can be done by using MySQL utilities. For the complete syntax of these utilities, you should refer to MySQL (http://www.mysql.com/doc.html)reference manual.

## Starting the Database Server

The Database Server mysqld is a daemon process; it creates a copy of itself and runs in the background. You can either start mysqld directly from the shell prompt or you can use shell script safe_mysqld, which starts the database server, and continuously verifies that mysqld is running. If the database server dies unexpectedly, then it restarts it.

There are set of tuning and configuration parameters that can be passed as command line arguments to mysqld. Any command line arguments passed to safe_mysqld are passed on to mysqld. If the values of these parameters are not specified in the command line then mysqld uses the default values. You should refer to the MySQL manual for the list of command line parameters and their default values.

```
# safe_mysqld -O key_buffer=16M -O table_cache=128 &
```

The database server mysqld should be started in the context of the user having read/write permissions on all the directory and files within the root data directory.

## Getting the Status of the Database Server

The mysqladmin utility can be used to monitor mysqld daemon.

For viewing the status of mysqld server, type:

```
# mysqladmin status
Uptime: 52927  Threads: 12  Questions: 212  Slow queries: 0  Opens: 10
Flush tables: 1  Open tables: 6
```

The values returned by `mysqladmin status` output have the following meanings:

❑   `Uptime:` – the number of seconds the server has been running

❑   `Threads:` – the number of threads that are interacting with `mysqld`

❑   `Questions:` – the number of SQL queries that have been sent to `mysqld` for execution

❑   `Slow queries:` – the number of queries which have taken more than `long_query_time` seconds (`long_query_time` is a configuration parameter passed to `mysqld` as command line argument)

❑   `Opens:` – the number of tables opened by `mysqld`, since it started

❑   `Flush tables:` – the number of times flush, reload, refresh commands are executed

❑   `Open tables:` – the current number of tables opened by `mysqld`

The `mysqld` daemon creates a new thread for each database connection. The database administrator can view the details of all the active threads with the `mysqladmin processlist` command. The output of the `mysqladmin processlist` command is this:

```
Id   User   Host        Db      Command    Time
2    root   localhost   Mysql   Sleep      756
4    root   localhost           Processes  0
```

The values returned by `myqladmin processlist` output have the following meanings:

❑   `Id:` – The internal identification number for the thread.

❑   `User:` – The database user connected with this thread.

❑   `Host:` – The host from which the user is connected.

❑   `Db:` – The database to which the user is connected.

❑   `Command:` – The type of command being executed by the thread.

## Shutting Down the Database Server

The following command should be used to do a clean shutdown of the database:

```
# mysqladmin -p shutdown
```

The standard UNIX command `killall -9 mysqld` can also be used to kill the running instance of `mysqld`, but it should generally be avoided.

## Database Creation

The `mysql_install_db` script, which is executed after installing MySQL, creates two databases `mysql` and `test`. The `mysql` database contains tables that store privileges of database users. You can create database objects (tables, indexes) in these databases, but generally all database objects within an application should be stored in a separate database, which helps in easy management of the application.

You can create new databases with the `mysqladmin` utility or by executing the SQL command `CREATE DATABASE` through the `mysql` utility.

```
# mysqladmin -p CREATE documents ;

# mysql -u root
# CREATE DATABASE documents ;
```

The database user executing these commands should have `CREATE` privileges, or else the above commands will fail. We will be covering database privileges shortly.

## Database Destruction

The administrator can drop a database with `mysqladmin` utility, or by executing the SQL command `DROP DATABASE` through the `mysql` utility.

```
# mysqladmin -p DROP <databasename> ;

# mysql -u root
# DROP DATABASE documents ;
```

These commands should be used with care, because the data in the dropped database cannot be recovered later. As with the `CREATE` command, the database user executing these commands should have `DROP` privileges or else the above commands will fail.

## Security and Access Control

MySQL implements a simple security/access control system that is used to authenticate a user connecting from a given host, and to associate that user with appropriate privileges on a database. For example, the system administrator should have privileges to shut down the database, flush the update logs, etc. A normal user should not have the administrative privileges, and should be given `SELECT`, `INSERT`, `DELETE` and `UPDATE` privileges only on the pre-selected list of tables that the user will be accessing. The following table list the privileges supported by MySQL.

| Privilege | Context | Description |
| --- | --- | --- |
| SELECT | Tables | Allows the user to perform select operations on the table |
| INSERT | Tables | Allows the user to perform insert operations on the table |
| UPDATE | Tables | Allows the user to perform update operations on the table |
| DELETE | Tables | Allows the user to perform delete operations on the table |
| INDEX | Tables | Allows the user to create and drop indexes from the table |

*Table continued on following page*

| Privilege | Context | Description |
|---|---|---|
| ALTER | Tables | Allows the user to execute 'alter table' commands on the table |
| CREATE | Databases, tables or indexes | Allows the user to create new databases and tables |
| DROP | Databases or tables | Allows the user to drop the existing databases and tables |
| GRANT | Databases or tables | Allows the user to give the privileges they possess to other users |
| RELOAD | Server administration | Allows the user to execute the following commands from the mysqladmin utility:<br><br>reload, refresh, flush-privileges, flush-hosts, flush-logs, flush-tables. |
| SHUTDOWN | Server administration | Allows the user to execute the shutdown command that shuts down the database server from the mysqladmin utility |
| PROCESS | Server administration | Allows the user to execute the process list and kill commands from the mysqladmin utility |
| FILE | File access on the server | Allows the user to read/write files on the server using LOAD DATA INFILE and SELECT … INTO OUTFILE statements |

Users should be granted the minimum privileges possible. For example, the server administration features should be granted only to the database administrator.

The privilege information is stored in the user, db, host, tables_priv and columns_priv tables in the mysql database. These tables get modified implicitly when GRANT, REVOKE or SET PASSWORD statements are executed, and they can also be modified directly. The database server reads them when it starts up. The server notices changes made through the above commands immediately; manual modification using INSERT, UPDATE, etc. requires that the SQL command FLUSH PRIVILEGES or the command mysqladmin flush-privileges should be executed.

| Table Name | user | db | Host | tables_priv | columns_priv |
|---|---|---|---|---|---|
| Scope fields | host | host | Host | host | host |
| | user | db | Db | db | db |
| | password | user | | user | user |
| | | | | table_name | table_name |

| Table Name | user | db | Host | tables_priv | columns_priv |
|---|---|---|---|---|---|
| | | | | | column_name |
| Privilege fields | select_priv | select_priv | select_priv | table_priv | column_priv |
| | insert_priv | insert_priv | insert_priv | column_priv | |
| | update_priv | update_priv | update_priv | | |
| | delete_priv | delete_priv | delete_priv | | |
| | index_priv | index_priv | index_priv | | |
| | alter_priv | alter_priv | alter_priv | | |
| | create_priv | create_priv | create_priv | | |
| | drop_priv | drop_priv | drop_priv | | |
| | grant_priv | grant_priv | grant_priv | | |
| | reload_priv | | | | |
| | shutdown_priv | | | | |
| | process_priv | | | | |
| | file_priv | | | | |
| Other Fields | | | | timestamp | timestamp |
| | | | | grantor | |

All the privilege fields in the user, db and host tables are declared as ENUM('N', 'Y'), with default value being 'N'. In the tables_priv and columns_priv tables, the privilege fields are declared as SET fields.

| Table Name | Field Name | Possible set elements |
|---|---|---|
| tables_priv | Table_priv | SELECT, INSERT, UPDATE, DELETE, CREATE, DROP, GRANT, REFERENCES, INDEX, ALTER |
| tables_priv | Column_priv | SELECT, INSERT, UPDATE, REFERENCES |
| columns_priv | Column_priv | SELECT, INSERT, UPDATE, REFERENCES |

The user table's scope fields determine whether to allow or reject the incoming connections. For allowed connections, the privilege fields of the user table indicate the user's global privilege. The db table's scope fields determine which users can access which databases from which hosts. The privilege fields of the db table, however, determine which operations are allowed. The host table is an extension of the db table, used when you want a given db table entry to apply to several hosts. The tables_priv and columns_priv tables are similar to the db table, but are more fine-grained – they apply at the table and column level rather than at the database level.

MySQL access control involves two stages:

❑   Stage 1: The server checks whether the user is allowed to connect. The identity of the user is based on the user name and the host from which they connect. The server uses the user table for username, hostname and password verification.

❑   Stage 2: For each request issued by the user, the server checks to see whether the user has sufficient privileges to perform the request. The server uses the user, db, host, tables_priv and columns_priv tables for privilege verification.

The database administrator should create users, grant and revoke privileges using the commands GRANT and REVOKE, instead of directly updating the tables.

## Creating Users

As mentioned in the previous section, the system administrator should use the GRANT and REVOKE commands for creating users, granting and revoking privileges of a user.

The syntax of the GRANT command is as follows:

```
GRANT priv_type [(column_list)] [, priv_type [(column_list)] ...]
    ON {tbl_name | * | *.* | db_name.*}
    TO user_name [IDENTIFIED BY 'password']
        [, user_name [IDENTIFIED BY 'password'] ...]
    [WITH GRANT OPTION]
```

And the syntax of REVOKE command is:

```
REVOKE priv_type [(column_list)] [, priv_type [(column_list)] ...]
    ON {tbl_name | * | *.* | db_name.*}
    FROM user_name [, user_name ...]
```

For example, you can create a user with All privileges for the document database. The following command creates a database user bob will all privileges on the document database. The password of bob is bob123.

```
mysql># GRANT all ON document.* TO bob@"%" IDENTIFIED BY 'bob123';
```

Alternatively we can do the same thing by directly updating access control tables

```
mysql># INSERT INTO mysql.user (Host, User, Password ) VALUES ('%', 'bob',
password('bob'));
```

And:

```
mysql># INSERT INTO mysql.db (Host , Db, User, Select_priv, Insert_priv,
Update_priv, Delete_priv, Create_priv, Drop_priv, Grant_priv, References_priv,
Index_priv, Alter_priv ) VALUES( '%', 'document', 'bob', 'Y', 'Y' , 'Y', 'Y', 'Y',
'Y', 'N', 'Y', 'Y' ,'Y');
```

The password field of the user table stores the encrypted password of user. If you are directly updating the user table, then the password function should be used to get the encrypted password.

Now let's revoke insert privileges for bob on the document database:

```
mysql># REVOKE INSERT ON document.* FROM 'bob';
```

Alternatively, we can directly update the db table

```
mysql># UPDATE mysql.db SET Insert_priv= 'N' WHERE user='bob' AND db='document';
```

## Backup and Recovery

The database storing production data, should be backed up regularly to prevent data loss from power outages, disk crashes and so on. If the database is backed up regularly then the lost data can be recovered in a very short time after any catastrophe. Complete backup of the database can be taken daily. But if the size of the database is large, then lots of space would be required to store complete backups, and moreover the system performance will go down during the backup time. See Appendix C for more information on how to back up files.

In MySQL, a full backup of the database can be done by one of two methods:

❑    Shutting down the mysqld server and copying all the table files (*.frm, *.ISD and *.ISM).

❑    Using the mysqldump utility with the --lock-tables option. With this, mysqldump locks all the tables before dumping them, giving a consistent backup of the database tables.

When taking incremental backups, start mysqld with the --log-update=filename option. mysqld will now log all SQL statements that update data in log files of the form filename.n. The value of n gets incremented after a mysqladmin refresh or a mysqladmin flush-logs command, if the SQL command FLUSH LOGS is executed, or when the mysqld server is restarted:

```
# safe_mysqld -log-update=logs
```

Let's look at an example backup mechanism. In this setup, full backups are taken every week, and incremental backups are taken on a daily basis, assuming that `mysqld` is started with the `--log-update` option. This mechanism uses `cron` to take full and incremental backups.

First, create a file called `mysql.i_bkup` in the `/etc/cron.daily` directory. The contents of the file is simply this:

```
mysqladmin refresh
```

Now add a second file called `mysql.c_bkup` to the `/etc/cron.weekly` directory. Once again the file consists of one line:

```
mysqldump --lock-tables mysql >/backup/weekly/mysql.c_bkup
```

Now, `cron` will refresh the database on a daily basis and do a full backup weekly.

To restore the tables after a crash, you can use the `isamchk` utility. This command will work in the majority of cases.

```
# isamchk -r <table_name>
```

If `isamchk` fails, try the following steps:

❑   Restore the full backup.

❑   Apply all the update logs, i.e. incremental backups, on the restored database. This can be done using the `mysql` utility:

```
# mysql < updatelog_file
```

## The Replication or StandBy Database

A **primary database** is the database that contains production data, and all updates are done on the primary database. The **standby database** is a copy of the primary that can be activated if the primary database goes down, which should hardly ever happen if the system is robust enough. The standby database is used as a backup database for the primary database.

In MySQL, the standby database can be configured. For this, the primary database server should be started with the `--log-update=file_name` option. The update log generated on the primary server should be applied to the standby database. This can be done with:

```
# mysql < updatelog
```

This will execute all the SQL commands in the `updatelog` file on the standby database. Now the standby database will be synchronized with the primary database.

## Table Maintainence

We have already shown how to use the isamchk utility to restore a database after a crash. In this section we will look at few more the capabilities of this versatile tool; for a full list of isamchk utility options, refer to the MySQL man pages.

### Description of a Table

To get a description of a table, type:

```
# isamchk -dv music_shop
```

This command displays statistics about the table like percentage of space wasted, degree of fragmentation etc.

### Checking Tables for Corruption

Tables in the MySQL database should be checked on a regular basis for any corruption, due to hardware failures, system crashes etc. The tables can be checked every time the system boots up, or can be done at preset times using cron. The command to use is this:

```
# isamchk -s /var/lib/mysql/mysql/*.ISM
```

### Optimizing Table Layout for Space and Performance

Over a period of time, update and delete operations carried out on a table result in fragmentation, which leads to lots of wasted space and performance degradation. To optimize table layout for space and performance, isamchk can be run in recovery mode, using the -r switch as for restoring tables:

```
# isamchk -r music_shop
```

For large databases, isamchk might take a long time to complete. For a faster response, the size of buffers that isamchk uses can be changed to larger values with the -O option, depending on the available memory in the machine. These variables can be changed; the default values are in brackets:

| Variable Name | Description (with defaults in parentheses) |
|---|---|
| key_buffer_size | Size of the buffer used for buffering index blocks (520192 bytes) |
| read_buffer_size | Size of the buffer used to store data read from the files (262136 bytes) |
| write_buffer_size | Size of the buffer used for storing data to be written (262136 bytes) |
| sort_buffer_size | Size of the buffer used for performing sorts (2097144 bytes) |
| sort_key_blocks | Number of blocks of keys used for sorting keys (16) |
| decode_bits | Number of bits used for generating certain internal tables (9) |

The size of these variables can be changed by specifying new values at the command line:

```
# isamchk -O read_buffer_size=1M write_buffer_size=1M music_shop
```

## Tuning the Database Server

One of the important tasks of database administrator is to tune the database server, to get maximum performance out of hardware. The MySQL database server mysqld uses a set of variable parameters that can be configured according to the needs to the database. The current values of these tunable parameters can be viewed with the following command:

```
# mysqladmin variables
```

If these parameters are not specified, mysqld uses default values that can be changed by specifying the new values as command line arguments to safe_mysqld, for example:

```
# safe_mysqld -O key_buffer=16M -O table_cache=128
```

In Linux, where the MySQL server is started from the startup scripts, you need to modify the appropriate startup file ( for example /etc/rc.d/init.d/mysql or /etc/rc.d/init.d/mysql.server).

Here we will cover few important tunable parameters.

| | |
|---|---|
| join_buffer_size | The size in bytes of the buffer allocated for a full join (joins that do not use indexes) between two tables. If the database applications installed in the database, do lots of full joins, then you should increase the size of this parameter. |
| key_buffer_size | The size of the buffer used for buffering index blocks. The buffered index blocks are shared by all the threads. |
| record_buffer | The size of the buffer allocated for reading data from the table, when doing a sequential scan. |
| sort_buffer | The size of the buffer allocated for sorting the table data. |

Increasing the size of these buffers will result in better performance, because with larger buffers, most of the data required for executing a SQL command will be available in the buffer. So the number of read and write operations will get reduced.

On machines with a large RAM, the size of buffers should be increased according to the database application needs. If these values are not changed, then there are no performance gains even if the RAM size of machine is increased. Arbitrarily increasing the size of buffers might lead to performance degradation; if the buffers are too large on a machine with less physical RAM, then this can lead to an increase in swapping activity. After changing the values of the buffer sizes, the administrator should monitor the swapping activity using tools like vmstat.

# Important MySQL Utilities

There are some important utilities included with the MySQL distribution. For a complete description of them, refer to the MySQL reference manual (www.mysql.com/doc.html); we'll just provide a quick list here:

❑   isamchk is a utility to describe, check, optimize and repair MySQL tables.

❑   mysqlaccess is a script that checks the access privileges for a host, user and database combination.

❑   mysqladmin is a utility for performing administrative operations. It supports the following commands:

| | |
|---|---|
| CREATE <database name> | Create a new database |
| DROP <database name> | Delete a database and all its tables |
| EXTENDED-STATUS | Gives an extended status message from the server |
| FLUSH-HOSTS | Flush all cached hosts |
| FLUSH-LOGS | Flush all logs |
| FLUSH-TABLES | Flush all tables |
| FLUSH-PRIVILEGES | Reload grant tables (same as reload) |
| KILL ID, ID . . . | Kill mysqld threads |
| PASSWORD | Change old password to a new password |
| PING | Check if mysqld is alive |
| PROCESSLIST | Show list of active threads in the server |
| RELOAD | Reload grant tables |
| REFRESH | Flush all tables and close and open log files |
| SHUTDOWN | Shut down the mysqld server |
| STATUS | Give a short status message from the server |
| VARIABLES | Prints available variables |
| VERSION | Get the version information from the server |

Some of these we have already covered in this section.

❑   mysqldump dumps the MySQL database into a file as SQL statements or as tab-separated text files. It is used for backing up a database, as we saw earlier.

❑   mysqlimport imports text files into their respective tables using LOAD_DATA_INFILE.

❑   mysqlshow displays information about databases, tables, columns and indexes.

❑ `mysql_install_db` creates the MySQL grant table with default privileges. This script is executed after installing MySQL. In Linux, this script gets executed automatically, as part of the installation.

❑ `safe_mysqld` is a script that starts the `mysqld` daemon with some safety features such as restarting the server when an error occurs, and logging runtime information in a log file.

❑ `pack_isam` compresses read only tables.

# Unsupported Features in MySQL

MySQL does not support a few database features, which are available in other commercial databases like Oracle, Informix and Sybase, which we will look at in this section. However, some of these features will be implemented in future versions of MySQL.

## Sub-selects

Sub-selects, that is SELECTs within a SELECT statement, are not supported in version 3.22.27 of MySQL. For example, the following statement returns data about employees whose salaries exceed their department's average:

```
SELECT deptno, ename, sal
    FROM emp x
        WHERE sal > (SELECT AVG(sal)
                        FROM emp
                            WHERE x.deptno = deptno)
    ORDER BY deptno;
```

Most SQL statements that would use sub-selects can be rewritten otherwise. For complex SQL statements that cannot be rewritten, you can create and store the value of the sub-query in a temporary table, and access the temporary table in the main query.

## Transactions

A **transaction** is a logical unit of work that comprises of one or more SQL statements executed by a single user. A transaction ends when it is explicitly committed or rolled back by that user. A transaction is automatically rolled back if it fails at any point.

In a banking application, when a bank customer transfers money from a savings account to a checking account, the transaction might consist of three separate operations: decrease the savings account, increase the checking account, and record the transaction in the transaction journal. When something prevents one of the statements in the transaction from executing (such as a hardware failure), the other statements of the transaction must be undone.

Committing a transaction makes permanent the changes resulting from all SQL statements in the transaction. Rolling back a transaction retracts any of the changes resulting from the SQL statements in the transaction. After a transaction is rolled back, the affected data is left unchanged as if the SQL statements in the transaction were never executed.

Transactions are not currently supported in MySQL. However, MySQL does support LOCK_TABLES and UNLOCK_TABLES commands that can be used by the thread to prevent interference by other threads.

LOCK_TABLES can lock multiple tables with the specified access – that is, read or write. Locks on a table get released when the thread holding the lock executes UNLOCK_TABLE command, or when the thread holding the lock dies.

The lack of transaction support in MySQL can be taken care of by designing your applications carefully. The atomicity of a set of related SQL commands can be guaranteed by using LOCK_TABLES and UNLOCK_TABLES. However a situation that needs careful attention is where the thread holding the locks on a table dies the execution of the sequence of SQL commands is complete. In that case, the tables on which the changes are made by the existing threads will be in an inconsistent state. So you should take the following steps while updating the tables:

❑ Lock all the tables that will be accessed

❑ Test if the tables are in a consistent state; if not then bring the table into a consistent state

❑ Update the tables

❑ Mark the tables as consistent

❑ Unlock the locks on the tables

One of the principal design goals of MySQL was to have a high performance database server. The reason why transactions are not supported is that adding such support does introduces a lot of overheads – you need extra logs to maintain changes, and extra threads for cleanup and flushing of data.

## Stored Procedures and Triggers

A stored procedure is a set of SQL commands that are compiled and are stored on the server. Clients can refer to the stored procedure instead of reissuing entire SQL commands. You get performance benefits by using stored procedures, because the SQL statements are already parsed and compiled in the server, and less data needs to be sent to the server from the client.

A trigger is a stored procedure that's invoked when a particular event occurs. For example, a trigger can be set on a stock price table – it would get fired after any UPDATE operation was done on the table. The trigger sends e-mail to any interested people (taken from another table) if the stock prices of any of the updated row changes by 20%.

MySQL does not as yet have support for stored procedures or triggers.

## Foreign Keys

A foreign key is a column in a table which corresponds to a primary key in another table and must contain compatible data. For example, suppose a database schema contains two tables Employee and Department. The Employee table contains details of employees, and the Department table contains details about the departments of the organization. The business rule that *each employee of the organization must work for one of the departments of the organization* can be implemented by using foreign keys.

The dept column of the `Employee` table can be defined as foreign key that refers to the dept column of `Department` table. Now any `INSERT` done on the `Employee` table with wrong value of for the department column (i.e. the corresponding value in the `Department` table does not exist) will fail. It means that there will be no employee entry in the `Employee` table, which will have a department that does not exist.

MySQL does not support foreign keys for reasons of overhead. The foreign key syntax in MySQL exists only for compatibility with other database vendors; it doesn't do anything.

## Views

A view is a tailored presentation of the data contained in one or more tables, or even other views. It takes the output of a query and treats it as a table; therefore, it can be thought of as a "stored query" or a "virtual table". However, no storage is allocated to views.

For example, in an `Employee` table, you want all the users to see only the name, and employee ID fields of the table. Then you can create a view on the table with the following SQL statement:

```
CREATE VIEW Employee_View AS SELECT name, employee-id FROM Employee
```

All the users can be given `SELECT` privilege on the `Employee_View`. Now they will only be able to access name, and employee-id fields of the Employee table.

MySQL version 3.22.27 does not support views.

## Data Format in Tables

In the current version of MySQL, data in tables is stored in machine format not binary format. For that reason, the tables are not portable across operating systems. However, a new table type MyISAM is implemented in the 3.23.x (alpha) release of MySQL, which stores data in neutral format.

# Conclusion

Because of the lack of features like transactions, stored procedures and triggers, it will be quite difficult to implement complex database applications like a Banking System using MySQL. However it is ideal for implementing applications that do not require transaction support, and any application having performance as a critical requirement. These are some of the applications which can be developed using MySQL:

❏   Search engines

❏   Bulletin boards

❏   Back-end of an LDAP Server (see the next chapter for more details on LDAP)

❏   Other web based applications like a scheduler, which need persistent storage.

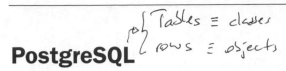

# PostgreSQL

If MySQL's lack of transactional capabilities feels too limiting, but you don't want to pay for the sophistication of Oracle, PostgreSQL might be worth a look. So, what is PostgreSQL?

In 1984, researchers at the University of California at Berkeley started working on the development of an object-relational database known as Postgres (**Post**-In**gres**, since the same team had worked on the very successful Ingres database). "Object-relational" means that, rather than being a completely object-oriented database, Postgres essentially added some features of object-orientation to the well-understood and effective relational model, with rows taking on some aspects of objects in programming languages such as Java or C++, and tables behaving as class definitions. The next major step in the life of the project was the addition of SQL capabilities in about 1995 (followed by the rather obvious name change), and shortly after the whole project was offered as open source. Since then, it is still essentially a project for researching into database engine technology, and there have been fewer radical changes in functionality. Instead the code has stabilized and a significant amount of effort has been put into bug fixing, improvements in robustness, efficiency and, very significantly, documentation. As an open source project, there are no restrictions on the deployment of PostgreSQL, and no charge for its use, although you may wish to pay for commercial support – see later.

PostgreSQL provides standard relational database mechanisms and supports an extended subset of SQL-92, which means in reality that it supports virtually all of the commonly used facilities of typical relational databases, but some less used features have been omitted or replaced by object-oriented equivalents. In other words, unless you are tackling something fairly obscure, PostgreSQL will provide all the features you need. Two of the main object-oriented additions to the relational model are:

- ❏ class inheritance – as has been mentioned, a database table fulfils a role as a class, and new classes can be created by extending already defined ones, just as classes can be derived from others in object-oriented programming languages such as Java and C++.
- ❏ types – most databases have a fixed set of data types (integer, string, etc.) but PostgreSQL lets you define your own and manipulate them exactly like the standard ones.

In this section, we will be approaching PostgreSQL as an alternative **relational** database implementation, and will not discuss the object facilities any further.

## Where to Find PostgreSQL

The main PostgreSQL web site is www.postgresql.org and the source code may be downloaded from one of the mirror sites listed there. PostgreSQL runs on a large number of platforms including Solaris, AIX, HP/UX, SCO UNIX and, fortunately for this book, Linux – there is a complete list on the PostgreSQL web site. Some precompiled binaries are available, but you may wish to build it yourself anyway.

*The client tools have been running on Windows 9x and NT for quite a while, but the server has only just become available on Windows machines and work is still in progress to get it to run reliably.*

If you use Red Hat Linux, your installation job is particularly easy; one of the supplied packages is PostgreSQL. However, to get the latest version and bug fixes, pay a visit to the PostgreSQL web site.

To supplement the documentation that is installed along with PostgreSQL, the PostgreSQL web site includes further documentation, and links to other sources, as well as a support mailing list (pgsql-general@postgresql.org) and bug and development mailing lists. There are also some newsgroups devoted to PostgreSQL (news:comp.database.postgresql.*) and various levels of commercial support are available from Wolfville, NS (see the PostgreSQL web site for details).

# Installation

As was mentioned earlier, if you are running Red Hat Linux, installing the version supplied is merely a job of unpacking the RPMs – well, almost. There is a minor bug with the automatic startup, which will be explained later in the section on starting the postmaster. There are a number of RPMs, shown in the table below – only the two are actually essential and you select the others depending on your intended use of PostgreSQL.

| | |
|---|---|
| Client applications and documentation | postgresql-6.5.2-1.i386.rpm |
| Server application and administration tools | postgresql-server-6.5.2-1.i386.rpm |
| Development libraries, such as the C interface | postgresql-devel-6.5.2-1.i386.rpm |
| Java database interface | postgresql-jdbc-6.5.2-1.i386.rpm |
| ODBC interface | postgresql-odbc-6.5.2-1.i386.rpm |
| Perl interface | postgresql-perl-6.5.2-1.i386.rpm |
| Python interface | postgresql-python-6.5.2-1.i386.rpm |
| TCL interface | postgresql-tcl-6.5.2-1.i386.rpm |
| Test suite | postgresql-test-6.5.2-1.i386.rpm |

Of course, your version numbers may vary – these are from Red Hat 6.1 – and other distributions may split the packages up differently. You can install them using GnoRPM or, if you prefer command lines to GUIs, the command:

```
# rpm -i postgresql-6.5.2-1.i386.rpm postgresql-server-6.5.2-1.i386.rpm ...
```

On the other hand, if you do not have the RPMs to hand, or would like to upgrade to a newer version of PostgreSQL, your first port of call is the PostgreSQL web site – if you're lucky, someone may have provided a binary package which you can download and unpack. However, you may have no option but to build it yourself.

The source is supplied as a file of around 6 MB in size, called postgresql-6.5.tar.gz (depending on the version), to be unpacked using the following command sequence:

```
# cd /usr/local/src
# tar xfz postgresql-6.5.tar.gz
```

This produces the source tree `/usr/local/src/postgresql-6.5.3` (or similar) containing all the source code and regression test suite. As with most source builds, the process breaks into three steps: configure, make and install. Change to the `postgresql-6.5.3` directory and run:

```
# ./configure
```

The default is acceptable for most installations, but you may wish to give configure some options, for example `--prefix=<some dir>` to place the installed code in some particular directory instead of `/usr/local/pgsql`. `./configure --help` will list all the available options.

After this, build the database executables with:

```
# make all
```

This will produce the PostgreSQL executables and libraries within the `postgresql-6.5.3` directory, and the final step to copy them to their final locations is:

```
# make install
```

Any user can execute the first two steps, but you have to be the super-user to execute the final one. All of this is covered in detail in the `INSTALL` file, as are suggestions for what to do should the process fail.

Each user may have to add the PostgreSQL executable and library directories to his/her setup: this is not always necessary and depends on how PostgreSQL has been configured. For example, Red Hat's PostgreSQL installation has been built to place the binaries in `/usr/bin` and shared libraries in `/usr/lib` which are already on the users' paths, but the default configuration places them in `/usr/local/pgsql/bin` and `/usr/local/pgsql/lib` respectively. While the first is more convenient, the latter is more flexible in that it simplifies the job of running several different versions of PostgreSQL, which you may want to do during upgrades in the future. You may have to alter the users' `.bash_profile` or similar files to extend the path and library path, with lines such as:

```
PATH=$PATH:/usr/local/pgsql/bin
export LD_LIBRARY_PATH=/usr/local/pgsql/lib
```

It is also very useful, and in the case of some PostgreSQL tools essential, to add a couple of other variable definitions for PostgreSQL tools to locate some of the internal libraries and data files. If you performed a default install, as described above, you need:

```
export PGLIB=/usr/local/pgsql/lib
export PGDATA=/usr/local/pgsql/data
```

In a pre-installed Red Hat system, these should be replaced with:

```
export PGLIB=/var/lib/pgsql
export PGDATA=/usr/lib/pgsql
```

*The latter directory is where the PostgreSQL database files will reside. It is available as a variable definition so that you can place it in any convenient location but note that the Red Hat install has the path hard coded in one of the initialization scripts so you need to change that too if you move the database files.*

Before you can create and use any PostgreSQL databases, you need to take one extra step: start the postmaster.

# Postmaster

PostgreSQL operates as a client-server system, and the postmaster process is the main PostgreSQL server, controlling access to any locally hosted database, either from other processes on the local machine or from any remote client. As this suggests, it must be running all the time that any application wants to use a PostgreSQL database. To enhance security, the postmaster should not be run by the super-user, since that would provide too many security holes for unscrupulous users to access parts of the system outside PostgreSQL databases. Conventionally, a user called postgres needs to be created specifically for running the postmaster. This has already been done in Red Hat systems.

The postmaster requires the data directory $PGDATA to be initialized. Log on as user postgres, create this directory if it does not already exist and execute the following command to initialize the contents of directory $PGDATA:

```
$ initdb
```
→ /usr/lib/postgres/8.3/bin

Now you can run the postmaster, again as user postgres:

```
$ postmaster &
```

You need to execute initdb once only, whereas you need to execute postmaster every time you boot. That's it: now you can create, use and delete PostgreSQL databases.

Incidentally, the PostgreSQL source distribution includes a number of regression tests which you may wish to build and run to increase confidence in your installation: see the postgresql-6.5.3/test/regress directory for details.

# Automatic Startup

It is not very convenient to have to log on as user postgres and start the postmaster every time you reboot – not that that should be very often on a well maintained system! You can insert a command in your startup files to perform the startup. The rc files are covered in Appendix C and all you need to do for PostgreSQL is create an initialization file like the existing ones. Life is easier on a Red Hat system since the file already exists and has been appropriately linked.

It is equally important to close PostgreSQL before shutting down the system, by stopping the postmaster process. If you omit this step, you may find that you have to perform a file system check, or to be more exact, it will happen automatically when you next boot, since the postmaster had some files open when the system killed it off without warning.

If you need to write your own, create the file /etc/rc.d/init.d/postgresql with the following contents:

For ubuntu 8.10 the file is /etc/init.d/postgresql-8.3

```
#!/bin/sh
# PostgreSQL postmaster startup

case "$1" in
  start)
    echo "Starting postgresql"
    su -l postgres -c '/usr/local/pgsql/bin/postmaster
                                        -S -D/usr/local/pgsql/data'
    ;;
  stop)
    echo "Stopping postgresql"
    killall postmaster
    ;;
  *)
    echo "Usage: postgresql [ start | stop ]"
    ;;
esac

exit 0
```

The -D argument to postmaster specifies the data directory; so adjust this appropriately for your installation – probably /usr/local/pgsql/data if you installed afresh, or /usr/lib/pgsq/data if pre-installed on a Red Hat system.

Link this to the startup and shutdown files in rc3.d:

```
$ cd /etc/rc.d/rc3.d
$ ln -s ../init.d/postgresql S70postgresql
$ ln -s ../init.d/postgresql K70postgresql
```

Earlier we mentioned a Red Hat installation bug; it is that a startup script is installed, but the PostgreSQL data directory is not initialized. You will see the following error message every time you boot until you initialize it with initdb:

```
Starting postgresql service: /usr/bin/postmaster does not find the database
system.  Expected to find it in the PGDATA directory "/var/lib/pgsql", but unable
to open file with pathname "/var/lib/pgsql/base/template1/pg_class".

No data directory -- can't proceed.
postmaster []
```

# Using Databases

The easiest way to create a database is to use the createdb command, for example:

```
$ createdb booksdatabase
```

Where booksdatabase is the name of the database. Destroying one is similarly simple:

```
$ destroydb booksdatabase
```

By default, only the postmaster owning user, in other words `postgres`, can create and destroy databases (and users and groups), but other users can be given the appropriate permissions, as will be explained shortly.

To do anything else, you need to execute some SQL commands. PostgreSQL has a large number of client bindings, from libraries that can be invoked from C and Perl, to industry standards such as ODBC and JDBC, as well as special purpose interpreters such as the command line interpreter `psql` and its graphical cousin `pgaccess`. We will cover just `psql` here.

`psql` is started and attached to a particular database with the command:

```
$ psql booksdatabase
```

`psql` supports two sorts of command: anything starting with a backslash is a system command and anything else is interpreted as SQL. The three most important system commands are:

- ❏  \? – lists all available system commands
- ❏  \h – lists all available SQL commands
- ❏  \q – quit `psql`

The following table lists all of the system commands:

| | |
|---|---|
| \a | toggle field-alignment |
| \C [<caption>] | set HTML caption |
| \connect <dbname\|-> <user> | connect to new database |
| \copy table {from \| to} <fname> | copy table to/from a file |
| \d [<table>] | list tables and indices, or columns in <table> |
| \da | list aggregates |
| \dd [<object>] | list comment for table, field, type, function, or operator. |
| \df | list functions |
| \di | list only indices |
| \do | list operators |
| \ds | list only sequences |
| \dS | list system tables and indexes |
| \dt | list only tables |
| \dT | list types |
| \e [<fname>] | edit the current query buffer or <fname> |
| \E [<fname>] | edit the current query buffer or <fname>, and execute |

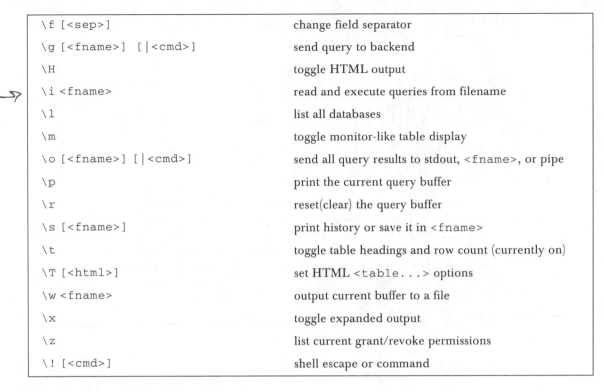

| | |
|---|---|
| \f [<sep>] | change field separator |
| \g [<fname>] [\|<cmd>] | send query to backend |
| \H | toggle HTML output |
| \i <fname> | read and execute queries from filename |
| \l | list all databases |
| \m | toggle monitor-like table display |
| \o [<fname>] [\|<cmd>] | send all query results to stdout, <fname>, or pipe |
| \p | print the current query buffer |
| \r | reset(clear) the query buffer |
| \s [<fname>] | print history or save it in <fname> |
| \t | toggle table headings and row count (currently on) |
| \T [<html>] | set HTML <table...> options |
| \w <fname> | output current buffer to a file |
| \x | toggle expanded output |
| \z | list current grant/revoke permissions |
| \! [<cmd>] | shell escape or command |

The complete range of SQL commands is:

| | | | |
|---|---|---|---|
| ABORT TRANSACTION | ALTER TABLE | ALTER USER | BEGIN WORK |
| CLUSTER | CLOSE | COMMIT WORK | COPY |
| CREATE | CREATE AGGREGATE | CREATE DATABASE | CREATE FUNCTION |
| CREATE INDEX | CREATE OPERATOR | CREATE RULE | CREATE SEQUENCE |
| CREATE TABLE | CREATE TRIGGER | CREATE TYPE | CREATE USER |
| CREATE VIEW | DECLARE | DELETE | DROP |
| DROP AGGREGATE | DROP DATABASE | DROP FUNCTION | DROP INDEX |
| DROP OPERATOR | DROP RULE | DROP SEQUENCE | DROP TABLE |
| DROP TRIGGER | DROP TYPE | DROP USER | DROP VIEW |
| END WORK | EXPLAIN | FETCH | GRANT |
| INSERT | LISTEN | LOAD | LOCK |
| MOVE | NOTIFY | RESET | REVOKE |
| ROLLBACK WORK | SELECT | SET | SHOW |
| UNLISTEN | UPDATE | VACUUM | |

Having created the books database above, you could create titles and authors tables and populate them with some data with the following statements in `psql`:

```
CREATE TABLE author ( authorid int, name varchar(100) );
CREATE TABLE title ( authorid int, name varchar(100), isbn varchar(10) );

INSERT INTO author VALUES ( 100, 'Horton, Ivor' );
INSERT INTO author VALUES ( 101, 'Grimes, Richard' );

INSERT INTO title VALUES ( 100, 'Beginning Java 2', ' 1861002238' );
INSERT INTO title VALUES ( 100, 'Beginning C++', ' 186100088X' );
INSERT INTO title VALUES ( 101, 'Professional DCOM Programming', '186100060X' );
```

Note that these commands are not actually executed until the semi-colon at the end is processed. In addition, you don't have to enter these commands interactively; you can place them in a text file and import them into `psql` with the `\i` command. If, on the other hand, you have been tinkering with `psql` interactively, you can create a text representation of the database with the `pg_dump` command and import it into `psql` later; this could even be used as a crude backup mechanism. However, this procedure may be necessary when making a major PostgreSQL upgrade, especially where internal formats have changed, for example, from a 5.x version of PostgreSQL to a 6.x one.

Having created the tables, you can execute some fairly obvious SQL queries. For example, this command dumps the following table to standard output:

```
SELECT author.name, title.name FROM author, title
                          WHERE author.authorid = title.authorid;
```

```
name           |name
---------------+----------------------------
Horton, Ivor   |Beginning Java 2
Horton, Ivor   |Beginning C++
Grimes, Richard|Professional DCOM Programming
(3 rows)
```

The `psql` program has a number of facilities for changing the print format, for example, renaming or removing the column titles; you can write special purpose programs in your favorite programming language, or even use PHP or Perl to present a web interface.

It is interesting to note that the `createdb` and `destroydb` commands are in fact not much more than sequences of `psql` commands.

To let someone else access this database, extra users have to be created with appropriate privileges, and for this very purpose, there is a convenient `createuser` command. As with `createdb`, this is a script which populates PostgreSQL system tables with the required data. The following illustrates the procedure followed when creating a user `andrew`. The command is run from user `postgres`:

```
$ createuser andrew                    ← use CREATE USER instead after loging into the
Enter user's postgres ID or RETURN to use unix user ID: 534 ->      database.
Is user "andrew" allowed to create databases (y/n) y
Is user "andrew" allowed to add users? (y/n) y
createuser: andrew was successfully added
```

As you can see, `createuser` lets you specify whether users can create further users or databases. Database user names need not correspond to UNIX users and are merely human-friendly ways to refer to the PostgreSQL ID. However, if the name is the same as an existing UNIX user, `createuser` defaults to that user's UNIX ID.

Databases can be individually protected from users, and PostgreSQL supports a user group system in a similar way to the operating system itself.

# Transactions

This book is not intended to include a SQL tutorial, so please consult the PostgreSQL documentation and web site for further information. However, before passing on, transaction processing deserves a brief mention.

As we discussed earlier, a **transaction** is a logical unit of work that comprises of one or more SQL statements executed by a single user. The sequence of operations with the transaction occur as a single uninterruptible unit, that is all the commands must be run in sequence. Unless you specify otherwise, each individual SQL statement is a single transaction.

As you saw in the MySQL section, transaction processing in that database has to be approximated by explicitly locking and unlocking tables, but the process is much simpler in PostgreSQL (and, as we shall see, Oracle); just use the SQL BEGIN TRANSACTION and END TRANSACTION statements. For example, a banking transaction could be expressed as the following (rather simplified) pseudo-code:

```
BEGIN TRANSACTION
SELECT savingsAmount FROM savings WHERE customer = customerA
if savingsAmount < transferAmount )
  ROLLBACK TRANSACTION
else
  newSavingsAmount = savingAmount - transferAmount
  UPDATE savings SET savingsAmount = newSavingsAmount
                                          WHERE customer = customerA
  SELECT checkingAmount FROM checking WHERE customer = customerA
  newCheckingAmount = checkingAmount + transferAmount
  UPDATE checking SET checkingAmount = newCheckingAmount
                                          WHERE customer = customerA
COMMIT TRANSACTION
```

There is an added benefit to transaction processing. Without transactions, each SQL statement is processed individually, with repeated calls to the database made if necessary. Incorporating the commands into transactions permits a degree of batching, reducing the number of times the client and server have to communicate, which could benefit performance.

# Administration

As with any database system, good performance and reliability rely on active administration. As far as performance is concerned, the best results are achieved by judicious application of table indices. The use of indices is beyond the scope of this section; however, there are a few other things you can do to speed up the PostgreSQL server:

- ☑ Persuade your users (or client application programmers) to perform batch operations instead of individual queries or updates, thus reducing the amount of traffic between client and server
- ☑ By default, the server flushes the disk after each transaction and, while this increases reliability, it does impose a performance penalty. You can start the `postmaster` with the `-o` `-F` options to reduce the frequency of flushing.
- ☑ Change the amount of memory used for buffers using the `-B` and `-S` options with the `postmaster` command
- ☑ Investigate data clustering, that is matching data storage with the associated index

See the man pages on `postmaster` and `cluster` for more information on these techniques.

PostgreSQL supports the SQL `VACUUM` command, to remove junk and unnecessary padding from your database: this will make it smaller and slightly faster, and is worth doing, at the very least, before performing a backup, so that space and time are not wasted backing up unwanted material.

Reliability is enhanced by ensuring your Linux machine has as few extraneous processes as possible (which are usually started automatically by `rc` files). For example, do you really need that FTP server running on your database machine? This may give you some security benefits too, as there will be fewer routes into your machine. Check that you have the most up to date patches for any of your tools (making the optimistic assumption that "latest" means most reliable, though this has not been proved incorrect that many times with Linux). As mentioned above, you can increase performance by reducing the level of disk flushing. Unfortunately, doing so may open you up to more problems if there is a system failure.

Regardless of your apparent level of system reliability, you do need to take periodic database backups, just in case. As was mentioned earlier, the pg_dump command produces a textual representation of the database, which can be used as a final fallback should everything else fail. (There is a similar command, `pg_dumpall`, to perform this for every locally hosted PostgreSQL database.) A more efficient technique is to simply backup all the files in the `$PGDATA` directory, having stopped the `postmaster` first to prevent database updates from occurring while the backup is taking place. You can use any UNIX mechanism for the backup since the data files are just normal UNIX files. Restoration of the database is the reverse; copy the backed up files back and restart the `postmaster`.

*postmaster s/b stopped*

# Summary

PostgreSQL is a very respectable and powerful database system. It is really a research engine, but that does not stop it being very useful as a low cost alternative to database systems such as Oracle. There is nothing to stop you ignoring the post-relational extensions (as, in fact, we have done in this section) and executing standard SQL commands.

There is a large number of client interfaces, though we described only one tool here – `psql`. This is sufficient for examining a database and carrying out SQL queries, but you may require other interfaces, such as the C library to perform more sophisticated processing. There are a number of mechanisms for tuning the database, though not as many as for Oracle.

Finally, as well as the Internet based support typical of open source projects, commercial support is available for the nervous IT director.

# A Commercial Database On Linux: Oracle 8

Among many other shortcomings attributed to Linux, none was more disparaging than the claim that it did not support enterprise class products. However, with Oracle Corporation announcing version 8 of its industrial-strength RDBMS for Linux in early October 1998, and many other enterprise-class database vendors throwing their weight behind Linux, these criticisms have been silenced.

While the Linux community is unsure of what to make of these commercial database offerings on Linux, mainly because such solutions do not fall into the open source domain, the fact remains that the entry of database majors into the Linux world has changed the landscape overnight. We shall not attempt to go into a lengthy debate; rather, we'll examine how the arrival of the enterprise database for Linux can be used for our purposes.

Oracle on Linux – or Oracle 8.0.5 to be precise – is available in *standard* and *enterprise* versions, and they exhibit a number of differences in their feature sets. At the time of writing, the Oracle Corporation claims to have an established commercial base of 800 customers, half of which are business or commercial users. Developers can download a single-user development version of the RDBMS free of charge from the Oracle Technical Network web site at http://technet.oracle.com/software/. This version does not have an expiry date but cannot be used for commercial prurposes.

## Oracle versus the Free World

It should be noted, right from the onset, that the three database solutions covered in this chapter each have their own place in your business enterprise. We have seen how MySQL and PostgreSQL can be used for small to medium sized applications. Now we come to Oracle, a highly complex but equally powerful system that can handle situations where the volume and scale of data is large.

In terms of cost, obviously Oracle is not free since it is a proprietary solution. Also, Oracle may be slower and more memory-intensive than a competing open source product like PostgreSQL using the same hardware configuration. This is because Oracle is a much more general-purpose product than the other freeware offerings that we discussed. MySQL is also faster than Oracle, when performing simple search and update operations.

Whereas MVCC locking in PostgreSQL is supposedly as good as or better than that of Oracle, the Oracle code has been tested and debugged far more than PostgreSQL. Oracle seems to handle overflow conditions of data vectors better than PostgreSQL, while handling large binary objects PostgreSQL seems to give better performance than Oracle with the same hardware configuration. More performance information comparing database products can be seen at the use Transaction Processing Performance Council web site at www.tpc.org.

Oracle's more advanced features such as replication, stand-by databases, parallel query processing cannot yet be used in a Linux environment, because Linux itself does not yet have the tools to carry out these operations. Consequently, the versions of Oracle ported to Linux do not have these high-end features.

## Installing Oracle 8 On Linux

Oracle installations have typically consumed much time and a lot of patience, and the release on Linux is no exception to the rule

*Get version 8.05 rather than 8i !*

At the time of writing, Oracle has just released version 8*i* of the RDBMS, but we do not attempt to cover it here for several reasons. For a start, it currently contains too many bugs to be of any serious use, and secondly the Java-based GUI installer does not work too well on Linux. Furthermore, many of the *i* (Internet) features of Oracle 8*i* are missing in the Linux version. If you are looking for a working version that you can tweak and experiment with – and ultimately get some productive work out of – the choice at this point of time is Oracle 8.0.5. Hopefully, in the not-too-distant future, these problems will be sorted out and we will have a reliable version of Oracle 8*i* to use.

With some of the newer Linux distributions moving to glibc as the standard C library, Oracle 8.0.5 on Linux was developed using the older libc library. This may lead to some quirks in the installation procedure for certain versions of these distributions. For version-specific installation instructions please refer to the web sites below:

❑ Oracle on Linux, for SuSE distributions: http://www.suse.de/en/support/oracle/

❑ Oracle on Linux, for Red Hat distributions: http://jordan.fortwayne.com/oracle/

# Configuring and Customizing Oracle on Linux

The task of customizing Oracle is quite daunting, due to the sheer number of parameters that are needed to achieve it – there are whole books dedicated to this topic. Our goal here is not to duplicate that work, but to cover those configuration and customization issues typical of Linux in general, and of Oracle on Linux in particular. To preserve the thread of the discussion, some general Oracle customization and configuration issues have also been addressed. By configuring and customizing in this context, we assign sensible parameters for a general installation, and then tailor the installation to fit our particular requirements.

## The initsid.ora File

A good place to start is the `initsid.ora` file, where the "`sid`" part of the name corresponds to the value of the `ORACLE_SID` variable. The Oracle server initializes several internal parameters from this file as it starts up, which means that changes to this file will only take effect after a server is shut down and restarted.

You must pick the values corresponding to the size of your installation and comment out the other two. Let us look at a sample:

```
  db_block_buffers = 100          # SMALL
# db_block_buffers = 550          # MEDIUM
# db_block_files = 3200           # LARGE
```

`db_block_buffers` is a parameter that fixes the number of database block buffers used internally by Oracle. Usually, the size of the individual data block buffer is set to the size of the underlying file system block size.

For information regarding the other parameters in the `initsid.ora` file, you should consult a standard book on Oracle tuning, such as *Oracle Performance Tuning Tips & Techniques (Oracle Series)* published by Osborne McGraw-Hill (ISBN 0078824346).

## Setting A Common Set Of Environment Variables For Users

The `oraenv` file is used for setting variables whose values get propagated to all users of the database. Usually, the `oraenv` file resides in the `/usr/local/bin` directory. You may have the situation where multiple instances of the database are running; this file can be used to switch between multiple database instances. Below is an example of this behavior:

```
$ export ORAENV_ASK=YES
$ source /usr/local/bin/oraenv
ORACLE_SID= [default] ? newsid
```

Where `newsid` is the SID of the database that you want to switch to.

To make changes pertaining to the installation that apply to all users, the `oraenv` file has to be updated. Then the following needs to be appended to all the users' `.profile` files:

```
ORAENV_ASK=NO; export ORAENV_ASK
source /usr/local/bin/oraenv
ORAENV_ASK= ; export ORAENV_ASK
```

The aim here is only to introduce you to the possibilities of the `oraenv` file. As mentioned earlier, you should consult a book on Oracle database administration to explore this file further.

## Tweaking Oracle Environment Variables

There are several variables pertaining to Oracle that can either be set from the shell (effective only during the lifetime of the shell) or in the `.profile` (so that it is effective even after logout). We won't look at an exhaustive list of such variables; instead we'll focus on a few that are of particular significance from the Linux perspective.

| Variable | Description |
|----------|-------------|
| ORACLE_BASE | Directory path that specifies the base of the Oracle directory structure. |
| ORACLE_HELP | Specifies the directory containing Oracle help documentation. |
| ORACLE_PATH | List of directories to look for Oracle executables. |
| ORACLE_HOME | Directory path to the Oracle software distribution. |
| ORACLE_TERM | Variable used by the Oracle installer to specify the terminal type of the system. |
| ORAENV_ASK | Determines whether the `oraenv` program asks the user for interactive input. |
| ORACLE_SID | Specifies the Oracle System Identifier. |

# Tuning Oracle on Linux

Frequent tuning optimizes system performance and prevents data bottlenecks. The load on the whole system is not always constant, so tuning is necessary to keep the system running at optimum performance. This section focuses on what can be tuned and how tuning can be achieved.

## Monitoring Tools on Linux

Most of the parameters that need to be tuned can be monitored using standard commands that come with Linux itself. We use these tools for monitoring parameters such as CPU usage, interrupts, swapping, paging, and context switching for the entire system. For example, the vmstat utility reports the parameters generally associated with the virtual memory subsystem:

```
$ vmstat -n 2
     procs                      memory      swap        io     system         cpu
   r  b  w   swpd   free  buff  cache  si  so   bi   bo   in    cs  us  sy  id
   1  0  0  32000    239   524  29904   2  14    1   61  118     3   9   3  97
   1  0  0  32000    393   301  40       0   0    2    0  116  1763   3   2  88
   1  0  0  32000    632   524  29904    0   0    0    0  886  1894   5   7  87
   0  0  0  32000    112   524  29624    0   0    1    5  344  1586   8   5  84
   1  0  0  32000    356   520  28296    0   0  211    0  797  1395  24  11  73
   0  0  0  32000    340   520  29060    0   0   48    0  621  1287   1   6  92
   0  0  0  32000    556   520  29196    0   0    0    0  127  1395   4   5  92
   0  0  0  32000    608   520  29288    0   0    1    0  238  1287   5   5  92
```

The w column indicates the number of processes swapped out. A non-zero value indicates swapping activity, and may indicate a memory crunch. You could verify this by using free, and then try to increase swap space by using the swapon command after creating a swap partition. The columns si and so indicate the number of swap-ins and swap-outs per second, respectively – the pages brought into the main memory from the swap device and vice versa. Swapping activity is usually associated with application response time; less swapping means better response time.

## Disk Or I/O Performance

Oracle recommends that the block sizes used by the database should either match or be a multiple of disk block sizes. To get the details about the disk block size, run the df command. If the block size does not conform to the recommendation, it would not be a bad idea to run the newfs command and create a new file system with the right block size. However if you use newfs, all existing data on the particular file system will be lost. However, a freshly created file system has no fragmentation. Another recommendation by Oracle is to distribute disk I/O as evenly as possible across disk drives and maintain the database files and the log files on different partitions, or better still, on different disks.

## Memory Management

Tuning for memory management involves monitoring and controlling swapping and paging activities. We also need to monitor shared memory availability, because the System Global Area (SGA) of the Oracle RDBMS is implemented using shared memory. Oracle maintains a buffer for data that is frequently read or written, which means less disk I/O operations take place and thus improves overall performance.

As mentioned earlier, you can monitor swap space availability and swapping activity using the `free` and `vmstat` commands. If you see that swap space is quickly and easily filling up, then it is time to add more.

## Process Priority

This involves making sure that we don't run into bottlenecks resulting from process priorities. It is common practice to use the `nice` command to bump up the priority of an application that is more performance intensive. In the case of the Oracle RDBMS, however, there is not one but many processes. If we increase the priority of one process, the others may run less frequently, causing them to be the performance bottlenecks. This means it's important to make sure that all Oracle processes have the same priority, and the simplest way to do this is not to change the default priority settings.

## File System Tuning

Now we come to tuning file system parameters such that they can complement parameters specific to Oracle, such as the block size. This can be set to an even-numbered value between 2KB and 16KB. In order to change the block size, change the value of the `db_block_size` parameter in the `initsid.ora` file. The ideal block size to set this to is same as the block size of the underlying file system, which can be found by running the `df` command.

# Summary

In this chapter we built up a case for Linux as a database deployment solution for the enterprise by examining various criteria that determine this choice. We then went on to take a look at various vendor offerings, both commercial and open source in terms of database solutions on Linux:

❑ We examined MySQL by way of features, installation, configuration, administration and its shortcomings (such as no transaction support).

❑ We looked at the more advanced open source product PostgreSQL, which offers, as well as standard database operations, the ability to carry out transactions.

❑ Finally we had an overview of Oracle, a commercial database solution, comparing it with the open source solutions and touching upon issues related to installing, configuring and tuning Oracle on Linux.

# References

*MySQL website* – www.mysql.org
*PostgreSQL* – www.postgresql.org
*Oracle Technical Network* – http://technet.oracle.com
Kreines, David et al, *Oracle Database Administration : The Essential Reference*, O'Reilly & Associates, ISBN 1565925165
Laird, Cameron, *Linux Vs. NT: Are you getting the most from your OS* – Sunworld article: http://www.sunworld.com/sunworldonline/swol-08-1998/swol-08-linuxvnt.html
Niemiec, Rich et al, *Oracle Performance Tuning Tips & Techniques (Oracle Series)*, Osborne McGraw-Hill, ISBN 0078824346
Wong, Brian L., *The TPC-C database benchmark – What does it really mean?*, Sunworld article: http://www.sunworld.com/swol-08-1997/swol-08-database.html

# Using Directory Services and LDAP

Following on from the discussion in the previous chapter about adding database support to your Linux system, we come to the related issues of directories and directory services. When compared to traditional databases, which have been around for many years, web-based directories are a relatively new concept, but they are fast becoming an integral part of the standard web architecture.

Before we continue, however, a few key definitions are required. In this context, a **directory** is a database-like application consisting of an indexed list of uniquely named entries or objects. Each entry consists of a collection of attributes defined by (name, value) pairs, and the user can search the directory for entries by specifying one or more of these attributes. Note that this is in contrast with the usual definition of 'directory', which is a container for files and/or other directories. Just as the Linux file system is arranged in a hierarchical fashion, so too are the directories we'll encounter in this chapter: directory entries can act as containers for other entries, as you'll see later.

A **directory service** provides access to a directory over the network; it consists of various tools and APIs to search a directory hierarchy, add new entries, or modify or delete existing entries.

These definitions might look similar, but there is a fundamental difference between them: a directory stores the information, while the directory service offers the means of accessing it. For example, a directory service could be used to manage which users are authorized to access a server; once a user has been authenticated, they can use the search tools to find the information they require from the directory. This could be a company's address, a colleague's e-mail address, or data about the availability of networked printers.

In this chapter, we're going to discover exactly what directories are (and what makes them so useful), before discussing the various directory services that are currently available. Then we'll look at **LDAP** (Lightweight Directory Access Protocol), which is the standard protocol for accessing web-based directories. Finally, the last part of the chapter will show you how to implement LDAP software on your Linux server.

# Directories, and Why We Need Them

Every web-based directory application has the following general characteristics:

❑   It is comprised of uniquely named entries.

❑   Entries are made up of one or more attributes.

❑   It has a hierarchical data representation.

❑   It will be read from much more often than it will be written to. Because of this, directories are optimized for lookup.

❑   Directories can be distributed – that is, the data can be split among several different machines.

At this point, you may be wondering why we need a separate directory application, when a normal database application could be made to achieve the same result. The simple answer is that directories and databases are designed for quite different purposes, and neither can perform the work of the other without incurring very serious performance hits, as you'll see over the course of this chapter.

# Problems and Solutions

Directories are not meant to be data repositories. They exist to help manage a network infrastructure. Just as a good book requires an index to help the reader find the required page, so a network needs a directory to provide fast access to any of its constituent utilities. To illustrate this, and some other very useful features of directories, let's look at some problems commonly encountered when administering a network, and then show how they can be solved using directories.

## Single Sign-on

In an average organization, a single user has to use several different user IDs and passwords in order to access different parts of the network: one for the database, another to access the web server, and so on. It is up to the user to remember each and every one of them, but passwords are easily forgotten, and it's tempting to pick simple ones that would be easy for someone else to guess. It would be far better to have a single user ID and password that allow the user to gain access to any system requiring them, and this is where the directory comes in. The directory provides single sign-on by placing the user ID and password in one location on the network, and authenticating the user at just one point. This can improve the security of the network while also improving user comfort – that is to say, the user need only remember one password that can be set by the system.

There is another aspect of single sign-on that makes the system administrator's task easier. In a networked system *without* an up-and-running directory service, individual applications tend not to share user databases (or user administrators for that matter), and it's possible for the system to contain user accounts that are not connected to anyone currently employed by the organization (so-called orphan accounts). Having the user ID and password stored in a single location eliminates this possibility: once an employee leaves an organization, the directory entry containing their user ID and password can easily be removed.

Because a directory service is available over a network, you can look up IDs and passwords from any networked machine, which means you will no longer have to manage multiple ID databases. The authentication process is also quick, a result of the directories being configured for fast read access. By contrast, authentication is slower for a traditional relational database, because those are optimized for transactional write operations.

## Certificate Management

As we have seen, simple authentication of users using an ID and password is made easier using directories. However the process of authentication itself has another problem that has nothing to do with the choice of password at all. In a network, the transfer of data occurs in the clear – that is, the bytes are transferred one after another without modification, which means anyone can intercept and read a data stream between two machines. **Encryption** is the ability to encode your network traffic so that only users who are authorized to see the data are able to do so. One form of encryption – public key encryption – allows us to provide more secure authentication by encrypting all network communications; a popular form of public key encryption on the Internet is through the use of **X.509 certificates**.

Because certificates are always issued to verify a single entity (either a user or a machine), and are nearly impossible to duplicate, they are often used to improve authentication control. Now, you might be wondering why certificate management has not been included in the above discussion about single sign-on. The reason is that while certificate management *can* be a part of a single sign-on solution, it is not a *requirement* – certificates are only necessary when a higher level of security is needed. They must be matched to a single entity and stored; your web browser, for example, will use a simple database for this purpose. However, the certificate standard X.509 is part of the X.500 OSI directory management suite, which means that X.509 certificates are supposed to be managed by a directory service.

*For more information about public key encryption, take a look at Chapter 11.*

## Computer Resource Management

Resources are continually being added to our networks, and we need the ability to manage these resources in an effective manner. Because most systems now have networking capabilities out of the box, and with the growth of bandwidth-hogging systems, such as streaming video, it is necessary to improve the network's management capabilities. Here are a few examples of resource management, in order of complexity:

❑   The ability to track which computers and printers are connected to the network.

❑   Auto-discovery capabilities, where a user can configure his machine to locate which printer is physically closest to where he is, or to find a networked printer that matches his printing requirements (a graphic plotter for a CAD application, for example).

❑   The ability to add or remove applications dynamically, allowing the system to be set up so that users can only run certain applications at certain times of day, for example.

❑   The management of bandwidth.

The last of these can be illustrated using an example of a project at the university where I work. The university dormitories have all been wired for network access from each of the rooms. However, we only want the students to be able to access the network once they have paid the required fees. Instead of having the data communications personnel activate each port in the wall one by one, it would be better to activate or deactivate access at the router. Initiatives such as Directory Enabled Networking are going to enable network managers to control resource management and network security via a common directory service.

### Address Books

Another commonly used and popular network application is the e-mail addresses book. Many different address book protocols and systems have been released and replaced over the ages, and all are largely incompatible with each other. They could all be rendered obsolete by standard e-mail directories. Not only would lookup be extremely fast, but also existing e-mail packages now support directory service lookup. It is likely to be only a matter of time before directories are the main place of storage for e-mail addresses.

# Directories Versus Databases

While it's true that all of the solutions discussed above could be implemented using a traditional relational database system, you would not want to do so. This is because there is no standard mechanism to exchange data between different database systems without a lot of work – most of the commonly used database systems use proprietary formats. Directories have a distinct advantage over databases in that they utilize a standard access protocol; they can exchange data with each other much more easily. Multiple vendors are beginning to implement standardized directory solutions in their products, and they're using LDAP.

Remember that a relational database is a powerful tool. Think of it like a traditional power saw: you can cut up all types of wood with it. A directory service is more like a jigsaw, and while you *could* emulate the abilities of a jigsaw with a traditional saw, it would take at least twice as much effort, and you probably couldn't achieve the same degree of finesse. A directory is a special kind of database, specifically designed with one purpose in mind: providing fast access to data in a standardized way.

# Examples of Directories

To this point, you've seen only a very broad overview of what directories are and what they can be used for. Now we are going to go into more depth and look at the internal structure of a directory. We start by discussing the most familiar of directories: a telephone directory. In many ways, a telephone directory typifies exactly what we mean by a directory service.

### The Telephone Directory

A physical telephone directory can be organized into two sections: the first lists residential numbers; the second lists business numbers. Every entry has this standard set of attributes:

❑   A name (of person, company, etc.)

❑   An address

❑   A telephone number

If the entry is in the business section, it will also have at least one extra attribute that describes the type of business (carpet cleaning, Java programming, etc.).

You will know, from personal experience, that telephone directories are organized for fast lookup – they're arranged in alphabetical order by surname for the residential section, or by the type of business. A system like this allows for multiple points of access – that is, a single number can be accessed in more than one way. If the telephone directory is available electronically (via a web site or on CD-ROM, perhaps), there are usually other ways to access a particular number or set of numbers. For example, you can find an address by just using the phone number, or discover the typical number prefix of a given zip code. All this, and more, is possible using directory services.

The listings by name and business types in a physical telephone directory are called **indexes**, and similar devices are used by electronic directory services to increase the speed of lookup for popular searches.

## The Domain Name Server (DNS)

When you use the Internet, you actually use a directory service regularly – and you may not even know it. This directory service is the **Domain Name Server**, or just **DNS**. On the Internet, each machine or service is typically given a human-friendly name such as www.yahoo.com or www.mypages.net. These are called **hostnames**, and they exist because humans can remember names much better than they remember numbers. At some point, however, those names have to be converted to IP addresses, and it is the task of the DNS to match hostnames with their corresponding addresses.

> *You'll learn more about DNS in Chapter 9; this discussion is simply intended to demonstrate that DNS is a type of specialized, distributed directory service.*

When you select a web site to visit (say, www.yahoo.com), the first thing the browser will do is look for the IP address of the computer by that name in its local 'cache' or 'hosts' file. If it fails to find the address there, it will consult the network's DNS server. If that server does not contain the IP address of the requested computer, then it will set about finding the address by contacting the DNS server of the computer's top domain (.com). That request will be subsequently routed to yahoo.com, and then finally to www.yahoo.com, if the site is available. Only when the IP address is passed back to the browser can it go on to request the web page.

All this activity between various DNS servers occurs in those first few seconds following a URL request. Because the DNS servers all communicate according to a standard protocol, the process of relaying requests from server to server is quite fast, even if they are physically scattered across the globe. The same is potentially true for the directory services we'll be discussing later in this chapter. If a particular directory service doesn't have the information stored in its directory, it can always pass the request on to a different server.

The telephone directory and DNS are both examples of directory services, but neither fulfills the notion of a *general-purpose* directory service. The telephone directory has obvious limitations in this respect in that it is published by telecommunications companies or other businesses, for their own purposes. DNS, as we have seen, is not a repository for general information – it exists to supply IP addresses from its databanks. In this section we will see what different types of *general* directory services are already available.

# X.500

X.500 is a directory service standard that was originally created by the International Telephone Union (ITU) to run over the Open Systems Interconnection (OSI) definition, which is a competing protocol to TCP/IP that is not commonly used. X.500 provides both a full data model and a communications protocol (the **Directory Access Protocol** or **DAP**). The data model has found great success since its inception (it has been implemented in various other directory services), but the X.500 DAP protocol has not seen widespread everyday use because of its complexity, even though it does now run over TCP/IP. However, X.500 retains an important place in history as its developers worked through many of the problems of establishing a directory services standard, and its communications protocol DAP is the forerunner of the simplified (or *lightweight*) protocol, LDAP. There are not many X.500 servers available for Linux, although MessagingDirect (http://www.messagingdirect.com/m-vault) sell one such product.

# NT/Active Directory

Windows NT 4.0 provides a very simple directory service called the **domain service** (not to be confused with Internet domains), which is not a true directory service in that the data is not stored in one place, or even in one format. Windows NT gathers the data from across its system and presents it to the user as if it were a single source. However, Windows 2000 comes with an entirely new directory service called Active Directory, which is based on the LDAP specification. We mention it here because you will likely have to interact with it in your network; furthermore, Cisco (http://www.cisco.com) is reported to be porting Active Directory to UNIX, so you might someday see an Active Directory server for Linux.

# Novell Directory Services (NDS)

One of the first directory service mechanisms to be released was Novell's NDS, introduced with Novell Netware version 4. It was originally developed as a proprietary protocol that only ran on Novell's Netware platform, and while it was supposed to be ported to other systems, that never happened. NDS was heavily inspired by X.500 (it used the same data model), but it was never an X.500 server.

Around the second half of 1997, Novell began to reinvent itself as a specialist in directory services. Instead of trying to get people to move to Netware, they focused on trying to get people to use NDS as their directory server. NDS is supposed to run on a variety of platforms, including Linux. The latest version is a native LDAP server (rather than an NDS server that's capable of speaking LDAP), but it can still use Novell's existing management tools. For more information, take a look at http://www.novell.com/products/nds.

# NIS/NIS+

The most popular directory service for UNIX/Linux is the Network Information System (NIS) protocol. This protocol was originally invented by Sun Microsystems, but it has always been an open standard for implementation. Unlike Novell Directory Services, NIS does not use X.500 as its data model. Instead, NIS is a flat-file database system, used mainly to manage centrally the standard configuration files in a server (password file, group files, disk mountings, etc).

NIS has provided a steady directory service for many years, but it does have problems:

❑  Its flat-file namespace does not make it very manageable.

❑  Because of the database technology it uses in its native form, NIS can only scale to about 30,000 entries.

❑  It's network-inefficient, because any transaction requires the entire database to be transferred over the network.

❑  It's insecure, because NIS does not use any encryption, even when it's moving the password database over the network.

NIS+ was released as an improvement on NIS; a significant revision is that it does not transfer the entire NIS database across the network for each lookup. However, it has not seen widespread use. Many NIS users are planning on (or are in the process of) migrating from NIS straight to LDAP, bypassing NIS+ altogether.

# Lightweight Directory Access Protocol (LDAP)

It's high time we looked more closely at the core of the standardized directory service: the protocol that makes it all happen – the Lightweight Directory Access Protocol (LDAP). You'll see how to set up an LDAP server on your Linux system, and learn how to use the search tools and simple scripts to access and manipulate LDAP data.

## Why LDAP?

Here are four reasons why you should choose LDAP:

❑   LDAP is an open directory standard that is available over TCP/IP.

❑   LDAP has a flexible data model – there is very little that you can't store in an LDAP server.

❑   LDAP has an inbuilt security model that makes use of Access Control Lists (ACLs), and support for other security technologies such as SSL and Kerberos.

❑   LDAP has been accepted as a standard by many different vendors and software suppliers.

## LDAP Fundamentals

LDAP is a standardized, high-level directory service protocol. Originally, it was designed to be a TCP/IP gateway to X.500 servers for PC and Macintosh computers that couldn't use the OSI communications protocol. It has now become the most popular directory standard, and all of the popular directory services (Active Directory, Netscape Directory Server and NIS) can talk LDAP.

LDAP is defined in several RFCs; the two most important are RFC 1777 (LDAP version 2 protocol) and RFC 2251 (LDAP version 3 protocol).

> **RFCs ('Requests For Comments') are documents that contain the written definitions of the protocols and policies of the Internet. The full list can be accessed at http://www.cis.ohio-state.edu/htbin/rfc/INDEX.rfc.html.**

LDAP is a high-level protocol in the same vein as SMTP (for e-mail), HTTP (for the Web), and NNTP (for news). Like these protocols, it currently uses TCP as its transport protocol. The default LDAP port is 389, though the secure port 636 is used when employing the SSL (Secure Sockets Layer) protocol.

There has been work, however, on developing an LDAP implementation that uses UDP (User Datagram Protocol) as its transport protocol. The reason why you might want UDP instead of TCP is one of speed: a TCP connection is considered more reliable than a UDP connection, but there is a great deal of overhead incurred when setting one up. This overhead is relatively small for most applications, but in certain cases it can be a performance hit. For example, if you wanted to use a directory service as a registry of network devices (as in Sun's JINI), you want the device to know what's available as soon as it comes online. Being a consumer device, this needs to happen in just a few seconds – not the minute or so we're accustomed to in our business environments. A directory service running over UDP could, in theory, provide a much faster service than one running over TCP. (This is why DNS normally uses UDP instead of TCP for providing lookup services to the Internet.)

*Even if services like JINI or DNS require specialized UDP-based directory services, they still may use LDAP – it's an access protocol, not a transport protocol. Microsoft's dynamic DNS, which comes with Windows 2000, uses LDAP to manage information stored on a DNS server. The LDAP server is used to update the information on the DNS server on a regular basis, while the DNS server continues to do its normal work.*

As the words 'directory' and 'domain' can have different meanings in different contexts, the same is true for 'LDAP'. When the term is used, it can actually be referring to any one of the following:

❑ An information model

❑ A naming model

❑ A functional model

❑ A security model

## Information Model

This model describes the type of information that you can put into your directory – LDAP can store either textual or binary data. As a further option, because LDAP is network-aware (by which I mean that it is understood the clients who interact with an LDAP server are on the network), you can embed information in the LDAP server in the form of URLs.

The beauty of this last approach is that your LDAP directory can very easily become a meta-directory. Let's say that you decide to implement an enterprise-wide directory service that consists of a standardized telephone and e-mail directory. The e-mail addresses will be stored as part of an individual's entry on the LDAP server, but the telephone numbers are already managed by your organization's PBX system. Instead of storing the phone numbers on the LDAP server, you could provide a reference (via a URL or similar network location description) to where they are *actually* located. The LDAP directory is then linked to an external directory; the linking of separate directories in this way forms the basis of a **meta-directory**.

### Attributes, Entries and Objectclasses

The basic elements of LDAP are **attributes**, which are also referred to as (name, value) pairs. Attributes can be single or multi-valued; you can think of them as the equivalents of the fields in a database.

The next level above an attribute is an **entry**. An entry is made up of one or more attributes, and can be compared to a record in a traditional database.

However, there is a special attribute called an **objectclass**. An objectclass defines what attributes are required (mandatory) and what attributes are simply allowed (optional) in an entry. You can think of it as being a little like a database table, if you wish.

*A listing of the main objectclasses with their required and optional attributes can be found in the* slapd.oc.conf *file. Likewise, a list of some common attributes can be found in the* slapd.at.conf *file.*

The difference between an average database table and an LDAP objectclass is that the latter can be extended. For example, you can imagine that an objectclass called `person` could have three mandatory attributes: the individual's last name, first name and telephone number. An objectclass called `employee` could then *extend* the `person` objectclass by containing the same three attributes as `person`, and additional attributes of its own (say, e-mail address, user ID and password). The `employee` objectclass is thus *derived* from `person`, and is said to *inherit* from the `person` objectclass.

It follows that `person` is the *parent* of `employee`, in that every entry in the database of objectclass `employee` is also of objectclass `person`. Therein lies the hierarchical nature of the LDAP data source: every entry is contained within an entry one place higher up in the hierarchy.

This information model is very flexible. When implemented in an LDAP server, it allows for very quick lookup, and is designed to complement (not replace) traditional database systems. However, LDAP does not support *ad hoc* queries and the like, so don't throw out your traditional database just yet!

The hierarchical system outlined here is very similar in structure to your file system, and it's referred to as a **directory information tree** (**DIT**). Each directory will have one or more roots; a directory with more than one root is sometimes called a directory forest.

## Naming Model

Entries in an LDAP server all have a unique name called a **distinguished name**, or **DN** for short. Like a full path name in your file system (`/usr/local/myfile.txt`, for example), a DN refers to the exact location of a particular entry in the directory. However, where a file system places its root to the *left* of the pathname (in this case, `/`), a DN places its root on the *right* side. In the example DN below:

```
uid=scarter,ou=people,o=airius.com
```

The root is `o=airius.com`.

> *Here, the* `uid` *attribute contains the value for the user ID,* `ou` *represents an organizational unit (a sub-division of an organization), and* `o` *represents the organization itself. Note that these three attributes are standard LDAP attributes.*

A DN is normally made up of attributes contained in the entry itself. The leftmost part of the DN (`uid=scarter` in the above example) is called the **relative distinguished name** (RDN) and refers to the part of the DN that is unique in this section of the directory information tree. In other words, there will be no other entries in the section of the DIT specified by the `ou=people` entry with a `uid` of `scarter`.

## Functional Model

This is how the process of accessing the LDAP directory is defined. To use an LDAP directory correctly, five steps are involved:

- ❑ Connect to the LDAP server
- ❑ Bind to (that is, be authenticated by) an LDAP server
- ❑ Perform operations (search, compare, update, etc.)
- ❑ Unbind
- ❑ Close the connection

The operations you can perform on an LDAP server are the following:

- ❑ **Search** – query the LDAP server to retrieve entries that match your criteria
- ❑ **Compare** – determine whether an entry contains an attribute of a particular value
- ❑ **Add** – add a new LDAP entry
- ❑ **Modify** – modify an LDAP entry
- ❑ **Delete** – remove an LDAP entry
- ❑ **ModRDN** – change the RDN of an entry

## Security Model

LDAP also has its own security model, and this is very important when you consider that your directory may contain some of the most sensitive information of any system on your network. Security can be broken down into four distinct areas:

- ❑ **Authentication** – verifying that users are who they say they are
- ❑ **Access control** – verifying access permissions for a user on the system
- ❑ **Encryption** – encoding transactions so only the parties involved can view or modify the data
- ❑ **Physical** – protecting the hardware

We will discuss only the first two of these here. Encryption is mentioned in the context of authentication, and discussed in more detail in Chapter 11.

### Authentication

When we talk about authentication, we're referring to the process used to determine who the client is. In LDAP, this is through the 'bind' operation. When you bind to the server, you do so as one of the entries in the directory. The access controls of the directory are all determined by the way you are bound.

In LDAP version 3, you have four options for authentication:

- ❑ **Anonymous** – that is, you don't provide a DN
- ❑ **Simple** – you provide a DN and a plain-text password
- ❑ **Client Certificate** – you provide a DN and an X.509 certificate via SSL
- ❑ **Simple Authentication and Security Layer (SASL)** – DN and negotiated authentication

Many directory servers will allow anonymous authentication, but with extremely limited rights. We'll talk more about this when we discuss access control.

The next level of authentication – simple – only requires the DN of an entry and its corresponding plain-text password. This is the default and most popular form of authentication.

> **If you attempt to bind to the server and pass a null or blank password, you will be authenticated successfully as an anonymous user. This is an important point to remember if you are using LDAP as an authentication system.**

If you want a more secure form of authentication, you can use client certificates or the SASL authentication mechanism. As you discovered earlier in this chapter, client certificates are defined in the X.509 standard. They use a public key infrastructure, as found in the Secure Sockets Layer (SSL). However, whereas SSL server certificates are used to help identify which server you are talking to before setting up SSL encryption, client certificates are a more secure mechanism of user authentication. This is because client certificates must be presented to the requesting server, either via a file stored on the user's computer, or on a smart card.

The Simple Authentication and Security Layer (SASL) protocol is an Internet standard (RFC 2222) for defining authentication systems besides simple passwords and client certificates. SASL isn't so much a single standard but a definition of how a client and a server can use a variety of other mechanisms. The two most common SASL providers are CRAM-MD5 and Kerberos, defined in RFC 2195 and RFC 2222 respectively. You can look up more about SASL and these two common systems at http://www.isi.edu/in-notes/iana/assignments/sasl-mechanisms.

## Access Control

After you have been authenticated onto the LDAP server, the directory's **Access Control List** or **ACL** defines your access rights. By default, nobody has any access rights except the root DN account, which is normally referred to as the Directory Manager. The Directory Manager account has unlimited access to data stored in the directory, and restrictions that apply to other users do not apply to the Directory Manager account.

ACLs let you define the fields that specified users are able to view and update. For example, you can set up your directory so that anonymous users only view very basic details on an individual, such as name, telephone number and e-mail address (this is a type of access you might want to provide for a public directory service). Those users would not even be aware that other attributes exist. Next, you might say that any authenticated users from within the organization will be able to see the building number or room number for the individual's place of work. Such information would not be available in the public domain. You might also allow authenticated users the right to change their passwords, but nothing else. Then, you might relax restrictions further by allowing administration assistants the right to change a user's telephone number, e-mail address or room number. Beyond that, you could create a management group for each part of the organization (marketing managers, human resource managers, etc.) that has the right to change people's user IDs and passwords. Finally, a small, select group of directory administrators would have the right to change *any* attribute in *any* entry. Only they would be allowed to add and delete entries.

ACLs are one of the best things about LDAP. They provide a great deal of access control flexibility, with a minimum of fuss. Unfortunately there is no standard for ACLs, so if you exchange data between different LDAP servers, the ACLs will most likely be ignored. This is not a fault in LDAP, and the LDAP development group (and other directory standards groups) is working on a standard for ACL information, but that's still in the future. For the time being, the incompatibility of ACLs issued by different companies is a limiting factor when it comes to LDAP security.

Configuring ACLs is a relatively advanced topic that is beyond the scope of this chapter. If you want to know more, look up the FAQ and information pages at the web sites of LDAP service providers (e.g. www.openldap.org, www.iplanet.com).

# What Can I Do With LDAP?

In this section, we're going to look at some of the standard LDAP applications that are already available for use with Linux. There are three popular uses for LDAP, and with Linux you can take advantage of all of them today.

## White Pages Service

A **white pages** service can be implemented to provide a public directory of the people in your organization over the Internet. There are many ways of doing this. Most of the LDAP servers available to you, including iPlanet Directory Server (formerly Netscape Directory Server) and OpenLDAP, are provided with web gateways that you can set up for use via a web browser. (You'll be shown how to do this at the very end of the chapter.) Many e-mail packages, including Eudora, Netscape Communicator and Microsoft's Internet Explorer, come with LDAP-capable address books. There are also a number of open-source clients available for other services, such as a `finger2LDAP` gateway that enables you to use the `finger` protocol to search an LDAP server. Many of these utilities come with the OpenLDAP server, which we will be using later on in this chapter.

Using a program like `mail500`, you can set up `sendmail` to use LDAP as one of its alias gateways. By properly configuring your LDAP server and the `mail500` program, you can use LDAP to manage your e-mail lists.

## User Authentication

LDAP is being looked at to provide the solution to the single sign-on problem. Many operating systems (including Linux and most UNIX variants) have versions that boast native LDAP authentication support. A number of other applications (such as the Apache and Netscape Enterprise web servers) also support the ability to use LDAP as an authentication system. Because X.509 certificates belong to the same information model as LDAP, it is also being used as the database for certificate management, which is extremely important in e-commerce.

To use LDAP for your authentication system in Linux, you need **Pluggable Authentication Modules**, or **PAM**.

### Pluggable Authentication Modules (PAM)

The concept of PAM was created in response to a need to standardize authentication APIs in the UNIX environment. Before PAM, if you wanted to change the user authentication mechanism (from a `crypt()` to an MD5 system, for example), you would have to recompile all of the utilities that used the previous system. Needless to say, this was a tedious and time-consuming task.

PAM provides a standard API to create an authentication interface with the operating system. For example, you could configure PAM to use Kerberos, the standard UNIX password system, or LDAP. Furthermore, you can generally switch these systems around without the operating system or other user-level applications knowing that you've changed your user authentication system. Most recent Linux distributions come with the ability to use PAM, and there are at least two ways of using PAM and LDAP on Linux.

❑ **Pam_ldap** is a free software product from Padl Software (http://www.padl.com) and should work with any LDAP server, whether that server resides on Linux or not.

❑ **Novell NDS** for Linux enables you to access an NDS server via PAM on Linux.

### Replace Other Directory Services

You can also use LDAP as the storage mechanism for other directory information, such as the **Name Services Switch (NSS)** or NIS systems.

#### Name Services Switch (NSS)

NSS is used to map the location of data that pertains to users, groups, computers, etc. For example, if you have a network of systems and you want your users to have the same shell and home location, regardless of what system they are logged into, you can store these attributes in a directory service. In the past this has been NIS on UNIX-based systems, but with NSS and Padl Software's `nss_ldap` program you can store this information in LDAP. There is even an RFC on the subject: RFC 2307.

The benefit of this is that by combining PAM/LDAP and NSS/LDAP, you can manage all of your user information in a centralized, open standard directory instead of storing it in a closed proprietary directory service or static local files.

#### Network Information System (NIS/NIS+)

Network Information Services (NIS) is a directory service originally developed by Sun Microsystems but used by every UNIX-based system. If you are bringing your Linux server into an existing UNIX-based network, it is possible that you already have a NIS system in place.

Unfortunately, there isn't an LDAP/NIS gateway for UNIX. However, Padl Software makes a commercial product called `ypldapd` for Solaris and Linux that replaces your standard NIS server with one that uses an LDAP server as its data store. This gives you the ability to phase out your NIS system gently, while getting some of the benefits of an LDAP based system.

## LDAP-Aware Tools

While LDAP can and will be used to manage all sorts of information for an application, most applications that say they have LDAP support mean they can use LDAP as an authentication system. Here are some samples of LDAP-aware tools:

❑ **FTP** – any FTP server can be made LDAP-aware for authentication via PAM

❑ **NSS** – you can use `nss_ldap` to use LDAP to manage your aliases and user profile information

❑ **Samba** – has support for LDAP in its CVS tree

❑ **Apache** – has several modules that can be used to communicate with an LDAP server

# LDAP Installation on a Linux Server

Now we come to installing an LDAP server on your Linux machine. There are a number of applications that you can use, and both open- and closed-source software are represented. Some of the main options available to you are described here.

## Open Source

The original LDAP server was developed by the University of Michigan, and while it is no longer actively maintained, it is still available from http://www.umich.edu/~dirsvcs/ldap/ldap.html. Its successor, **OpenLDAP**, is certainly still in development – version 1.2.7 supports LDAP v2. (The developers are working on compliance with the LDAP v3 specification at the time of writing.) You might find this server included among the various utilities that come with the latest Linux distributions, but the most up-to-date version can always be downloaded from http://www.openldap.org.

OpenLDAP also comes with a bundle of client tools that enable you to provide access to your LDAP server via various existing utilities, including `finger`, e-mail, and the Web.

## Proprietary Applications

The iPlanet (Netscape) Directory Server is perhaps the premier LDAP server on the market. It supports the full LDAP v3 specification, is extremely scalable (up to 50 million entries), and sports a GUI interface to LDAP via a Java console. The iPlanet DS also supports SSL out of the box, where the open-source LDAP servers require some programming to get them to communicate via SSL. Of course, this does come at a cost: iPlanet Directory Server is not cheap and, like any enterprise database system, requires some serious hardware. There is a 90-day evaluation application for Linux available for download from the iPlanet web site at http://www.iplanet.com/downloads/testdrive.

The fact that iPlanet Directory Server (along with other enterprise applications such as iPlanet Enterprise web server and Oracle database system) has been ported to Linux is yet another reason to believe that you can now take Linux seriously in the enterprise market. That Oracle and iPlanet (through its parents Sun and Netscape) would even release a version of their software for Linux gives Linux a very large credibility boost.

# Working with LDAP

We'll spend the rest of this chapter working with a real LDAP server. Obviously, we won't be able to go into all of the details of how to use it; if you want more information you might like to check out *Implementing LDAP* (Wrox Press, 1-861002-21-1).

## Installing OpenLDAP

The first step is to download a copy of the latest version of the software from www.openldap.org. The homepage will also have a link to the OpenLDAP FAQ, which now has a quick-start guide; you might want to check there before installing the software to get the latest information. Put the `gzip`'ed file into the directory from which you wish to unpack it (`/usr/local`, for example) and unzip it as follows:

```
$ tar xvfz openldap-release.tgz
```

This will expand and unpack the server source files, documentation and example utilities. You will need about 4 MB of disk space.

All of the files that have been unpacked will be put into a directory called `ldap`. Change into that directory. Like many other open-source packages, OpenLDAP uses the GNU `autoconf` utility via a `configure` script that has made installing software a lot less painful than it used to be on UNIX systems. In the `ldap` directory, type the following commands:

```
# ./configure
```

This may take a while, depending on your machine. Furthermore, the script could fail to finish if you don't have (say) the `gcc` compiler or the standard C headers installed.

```
# make depend
```

This command will build all of the libraries that the rest of the software depends on.

```
# make
```

Finally, this command will compile all of the software. After you've done this, you are ready to test out the server.

Change into the `ldap/tests` directory, type `make` again, and watch the tests run. This will test all of the various components of the LDAP server, which goes by the strange name of `slapd`. These tests include starting and stopping the server, loading, searching and modifying data, and finally server replication. The screen will scroll as every command is echoed as it is carried out. The output can be redirected to a text file to be viewed at your leisure. If the tests worked, you will see this line after each one:

```
>>>>> Test succeeded
```

Finally, you need to actually install the software. Type the following command from the `ldap` directory:

```
# make install
```

This will put all of the server binaries and scripts in the places specified during the configuration steps.

## Loading the Server

Now that you've installed the server, it's time to give it some data, start it up, and begin working with it.

### Getting Data

In a real world LDAP setting, you would have existing data sources to draw from. These might be your human resources databases, e-mail, existing network directories, or even the organization's phone book. To get an example running as quickly as possible, however, we're going to play with some fake data. We'll be using a very simple script called `wrox.ldif` that you can download from the Wrox web site.

> *Alternatively, you could use the example data file from one of the latest Connectathons. The Connectathon is a contest each year that tests how different systems actually interact with each other — or more specifically, how they connect between different clients and servers. Among the tests are NIS, NFS and, of course, LDAP. Go to* http://www.connectathon.org/ldaptests *and download a copy of the* ldif for basic tests *under* For DC naming. *Note that file* dc-names.ldif *is very large — 1.7 MB.*

You'll have noticed a new term here: **LDIF** stands for **LDAP Data Interchange Format**, and you can think of LDIF files as being human-readable LDAP information. It is the standard for presenting and transmitting LDAP data.

Before we can move on, you need to verify that the very first entry in the LDIF file looks like this:

```
dn: dc=IMC, dc=org
dc: IMC
o: IMC
objectclass: top
objectclass: organization
objectclass: dcobject
```

You will also need to edit your `slapd.conf` file, located in the `/usr/local/etc/openldap` directory, so that it looks something like this:

```
database        ldbm
suffix          "dc=IMC, dc=org"
#suffix         "o=Your Organization Name, c=US"
directory       /usr/tmp
rootdn          "cn=root, dc=IMC, dc=org"
#rootdn         "cn=root, o=Your Organization Name, c=US"
```

The `rootdn` account is the Directory Manager account – that is, the superuser of the LDAP server. If you want use your domain in place of `IMC.org`, simply replace all occurrences of `IMC` with your domain name (such as `WROX`) and `org` with your root domain (such as `com`). Any time you make any changes to the `slapd.conf` file, you need to restart the server, which is achieved with the same command as the one used to start it in the first place...

### Starting The Server

To start (or restart) the `slapd` server daemon, type:

```
$ /usr/local/ldap/servers/slapd/slapd -p 389 /usr/local/etc/openldap/slapd.conf
```

(Of course, the paths to `slapd` and `slapd.conf` might be different for your Linux distribution.)

## LDAP Command Line Tools

The OpenLDAP distribution ships with a set of simple LDAP clients, usually referred to as the LDAP command line tools. These clients were created for the original reference implementation of LDAP, and variants of them come with just about every LDAP server. They are:

❑　`ldapadd` – a client that adds new entries to your LDAP server

❑　`ldapdelete` – a client that deletes existing entries in your LDAP server

❑　`ldapmodify` – a client that adds, modifies and deletes entries in your LDAP server

❑　`ldapmodrdn` – a client that can modify the relative distinguished name (the leftmost part of a DN) of an entry in your LDAP server

❑　`ldapsearch` – a client that can search your LDAP server

*A* man *page on each of these clients ships with OpenLDAP, and information about them is also available on the OpenLDAP web site.*

We're now ready to add some entries to the LDAP server, using the `ldapadd` tool. (Using the `ldapadd` command is exactly the same as using `ldapmodify` with the `-a` switch.) By default, `ldapadd` and all the other tools are found in the `ldap/clients/tools` directory.

To add users to the LDAP server, type:

```
$ /path/to/ldapadd -h your.host.name -p 389 -D "cn=root,dc=IMC,dc=org" -W <
/path/to/your.ldif.file
```

Obviously, you replace `/path/to/` with the full paths of the `ldapadd` tool and the `Wrox.ldif` file respectively. An option you might want to use is `-c`, which will continue to add entries even if the server returns an error. If this is not specified, `ldapadd` will stop when the first error is encountered. Also, the `-v` option will display detailed information about the interactions between your client and the server.

If it is different, you will need to replace `"dc=IMC,dc=org"` with whatever you have specified in your `slapd.conf` file.

At this point, you will be prompted for your Directory Manager password, which is set in the `slapd.conf` file. The default is `secret`, which of course you must change before using the OpenLDAP server for real. You should begin to see something like this on your screen:

```
adding new entry dc=IMC, dc=org

adding new entry dc=Acmewidgets, dc=IMC, dc=org

adding new entry dc=Plastico, dc=IMC, dc=org

adding new entry dc= Main Office, dc=Acmewidgets, dc=IMC, dc=org

adding new entry dc=Admin, dc=Acmewidgets, dc=IMC, dc=org
```

If you don't, the most likely problem is one of the following:

❑ You entered the wrong password or Directory Manager DN

❑ The LDAP server is not on

❑ The `slapd.conf` suffix is not the same as the base suffix in your LDIF file

If you used the `Wrox.ldif` file, and if all goes well, the process will complete in less than a minute. However, if you have a low-end machine, and you decide to use the 1.7 MB `dc-names.ldif` file, be prepared to wait a long, long time for `ldapadd` to finish its work. Unless the program breaks down in the first few minutes, it will grind on, adding one entry after another for up to 12 hours. This illustrates just how slow LDAP write operations are – they are always several orders of magnitude slower than read operations.

For LDAP to provide quick read access, which is its primary purpose, it must be able to find entries quickly. To do this, it indexes each and every entry as it is added – or to be more precise, it indexes particular attributes within the entries, which you can configure. The indexing process slows updates and can be very tedious to set up, but the benefit is that once the LDAP database and the indexes have been set up, searching becomes very easy indeed.

## Testing the Server

After the server has finished loading, you can test to see whether it worked by using the `ldapsearch` tool. This is located in the same place as the `ldapadd` command line tool. One of the entries in the server is for Pablo Picasso, and we would like to see what we have stored for him. This is the syntax for a simple search, which looks for Picasso's `sn` attribute (that is, his surname) from the LDAP source:

```
$ /path/to/ldapsearch -h server.name -p 389 -D "cn=root,dc=IMC,dc=ORG" -W -b
"dc=IMC, dc=ORG" "sn=Picasso"
```

You should see the following results in LDIF format. If you're running your OpenLDAP server on a simple workstation, you may see a delay as the operating system swaps back and forth. If you're running the OpenLDAP server on a real server, then you should see a much quicker result:

```
cn=Pablo Picasso, dc=Acmewidgets, dc=IMC, dc=org
cn: Pablo Picasso
sn: Picasso
givenname: Pablo
uid: 00123456789
mail: Pablo.Picasso@connectathon.org
userpassword: guernica
title: Cubist
objectclass: top
objectclass: person
```

A quick explanation of this output is given in the table below.

| Attribute name | Meaning |
| --- | --- |
| cn | Common name |
| sn | Surname or last name |
| givenname | First name |
| uid | User ID |
| mail | The e-mail address of the entry |
| userpassword | The password for this entry |
| title | The title of the entry |
| objectclass | The objectclass of the entry |

# Programming LDAP

Once you have an LDAP server installed and loaded with some data, the next thing you're going to want to do is access it from other applications. The reasons for this can range from providing a web-based white pages directory using LDAP authentication, to using directory-based preferences for workstations. In this section we will cover how to develop LDAP-aware applications. Space dictates that we won't be able to go into great detail; for more information look up the Wrox book *Implementing LDAP*.

We will demonstrate the five main LDAP operations programmatically: connecting, binding, carrying out an LDAP activity, unbinding and disconnecting. You will learn how to use simple scripts to search the directory, and how to add, modify and delete an entry. To simply things, we will cheat authentication by hard-coding the password into the script.

# Installing Net::LDAP

The examples we'll use in this section are going to be written in Perl, which is installed by default on most Linux distributions and available on a large number of other operating systems, including MS Windows. There are two primary LDAP APIs available to you for use with Perl: the Netscape PerLDAP module (available from www.mozilla.org), which is a wrapper around the Netscape C SDK; and Net::LDAP, which is a pure Perl module that doesn't use any C code and is therefore very portable. We'll be using Net::LDAP in this chapter.

If you have a version of Perl 5 or later, you will be able to install Net::LDAP without any problems – you can download it from http://www.perl.com/CPAN. You will also need the Convert::BER module, which has to be installed first. The reason why we need Convert::BER is that LDAP, unlike many other TCP/IP protocols, is a binary-only protocol. The binary structures are described using a special set of rules called Abstract Syntax Notification One (ASN.1), and they're encoded via another set of rules called **basic encoding rules** or BER. Convert::BER takes care of encoding the LDAP commands into BER, and also decoding BER back into data structures that Perl programmers can use.

## Installing Perl Modules

Installing these two Perl modules requires you to follow the same basic steps. First, you need to unzip and extract the module:

```
$ tar xvfz module.version.gz
```

Then you can change into the module's directory, in which there will be a file called Makefile.PL. This is a 'magic' Perl script that will generate the makefile needed to install the module. You can configure how you want to install the module by passing parameters to the Makefile.PL script; these are described in the Perl documentation.

The first step is to run the Makefile.PL script by typing:

```
$ perl Makefile.PL
```

This will create a makefile that matches the parameters of your Perl installation. (Don't worry if, when running this for Net::LDAP, you get an error displayed telling you that Digest::MD5 was missing. It will not affect the outcome of the installation.)

Now type these three commands:

```
$ make
```

This will build the basic module for you. Some Perl modules are actually wrappers around C code; were that the case, this step would compile any C code and link it to the Perl code.

```
$ make test
```

This will run any test scripts that might be shipped with the module. These tests enable you tell if you have all of the pieces necessary to run the module correctly.

```
# make install
```

With this, the modules are at last installed, and you are ready to start running Perl scripts.

# Search Parameters

The most common LDAP operation to be performed by any application will be to search an LDAP server. Essentially, all search functions take:

❑   An LDAP connection handle

❑   The base from which the search should start

❑   The scope of the search

❑   A search filter

The reason for and nature of the first of these is obvious, but the other three require more detailed explanation, which we shall do in this section.

## LDAP Search Base

An LDAP search base is how we tell the LDAP server which part of its directory we want to search. By narrowing a search base (thereby reducing the number of entries it must look through to find matches), you can improve search performance.

## *Determining LDAP Scope*

The scope of an LDAP search defines exactly how much of the tree you want to examine. There are three levels of scope:

❑   sub (sub-tree) – the scope starts at the base entry and searches everything below it, including the base entry:

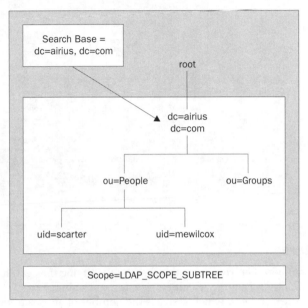

❑   onelevel – the scope searches the immediate children of the base entry. It does not include the base entry:

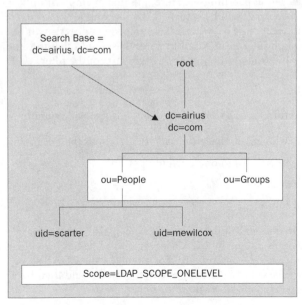

❑   `base` – the scope searches only the base entry, which is useful if you only want to get the attribute values for a single entry:

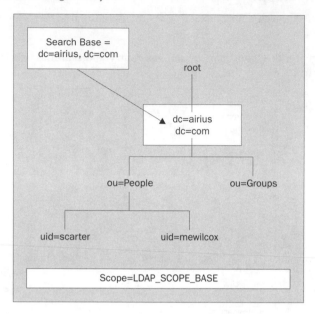

## LDAP Search Filters

Having limited the number of entries to be searched by specifying the search base and the scope, we can fine-tune our search by specifying which entries we want pulling out of the directory and displayed. We do that by using a search filter, which restricts the number of entries to those that match the filter. Example of search filters are `(sn=Carter)` and `(&(sn=Carter)(ou=People))`.

Filters are always enclosed in parentheses. Here, the first example simply specifies that only entries with `sn` (surname) equal to `Carter` will be returned. The second looks more complicated, but it really only means that entries with `sn=Carter` within the group `ou=People` will be returned. Note that each attribute within the search filter is enclosed in parentheses, and that the Boolean operator `&` (AND) is placed to the left of (rather than in between) the two parts of the filter.

## The Search Result

A search will always return an LDAP message. The message will contain:

❑   A result code, which contains either an error code or the number of entries returned

❑   Zero or more entries, listed one attribute per line

❑   Zero or more referrals

❑   Zero or more controls

**Referrals** are entries that point to other servers that can also hold entries that match the given search criteria. **Controls** are extra things the LDAP server sends back to provide more information about the search, or to supply additional functionality. For example, the LDAP server might send back a control that says that the user's password is to expire, and the user would then be warned. Further discussion of referrals and controls is beyond the scope of this chapter.

## Searching with Net::LDAP

Now that we have a better idea about what we're doing, let us perform a simple search. The first thing you need to do is open your favorite text editor and create a file called `search.pl`. (Alternatively, you can download `search.pl` (and all subsequent Perl scripts) from the Wrox web site.)

*For instructions on how to use some of the more popular text editors, look up Appendix B.*

The first line (called the "shebang" line) tells the operating system the location of the Perl interpreter, and tells the interpreter to run the script. Note that different distributions of Linux will have the Perl binary file in a different location.

```
#!/usr/local/bin/perl
```

Now we need to import the `Net::LDAP` module.

```
use Net::LDAP;
```

Next, we initialize a `Net::LDAP` object. You can replace `localhost` with the name of your LDAP server.

```
my $ldap = new Net::LDAP('localhost');
```

Next we bind to the LDAP server. On this occasion we will bind as the Directory Manager account, and hard-code the password into the script (which we shouldn't really do). The `$mesg` variable stores the results of our LDAP operation; if an LDAP operation succeeds it will return zero.

```
my $mesg = $ldap->bind("cn=root,dc=IMC,dc=org", password=> "secret");
```

Because we know that all successful LDAP operations will return zero, and that `true` in Perl is considered to be any non-zero value, we can easily code error message operations like the one on the next line. This will stop the program and print out the LDAP result code:

```
die("failed to bind: ",$mesg->code(),"\n") if $mesg->code();
```

We are now ready for our search operation. It is very simple: the search will start at the base of the `dc=IMC,dc=org` tree, using a scope of `subtree`, with the search filter `sn=picasso`:

```
$mesg = $ldap->search(base => "dc=IMC,dc=org",
                      scope => "sub",
                      filter => "sn=picasso"
                     );

die("failed to search: ",$mesg->code(),"\n") if $mesg->code();
```

Besides containing the result code of the operation, the Net::LDAP::Message object returned by the search routine also contains the number of entries found. We print out that number in the next line.

```
print "message count is ",$mesg->count(),"\n";
```

Finally, we step through all of the returned entries and dump them to standard output. This is the easiest way to return the values from a search.

```
for $entry ($mesg->all_entries) { $entry->dump; }
```

As with all shell programming languages, there are two ways to execute this application. The first way is like this:

$ **perl search.pl**

The second way is to call the script as if it were a compiled executable – that is, like a Windows batch file. First, you need to set the execute bit on the application, like this:

$ **chmod 700 search.pl**

Then you can call the script directly:

$ **./search.pl**

Here is an example of the resulting output on running this script:

```
message count is 1
------------------------------------------------------------------
dn:cn=Pablo Picasso, dc=Acmewidgets, dc=IMC, dc=org

cn=Pablo Picasso, dc=Acmewidgets, dc=IMC, dc=org
cn: Pablo Picasso
sn: Picasso
givenname: Pablo
uid: 00123456789
mail: Pablo.Picasso@connectathon.org
userpassword: guernica
title: Cubist
objectclass: top
objectclass: person
```

# Adding An Entry

Our next example, add.pl, will demonstrate how to add a new entry to the LDAP server. The first few lines of the script are exactly the same as our search sample.

First, we will define the distinguished name (DN) of the entry. (Remember that each entry in the LDAP server must have a DN.) You can change the DN to match the directory base of your organizational tree; I'm basing my entry here on the example tree that we installed earlier in this chapter.

```
die("failed to bind: ",$mesg->code(),"\n") if $mesg->code();
```

```
my $dn = "uid=mewilcox,dc=IMC,dc=org";
```

Next, we will provide values for the attributes we want in the entry. Remember that each entry must have at least one value for the `objectclass` attribute, which specifies what other attributes are required and allowed in the entry.

```perl
# Create variables to store new information
my @objectclass = ['top','person','organizationalperson','inetorgperson'];
my @sn = ['Wilcox'];
my @cn = ['Mark Wilcox'];
my @givenname = ['Mark'];
my @ou = ['People', 'Jedi Knight'];
```

The following lines constitute the actual addition operation. We must pass the DN of the entry as well as the attributes and their values:

```perl
# Add entry, attribute by attribute
$mesg = $ldap->add($dn,
                    attrs => [
                        'objectclass' => @objectclass,
                        'sn' => @sn,
                        'cn' => @cn,
                        'givenname' => @givenname,
                        'uid' => mewilcox,
                        'mail' => "mewilcox\@imc.org",
                        'userpassword' => "bobafett",
                        'ou' => @ou
                        ]
                  );

# Report on success of failure of addition
die("Failed add: ",$mesg->code(),"\n") if $mesg->code();

print "$dn added\n";
```

*Note that the @ symbol denotes an array in Perl, so we must use \@ if we wish to use it in a string, as in an e-mail address.*

Next, we will search the server so that we can print out the new entry. This search is slightly different from our original example. Here, we are restricting the attributes we want returned from the server. If you don't specify any attributes, then the server will return all the attributes allowed by the ACL.

```perl
# Search for and display added entry
my @attrs = ['cn','mail'];

$mesg = $ldap->search(base => "dc=IMC,dc=org",
                      scope => "sub",
                      filter => "uid=mewilcox",
                      attrs => @attrs
                     );

die("failed to search: ",$mesg->code(),"\n") if $mesg->code();

print "message count is ",$mesg->count(),"\n";

for $entry ($mesg->all_entries) { $entry->dump;}
```

Here is the result of the add operation:

```
uid=mewilcox,dc=IMC,dc=org added
message count is 1
----------------------------------------------------------------------
dn:uid=mewilcox,dc=IMC,dc=org

  cn: Mark Wilcox
mail: mewilcox@imc.org
```

# Modifying An Entry

After you have loaded entries into the server, you might need to modify them, and our next example shows how to do this. An LDAP modify operation can take one of three forms:

❑ **Add** – this will add values to an existing attribute

❑ **Replace** – this will replace all of the values of an attribute, adding the attribute if it's not already populated

❑ **Delete** – this will remove all of the values of an attribute

You will need to create a new file called mod.pl, which will be based on the other examples in this chapter. First, we want to replace the values of the ou (organizational unit) attribute, and then add a second value to the mail attribute:

```perl
# Create a variable for the new ou attribute value.
my @ou = ['People', 'Jedi Master'];

# Replace the old value for the ou attribute with the new value stored in @ou:
$mesg = $ldap->modify($dn,
                      replace => {
                          'ou' => @ou
                          },

# Add a second value for the mail attribute
                      add => {
                          'mail' => "jedi\@imc.org"
                          }
                     );

# Report result, i.e. failure or success
die("Failed modify: ",$mesg->code(),"\n") if $mesg->code();

print "$dn modified\n";

my @attrs = ['cn','mail','ou'];

# Search for and display modified entry
$mesg = $ldap->search(base => "dc=IMC,dc=org",
                      scope => "sub",
                      filter => "uid=mewilcox",
                      attrs => @attrs
                     );
```

```
die("failed to search: ",$mesg->code(),"\n") if $mesg->code();

print "message count is ",$mesg->count(),"\n";

for $entry ($mesg->all_entries) { $entry->dump; }
```

Here's what happens when you run the mod.pl script:

```
uid=mewilcox ,dc=IMC,dc=org modified
message count is 1
----------------------------------------------------------------------
dn:uid=mewilcox,dc=IMC,dc=org

   cn: Mark Wilcox
 mail: mewilcox@imc.org
       jedi@imc.org
   ou: People
       Jedi Master
```

# Removing An Entry

Finally, you can remove an entry from the LDAP server via an LDAP delete operation. This script is called del.pl.

```
#!/usr/local/bin/perl

use Net::LDAP;

my $ldap = new Net::LDAP('localhost');

my $mesg = $ldap->bind("cn=root,dc=IMC,dc=org", password=> "secret");

die ("failed to bind: ",$mesg->code(),"\n") if $mesg->code();

my $dn = "uid=mewilcox,dc=IMC,dc=org";
```

The only difference between a delete and any other modify operation is that the delete method simply takes the DN of the entry to remove:

```
# Delete entry and report failure error or success
$mesg = $ldap->delete($dn);

die("Failed delete: ",$mesg->code(),"\n") if $mesg->code();

print "$dn deleted\n";

my @attrs = ['cn','mail'];
```

```
$mesg = $ldap->search(base => "dc=IMC,dc=org",
                      scope => "sub",
                      filter => "uid=mewilcox",
                      attrs => @attrs
                     );

die("failed to search: ",$mesg->code(),"\n") if $mesg->code();

print "message count is ",$mesg->count(),"\n";

for $entry ($mesg->all_entries) { $entry->dump; }
```

Here is the result of running the del.pl script:

```
uid=mewilcox,dc=IMC,dc=org deleted
message count is 0
```

# Accessing LDAP Data from a Web Browser

So far we have learnt how to access LDAP data internally with the client and server on the same machine. However this is not what LDAP was meant to achieve. For it to be useful in the world at large, LDAP data has to be accessible over the network and the results viewable by standard web browsers. Since LDAP is a standardized web protocol, it was decided by the LDAP committee for the IETF to devise a URL standard for LDAP. The URL could then be typed in at the same place as a normal HTTP URL would go and the results displayed on screen in a readable format.

## LDAP URLs

The syntax for the LDAP URL, specified in RFC 2255, is shown below:

```
ldap://<hostname>/<base>?<attrs>?<scope>?<filter>
```

Where:

❑   ldap:// – the protocol (this can be ldaps:// when using SSL)

❑   hostname – a named host or IP address

❑   base – the search base

❑   attrs – a comma-separated list of required attributes

❑   scope – the search scope (sub, one or base)

❑   filter – the search filter, enclosed in brackets, which can include the * wildcard.

Note that all the information after the hostname comprises the same LDAP search information that we have seen before. However the LDAP URL syntax requires each field to be separated by a ?.

The URL can be typed in the **Address** or **Location** box of the browser, making sure you make no typing errors or include spaces (which can confuse the server). Leave the LDAP server to carry out the search and send back the results. Obviously, if you are accessing the LDAP server from a Windows installation, then you will need Samba up and running on your server machine. What will be displayed will depend on the browser. For instance, Netscape Communicator is able to present LDAP data as a web page, complete with captions. On the other hand, Microsoft's Internet Explorer will display the search results in an address book format.

This is the result of typing the following URL into Netscape Communicator:

```
ldap://hostname/dc=Acmewidgets,dc=IMC,dc=org?cn,sn,givenname,mail?sub?(sn=Small)
```

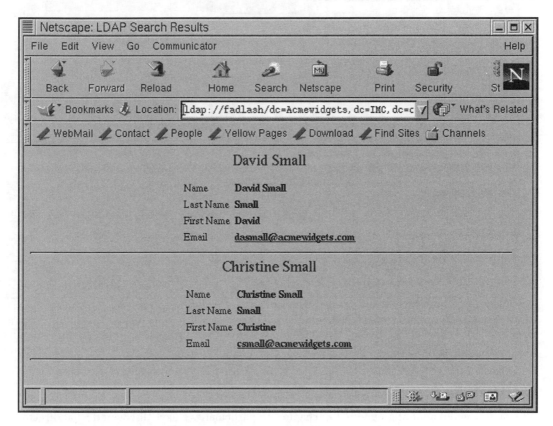

And this is what you get by typing the following URL in Microsoft IE5:

```
ldap://hostname/dc=Acmewidgets,dc=IMC,dc=org?cn,sn,givenname,mail?sub?
```

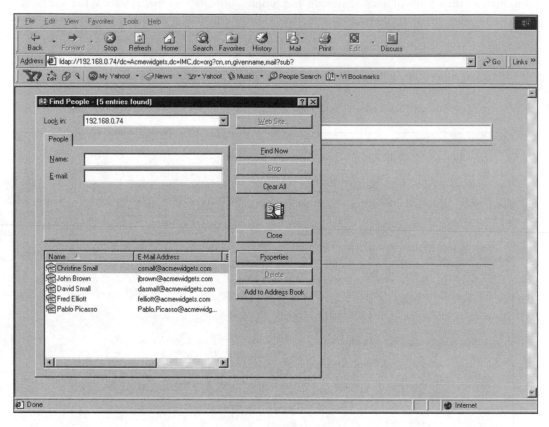

Note that there in no filter specified here – the URL ends in a ? – so the server sends all the entries back that are under the search base. Double-click on any of the entries to see the data for that entry.

# Summary

We have covered a lot of ground in this chapter. In particular, we have discovered what directory services are and why they are an important part of any networked organization. We looked into the different types of directory services, and why it could be important to move to an LDAP-based directory service. Next, we learned how to install an LDAP server on a Linux system and demonstrated how to use some simple Perl scripts that could interact with the LDAP server. Finally, we were shown how to access LDAP data from common web browsers.

LDAP and directory services will play an important role as the use of Internet technologies continues to grow. The ability to use LDAP with Linux, both for authentication and directory services, will help you to increase the return of investment in your Linux based operations.

# References

### Web

```
Novell Directory Services
```
http://www.novell.com/products/nds

Open LDAP web pages
www.openldap.org

### Books

Mark Wilcox, *Implementing LDAP*, Wrox Press, ISBN 1861002211

# Linux as an Internet Gateway

There are an increasing number of small, and not so small, companies looking at Linux as a method of connecting their internal systems to the Internet and supplying their e-mail and web services on a Linux based system. There are many advantages to doing this, which make it a sensible approach, including the relatively low cost of the Linux based solution when compared to the commercial competition. The difference in cost between a small Microsoft BackOffice solution and an equivalent Linux/Apache/Sendmail solution, particularly if the relative cost of hardware is considered, is around $5,000 to $8,000. If there is a need for training staff to maintain the Internet systems, then this difference is sufficient to cover the cost of that training. The Linux based system's price is so low that developing a second software and hardware setup as a development and test system is perfectly possible, something which can be a major cost for a more commercial based system. In addition to supplying services, Linux can also be used as a router for connecting small organizations to their service provider via a dial-up line or even a leased line, although the quite low cost of routers makes this less common.

In this chapter, I shall consider the possible configurations for a Linux based gateway system and discuss the strengths and weaknesses of each. There will be a detailed look at the hardware and software configuration required for the most common gateway setups. I shall also look at what is needed to install and configure the services a company would need on such a gateway including a domain name system and a `sendmail` based mail system. First, I will spend a couple of pages discussing some different methods of connection to your ISP.

# Gateway Configurations

All that is really needed to start building a gateway is a Linux based computer with two network interfaces. These interfaces can be Ethernet network interfaces, serial ports with attached modems or any device that lets the computer connect to a network. The simplest setup of a Linux based gateway is a machine with a serial port and modem plus telephone line as one network interface (to the Internet Service Provider, or ISP) and an Ethernet port to the local LAN.

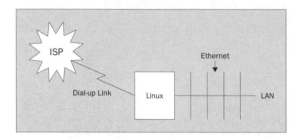

This is a good configuration for a small to medium-sized organization. The Linux machine runs a PPP link to the ISP and this is set up as a dial-on-demand line. By running a proxy server and configuring e-mail to connect only at extended intervals, telephone line use can be limited. If a better connection is required the line can be replaced with an ISDN link. This could be handled by replacing the modem on the Linux system with a suitably supported ISDN terminal adapter, but it would be sensible to discuss this with your ISP to be sure that they will support you with this configuration. Many telecommunications suppliers only have a limited number of staff with experience in supporting their own ISDN services, and ISPs are often left carrying most of the support load for both the service and connection when this happens. As a result, your ISP may be happier if they know exactly what is at both ends of the line. In any case, a business that needs the 64K or 128K bandwidth of ISDN may be better served by a leased line and router connection. This can be expensive, but support from both the telecommunications supplier and ISP will be better, and you may find the cost of the permanently open line is lower than the cost of an ISDN line with a per-bit charge for network traffic. Your choice will be determined by how much you have to spend and how much data you want to transfer across the link each day.

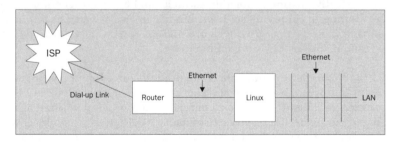

Routers designed to connect a small LAN to the Internet are now relatively inexpensive and the combination of router, to support the ISDN link, and Linux based gateway can be a better choice than a Linux box alone. One important strength is the ease of support, particularly if you have to solve problems in connection with your ISP (who will probably recommend a preferred make and model of router), as ISPs are traditionally, and sometimes correctly, suspicious of mis-configured routers. If they wish to do it, and you are willing, you should allow your ISP Telnet access to your router for debugging problems. This can make life easy and your supplier much happier.

This router and gateway configuration also allows an increase in security, as you can set up the security on the router and on the gateway separately. This security improvement becomes essential if you decide to host your own web server and FTP, and move to a configuration that has a leased line between you and your ISP.

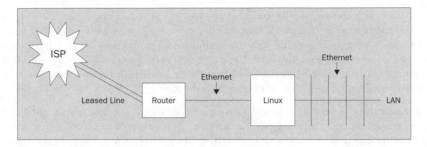

As in the previous configuration, you would be best advised to install a router with the gateway to connect. The router for this will be a little more expensive, and you will need a more expensive modem to go with it, but the costs are not excessive and you will have no difficulty in justifying the expenditure in any cost-benefit analysis (where the recurring costs of the line will be greatest component) if you really need to keep your line open all the time. It is possible to do this without a router (see below), and organizations have supported e-mail for one thousand or more users through a gateway of this type based on Linux and FreeBSD servers. Router costs are now so low, however, that the advantages of having a router operating system handling a leased line link far outweigh the expenditure on the extra component.

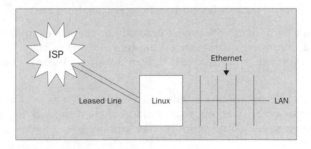

# The Link — Dial-up or a Leased Line

The choice between the two types of connection is technically very easy to make, as it is determined by a small set of criteria. If you are part of even a small organization, the problem will come in justifying the costs for implementing the choice. It is not uncommon to spend longer carrying out that process than it takes to install and configure the chosen solution.

Difficulty arises in assigning a weight to each of the options, as each will have different importance for different people in your organization; you may have to emphasize different areas in presenting the justification of your choice to different people. Depending on your experience, you may have made these decisions already.

❑ Do you need a connection that allows people to come to you, or is it simply to allow your internal users out? If it is the former then you are going to have to install a leased line – dial-up won't let people come to you. If the need is driven by the desire to supply services then the cost will be less important and the marketing and services people will drive the development to a leased line. A need for more bandwidth for internal use will be harder to justify and will need a lot of research and coating.

❑ How much traffic do you expect? This can be difficult to estimate, as until the link is in place, you can't be sure what people will do. You can talk to them, test connections for individuals doing what they say they will do to get some numbers, make estimates, guess, and then double everything. Do put in some time investigating what business gains could be made, or what improvements could be made to MIS systems by increased information flow in and out. You may find that it may be up to you to suggest possible business developments, which help justify the case for the link.

❑ How fast do you need the transfer to be? In reality you can get some data on your needs for speed quite easily by looking at what the users are likely to do and calculating transfer sizes and the time that is acceptable for the transfers. Again, you may have to indicate possible advantages to the business that are not the immediate driving forces for the link.

❑ Where are you? If you are in a remote site, you may be struggling to find a supplier who will install an ISDN line or a leased line for a reasonable cost.

❑ What can you afford? This will almost certainly be the most important consideration in the real world. Build large spreadsheets to see where ISDN starts to be cheaper than dial-up, and leased lines cheaper than ISDN, then develop a business case.

Do look at the business advantages as a whole and plan for a few years ahead when justifying the link. At the same time be realistic about what could be done if the link is put in place. You will not help yourself if you suggest you could support large number of connections moving large amounts of data across a 64K link.

# Point to Point Protocol

In general you will be making a Point to Point Protocol connection to your ISP and for this you will need to retrieve some important information. You need to know if you will be making a link in which you will be issued with a dynamic IP address or if you will be issued with a static address on signing up with the ISP, which will always be used to identify your link. You should also get the IP address of the gateway on your ISP's network (which will become the default gateway for this port), the subnet mask for the ISP's network to which you are connecting and, useful but not essential for more recent versions of PPP, the addresses of one or more name servers on the ISP's network. If you are assigned an IP address dynamically then much of this information may be assigned from the configuration file on your ISP machine, but having it as part of your configuration will make life easier when it comes to debugging connections. You also need the ISP's phone number for a dial-up link and your dial-up username and password, but I guess you had worked that out.

The first thing you must do is get the latest version of PPP. The sources for the latest version can be found at ftp://sunsite.unc.edu/pub/Linux/system/network/serial/ppp/ and its mirrors. The directory also contains a number of useful PPP related utilities and scripts. The sources also contain the information needed to install the PPP software on your system – check the README-Linux file for the necessary details. The process first installs the necessary files for the kernel and then instructs you to reconfigure your kernel to ensure that PPP support is included. The best method of configuration is to configure PPP as a loadable module. While this is not the place to discuss the configuration of the kernel, you can do this by using make config and selecting the following options. When using loadable module support:

```
*
* Loadable module support
*
Enable loadable module support (CONFIG_MODULES) [Y/n/?] Y
```

and:

```
*
* Network device support
*
(…Lines omitted…)
PPP (point-to-point) support (CONFIG_PPP) [M/n/y/?] M
```

*If you normally use* make menuconfig *then choose the **Enable loadable module** support option under **Loadable module support** and set* PPP (point-to-point) support *to* M *under the Network device support option.*

The PPP programs should then be built and installed and the system rebooted to the new kernel. The relevant PPP modules must be loaded. These are, in the order in which they should be loaded, slhc.o (VJ header compression), ppp.o (PPP driver) and bsd_comp.o (BSD compression for PPP's compression protocol). The README.linux file identifies these, it is sensible to check for changes in the version you have.

Check the settings of your modem to ensure that it is ready to run with PPP. For most modems the standard factory settings will suffice, but ensure that the Hardware Flow Control (RTS/CTS) is on. The manual for your modem should give you the information needed to check the settings. It is also sensible to set autoanswer to off to stop people dialing in on the modem line. Most modems can store the required initialization settings but it is also possible to initialize the modem as part of the PPP startup.

The program which starts a ppp connection is /usr/sbin/pppd. This program uses a number of files to start configure and stop the connection, normally used for automating the making and breaking of the link. These are options, ppp-on, ppp-off, and ppp-on-dialer. These will be found in /etc/ppp/scripts (or somewhere off that directory), and /usr/doc/ppp-<ver>/scripts in Red Hat Linux (where <ver> is the version number of the ppp release – remember to move your working scripts if you install a new version of ppp on Red Hat). The ppp-on script initiates the connectionwith entries for the account name, password, IP addresses, and telephone numbers. The parameters are passed to the pppd process, and then, to the second part of the connect script as a set of environment variables.

The second part is `ppp-on-dialer`. It executes the `chat` program (which is part of the `ppp` distribution) to connect the user with a standard UNIX style `getty`/`login` connection sequence. `ppp-off` terminates the active `ppp` connection. The `options` file contains the configuration options as an alternative to adding them to the command line `pppd`. A set of sample files are distributed with the `ppp` sources although the latest distributions seem to omit the full `options` template file. This can be recreated from the `pppd` man page but a sample is given here for ease.

```
# /etc/ppp/options -*- sh -*- general options for pppd
# created 9-Sept-1999 id

# Add a default route to the system routing tables, using the peer as
# the gateway, when IPCP negotiation is successfully completed. This
# entry is removed when the PPP connection is broken
defaultroute

# Use hardware flow control (i.e. RTS/CTS) to control the flow of data
# on the serial port.
crtscts

# Specifies that pppd should use a UUCP-style lock on the serial device
# to ensure exclusive access to the device.
lock

# Use the modem control lines - this option implies hardware
# flow control
modem

# Set the interface netmask to <n>, a 32 bit netmask in "decimal dot"
# notation (e.g. 255.255.255.0). ***Set this to suit your ISP***
netmask 255.255.255.0

# Don't fork to become a background process (otherwise pppd will do so
# if a serial device is specified).
-detach

# Don't agree to authenticate using PAP.
-pap

# Require the peer to authenticate itself using CHAP [Cryptographic
# Handshake Authentication Protocol] authentication.
# This requires TWO WAY authentication - do NOT use this for a standard
# CHAP authenticated link to an ISP as this will require the ISP machine
# to authenticate itself to your machine (and it will not be able to).
+chap

# Set the name of the local system for authentication purposes to <n>.
# This will probably have to be set to your ISP user name if you are
# using PAP/CHAP.
name <n>
```

This script assumes that you are using authentication via the Challenge Handshake Authentication Protocol (CHAP). You need to know if the connection will be authenticated using a standard login/password pair, a Password Authentication Protocol (PAP) login/password, or a CHAP login/password. PAP is like a normal login, in that the login and (optionally encrypted) password, taken by the machine logging in from its `/etc/ppp/pap-secrets` file, is passed to the server and compared with its database. Someone listening on the line could break this. CHAP is a stronger system, in that the machine that is being connected to establishes the connection. The server sends a random string and its hostname to the connecting machine, the client. The client looks up the password it has to use for that host in its secrets file `/etc/ppp/chap-secrets`, encrypts it using the random string and a one-way hash function, and returns the encrypted version with its own host name. The server then repeats the hash process using the password from its own secrets database and compares the result. This is harder to eavesdrop and break, and, for a further increase in security, the CHAP authentication is repeated a number of times each connection to ensure that the established link has not been taken over by another machine. The secrets files have the format:

```
# Secrets for authentication using CHAP
# client    server     secret              IP addresses
foobar1     foobar5    AgFX2527
foobar1     foobar2    Qrt2GHui
foobar4     foobar1    ni690fue            192.168.100.192
```

In this case, the file is taken from a machine called `foobar1`, which uses the password `AgFX2527` to connect via PPP/CHAP to a machine called `foobar5`, a password of `Qrt2GHui` to connect to `foobar2`. It also acts as a server for `foobar4`, which should authenticate itself with the password `ni690fue` and, if successful, is issued with the IP address `192.168.100.192` for that link. The `/etc/ppp/pap-secrets` file has the same format. If your ISP supports CHAP then use that. This will of course not work for ISP systems where there are multiple machines to which you are connected, depending on the line that picks up your call. In this case, put a name option in the `options` file:

```
# Set the name of the local system for authentication purposes to <n>.
# This will ave to be set to your ISP user name if you are
# using PAP/CHAP.
name ISPloginname
```

and also an assumed name for the remote server:

```
# Set the assumed name of the remote system for authentication purposes
# to foobar.
remotename foobar
```

Use these in your chap-secrets file for client and server names.

PPP normally tries a CHAP authentication before falling back on failure to PAP so if you have a number of connection options, then it is possible to select the authentication for a server by including the relevant line only in the appropriate secrets file for that protocol. If you are connecting to a Windows NT machine via a dial-up connection you may need to look at the `README.MSCHAP80` file in the PPP distribution, if the Microsoft extensions to CHAP are being used.

If your ISP also uses dynamically assigned IP addresses, then you will also need to add the following to the `options` file:

```
# Disables the default behaviour when no local IP address is specified,
# which is to determine (if possible) the local IP address from the
# hostname. With this option, the peer will have to supply the local IP
# address during IPCP negotiation (unless it specified explicitly on the
# command line or in an options file).
noipdefault
```

The address will be assigned on connection and dropped when the connection is lost.

Once configuration is complete, then a manual connection should be tried, specifying the options on the command line. The command line should be as sparse as possible for the first test. Try using:

```
pppd connect 'chat -v "" ATDT12345678 CONNECT "" ogin: username word: password
otocol: ppp' /dev/ttyS0 38400 debug noipdefault crtscts modem defaultroute
10.1.1.254
```

This command should be all on one line, ignore the breaks caused by the typesetting process. `connect 'chat ...'` gives a command to run to contact the PPP server using the supplied `chat` program modified with the options given inside the single quotes. The whole command is enclosed in single quotes because `pppd` expects a one-word argument for the `connect` option. This dials the remote computer and logs in.

The options to `chat` are:

| | |
|---|---|
| `-v` | Verbose mode, logging to syslog |
| `" "` | Send a return, don't wait for a prompt |
| `ATDT12345678` | Instruct the modem to dial `12345678` |
| `CONNECT` | Wait for this string to be received |
| `" "` | Then send a return |
| `ogin: username` | Send `username` when the *Login* or *login* prompt is received |
| `word: password` | Send `password` when the *Password* or *password* prompt is received |
| `otocol: ppp` | Send `ppp` when the *Protocol* or *protocol* prompt is received |

You may not need all of these options, or you may need others, to connect to your ISP. Use a package like `minicom` to make the connection interactively and establish what is required to make the connection. The options for `pppd` itself are:

| | |
|---|---|
| `/dev/ttys0` | Specify the callout serial port COM1: |
| `38400` | Specify baud rate |
| `debug` | Log status in `syslog` |
| `noipdefault` | IP address will be dynamically assigned |
| `crtscts` | Use hardware flow control between computer and modem |
| `modem` | Indicate that this is a modem device; `pppd` will hang up the phone before and after making the call |
| `defaultroute 10.1.1.254` | Once the PPP link is established, make 10.1.1.254 the address of the default route. |

If this runs correctly you will see the following output if you invoke `ifconfig`

```
$ ifconfig
lo        Link encap Local Loopback
          inet addr 127.0.0.1  Bcast 127.255.255.255  Mask 255.0.0.0
          UP LOOPBACK RUNNING  MTU 2000  Metric 1
          RX packets 0 errors 0 dropped 0 overrun 0
          TX packets 0 errors 0 dropped 0 overrun 0

ppp0      Link encap Point-to-Point Protocol
          inet addr 10.1.1.3  P-t-P 10.1.1.165  Mask 255.255.255.0
          UP POINTOPOINT RUNNING  MTU 1500  Metric 1
          RX packets 33 errors 0 dropped 0 overrun 0
          TX packets 42 errors 0 dropped 0 overrun 0
```

If this is the case check the output from `netstat -nr` to see if the default route has been established (the 0.0.0.0 route)

```
$ netstat -nr
Kernel IP routing table
Destination     Gateway         Genmask           Flags Window  irtt Iface
192.168.42.0    0.0.0.0         255.255.255.0     U     0        0 eth0
127.0.0.0       0.0.0.0         255.0.0.0         U     0        0 lo
10.1.1.3        0.0.0.0         255.255.255.255   UH    0        6 ppp0
0.0.0.0         10.1.1.254      0.0.0.0           UG    0        0 ppp0
```

This means you have a connection and can test other network connections using tools such as `ping`, or make HTTP connections.

If it doesn't work the output from `ifconfig` will have a line like:

```
ppp0        Link encap Point-to-Point Protocol
            inet addr 0.0.0.0  P-t-P 0.0.0.0  Mask 0.0.0.0
            POINTOPOINT MTU 1500  Metric 1
            RX packets 33 errors 0 dropped 0 overrun 0
            TX packets 42 errors 0 dropped 0 overrun 0
```

showing that the connection has not been successfully made. Look to the output from `syslog` for the following entries

| | |
|---|---|
| `pppd[NNN]: Connected...` | Means that the connect script has completed successfully. |
| `pppd[NNN]: sent [LCP ConfReq` | Means that `pppd` has attempted to begin negotiation with the remote end. |
| `pppd[NNN]: recv [LCP ConfReq` | Means that `pppd` has received a negotiation frame from the remote end. |
| `pppd[NNN]: ipcp up` | Means that `pppd` has reached the point where it believes the link is ready for IP traffic to travel across it. |

The missing entry should indicate where the process has fallen down. If you never see a `recv` message then there may be serious problems with your link, such as not passing all 8 bits. To gather the maximum amount of information from the debug option, you need to change the way `syslog` is gathering data. To gather all the bytes being passed between your computer and the remote PPP server, alter your `/etc/syslog.conf` lines to contain the entries:

```
daemon.*,kern.*       /dev/console
daemon.*,kern.*       /usr/adm/ppplog
```

Then restart the `syslog` daemon. Restart `pppd` with the option `kdebug 25`. The output from this should indicate where the problem lies, but if you need more help, the Usenet news group `comp.protocols.ppp` is probably the best place to start, the FAQ ID at http://cs.uni-bonn.de/ppp/faq.html

To automate the connection process it is necessary to create the `ppp-on`, `ppp-on-dialer` and `ppp-off` script files. The sample scripts supplied with the `ppp` source are usable, after a little editing.

The `ppp-on` script:

```
#!/bin/sh
#
# Script to initiate a ppp connection. This is the first part of the
# pair of scripts. This is not a secure pair of scripts as the codes
# are visible with the 'ps' command. However, it is simple.
#
# These are the parameters. Change as needed.
#
TELEPHONE=<your ISP number>     # The telephone number for the connection
ACCOUNT=<your ISP login>        # The account name for your account
PASSWORD=<your ISP password>    # The password for this account
LOCAL_IP=0.0.0.0                # Local IP address if known. Dynamic = 0.0.0.0
REMOTE_IP=0.0.0.0               # Remote IP address if desired. Normally 0.0.0.0
NETMASK=255.255.255.0           # The proper netmask if needed
#
# Export them so that they will be available at ppp-on-dialer time.
export TELEPHONE ACCOUNT PASSWORD
#
# This is the location of the script which dials the phone and logs
# in. Please use the absolute file name as the $PATH variable is not
# used on the connect option. (To do so on a 'root' account would be
# a security hole so don't ask.)
#
DIALER_SCRIPT=/etc/ppp/ppp-on-dialer
#
# Initiate the connection
#
# I put most of the common options on this command. Please, don't
# forget the 'lock' option or some programs such as mgetty will not
# work. The asyncmap and escape will permit the PPP link to work with
# a telnet or rlogin connection. You are welcome to make any changes
# as desired. Don't use the 'defaultroute' option if you currently
# have a default route to an ethernet gateway.
#
exec /usr/sbin/pppd debug lock modem crtscts /dev/ttyS0 38400 \
        asyncmap 20A0000 escape FF kdebug 0 $LOCAL_IP:$REMOTE_IP \
        noipdefault netmask $NETMASK defaultroute connect $DIALER_SCRIPT
```

This calls the `ppp-on-dialer` script. The sample given is for a user/password connection. For a PAP/CHAP connection this is simplified to:

```
#!/bin/sh
#
# This is part 2 of the ppp-on script. It will perform the connection
# protocol for the desired connection.
#
exec /usr/sbin/chat -v                                      \
        TIMEOUT         3                                   \
        ABORT           '\nBUSY\r'                          \
```

```
          ABORT                '\nNO ANSWER\r'                          \
          ABORT                '\nRINGING\r\n\r\nRINGING\r'            \
          ''                   \rAT                                     \
          'OK-+++\c-OK'        ATH0                                     \
          TIMEOUT              30                                       \
          OK                   ATDT$TELEPHONE                           \
          CONNECT              ''                                       \
```

The `ppp-off` script tidies up when the connection is broken.

```
#!/bin/sh
######################################################################
#
# Determine the device to be terminated.
#
if [ "$1" = "" ]; then
        DEVICE=ppp0
else
        DEVICE=$1
fi


######################################################################
#
# If the ppp0 pid file is present then the program is running. Stop it.
if [ -r /var/run/$DEVICE.pid ]; then
        kill -INT 'cat /var/run/$DEVICE.pid'
#
# If the kill did not work then there is no process running for this
# pid. It may also mean that the lock file will be left. You may wish
# to delete the lock file at the same time.
        if [ ! "$?" = "0" ]; then
                rm -f /var/run/$DEVICE.pid
                echo "ERROR: Removed stale pid file"
                exit 1
        fi
#
# Success. Let pppd clean up its own junk.
        echo "PPP link to $DEVICE terminated."
        exit 0
fi
#
# The ppp process is not running for ppp0
echo "ERROR: PPP link is not active on $DEVICE"
exit 1
```

Once these are in place, the connection can be automated. What we really want is for the link to be made when data transmission is required and to be dropped when it is no longer required. To do this, the following three `options` need to be added to the options file:

```
# Initiate the link only on demand. Initially configure the interface
# and enable it for IP traffic without connecting to the peer.
# When traffic is available, pppd will connect to the peer and
# perform negotiation, authentication, etc.
demand

# Specifies that pppd should disconnect if the link is idle for
# n seconds. The link is idle when no data packets (i.e. IP packets)
# are being sent or received.
idle 120

# Specifies how many seconds to wait before re-initiating the link
# after it terminates.
holdoff 120
```

With these in the `options` file, `pppd` should be invoked from the start-up file and it will make connections when required. To ensure this works properly set the default route to be the `ppp` link and add a static route for any internal networks.

# Setting up Routing

Which ever option is used, it is important that you consider carefully how you set up routing. In most sites, unless internal network topology is very complex, there is no need to use the `routed` program to discover routes to networks. The `routed` utility is a very trusting program; it accepts information about routes to hosts with little or no checking. It should certainly not be running on a gateway system that only needs to know how to send packets to your ISP (on the way out), and to your internal network (on the way in). These are best configured by adding `route` commands to your `/etc/rc.d/rc.local` file (or your distribution's equivalent). The syntax for adding static routes with `route` is:

```
/sbin/route  add [-net|-host] target [netmask] [gw gateway] dev If
```

This example will add a route for Class C network 192.168.100.0 via the interface `eth0`:

```
/sbin/route  add -net 192.168.100.0 netmask 255.255.255.0 dev eth0
```

This will add a route for the specific host 192.168.101.1 via interface `eth1`:

```
/sbin/route  add -host 192.168.101.1 dev eth1
```

This sets the default route via interface `eth0` and the local gateway:

```
/sbin/route  add -net 0.0.0.0 gw 192.168.100.254 dev eth0
```

This means that a packet addressed to a network for which no route is defined will be sent out via this interface to the gateway 192.168.100.254. The kernel routing table, which stores the information, looks like this after the above commands are run:

```
# /sbin/route
Kernel IP routing table
Destination       Gateway          Genmask            Flags Metric Ref  Use  face
192.168.101.1     0.0.0.0          255.255.255.255 UH    0      0    0    eth1
192.168.100.0     0.0.0.0          255.255.255.0   U     0      0    0    eth0
127.0.0.0         0.0.0.0          255.0.0.0       U     0      0    4    lo
0.0.0.0           192.168.42.254   0.0.0.0         UG    0      0    27   eth0
```

In a situation where all packets are being routed via the ISP, then the routing tables on the gateway will be relatively simple. All the hosts on the internal network need only have a default host directed to the internal network interface of the gateway. The routing table is dynamic because it is held in memory, hence the need to regenerate it each time the server is restarted.

*When you define an IP address and subnet mask for an interface, ifconfig automatically sets up the routing for that network. Also, remember when you use a dial-on-demand connection, it can be set up to define the default route when you are connected to your ISP.*

# Considerations for Connecting to the Internet

It is important to talk to your ISP when planning and setting up your connection. This is particularly true if you are moving from a single computer connection to the connection of a LAN.

The first consideration is the precise terms of the contract you have with your ISP. Many ISP contracts differentiate between connections supporting multiple users of a single machine and multiple users making connections through a single machine acting as a gateway. You may even find that your provider will not wish to support such a connection and you will find yourself having to change ISP. Ensure that both of you are clear about the connection type and that the contract and costs are correct. Ensure that your relationship with your ISP is kept friendly as you may find yourself having to talk to them regularly as you debug your connection.

You will have to discuss the location and setup of the Domain Name Server (DNS), your web pages, mail forwarding, and other issues related to network traffic to you and from your system. I will consider the options for these below so that you can make an informed decision but you should be careful that your ISP understands exactly what you wish to happen with each service and to define where the responsibility lies. It is also essential that both you as the user and the ISP as the supplier are clear about how changes are to be made to things such as host table administration for DNS.

Since you are reading this book, I can assume that you are at least considering using Linux for that connection. This is not an obvious choice to most of the world currently using Microsoft Windows NT or a commercial UNIX, but there are a number of advantages. Cost is the most obvious of these but it is not the only factor. A Linux system is much easier to monitor and maintain than an NT system in which much of the detail of what is happening is difficult to uncover. A Linux system also handles its network configuration in a more elegant manner, allowing quite complex configurations to be set up and controlled with little difficulty. Most importantly, it is easy to identify what a Linux system is doing and ensure that it doesn't do something you don't want, either by configuring the kernel or ensuring that programs don't run, whereas NT has a deserved reputation for software bloat that leads to many unidentified programs running in the background. For this reason, it should be obvious that Linux makes for a more secure connection.

If you are connecting fewer than five machines to the Internet, you can ask your ISP for a range of IP addresses for your machines, although you would wish to do this only if you have a very small number of machines to connect. With a larger number of machines it is possible to give each machine its own IP address and allow it to appear fully as a host on the Internet, or to ask for a range of addresses which is smaller than the number of machines you have (or even just one address) and use Network Address Translation, or IP masquerading, to allow the machines behind the gateway to access resources outside. This latter option has many advantages, not least the reduction in pressure on the global pool of available IP addresses, but the most important is the control it gives you over what resources your users can access and the way in which they can be accessed.

It is important to note the difference between IP masquerading and Network Address Translation (NAT) – the former is a one-to-many system and the latter is a many-to-many system. With IP masquerading there is only one IP address available and users connect to the gateway machine and share the address in the outside world. This is a sensible configuration where a dial-up line is being used and bandwidth is limited to about 30,000bps, although it means that a number of users connected at once will only receive a share of this bandwidth. With a large number of users the bandwidth can be subdivided until nothing effective can be done with it. IP masquerading is best used for a situation where traffic is limited to that generated by a maximum of five light concurrent users (occasional mail transfer and a little web browsing or Telnet sessions), or two or three heavy users (such as a mail hub and a proxy web server for a couple of dozen users). It is not a good configuration for an organization requiring access from the outside world into a server inside. NAT uses a pool of *real* IP addresses and assigns one to each connecting internal user. With this, you can make static assignments for some internal systems such as mail servers, so that they will be given the same address translation each time they connect through the gateway, which can make your mail system more secure, as it allows your ISP to accept mail only from specific IP addresses or servers. You can also make dynamic assignments for most users who have a random IP address from your pool assigned to them each time they connect. The downside of this is that you have a finite pool of addresses and when they have been exhausted no further users can connect to your site until someone disconnects and frees a pool address.

Looking at the real world, IP masquerading and network address translation can both be implemented on Linux gateways but I would recommend that you do not consider implementing NAT on a commercially important system with the currently available software. There are several reasons for this. IP masquerading is a well-defined and supported implementation and it will supply a very effective service to a small number of users. It can be expanded, if you have a number of real IP addresses, by setting up a number of separate masquerading machines. This allows you to increase your dial-up bandwidth at the cost of a separate modem and phone line for each group of users. NAT has strengths, but, as of December 1999, there is no current Linux implementation that offers a full set of features without an unreasonable amount of work. If we consider the specification of a PC which would be needed to support the number of users which could not be economically supported by the multiple IP masquerade option, then we are creeping very close to the cost of a Cisco router and a leased line, which would offer an excellent implementation of NAT *and* a number of other features which will make your life easier. I am a great believer in using Linux, where possible, but there comes a point where you can make your life easier by realizing that a Swiss Army knife isn't the best tool for building a wall. This does not mean that NAT will not be an effective solution in future, so it is sensible to monitor what is available as Linux implementation of NAT develops.

By enabling IP masquerading on your Linux gateway machine you can allow machines on your network, using a private address range, to access the Internet through the gateway using a single address. There is a HOWTO that discusses the detail of setting up IP masquerading, and this is strongly recommended as a clear and fairly complete technical guide to setting up masquerading. The HOWTO also refers readers to the IP Masquerade Resources web page at http://ipmasq.cjb.net/, which contains pointers to other resources related to modifying applications (both Linux-based and for other operating systems) to operate through an IP masquerading gateway. The IPCHAINS-HOWTO also discusses IP masquerading, as ipchains is the tool that should be used to set it up. The use of ipchains is discussed in some detail in the next chapter.

To get a full description of what is currently possible with network address translation, how it works and how complex it is, I suggest you look at the web pages below, some of which also have pointers to the relevant software. One problem with this software is that it is set up to allow static address translation only, which means the external range of real IP addresses must be the same size as the internal range (although you can cheat by splitting your internal network with sensible sub-netting until each subnet is the same size as the external range), but there are some situations where this may be of use and these are covered in the documentation supplied with the sources.

### References for NAT and IP Masquerading

| | |
|---|---|
| An article explaining NAT | http://www.computerbits.com/archive/9708/lan9708.htm |
| An article on the uses of NAT on Linux | http://linas.org/linux/load.html |
| Information and code for existing Linux NAT implementations | http://www.suse.de/~mha/HyperNews/get/linux-ip-nat.html |
| IP masquerading HOWTO | http://mirrors.indyramp.com/ipmasq/ipmasq-HOWTO.html |

# Setting up Domain Name Resolution

The DNS system allows the Internet to function by permitting resources to be referred to by name rather than IP address. It is likely that your ISP will be carrying out domain name resolution for your system whether you have your own domain name or appear as a host on in your ISP's domain – whether you are yourdomain.com or yourdomain.ispdomain.com. This is necessary, as your ISP will have to, if it does nothing else for you, be able to advertise that it is the host to which your mail is sent. If you also have a web page, then the ISP will also have to have an entry in their Domain Name Server (DNS) for that, whether it is hosted by the ISP or running on a server at your own site. There is a sensible precedent for running an internal DNS that serves home users and a separate external DNS for the rest of the world. The servers that have to be accessible from the outside must be in the external DNS, which could be hosted by the ISP, or on your own network, but the full listing of machines you run for internal users should only be in the internal DNS. There are many advantages in doing this and it is relatively simple. The greatest advantage you will get is the ability to run your own network independently of the outside world while maintaining the same service of name resolution for your users.

Imagine a configuration in which the Foobar website, www.foobar.co.uk is hosted by its ISP but it also has an Intranet server intranet.foobar.co.uk and a private FTP server ftp.foobar.co.uk which, along with resources held on individual users' computers, are available to internal users only. The ISP's DNS server will normally only holds information for www.foobar.co.uk, and without an internal DNS server, any user requesting access to ftp.foobar.co.uk will get an Unknown Host error. We want to be able to keep this response for external users, but we would like to make the server available for internal users without them having to keep a note of the IP address of the machine. This can be done by setting up a `/etc/hosts` file on each machine, but this soon becomes a problem if you have to move the FTP or intranet server to another machine, as updating all the host files becomes a chore. By using a machine as a DNS server and making it the first `nameserver` entry in the `/etc/resolv.conf` file on each machine, then maintaining the table becomes a simple exercise. It could even be a service running on one of your more powerful machines, which is handling other tasks, such as mail – the actual overhead of DNS is relatively low. In case of problems with that DNS server, there can be multiple `nameserver` entries (normally up to three) in `/etc/resolv.conf`, one of which should be the name server at the ISP which would be used as an emergency backup. A request for name resolution is addressed to each listed server, in the order listed, until a working machine responds. The details of the format of the `/etc/resolv.conf` file is to be found on the `resolver(5)` man page but a sample is shown below:

```
$ more /etc/resolv.conf
search foobar.co.uk develop.foobar.co.uk
nameserver 192.168.100.254
nameserver 192.168.100.253
nameserver 195.195.217.1
```

This shows two name servers on the local (private IP) network and one externally on the ISP's network. The `search` keywords are the domains to add to any hostname with no domain portion – an entry of `intranet` is interpreted, using this line, as `intranet.foobar.co.uk` then, if that fails to be found, as `intranet.develop.foobar.co.uk`. It will also interpret `rtfm.mit.edu` as `rtfm.mit.edu.foobar.co.uk` and `rtfm.mit.edu.develop.foobar.co.uk` and search for these before searching for `rtfm.mit.edu`, so don't enter too many domains in this line or you'll introduce unnecessary delays.

Setting up the name service is a little more complicated but not as difficult as many system managers believe. There is, again, a DNS-HOWTO, which will help you through most of the technical aspects of setting up the system, and this is an excellent guide. The Berkley Internet Name Daemon, or **BIND** supplies the DNS service, and this has undergone a change between the more common version 4 and the newer version 8. The first change is that version 4 by default used a file called `/etc/named.boot` as its configuration file, and version 8 now uses `/etc/named.conf` script that acts as a conversion utility for moving files created in version 4 to version 8, but it is sensible to use version 8 if you are setting up DNS from scratch. The `/etc/named.conf` file looks like this

```
options {
        directory "/var/namedb";
};

zone "." {
        type hint;
        file "named.root";
```

```
};

zone "0.0.127.in-addr.arpa" {
       type master;
       file "127.0.0";
};


zone "foobar.co.uk" {
       type master;
       file "foobar.co.uk";
};

zone "100.168.192.in-addr.arpa" {
       type master;
       file "192.168.100";
};
```

The first section, headed `options` defines the directory that holds the data that the `BIND` service daemon, `named`, needs. All the lines that follow, which are labeled as `file`, refer to files held relative to that directory. The following `zone` options tell `named` about which file holds information about which domain. The `in-addr.arpa` zones allow the opposite of the normal DNS process – they resolve machine IP addresses to names. These are needed for full operation on the Internet but if you are setting up a local DNS they are less important. I suggest putting them in regardless of this; try to make your local system as close to the standard as possible. The `type` option, listed as `master` means that these files are the authoritative listing of hosts and IP addresses for these zones. The files listed are:

### /var/namedb/named.root

```
;          This file holds the information on root name servers needed to
;          initialize cache of Internet domain name servers
;          (e.g. reference this file in the "cache  . <file>"
;          configuration file of BIND domain name servers).
;
;          This file is made available by InterNIC registration services
;          under anonymous FTP as
;               file                    /domain/named.root
;               on server               FTP.RS.INTERNIC.NET
;          -OR- under Gopher at     RS.INTERNIC.NET
;             under menu                InterNIC Registration Services (NSI)
;                 submenu               InterNIC Registration Archives
;              file                     named.root
;
;       last update:    Aug 22, 1997
;       related version of root zone:    1997082200
;
;
; formerly NS.INTERNIC.NET
;
.                      3600000   IN   NS    A.ROOT-SERVERS.NET.
A.ROOT-SERVERS.NET.    3600000        A     198.41.0.4
; formerly NS1.ISI.EDU
;
```

```
.                       3600000         NS      B.ROOT-SERVERS.NET.
B.ROOT-SERVERS.NET.     3600000         A       128.9.0.107
;
; formerly C.PSI.NET
;
.                       3600000         NS      C.ROOT-SERVERS.NET.
C.ROOT-SERVERS.NET.     3600000         A       192.33.4.12
;
; formerly TERP.UMD.EDU
;
.                       3600000         NS      D.ROOT-SERVERS.NET.
D.ROOT-SERVERS.NET.     3600000         A       128.8.10.90
;
; formerly NS.NASA.GOV
;
.                       3600000         NS      E.ROOT-SERVERS.NET.
E.ROOT-SERVERS.NET.     3600000         A       192.203.230.10
;
; formerly NS.ISC.ORG
;
F.ROOT-SERVERS.NET.     3600000         A       192.5.5.241
;
; formerly NS.NIC.DDN.MIL
;
.                       3600000         NS      G.ROOT-SERVERS.NET.
G.ROOT-SERVERS.NET.     3600000         A       192.112.36.4
;
; formerly AOS.ARL.ARMY.MIL
;
.                       3600000         NS      H.ROOT-SERVERS.NET.
H.ROOT-SERVERS.NET.     3600000         A       128.63.2.53
;
; formerly NIC.NORDU.NET
;
.                       3600000         NS      I.ROOT-SERVERS.NET.
I.ROOT-SERVERS.NET.     3600000         A       192.36.148.17
;
; temporarily housed at NSI (InterNIC)
;
.                       3600000         NS      J.ROOT-SERVERS.NET.
J.ROOT-SERVERS.NET.     3600000         A       198.41.0.10
;
; formerly NIC.NORDU.NET
;
.                       3600000         NS      I.ROOT-SERVERS.NET.
I.ROOT-SERVERS.NET.     3600000         A       192.36.148.17
;
; temporarily housed at NSI (InterNIC)
;
.                       3600000         NS      J.ROOT-SERVERS.NET.
J.ROOT-SERVERS.NET.     3600000         A       198.41.0.10
;
;
```

```
.                            3600000      NS     K.ROOT-SERVERS.NET.
K.ROOT-SERVERS.NET.          3600000      A      193.0.14.129
;
; temporarily housed at ISI (IANA)
;
.                            3600000      NS     L.ROOT-SERVERS.NET.
L.ROOT-SERVERS.NET.          3600000      A      198.32.64.12
;
; housed in Japan, operated by WIDE
;
.                            3600000      NS     M.ROOT-SERVERS.NET.
M.ROOT-SERVERS.NET.          3600000      A      202.12.27.33
```

Any printed version of this file will be out of date; I have used it here because it is the complete version with explanatory comments including the sources where the latest versions can be found (ftp://ftp.internic.net/domain/named.root). The file does change quite regularly (you will notice the temporarily housed comments) and I suggest that you check for updates regularly. There is a script for automating monthly updates in the DNS-HOWTO that you may find useful. I prefer to make bi-monthly checks myself, as it is a good reminder to have a quick check of the other documents at the InterNIC FTP site to see what is changing.

### /var/namedb/127.0.0

```
0.0.127.in-addr.arpa. IN SOA foobar3.foobar.co.uk. root.foobar3.foobar.co.uk. (
                            19990518   ; Serial (yymmdd)
                            3600       ; Refresh (1 hour)
                            900        ; Retry (15 minutes)
                            3600000    ; Expire (1000 hours)
                            3600 )     ; Minimum (1 hour)


0.0.127.in-addr.arpa. IN NS    foobar3.foobar.co.uk.


1.0.0.127.in-addr.arpa. IN PTR localhost.
```

This is the name server information for the localhost loopback. We shall use this file to discuss the heading information. The first line actually runs from "0.0.127…" to "; Minimum" (there is no newline character after the ".foobar.co.uk."). This is the Start of Authority (SOA) resource record. This identifies the zone as 0.0.127.in-addr.arpa. – which means it is the reverse lookup file for the localhost. It also identifies it as the SOA (there should be one and one only SOA in each zone file). Finally, it identifies its source (foobar3.foobar.co.uk.), and the person responsible for maintaining it (root.foobar3.foobar.co.uk.). The bracket then opens into the information that tells the system how long to hold information that it discovers as part of the DNS service, and the information that allows multiple DNS servers to support a single zone. The former role is supported by the Refresh, Retry, Expire, and Minimum fields (whose values are in seconds). The values given here are fairly standard and will probably work for most people.

The `Serial` entry is used to maintain multiple copies of the DNS information on multiple servers while maintaining only the original version. In systems with a large number of machines, or where you are solely responsible for maintaining the information for your domain (that is, your ISP has delegated that fully to you), it is normal, even essential, to define a single server as the primary DNS server and others as secondary servers. The primary server is the only server that has to be maintained, the secondary servers use the information held here to maintain themselves by a process known as **zone transfer**. The secondary server compares the `Serial` value in its SOA record with that in the primary server. If the value in the primary server is larger than the secondary server, it replaces the name server data in its files with those in the primary server's files. The secondary server's files don't have the same tidy layout as the primaries, although they are humanly readable, which makes it easy to identify which is the primary server if you are unsure. Many people use a simple 1, 2, 3 series for serial numbers. For each change you make, you simply have to ensure that the date is updated in the primary files and the zone transfer process will update the others.

A PTR record is a domain name pointer and it points to the domain name for that IP address.

**/var/namedb/foobar.co.uk**

```
@        IN   SOA foobar3.foobar.co.uk. root.foobar3.foobar.co.uk. (
                                19990518 ; Serial
                                3600     ; Refresh
                                900      ; Retry
                                3600000  ; Expire
                                3600 )   ; Minimum
;
;        Name Servers
;
foobar.co.uk. IN      NS       foobar3.foobar.co.uk.
;
;        MX Records
;
foobar.co.uk. IN      MX       0         foobar3.foobar.co.uk.
;
;        Canonical Names
;
foobar1.foobar.co.uk. IN A     192.168.100.201
foobar2.foobar.co.uk. IN A     192.168.100.202
foobar3.foobar.co.uk. IN A     192.168.100.203
foobar4.foobar.co.uk. IN A     192.168.100.204
foobar5.foobar.co.uk. IN A     192.168.100.205
```

The lines starting with `;` are comments and are in here for the administrator's benefit only. Also note that machine names are fully qualified, ending in a period – if you miss this out things don't work and it can be infuriating trying to debug this simple typographical error. The `Name Servers` entry (`NS`) defines where the information can be found – if you have more than one there will be a number of entries here. The `MX Records` line (`MX`) is a pointer to the central mail server used by `sendmail` for mail distribution. This is another thing which can be infuriating when debugging – a typo in this line can make `sendmail` fail, and I can guarantee that you will not think to check `named` when working with mail. The actual list of servers in the domain, with their addresses, is under the `Canonical Names` entry.

**/var/namedb/192.168.100**

```
100.168.192.in-addr.arpa. IN SOA foobar3.foobar.co.uk. root.foobar3.foobar.co.uk.
(
                              19990518 ; Serial
                              3600     ; Refresh
                              900      ; Retry
                              3600000  ; Expire
                              3600 )   ; Minimum
;
;       Name Servers
;
100.168.192.in-addr.arpa. IN NS  foobar3.foobar.co.uk.
100.168.192.in-addr.arpa. IN NS  router.foobar.co.uk.
;
;       Address Pointer to Canonical Names
;
1.100.168.192.in-addr.arpa. IN PTR foobar1.foobar.co.uk.
2.100.168.192.in-addr.arpa. IN PTR foobar2.foobar.co.uk.
3.100.168.192.in-addr.arpa. IN PTR foobar3.foobar.co.uk.
4.100.168.192.in-addr.arpa. IN PTR foobar4.foobar.co.uk.
5.100.168.192.in-addr.arpa. IN PTR foobar5.foobar.co.uk.
```

This is the reverse lookup file for the actual domain, allowing `192.168.100.1` to be reported as belonging to `foobar1.foobar.co.uk`.

If your network is fairly simple, if, in effect you are using only one network internally then this information should help you put a DNS service together. If you have a more complicated setup then you should spend more time designing your files and test them hard before committing to them. In particular, if you have a large domain you may wish to delegate administration for sub-domains to separate departments. Specifying nameservers for that sub-domain in the `foobar.co.uk` file does this:

```
@       IN  SOA foobar3.foobar.co.uk. root.foobar3.foobar.co.uk. (
                              19990518 ; Serial
                              3600     ; Refresh
                              900      ; Retry
                              3600000  ; Expire
                              3600 )   ; Minimum
;
;       Name Servers
;
foobar.co.uk.     IN    NS     foobar3.foobar.co.uk.
qux.foobar.co.uk. IN    NS     foobar4.foobar.co.uk.
                               foobar3.foobar.co.uk.
;
;       MX Records
;
foobar.co.uk. IN      MX     0       foobar3.foobar.co.uk.
;
;       Canonical Names
;
```

```
foobar1.foobar.co.uk.  IN A    192.168.100.201
foobar2.foobar.co.uk.  IN A    192.168.100.202
foobar3.foobar.co.uk.  IN A    192.168.100.203
foobar4.foobar.co.uk.  IN A    192.168.100.204
foobar5.foobar.co.uk.  IN A    192.168.100.205
www.qux.foobar.co.uk   IN A    192.168.100.100
```

This will set the primary name server for the sub-domain `qux.foobar.co.uk` to be `foobar4` but leave `foobar3` as a name server in case `foobar4` crashes out. This is a sensible precaution and only requires the important servers, such as `www.qux.foobar.co.uk`, to be listed in the main domain server for emergencies.

The software for DNS, BIND, is found at the Internet Software Consortium (http://www.isc.org), which supplies the latest version of the software and offers documentation and configuration information. Both versions at 8.x and 4.x are available, and there is, at the time of writing, talk of a version 9.x that will be *a major architectural revision of the software ... offered as a public beta release in January 2000* – note that this delivery date has dropped back four months in since the announcement appeared in mid-1999. A final, usable version is unlikely to be in place before mid-2000, and a cautious system administrator will defer deploying this until 2001 at the earliest.

# Sendmail

If you are using electronic mail on a Linux based system you are, almost certainly, currently using `sendmail` to route your e-mail around. You may even have a number of machines all running `sendmail` in various versions to pass mail internally. The `sendmail` program is fairly ubiquitous in the UNIX and UNIX-derived world. What I will do here is show how `sendmail` can be configured to run as a mail hub for an organization, delivering to a number of machines running POP3 (although it could be IMAP) based e-mail clients and gathering mail that will be routed around within the organization and eventually out in a more controlled manner. This can allow you more control over both the mail being sent and the on-line time consumed in sending mail.

Sendmail originated with Eric Allman at the University of California at Berkeley and was developed, over a number of versions, and at least one name change, to be a program that could route mail over a number of different networks using different transmission protocols from UUCP (UNIX to UNIX CoPy) to SMTP (Simple Mail Transfer Protocol). In all versions, the philosophy has been to make the mail *work* rather than to reject messages, for the standard in one system may cause an error in another – to quote Allman "...the goal was to communicate, not to be pedantic". Sendmail, as a program, does not send or read mail from a user – it passes mail from one machine to another. Other software, such as `elm`, `pine`, Qualcomm's `Eudora`, and Microsoft's `Outlook`, or your own favorite mail client, do that end of the business; each in their own way in their own environment. Sendmail has survived and grown because it is flexible, and to maintain its flexibility, it has been forced to become increasingly complex. Sendmail is now owned and distributed by Sendmail Inc, who also offers commercial support for the product. There is still some question over the precise status of the license for `sendmail` version 8.9 which states that it cannot be redistributed unless the original source code *and all modifications to it* are also distributed. For this reason commercial suppliers, and even some versions of free UNIX, are still distributing version 8.8.x, although 8.9.x is now starting to appear. There are some big security and anti-spam improvements in 8.9.3 and I strongly suggest you use that or a later version. Note that the license puts no restriction on system administrators downloading the latest version and compiling it themselves.

A configuration file controls `sendmail`'s behavior, by default called `sendmail.cf`, which has syntax only a programmer could love. When it first appeared, direct editing of a sample version of this file was the only way to set up and configure `sendmail`, but now the procedure creates a smaller configuration file and runs a processor program against that. This does not mean that you can now ignore the `sendmail` configuration file. If you are going to be administering the mail for your organization then you will need to have at least a working familiarity with the file and its contents. Given that the recommended `sendmail` text (*sendmail*, by Brian Costales with Eric Allman, published by O'Reilly and Associates) runs to 800 pages plus bibliography and index we won't be going into this in any great depth.

If you are running e-mail for a number of users then it can be much simpler to do so by supplying users with a central mail hub to handle all their incoming and outgoing mail. Doing this can also simplify matters if your mail is being processed as *store and forward* by your ISP, and if you have a dial up link. The hub should fulfill the following roles:

❑ It should handle all mail for all internal users, with the accounts of all users residing on that machine for small organizations or, in a larger organization, distributing mail for separate departmental mail hubs on which accounts are housed. The main hub should hold a record of the addresses of all users on the system

❑ It should be the only machine permitted to connect to the Internet to send or receive mail.

These two options will make mail administration much easier for the main system administrator. On a dial-up system this mail hub configuration should reduce the cost of sending mail, as the hub can be configured to deliver mail only in low cost periods, or to spool mail until the queue reaches a length that can be sent economically. If your telecom provider charges by the minute, but there is a minimum charge of five minutes per call, you do not want five one minute connections in a five minute period, or you could end up paying for 300 minutes of connection time for each hour. Individual users sending mail via their own connections can cause this to happen. By spooling mail until cheap rate, or until there is enough mail to make economical sense, you can drastically cut your telecom bills.

# Getting Sendmail

The Sendmail Consortium, who can be found at www.sendmail.org/, distributes `sendmail`. All distributions of Linux have a version of `sendmail` included, but the nature of the program and possible security issues mean that it is sensible to be sure that you have the latest version, which can be found through the Sendmail Consortium's web page. The software comes as a source distribution in `tar.gz` format. I will explain what to do step by step. This example is run assuming version 8.9.3.

❑ FTP the latest version to your machine and place it in the `/usr/local/src/` directory, or whatever your site standard says for new source.

❑ Unzip and untar the file, creating the directory `/usr/local/src/sendmail-8.9.3`, by entering:

```
$ tar zxvf sendmail.8.9.3.tar.gz
```

❑ Read the top level `sendmail-8.9.3/README` file, it contains a lot you will probably need to know.

❑ Change into the `src` directory and run the `Build` script, by typing `sh Build`; this should do all the hard work for you. The result is:

```
Configuration: os=Linux, rel=2.0.36, rbase=2, rroot=2.0, arch=i586, sfx=
Using M4=/usr/bin/m4
Creating obj.Linux.2.0.36.i586 using ../BuildTools/OS/Linux
Making dependencies in obj.Linux.2.0.36.i586
cc -M -I. -DNEWDB   *.c >> Makefile
Making in obj.Linux.2.0.36.i586
cc -O -I. -DNEWDB    -c alias.c -o alias.o
cc -O -I. -DNEWDB    -c arpadate.c -o arpadate.o
…
and so on for several lines
…
cc -O -I. -DNEWDB    -c version.c -o version.o
cc -o sendmail   alias.o arpadate.o clock.o collect.o conf.o control.o convtime.
o daemon.o deliver.o domain.o envelope.o err.o headers.o macro.o main.o map.o mc
i.o mime.o parseaddr.o queue.o readcf.o recipient.o safefile.o save-mail.o snprin
tf.o srvrSMTP.o stab.o stats.o sysexits.o trace.o udb.o userSMTP.o util.o versio
n.o  -ldb -lresolv
cp /dev/null sendmail.st
groff -Tascii -mandoc aliases.5 > aliases.0
groff -Tascii -mandoc mailq.1 > mailq.0
groff -Tascii -mandoc newaliases.1 > newaliases.0
groff -Tascii -mandoc sendmail.8 > sendmail.0
```

This creates a directory in /usr/local/src/sendmail-8.9.3/src/ called, on my system running kernel 2.0.36 on a Pentium based system, obj.Linux.2.0.36.i586. The directory name will be different depending on your particular configuration, but it will always start obj... and will be listed in the output from the Build command so you won't have problems finding it.

❑ In that directory there will be a new sendmail binary. Copy the existing /usr/sbin/sendmail to /usr/sbin/sendmail.old to make sure you have a backup.

❑ Change directory into the /usr/local/src/sendmail-8.9.3/src/obj.Linux.2.0.36.i586 directory and run make install

This copies the sendmail binary into the /usr/sbin directory, sets the necessary permissions and creates essential links such as mailq and installs the manual pages. To make sure that everything works you can check sendmail's version number with a debugging command line option:

```
$ /usr/sbin/sendmail.old -d0.1 < /dev/null
Version 8.8.7
Compiled with: LOG MATCHGECOS MIME7TO8 MIME8TO7 NAMED_BIND NETINET
               NETUNIX NEWDB NIS QUEUE SCANF SMTP USERDB

============ SYSTEM IDENTITY (after readcf) ============
      (short domain name) $w = linux
  (canonical domain name) $j = linux.foobar.co.uk
         (subdomain name) $m = foobar.co.uk
             (node name) $k = linux.foobar.co.uk
========================================================

root... Recipient names must be specified
```

```
$ /usr/sbin/sendmail -d0.1 < /dev/null
Version 8.9.3
 Compiled with: LOG MATCHGECOS MIME7TO8 MIME8TO7 NAMED_BIND NETINET
                  NETUNIX NEWDB QUEUE SCANF SMTP USERDB XDEBUG

============ SYSTEM IDENTITY (after readcf) ============
       (short domain name) $w = linux
  (canonical domain name) $j = linux.foobar.co.uk
          (subdomain name) $m = foobar.co.uk
               (node name) $k = linux.foobar.co.uk
========================================================

root... Recipient names must be specified
```

You now need to build a new sendmail.cf file. The data in the "SYSTEM IDENTITY" box above derives from the default version, which is created during Linux installation. You won't want to run with those options if you wish to run a mail hub.

# Configuring Sendmail

Return to /usr/local/src/sendmail-8.9.3 and cd into the cf/cf directory. In here you will find a number of files with .mc and .cf suffixes – these are sample configuration files from which you can create your sendmail.cf file. The system administrator uses the .mc files, known as macro files, as templates to create a file specific to their machine and site. The m4 macro program is then invoked using the new file name as an argument and m4 creates the sendmail.cf file. Start by copying tcpproto.mc (because we wil be transferring mail via TCP) to yourdomain.mc, the example below uses foobar.mc. For sendmail v8.9.3 this will look like:

```
divert(-1)
#
# Copyright (c) 1998 Sendmail, Inc. All rights reserved.
# Copyright (c) 1983 Eric P. Allman. All rights reserved.
# Copyright (c) 1988, 1993
#       The Regents of the University of California. All rights reserved.
#
# By using this file, you agree to the terms and conditions set
# forth in the LICENSE file which can be found at the top level of
# the sendmail distribution.
#
#


#
#   This is the prototype file for a configuration that supports nothing
#   but basic SMTP connections via TCP.
#
#   You MUST change the 'OSTYPE' macro to specify the operating system
#   on which this will run; this will set the location of various
#   support files for your operating system environment. You MAY
#   create a domain file in ../domain and reference it by adding a
#   'DOMAIN' macro after the 'OSTYPE' macro. I recommend that you
#   first copy this to another file name so that new sendmail releases
#   will not trash your changes.
```

```
#

divert(0)dnl
VERSIONID('@(#)tcpproto.mc        8.10 (Berkeley) 5/19/1998')
OSTYPE(unknown)
FEATURE(nouucp)
MAILER(local)
MAILER(smtp)
```

Change the file to look like this:

```
divert(-1)
#
# Copyright (c) 1998 Sendmail, Inc. All rights reserved.
# Copyright (c) 1983 Eric P. Allman. All rights reserved.
# Copyright (c) 1988, 1993
#        The Regents of the University of California. All rights reserved.
#
# By using this file, you agree to the terms and conditions set
# forth in the LICENSE file which can be found at the top level of
# the sendmail distribution.
#
#


#
#   This is the prototype file for a configuration that supports nothing
#   but basic SMTP connections via TCP.
#
#   You MUST change the 'OSTYPE' macro to specify the operating system
#   on which this will run; this will set the location of various
#   support files for your operating system environment. You MAY
#   create a domain file in ../domain and reference it by adding a
#   'DOMAIN' macro after the 'OSTYPE' macro. I recommend that you
#   first copy this to another file name so that new sendmail releases
#   will not trash your changes.
#

divert(0)dnl
VERSIONID('@(#)foobar.mc          1.0 6/18/1999')
OSTYPE(linux)
FEATURE(nouucp)
MAILER(local
MAILER(smtp)
MASQUERADE_AS('foobar.com')
FEATURE('masquerade_entire_domain')
FEATURE('masquerade_envelope')
define('SMART_HOST', mail.isp.com)
define('confTO_QUEUEWARN', '24h')
define('LOCAL_MAILER_PATH', '/usr/bin/procmail')
```

We will use /usr/bin/procmail as the local delivery agent. MAILER declares the delivery agent you will be using – local and smtp are pretty standard, (local defaults to /bin/mail) but you should redefine the local mailer program by using the option, define('LOCAL_MAILER_PATH', '/usr/bin/procmail') as this is installed as a default in most Linux systems and performs better in this role than the standard /bin/mail delivery mechanism. Besides, it is not possible to use /bin/mail with Red Hat and SuSE.

I had better explain the other options used here. Refer to http://www.sendmail.org/m4/readme.html for an up-to-date full list of options and their usage.

divert is a mechanism for dividing the output from the m4 macro so that it is logically structured. The two values here are (-1) to ignore all the following lines until a new divert statement is found, and (0) tells m4 to stop diverting and output immediately.

dnl is used to suppress blank lines which m4 inserts where there is a statement in the configuration file which does not produce output. The two divert statements would have produced blank lines in the final file if they did not have the dnl statement appended. This is a sensible thing to do with lines that you are sure do not produce output, the .cf file will be hard enough to read without extra blank space breaking it up, although you will get some blank lines anyway.

VERSIONID puts a version identifier into the output file that can, but need not, be the version information for the RCS or similar revision system. It cannot contain a newline character as it appears as a comment in the output file. The above line will create an entry in the output file of:

```
#####  @(#)foobar. mc      1.0 6/18/1999  #####
```

OSTYPE allows you to add specific support for your OS, in this case Linux. The options are found in the directory /usr/local/src/sendmail-8.9.3/cf/ostype choose filename closest to the system you are using, in this case linux.m4 is an easy choice, and enter the filename, less the .m4, in this line.

FEATURE includes a standard feature defined in files held elsewhere under the cf directory. The nouucp option simply excludes any support for UUCP, which you will want to do unless you send mail via UUCP. UUCP is an older protocol for the Internet and is generally not used anymore. If you are using UUCP consider using uucpprot.mc as your start point. Note that FEATURE options are bracketed and quoted with a grave accent ', and an acute accent '.

MAILER declares the delivery agent you will be using. local and SMTP are pretty standard (local defaults to /bin/mail) but you can define the local mailer program by using the option, define('LOCAL_MAILER_PATH', '/usr/bin/procmail').

MASQUERADE_AS means that all the mail from this machine is labeled as having come from the listed server, or in this case domain.

FEATURE('masquerade_entire_domain') makes sure that in combination with the MASQUERADE_AS option, mail from all the hosts in the domain are transformed.

FEATURE('masquerade_envelope') means that the *envelope* of the message will also be masqueraded. Without considering the detail of what happens, this ensures that all mail, including some error messages which look at the envelope data to identify the return address, come back to the central mail hub.

define('SMART_HOST', mail.foobar.com) should be used if you send all your mail out via a mail gateway. If this was your ISP's mail server this can be the fastest way to get your mail as it is, in effect, a local SMTP transfer. It is often used to direct mail to an internal hub for forwarding, en masse, to an external mail hub at your ISP or elsewhere. In the internal mail hub this entry in the sendmail configuration file would refer to the ISP mail hub.

define('confTO_QUEUEWARN', '24h') stops sendmail complaining for the first 24 hours that mail is not moved out of the queue. If you are using a dial-up link and only connecting to send and receive a couple of times a day, this will allow for a couple of failures to connect before errors start reporting.

Once you have the file ready then it is time to run the m4 command. Ensure you are in the /usr/local/src/sendmail-8.9.3/cf/cf directory and run the command below (adapted for your own site, of course)

```
m4 ../m4/cf.m4 foobar.mc > foobar.cf
```

All that happens is the prompt comes back and you get a foobar.cf file in the /usr/local/src/sendmail-8.9.3/cf/cf directory. Take a look in the file and you will see a lot of fairly incomprehensible data like:

```
# handle locally delivered names
R$=L                    $#local $: @ $1              special local names
R$+                     $#local $: $1                regular local names
```

However, you should look for the following lines to make sure the configuration has happened correctly (they don't appear together as they do here but they will be in the first half of the file...)

```
# "Smart" relay host (may be null)
DSmail.isp.com


...


# who I masquerade as (null for no masquerading) (see also $=M)
DMfoobar.co.uk
```

Now it's time to get it running and test mail. Make sure that there is no copy of sendmail running with a ps ax command, kill the "accepting connections" program with a -SIGTERM option. Check the program has gone with a further ps ax.

```
# ps ax | grep sendmail
    308   ?    S    0:00 sendmail: accepting connections on port 25
  11698   ?    S    0:00 /usr/sbin/sendmail -bd -q30m
# kill -SIGTERM 308
# ps ax | grep sendmail
  11705   p0   S    0:00 grep sendmail
```

Copy /etc/sendmail.cf to /etc/sendmail.cf.old and then copy your new file to /etc/sendmail.cf. Restart sendmail with a /usr/sbin/sendmail -bd -q30m, which starts sendmail running as a daemon, and tells it to process the queue every 30 minutes. If the sendmail.cf file has errors, the program will list them at this point. A common error is for a blank line in the file to actually contain a number of space characters. This normally happens in the comment section at the top of the file. If you get an error like the following check to see where the line is in the file:

```
/etc/sendmail.cf: line 45: unknown configuration line " "
```

If, as suspected, it is amongst the comments at the top of the file, I suggest you simply compact that section (all the lines starting with #####) by deleting any blank lines in it. Stop when you get to the following lines:

```
# level 8 config file format
V8/Berkeley
```

This marks the start of the actual configuration information and sendmail can be touchy about blank spaces. Most of the whitespace characters you see are tab characters and they need to be there for correct interpretation of the file. Don't take chances.

Start by sending mail between local users. If this is successful, go to another machine on the local network and send mail to users on the hub machine. At this point, you should set up an MX record in the DNS for the hub machine. A sample of this was shown earlier in the chapter when we discussed DNS. The mail hub should have a normal set of DNS records so that it can be identified and resolved by name or by IP address. In the zone file for the domain you also need the following entry to indicate which machine is handling mail for foobar.co.uk:

```
;
;       MX Records
;
foobar.co.uk. IN      MX      0         foobar3.foobar.co.uk.
```

The numerical entry in the fourth column allows you to set up fallback hosts in case of failure. If the DNS is set up to look like the following. Then incoming mail for foobar.co.uk will first be routed to foobar3.foobar.co.uk:

```
;
;       MX Records
;
foobar.co.uk. IN      MX      10        foobar3.foobar.co.uk.
foobar.co.uk. IN      MX      20        foobar2.foobar.co.uk.
foobar.co.uk. IN      MX      30        foobar.backup.infobiz.com.
```

If that fails then foobar2.foobar.co.uk is tried and finally foobar.backup.infobiz.com. If your ISP handles your DNS for external users, you will have to be careful that any changes that you make are reflected in their files. DNS errors can cause sendmail to generate some error messages that can be difficult to debug.

Back to testing. If you have a second machine running `sendmail`, set up an MX record for it and try sending mail to it. You'll have to remove your "Smart host" line from the `sendmail.cf` file to do this – copy the line, edit the original and comment out the copy so that you know how to recover it.

Changing from:

```
# "Smart" relay host (may be null)
DSmail.isp.com
```

to:

```
# "Smart" relay host (may be null)
DS
#DSmail.isp.com
```

should do it.

Once you are happy that mail is moving around correctly try sending some mail that should generate errors and ensure that those are handled correctly. Then, and only then, should you try connecting your mail server to the Internet and mailing external hosts. If you have a leased line, and there appears to be no problem with capacity, then invoking `sendmail` with the command line is a good option. If you have a dial up line then you may wish to have more control. Invoke `sendmail` as a daemon, but don't set it up to process the queue. On the command line this is done by running `/usr/sbin/sendmail -bd -odq`, but if you start `sendmail` on system start-up (as most people do) then you should edit the `/etc/rc.d/init.d/sendmail` file so that there is no option for any other start-up. Make it look like:

```
#!/bin/sh
#
# sendmail      This shell script takes care of starting and stopping
#               sendmail.
#
# chkconfig: 2345 80 30
# description: Sendmail is a Mail Transport Agent, which is the program \
#              that moves mail from one machine to another.
# processname: sendmail
# config: /etc/sendmail.cf
# pidfile: /var/run/sendmail.pid

# Source function library.
. /etc/rc.d/init.d/functions

# Source networking configuration.
. /etc/sysconfig/network

# Source sendmail configuration.
if [ -f /etc/sysconfig/sendmail ] ; then
        . /etc/sysconfig/sendmail
else
```

```
        DAEMON=yes
        QUEUE=1h
fi

# Check that networking is up.
[ ${NETWORKING} = "no" ] && exit 0

[ -f /usr/sbin/sendmail ] || exit 0

# See how we were called.
case "$1" in
  start)
        # Start daemons.
        echo -n "Starting sendmail: "
        /usr/sbin/sendmail -bd -odq
        echo
        touch /var/lock/subsys/sendmail
        ;;
  stop)
        # Stop daemons.
        echo -n "Shutting down sendmail: "
        killproc sendmail
        echo
        rm -f /var/lock/subsys/sendmail
        ;;
  restart)
        $0 stop
        $0 start
        ;;
  status)
        status sendmail
        ;;
  *)
        echo "Usage: sendmail {start|stop|restart|status}"
        exit 1
esac

exit 0
```

Restart the `sendmail` program and check that the daemon is running correctly by connecting via `telnet` into the SMTP port. This can be done initially on the `localhost` and then checked from remote hosts. Finish the session with a `quit` command.

```
$ telnet localhost 25
Trying 127.0.0.1...
Connected to localhost.
Escape character is '^]'.
220 linux.foobar.co.uk ESMTP Sendmail 8.9.3/8.9.3; Sat, 19 Jun 1999 09:58:14 GMT
quit
221 linux.foobar.co.uk closing connection
Connection closed by foreign host.
```

Once we've done that we then have to process the queue. Set up an entry in the root crontab to ensure that cron will cause a regular execution of /usr/bin/sendmail -q, as often as you wish to process your mail queue. See man cron and man crontab for the details of how to do this on your system. By sensible use of the options in cron, you can manage your mail costs very easily as each processing of the mail queue will cause a connection to your ISP, ensure that it only occurs when connection costs are lower.

# Sendmail and Avoiding Spam

One of the main reasons for choosing versions of sendmail after 8.9 is the great improvement in protection against misuse and unsolicited mail. There are a number of options that can be included in the .mc file, before the m4 program is used to create the .cf file. They are included here rather than earlier because they are complicated to explain. I shall discuss each of the options you should put in place, along with the approriate entry in the .mc file. However, be careful. Although some of these options help prevent spamming, they may also stop you from doing other essential tasks. I suggest you start with a relatively simple .mc file (like that described above) to make sure that your general mail works and then add a line or so at a time to the file, recreate the.cf file with m4, then test the system again. Take time to do this; if you get it right then sendmail will run quite happily with only a short, daily perusal of logs and little other intervention for a long time.

FEATURE(promiscuous_relay) supplies a feature known as *blind relaying* and should be disabled by default in version 8.9 – you may see it if you are transferring from and upgrading a version 8.8 .mc file. Blind relay allows any external domain to use your mail server to send mail to another domain. If you have internal domains, or other systems are genuinely permitted to use your system in this way then you may need to run with blind relay enabled for a while and watch your logs to identify which sites are using you in this way. After this you can disable universal relaying and be specific about which domains have to be permitted, denying all others. The simplest way to do this is to list the domains you are willing to relay in the file /etc/mail/relay-domains. To be specific about hosts which can be relayed, add the option FEATURE(relay_hosts_only). Full details on the possibilities available for protecting yourself from spammers, using yourself as a relay host, can be found at http://www.sendmail.org.

In general, a sendmail system running in its operational mode should have a .cf file created from a .mc file, which contain *no* FEATURE(promiscuous_relay) statements. FEATURE(accept_unresolvable_names) should also be excluded from the .mc file as this insists that the hostname supplied via SMTP is checked against DNS. If the domain doesn't exist the mail will be rejected as it is assumed that the named host is a fake. If you do this you can be a little more confident that the incoming link comes from where it says. A similar option to be avoided is FEATURE(accept_unqualified_senders) which permits sendmail to accept mail from a sender without a domain attached; for example, user instead of user@foo.bar.com.

The most useful way to control access is to develop a database of acceptable and unacceptable hosts and domains. To do this use the .mc entry FEATURE('access_db') to define the file used for this database; the format is FEATURE('access_db','hash -o /etc/mail/access'), where the second entry is the keyfile definition for the database. This is a text file and if you make changes to it you will need to recreate the database map with:

```
makemap hash /etc/mail/access < /etc/mail/access.txt
```

The format of the table is simple, allowing you to define rules in terms of addresses, domains and network numbers. For each there are five possible options:

| OK | Override other rules that would cause the mail to be rejected and allow it to be accepted, even if it fails to meet those rules. |
| --- | --- |
| RELAY | Accept mail for the domain indicated so that it may be relayed. Override other rules that would cause the mail to be rejected. |
| REJECT | Reject with a general rejection message. |
| DISCARD | Discard the message completely. |
| number text | Reject with an RFC 821 compliant error code and the text specified. |

To illustrate with examples, consider the following `/etc/mail/access` file:

```
spammbox.infobiz.com      550 Mail not acceptable from your host
spammers.spamcorp.com     550 Bug out and stick your mail
enemies.com               DISCARD
spies.enemies.com         OK
192.168.200              RELAY
192.168.201              REJECT
```

Mail from spammbox.infobiz.com has caused us problems before in our company, but the mail administrator there is not permitted to help us out so we reject it firmly but politely by returning it to sender with this error message attached. The mail administrator at spammer.spamcorp.com has refused to help when we told him of our problems with his site, so he gets a less polite message as the error on their returned mail. Mail from enemies.com is simply dropped, without being returned, so that the error message doesn't tell them very much, because the next line permits mail from spies.enemies.com to come in with no problems, and we don't want them to be suspicious. Mail for machines on network 192.168.200 is relayed because it belongs to us; mail from 192.168.201 is rejected and returned with a REJECT error message because they've been told to use another mailer but it is taking them time to adjust to this.

That should give some idea of the control that the access database allows you, and I recommend using it for most of your spam control, because of the fine granularity it allows you in acceptance and rejection.

## Using Different Mail Clients

If you want to use various mail clients to collect mail from a Linux server on different systems, such as Windows 98 or even other Linux computers, you should add a POP3 or IMAP server to your system to deliver messages. Most e-mail clients are now configured to use POP3 or IMAP as transfer mechanisms rather than the traditional UNIX SMTP. Of the two, IMAP based solutions are more secure, but there are fewer clients able to handle IMAP, but POP3 is wider supported. Collecting mail via a non-SMTP protocol is a little more complex than simply using sendmail and local delivery such as /bin/mail. Sendmail delivers mail to /var/spool/mail/<username> and when the user connects via the IMAP or POP3 port, then the relevant daemon will authenticate the username and deliver the mail from the /var/spool/mail/<username> file to the user's local machine using the IMAP or POP3 protocol. Sending mail still uses the SMTP protocol to deliver mail from the user's local machine to the mail hub.

The best freeware IMAP and POP3 servers are available as a set of daemons (imapd, ipop2d and ipop3d) and can be found at The University of Washington website at ftp://ftp.cac.washington.edu/imap/imap.tar.Z. The license for this software currently has no restrictions on use and it offers POP2, POP3 and IMAP4rev1 server support.

It has been my experience that the IMAP server offers much greater reliability and security than the POP3 server and for that reason I have concentrated on that. If your current mail clients do not support IMAP, you will gain much from moving to such a client. A list of IMAP-enabled clients can be found at The IMAP Connection at http://www.imap.org/products/database.msql, which will allow a search for clients for a number of operating systems.

# Installing the IMAP Server

Again we shall be working with the source in /usr/local/src.

Uncompress and unpack the tar file with: uncompress -c imap.tar.Z | tar x. This creates the imap-4.5 directory; which contains:

```
-rw-r--r--    1 104       root         1940 Dec  1  1998 CONTENTS
-rw-r--r--    1 104       root        13399 Jan 27 22:40 Makefile
-rw-r--r--    1 104       root         2144 Sep  8  1998 README
drwxr-xr-x    3 104       root         1024 Dec 16  1998 docs
-rw-r--r--    1 104       root         2132 Apr 28  1998 makefile.nt
-rw-r--r--    1 104       root         2133 Apr 28  1998 makefile.ntk
-rw-r--r--    1 104       root         1956 Apr 28  1998 makefile.wce
drwxr-xr-x    9 104       root         1024 Dec  1  1998 src
drwxr-xr-x    2 104       root         1024 Nov 10  1998 tools
```

The source for this program is usable on many systems so it is essential that you configure the make process correctly. Check the README file for details of the compile process. The program's authors have simplified this for you by offering a command line option to make defined by system. grep for lines containing Linux in the Makefile and you will see the possible options:

```
# lnx    Linux with traditional passwords and crypt() in the C library
# lnp    Linux with Pluggable Authentication Modules (PAM)
# sl4    Linux using -lshadow to get the crypt() function
# sl5    Linux with shadow passwords, no extra libraries
# slx    Linux using -lcrypt to get the crypt() function
```

On Red Hat 5.2 the option is make lnp. A number of new directories are created – the new imapd program is in the imapd directory, the ipop3d and ipop2d programs are in the new ipopd directory:

Copy any existing `imapd`, `ipop2d` and `ipop3d` programs in `/usr/sbin` to `*.old` versions and move these new versions into `/usr/sbin`. Then you should check that the relevant lines are in the `/etc/services` file:

```
pop-2           109/tcp                         # PostOffice V.2
pop-3           110/tcp                         # PostOffice V.3
...
imap            143/tcp                         # imap network mail protocol
```

Check that the `/etc/inetd.conf` invokes the relevant daemons on those services.

```
# Pop and imap mail services et al
#
pop-2    stream   tcp     nowait   root    /usr/sbin/tcpd   ipop2d
pop-3    stream   tcp     nowait   root    /usr/sbin/tcpd   ipop3d
imap     stream   tcp     nowait   root    /usr/sbin/tcpd   imapd
```

Restart the system and `telnet` into the relevant port to make sure that the daemons for each of the services are responding correctly. The daemon only runs in response to a connection to the port so will not show on the output from `ps ax` unless a connection is in progress.

```
$ telnet localhost 143
Trying 127.0.0.1...
Connected to localhost.
Escape character is '^]'.
* OK localhost IMAP4rev1 v12.250 server ready
^]
telnet> close
Connection closed.
```

Note that the easy way out if you don't know the closing command, is to close the session interactively. It is a Telnet session so escaping to the `telnet` prompt, with control and right square bracket (^), and then issuing a `close` command for the session releases you. When these are running you are ready to test transfer mail using combinations of SMTP for sending and POP3/IMAP for receiving between local machines, and then testing by sending to and receiving from external systems.

To configure the client to collect mail via IMAP, it is necessary to tell the client where the mail will be found on the server. The normal behavior of IMAP is to use the user's home directory (that is, the directory defined by the environment variable HOME). Any client which you use to collect your mail should have an option to define the IMAP mailbox location: for a user *foo* on the system described here this should be `/var/spool/mail/foo`. The username, which is set up, is your username on the mail system and the password for that user. By running a mail hub and collecting mail from it via IMAP, it is possible to set up users on the mail server, which can have a different password from the login, offering increased security, if used correctly. Such a system means that using your mail password, which you will use in the outside world in insecure environments such as cyber-cafes, will not compromise your login to the system. All that is necessary is to bar access to other non-mail services from the Internet using a firewall – details are available in the next chapter.

# /etc/aliases

The final thing you should do if you are running a mail hub is to give each of you users an entry in the /etc/aliases file. The file has the format local:alias where local is the mail address given to the outside world and alias indicates what is to be done with the incoming message. The alias can be a user on the local or a remote machine; a file (just give the path), in which case the mail is appended to that file (to keep a record of people sending mail for a particular reason); a program (prefix the program path with |) the in which case the program is executed (which could be used as an auto-response option) or an include statement which can point to a list of aliases in another file as a mailing list. In general the list will contain user names:

```
fred : fred@foobar3
mary : mary@foobar4
stan : stan@smallcopr4
```

When you make changes to the aliases file you must run newaliases to load these changes into the aliases database, which sendmail uses to deliver mail addressed globally to local users.

# Fetchmail and Other Alternative Mail Programs

Eric S Raymond's famous paper *The Cathedral and the Bazaar* discusses some of the philosophy behind the development of Open Source software in general and the development of fetchmail in particular. The paper itself is worth reading and can be found by an Internet search for the title – which will probably get you to Raymond's home page – and also the sources for fetchmail. Many small, and not so small, sites are using this program as an alternative to sendmail. It has advantages for sites which have dial-up links or whose ISP delivers mail via POP3 or IMAP rather than SMTP (for which sendmail is not an option). It is a mature, fully featured, "industrial strength", program which can be used with confidence, not "a toy or a coder's learning exercise". I would recommend it for anyone who wishes a functional mail program but who does not wish to dig too far through sendmail (although you will still need to run sendmail to send your mail; it is easier to configure for this).

The fetchmail utility is a mature product with a great deal of work put in by a large number of open source contributors. If you are using a less than helpful ISP via a dial-up link then it may be the best solution for gathering and redistributing mail. The best source of information on its use and configuration is *The Fetchmail FAQ*, which contains information on using fetchmail with a number of ISPs from Compuserve, through Hotmail to Demon Internet, and explains how it can be connected to almost every normal mail program available from sendmail to Lotus Notes. The *FAQ* can be found at http://www.tuxedo.org/~esr/fetchmail/fetchmail-FAQ.html.

There are other alternatives such as **smail** and **qmail**. If you wish to investigate these further I suggest you look at the Linux Electronic Mail HOWTO, which cover these options. The advice I would give is simple; use sendmail as a first choice if you are a large site or you wish to create a hierarchy of hubs for sites or departments; use fetchmail if you need to pick mail up from an ISP via POP3 or IMAP and for delivery mechanism on local Linux machines receiving mail from your central hub; use smail or qmail if you know them or don't wish to spend time learning the other options. Sendmail is a complex application but documentation and support for it outstrips the alternatives.

# Summary

Connecting your internal network to the outside world and the Internet is not an inherently difficult procedure, but you will need to put some effort into planning and investigating the software you need before going ahead. Making sure that you have the correct expertise available is probably the most important factor. By connecting to the outside world you are exposing yourself to the world and, just as importantly, you are exposing them to you. You will not maintain a good relationship with your ISP if you cannot maintain your link correctly. This is true of all links, not just those supported by a Linux gateway, and by choosing Linux you will be putting in place a gateway that is much easier to configure and monitor than the systems many organizations are using. It is a good idea to give your staff some time to plan and test configurations before going live with them – many of the packages discussed here are outside the normal experience of many professionals. In particular, ensure that you have a good knowledge of TCP/IP as this will be the source of many of the problems you will hit in trying to make it work.

Perhaps the most important thing to remember is that the Internet was originally built on UNIX gateways such as these and that it ran, in many cases is still running, on them with no problems.

# References

## *Web*

| | |
|---|---|
| ftp://sunsite.unc.edu/pub/Linux/system/network/serial/ppp/ | PPP sources for the latest version will be found in this directory. |
| http://cs.uni-bonn.de/ppp/faq.html | FAQ for `comp.protocols.ppp`. |
| http://www.isc.org | Internet Software Consortium – suppliers of BIND. |
| ftp://ftp.internic.net/domain/named.root | DNS root server information file. |
| http://www.tuxedo.org/~esr/writings/cathedral-bazaar/cathedral-bazaar.html | *The Cathedral and the Bazaar* – article on open source software. |
| http://www.sendmail.org | Sendmail's home page. |
| http://www.harker.com/sendmail/sendmail-ref.html | A Sendmail Reference page. It also enables you to create your own `sendmail.cf` file via a web page. |
| http://www.tuxedo.org/~esr/fetchmail/ | Fetchmail's home page. |

*HOWTOs*

| | |
|---|---|
| Mail-Queue-mini-HOWTO | Instructions on how to queue remote mail on a dial-up connection. |
| Mail-HOWTO | Information on mail servers and clients. |
| ISP-Connectivity-mini-HOWTO | How to set up PPP and `fetchmail` to retrieve mail from your ISP. |
| DNS-HOWTO | Information on setting up a DNS server. |
| PPP-HOWTO | A large document explaining the intricacies of `pppd`. |
| Diald-mini-HOWTO | A small document explaining how to use Diald to connect to your ISP. |

*Books*

Costales, Allman & Rickett; *sendmail* (2nd Edition); O'Reilly & Associates

# Configuring Linux as a Firewall and Proxy

## Introduction

Utilizing the Linux platform as a gateway has already been discussed, but the security of that system and also the facilities it can perform are of importance. In this chapter we will discuss how you can set up your gateway server to be a proxy and web cache, and also how you can configure the gateway (and indeed any networked Linux box) to be a firewall.

There are three levels we will deal with here:

❏ **Firewall**: Preventing unauthorized access and security compromises. The firewall should be the only way to get in and out of your network – effectively a guard-tower.

❏ **Proxy**: Making the gateway act as the "middle man" for network connections: proxies may also include such facilities as content filters and suchlike.

❏ **Cache**: Improving web browsing response times using features of the proxy facility.

By the end of the chapter, you will be able to configure your Linux servers to carry out all three of these functions.

# Firewalls

Just as a traditional bricks-and-mortar firewall prevents the spread of fire throughout a building, its computer namesake prevents the spread of unauthorized access between computer networks. We're only going to deal with network-level firewalls here since they tend to be the most useful and are certainly the easiest to configure.

There are two main types of network-level firewall:

❑ **IP-based Filtering**
Every incoming connection's source and destination address is checked against a list of allowed and denied addresses. If the address is denied, then the packet is dropped; conversely if it is allowed, then the packet is passed to the next hop on the way to its eventual destination.

❑ **Port-based Filtering**
The source and destination ports are scanned instead of the IP address.

In many cases you may wish to configure both IP and port-based firewalls, especially in the case of servers, which carry out several functions such as serving mail, web hosting, etc.

# Scenario

So let's consider an example here: System Administrator Bob Smith has a company network and three main servers, which are based on a company Internet connection with IP block 195.82.125.0/24.

❑ Server 1 (www) is a public web server, which must only allow incoming connections to its web server, and permit outgoing SMTP mail connections.

❑ Server 2 (intra) is an Intranet server which must only allow connections from the networks 195.82.125.0/24 and 192.168.1.0/24, and then only to the httpd daemon on port 80.

❑ Server 3 (Bastion) is a gateway so that no external Internet user can see the internal network. This server must also be a cache to allow internal users access to web pages. While configuring as a gateway is outside the scope of this chapter, we will assume that *Bastion* handles external e-mail transactions and internal POP3 connections.

There are also twenty desktop machines, all of which must have web and mail access.

The network topology looks like this:

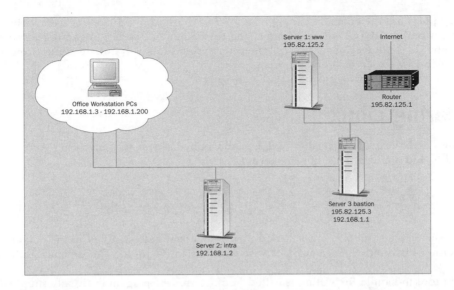

*Bastion* is a simple gateway that has two Ethernet interfaces: one allows access to the 192.168.1.0/24 network, and the other deals with access to the outside world.

Ideally, the situation we want to be in is this:

| Machine | Access Level |
| --- | --- |
| Server 1 (www)<br>195.82.125.2 | Incoming public access to port 80 (www) |
| | Outgoing access from arbitrary ports to port 25 (SMTP) on any other server, in order to deliver mail |
| | DNS access |
| Server 2 (intra)<br>192.168.1.2 | Access to port 80 (www) from 192.168.1.0/24 |
| | Access from arbitrary ports to port 25 (SMTP) on anything |
| | DNS access |
| Server 3 (bastion)<br>192.168.1.1<br>195.82.125.3 | Access from arbitrary ports to ports 25 (SMTP), 53 (DNS) and 80 (Web) on anything. |
| | Access to port 25 (SMTP) from anything |
| | Access to port 53 (DNS) from 192.168.1.0/24 |
| | Access to port 110 (POP3) from 192.168.1.0/24 |
| | Access to port 8080 (Web proxy) from 192.168.1.0/24 |
| | This server also serves DNS to 192.168.1.0/24 |

**Arbitrary ports** are the common name given for TCP ports above 1023 – these unprivileged ports are used for outbound TCP/IP connections and for some non-standard incoming services (such as proxies, etc). It is not feasible to firewall them for systems that will initiate connections to other systems such as web servers or mail hosts.

# Preparing Linux

Assuming you have a kernel version of 2.2 or above, before you start installing your firewall, you will need to add a few options into the kernel:

```
CONFIG_FIREWALL=y
CONFIG_IP_FIREWALL=y
```

If you are using Red Hat 6.0, you will find that these are already enabled in the default server kernel. Other distributions such as Slackware and Debian do not have these enabled by default.

The main tool to handle firewalling is called `ipchains`, which again is already supplied with the default Red Hat 6.0 installation. The `ipchains` program performs the task of inserting and removing filtering options from network interfaces on a port and IP address basis. You can get the latest version of `ipchains` from http://www.rustcorp.com/linux/ipchains/.

Versions of Linux prior to kernel 2.2 used a system called `ipfwadm`, which has now been deprecated.

# The ipchains Concept

Before we dive headlong into configuring a firewall, we will take a moment to cover the concept of `ipchains`. If you have previously been using `ipfwadm` as supplied with pre-2.2 versions of Linux, you will need to re-learn from first principles rather than attempt to upgrade.

The `ipchains` program is hierarchical in its approach. Each link is added at the bottom of a chain to give a whole series of rules by which network packets may be allowed or denied transit to the next hop on the way to their destination.

| Link | Description | Notes |
|------|-------------|-------|
| 1 | Deny all packets | The first step is to deny everything. |
| 2 | Allow access to web port (`httpd`) | This will allow the web port through, but from link 1 this still denies everything else. |
| 3 | Allow access to incoming mail (`smtp`) | Now we have allowed both web and smtp ports through, but everything else is still blocked. |

But conversely, if we were to do this in the following order, we would deny everything:

| Link | Description | Notes |
| --- | --- | --- |
| 1 | Allow access to web port (`httpd`) | This will allow the web port through, but since we didn't do anything before (default is to *allow* traffic) this has no net effect. |
| 2 | Allow access to incoming mail (`smtp`) | Still everything is allowed – there is nothing blocked. |
| 3 | Deny all packets | Now we've blocked everything, since this is at the bottom of the chain! |

You must remember that when using `ipchains`, *order is important.*

There are several different built-in chains, which are traversed, although advanced users may wish to create their own chains. The built-in chains are (in order of traversal):

❑ **Input**: The first chain that is traversed, deals with packets input to the system. The result may be either DENY, REJECT or ALLOW – if the latter condition is met, the packet continues.

❑ **Forward**: This chain is traversed for packets that are using this server as a hop en route to another machine. If you are using a Linux box as a router this is the chain you will need to modify.

❑ **Output**: This chain is traversed for all packets prior to being sent outwards.

# Basic Firewall

We'll start with the simplest server of the group, www. The `ipchains` application is hierarchical, so what we need to do first is deny all IP traffic and then gradually enable the services we need, one by one. While all these commands may be issued on the command line, it's invariably a good idea to put all the commands in one script for clarity of how your chains are configured.

> **A brief warning at this point: it is strongly recommended that you carry out any changes to allow/deny chains on the console rather than from a `telnet`/`rsh` session — disabling the wrong service, on the input or output chain, can prevent any remote access!**

First we deny every incoming and outgoing connection:

```
ipchains -A input -s 0.0.0.0/0 -j DENY
```

Here, we have specified the internal chain `input` with option `-A`, stated that the source address (`-s`) can be anything (`0.0.0.0/0`), and then denied it with `-j`. This has the effect of disconnecting this computer from the network. By not specifying the packet type, we have also stopped any type of packet (e.g. TCP, UDP) – thus a `ping` will fail.

For local use it is always a good idea to enable full access for the local (loopback) interface:

```
ipchains -A input -i lo -j ACCEPT
```

The `-i` switch specifies an interface for which this rule is valid.

You can now list the contents of a particular chain:

```
# ipchains -n -L input
Chain input (policy ACCEPT):
target      prot opt      source              destination           ports
DENY        all  ------   anywhere            anywhere              n/a
ACCEPT      all  ------   anywhere            anywhere              n/a
```

Note the structure of the chain – the `DENY` comes *before* the `ACCEPT`, thus incoming packets will be compared to this chain and match the first clause on the list (`DENY`).

To list all chains, omit the chain name. The `-n` switch prevents host-name lookups on the list, since you may be blocking DNS traffic and the list will appear to freeze until the DNS resolution times out.

It is worth noting at this point if you run into trouble that the entire chain can be cleared (or flushed) with the `-F` option, like so:

```
ipchains -F input
```

## Packet Logging

By appending `-l` to a particular chain addition, you can log `DENY` events via `syslog`'s `info` priority. This is very useful in debugging firewall scripts; resultant logs look like this:

```
Oct 16 14:04:14 localhost kernel: Packet log: input DENY eth0 PROTO=17
192.168.1.5:138 192.168.1.255:138 L=236 S=0x00 I=53781 F=0x0000 T=32 (#9)
Oct 16 14:04:14 localhost kernel: Packet log: input DENY eth0 PROTO=17
192.168.1.5:137 192.168.1.255:137 L=78 S=0x00 I=54037 F=0x0000 T=32 (#9)
```

This particular log shows an attempt by a Windows machine (`192.168.1.5`) to find other machines on a network using a TCP/IP broadcast (`192.168.1.255`) – we can tell this through the use of broadcasting and ports 137 and 138 – NetBIOS name service and NetBIOS datagrams respectively.

Of the log lines, the following details are the most useful:

❏  `input` is the chain name which was matched.

❏  `DENY` is the rule which was applied to this packet (if this is '–' then no rule was applied – an accounting rule)

❏  `eth0` is the interface name.

❏  `192.168.1.5:138` is the source of the packet and the port number (138). For ICMP packets, the port number would be replaced by the ICMP code.

❏  `192.168.1.255:138` is the destination address of the packet and the port number (you may note that this is a broadcast packet).

❏  `L=236` means that the packet was 236 bytes long.

❏  `T=32` is the Time-To-Live of the packet (1 is subtracted per hop, until Time-To-Live equals zero and the packet dies).

More detailed information regarding log format is given in the `ipchains` HOWTO.

## Server 1: Web & Outgoing Mail Services

A firewall, which blocks absolutely everything, would be useless – you may as well just unplug the server from the network; the next stage is to let the various permitted services through. To do this, we will create a chain called `firewall`, and place all our permissions within that:

```
ipchains -N firewall
ipchains -A input -s 0.0.0.0/0 -j DENY -l
ipchains -A input -i eth0 -j firewall
ipchains -A firewall -s 0.0.0.0/0 -j DENY -l
```

We're stating that the name of the chain is `firewall`, and it will only apply to input packets through interface `eth0` (you can just as easily state other interfaces). We also start by blocking all network traffic on both chains and logging it to `syslog`.

Next we can add the various filter exceptions for services that this machine supports. We need to let connections to port 80 through of course, since this is the port on which our web server resides; incoming connections will come from arbitrary ports (1024 and above) so we can also specify this:

```
ipchains -A firewall -p TCP -s 0.0.0.0/0 1024: -d 195.82.125.2 www -j ACCEPT
```

The options we're passing here are:

| | |
|---|---|
| `-A firewall` | The chain name (`firewall`) |
| `-p TCP` | This rule is specific to TCP packets |
| `-s 0.0.0.0/0 1024:` | Allow any source address, with any arbitrary port 1024 and above. Ranges are specified using : as a delimiter, so if we wanted to specify ports 1500 to 2000, we'd write `1500:2000`. |
| `-d 195.82.125.2 www` | The destination is only 195.82.125.2, on the www port (port 80) |
| `-j ACCEPT` | ACCEPT the packets. |

Now comes the SMTP traffic, originating from an arbitrary port on this server but always with a destination of port 25 on any server (and of course the converse, for the reply):

```
ipchains -A firewall -p TCP -s 195.82.125.2 1024: -d 0.0.0.0/0 smtp -j ACCEPT
ipchains -A firewall -p TCP -s 0.0.0.0/0 smtp -d 195.82.125.2 1024: -j ACCEPT
```

Finally, a vital service to have is DNS. The name service talks on UDP for small requests, but for anything over 512 bytes it speaks TCP. Therefore we have to add rules in for both UDP and TCP.

Assuming that we are going to talk to the ISP's DNS server 195.82.96.40, we would use the following:

```
ipchains -A firewall -p TCP -s 195.82.125.2 1024: -d 195.82.96.40 domain -j ACCEPT
ipchains -A firewall -p TCP -s 195.82.96.40 domain -d 195.82.125.2 1024: -j ACCEPT
ipchains -A firewall -p UDP -s 195.82.125.2 1024: -d 195.82.96.40 domain -j ACCEPT
ipchains -A firewall -p UDP -s 195.82.96.40 domain -d 195.82.125.2 1024: -j ACCEPT
```

So, for our web server the basic firewall script looks like this:

```
# Set up the chain
ipchains -N firewall

# Deny everything, and log it to syslog
ipchains -A firewall -s 0.0.0.0/0 -j DENY -l
ipchains -A input -s 0.0.0.0/0 -j DENY -l

# Divert all traffic from the ethernet card to the firewall chain
ipchains -A input -i eth0 -j firewall

# Accept the loopback interface
ipchains -A firewall -i lo -j ACCEPT

# Allow web traffic
ipchains -A firewall -p TCP -s 0.0.0.0/0 1024: -d 195.82.125.2 www -j ACCEPT
```

```
# Allow incoming DNS traffic to resolve names and addresses
ipchains -A firewall -p TCP -s 195.82.125.2 1024: -d 195.82.96.40 domain -j ACCEPT
ipchains -A firewall -p UDP -s 195.82.125.2 1024: -d 195.82.96.40 domain -j ACCEPT
ipchains -A firewall -p TCP -s 195.82.96.40 domain -d 195.82.125.2 1024: -j ACCEPT
ipchains -A firewall -p UDP -s 195.82.96.40 domain -d 195.82.125.2 1024: -j ACCEPT

# Allow outgoing SMTP connections for sending mail
ipchains -A firewall -p TCP -s 195.82.125.2 1024: -d 0.0.0.0/0 smtp -j ACCEPT
ipchains -A firewall -p TCP -s 0.0.0.0/0 smtp -d 195.82.125.2 1024: -j ACCEPT
```

And the resulting chain list looks like this:

```
# ipchains -L -n
Chain input (policy ACCEPT):
target      prot opt   source           destination          ports
firewall    all  ------ 0.0.0.0/0        0.0.0.0/0            n/a
DENY        all  ------ 0.0.0.0/0        0.0.0.0/0            n/a
Chain forward (policy ACCEPT):
Chain output (policy ACCEPT):
Chain firewall (1 references):
target      prot opt   source           destination          ports
ACCEPT      all  ------ 0.0.0.0/0        0.0.0.0/0            n/a
ACCEPT      tcp  ------ 0.0.0.0/0        195.82.125.2         1024:65535 ->     80
ACCEPT      tcp  ----1- 195.82.125.2     195.82.96.40         1024:65535 ->     53
ACCEPT      udp  ----1- 195.82.125.2     195.82.96.40         1024:65535 ->     53
ACCEPT      tcp  ----1- 195.82.96.40     195.82.125.2         53 ->     1024:65535
ACCEPT      udp  ----1- 195.82.96.40     195.82.125.2         53 ->     1024:65535
ACCEPT      tcp  ----1- 195.82.125.2     0.0.0.0/0            1024:65535 ->     25
ACCEPT      tcp  ----1- 0.0.0.0/0        195.82.125.2         25 ->     1024:65535
DENY        all  ----1- 0.0.0.0/0        0.0.0.0/0            n/a
```

### A Brief Note Regarding Setup

If you are building a firewall into a system, the moment you reboot the system it will lose its settings. To prevent this it is a good idea to place the setup script into the start up script (/etc/rc.d/init.d/rc.firewall), and make a symbolic link from rc2.d/S15firewall or similar.

## System 2: Intranet Server

For this server we are going to rely on the fact that the *Bastion* server (192.168.1.1) will be protecting us from the outside world, and utilize almost exactly the same script as we did for the first server:

```
# Set up the chain
ipchains -N firewall

# Deny everything, and log it to syslog
ipchains -A firewall -s 0.0.0.0/0 -j DENY -l

# Divert all traffic from the ethernet card to the firewall chain
ipchains -A input -i eth0 -j firewall

# Accept the loopback interface
ipchains -A firewall -i lo -j ACCEPT

# Allow web traffic from the internal network
ipchains -A firewall -p TCP -s 192.168.1.0/24 1024: -d 192.168.1.2 www -j ACCEPT

# Allow incoming DNS traffic to resolve names and addresses
ipchains -A firewall -p TCP -s 192.168.1.2 1024: -d 192.168.1.1 domain -j ACCEPT
ipchains -A firewall -p UDP -s 192.168.1.2 1024: -d 192.168.1.1 domain -j ACCEPT
ipchains -A firewall -p TCP -s 192.168.1.1 domain -d 192.168.1.2 1024: -j ACCEPT
ipchains -A firewall -p UDP -s 192.168.1.1 domain -d 192.168.1.2 1024: -j ACCEPT

# Allow outgoing SMTP connections for sending mail to the relay (192.168.1.1)
ipchains -A firewall -p TCP -s 192.168.1.2 1024: -d 192.168.1.1 smtp -j ACCEPT
ipchains -A firewall -p TCP -s 192.168.1.1 smtp -d 192.168.1.2 1024: -j ACCEPT
```

Effectively this chain setup relies on the *Bastion* server processing SMTP relaying and DNS requests on behalf of the network. By assuming this setup, we have taken the first step towards *Bastion* becoming a proxy – but more about that later.

## Server 3: The Bastion Server

From now on, things get a little more complex. We want *Bastion* to act as a firewall for the internal network and only allow certain traffic through. It will also deal with masquerading (see later on for a proper explanation), effectively acting as a router.

*Bastion* also has two Ethernet ports:

❑　eth0 has the address 195.82.125.3, and is visible to the outside world only.

❑　eth1 has the address 192.168.1.1, and is visible to the internal network only.

Let's consider the situation:

❑　Access from arbitrary ports to any port on anything.

❑　Access to port 25 (SMTP) from anything

❑　Access to port 53 (DNS) from 192.168.1.0/24

❑　Access to port 110 (POP3) from 192.168.1.0/24

❑　Access to port 8000 (Web proxy) from 192.168.1.0/24

❑　This server also serves DNS to 192.168.1.0/24

First of all we'll deal with the firewall on the *Bastion* server itself. This is fairly trivial considering what we've done on the first two servers, and a typical chain like this will do quite adequately:

```
# Set up the firewallchain
ipchains -N firewall

# Deny everything, and log it to syslog
ipchains -A firewall -s 0.0.0.0/0 -j DENY -l

# Divert traffic from eth0, which is the outside-facing interface
ipchains -A input -i eth0 -j firewall

# Accept the loopback interface
ipchains -A firewall -i lo -j ACCEPT

# Allow incoming DNS traffic to resolve names and addresses
ipchains -A firewall -p TCP -s 195.82.125.3 1024: -d 195.82.96.40 domain -j ACCEPT
ipchains -A firewall -p UDP -s 195.82.125.3 1024: -d 195.82.96.40 domain -j ACCEPT
ipchains -A firewall -p TCP -s 195.82.96.40 domain -d 195.82.125.3 1024: -j ACCEPT
ipchains -A firewall -p UDP -s 195.82.96.40 domain -d 195.82.125.3 1024: -j ACCEPT

# Allow outgoing SMTP connections for sending mail to the world
ipchains -A firewall -p TCP -s 195.82.125.3 1024: -d 0.0.0.0/0 smtp -j ACCEPT
ipchains -A firewall -p TCP -s 0.0.0.0/0 smtp -d 195.82.125.3 1024: -j ACCEPT

# And allow incoming SMTP connections from people who want to send us mail
ipchains -A firewall -p TCP -s 0.0.0.0/0 1024: -d 195.82.125.3 smtp -j ACCEPT
ipchains -A firewall -p TCP -s 195.82.125.3 smtp -d 0.0.0.0/0 1024: -j ACCEPT
```

For the internal system, interface `eth1` is only for internal traffic, so we can re-use the stock configuration file yet again:

```
# Set up the chain on eth1, which is the internally-facing interface
ipchains -N internal

# Deny everything, and log it to syslog
ipchains -A internal -s 0.0.0.0/0 -j DENY -l

# Divert all traffic from the ethernet card to the internal chain
ipchains -A input -i eth1 -j internal

# Accept the loopback interface
ipchains -A internal -i lo -j ACCEPT

# Allow incoming DNS traffic to resolve names and addresses
ipchains -A internal -p TCP -s 192.168.1.0/24 1024: -d 192.168.1.1 domain -j
ACCEPT
ipchains -A internal -p UDP -s 192.168.1.0/24 1024: -d 192.168.1.1 domain -j
ACCEPT
ipchains -A internal -p TCP -s 192.168.1.1 domain -d 192.168.1.0/24 1024: -j
ACCEPT
ipchains -A internal -p UDP -s 192.168.1.1 domain -d 192.168.1.0/24 1024: -j
ACCEPT
```

```
# And allow incoming SMTP connections from people who want to send us mail
ipchains -A internal -p TCP -s 192.168.1.0/24 1024: -d 192.168.1.1 smtp -j ACCEPT
ipchains -A internal -p TCP -s 192.168.1.1 smtp -d 192.168.1.0/24 1024: -j ACCEPT

# Users will need to check their POP3 email
ipchains -A internal -p TCP -s 192.168.1.0/24 1024: -d 192.168.1.1 pop3 -j ACCEPT
ipchains -A internal -p TCP -s 192.168.1.1 pop3 -d 192.168.1.0/24 1024: -j ACCEPT

# And they'll need to get to the web proxy on port 8000
ipchains -A internal -p TCP -s 192.168.1.0/24 1024: -d 192.168.1.1 8000 -j ACCEPT
ipchains -A internal -p TCP -s 192.168.1.1 8000 -d 192.168.1.0/24 1024: -j ACCEPT
```

That's taken care of internal and external access from the box, but what about internal forwarding? We're going to need to make sure that the box can do what's called **masquerading**, which effectively hides one network behind a single IP address.

The first step here is to stop any forwarding of TCP/IP packets. This disables the 192.168.1.0/24 network from being copied to the 195.82.125.0/27 network, and vice-versa:

```
ipchains -P forward DENY
```

Secondly, we set up a rule to carry out the internal/external forwarding, but in a masquerading capacity:

```
ipchains -A forward -s 192.168.1.0/24 -d 0.0.0.0/0 -j MASQ
```

This now gives the whole of the internal network full access to the Internet, subject to the workstation settings.

Likewise some streaming software will require you to compile and install the kernel modules for masquerading, called `ip_masq_real.o` and suchlike. In order to use these enable masquerading in your kernel configuration, and create the modules from your kernel source directory:

```
make modules
make modules_install
```

Then reboot to enable self-installation of the modules.

## Forwarding: Restricting User Access

Now we have a situation where the *Bastion* server will pass any packet through its interfaces, but restricts access directly to itself. The final stage of the firewall process is to restrict user access to services that will not form part of their work requirement – such as RealAudio, IRC, ICQ, etc.

As the workstations will only require web, mail and DNS access (and the latter two of these services are provided by the *Bastion* server itself), we can construct appropriate `ipchains` rules specifically for forwarding. We can add to the masquerading rules earlier to restrict the destination port to the web port.

```
ipchains -A forward -s 192.168.1.0/24 -d 0.0.0.0/0 www -j MASQ
```

This stops all access to any port except a destination port of 80 – effectively restricting any gateway traffic to web access.

We shall now look at the TIS firewall toolkit, which is an alternative or complementary method of setting up a firewall.

## The TIS Firewall Toolkit

The source for the toolkit comes directly from Trusted Information Systems and the latest version is always available from them. To get the software, it is necessary to read and to agree to the licensing information at the above web page and then send e-mail to `fwtk-request@tislabs.com` with the single word *accepted* in the body of the text (this changes so *do* check the page and read the license before sending the mail). You receive in return, a pointer to a hidden directory on `ftp.tislabs.com` where a copy of the source and documentation are available for about twelve hours, so don't send the mail last thing before the weekend and expect to follow up on the following Monday.

As is correct for a security conscious firm, if you have problems connecting to the FTP server then "*your IP address may not have the appropriate reverse mapping of address to hostname in the Domain Name System. As a security precaution, we do not allow connections to our FTP server that do not have this DNS information properly configured.*" (a direct quote from the return email from `fwtk-req@tislabs.com`). You need to get both `fwtk2_1_tar.Z` and `fwtk-doc-only_tar.Z` (or the equivalent for the current release) – each file is less than 500KB. As usual, put them into the `/usr/local/src` directory, uncompress and untar them both. An `fwtk` directory is created under there, containing:

| | |
|---|---|
| `Makefile` | Top level Makefile |
| `auth` | Authentication server and libraries (optional) |
| `config` | Sample configuration/permissions tables |
| `doc` | Documentation |
| `firewall.h` | Compile-time configuration |
| `ftp-gw` | Sources for FTP proxy server |
| `http-gw` | Sources for http/gopher proxy |
| `lib` | Sources for library routines |
| `netacl` | Sources for TCP/IP access control "wrapper" |
| `plug-gw` | Sources for plug-board proxy server |
| `rlogin-gw` | Sources for rlogin proxy server |
| `smap` | Sources for sendmail wrapper client |
| `smapd` | Sources for sendmail wrapper daemon |
| `tn-gw` | Sources for TELNET proxy server |
| `tools` | Miscellaneous/unsupported tools |
| `x-gw` | X11 proxy (for use with X servers) |

In addition, there are a number of `makefile.config.OS` files for various operating systems, including Linux. Although that `makefile` was copyrighted in 1993 and discusses Slackware 2.3 it ran perfectly well on Red Hat version 5.2. One advantage for the FWTK is that the sources are relatively small and readable. This is an advantage if you want to know exactly what is loaded on your system, what it is doing, and how it does it.

Rename `makefile-config.linux` to `makefile.config` and then run `make` and `make install`. The gateway programs are installed at `/usr/local/etc` – you may want to change the access rights in this directory to `drwx------` with a `chmod 700 /usr/local/etc`.

To work with these files you will have to make changes to three files – `/etc/services`, `/etc/inetd.conf` and `/usr/local/etc/netperm.table`.

The `/etc/services` file allows the system to match ports with services. These will have to be changed to reflect the new FWTK tools that we want to work on these ports. For example the `telnet` and `ftp` lines will have to be changed from:

```
ftp             21/tcp
telnet          23/tcp
```

to:

```
ftp-gw          21/tcp
tn-gw           23/tcp
```

The `/etc/inetd.conf` file controls which program responds to a connect request on a specific port – this will have to be edited to ensure that the program which responds to the request is one of the FWTK programs. Again, considering the `ftp` and `telnet` programs:

```
#
# These are standard services.
#
ftp      stream  tcp     nowait  root    /usr/sbin/tcpd  in.ftpd -l -a
telnet   stream  tcp     nowait  root    /usr/sbin/tcpd  in.telnetd
```

becomes:

```
#
# These FWTK gateway services.
#
ftp      stream  tcp     nowait  root    /usr/local/etc/ftp-gw   ftp-gw
telnet   stream  tcp     nowait  root    /usr/local/etc/tn-gw    tn-gw
```

/usr/local/etc/netperm.table is the configuration file for the FWTK tools. The authors of the toolkit supply a sample and, as suggested in the comments in the file, changing the networking settings to echo your environment setup will provide a "*good sample working* netperm-table *file*". The file looks like this:

```
#
# Sample netperm configuration table
#
# To get a good sample working netperm-table, just globally
# substitute YOURNET for your network address (e.g.; 666.777.888)
#

# Example netacl rules:
# ----------------------
# if the next 2 lines are uncommented, people can get a login prompt
# on the firewall machine through the telnet proxy
#netacl-telnetd: permit-hosts 127.0.0.1 -exec /usr/libexec/telnetd
#netacl-telnetd: permit-hosts YOURADDRESS 198.6.73.2 -exec /usr/libexec/telnetd
#
# if the next line is uncommented, the telnet proxy is available
#netacl-telnetd: permit-hosts * -exec /usr/local/etc/tn-gw
#
# if the next 2 lines are uncommented, people can get a login prompt
# on the firewall machine through the rlogin proxy
#netacl-rlogind: permit-hosts 127.0.0.1 -exec /usr/libexec/rlogind -a
#netacl-rlogind: permit-hosts YOURADDRESS 198.6.73.2 -exec /usr/libexec/rlogind
-a
#
# if the next line is uncommented, the rlogin proxy is available
#netacl-rlogind: permit-hosts * -exec /usr/local/etc/rlogin-gw


#
# to enable finger service uncomment these 2 lines
#netacl-fingerd: permit-hosts YOURNET.* -exec /usr/libexec/fingerd
#netacl-fingerd: permit-hosts * -exec /bin/cat /usr/local/etc/finger.txt

# Example smap rules:
# -------------------
smap, smapd:    userid 6
smap, smapd:    directory /var/spool/smap
smapd:          executable /usr/local/etc/smapd
smapd:          sendmail /usr/sbin/sendmail
smap:           timeout 3600

# Example ftp gateway rules:
# --------------------------
#ftp-gw:         denial-msg      /usr/local/etc/ftp-deny.txt
#ftp-gw:         welcome-msg     /usr/local/etc/ftp-welcome.txt
#ftp-gw:         help-msg        /usr/local/etc/ftp-help.txt
ftp-gw:          timeout 3600
# uncomment the following line if you want internal users to be
# able to do FTP with the internet
```

```
#ftp-gw:                  permit-hosts YOURNET.*
# uncomment the following line if you want external users to be
# able to do FTP with the internal network using authentication
#ftp-gw:                  permit-hosts * -authall -log { retr stor }

# Example telnet gateway rules:
# ----------------------------
#tn-gw:          denial-msg     /usr/local/etc/tn-deny.txt
#tn-gw:          welcome-msg    /usr/local/etc/tn-welcome.txt
#tn-gw:          help-msg       /usr/local/etc/tn-help.txt
tn-gw:           timeout 3600
tn-gw:           permit-hosts YOURNET.* -passok -xok
# if this line is uncommented incoming traffic is permitted WITH
# authentication required
#tn-gw:          permit-hosts * -auth

# Example rlogin gateway rules:
# ----------------------------
#rlogin-gw:      denial-msg     /usr/local/etc/rlogin-deny.txt
#rlogin-gw:      welcome-msg    /usr/local/etc/rlogin-welcome.txt
#rlogin-gw:      help-msg       /usr/local/etc/rlogin-help.txt
rlogin-gw:       timeout 3600
rlogin-gw:       permit-hosts YOURNET.* -passok -xok
# if this line is uncommented incoming traffic is permitted WITH
# authentication required
#rlogin-gw:      permit-hosts * -auth -xok

# Example auth server and client rules
# -----------------------------------
authsrv:         hosts 127.0.0.1
authsrv:         database /usr/local/etc/fw-authdb
authsrv:         badsleep 1200
authsrv:         nobogus true

# clients using the auth server
*:               authserver 127.0.0.1 7777

# X-forwarder rules
tn-gw, rlogin-gw:        xforwarder /usr/local/etc/x-gw
```

Replacing YOURNET and YOURADDRESS will give a sensibly working file, but as with most protection regimes, it is important that the system is monitored to be sure that the Firewall Toolkit is giving the protection you need.

We can restrict the access even further though, through use of a **proxy**.

# Proxies

A proxy acts as an intermediary, fetching data from one location to hand to another. It is a form of security that allows access based upon everything from document type to domain name. In our case we can place the proxy either on the *Bastion* server, the *intra* server, or on a completely separate box. For our purposes we will assume it is installed on the *Bastion* server.

It's easy to configure Apache up to be a proxy server and fetch web pages on behalf of an internal workstation. The default Apache which ships with Red Hat should have the following line uncommented in the file `httpd.conf`:

```
LoadModule proxy_module    modules/libproxy.so
```

You will also need to ensure that the `mod_proxy.c` code is included in the module list by un-commenting the following line:

```
AddModule mod_proxy.c
```

Finally, enable the server for proxy requests by un-commenting the line:

```
ProxyRequests On
```

Apache will now serve proxy requests.

# Cache in Hand

What is a cache? Put simply, it's a storage space for frequently fetched web pages, such as search engines, portals, and other documents; by storing the pages on a local server this alleviates some traffic from the upstream link.

If four people are reading the main page of *Yahoo!*, they're going to each be fetching a document which is about 4KB in size – that adds up to 16KB of line usage. If you have an office full of users who are all using the same portal or search engine, then that tends to add up. By caching the document on the server the first time it is read, it's usually only fetched once – although exceptions to this rule are inevitably sites which provide *No-Cache* and *Expiry* style headers.

Since your proxy server already deals with all the web pages that are requested by the workstations, it is an ideal place to enable a web-cache and luckily for us, Apache has a cache facility.

## Using Apache as a Cache

Apache comes with its own inbuilt caching facility, and enabling it is quite trivial by adding the following configuration directives:

```
CacheRoot /var/cache/httpd
```

This is where we place the cached files. This should be on a mount with plenty of disk space and fast access.

This is the size of the cache in 1KB blocks. Setting this to fill the partition is a bad idea, as it actually uses 20%-40% more space on indexing the cache. A size of 250 MB is usually quite adequate for small networks:

```
CacheSize 250000
```

This checks the cache size every n hours – here it checks the size every four hours against the amount given in the `CacheSize` option:

```
CacheGcInterval 4
```

This keeps the document for this maximum amount of time (in hours). Thus a document will be forced to expire here after 72 hours (although you can override this for specific sites as below):

```
CacheMaxExpire 72
```

This prevents documents from these domains from being cached. While this shouldn't be required, not every site uses the correct headers to expire old documents:

```
NoCache cnn.com news.bbc.co.uk
```

Thus the Apache cache is configured. While it is adequate for small networks and applications, there may be times when you do not require an `httpd` daemon on the server itself, and require far more control over the cache and proxy settings. This is where custom-caching software is required; enter **Squid**.

# Squid Proxy Server

Squid provides a much more controllable solution for proxy and caching of HTTP, FTP, and SSL requests. It features extensive access controls and is used by many service providers and system administrators to carry out the job of monitoring and controlling web access by users.

The Squid distribution may not come with your Linux distribution, in which case you will need to obtain a copy of the source and compile it yourself.

- ❑ Download the latest version of Squid from http://squid.nlanr.net/
- ❑ Unpack into /usr/src and un-tar it with:
  tar xvfz squid-2.2.tar.gz
- ❑ Enter the created directory: cd /usr/src/squid-2.2
- ❑ ./configure --prefix=/usr/local/squid
- ❑ make
- ❑ make install

Squid Proxy Server will now be installed in /usr/local/squid.

## Configuring Squid

Squid's configuration file lives in /usr/local/squid/etc/squid.conf and may be quite minimal. Rename the existing file, which is there since it is highly complex and over specified for our needs – we shall start from scratch with a new file.

Squid bases its access on **Access Control Lists** (**ACLs**). This prevents unauthorized access to your proxy server, and also controls what sites the proxy can fetch pages from. Access control is split into two sections:

❑   Definition of the access list

❑   How and what to actually control (allow/deny)

The first line of the configuration file will be a definition as to what IP range belongs to our internal network, assuming we are proxying for internal users:

```
# Firstly we define the internal network as "ournet"
acl ournet src 192.168.1.0/255.255.255.0
```

Strictly speaking this is unnecessary, as nobody from the outside can connect inwards (assuming the firewall is in place of course). However, we will place it here for added security. Multiple network addresses can be defined using multiple acl src directives.

The line specified defines the 192.168.1.0/24 address space as an access control list called ournet. The syntax is in the form of:

```
acl <name> <type> <addresses>
```

The second ACL will define the rest of the world; as for the moment we will allow any page to be fetched by our users:

```
# Define an ACL including all IP addresses
acl all src 0.0.0.0/0.0.0.0
```

Those two ACL entries alone simply define the IP ranges that we shall use, and associates names with them. The next stage is to allow and deny the specific networks:

```
# Allow "ournet" sites to connect to us via HTTP, but deny everyone else.
http_access allow ournet
http_access deny all
```

It is important to note at this stage that access control statements (such as http_access above) are evaluated in the order in which they appear in the configuration file. Thus the following would not work, and cause everyone to be denied access to the proxy, as the first line is matched on *any* address:

```
http_access deny all        # Putting this first is bad!
http_access allow ournet
```

In this example, the second line is never reached since the first line (deny all) evaluates all to the entire Internet.

We'll find out more about access control lists in a moment, but continuing on with the configuration file we come upon the concept of Internet Cache Protocol (ICP) access:

```
icp_access  allow  all
```

ICP is used to communicate between our cache and other caches: we don't ordinarily need it unless we are talking to an *upstream* cache (such as your own ISP's cache), though it is a good idea to configure it so that connections can be optimized if possible.

Finally, we shall add in a line to ensure that Squid itself does not run as a user with any permissions, in order to minimize any security issues:

```
# Run as a user with little permissions (for security reasons)
cache_effective_user nobody nobody
```

That is the minimal configuration file for Squid, and will set up a default cache and proxy operating on your intra server, and clients will need to set up their proxies to talk to port 3128. The default cache size is 100 MB, and 8 MB of server memory will be used.

## Starting Squid

If this is the first time you are starting Squid, then you need to set up the directory structure. Assuming we are using the user nobody, together with the group nobody, the command structure will go as follows:

❑  Go into the directory where you installed Squid: cd /usr/local/squid

❑  Make the Squid cache directory: mkdir cache

❑  Make the Squid logs directory: mkdir logs

❑  Now check both these are set to user nobody, group nobody:
   chown nobody.nobody cache logs

❑  Finally, create Squid's cache directories by running: ./bin/squid -z

*Note: If you have been using Apache as a proxy cache as described earlier, it is a good idea to turn it off so that the two systems do not clash.*

Setting the proxy going is simple, as a script is thoughtfully provided which will run the entire system as a proxying cache:

```
/usr/local/squid/bin/RunCache &
```

This starts Squid up in the background, and appends activity logs to `/usr/local/squid/logs/cache.log`.

## Client Configuration

As a quick parenthesis, it is worth noting the two major Windows-based desktop browsers have support for proxies built in.

- ❑ Under *Netscape*, you will find proxy configuration details in the Advanced section of the Preferences window.

- ❑ Likewise, *Internet Explorer* has the proxy section under Internet Options | LAN Settings.

For both of these browsers, give the name or IP address of the proxy server, followed by a port number of 3128. It will proxy all of the usual URLs, including HTTP, HTTPS, and FTP.

It is unlikely that you will find modern browsers – on any platform – without proxy facilities.

## More about Access Control Lists

Let's assume now that your users are spending all their time looking at playboy.com and hotmail.com. We can add in an ACL for those domains to prevent access to them:

```
acl badsites dstdomain www.sexsite.com www.spam-domain.com
```

This has defined an ACL called `badsites`, which will match on any sub domain of either www.sexsite.com or www.spam-domain.com. The `dstdomain` directive is used to evaluate destination domains (as opposed to source domains, who are the users connecting to the proxy).

The second part is an addition into the `http_access` hierarchy so that it looks like this:

```
http_access deny badsites
http_access allow ournet
http_access deny all
```

Remember that the access controls in this section are evaluated in order, so www.hotmail.com would match on the first access control. The second control checks that the user requesting the page is on our internal network, and if not the third control denies access.

Access Control Lists can carry out a variety of tasks and are not simply restricted to what sites a user may or may not look at: there are a variety of options based upon local time, network access, protocol, etc. Each access control method follows the same format as we have seen. Look at Squid's own documentation for more advanced information.

### Logging Proxy Requests

By default, Squid logs all requests to the proxy into the file
`/usr/local/squid/logs/access.log`. This file is in a specific format to Squid:

```
940591681.803  12521 192.168.1.23 TCP_MISS/200 5319 GET
    http://www.bob.com/picture.jpg - DIRECT/bob.com image/jpeg
```

The log entry here tells us:

- ❏ The requester was a machine on our network with IP address 192.168.1.23

- ❏ The TCP_MISS refers to the failure of Squid to find a matching page within its cache.

- ❏ We can see that the request was made for http://www.bob.com/picture.jpg, and it is of type image/jpeg

While raw log files of this type are useful to a certain extent, you may find that you require statistics that give you a better idea of what's going on. Log analysis systems are outside the scope of this chapter. However, there are several on the market that are worth looking into if you wish to keep a closer eye on user browsing. Examples are Calamaris and Squeezer, both of which are available from sites detailed below in the *References* section. The other kind of proxy you can use is the SOCKS proxy.

# Bringing it Together

To allow me to bring in as many options as possible we shall design the company for whom we are installing the gateway first. *Foobar Computers Ltd* is a small United Kingdom company with around fifty employees all involved in the design, marketing, and sales of eclectic doodads. They are specialist suppliers and as such have customers world-wide with whom they wish to communicate electronically (although sales are all carried out via fax and telex), both by e-mail and by supplying a catalogue on the World Wide Web, and also by allowing customers to access detailed technical specification via FTP. They would like to put more private customer information on an Intranet server for their internal staff and use more e-mail and distributed applications inside, but they are worried about who can access them. Having looked at the options, they have decided to buy a leased line connection to their ISP, terminated at a router at their ISP's insistence, and they will manage their own Web server, as they believe this will make it easier to keep it up to date. They have a number of operating systems in use and their system administrators have a number of Linux systems as common denominators providing internal services such as DNS, and internal e-mail.

There are a number of things that they could do, but the sensible thing to look at here is what needs to protected and from whom. We will need a gateway in place between the router and the network and this makes the basic configuration look something like

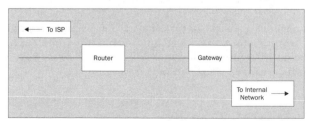

So now the question is how to place and protect services. The web server, the security of which worries many people, is actually the easiest to place. If you place it behind the gateway, you have to open a hole in your protective firewall to allow www services through, which is fine if you do not have another web server running, but can cause a problem if you have an intranet server as it will be potentially open to external users too. Given that the web server will be closed down to offer nothing but the web services, it is pretty well protected already, so why not connect it between the router and the gateway? This makes it a bit of a sacrificial lamb but keeping good backups and monitoring the server regularly means that you don't have to open a hole in your firewall for people coming in to the server, just for internal users going out. The same may be true of the FTP server – which you will probably want to run on the same machine as the web server, if budgets are tight – and so long as you are careful, this doesn't need to be a problem. If you wish to offer some security, I strongly recommend installing some packet filtering rules on your router to block problem sites and hosts.

A server running Squid also routes all web requests from the internal network. Traffic to and from external servers through the gateway will all then be passed via this server and can therefore be better controlled. If, as is usual, there are sites commonly used by a number of users then they should also see an improved performance, as the cache will supply the page.

Your mail server should be behind the gateway, with a hole or a proxy to allow SMTP to pass through to it. If you want users to be able to access mail from outside you will also need to open a POP3 or IMAP hole for them to get in. If you can discourage this then do so. Consider a separate mail account with an ISP and forwarding mail for them to that account via SMTP if it is very important that they don't lose access (an alias can be set up to send copies of mail to both an internal account and an external account so nothing is lost). Remember to set up a backup mail server and the MX record for it, if you want some resilience.

To be a good Internet user, install some form of network address translation or masquerading either in the router or the gateway, and reduce the number of IP addresses you need (count one or two addresses for each service you offer to the external world, one for the router or gateway's external port, and a couple for sudden expansion). Put a DNS server both outside the gateway, although this may be handled by your ISP, and behind the gateway to handle requests from your users for internal machines that are not handled externally. This allows you to make your internal servers easily available to home users but only those servers that need to be available to the outside world, such as your Web and mail servers, are advertised globally. You'll need to open a hole to allow DNS requests from your internal DNS server get out to root servers. This will involve allowing connections on port 53 through to your DNS server from external name servers, that is if you are handling some of your Internet domain name service requests.

With a router you will be able to control packet filtering there, and again at the gateway itself. I recommend using the router to do an initial packet filter based on ports and denial based on network addresses, leaving the gateway to do more precise filtering based on hosts and any other criteria. You should duplicate the filters in place on the router in addition, as a *belt and braces* approach to security won't do any harm. Given that you have your web server outside the gateway, and it contains stuff you want everyone to see, it is a good idea to put fewer limits on access to that than you do to other parts of your network. I also think that packet filtering with ipchains is easier to monitor and configure than the router based applications so put definite, tested, fixed, build once and keep, rules on the router, and make your changes at the gateway level where backtracking to a working version is easier if it all goes wrong.

All these rules could be installed on the gateway if you don't want to install a router. In the latter case it is a little more difficult to put the Web server outside the gateway, so you will have to install it inside and open a hole to let packets in and out. In general, configure it to be as closed as possible regardless of its position. I have seen web servers run happily with the only access being via the system console and the www ports on the network, although there was some fancy CGI programming which allowed a request (from a specific IP address only), access to a page which contained a number of scripts for shutting down or restarting the server, opening a Telnet port, and running a backup to tape – just because there was a possibility that the console might freeze. The last time I saw it they were writing a Perl script to identify the getty for the console, stop it, and start a fresh one.

# A Summary Diagram

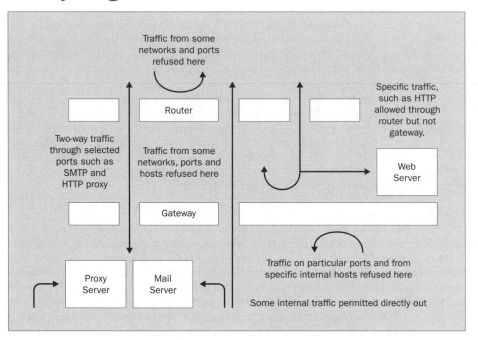

# References

| The ipchains utility Homepage | http://www.rustcorp.com/linux/ipchains/ |
| Internet Firewalls FAQ | http://www.clark.net/pub/mjr/pubs/fwfaq/ |
| Apache Project Homepage | http://www.apache.org/ |
| Squid Homepage | http://squid.nlanr.net/ |
| Calamaris, a Squid logfile analyser | http://calamaris.cord.de/ |
| Squeezer, a Squid cache profile utility | http://www.uck.uni.torun.pl/~maciek/w3cache/ |
| The TIS Firewalling Toolkit Homepage | http://www.tis.com/research/software/ |

# Cryptography and the Linux Connection

The Internet is an open, insecure medium, but increasing amounts of sensitive information are now flowing through it. We need a way to protect such information while still using the tremendous flexibility afforded by the Internet. Cryptography is the answer. There are several types of cryptography, but what we normally understand by the term is the ability to convert a message (called *cleartext*) into an unintelligible form (called *ciphertext*) and transport it in that form to the intended recipient who alone is able to read it. That's a rather naive and limited definition of cryptography, but it will suffice for now. As we go along, we will see other aspects of cryptography, and many open source products that make our applications more secure.

## A Simple Example of Cryptography

You know the old childhood technique of sending "secret" messages. Just replace all occurrences of "a" with "b", all occurrences of "b" with "c", and so on, finally wrapping around by replacing all occurrences of "z" with "a". So a message such as:

```
Meet me at the library.
```

is transformed into:

```
Nffu nf bu uif mjcsbsz.
```

Though such a message appears incomprehensible at first glance, almost anyone can crack it in a couple of minutes because the technique is so simple. Just replace every letter by the one just before it in the alphabet ("a" wraps back around to "z", of course), and the secret is out.

# The Concept of a Key

One of the reasons why this technique of "encrypting" (scrambling) messages is so simple is that it requires very little computation to perform. Anyone can tell the next (or previous) letter in the alphabet without much thinking. More sophisticated practitioners would vary the distance between a letter and its replacement to make the message harder to decrypt (unscramble). For example, a distance of 2 would mean that all occurrences of "a" are replaced by "c", all occurrences of "b" are replaced by "d", and so on. A distance of 3 would mean that the replacement for "a" is "d", and so on. With a distance of 3, therefore, our secret message:

    Meet me at the library.

becomes:

    Phhw ph dw wkf oleudub.

Notice that the "y" in "library" has wrapped around to "b".

This scrambled message, or *ciphertext*, is harder to decrypt than the one in our first example, because the distance chosen by the scrambler of the message is not known. If we assumed that the distance is 1, we would unscramble it to yield:

    Oggv og cv vje nkdtcta.

This makes no sense either. Our attempt at decryption has failed, and that's because we didn't have a crucial piece of information – the distance used by the scrambler. (Yes, we could try every distance from 1 to 25 until the resulting *cleartext* made sense, but that's too tedious; cryptography is all about making the cost of retrieving a message higher than the value of the message.) The distance used to scramble the message can be called the **key**. Most techniques of scrambling, or encryption, rely on the knowledge of a key like this one. Without knowledge of the key, someone attempting to unscramble the message has to try out all possible keys, in what is known as a brute-force attack. If the number of possible keys is very large, the attacker will need to spend an inordinately long time trying to crack the message.

# Keys and Algorithms

It's useful at this stage to clarify the difference between a key and an algorithm. An algorithm is a step-by-step recipe of the logic used to do something. The fact that we replace every letter by another letter $n$ places ahead of it in the alphabet is the algorithm for encryption. Similarly, the algorithm for decryption is that we replace every letter by another letter $n$ places behind it in the alphabet. It isn't possible to execute the algorithm as it is because we don't have a value for $n$. The key, on the other hand, is an actual value that we can use in place of a general term like $n$ to actually implement the algorithm. In our example, a key of 3 makes it possible to actually carry out the encryption (or decryption) by replacing each letter by another one 3 places ahead of it (or behind it) in the alphabet.

An algorithm is therefore general. A key makes it specific.

It's possible to have algorithms that are not general, of course. For example, our algorithm could *specifically* state that we must always replace a letter by another one 3 places ahead of it in the alphabet. If we adopt this approach, however, it will become imperative to keep the entire algorithm secret because it contains this crucial information. One of the lessons learnt in cryptography is that it's not worthwhile using algorithms that need to be kept secret. Once the algorithm is known, all messages encrypted with that algorithm can be cracked. What's more, that algorithm can never be used again. It's far better to use *general* algorithms (algorithms that don't contain specific information) and only keep the actual keys secret. That way, if a key is ever revealed or compromised, another key can be chosen with ease and the same algorithm can still be employed. Eavesdroppers will gain only a temporary advantage because the knowledge of a key will only allow them to crack messages encrypted with that key, and not with any other.

This may surprise you, but algorithms don't need to be secret at all. Some of the world's most powerful algorithms are actually well known. Messages encrypted with such algorithms remain virtually unbreakable as long as their keys are secret. Knowledge of the algorithm alone does not help someone trying to unscramble a message. In fact, well-known algorithms are now felt to be more secure than secret algorithms because more minds work at trying to find flaws and weaknesses in them. (The DES algorithm, for instance, has been studied so thoroughly that researchers have found several weak and semi-weak keys that make it easy to crack. Paradoxically, the DES algorithm is now stronger thanks to the discovery of such weaknesses because users now steer clear of the weak and semi-weak keys and thus keep their data more secure.)

# The Problem with Single-Key Encryption

The algorithms we have been talking about so far, are examples of *single key encryption* algorithms. Single-key encryption means that the same key is used for encryption and for decryption. If the sender of the message uses a key of 3 to scramble the message, the receiver must also use the same key to unscramble it. Now consider a problem. If A sends such an encrypted message to B, how does B know the key that was used? Simple, you might think. A and B must have already agreed upon the key (3 in this case), and so B can decrypt the message very easily, while anyone else will find it much tougher. Well, it's not so simple. A and B are forced to communicate in code because they want to hide the contents of their messages from eavesdroppers. In other words, the channel of communication between them is untrusted. If that is so, A and B cannot at any time discuss the key to be used for encrypting messages, because that piece of information must also travel through the same untrusted channel, open to eavesdroppers.

It's a catch-22 situation. If A tells B which key to use, an eavesdropper can pick it up and decrypt the message as fast as B. If A doesn't tell B the key, B will struggle with the message just like any eavesdropper. And, most importantly, if you assume that there is some way that A can securely communicate the key to B without the danger of that information being picked up by eavesdroppers, then there's really no need to send scrambled messages in the first place! A can simply send messages to B (in *cleartext*) through this other, secure channel. (In certain cases, this may still make sense, such as if A and B meet personally at intervals and decide on what keys to use, but in general, this is a weakness.)

This catch-22 is an unavoidable evil in all **single-key** encryption schemes like this one. Single-key encryption requires the key to be communicated between sender and receiver in addition to the actual message. That's why it is often said in cryptographic circles, "Encryption is easy; key management is tough".

# How Dual-Key Encryption Solves the Problem

The breakthrough in cryptography has come about through what are known as **dual-key** encryption schemes. In these schemes, there are special key-pairs; such that what is encrypted using one key can only be decrypted using the other. What's more, neither key can be derived from the other (without inordinate computing effort), so knowledge of one key will not allow an eavesdropper to determine the other. Let's say that B discovers such a pair of keys (call them *x* and *y*). B would then ask A to send him a message encrypted using one of these two keys (say, *x*). The channel is untrusted, of course, so our sharp-eared eavesdropper picks up this piece of information immediately, and knows that A is going to use key *x* to scramble the secret message. When A sends the encrypted message to B, B uses the other key *y* to decrypt it. The eavesdropper also manages to grab a copy of the encrypted message when A sends it to B, but alas for him, he cannot decrypt the ciphertext because he needs key *y* to do that. Knowledge of *x* is of no use, even to decrypt something encrypted with *x*. And since *y* cannot be derived from *x*, there's nothing the eavesdropper can do. A and B have managed to send a message securely through an untrusted channel.

How did B arrive at *x* and *y* in the first place? Let's just say there are mathematical techniques to derive such pairs of keys. These need not concern us right now, though interested readers will find more details at the end of this chapter.

# A Simple Example of Dual-Key Encryption

Let's take a simplistic and somewhat flawed example to illustrate dual-key encryption. We used a key of 3 to convert the cleartext:

```
Meet me at the library.
```

into the ciphertext:

```
Phhw ph dw wkf oleudub.
```

Now, let's say that to convert the ciphertext back into the cleartext, we don't use the key 3 again. What else could we do to unscramble the code? Well, we could use a key of 23 and use the same *scrambling* technique that was used to convert the cleartext into the ciphertext. This means that instead of replacing each letter by one 3 places *before* it, we replace it by one 23 places *after* it. This is of course, the same thing, because $3 + 23 = 26$, the number of letters in the alphabet. Our logic of wrapping around the end of the alphabet ensures that as long as the sum of the two keys equals 26, scrambling with one key and then scrambling it again with the other transforms each letter back into itself, returning the original cleartext.

That's an example of dual-key cryptography. We have two keys, and what is scrambled with one can only be unscrambled with the other, not with itself. For example, if we apply the key of three *twice*, we are not unscrambling the message the second time but are effectively using a key of six!

This is admittedly a flawed example. It is trivially possible to derive one key from the other, and nothing prevents an eavesdropper from using the encryption key itself to decrypt the message by applying the encryption logic backwards. But true dual-key cryptography makes both these things extremely difficult. The mathematical relationship between the two keys is not so simple that one can be derived from the other by just subtracting it from 26, as we did. And the actual scrambling logic that is used (the algorithm) is such that it cannot be applied in reverse. There are so-called one-way mathematical algorithms that can only be applied in one direction. If such mathematical properties seem like magic, consider this: it is relatively easy for someone to multiply two large prime numbers together to get their product, but it is not so easy for someone else to break this product back into its prime factors. The scrambling algorithms used in dual-key cryptography are related to this property. Some things are easy to do in one direction, but not easy to do in reverse.

So you see that if it is not possible to derive 23 from 3, and if it is not possible to use the number 3 and step *backwards* 3 places, then we have achieved dual-key cryptography in our example. A message encrypted with key 3 cannot be decrypted with 3 at all, only with 23. And if 23 cannot be derived from 3, then no one else can crack the message.

Now anyone can use the same algorithm, but use different keys. Let's say that A arrives at a key pair 5 and 21, and asks B to send him a message using the key 5. B does this, and A unscrambles it easily using the other key 21, (which is 26 minus 5, of course, but we assume it was derived through some other very complex process!). The poor eavesdropper on the other hand, has managed to intercept the encryption key of 5, and the ciphertext, but is unable to decrypt the message because he has no way to derive 21 from 5, and the encryption algorithm is one-way. It is not possible to replace a letter by something *before* it in the alphabet.

This is really all there is to dual-key cryptography, but we shall see in the following sections that some really useful features emerge from a judicious use of this technique.

# Public Key Cryptography

Let's say A and B decide to use their newfound cryptographic tools to send messages to each other. They decide upon a scheme like this: A creates a pair of keys 5 and 21 through a complex mathematical process. He gives the key 5 to B, and neither of them cares if eavesdroppers see it too. He just guards the key 21 very jealously and doesn't let anyone (not even B) know what it is. Similarly, B creates a pair of keys 3 and 23 and gives the key 3 to A in full view of eavesdroppers. He keeps the key 23 secret, even from A.

Let's say that A now sends two messages to B. He encrypts one of them with the key 3, which B had given him. He encrypts the other with his own key 21, which he has kept secret from everyone. What has been achieved? Is the result the same in both cases? We shall see.

In the first case, the message was encrypted using B's key 3, so it can only be decrypted using B's other key 23, which only B knows. Such a scheme of encrypting a message using a key given by another person has the effect of protecting it from the eyes of everyone but that person.

The second message, on the other hand, was encrypted with A's own key 21, which no one knows but A. It can only be decrypted with the corresponding key 5, which A gave to B. However, when A sent the key 5 to B, he did it in full view of any eavesdroppers. That means an eavesdropper also knows the key 5 and is equally capable of decrypting the second message. So this second form of encryption is of no use, or so it would seem.

Certainly, encrypting something with your own, secret key doesn't keep it secret, because anyone can pick up the other key and decrypt it. But this encryption does achieve something, after all. B knows when he decrypts the message that it could not have come from anyone other than A! No one else could have impersonated A and sent this message because no one else knows the secret key corresponding to the key 5.

There are special terms in cryptography for these two situations. If I send you a message, **privacy** means that no one can read it except you, and **authentication** means that you know the message came from me and not from someone else pretending to be me. Authentication can be as powerful a requirement as encryption. After all, if you received a message saying, "I made a mistake on the sales figures, change outgoing figures from 1200 to 12000. – Bill", is it a genuine message, or is someone trying to fiddle the figures? Authentication is the means of telling whether a message really came from the person it claims to be from. In a business context, an order to sell 10,000 shares, for example, requires authentication before it can be executed.

To recapitulate, you achieve privacy by encrypting a message with the key that someone else gave you. You achieve authentication by encrypting it with your own key that you keep secret. So dual-key cryptography yields these features, provided every party to a transaction creates two keys, a secret or private key, which is revealed to no-one, and a public key, which can be freely publicized. For this reason, dual-key cryptography in the form in which it is practiced is also called **public-key cryptography**. Encryption with one's own secret key is also called **signing**, and we will use the word from now on to distinguish it from encryption, though the actual mathematical algorithms used for encryption and signing are in fact identical. The word signing is useful because it tells you that it provides authentication. If you receive a letter signed by a close friend, and you recognize the signature, you are satisfied that it came from your friend. For this reason, a signed message (a message encrypted with the sender's private key) is also sometimes referred to as a **digital signature**.

Public-key cryptography is resource-intensive and is not really suitable for encrypting large amounts of data. So single-key encryption is used to encrypt the actual data, while public-key encryption is used to securely transfer the **session key** used for the single-key encryption. It's called a session key because typically, it is randomly generated and used only for that session.

# Notation

We adopt the following notation to explain cryptographic concepts. A cleartext message is printed as normal. An encrypted message using a key is denoted by {Message}$_K$.

This is a cleartext message:

    Message

This is a message encrypted using a key:

    {Message}$_K$

The curly braces represent the encryption algorithm that transforms the message, and the letter K represents the actual key used for the encryption. A public key is represented by PK, and a secret key by SK. The public and secret keys of A are represented by PK(A) and SK(A). Similarly, the public and secret keys of B are PK(B) and SK(B).

Here's how we show A sending an encrypted message to B (encrypted with B's public key):

```
A -> {Message}_PK(B) -> B
```

When B decrypts A's encrypted message (with his secret key), we show it like this:

```
{{Message}_PK(B)}_SK(B) => Message
```

This shows that the same encryption algorithm applied twice, once with B's public key and then with B's secret key, returns the original cleartext.

When A sends a signed message to B (signed with his own secret key), we represent it like this:

```
A -> {Message}_SK(A) -> B
```

And when B verifies that A's signed message has really come from A (using A's public key), we show it like this:

```
{{Message}_SK(A)}_PK(A) => Message
```

Once again, the same encryption (or signing) algorithm applied twice, once with A's secret key and then with A's public key, returns the original cleartext.

# Message Integrity and Checksums

There is yet another important concept in cryptography, quite apart from privacy and authentication. We very often want to be sure that a third party did not modify a message from A to B. This becomes very important in situations like electronic banking. If a customer tells his bank (electronically, of course) that he wishes to transfer $1000 to the account of another customer, what is to prevent someone from modifying that message to make it a million dollars instead? We need a foolproof way to guarantee that a message has not been tampered with in transit. In other words, we need a way to guarantee message integrity.

Fortunately, there is a simple way to do this. Checksums have been around for a long time, and are ideal for this sort of requirement. In case you have never come across a checksum algorithm, you can just assign a number to every letter (or character) of the message, and add them all up, perhaps dividing the result by a prime number and taking the remainder. This technique ensures that a change to the message will result in a very different number at the end of the checksum process; although this is not a particularly good example of a hashing algorithm. When we want to guarantee that a message has not been tampered with, we calculate the checksum and send it along with the message itself. The recipient calculates the checksum of the received message independently and checks to see if it matches the one sent by the creator of the message. If the two checksums don't match, it means the message was tampered with.

Let's take a simple example. Let's assign a number to each letter of the alphabet, starting with 1 for A and ending with 26 for Z. Then a message such as:

CAT

results in a total of 24. Divide this number by a prime number, 11, and take the remainder. The remainder in this case is 2.

Now, if the message is altered to make it:

CAR

the total is now 22 (3+1+18). The remainder after dividing by 11 is 0. So a glance at the checksum is sufficient to show that the text has changed. This is useful for large messages, in which a small change is not easily visible. The checksum makes even minor changes obvious.

Is it possible that two different messages could have the same checksum? In theory, it is possible. In practice, the probability of two *meaningful* messages having the same checksum is negligibly low, if the checksum algorithm is well designed. More importantly, two messages that are *almost* identical will never have the same checksum, again, if the checksum algorithm is well designed.

The method we described above has a loophole that can let someone modify a message in a way that cannot be detected. Remember that we need to send the checksum along with the message. We also implied that the checksum algorithm is well known, so that the recipient can independently verify it. If the sender of a message *signs* the checksum with his secret key and sends the signed checksum along with the message then the security is assured, as you will see. The recipient needs to do three things:

❑ Independently calculate the checksum of the received message.

❑ Decrypt (verify) the signed checksum using the sender's public key.

❑ Compare the newly calculated checksum in step 1 with the checksum sent by the sender.

If the two checksums match, it means the message was certainly not tampered with in transit. We know this because if someone did tamper with the message, and they also managed to generate the checksum of the modified message, then the one thing that they would not be able to do is *sign the checksum using the secret key of the sender*, because they don't know the sender's secret key. If they sign it using their own secret key, the recipient will be unable to verify (decrypt) it using the sender's public key, because these two keys are not part of the same pair. So the use of signed checksums makes it impossible for messages to be imperceptibly changed. Any tampering will be immediately obvious.

Checksums are also sometimes called **hashes** or **message digests**. Checksum algorithms are called "hashing" algorithms. Most hashing algorithms today are designed to yield checksums of the same length, regardless of the length of the message they hash, which is really convenient. The hash algorithm of choice today is called SHA-1, and produces an output of 160 bits, no matter what the length of the message may be.

The notation we will use for hashing is simply a "hash" character (#) on either side of the message, as follows: #Message#. Signed hashes look like this: {#Message#}$_{SK}$ where SK is the sender's secret key.

# Clearsigning, Legal Documents and Non-Repudiation

Going back to our earlier discussion of privacy and authentication, you can readily see that their requirements are very different, though we use the same algorithm for both. Is this really appropriate? When we need privacy, we need the message to be horribly jumbled, so that no one can tell what the message really says. But when we only want authentication, it's not necessary to jumble up the message. The message can even remain in cleartext, open to anyone to read. We just need to know that it came from the person who claimed to have sent it. Unfortunately, the signing process jumbles it as badly as the encryption process, because the algorithm is the same, after all. Is there any way to avoid this?

Hashing comes to our rescue. We don't have to sign the message itself, just its hash (checksum). The message itself can remain in cleartext. The purpose is still achieved. We can readily read the message because it isn't jumbled. We aren't unduly worried about other people reading it because, as we said, privacy isn't the issue here. No one can tamper with the message because the signed hash lets us detect such tampering immediately. And we know it really came from the sender, because we can verify the signed hash using the sender's public key. This is known as **clearsigning**, because we are able to effectively sign a message and achieve authentication, while keeping the message itself in cleartext.

When A sends a clearsigned message to B, we denote it like this:

A -> Message + {#Message#}$_{SK(A)}$ -> B

Let's say an attacker replaces the message with NewMessage. What B receives is this:

NewMessage + {#Message#}$_{SK(A)}$

The deception is therefore detected, because the two hashes are not the same. If the attacker had instead tried sending a signed hash of the new message, this is what B would have received:

NewMessage + {#NewMessage#}$_{SK(Attacker)}$

Notice that the attacker doesn't have access to A's secret key, and is therefore forced to use some other key! This deception is detected also, because verifying the signed hash using the sender's public key like this:

{{#NewMessage#}$_{SK(Attacker)}$}$_{PK(A)}$

fails because nothing readable is produced, and you realize it when the checksums won't match. That's because the attacker's secret key and the sender's public key don't match.

Obviously, the technique of clearsigning has enormous legal implications for the digital transmission of documents and transactions. It is possible to *prove* that a certain person in fact sent a document and that it was not altered in transit. The sender cannot at a later date deny, or *repudiate* the contents of the document or the fact that he sent it. This property is known as **non-repudiation**. Non-repudiation, along with privacy, authentication, and message integrity, lays the foundations of an economy that can now be conducted entirely electronically. A little thought will show that non-repudiation is not an independent property but a natural corollary of authentication and message integrity.

# Digital Certificates

All of what we just discussed must seem very impressive and a complete infrastructure for a digital economy, but we still haven't plugged one loophole. We trust that a message came from a sender if we are able to verify it using the sender's public key, but how can we trust the public key in the first place?

Let's say you receive e-mail from a friend with his public key attached. How do you know that this e-mail message really came from your friend, and that the key is really his? If someone *spoofed* the message (impersonated the sender), then you get fooled into trusting that the public key you received is really your friend's. You are then led to believe that any message signed with the corresponding secret key was really sent by your friend, because you are able to verify it with this key. But the whole thing could be a deception. How can we safeguard against such a fundamental attack on our security system?

Let us say that A and B exchange public keys in person. They then know that no one could have tampered with the keys. However, this face-to-face approach to exchanging keys isn't practical in many situations. If A wants to introduce B and C to each other, and get them to exchange their public keys, it is not easy because they may all now be in different cities. We know that e-mail messages can be spoofed and are not to be trusted. Is there no way to trust a public key without receiving it in person?

We can use the concept of clearsigning to help us here. Let's say that A has received the public keys of both B and C in person, so he knows they are both genuine. B and C also have received A's public key in person, so they trust it, too. However, B and C have never met. How can they send their public keys to each other without having to actually travel to a common meeting place? Their common friend, A, can compose a message to B saying something like, "This is my good friend C, and here is her public key: KJYU87878KJHJ5KJ0SF2JH656JG..." with a long sequence of nonsense characters that form C's public key. A composes a similar message to C containing B's public key. A then clearsigns both messages using his secret key.

B receives his message and can readily read it and see C's public key. B can also verify that the message is genuine, because he has A's public key, and the message is clearsigned, so any tampering can be instantly detected. With this system, two people with a common acquaintance can be introduced to each other without the danger that someone could tamper with their public keys.

In cryptographic terminology, such a clearsigned message is called a **digital certificate**, and the introducer is called a **certifying authority**. Obviously, if you must accept a digital certificate, you must already possess and trust the public key of the certifying authority. If you don't trust the public key of the certifying authority, it must come to you inside a digital certificate signed by another certifying authority that you trust. The process has to end somewhere, of course. You cannot claim to trust no one, because you then cannot believe anything that is sent to you.

One of the major certifying authorities that have emerged in recent years is Verisign. Verisign's public key is well known. If someone sends you their public key in a certificate signed by Verisign, you can be fairly certain that the public key really belongs to them. It is Verisign's responsibility, of course, to check this fact before signing the certificate.

Actually, there is another way to check if someone's public key is really his or hers. It is possible to extract what is called a fingerprint of a public key, which is nothing but a shortened and readable string of characters (usually 40 characters long). You can read this out over the phone to confirm with the sender that the public key you have received through e-mail is really theirs, because the chances of two keys having the same fingerprint are extremely low.

We have covered the basic concepts required to understand cryptographic products and systems. We can now study some of the good cryptographic software available for Linux and other systems.

# PGP (Pretty Good Privacy)

If you need just one piece of proof that free, open source software is as good as (or better than) commercial software, PGP is it. Developed by Phil Zimmerman, PGP (for Pretty Good Privacy) turned out to be more than just pretty good. It proved to be such a strong, cheap, and easy-to-use package that Zimmerman was even the target of a US government investigation; because the US government views the proliferation of strong cryptography products with alarm (http://www.pgpi.org).

PGP is useful for anyone wishing to keep his or her correspondence and documents confidential. Using PGP does not imply a guilty secret. Organizations like Amnesty International and Greenpeace require that their communications are protected from hostile governments, and PGP can give them this at little cost. It helps to protect the identities of witnesses who give evidence against dictatorships. Without PGP, the seizure of documents from human rights activists could mean the unmasking of such witnesses' identities, and their exposure to great danger. Even ordinary citizens in democracies, who have nothing to fear, can use PGP to protect their confidential information.

Today, PGP has become the *de facto* standard for public-key cryptography. In July 1999, Republican legislators submitted a bill to President Clinton through e-mail, and Congress used PGP to digitally sign the bill. There is now a proposed Internet standard (RFC2440) called **OpenPGP**, which is a specification that any public-key cryptographic software must comply with to be considered PGP-compatible.

> *The US government has recently (December 1999) allowed PGP to be exported to most of the world, excepting countries like Cuba and Libya. This could either mean that they believe they can crack the messages now, which is very unlikely considering Washington uses it, or they have realized that it is pointless restricting the export of such a product as consumers just get it from another country.*

# GnuPG (GNU Privacy Guard)

**GnuPG** (also called GPG), the GNU Privacy Guard, is one such software package that conforms to the OpenPGP standard. PGP has a few limitations (commercial/legal as well as technical), which GnuPG seeks to address. These are described on the GnuPG website (http://www.gnupg.org). GnuPG is a completely free public-key cryptography package, in four senses of the term.

- ❏ It is available free of charge, like all other GNU products.

- ❏ Its source code is available, and anyone is free to modify and redistribute it, under the terms of the GNU Library General Public License (LGPL). The LGPL, unlike the General Public License (GPL), also allows commercial vendors to write proprietary software products that build upon GnuPG, without forcing them to release their source code.

- ❏ It avoids patent-restricted algorithms like IDEA and RSA, so it can be used worldwide without the need to pay license fees to any party.

- ❏ GnuPG was developed in Germany, so it escapes current US export restrictions.

We will cover GnuPG in this book, since it is the same as PGP for all practical purposes. It is also written to work like a standard Unix utility, which means you can pipe data in and out of it. It is quite possibly the best personal cryptography package available. We will spend some time discussing GnuPG, not just because it is a useful product, but because some examples will help to internalize the public-key cryptography concepts we just covered. As we shall see, other cryptographic systems like SSL and IPSec are also based on public-key cryptography, and it will be far easier to understand how they work once the basic concepts are clear. **Geheimnis** is a graphical front-end for GnuPG which you can use with the K Desktop Environment. **GnomePG** is the equivalent front-end for the GNOME Desktop environment. Both these products are still under development, but are already fairly usable. It is just a matter of time before GnuPG can be used entirely within a graphical environment.

## Downloading and Installing GnuPG

GnuPG can be downloaded from many sites on the Internet, and these are listed on the GNU web site, http://www.gnu.org/software/gnupg. You can also download it from ftp.gnupg.org. None of these sites are in the US, so a download is legal, no matter where you are in the world. The latest version at the time of writing is 1.0.0, and the file is gnupg-1_0_0_tar.gz.

Copy the file gnupg-1_0_0_tar.gz to /usr/src, then follow the standard Linux steps to install the software. It involves a compilation of the source code. First decompress and extract the files into a directory called gnupg-1.0.0:

```
# tar -zxvf gnupg-1_0_0_tar.gz
```

Enter this directory and take a look at the files there. You can read the README and INSTALL files if you wish, but all you need to do is type the following three commands, one after the other.

```
# ./configure
# make
# make install
```

GnuPG is now installed.

# GnuPG Quick Reference

Here's a quick reference of some of the more common GnuPG commands. We will encounter many of them in our examples that follow. We will use the "long form" of all the command-line arguments here for the sake of clarity, but you can use the shorter equivalents when you become more comfortable with the tool. The long form usually uses two hyphens and full words, rather than single hyphens and single-letter codes. Parameters shown in square brackets are optional.

To get help on GnuPG commands:

```
# gpg --help | more
```

To generate a key-pair:

```
# gpg --gen-key
```

To extract the public key and display it on the screen:

```
# gpg --export
```

To extract the public key into a file my_public_key:

```
# gpg --export > my_public_key
```

To extract the public key into a file using only printable (ASCII) characters:

```
# gpg --export --armor > my_public_key
```

To import someone else's public key from a file their_public_key:

```
# gpg --import their_public_key
```

To list out all the keys in my public key ring:

```
# gpg --list-keys
```

To list out all the keys in my public key ring along with any signatures (certificates):

```
# gpg --list-sigs
```

To list out all my secret keys (I could have more than one):

```
# gpg --list-secret-keys
```

To extract a fingerprint of a public key:

```
# gpg --fingerprint [user]
```

To perform many operations on a user's key (help at this prompt lists the options):

```
# gpg --edit-key user_name
```

To encrypt a message in `message_file` for the eyes of a recipient `my_friend` only:

```
# gpg --encrypt --armor --recipient my_friend message_file
```

To decrypt a message I have received (in `encrypted_message_file`):

```
# gpg --decrypt encrypted_message_file
```

To sign a message with my private key and make the output printable:

```
# gpg --sign --armor message_file
```

To verify that a signed message I have received is from a recognized user:

```
# gpg --verify signed_message_file
```

To clearsign a message with my private key (keeping the message readable):

```
# gpg --clearsign message_file
```

To sign and encrypt a message and make the output printable:

```
# gpg --recipient my_friend --sign --encrypt --armor message_file
```

GnuPG can also run as a filter like any UNIX command, for example:

```
# cat signed-file | gpg --verify | wc -1
```

This will check the signature of a signed file and display the number of lines in the original file. You can encrypt a piece of text for the use of a recipient, and mail it to that person, all in one command:

```
# echo "Meet me at the library" | gpg --encrypt --armor --recipient tom |\
> mail tom@fictitious.address.com
```

# Key Generation Using GnuPG

Let's say we have 3 people called Tom, Dick and Harry who use GnuPG. Each of them installs GnuPG on his Linux computer and then creates a key-pair for himself. Let's take Tom as an example. First, Tom types

```
# gpg --gen-key
```

GnuPG prompts him a few times for different pieces of information, and Tom just hits the return key each time to choose the default.

```
What kind of key do you want?
...
    DSA and El Gamal (default)
...
    default keysize is 1024.
...
What keysize do you want?
...
Please specify how long the key should be valid.
...
    0 = Key does not expire
...
Is this correct y/n?
```

He answers y to confirm that all the information he has selected is correct.

GnuPG then prompts him for his real name, e-mail address, and an optional comment. Once he confirms all of these, it prompts him for a passphrase, which is a very important and necessarily secret word, or set of words. (A phrase is less "guessable" than a word, and should therefore be preferred.) This is what unlocks the secret key used for signing and decrypting messages. After Tom confirms the passphrase, GnuPG starts generating a random seed for the key generation, during which time Tom must either type idly on the keyboard or move the mouse aimlessly about just to make the seed really random. After a few seconds, GnuPG announces that the key-pair has been generated and Tom is now in business!

Dick and Harry do pretty much the same thing on their computers.

# Exchanging Public Keys

Tom now extracts his public key into a file to give to his friend Dick. Being a considerate sort, he chooses the ASCII armor option, so that the key is written out using printable characters, otherwise the file will contain control characters.

```
# gpg --export --armor > toms_key.asc
```

This is what the file toms_key.asc now contains:

```
-----BEGIN PGP PUBLIC KEY BLOCK-----
Version: GnuPG v1.0.0 (GNU/Linux)
Comment: For info see http://www.gnupg.org

mQGiBDfyvLERBACAPSp4vM4OnWFhnqEeInUkGz3bpHqRJ7UA6yOCxCJwc5O4/xhy
O9t+IND+elBVL+XvxnGN0/E4/LHKqPUkwDL/T6uDhpstnnte/zl0k8qOCYXF1pqK
WjPxSdUPakBInhzHg3n/4JanduyObpub5L5NodlDP0JOwOIF9okAsphHnwCgob7I
Bsqgbwz/wt2BfssxZCaW71sD/2CabutBkawZNM/ETXGnEF3zRofrKVzmBplkfwOX
7b7pF6xfXuJ2n1u05SbMJQCLEjFAdRDHyL67wCxaaEq3mb+O3DJonsR7yM89cZL7
+7qDrcgDAR8K/6LltzpY1nQZbXdjbeM4mjhWJLhm3pyKFo+r8Wa9/GG6UjkNnhjU
BC7XA/0eo4WZjbt5P4qxFzxGJHxXne7yH+Wdq/3nChYE47jW22EqFQTjI2lUOk9H
xvVpkw/YKZNo7gOMxaWBqEeLKiW1VQISvx7ZPL5jzVzC2PSz9FQ7hSVJGOLf+U5S
mPST9b1+rL4eOeHr6m6wpgUH0fVToG2WzP+5bD+iUqdaRQ7Qy7Q1VG9tIFVzZXIg
PHRvbUBmaWN0aXRpb3VzLmFkZHJlc3MuY29tPohVBBMRAgAVBQI38ryxAwsKAwMV
AwIDFgIBAheAAAoJEG4l3J4cwn1xF6MAn0/9GAwii9mDYhJRmqx9EAdjNU1IAJ9w
THD/ABDFoeXV7Hd7OwVllurM5LkBDQQ38ry5EAQAtp+l77nwySF8wvNWXTw+rNIY
e+xzrtvimmLOe0ZBNsKqAlTGTEr/GmpVv9RZufZZF10teskY+6b8QGG/AnGm3/wL
UsvM48NY9rZx35X5RVMjOUIUZjTid7GlkvAZkFPpX2qOHOtiVzKn3maJmLg+/ijr
C4SDZ1+Zd+AVpUIdHJ8AAwUEAIxPNKtbglyktxbm5FX9nQlKFpuVpFKlEZLiWmo+
QIPz8BTHOcTG9qrCQvMQf5W0HOfIJa99HV506QMuMYN7wWteyzfkVlU54uKMZaM0
a3gx9Wyx8JV6vbC3HjDys7uj/jS2AANVjp3FEaeBztzYA6v3TPWt1tSXnxTx75c4
I+JCiEYEGBECAAYFAjfyvLkACgkQbiXcnhzCfXF3MgCfbelXiDqxAVVJC/TZjsJ5
TPLK1poAn2tZkQtBfuYa7ug20Bhd2O3h9R6J
=4qy+
-----END PGP PUBLIC KEY BLOCK-----
```

As you can see, making the public key printable doesn't make it intelligible!

Meanwhile, Dick has extracted his public key into a file called dicks_key.asc and when the two friends next meet, they exchange floppy disks containing their public keys. When Tom goes back to his computer, he imports Dick's public key as follows:

```
# gpg --import dicks_key.asc
```

GnuPG, like any good UNIX command, *silently* imports Dick's public key and returns to the command prompt without reporting a thing. That's good news. It means the key was successfully imported. Tom is curious to see if Dick's public key has really been imported into his public key ring, so he types:

```
# gpg --list-keys
```

GnuPG responds with this list:

```
/home/tom/.gnupg/pubring.gpg
---------------------------
pub   1024D/1CC27D71 1999-09-30 Tom <tom@fictitious.address.com>
sub   1024g/3DF0858E 1999-09-30

pub   1024D/5085F3C3 1999-09-30 Dick <dick@fictitious.address.com>
sub   1024g/8AC9AC53 1999-09-30
```

Tom has two public keys in his key-ring – his own and now Dick's. Don't worry about the sub keys for now. Tom then wants to see the signatures (certificates) on the public keys he has. He types:

```
# gpg --list-sigs
```

GnuPG lists this:

```
/home/tom/.gnupg/pubring.gpg
---------------------------
pub  1024D/1CC27D71 1999-09-30 Tom <tom@fictitious.address.com>
sig         1CC27D71 1999-09-30  Tom <tom@fictitious.address.com>
sub  1024g/3DF0858E 1999-09-30
sig         1CC27D71 1999-09-30  Tom <tom@fictitious.address.com>

pub  1024D/5085F3C3 1999-09-30 Dick <dick@fictitious.address.com>
sig         5085F3C3 1999-09-30  Dick <dick@fictitious.address.com>
sub  1024g/8AC9AC53 1999-09-30
sig         5085F3C3 1999-09-30  Dick <dick@fictitious.address.com>
```

*Every Diffie-Hellman/DSS key is actually two keys: a DSS signing key and a Diffie-Hellman encryption subkey. PGP and GnuPG provide the ability to create and revoke new encryption keys without sacrificing your master signing key and the signatures collected on it. One of the most common uses for this feature is to create multiple subkeys that are set to be used during different periods of the key's lifetime. For example, if you create a key that will expire in three years, you might also create 3 subkeys and use each of them for one of the years in the lifetime of the key. This can be a useful security measure and provides an automatic way to periodically switch to a new encryption key without having to recreate and distribute a new public key.*

# Signing and Verification with GnuPG

Let's see how authentication works with this scheme in place. Tom creates the following message in a file auth_message1:

```
Hi,

This is a message from Tom.

Tom
```

He then clearsigns it by typing:

```
# gpg --clearsign auth_message1
```

GnuPG prompts him for his passphrase and then clearsigns the message, putting the output into the file auth_message1.asc, which looks like this:

```
-----BEGIN PGP SIGNED MESSAGE-----
Hash: SHA1

Hi,

This is a message from Tom.

Tom
-----BEGIN PGP SIGNATURE-----
Version: GnuPG v1.0.0 (GNU/Linux)
Comment: For info see http://www.gnupg.org

iD8DBQE381VIbiXcnhzCfXERAib3AJ92KJDAMSXMEos3jdq7aaLJcTp3nwCglcYF
9/ScfnrqI2RiFWT07xCezcE=
=hP8/
-----END PGP SIGNATURE-----
```

When Dick receives this message from Tom, he decides to verify it.

```
# gpg --verify auth_message1.asc
```

This is what GnuPG shows him:

```
gpg: Signature made Thu Sep 30 22:19:20 1999 EST using DSA key ID 1CC27D71
gpg: Good signature from "Tom <tom@fictitious.address.com>"
Could not find a valid trust path to the key.  Let's see whether we
can assign some missing owner trust values.

No path leading to one of our keys found.

gpg: WARNING: This key is not certified with a trusted signature!
gpg:           There is no indication that the signature belongs to the owner.
gpg: Fingerprint: A070 AA7F 83AF 3DD7 FF84  7E42 6E25 DC9E 1CC2 7D71
```

Note that GnuPG reports that the signature is valid (Good signature from Tom), but also warns Dick that the key is not certified with a trusted signature.

Dick knows that the public key in his key-ring is really Tom's, because Tom gave it to him in person, so he decides to vouch for it by signing it. He types:

```
# gpg --edit-key Tom
```

GnuPG responds with a terse prompt:

```
Command>
```

Dick isn't sure of what command to type, so he types help. GnuPG helpfully responds with:

```
quit      quit this menu
save      save and quit
help      show this help
fpr       show fingerprint
list      list key and user IDs
uid       select user ID N
key       select secondary key N
check     list signatures
sign      sign the key
lsign     sign the key locally
deluid    delete user ID
delkey    delete a secondary key
delsig    delete signatures
pref      list preferences
trust     change the ownertrust
revsig    revoke signatures
disable   disable a key
enable    enable a key
```

Dick types sign, and confirms that he really wants to sign Tom's public key. He enters his passphrase when prompted. GnuPG obediently records Dick's signature, and when he next types:

```
# gpg --list-sigs
```

And this is what he sees:

```
/home/dick/.gnupg/pubring.gpg
-----------------------------
pub  1024D/5085F3C3 1999-09-30 Dick <dick@fictitious.address.com>
sig        5085F3C3 1999-09-30  Dick <dick@fictitious.address.com>
sub  1024g/8AC9AC53 1999-09-30
sig        5085F3C3 1999-09-30  Dick <dick@fictitious.address.com>

pub  1024D/1CC27D71 1999-09-30 Tom <tom@fictitious.address.com>
sig        1CC27D71 1999-09-30  Tom <tom@fictitious.address.com>
sig        5085F3C3 1999-09-30  Dick <dick@fictitious.address.com>
sub  1024g/3DF0858E 1999-09-30
sig        1CC27D71 1999-09-30  Tom <tom@fictitious.address.com>
```

As you can see, an extra line has been added under the entry for Tom's public key, showing that Dick has signed this key.

Now when Dick verifies Tom's message again, the story is different:

```
# gpg --verify auth_message1.asc
```

This results in this output:

```
gpg: Signature made Thu Sep 30 22:19:20 1999 EST using DSA key ID 1CC27D71
gpg: Good signature from "Tom <tom@fictitious.address.com>"
```

No warnings here, because Tom is now *trusted*.

Let's say that someone tampered with Tom's clearsigned message in transit. When Dick verifies it using:

   # **gpg --verify auth_message1.asc**

GnuPG detects the deception immediately:

```
gpg: Signature made Thu Sep 30 22:19:20 1999 EST using DSA key ID 1CC27D71
gpg: BAD signature from "Tom <tom@fictitious.address.com>"
```

Consider another situation. Dick does not have Harry's public key at all. Let us say Harry creates a similar message and puts it into a file auth_message2:

```
Hi,

This is a message from Harry.

Harry
```

He clearsigns it just as Tom did, with:

   # **gpg --clearsign auth_message2**

And the clearsigned message is now in the file auth_message2.asc:

```
-----BEGIN PGP SIGNED MESSAGE-----
Hash: SHA1

Hi,

This is a message from Harry.

Harry
-----BEGIN PGP SIGNATURE-----
Version: GnuPG v1.0.0 (GNU/Linux)
Comment: For info see http://www.gnupg.org

iD8DBQE382ZdcA/kAwBdmOoRAgpVAJ0VFNgR1/MF5NsgSkQ5OCMQYzWb5ACffDv/
+jc/le6xZ43fgiHEv0/S/bI=
=C1BB
-----END PGP SIGNATURE-----
```

When Dick receives this message and tries to verify it using:

   # **gpg --verify auth_message2.asc**

GnuPG displays this:

```
# gpg: Signature made Thu Sep 30 23:32:13 1999 EST using DSA key ID 005D98EA
# gpg: Can't check signature: public key not found
```

That's because Harry's public key isn't on Dick's key ring at all. The authentication fails.

# Encryption and Decryption with GnuPG

Now let's see how encryption works. Tom writes a secret message intended for Dick into a file secret_message:

```
Hi Dick,

This is a secret message.

Tom.
```

He then encrypts it with Dick's public key:

```
# gpg --encrypt --recipient Dick --armor secret_message
```

GnuPG puts it into the file secret_message.asc:

```
-----BEGIN PGP MESSAGE-----
Version: GnuPG v1.0.0 (GNU/Linux)
Comment: For info see http://www.gnupg.org

hQEOA9MD/YKKyaxTEAP+LK5E4bdZ14uf21NPSKGArGj2wo9ozaSY/mqud8LR4E/H
WWtzktf0Y2AHm87dxr7CdGKWmJbw77natZK/FRayIp90eFkqqcH8qaBCs9Xe1y9T
OIBGK73h1bM7NekQa1SgYogOHkA2db5khbL8a7wdrpfTJ8Pm40nMWnDNR8wK0MAD
/iVgiuzUIIwKtgIy+bUOdzIggtp28kcahpzwCLVpjXZ+QMEZTDgP/+BK+XqedYj0
WDtCrbrntTf6vsOk9t1tpMWUfWw9RG/Iujcu6hG6Ndj6M1KQJlU0z6fhUpozoT9B
qZhY7V+QOLnc4DbzZ7Iex38U+xuYtXEAR4e/I9gG7l5YyUj1hInui+v/XtK32aYZ
+5CTe7+4ispcshpylEMqUZluWHahxBUGdS2KqONu/sWSmEKMtJjr7/BQGaQx/q6f
gnpiBXbOgbZNN4I=
=gqS4
-----END PGP MESSAGE-----
```

As you can see, encryption, even with the ASCII armor option, does not reveal the contents of the message. It only makes the characters printable. Dick receives this message and decrypts it as follows:

```
# gpg --decrypt secret_message.asc
```

GnuPG prompts him for his pass phrase and then displays the contents of the message:

```
Hi Dick,

This is a secret message.

Tom.
```

Let's say Harry stumbles upon the file `secret_message.asc`. He knows Dick and even has Dick's public key in his key ring, but he doesn't have Dick's private key. Can he decrypt something intended for Dick's eyes only? He tries:

```
# gpg --decrypt secret_message.asc
```

This is what he sees:

```
gpg: encrypted with 1024-bit ELG-E key, ID 8AC9AC53, created 1999-09-30
     "Dick <dick@fictitious.address.com>"
gpg: no secret key for decryption available
gpg: decryption failed: secret key not available
```

Obviously, though GnuPG has Dick's details in the public key ring, this is not sufficient to decrypt the message, and the attempt fails.

# Building a Web of Trust

We know that Dick has signed Tom's public key in his own (Dick's) key-ring, so that messages signed by Tom with his secret key can be verified without any annoying warnings. Dick then decides to give Tom back his public key with his (Dick's) signature attached, so that Tom can then introduce himself independently to Dick's other friends. Since they have (and trust) Dick's public key, they will trust the contents of any message signed with Dick's private key. Tom's public key, when signed with Dick's private key, is the digital equivalent of Dick saying, "Hey guys, this is my friend Tom, and I assure you this is his public key."

Dick now extracts Tom's signed public key from his key ring:

```
# gpg --export --armor Tom > toms_signed_key.asc
```

Observe carefully the differences between Tom's public key as Tom gave it to Dick, and the new one with Dick's signature added.

The original `toms_key.asc`:

```
-----BEGIN PGP PUBLIC KEY BLOCK-----
Version: GnuPG v1.0.0 (GNU/Linux)
Comment: For info see http://www.gnupg.org

mQGiBDfyvLERBACAPSp4vM4OnWFhnqEeInUkGz3bpHqRJ7UA6yOCxCJwc5O4/xhy
O9t+IND+elBVL+XvxnGN0/E4/LHKqPUkwDL/T6uDhpstnnte/zl0k8qOCYXF1pqK
WjPxSdUPakBInhzHg3n/4JanduyObpub5L5NodlDP0JOwOIF9okAsphHnwCgob7I
Bsqgbwz/wt2BfssxZCaW71sD/2CabutBkawZNM/ETXGnEF3zRofrKVzmBplkfwOX
7b7pF6xfXuJ2n1u05SbMJQCLEjFAdRDHyL67wCxaaEq3mb+O3DJonsR7yM89cZL7
+7qDrcgDAR8K/6LltzpY1nQZbXdjbeM4mjhWJLhm3pyKFo+r8Wa9/GG6UjkNnhjU
BC7XA/0eo4WZjbt5P4qxFzxGJHxXne7yH+Wdq/3nChYE47jW22EqFQTjI2lUOk9H
xvVpkw/YKZNo7gOMxaWBqEeLKiW1VQISvx7ZPL5jzVzC2PSz9FQ7hSVJGOLf+U5S
mPST9b1+rL4eOeHr6m6wpgUH0fVToG2WzP+5bD+iUqdaRQ7Qy7QlVG9tIFVzZXIg
PHRvbUBmaWN0aXRpb3VzLmFkZHJlc3MuY29tPohVBBMRAgAVBQI38ryxAwsKAwMV
AwIDFgIBAheAAAoJEG4l3J4cwn1xF6MAn0/9GAwii9mDYhJRmqx9EAdjNU1IAJ9w
THD/ABDFoeXV7Hd7OwVllurM5LkBDQQ38ry5EAQAtp+l77nwySF8wvNWXTw+rNIY
e+xzrtvimmLOe0ZBNsKqAlTGTEr/GmpVv9RZufZZFl0teskY+6b8QGG/AnGm3/wL
UsvM48NY9rZx35X5RVMjOUIUZjTid7GlkvAZkFPpX2qOHOtiVzKn3maJmLg+/ijr
C4SDZ1+Zd+AVpUIdHJ8AAwUEAIxPNKtbglyktxbm5FX9nQlKFpuVpFKlEZLiWmo+
QIPz8BTHOcTG9qrCQvMQf5W0HOfIJa99HV506QMuMYN7wWteyzfkVlU54uKMZaM0
a3gx9Wyx8JV6vbC3HjDys7uj/jS2AANVjp3FEaeBztzYA6v3TPWt1tSXnxTx75c4
I+JCiEYEGBECAAYFAjfyvLkACgkQbiXcnhzCfXF3MgCfbelXiDqxAVVJC/TZjsJ5
TPLK1poAn2tZkQtBfuYa7ug20Bhd2O3h9R6J
=4qy+
```

The signed version `toms_signed_key.asc`:

```
-----BEGIN PGP PUBLIC KEY BLOCK-----
Version: GnuPG v1.0.0 (GNU/Linux)
Comment: For info see http://www.gnupg.org

mQGiBDfyvLERBACAPSp4vM4OnWFhnqEeInUkGz3bpHqRJ7UA6yOCxCJwc5O4/xhy
O9t+IND+elBVL+XvxnGN0/E4/LHKqPUkwDL/T6uDhpstnnte/zl0k8qOCYXF1pqK
WjPxSdUPakBInhzHg3n/4JanduyObpub5L5NodlDP0JOwOIF9okAsphHnwCgob7I
Bsqgbwz/wt2BfssxZCaW71sD/2CabutBkawZNM/ETXGnEF3zRofrKVzmBplkfwOX
7b7pF6xfXuJ2n1u05SbMJQCLEjFAdRDHyL67wCxaaEq3mb+O3DJonsR7yM89cZL7
+7qDrcgDAR8K/6LltzpY1nQZbXdjbeM4mjhWJLhm3pyKFo+r8Wa9/GG6UjkNnhjU
BC7XA/0eo4WZjbt5P4qxFzxGJHxXne7yH+Wdq/3nChYE47jW22EqFQTjI2lUOk9H
xvVpkw/YKZNo7gOMxaWBqEeLKiW1VQISvx7ZPL5jzVzC2PSz9FQ7hSVJGOLf+U5S
mPST9b1+rL4eOeHr6m6wpgUH0fVToG2WzP+5bD+iUqdaRQ7Qy7QlVG9tIFVzZXIg
PHRvbUBmaWN0aXRpb3VzLmFkZHJlc3MuY29tPohVBBMRAgAVBQI38ryxAwsKAwMV
AwIDFgIBAheAAAoJEG4l3J4cwn1xF6MAn0/9GAwii9mDYhJRmqx9EAdjNU1IAJ9w
THD/ABDFoeXV7Hd7OwVllurM5IhGBBARAgAGBQI384EbAAoJEKISueJQhfPDF8MA
n1c1VGIylBjKIFbW+389ErJ83CCYAJ9gd2EkWnif/dOb+4rlmVJpt4c2RLkBDQQ3
8ry5EAQAtp+l77nwySF8wvNWXTw+rNIYe+xzrtvimmLOe0ZBNsKqAlTGTEr/GmpV
v9RZufZZFl0teskY+6b8QGG/AnGm3/wLUsvM48NY9rZx35X5RVMjOUIUZjTid7Gl
kvAZkFPpX2qOHOtiVzKn3maJmLg+/ijrC4SDZ1+Zd+AVpUIdHJ8AAwUEAIxPNKtb
glyktxbm5FX9nQlKFpuVpFKlEZLiWmo+QIPz8BTHOcTG9qrCQvMQf5W0HOfIJa99
HV506QMuMYN7wWteyzfkVlU54uKMZaM0a3gx9Wyx8JV6vbC3HjDys7uj/jS2AANV
jp3FEaeBztzYA6v3TPWt1tSXnxTx75c4I+JCiEYEGBECAAYFAjfyvLkACgkQbiXc
nhzCfXF3MgCfbelXiDqxAVVJC/TZjsJ5TPLK1poAn2tZkQtBfuYa7ug20Bhd2O3h
9R6J
=P0pD
-----END PGP PUBLIC KEY BLOCK-----
```

Both are unintelligible of course, but a little examination will show that the last few lines have changed. The signed key is also a little longer than the original. Dick sends this file to Tom, and Tom imports his own public key just as he would anyone else's:

```
# gpg --import toms_signed_key.asc
```

When he next types:

```
# gpg --list-sigs
```

GnuPG displays an additional signature line under his public key:

```
pub   1024D/1CC27D71 1999-09-30 Tom User <tom@fictitious.address.com>
sig           1CC27D71 1999-09-30  Tom User <tom@fictitious.address.com>
sig           5085F3C3 1999-09-30  Dick User <dick@fictitious.address.com>
sub   1024g/3DF0858E 1999-09-30
sig           1CC27D71 1999-09-30  Tom User <tom@fictitious.address.com>
```

Tom can use the certificate file that Dick gave him, or generate one afresh using:

```
# gpg --export --armor > toms_signed_key.asc
```

This is his introduction to all of Dick's friends.

Meanwhile, Dick's other friend Harry has decided to trust Dick to introduce people and their public keys to him. He decides to update his opinion of Dick in his GnuPG database and register him as someone who can be trusted to introduce others. In addition to signing Dick's public key (just as Dick signed Tom's public key), he types:

```
# gpg --edit-key Dick
```

At the command prompt, types trust:

```
Command> trust
```

GnuPG displays Dick's details and asks Harry to what extent he is willing to trust Dick to correctly verify other users' keys. GnuPG will keep such trust information discreet and not let it form part of any output that is sent to other users, otherwise it could be responsible for some lost friendships! In our case, Harry says he is willing to trust Dick fully:

```
pub  1024D/5085F3C3  created: 1999-09-30 expires: never     trust: -/q
sub  1024g/8AC9AC53  created: 1999-09-30 expires: never
(1)  Dick User

Please decide how far you trust this user to correctly
verify other users' keys (by looking at passports,
checking fingerprints from different sources...)?
```

```
1 = Don't know
2 = I do NOT trust
3 = I trust marginally
4 = I trust fully
s = please show me more information
m = back to the main menu

Your decision? 4
```

At that, GnuPG displays Dick's updated records:

```
pub  1024D/5085F3C3  created: 1999-09-30 expires: never     trust: f/q
sub  1024g/8AC9AC53  created: 1999-09-30 expires: never
(1)  Dick User
```

Notice that the `trust` entry has changed from -/q to f/q. Some time after this, Harry receives e-mail from Tom introducing himself and attaching his public key signed by Dick (`toms_signed_key.asc`). Harry imports Tom's public key:

```
# gpg --import toms_signed_key.asc
```

Then, to check the signatures (certificates) in this public key ring, he types:

```
# gpg --list-sigs
```

This is what he sees:

```
/home/harry/.gnupg/pubring.gpg
------------------------------
pub  1024D/005D98EA 1999-09-30 Harry User <harry@fictitious.address.com>
sig       005D98EA 1999-09-30  Harry User <harry@fictitious.address.com>
sub  1024g/70A5A677 1999-09-30
sig       005D98EA 1999-09-30  Harry User <harry@fictitious.address.com>

pub  1024D/1CC27D71 1999-09-30 Tom User <tom@fictitious.address.com>
sig       1CC27D71 1999-09-30  Tom User <tom@fictitious.address.com>
sig       5085F3C3 1999-09-30  Dick User <dick@fictitious.address.com>
sub  1024g/3DF0858E 1999-09-30
sig       1CC27D71 1999-09-30  Tom User <tom@fictitious.address.com>

pub  1024D/5085F3C3 1999-09-30 Dick User <dick@fictitious.address.com>
sig       5085F3C3 1999-09-30  Dick User <dick@fictitious.address.com>
sig       005D98EA 1999-10-03  Harry User <harry@fictitious.address.com>
sub  1024g/8AC9AC53 1999-09-30
sig       5085F3C3 1999-09-30  Dick User <dick@fictitious.address.com>
```

As you can see, Dick's public key is vouched for by Harry himself, and Tom's signature is vouched for by Dick. Besides, Harry trusts Dick to vouch for other people's signatures, so GnuPG will now verify messages signed with Tom's private key without any fuss.

This is how you build a web of trust, using any OpenPGP-compliant public-key cryptography package. You do this by signing the public key of a person when you are sure it really belongs to him. This person can then introduce himself to your friends without your direct intervention, using the digital certificate that you have given him. Your friends will be able to trust the authenticity of this man's public key because of your certificate (his public key is signed using your private key, and they have your public key to verify it). After that, they can trust messages signed using his private key. As people vouch for the public keys of other people, it gradually builds a web of trust. PGP and GnuPG are therefore grassroots structures, whereas the system dominated by Verisign is a hierarchical one, with Verisign at the top and a long hierarchy of other certifying authorities all ultimately vouched for by Verisign. There are also other top-level certifying authorities, such as the current runner-up, Thawte Digital Certificate Services http://www.thawte.com. What a hierarchical scheme means is that everyone subscribing to that hierarchy trusts the top-level authority without question, and all others, directly or indirectly, derive their trust levels from that authority.

The web of trust and the hierarchy of trust are two different trust models, but they are not really as different as they seem. Both are valid implementations of what are called **PKI**, a **Public-Key Infrastructure**. As e-commerce becomes more widespread, the need for a PKI will increase. It remains to be seen which PKI model will ultimately win out, the grassroots web of trust, or the top-down hierarchy of trust, or whether they will continue to co-exist.

With this fairly lengthy introduction to cryptography and examples using GnuPG, we are in a comfortable position to understand the security underpinnings of most Internet-based systems today.

GnuPG page: http://www.gnupg.org

# Incorporating PGP/GnuPG into an E-mail Client

In general, it is not good policy to store one's secret keys on a multi-user system, because other users, and certainly the superuser, may have access to it. Always keep your secret keys on a floppy (with a backup), and keep both locked up when not in use.

With that in mind, let us look at integrating a PGP/GnuPG system with an e-mail client. We will first consider a graphical e-mail client and then a text-based one.

Incorporating PGP into the KMail e-mail client (part of KDE) is simplicity itself, though GnuPG isn't well supported yet. Assuming that PGP has already been set up, all that you need to do in KMail is select File | Settings and click on the PGP tab. Enter your PGP user name and save it. That's it.

The next time you open the composer to create a new mail message, you will find two additional icons enabled – a quill icon to sign your mail, and a key icon to encrypt it. If you press one or both of these buttons and leave them "selected", KMail will prompt you to sign and/or encrypt your mail when you are about to send it. Signing requires you to enter your pass phrase to unlock your secret key. Do not let your e-mail client store your passphrase, even if it seems convenient, because it's a security risk.

KMail looks for PGP, not for GnuPG, so defining a symbolic link pgp pointing to gpg does part of the trick. However, encrypting with a recipient's public key is still a problem. Signing with your own private key is, however, possible. Hopefully, GnuPG support will appear soon in KMail.

To incorporate GnuPG into a text-based e-mail client such as `pine`, you need to put the following lines into the `.pinerc` file:

```
display-filters=_LEADING("-----BEGIN PGP")_    /usr/local/bin/gpg  -

sending-filters=/usr/local/bin/gpg --armor --sign,
     /usr/local/bin/gpgencrypt.sh _RECIPIENTS_,
     /usr/local/bin/gpgsignencrypt.sh _RECIPIENTS_
```

Where `gpgencrypt.sh` is an executable file containing the lines:

```
#!/bin/sh
/usr/local/bin/gpg --armor -r `echo $* | sed 's/ / -r /g' ` --encrypt
```

*(Note that the characters immediately after "`sed`" are enclosed in single quotes and it means that all blanks between recipient names are substituted by " `-r` " (Don't omit the blanks around `-r`). That's because `gpg` wants the name of each recipient prefixed by a "`-r`". The `pine` variable "`_RECIPIENTS_`" lists all recipient names separated by blanks, which is why we need to do the substitution before passing the list to GnuPG. The "`echo`" and everything up to the "`--encrypt`" are enclosed in backquotes (`). This basically substitutes the output of the replacement in place within the outer `gpg` command, so that GnuPG can encrypt the message for all recipients.)*

The `gpgsignencrypt.sh` file is an executable file containing the lines:

```
#!/bin/sh
/usr/local/bin/gpg --armor -r `echo $* | sed 's/ / -r /g' ` --sign --encrypt
```

When you attempt to send a mail through `pine`, you will be prompted to choose one of the three send filters you have specified in the `.pinerc` file. Depending on which one you choose, `pine` will either sign the message with your secret key, encrypt the message with each recipient's public key, or do both. If you need to sign a message, you will of course be prompted for a pass phrase. When specifying encryption with multiple recipients, ensure that you have public keys for all of them, or the process will fail.

# SSL (Secure Sockets Layer)

SSL is a technology developed by Netscape to enable browsers and web servers to communicate securely, with both encryption and authentication. Encryption hides the actual data from prying eyes, and this is done through a single-key algorithm such as Triple-DES. The key used for the single-key encryption is generated once per session and then discarded. To get around the key management problem inherent in single-key systems, a public-key mechanism such as RSA or Diffie-Hellman is used. The client (browser) generates the session key that is used to encrypt all data, and it sends the session key to the server after encrypting it with the server's public key. Obviously, only the server has the corresponding private key, so no one else can determine the session key. If they can't get the session key, they can't break the messages traveling between client and server.

How does the client browser trust the server's public key? The server sends it down in the form of a certificate, which is nothing but a clearsign of the name of the server and its public key, using the secret key of a certifying authority. In most cases, this certifying authority is Verisign. All browsers come with the public key of Verisign (and other certifying authorities) built in, so those keys are trusted by default. The user doesn't have to do anything special to enable SSL. The process is quite transparent.

The actual sequence of messages is as follows:

❑ The client browser requests a connection with the web server. It sends a random challenge message to the server, the purpose of which we shall see very soon.

❑ The server sends back its certificate signed by Verisign, or another well-known certifying authority for whom the public keys are already built into the browser.

❑ One of the pieces of information in the certificate is the Internet domain name of the server. If that doesn't match the actual domain that the certificate was downloaded from, the browser pops up a warning, and the user has a chance to back away from that site.

❑ If the certificate is OK, the client generates a session key and sends it to the server after encrypting it with the public key of the server.

❑ If the server is the genuine article, it will have the corresponding private key and can therefore decrypt the session key. It then encrypts the challenge message sent to it in the first step using this session key (single-key encryption) and sends it back to the client.

❑ The client can decrypt the challenge because it was the one that generated the session key in the first place. If the decrypted challenge string matches what it sent, it means the server was able to decrypt the session key, and it could only do that if it had the private key. Obviously, the server can now be trusted, and a secure link is now established. All further communication is carried out using the session key with single-key encryption.

Even if the session key is ultimately cracked, it doesn't matter because a new one is generated for the next session.

## The Problem with Commercial Web Servers

The two leading commercial web servers, Microsoft's Internet Information Server (IIS) and Netscape's Enterprise Server (NES), both originate in the US and at time of writing are subject to US export control restrictions. Neither of them can provide strong encryption to users outside the US and Canada. The SSL that comes bundled with these servers is of diluted strength. Of the 128 bits used by the session key, 88 are sent in cleartext, and only 40 are encrypted by the server's public key. This effectively yields only 40-bit strength, because eavesdroppers can pick up 88 bits of the key.

# Apache-SSL

The shining exception to this mandated cryptographic weakness is the free Apache web server. Apache can also be downloaded from US sites, so it cannot legally provide strong cryptography. However, Apache is an open source product, so it is possible for people outside the US to patch it with cryptographic modules that will give it 128-bit strength SSL. A package known as OpenSSL is a free implementation of all the major cryptographic functions required by a public-key cryptosystem, such as signing, encryption, hashing, etc. A special Apache module called `mod_ssl` then integrates OpenSSL with Apache. When the modified source is recompiled, we get a 128-bit strength SSL web server, absolutely free, with no political restrictions attached. Of course, 40-bit browsers can only connect at 40-bit strength, so you might need to patch your browser to acquire 128-bit capability. That is available only for Netscape, from http://www.fortify.net.

## *Configuring Your Own Secure Web Server*

To install Apache with SSL capability, you need to download the following files in addition to Apache itself (`apache_1.3.9.tar.gz`):

❑   `mod_ssl-2.4.8-1.3.9.tar.gz`

❑   `openssl-0.9.4.tar.gz`

These are the latest versions at the time of writing, and can be obtained from the web sites www.modssl.org and www.openssl.org, respectively.

> **Details of installing Apache have already been provided in Chapter 5. However, if you want to add SSL support to your server, it must be recompiled and reinstalled using the following procedure:**

Decompress and extract the packages to `/usr/local/src`:

```
# tar xvfz mod_ssl-2.4.0-1.3.9.tar.gz
# tar xvfz openssl-0.9.4.tar.gz
```

Configure and build the OpenSSL library

```
# cd openssl-0.9.4
# sh config
# make
# cd ..
```

Configure Apache from `mod_ssl`'s configure script. This is the simplest way to do it, but this will not let you add more third-party Apache modules like `mod_php` and `mod_perl`. The `INSTALL` file included with `mod_ssl` details how to do that.

```
# cd mod_ssl-2.4.0-1.3.9
# ./configure --with-apache=../apache_1.3.9 --with-ssl=../openssl-0.9.4
--prefix=/usr/local/apache --enable-shared=ssl
# cd ..

# cd apache_1.3.9
# make
# make certificate
# make install
# cd ..
```

The `make certificate` step creates a trial, unsigned certificate after you fill in various details like your company name and country of origin. When it prompts you for a password, don't give it one yet as this is just for testing. Now try out Apache without SSL with the usual command `apachectl start`. Use the name of your host as it appears in the server certificate. After starting Apache in the normal way, type:

```
$ netscape http://<host-name>/
```

This should display the default `index.html` file that comes with Apache. Now stop Apache (with `apachectl stop`) and restart it with SSL enabled. Note that the syntax to start Apache with SSL is different from normal (`apachectl startssl`):

```
# apachectl startssl
$ netscape http://<host-name>/
$ netscape https://<host-name>/
```

You see the same `index.html` file, which is different from the usual, for both types of connections; but depending on whether you connect with HTTP or HTTPS, you will find that the lock icon at the bottom of the screen is either open or closed. The closed lock icon signifies a secure connection. If your browser supports 128-bit SSL, you will have a 128-bit SSL connection; otherwise the encryption will be of 40-bit strength. If you like, you can apply the Cryptozilla or Fortify patches to Netscape to get a 128-bit browser.

To get an official signed certificate, you need to visit Verisign's web site at: http://www.verisign.com/. Instructions on how to implement the certificates follow. Ensure that you have bought a domain name and are a registered business before applying for a certificate, and leave enough time between applying for your certificate and your site going live.

Firstly, fill in an on-line form at Verisign. Standard server certificates are available from: http://www.verisign.com/server/prd/s/index.html. *Global* certificates are available from: http://www.verisign.com/server/prd/g/index.html. Global certificates allow 40-bit browsers to step up to 128 bits, but are only issued to US companies and approved international financial institutions, so they are not available to everyone. You must first enter the exact domain name of your Web site and the exact name of your site's registered owner.

Now, either submit your DUNS (Dun & Bradstreet number) or mail/fax one of the following documents with a reference to your domain name:

❑ Articles of Incorporation

❑ Partnership Papers

❑ Business License

to Verisign's address:

```
Digital ID Center
VeriSign, Inc.
1390 Shorebird Way
Mountain View, CA 94043
United States of America

Fax: +1 (650) 961-8870
```

You then generate a private (secret) key and certificate signing request. Identify a file to use as a random seed for the key generation process. It could be any file at all, or even a number of files, and you just redirect its contents to a file called `random.seed`.

Generate a private key protected by a passphrase with the following command:

```
# ssleay genrsa -rand random.seed -des3 1024 > secret_key.pem
```

> **Note: Remember your passphrase. You will need it whenever you start up Apache.**

Back up your private key and store it safely. Do not send the private key to Verisign, or anyone else for that matter. Generate a Certificate Signing Request with the following command:

```
# ssleay req -new -key secret_key.pem -out csr.pem
```

`secret_key.pem` is the name of the file containing your secret key which you generated in the previous step, and `csr.pem` is the name of the output CSR file.

You will be prompted for the following information:

❑ Your two-character country code (e.g. *au* for Australia).

❑ The full name of your state or province. (e.g. *New South Wales*, not *NSW*).

❑ The name of your city, town, or locality.

❑ The name of your organization (The one that owns the domain name).

❑ The name of your unit within your organization (e.g. Marketing, Sales, MIS).

❑ Your common name (The fully qualified domain name of your site (e.g. www.mycompany.com). This must match the HTTPS URL that you are planning to use. It must also be a domain name that your organization owns.

Ignore any other attributes that you may be prompted for. The contents of `csr.pem` should look something like this:

```
-----BEGIN CERTIFICATE REQUEST-----
MIIBETCBvAIBADBXMQswCQYDVQQGEwJBVTETMBEGA1UECBMKU29tZS1TdGF0ZTEh
MB8GA1UEChMYSW50ZXJuZXQgV21kZ2l0cyBQdHkgTHRkMRAwDgYJKoZIhvcNAQkB
FgFgMFwwDQYJKoZIhvcNAQEBBQADSwAwSAJBAL6nPTy3avNgbubx+ESmD4LV1LQG
fcSh8nehEOIxGwmCPlrhTP87PaAOXvGpvRQUjCGStrlQsd8lcYVVkOaytNUCAwEA
AaAAMA0GCSqGSIb3DQEBBAUAA0EAXcMsa8eXgbG2ZhVyFkRVrI4vT8haN39/QJc9
BrRh2nOTKgfMcT9h+1Xx0wNRQ9/SIGV1y3+3abNiJmJBWnJ8Bg==
-----END CERTIFICATE REQUEST-----
```

Copy the entire contents of this CSR (including the `BEGIN CERTIFICATE REQUEST` and `END CERTIFICATE REQUEST` lines) and paste them into the enrollment form (No, there's no other way).

Fill out the application form with information about your organization and its contact people. Verisign will then send you a certificate, which could look like this:

```
-----BEGIN CERTIFICATE-----
JIEBSDSCEXoCHQEwLQMJSoZILvoNVQECSQAwcSETMRkOAMUTBhMuVrM
mIoAnBdNVBAoTF1JTQSBEYXRhIFNlY3VyaXR5LCBJbmMuMRwwGgYDVQ
QLExNQZXJzb25hIENlcnRpZmljYXRlMSQwIgYDVQQDExtPcGVuIElhc
mtldCBUZXN0IFNlcnZlciAxMTAwHhcNOTUwNzE5MjAyNzMwWhcNOTYw
NTE0MjAyOTEwWjBzMQswCQYDVQQGEwJVUzEgMB4GA1UEChMXU1NBIER
hdGEgU2VjdXJpdHksIEluYy4xHDAaBgNVBAsTE1BlcnNvbmEgQ2VydG
lmaWNhdGUxJDAiBgNVBAMTG09wZW4gTWFya2V0IFRlc3QgU2VydmVyI
DExMDBcMA0GCSqGSIb3DQEBAQUAA0sAMEgCQQDU/7lrgR6vkVNX40BA
q1poGdSmGkD1iN3sEPfSTGxNJXY58XH3JoZ4nrF7mIfvpghNi1taYim
vhbBPNqYe4yLPAgMBAAEwDQYJKoZIhvcNAQECBQADQQBqyCpws9EaAj
KKAefuNP+z+8NY8khckgyHN2LLpfhv+iP8m+bF66HNDUlFz8ZrVOu3W
QapgLPV90kIskNKXX3a
------END CERTIFICATE-----
```

Save this to a file called (say) `server.cert`. Add this lines to your apache configuration file `httpd.conf`:

```
SSLCertificateFile /path/to/certs/server.cert
SSLCertificateKeyFile /path/to/certs/secret_key.pem
```

Obviously, where `/path/to/certs` should be replaced by the actual path. Restart the server with `apachectl startssl`. You will be prompted for the passphrase. Enter it now.

Congratulations! Your Apache server is now not only capable of 128-bit SSL, but will provide this strong SSL without having the browser display warnings about unrecognized certificates. Of course, unless you have a Global Certificate, you will have 128-bit SSL only with 128-bit browsers (US domestic versions). To enable 128-bit SSL even with 40-bit (export) browsers, you can apply a patch from www.fortify.net, but this works only with Netscape Communicator.

### Resources

Apache server project homepage:
http://www.apache.org

OpenSSL homepage:
http://www.openssl.org

mod_ssl homepage:
http://www.modssl.org

# IPSec

Most security services provide encryption, authentication, etc. at the application level. For example, PGP and GnuPG provide security for e-mail; SSL provides security for web traffic, etc. However, it would be useful to have a common security layer irrespective of the type of application running on top. In other words, we need security at the IP (Internet Protocol) layer itself, the Network Layer.

IPSec (Internet Protocol Security) is an Internet standard that provides security based on public-key cryptography, and does this at the network layer (or more correctly, between the network and transport layers). Then all traffic above it is automatically protected. One of the modes in which IPSec is used is called **tunnel mode**. Each IP packet is encrypted and possibly also packed with authentication data, and the whole lot is wrapped up in another layer of IP. As far as the network is concerned, it's normal IP traffic, but the data in the payload is in fact encrypted.

IPSec is usually not an end-to-end security solution. It can however be implemented as a security solution between special gateways. Then it's only the two gateway machines that need to talk IPSec. Obviously, they need to exchange public keys, and then each one encrypts data by using a single-key algorithm such as Triple-DES in combination with a session key, which is sent across encrypted by the other machine's public key. Signing with a machine's private key authenticates the data, and the gateway at the other end can verify the signature because it has the sending server's public key. This should be familiar by now. It's the same set of concepts applied over and over. One's own private key for signing (authentication), and the other guy's public key for encryption (privacy), with hashing thrown in for message integrity, and a single-key encryption algorithm for faster encryption.

A system based on IPSec allows organizations to set up Virtual Private Networks (VPNs), because the entire communication between two LANs can be completely and transparently encrypted. Only the gateway machines need to be configured. The rest of the network doesn't even have to know!

# FreeS/WAN

Just as GnuPG provides a totally free implementation of public-key cryptography for personal use (usually for e-mail), the FreeS/WAN project has delivered an early version of an IPSec implementation that runs on Linux. It uses the tunneling mode of IPSec and needs to be set up only on gateway machines. Free software is now enabling VPNs in countries where current US export controls prevent the use of stronger cryptography. The FreeS/WAN homepage is http://www.xs4all.nl/~freeswan

All these examples go to show that the basic concepts of cryptography are very few and simple indeed. Once they are grasped, their application in a variety of different situations can be very easily understood. Open source and cryptography go well together because the best security systems are those that have undergone extensive peer review. Open source is built upon continuous peer review, and therefore squeezes out bugs faster. The quality of open source cryptographic software such as GnuPG, Apache-SSL and FreeS/WAN is making the Linux platform very attractive to organizations that need strong cryptography but are frustrated in their attempts by US export control restrictions.

Perhaps the best site for Linux-based cryptography products is the Munitions site hosted in Germany: http://munitions.vipul.net. Visit this site for legal access to all strong cryptography products for the Linux platform. You will find everything you need here.

# An IPSec-based VPN using FreeS/WAN on Linux

*This section is based on Kurt Seifried's excellent documentation at:*
*http://www.securityportal.com/lasg/*

To set up a VPN based on IPSec, the gateway machines need to have IPSec support built into the kernel itself. Currently, no US-based Linux distribution includes IPSec support in the kernel because of US cryptography export laws. So it is necessary to obtain the Linux kernel source code and FreeS/WAN separately, and compile the IPSec support into Linux yourself.

You will need four machines for this exercise. They will represent two organizations that wish to communicate securely over the Internet. Each organization has a machine on its internal network, and a gateway machine, which is connected to both the internal network and to the Internet. For simplicity, we can connect the two gateway machines together directly.

The network should look like this:

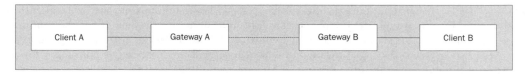

❑  Gateway A has its main Ethernet interface eth0 attached to the Internet and has the IP address 1.2.3.4. The other interface eth1 is attached to the internal network and has the private (Class A) IP address 10.0.0.1.

❑  Network A is the network behind Gateway A and consists of machines on the 10.0.0.* subnet (also denoted 10.0.0.0/24).

❑  Gateway B has its main Ethernet interface eth0 attached to the Internet and has the IP address 5.6.7.8. The other interface eth1 is attached to the internal network and has the private (Class C) IP address 192.168.0.1.

❑  Network B is the network 'behind' Gateway B and consists of machines on the 192.168.0.* subnet (192.168.0.0/24).

The broad steps to implement FreeS/WAN on this network are as follows:

❏ Obtain Linux kernel source code and compile it afresh, on the two connected gateway machines.

❏ Configure and restart the machines to check that they can communicate *without* FreeS/WAN.

❏ Recompile the kernels with FreeS/WAN.

❏ Configure the machines with new networking parameters.

❏ Restart the machines and test the VPN.

You can download the source code of the latest stable Linux kernel from your distribution CD or from http://www.kernel.org, and the latest stable version of FreeS/WAN from http://www.freeswan.org. It is best to follow the documentation that comes with the version of FreeS/WAN you download. What we describe here are the steps required for kernel 2.2.10 and FreeS/WAN 1.2 as documented at www.securityportal.com by Kurt Seifried.

## Compilation

Unpack the full Linux kernel source under /usr/src. Remove the existing symbolic link linux and recreate it to point to /usr/src/linux-2.2.10. Then configure the kernel, compile and install it. Use make bzImage, otherwise the kernel will fail to compile if it's too large (This is a kernel compilation problem, not a FreeS/WAN problem).

The steps to achieving this are as follows:

```
cd /usr/src/
rm linux
tar -zvvxf /path/to/tarball/linux-2.2.10.tar.gz
mv linux linux-2.2.10
chown -R root:root linux-2.2.10
ln -s linux-2.2.10 linux
cd linux
make menuconfig
make dep
make bzImage
make modules
make modules_install
cp /usr/src/linux/arch/i386/boot/bzImage /boot/vmlinuz-2.2.10
rm /boot/System.*
cp /usr/src/linux/System.map /boot/System.map
```

## *Configuration and Testing without FreeS/WAN*

Now check the Linux Loader (LILO) configuration file (`lilo.conf`) and ensure that it looks something like this:

```
boot=/dev/hda
map=/boot/map
install=/boot/boot.b
prompt
timeout=100
image=/boot/vmlinuz-2.2.10
label=linux
root=/dev/hda1
read-only
image=/boot/vmlinuz-2.2.5-12
label=linuxold
root=/dev/hda1
read-only
```

If you run LILO, the output should look like this:

```
linux *
linuxold
```

Some installations may say:

```
Adding linux
Adding linuxold
```

Now we need to edit the firewall rules on the two gateways, placing these lines at the end of the firewall script:

**Server A:**

```
# ipchains -P forward DENY
# ipchains -A forward -p all -j MASQ -s 10.0.0.0/24 -d 0.0.0.0/0
```

**Server B:**

```
# ipchains -P forward DENY
# ipchains -A forward -p all -j MASQ -s 192.168.0.0/24 -d 0.0.0.0/0
```

Next, enable packet forwarding by editing the file `/etc/sysconfig/network`, and replacing the line:

```
FORWARD_IPV4="no"
```

with the line:

```
FORWARD_IPV4="yes"
```

**334**

You should now be able to ping Gateway B from Network A (ping 5.6.7.8), and you should also be able to ping Gateway A from Network B (ping 1.2.3.4). If this does not work, something has gone wrong with the installation of the new kernel or the network configuration. Revisit the above steps and fix the problem before continuing with the FreeS/WAN installation. A possibility is that you haven't compiled the kernel to forward ICMP packets. It should be set up to do so, however that shouldn't be a problem. You can test if this is the case by attempting to connect to a service such as telnet or web – if the destination machine has a server running.

## Incorporating FreeS/WAN

Unpack FreeS/WAN into /usr/local/src or another convenient directory and run the install program by typing make menugo. This will patch the kernel files, run the kernel configuration, build the IPSec tools and rebuild the kernel. Actually, this command will fail at the last step (rebuilding the kernel) because it uses a make zImage and not a make bzImage, and the kernel is too large for this approach. But it's not a serious problem. You can either edit the Makefile or just run make bzImage yourself.

```
cd /usr/local/src/
tar -zvxf /path/to/tarball/snapshot.tar.gz
chown -R root:root freeswan*
cd freeswan*
make menugo

cd /usr/src/linux
make bzImage
cp /usr/src/linux/arch/i386/boot/bzImage /boot/vmlinuz-2.2.10-ipsec
```

Now once again edit lilo.conf, and see that it contains the following lines:

```
boot=/dev/hda
map=/boot/map
install=/boot/boot.b
prompt
timeout=100
image=/boot/vmlinuz-2.2.10-ipsec
label=linux-ipsec
root=/dev/hda1
read-only
image=/boot/vmlinuz-2.2.10
label=linux
root=/dev/hda1
read-only
```

When you next run LILO, you should see this output:

```
linux-ipsec *
linux
```

Now add /usr/local/lib/ipsec to your path. Then reboot. There will be a few errors, because IPSec is set up to use interface eth999 by default, which does not exist. Ignore these errors for now.

## Configuring with FreeS/WAN

Edit the `ipsec.conf` file. It contains the following lines:

```
conn sample
type=tunnel
# left security gateway (public-network address)
left=
# next hop to reach right
leftnexthop=
# subnet behind left (omit if there is no subnet)
leftsubnet=
# right s.g., subnet behind it, and next hop to reach left
right=
rightnexthop=
rightsubnet=
#
spibase=0x200
# (manual) encryption/authentication algorithm and parameters to it
esp=3des-md5-96
espenckey=
espauthkey=
```

You need to replace the `espenckey` and `espauthkey` values (encryption key and authentication key) with new keys (using `ranbits` to generate a number). The leading `0x` indicates that it is a hex number.

The `ipsec.conf` file would now look like this:

```
conn my-tunnel
type=tunnel
# left security gateway (public-network address)
left=1.2.3.4
# next hop to reach right
#
# Please note when the IPSec gateways are directly connected
# (i.e. neighbours) the rightnexthop and leftnexthop directives are
# completely optional. Including them is harmless however.
#
leftnexthop=5.6.7.8
# subnet behind left (omit if there is no subnet)
leftsubnet=10.0.0.0/24
# right s.g., subnet behind it, and next hop to reach left
right=5.6.7.8
#
# Please note when the IPSec gateways are directly connected
# (i.e. neighbours) the rightnexthop and leftnexthop directives are
# completely optional. Including them is harmless however.
#
rightnexthop=1.2.3.4
rightsubnet=192.168.0.0/24
#
```

```
spibase=0x200
# (manual) encryption/authentication algorithm and parameters to it
esp=3des-md5-96
espenckey=some_auth_key_here (ranbits 192)
espauthkey=some_other_key_here (ranbits 128)
```

Now copy the files `ipsec.conf` and `ipsec.secrets` from this machine to the other gateway securely.

*Options: (1) Physically transport information by hand on a floppy (not by post!). (2) Use PGP/GnuPG to send the data to the other end. (3) Use SSH to copy the files securely. (4) Build both machines in the same place and then (personally) transport one machine to the other site.*

Next add firewall rules so that packets do not get masqueraded (we simply want them forwarded).

On Gateway A, the firewall rules would look like this:

```
#
# FORWARD RULES
#
ipchains -P forward DENY
#
ipchains -A forward -p all -j ACCEPT -s 10.0.0.0/24 -d 192.168.0.0/24
ipchains -A forward -p all -j ACCEPT -s 192.168.0.0/24 -d 10.0.0.0/24
ipchains -A forward -p all -j MASQ -s 10.0.0.0/24 -d 0.0.0.0/0
```

On Gateway B, the rules would be:

```
#
# FORWARD RULES
#
ipchains -P forward DENY
#
ipchains -A forward -p all -j ACCEPT -s 192.168.0.0/24 -d 10.0.0.0/24
ipchains -A forward -p all -j ACCEPT -s 10.0.0.0/24 -d 192.168.0.0/24
ipchains -A forward -p all -j MASQ -s 192.168.0.0/24 -d 0.0.0.0/0
```

The forwarding rules should appear before the masquerading rule, as shown above.

## Testing the VPN

Now you should be able to bring up the `ipsec` tunnel on both machines manually and the machines on Network A should be able to talk to the machines on Network B with no problems.

Type:

```
# /usr/local/lib/ipsec/ipsec manual -up my-tunnel
```

on both Gateway machines.

The output will be like this:

```
/usr/local/lib/ipsec/spi: message size is 36
/usr/local/lib/ipsec/spi: message size is 132
/usr/local/lib/ipsec/spi: message size is 132
```

Try pinging 192.168.0.2 from the client on the 10.0.0.x network. If this works then you have set up your VPN correctly. Congratulations!

To set up such a network across the Internet, the `leftnexthop` and `rightnexthop` in the `ipsec.conf` file are no longer optional and must be given the right values.

# Summary

This chapter has detailed a number of cryptography products and how to obtain and use them. We started off with a description of how encryption and signing works. We then explained the GnuPG product, with its switches and options. After this we showed how it can be implemented into some mail clients. Using SSL with Apache was covered next, and we also showed you how to obtain a digitally signed certificate from Verisign and where to go to patch your browser to use 128 bit security. We ended with a description of how to set up a Virtual Private Network using IPSec, which could prove very useful to a number of organizations whose offices can only connect via the Internet.

You should now appreciate the value of cryptography and how it can be implemented with a strength that is so powerful, it should be hacker-proof for quite a while yet. Of course these tools are available for the Windows environment, created by different people, but you always suffer from the fact that you have to pay for licenses to use the products, and that in a commercial product, the security is likely to be only 40 or 56 bit strength.

# Appendix — The RSA and Diffie-Hellman algorithms

## The RSA Algorithm

The RSA algorithm is named after its creators – Rivest, Shamir and Adleman. It is a patented algorithm, but the patent expires on 20 September, 2000. The RSA logic for generating key-pairs is as follows:

1. Find two large primes $p$ and $q$.

2. Multiply the primes together to get their product $n$.

3. Choose a number $e$ that has no factors in common with the product $(p-1)(q-1)$.

4. Find another number $d$ such that $ed = 1 \bmod (p-1)(q-1)$.

5. Then the combination $\{n,e\}$ is the secret key, and the combination $\{n,d\}$ is the public key.

Looking at the relationship between $e$ and $d$, it is obvious that one cannot be derived from the other without finding $p$ and $q$ as well, but $p$ and $q$ cannot be obtained without factorizing $n$. The value of $n$ is of course known, because it is part of the public key, along with $d$, but the need to factorize it makes the entire exercise practically infeasible. Therefore, it is not possible to derive one key from the other. Plaintext P is encrypted to create ciphertext C. C is decrypted to create P.

```
P = C^e mod n
```

```
C = P^d mod n
```

This works because substituting for P in the second equation yields

```
C = (C^e mod n)^d mod n
```

```
= C^de mod n
```

i.e. `C = C mod n`, which is true if n is larger than C.

## The Diffie-Hellman Algorithm

The Diffie-Hellman algorithm is named after its inventors Whitfield Diffie and Martin Hellman. The patent on this algorithm expired on 6 September 1997, and that is why it is more popular than RSA today. The Diffie-Hellman algorithm is similar in purpose to RSA (key management), but is based on a very different mathematical premise.

1. Person A has a number $a$, which he transforms through a special algorithm into $a'$.

2. Similarly, person B has a number $b$, which he transforms using the same algorithm into $b'$.

3. Person A sends $a'$ to B.

4. Person B sends $b'$ to A.

5. Person A derives a key K by applying a special algorithm to $a$ and $b'$.

6. Person B derives a key K' by applying the same algorithm to $b$ and $a'$.

7. K and K' turn out to be the same!

So persons A and B have managed to agree on a single key without actually sending it across the untrusted channel. Note that an eavesdropper cannot generate K from $a'$ and $b'$, which are the only things he sees. (This scheme could be vulnerable to a so-called "man-in-the-middle attack", where an intruder interposes himself between the two parties and carries on conversations with both, impersonating each side to the other. In such a case, the "man in the middle" will end up sharing a key with A, and another key with B. He can decrypt everything that A sends, and re-encrypt it with the other key to send to B. A and B will be unable to tell that the channel has been compromised. Paradoxically, the best defense against this attack is openness. If A and B send the key components $a'$ and $b'$ through multiple public channels that are verifiable, instead of through a single secret channel that can be subverted, this kind of attack cannot occur.)

# 12

# Distributed Systems in the Linux Environment

## Introduction

The general concept of a distributed system is vague and discussions of the technology are often contentious. Everyone in the IT field generally has his or her own personal opinion of just exactly what a distributed system is and what it might be used for. Even though it is often the case that many of these opinions are divergent, it is also true that many of these opinions contain valuable insights into an ideal distributed system.

In this chapter, we will develop a simple definition of a distributed system which will also serve as a point of reference for further discussion. We will consider distributed systems in relation to classic single CPU systems and we will speculate on their future. Furthermore, we will discuss the types of distributed system that can be constructed with Linux and discuss their strengths and weaknesses. Finally, we will touch on other issues that will effect the function and operation of distributed systems including their strengths and weaknesses.

It should be noted that this chapter is not, nor could hope to be, a thorough discussion of all the relevant topics associated with distributed systems. Many key topics will be briefly discussed and other topics are beyond the scope of this book. It is up to the reader to research the topic further and to that end a bibliography has been included at the end of this chapter. It must be clearly understood that distributed systems technology is a very active area of research and hence is constantly improving. The installation of a distributed system is not as easy as just plugging in the cables and letting fly, it requires planning and perseverance. However, a well designed and implemented system is worth all the effort!

# The Concept of a Distributed System

Distributed systems have been with us for a very long time. In fact we can estimate their origins some hundreds of millions of years ago, in organic systems. Indeed, the simplest organic or biological system, such as an insect, can presently outperform any presently available silicon analogs.

The organic structures within a biological system do not have the communication or processing speed of silicon; but they can acquire, process, store, and retrieve data on a scale undreamed of by the most imaginative chip engineer. The fundamental nature of the performance of a biological system is due to **massive parallelism**, where every individual cell carries out its own function within the body as a whole. This behavior cannot be matched by our present silicon based technologies. This approach is used in not only neurological components like the brain or the optic nerve, but also for mechanical functions like muscle fiber in which individual muscles cells each pull at different times to produce a fluid and controlled muscle contraction. Again, this is all done through the use of billions of functionally weak cells which work together in ways that overcome their individual performance deficiencies. Biological organisms further illustrate the power of parallelism when considering problems with bodily function, such as what to do when the body is injured or is sick. Later on we will discuss what a similar problem might be for Linux based distributed systems, but for now bear in mind that capturing the full benefits of distributed systems and parallel processing depend strongly on the problems to which they are applied.

At this point, we have seen that nature has chosen to utilize distributed computing in order to solve problems that are well beyond the state of the art in the computing world. Furthermore, the human brain is an excellent model for distributed computing in that different portions of the brain specialize in different operations: vision, hearing, pattern recognition, systems repair, command control, etc. All of these components communicate with each other by passing data back and forth through a complex and highly integrated network, while allowing all components to operate independently of each other. Thus, providing a seamless interface that appears to the user as a single unit. This is the essence of distributed computing, to have a network of computers each doing what it does best and not interfering with its associates but contributing to the whole without the user being conscious of the operations.

# How Distributed Computing Helps

If we had unlimited resources we could just purchase new systems to meet the ever increasing performance requirements. Unfortunately, we face two limitations:

❑   A CPU's performance has an inherent limit – the speed of light

❑   Distributed systems can be costly to set up – financial resources are always limited.

IT professionals are always being asked to provide solutions for increasingly complex problems with limited resources. As stated previously, many of those problems fit the distributed processing paradigm. It is often the case that information from many different installations and applications feed into a centralized location which processes that information before redistributing it either back to the originator, or other client systems, or usually both. Historically, these systems use the client/server paradigm in which the bulk of the processing power takes place at the central location.

Unfortunately there is an inherent limitation on scalability with the traditional client/server concept. First of all, the more computing power that is required in the central location, the greater the cost. Second, concentrating all the processing on one machine could prove troublesome should that machine break down at any point. Finally there is always a limit on just how well a single central processor is able to perform. A decentralized or distributed system can make use of existing equipment, often with little or no additional resources in either hardware or software to achieve the superior results. This is because distributed systems push processing down onto the individual nodes, that is the individual components of a distributed system, while taking advantage of underutilized resources where they exist. When the low cost of individual PCs are factored in, distributed systems are simply much cheaper to acquire on a cost averaging basis, and the overall performance of the system is likely to increase as the performance of each additional node will increase over time.

What do we need to make this work? Arguably, the key starting point is determining what capability is needed to meet the present need – how many nodes will meet or exceed the required processing power, and in what configuration (RAM, mass storage, etc.). Next, we need to consider how the information is transferred; we need a means through which the systems can communicate with each other in a sufficiently efficient manner to make the system worth while. Finally, we have to have an operating system with sufficient power that it supports a truly distributed system. Of course, it would be helpful if there were specially developed applications for a distributed environment; such systems are at present rare, but generally there are workarounds as long as the applications are not too restrictive in a network environment.

# An Ideal Distributed System

This is what an ideal distributed system should look like. It would have the following characteristics:

❑ The primary requirement is that the *user does not know or need to know that he is on a distributed system*, hence he or she should not have to be at a dedicated terminal to use the system. This is actually rather challenging in a heterogeneous operating system environment hence the next point.

❑ The overall system should have a *consistent look and feel* independent of whether the users is at an active node or a dumb terminal.

❑ It should be *transparent*. This is sometimes referred to as a *virtual uniprocessor* or *single-system* image.

Frankly, the technology to achieve these things is simply not widely available yet, although great strides have been made in the last few years and it is reasonable to expect that within time all of these requirements will be achieved. For the moment though, the second and third are achievable as long as the following components are supported by the operating system:

❑ A common communication system so all processes on all processors can communicate with each other, even in a heterogeneous environment.

❑ System operations and environment must be consistent across all the nodes. This includes how processes and files are created and managed across all the systems. This essentially necessitates a single set of system calls, or a common protocol across all the nodes of the system.

The first requirement can be met reasonably well, as long as the operating system is consistent across all nodes or through the use of virtual machines. In this, and the next chapter we will discuss how this can be done using Linux.

# Definitions

At this point it is probably a good idea to introduce some definitions.

- ❑ **Network** – a collection of independent computers that are able to communicate with each other through some means.

- ❑ **Network Protocol** – a formal set of rules that govern how the computers communicate via a network.

- ❑ **Distributed System** – a network of independent computers which appear to the user of the system as a single computer

- ❑ **Cluster** – a subclass of distributed systems which are made up of similarly or identically configured computers.

- ❑ **Beowulf Cluster** – tightly integrated, set of Intel based nodes, running Linux, with multiple network communications pathways between the nodes in the cluster.

- ❑ **Parallel Computing** – the use of multiple processors, which are able to communicate through what ever means, to solve a single overarching problem.

- ❑ **Race Condition** – the situation in which the outcome of the running of two applications is not deterministic because it depends on which process is run first.

- ❑ **Concurrency** – when two or more copies exist of the same information and there is a potential for one to become out of sync with the other. This class of problems generally are found with stored files on hard drives, with file in memory (cached copies of other memory resident files) or a combination of the two.

- ❑ **Single Point of Failure** – this is the case where a single component or link will cause major disruptions for the entire network and distributed system.

- ❑ **Contention** – this is the situation in which two or more entities (processes or computers) want access to the same resource at the same time.

- ❑ **Hypercube** – a configuration of processors in which each processor is connected to every other processor within the system, that may be a simple connection so that a processor will have to pass communications requests through other processors to span the entire network of processors, or it may be a fully connected hypercube in which each processor is connected to every other processor. These systems are used primarily in Beowulf clusters and other tightly connected clusters.

- ❑ **Star Topology** – a network configuration in which a series of nodes all feed into a single hub, and the traffic from that hub feeds back to a central switch which distributes the traffic out to the other nodes through their respective hubs.

# The Advantages and Disadvantages of Distributed Systems

Everything in this world has strengths and weaknesses, and distributed systems are no different. The problem is that distributed systems, are an active area of research and arguments for and against distributed systems are shifting because of recent technological advances. This is compounded with the advent of Linux clusters since the extremely low entry costs of these systems has put them into the hands many more individuals. Nevertheless we will look at some of the more enduring issues.

## Advantages

The advantages of distributed systems can be divided into two categories: those over centralized mainframe systems and those over independent desktop PCs.

### Advantages over Centralized Mainframe Systems

#### Price and Performance

Historically the price to performance ratio has been governed by a single law first postulated by Herbert Grosch (a one-time IBM Vice President and subsequently the head of the U.S. Department of Commerce's National Bureau of Standards) that states:

> *Grosch's Law: The power of a CPU is proportional to the square of its price.*

Generally, what this means is that if you spend X dollars you get Y processing power, but if you spend 2X dollars you get 4Y processing power. The underlying concept of Grosch's Law is an economy of scale; the base cost of constructing a computer of power Y is actually most of the cost of constructing a machine of 4Y so if you want to upgrade to 4Y you have a scalable and predictable cost of 2X. This law held well for mainframes for years.

For workstations the law does not hold, because the increased point price associated with increased power could not be supported due to increased competition of the vendors. Mainframes are very expensive to design and manufacture using proprietary parts and software developed by the vendor. Workstations, on the other hand, are generally constructed in a facility that is substantially cheaper to construct and they are designed around components that are manufactured by a third party. This lower cost of entry leads to many more competitors, hence more downward pressure on prices, because the only hook a new competitor can use to gain market share is performance per unit cost.

The PC market has turned all of this into an art form. Major commodity PC vendors have literally been created in dormitory rooms (Dell) or renovated barns (Gateway) with equivalent components that were purchased in bulk from manufactures who were trying to gain market share or market dominance. In effect, Grosch's Law fails in the PC world because of its own underlying principle of economy of scale taken to an extreme. No vendor builds every single component of a system, hence they can easily change vendors or re-engineer their products in ways that are impossible for conventional mainframes or even workstations. Each manufacturer along the chain can only increase market share by increasing performance with respect to cost. Hence the base price of all entry level PCs is roughly constant, because of the unavoidable costs of the manufacture and distribution of the base product, while each year the performance of those systems increases. Higher priced systems only have marginally better performances with the costs increasing because CPU manufactures are trying to recoup their development costs as quickly as possible before a better chip is released. This scenario may change with the introduction of the Athlon chip by which AMD hopes to move from a low end processor manufacturer to a higher margin business quality machine. If AMD is successful we may see a shrinking in the margin between top performing processors and their entry level counterparts making PCs even more competitive with high performance workstations.

What does all this mean for clustered PCs running Linux? In general, the performance gain attained by moving from PCs to workstations to mainframes is negligible compared to the associated cost increases. With PCs and Linux you can attain a much finer grain control over your costs by matching the processor requirements more closely with your present needs and scaling up as required. This means that you can hold your capital in reserve and wait, secure in the knowledge that with each passing month, the base price of the processors you purchase will remain roughly stable while their performance will increase, hence maximizing you purchasing power and knowing that those new systems can be added into your existing cluster with ease.

## Portability

Many applications are, at their core, distributed. For example, most retail is inherently distributed by virtue of the fact that each store must keep track of its inventory even if it all comes from a central supplier or corporate warehouse. The central corporate headquarters will want to track sales trends, to identify which stores have a hot week, what products are particularly good in specific areas, as well as all personnel management issues that are common to all companies. In addition to the distributed nature of many problems, there is the fact that in the modern world, people tend to travel and work away from the office. With people traveling more and more, it becomes increasingly difficult to envision the fixed desktop computer as the principle computing tool that people will be working with in the future. This reality forces us to adopt models of distributed systems to allow people to work over great distances. Standard views of data and information consistent with traditional network configurations tend to fail under these circumstances, because among other things, you must deal with file concurrency issues, that is ensure that all files are kept consistent on all nodes of the system and any changes made are communicated to all systems. This is necessary in any network system even if you don't seek the full benefit of a distributed system.

## Reliability

Increased reliability is also a great advantage. When the mainframe is down, nothing gets done. Individual mainframe terminals do not have the computing power to perform many tasks, even assuming that the individual nodes would have the required files cached locally. This is not to say that distributed systems are immune from systems failure – far from it, but it does mean that in a reasonably well designed system, there is no single point of failure problem that plague most mainframe systems. One node within a distributed system going down is a problem for the user concerned. Fortunately, everyone else can work on, with perhaps only a slight degradation of overall system performance.

### Scalability

A particularly strong strategic advantage that distributed systems have over mainframes is scalability. It is theoretically possible for a system to start as a single machine and grow the system to tens of thousands with no disadvantage to the original system's user. Furthermore, if a company chooses a mainframe, it is likely that the company will at some point outgrow the system and it will essentially have to be thrown away. The reality is that often legacy mainframe hardware and software will not be compatible with the new system, essentially losing the value of the legacy equipment even if it still had some useful operational life.

Scalability, when combined with adaptability, is one of the real strengths of Linux in general. Linux is actually one of the only operating systems that can run on all of the major architectures available today, making it very unlikely that the evolution of technology will make Linux obsolete.

### Popularity of the PC

Finally, the major driving force behind distributed computing usurping the position presently handled by mainframes is the ubiquitous nature of the PC itself; they are essentially everywhere. These machines will be available and people will be using them. The users of PCs will want to communicate on joint projects, so they will need to be connected through a network, and over time, the network's capacity will be increased due to increased traffic. It is inevitable that people will want to work closely together without having technology get in the way, which will inevitably lead to a transparent distributed system.

## Advantages of A Distributed System over a Single PC

We can see how PCs could eventually lead to the death of the mainframe just as workstations did to the minicomputer, but why connect the PC into a distributed system? There are actually a significant number of arguments for building a distributed system within an existing network of desktop PCs and for building one from scratch.

### People Like To Communicate

People like to communicate; they need to share information, data, work product, all kinds of things that cannot be achieved by an isolated, non-networked PC. A networked environment is also ideal for using valuable, but infrequently employed resources like printers, scanners, etc. If we recognize that people will want to communicate via some electronic means (lets remember that at the time of writing, the bulk of Internet traffic is e-mail), then it is reasonable to assume that a networking infrastructure would be added to the existing PCs, even if a distributed system is not immediately envisioned. Unless the networking infrastructure is complete, it is likely that most, if not all, of the infrastructure for a distributed system will be in existence at no additional cost either in hardware or in network support.

### More Reliable, More Flexible

Distributed systems allow for greater flexibility and reliability. In a well designed system, the loss of an individual networked PC means that the user will only need to move to an unoccupied system to continue to work; this is in contrast with an isolated system in which a PC failure will likely shut that user down. Also, most hard drives on isolated PCs are never backed up, so the loss of work product and time due to a single failure might well be enough to justify the distributed system. In a distributed system it is easier to keep track of the status of individual PCs, to track utilization in order to make use of time, and to insure that hard drives are indeed maintained in a reasonable way. With the size of mass storage increasing so quickly, it is becoming an issue to maintain a backup methodology in consistent ways. It can be argued that a distributed system with multiple automatic backup to ultra high capacity storage locations such as RAIDs (Redundant Array of Inexpensive Disks) provide the only reasonable solution from perspective to the data loss problem faced by many organizations.

# Disadvantages

## *Software Availability*

A lack of software is the greatest obstacle that distributed systems presently face. Although there are some problems to be solved on the operating system side, the lack of application software that takes full advantage of the capabilities and strengths of distributed systems is the main challenge for Linux-based distributed systems. However, it is important to note that the this problem is being addressed by virtue of the proliferation of small and large scale distributed systems based on Linux.

Today there are many organizations, small and large, engaged in the development of software for distributed systems. Some of the applications will become commercially available, and others will be free. Because distributed systems are generally new to most organizations, we are currently working with the first generation of distributed applications. That is changing rapidly however; Microsoft has created DCOM which is really a foray into distributed computing, and incidentally has a flavor running on Linux bankrolled by Microsoft through another company – see Chapter 14 for more details. Remote Procedure Calls (RPCs) have long allowed a distributed system development capacity. Yet another technology is Common Object Request Broker Architecture (CORBA) which is intended to develop the basic technology required by applications developers to create distributed applications. With all the effort, it is likely that the lack of software for distributed systems will be short lived.

### *Network Saturation*

Network saturation is a headache that won't go away, whether you have a distributed system or not. Given that adding the additional traffic of a distributed system's overhead to an already brittle network is like having a migraine and then banging your head into a wall, you just make a bad situation worse.

Any additional strain caused by the distributed system's network traffic strongly depends on how the system is implemented. For example, a loosely connected virtual network running over a WAN will require much more security and reliability overhead than a set of nodes living on a tightly coupled LAN. On the LAN, it might well be possible to implement a distributed system using only portions of the network protocols, because of a reasonable expectation that most, if not all, packets will reach their destination – this is common in tightly coupled systems like Beowulf clusters. Whereas in the case of a WAN, that is not only impractical, but downright foolish – without a significant portion of the redundancy afforded by the complete protocol suite, information loss is inevitable.

It should be noted that the potential exists for network traffic to grow faster without a distributed system. This is because users tend to find ways to utilize a resource in ways that come as a complete surprise to system designers. Users may move files and information by a means that is logical to them, but which increase demands on the network by their nature.

Communications requirements never stop growing. During the last twenty years, US common carrier data transmission rates have increased two hundred fold, dedicated LAN speeds have increased even faster from 2.5 Mbps (Arcnet) to 1,200 Mbps (ATM) which is almost five hundred fold. All of this bounty has been consumed greedily by users with ever increasing demands for more as multimedia applications and web sites put ever increasing demands on bandwidth.

### Potentially More Bugs

To put it simply, something as complex as a distributed system or application is potentially a target for whole new classes of bugs and other problems that an independent PC just will not experience. For example, if the network were to be subject to spurious events through electric and electronic means, the interaction of those events with system hardware or application software might be difficult to predict, potentially causing unforeseen outcomes in systems that assume clean signals.

You might assume that this will inevitably mean more bugs than ever before. However that is not necessarily the case. A distributed system environment certainly places a high level of strain on the operating system, more than the most fragile of systems can withstand. However operating system design has become very advanced, certainly more advanced than PC operating systems of only a few year ago. With the development of more powerful software development tools as well as the advances in software engineering techniques that have already shown themselves able to dramatically reduce errors, the application developer will in all likelihood be able to hold the bug count to acceptable levels.

# Individual User Workstations

Regardless of whether a distributed system is implemented, users must be provided with a machine to work on. The exact nature and performance of these individual machines may vary depending on exactly how the overall system is configured. Nevertheless, there must be some machine for each user. Given this, there are some things to consider:

❑ Will faster chips buy you what you want?

❑ Are you getting maximum use of the existing systems?

❑ Are you going to make full use of the new systems?

❑ What are your short and long term needs?

❑ What is in your long term interest?

# Faster Chips

No single chip system can compete with a collection of CPUs that are able to work collectively to achieve the same goal as the single chip system. The old saying that "two heads are better than one" can be applied to the computer world as well. This reality has been recognized by the industry, which has begun to build multiprocessor systems using Symmetric Multi Processors (SMP) and helper chips such as video, audio, and I/O coprocessor chips.

There are limitations to performance which we can not overcome, the ultimate example being the speed of light. The maximum speed by which information can travel, and thus CPU speed, is the speed of light in the chip material. Let's assume we have a chip that can do say 10 MIPS (which is slow these days), that is $10^7$ operations per second, which is means the information has 0.0000001 sec to move across the chip. Remember, this is the maximum length information can travel per cycle, including memory, cache, CPU etc. Therefore, the chip cannot be any larger than 30 meters. Now 30 meters is huge and no technological challenge, but what if our performance requirements increase? The table below shows how the speed issue becomes a limit.

| Millions of Instructions Per Second (MIPS) | Seconds per Instruction | Maximum Information Path (meters) | Comparative Size |
|---|---|---|---|
| 10 | $10^{-7}$ | 30 | Small Building |
| 100 | $10^{-8}$ | 3 | Cubicle |
| 1000 | $10^{-9}$ | 0.3 | Dinner Plate |
| 10000 | $10^{-10}$ | 0.03 | Postage Stamp |
| 100000 | $10^{-11}$ | 0.003 | Pencil Eraser |
| 1000000 | $10^{-12}$ | 0.0003 | Pin Head |

We see that the physical size of a single CPU machine capable of 10,000 MIPs would require all information paths to fit within a space of a single postage stamp! Further, this performance is only a hundred times the performance of machines that are readily available today, yet the size would form a very significant technological problem. What is worse, is that these calculations use the speed of light in a vacuum. The speed of light will drop substantially depending on the materials the chips contain.

Having said that, it is likely that the performance of chips will continue to improve so that one day we may have desktop systems which near the maximum allowed performance. The next step will be machines with whole arrays of such CPUs, thus approaching the performance of mainframe super computers. This will essentially force the mainframes out of existence by leaving them without a niche.

None of this information should be taken as a reason to curtail investment in desktop systems. Although CPU performance is the ultimate limiting factor, other components of the system can have a dramatic effect on overall system performance. Over time, these other systems will become the focus of improving technologies. Essentially, even if the ultimate CPU were available, we would be periodically upgrading the systems to obtain more advanced support components, at least until all the components had reached their theoretical limits of performance.

# Low Utilization of Uni-Processor Systems

Historically, the initial cost of single processor machines is low and the price per performance has dropped since their introduction. With that fact firmly in place, most organizations have acquired systems for the majority of their personnel. However, most organizations rarely ask themselves how effectively they are using their computer resources.

Utilization is a complex factor to study, so we will stay with generalizations and suffer their inaccuracies. It is worth spending some time looking into this aspect of your problem, since it does have some bearing on the sizing of the resources need to solve the present problem, as well as provide some guidance of future development.

## Maximizing the Use of Existing Resources

In general, most desktop system cycles are lost. The majority of applications today are graphically and I/O intensive but this does not generally tax the resources of the CPU. It is also true that users view the performance of the system through the lens of the CPU's clock speed. Many systems are prematurely retired because of a mistaken belief that greater performance can only be achieved by acquiring a faster machine, when an upgrade in system resources (e.g. memory, hard drive performance, video subsystem) would produce greater results from the users stand point.

This means that:

❏ There are unused clock cycles going to waste on systems throughout every organization.

❏ There are capable antiquated systems that might be salvaged for reuse.

❏ Landfills are becoming clogged with millions of seemingly worthless computers.

It is also true that within any organization there are "power users" who challenge their system resources and would love to somehow recover those lost cycles, but they are the minority and might be the individuals you target for more frequent hardware upgrades.

## The Way Forward

You must decide whether to tailor the hardware acquisitions to users and hope their needs do not change too rapidly, or try and develop a system that will have the ability to accommodate all the users to some degree dynamically. Both approaches have their weaknesses and both have the potential for failure. But to be realistic, trying to constantly tailor each system to individual users needs is always a losing proposition.

Where does all this leave us? Firmly in the arena of distributed computing. With distributed systems you can approach full utilization in ways that are flexible enough to meet the ever-changing needs of virtually any organization. This flexibility has been accepted by many software and hardware manufactures and one in which Linux is particularly well positioned. Linux is one of the few available options (there is FreeBSD, Solaris and some other Unix flavors as well as NT), which is designed to be highly dynamic and flexible. With the possible exception of FreeBSD, Linux is the only one with such a rich supply of free or low cost tools as well as dedicated and knowledgeable individuals whose goal is the improvement of the operating systems itself.

# Flexibility of Application Movement

The ultimate dream of distributed systems is the automatic movement of processes to the most appropriate system, combined with some form of natural resource allocation that will make the best match between operations and systems.

Unfortunately the technology to fully achieve this does not exist at present. It takes a lot of knowledge about a process's lifetime resource needs in order to select which machine might be the most appropriate. It is usually difficult or impossible to do this, at least at the launch of an application, because those resource needs will generally change during execution. Alternatively, a process might request all its required resources at startup. This is difficult to imagine because it would essentially preclude any user interaction that would affect resource needs, which is far too restrictive.

However, all is not lost, because resource intensive applications will generally run for a sufficient length of time to be swapped out, which will enable a resource monitoring device to gather data on the behavior of the process. By tracking this behavior, it should be possible to implement an automatic process allocation scheme that uses the information to move processes based on their actual behavior rather than some anticipated activity. Don't lose hope though, this is a very active area of research and some significant advances are on the horizon.

# Determining System Requirements

There are a number of decisions that have to be made in order to build a distributed system. There is no way to create a 'one size fits all' solution, or even a set of solutions that will answer all the questions that will be asked. Every distributed system will be different and each topic has to be considered separately.

If you know what components you are considering for your distributed system, then you might just skim this section. It is intended to assist those who have to deal with others who will be impacted by the decision to move to a distributed system, although there might be some tidbit that will be of general interest as well. So take this section for what it is, background information mixed with advice. If you don't want it, move on to the next section.

## Create a Plan

It is important to keep in mind both the short and long-term goals of the project, in order to know when we have strayed from the original objectives. Or perhaps more importantly, to know when we have achieved the project goals. If you spend some time evaluating some of these questions and then creating a working plan for the systems development, then you will be happier with the results:

❏ Who is the system for?

❏ What will the system be asked to do?

❏ What are the short term goals?

❏ What are the long term goals?

❏ Are the long term goals the same as the short term goals?

❏ Do you have a clear picture of what you want the system to evolve into?

Your plan or vision should answer all of these questions, at least in general terms. Evaluate what resources are available for you now, and those you might need in the future, and leave some room for future unrecognized needs. Once you have that, you should be able to develop a road map on how to proceed with a distributed system project. We will see some of this in the discussion of the case studies in the next chapter. The plan will guide you and help you determine whether the problems you encounter are due to the addition of new stresses into your computer systems or there were problems there initially that were being overlooked. Either way, knowing where you are and where you want to go is crucial.

Finally, a word of caution concerning over-exuberance. Keep in mind that there is an inherent danger with any new technology. As computer professionals, we love the technology we work with. Because of this, there is always the danger that we are rationalizing our users needs in such a way as to allow us to play with new technology. Let's face it, a truly distributed system is the essence of what we have all dreamed about – computers being powerful, robust, transparent, and effortless. Presently, distributed systems are some, but not all, of these things, and it is only realistic to say that they may not be for everyone – well not just yet. It is very important that you keep your objectives in mind when deciding on how to proceed.

## Which Architecture to Use

This is a relatively limited choice, but it is important to at least have some feel for what options are theoretically available before we recognize the limitations we face. There are four different architectures that have been described for computers in general:

- ❏ **Single Instruction Stream - Single Data Stream (SISD)**: This is the classical von Neumann machine. This architecture is made up of a single processor with a single source of instructions and a single source of data. This is the traditional architecture for machines from mainframes to PCs

- ❏ **Single Instruction Stream - Multiple Data Streams (SIMD)**: This machine is made up of a single source of instruction feeding multiple processors. Such systems generally have a processor that controls the single instruction stream. The control processor feeds each instruction, from the instruction stream, to each member of the group of processors. Each processor will execute the instruction on their respective data sets. These machines are most useful for situations that would repeat the same operation on independent data objects such as identical operations on groups of vectors.

- ❏ **Multiple Instruction Streams - Single Data Stream (MISD)**: This is an architecture that has, to the authors knowledge, never been implemented. An MISD machine would require multiple instructions to be performed by a single processor.

- ❏ **Multiple Instruction Streams - Multiple Data Streams (MIMD)**: A MIMD system is made up of multiple independent asynchronous processors each able to execute their own applications at their own pace on their own data.

Given these definitions, distributed systems built around independent computers fall naturally into the MIMD camp. There are development efforts to create tools that will simulate a shared memory system (SIMD) architecture over a network. This has certain advantages in programming, but would potentially have performance issues associated with significantly higher communications overhead. The difficulty in synchronizing the processors so that operations would potentially be coordinated is a very great challenge. A further challenge is to ensure that race conditions or memory concurrency problems are avoided.

There are two ways to implement MIMD. The first is shared memory where processors are physically located with direct access to the same pool of memory that every other processor has access to, and distributed memory where each processor has its own memory and both live on some sort of communications medium like a network.

### Shared Memory MIMD

There are two architectures in shared memory (MIMD) systems:

❑ **Bus-Based Architecture**: The various CPUs are independent from the overall system memory modules. They are connected to the memory by a system bus with address, control, and data lines. This is a simple solution to implement, but bus contention strongly limits processor numbers. Contention for file access can be handled by local caching of memory.

❑ **Switch-Based Architecture**: The CPUs are connected to memory by a matrix of lines and switches. Through the switches, each CPU can reach any memory module through a dedicated line controlled by a single switch. The downside is the number and control of the switches. For M CPUs and N memory modules you need M*N switches which grows very quickly.

### Distributed Memory MIMD

There are two architectures in the distributed memory (MIMD) systems:

❑ **Static Network**: The independent CPUs are connected through a series of dedicated connections which allow for low communication latency and efficient transmission of data. The difficulty is the cost of so many connections.

❑ **Dynamic Network**: The independent CPUs are connected through a series of dynamically configured connections.

In the end, it is clear that a distributed system made up of independent machines which communicate over some sort medium must essentially be a Distributed Memory Multiple Instruction Streams - Multiple Data Stream (MIMD-DM).

## The Objective of the Distributed System

At this point we have some idea what our architectural options are, for the kind of distributed system we could build, but a vital question that has to be answered is what to do with the system once it is in place.

Keep your users in mind, they tend to be a nervous lot. There will be resistance if you do not carefully define and clearly illustrate the objectives of the effort and show the organization how it will benefit. On the other hand, if you are developing a system for a specific, clearly defined purpose that will have only marginal effect on others, you still need your plan.

## The Type of Distributed System that Meets your Needs

Generally speaking, this is usually clear from the outset if you know what type of problem you are going to be working with. Under Linux, you have three variations on the same theme:

❑ **Distributed System** – a general configuration that is loosely coupled over a general use network. Will have users at most nodes.

❑ **Cluster System** – a specialized system that is intended to focus on a single problem, the systems may or may not be identical and they may or may not communicate over a dedicated network. For example, this might be to act as a series of backup servers for a database. They may have a few users at terminals.

❏ **Parallel System** – a purpose built, highly integrated system that has a narrowly focused purpose. Generally these systems are made up of identical CPUs interconnected over a dedicated high bandwidth network that may have a simple bus or star topology or something as complex as a hypercube. This system is generally a sort of computer server providing a very limited and focused resource to the wider world through a single node.

## Resource Control

One of the key issues to be faced when planning a distributed system is who will actually control its resources.

Users who have control over resources feel very uneasy, to say the least, at the prospect of losing control of their resources. That means that if you need those resources you are going to have to go and find them. Start with a detailed survey of who has *physical* and *psychological* control of the systems and the various resources will be required in order to make the new system successful.

Always keep in mind that the system is only as good as the happiness level of the users. If you alienate your users, then the system will be a failure from the outset – the opinions and feelings of your users are important.

### Decentralized Control

If control is decentralized, it generally will mean that the local user has some significant control of the resources you are going to need. That could mean anything from keeping a copy of every single file the user has ever had cross his or her desktop, to aggressively deleting unrecognized files, or even remotely shutting the system down without thought of whose might also be using it.

### Centralized Control

If the system is centralized, you may not be better off unless you control the resources yourself. If you don't own the resources, check with the owner whether you can use them, or better yet assume responsibility for the resources. A great selling point is that centralized systems can be hard to maintain, and distributed systems have the capacity to improve maintenance by allowing more automatic support and by providing greater reliability, as we have already said.

Another question that might be asked is whether the centralized system is really needed in its current form. Why was it centralized in the first place? Are those reasons still valid in a distributed system or would those resources be better utilized in another way?

## Determining the Resource Utilization of the Present System

To successfully implement a distributed system, you need some understanding of how the resources are presently being used. This should be more than a cursory understanding, but a thorough survey of resource utilization. While this feedback might be helpful, and can give some degree of insight into resource use, hard numbers are better. You should endeavor to obtain some firm estimates on hard disk usage, mass storage, memory requirements, printer usage, network load – both Internet and intranet, and anything else you can find. You might have to do some research for a number of these points, depending on the type of setup you have and the tools available.

## Network Utilization

The most important data you will need to have available is network utilization. This data is so important, that you might well be served by spending some money here.

First, you will need a copy of your network topology map of your present system, your network administrator will have one if you don't. If he or she does not then convince them create one. If you are lucky, you will find that your present topology will serve the future system well, but more likely, you will find a need to make modifications to the topology and that will mean both physical and logical changes. If you are rather unlucky, you will have to make substantial modifications just to begin the process of building a distributed system. Network design is beyond the scope of this book, so we will not go into it here, but the primary focus is to try and isolate generators of large amounts of short distance traffic from the general users. The whole objective being to try and minimize network traffic in order to optimize bandwidth.

Next, you will need to try and get a handle on the level of traffic that the network presently supports. That can be done only through some sort of network monitor, placed at various point throughout the network based on possible choke points from the topology map. The choke points are generally things like routers, switches, concentrators of any kind, and often servers and specific nodes that generate or process large amounts of traffic. To get some idea of the expected network traffic, you can use a **sniffer**. A dedicated sniffer is a machine whose sole purpose is to watch packets go by, determine what type they are, and keep a log. With this sort of information, you can determine the overall network bandwidth utilization and determine what the predominant packet type, and hopefully, the source of those packets. Dedicated sniffers are rather expensive ($5,000 to $20,000 depending on what features it contains), but you can build a simple sniffer by loading one of several software packages onto a Linux box. The box does the same thing as a dedicated sniffer with a few performance issues that are generally not of great interest to the general user. You might want to try a software solution before you invest in a dedicated sniffer. Sometimes difficult network problems can only be discovered by specialized equipment like continuity testers and dedicated sniffers.

## Network Saturation

If you intend to use an existing network, you need to know how close you are to saturation of the network. Saturation really depends on the method and media of transmitting the information. For example, it is commonly held that Ethernet 10Base2/T will support 10 million bits per second (Mbps); this is purely fiction. Ethernet generally reaches saturation at 30% of the maximum theoretical performance. Hence, you are going to start having trouble with Ethernet if your utilization is over 3 Mbps. By contrast, token ring can approach 100% efficiency under heavy load at 16 Mbps. Research the kind of network you are using to determine just how close you are and what you can do about it within that system.

## CPU Utilization

The next question is CPU utilization. That is harder to determine, but there are applications that will monitor utilization and provide feedback to a central location for logging. These applications are only good for a rough guess, but they will give you some idea of the situation.

A detailed survey of all of the other resources that are presently in use will help you determine where they will fit into your plan. Take note that this survey, and subsequent modification of the plan, might well be the most difficult part of the design process. You do not want to jeopardize the operations by accidentally placing resources out of the reach of the users.

## Scaling to Fit

Here we are trying to focus on exactly what sort of problem you are trying to solve. Is this problem going to require many CPUs, much memory on each node, lots of fast hard drives, or all of the above? You have to consider a couple of points along the way, generally most problems fall into two scenarios:

❏ You know the exact application that you are trying to accommodate, which means that you should have some information on the resource requirements that will be involved. You will hopefully have had some hands-on experience with the application, but if not, you should try and find someone who has. Failing either of these, go over the documentation and your needs to try and make some educated guesses as to what you will need.

❏ You do not know the exact application that you are trying to accommodate and you are trying to build a general system that will more fully utilize present and future resources.

### A Specific Application

There are aspects of distributed systems that will strongly effect the type of problems that can be solved. Consequently you must have a clear understanding of the particular problem, not only what it does but also how it does it. The issue is that some applications will perform better with fewer processors than with more. This might make sense if you consider how distributed applications achieve their performance improvement. Generally, given a fixed data set, the total processing time for a particular problem is fixed. If we then break the problem up and disperse it to N processors you will have at least 2 * N communication steps – out and back. Now if the total processing time was M then each processor will be asked to do M / N of that work. If the total communications time per node is $e$ then as N increases M / N will approach $e$:

```
Calculation time/node = M/N + e υ e as N increases
```

> $e$ **is actually a combination of several factors including latency and the time required to process and transfer whatever information is required to a first approximation; it is a constant generally dominated by latency.**

Once the time per node approaches $e$ then you have reached the point of diminishing returns and further nodes will actually increase the time the overall computation will take.

Now that is all well and good, but what if you don't know anything about the communications of the application? That makes life more complicated, but not terribly so. It means that you have to do some research. You have to contact the developer or vendor of the application you're working with to see how the communications resources were allocated, and if you are lucky, you can determine if they have benchmarked the application on multiple processors and get that information. After all this, it is still largely up to your experience to optimize the operations of the system because your particular setup may be sufficiently different from others that your value of $e$ is very different from others. For example, if your application is doing lots of small communication tasks, then latency will dominate your value of $e$, hence you might wish to chose a lower bandwidth communication medium with smaller latency (serial port to serial port) over one with high data transfer rate, but much longer latency (Ethernet). The reverse situation would hold if you do fewer communication operations but transfer lots of data in the process, for example image processing for animation.

### A General Application

In this situation you are building the system to meet general needs and to improve overall reliability and resource utilization. If that is the goal of the system, then there are really very few ground rules to follow other than to prioritize your goals since you will probably find your goals will conflict with others and you will probably end up optimizing for your top priority objectives.

# Components of a Distributed System

There are several different types of components that might be brought into play in designing and building distributed systems. The core components will be discussed in the next few sections, but it is important to take into account other components may well be included in the system or introduced later. Things like input/output devices like scanners, printers, plotters, CCD cameras, video capture, and network devices like routers, bridges, firewalls, as well as all kinds of toys that we don't have yet will have an effect on your systems performance and you will have to include provisions in your design. However, the fundamental parts of a distributed system are made up of just a few key components: CPUs, a communication network, an operation system and software that can be used in a distributed environment.

# Key Components

These are the components that you have to have in order to build even the most rudimentary distributed system. Bear in mind that they are not all created equal, but they all do have fundamental affects on the performance of the complete system. The quality of hardware varies from manufacturer to manufacture. For example one vendor's 100BaseTX switching hub might work well for the office, but might not have enough internal bandwidth to support the traffic a highly integrated Beowulf cluster would put on it. Another example is that some motherboard vendors skimp on memory subsystem components to save a few dollars, which can have a profound affect on the motherboard's overall performance. Also, some versions of BIOS are have more problems with bugs than others. Stay with reputable vendors with good reputations and product reviews by real people (www.tomshardware.com is a great source of news, as well as www.overclockers.com for extreme workouts) and try and get as much information from the vendor as possible in order to research whether the components will be supported. Alternatively you could buy turnkey components.

### CPUs and Their Hardware

Of course this is the component that gets everything done. Without the CPU there is nothing to do but try and figure out why you bought all the other stuff. When discussing the CPU, we actually refer to the memory, BIOS, support chips including the cache, DMA controller, integrated storage controller, and ALU/FPU chip.

Each one of these components can have a very significant effect on the operations of the CPU and the overall system. The memory subsystem within the CPU is one of the most critical components of the system. For example, I am writing this on a Micron Millennia Mxe which has an excellent memory subsystem and has consistently benchmarked competitively with other 233 MHz machines. The actual performance difference was very noticeable when comparing general use with memory-intensive operations. Another example is that some motherboards do not implement complete cache for all the memory they are able to support. Consequently, there is a limit to performance improvement on certain boards based on the main memory to cache memory ratio.

In general, you will need to keep a careful eye on hardware compatibility no matter what operating system you select. This is because certain CPU chipsets are more reliable than others. As stated previously, the memory system may well be inferior, or the BIOS may well have bad habits that will cause you much trouble over time. Depending on which category you fall into, you may have more flexibility than others; conversely you should try to match your hardware requirements with those of the various Linux providers. This seems obvious but this is procedure is often overlooked and the outcome can be very frustrating. The best advice is to try and get some feedback from your Linux vendor and the relevant news groups to help you make your decisions on the architecture of the CPUs and the motherboard vendors

## Communication

If the cumulative CPUs are the brain cells, then the network is the central nervous system. Each of the nodes needs to communicate effectively and efficiently with each of the other nodes within the distributed system.

Beyond this, the communications system must be efficient and reliable. There is a certain amount of performance overhead associated with the communication between nodes in order to do distributed computing. This added traffic coordinates operations and passes information between processes and is required to make distributed applications run. It would be helpful if the applications' communication properties were known in advance in order to optimize the communications system for a particular project. On the other hand, if you do not know exactly what problems need to be addressed, then by all means go for the least expensive solution that provides the most bandwidth with the least latency you can afford.

## Operating System

Linux is particularly well suited for distributed system applications. Beyond a theoretical capability, Linux has a proven track record of deployment in very large clusters, hundreds and even thousands of CPUs running Linux in clusters all over the world. This real world success is impressive and should not be ignored

Keep in mind that there is no restriction on the number or type of communications methods that are used within your Linux cluster. For example, you might start with a traditional Ethernet network routed through a conventional hub. Then, you might augment the network later by adding multi-port Ethernet network cards that may be configured for point-to-point communications between nodes to simulate a hypercube configuration. Finally, if it is determined that the latency is too great, one could add a PAPERS serial port communication system (http://garage.ecn.purdue.edu/~papers). All of these communication systems can live together, each supporting different classes of problems thereby increasing the overall flexibility of the cluster.

## Applications Capable of Utilizing Multiple Processors

Applications that are specifically designed to take full advantage of distributed systems are relatively rare at the moment. There are a significant number of specialized applications which have been developed to capitalize on distributed systems, and most of these applications have been developed for dedicated or purpose built parallel systems for complex problems like weather prediction. This is not to say that there are no truly distributed system capable applications. There are several efforts to develop free applications for image processing, ray tracing image generators, numerical processing systems for modeling of all kinds, and lots more. In fact, there are several existing development models like Message Passing Interface and the older Parallel Virtual Machine as well as other industry standard technologies like CORBA.

### Application and Resource Utilization

Recognizing the limited number of truly distributed system applications, does not mean that distributed will not provide you any benefit. Neither does it mean that your present applications will not work for you. In fact, you will often improve the overall system performance, usability, and reliability by implementing a distributed system while running software that was originally designed for isolated systems.

Suppose you have a legacy word processor that your organization has been using for quite some time. One day you find that you need to upgrade that system and you send out an email asking the users to indicate who has the product, the version of the product and where the product is located. Unfortunately we all know that will be a failure. Users are busy, they don't receive or do not read e-mail, or simply may not have any idea how to answer the question. In a distributed system, you can build a common environment with access to common resources and software packages that you can control and upgrade as needed. You can set each system up so that no matter which terminal a user is using, he will have access to all his own files and applications, as well as proprietary resources, and do this in a transparent way. You simply cannot do that on isolated machines or those that simply have access to shared resources, because the user will need to know to much about the system to make it transparent.

Now, some of you might be saying that you can do all this with NIS, NFS and Samba. Well, the truth is, that these will be part of a Linux-based distributed system foundation, so if you already have them up and running, then so much the better. If not, well you had better start reading your man pages because you will be.

Finally, we are starting to see emulation and low-level virtual machines that will allow you to use legacy software on Linux systems. With each passing month these products become more viable and imaginative. It is true that you will probably not be able to run your favorite game on the Linux Windows emulator, but it is only a matter of time before there is a Linux version of all of them. Let's face it, software makers are nothing if not pragmatic. It is an odds on bet that once Linux is up to the same market share as Apple, we will see products for Linux being produced.

# Other Factors to be Considered

Now let us briefly discuss some of the other important factors that must be considered when planning a distributed system, such as concurrency, storage space, centralization and others. First however, there is more to say on communications.

## More on Communications

As we have seen, communication is critical to making the system work. The operations of the proposed or existing applications must be studied in order to determine what specific needs they have and what strain they will place on an existing system. Particular attention must be paid to the communications arena. The initiation, maintenance and operation of a single connection can be time consuming. For example Ethernet systems can take 100 milliseconds just to initiate a single connection which may pass only on mere kilobytes of data. One must keep that in mind and work diligently to match the communications with the problem.

## Concurrency

At the moment, implementing efficient concurrency is a major technological problem in the computing world, with relatively few solutions. Generally speaking, file locking is a solution in limited sized systems, but is the most widely available.

The technology of concurrency is improving, and with any luck we will find some sort of solution that will not adversely effect the performance of the system. If you have a large number of people working on the same projects or components at the same time, you are going to run into concurrency problems and you might as well start thinking about it early.

## Avoid Over-Centralization

The problem with over-centralization is that it has the potential of creating a point of failure weakness in your system. It has been said that distributed systems are defined as a system on which, 'no work can be done since an unknown server has just gone down'. Don't get yourself into that situation. You will need servers (NDS, NFS and NIS and potentially others) so you should always create and maintain backup servers even if you only have a couple of systems, same goes for all the other potential points of failure.

## Storage Space

Do you have enough storage space? If you say yes, you are probably wrong. Users have a way of consuming storage well beyond any reasonable scaling factor. It is a reasonable request for the system administrator to ask people to conserve space on the system, that is, until the cost of storage became roughly that of tissue paper.

### Fear and Terror

It is important to keep in mind, that the users of the system are transitioning with the system. Their level of anxiety is higher because they don't really know what is going on. You, as the IT guru, will have more control of the operation, more understanding of its status and you will see the light at the end of the tunnel and know that it is not a train. Your users don't have any of these luxuries. Even if you provide them with updates regularly they will not necessarily believe you. Be prepared for a significant amount of skepticism born form previous experience. You can make use of the design and implementation plan you created. One suggestion would be to publish it in layman's terms on the organization's intranet.

## Hardware Considerations

It should be clear that the quality and type of hardware is important to the success of a distributed system project. We have seen that communications are the most important overall component, but the other components reliability and compatibility is also an issue. Bear in mind that if you are trying to cobble together systems you saved from the dumpster before breakfast, don't expect to be doing computational fluid dynamics by lunch.

### Vendor Support of Parallel Systems

There is a growing number of companies providing turn key solutions of distributed systems. These companies will work with you on designing a system around their hardware of choice. They generally offer a limited number of options, because these companies usually do not have the resources to test every possible variation of available hardware and drivers. If you have sufficient funds and do not require special hardware integrated into the system, then this may well be an excellent way to experiment with distributed systems.

On the other hand, there are a number of consulting companies who are providing assistance to those who require short term technical expertise to those who are attempting to develop distributed systems as well as in house resources to support the project. These same companies will generally be able to provide personnel who are able to work with you on hardware support of generally any available Linux flavors and hardware configurations.

> *Just before publication of this book, several major Linux hardware developers have begun to market powerful rack-mounted systems with the capability to support dozens of CPUs. Other companies have begun to market and support products including professional grade compilers and other software tools that will substantially improve the likelihood of success in distributed system projects.*

## Programming Languages

It depends on what you already know. As you might guess Visual Basic will be of limited use in a Linux environment, at least for the present. On the other hand, if you are an experienced C, C++, or Fortran programmer, then you are in luck. In the next chapter we will discuss development tools including the two most prominent: Message Passing Interface (MPI) and Parallel Virtual Machine (PVM).

## Design and Implementation

There is no way to hide the fact that a distributed system is both physically and logically complex to design and implement. However, it is no more difficult to do with Linux than it would be with any other operating system. It is not a project to be entered into without recognizing the level of effort and quality of resources that will be required to be successful. That is not to say that a group of old machines and an extra hub could not be built into a nice little system for research. However, if you are serious about building a state of the art system to address an enterprise critical problem, then you must secure sufficient support from the outset or you will not be successful.

On the other hand, if you have experience with NIS, NFS, TFTP, and other basic Linux network tools and utilities then you are ready to go. A simple distributed system is essentially the judicious application of those very tools with a couple of extras.

Don't let all this scare you off. Distributed systems are more complex to build and maintain because they are generally dependent on more systems than just one box, but any IT professional that is willing to spend a little time adding to his or her bag of tricks will be able to master the material and build a successful project.

## Maintenance

A distributed system is no more difficult to maintain than a standard network with the same number of nodes and servers. It is true that a poorly designed system will be more sensitive to the failure of individual systems such as a NFS mounted partition, but a properly designed system will minimize this problem if not eliminate it. Distributed systems substantially reduce the level of effort involved in maintaining individual users environments, maintaining reliable and safe backups of mass storage, and can allow for easier maintenance of software in a consistent and dependable manner.

## Other Factors

The quality and type of personnel that will be charged with developing and maintaining a distributed system will have a significant impact on the overall success of the project. The project will require extensive knowledge of the key technologies like networking, computer architecture, and the Linux operating system.

If you plan to develop your own application, then of course you will need an individual or team familiar with distributed systems programming and the particular development tools (MPI, PVM, etc.). Although these tools are not difficult to learn, it does take time. Luckily there are several excellent references on the available tools and a few are listed in the bibliography at the end of this and the next chapter. If you acquire the standard distribution then you will receive several source code examples as well.

# Hardware Decisions

Hardware considerations are every bit as important to the overall system performance and reliability as a correct driver module or library version. Problems caused by hardware tend to be subtle, unlike those that plague software. However, software generally has the capacity to help diagnose its own faults. Often, the operating system, in conjunction with the underlying system hardware, will provide information and clues to the state of the software at the time of a failure. For example, applications that violate some memory access restriction will generate a segmentation fault in the hardware that alerts the operating system that a fault has occurred. At that point, the operating system takes some action to deal with the fault. With a properly configured hardware component supporting a functioning operating system, a user will still be able to retain useful control of the system even in the face of a badly behaved application.

A hardware component failure, on the other hand, may or may not reveal itself in an overt way. For example, let us consider a system that has a defective memory module. Presuming the module passes the cursory initial boot test, (which is common) and depending on where that module resides in the memory map (i.e. the exact address of the affected memory locations) for that particular system, it is possible the system will experience a diverse number of failures. Faulty memory modules produce corruption of working data, of modified application code, or even complete system failure. Memory subsystem failures can cause catastrophic events like system crashes, which are obvious effects. However, a faulty memory module can be masked if the module simply modifies some other information residing in memory, that the application or operating system is dependent on. Generally, neither failure mode will produce any sort of warning, nor will there be any assistance from the operating system or hardware in diagnosing what caused the failure. This is because there was no net to catch any memory faults or indications that might have been generated prior to when the system fails and throws a major system fault.

Something even more insidious may occur. Hardware may appear to be operating correctly, when, in fact, it is not. This may be due to errors of configuration, and may cause subtle problems that will not present themselves in an obvious way. Components, in this situation, may cause systems to behave erratically or in an inconsistent manner. Almost as serious is the situation where a piece of hardware may be functioning to the manufacture's specifications, but the quality of the design can strongly affect the operation of the system. The hardware might well be fine, but the software drivers may cause serious performance degradation.

At this point, it should be obvious that the hardware decisions you make now will strongly affect the results will be working with. We will further discuss all of the topics covered in the last section on the *Components of a Distributed System*, in particularly communications, as well as introduce some new ones.

Having said all that, this section can not hope to present all the relevant details and considerations, there are just too many potential variations in hardware to create a complete list anywhere. As always, it is up to you to dig deep and explore all of the options and determine what is right and necessary for your specific application.

**363**

# The Central Processor Unit (CPU)

In this section the various chips that are available at the moment are discussed, and reference will be made to new chips that are due to be released in the not-too-distant future. In particular we shall discuss the following:

❑    Alpha

❑    PowerPC

❑    SPARC

❑    The x86 series

Historically, the Intel line of processors has dominated the PC market. However, Intel's market dominance does not imply that you have no other alternatives, or that the Intel line is even a reasonable choice for your needs. This is particularly true if you have legacy hardware to incorporate into the system. With Linux, the number of supported processors is very broad and gives you the greatest latitude in distributed system development of any operating system available today.

In this section we will discuss in some detail, but by no means in *complete* detail, the other issues that you might consider. We will also discuss the state of the Linux operating system on these processors and whether you can enable your legacy systems to use Linux. Only those systems with mature Linux implementations will be discussed here. Some of these systems will not have as complete a version of Linux as others.

## Alpha

The future of the Alpha is in the balance. It has been reported that Digital Equipment was experiencing a serious brain drain in its Alpha R&D efforts even before the sale of Digital to Compaq. Compaq has taken steps to slow this loss, but the effects on the long-term future of the Alpha line are uncertain. The up side is that the prices of Alpha machines have dropped considerably, making them a much better buy than they once were. Furthermore, Compaq has become more forceful in marketing and supporting the Alpha CPU. It has been rumored that Compaq is in fact actively supporting the development and improvement of Linux on the Alpha in order to bring Alpha Linux in line with the present state of development of the Intel x86 systems, and then surpass it.

If you have an application that requires serious floating point computations you should give Alpha serious consideration. For floating point operations the Alpha runs generally about 4 times the speed of a comparable speed x86, including the newest models. These systems have a history of use in highly computationally intensive applications like image processing. A farm of Alpha chips running Linux was used in the movie *Titanic* as compute servers supporting SGI systems that operated as the primary rendering systems. Very large (1000+ nodes) are under development for NASA, MIT and a couple of other public entities. Depending on your computational needs, there are systems available with multiple parallel processors configured in a Symmetric Multi-Processor system. Systems of 16 processors as well as rack system of as many as 64 processors can be purchased. However, these systems are not cheap; The single CPU versions have come down in price but the SMP versions seem to still be very expensive.

Future Alpha releases include a 64-bit processor running a 64-bit version of Linux. In my opinion, the versions available are not quite as advanced as Intel versions of the operating system, but since Digital/Compaq have been assisting the Alpha flavor of Linux, it has improved rapidly. In addition, Compaq has announced that it will provide a Fortran and C/C++ compiler for Alpha Linux in the near future, but are not available at the time of this writing.

One issue to keep in mind is the cost of feeding these systems. The power consumption of an Alpha is not small. Generally the Alpha systems consume twice the power of a PC system. That may sound small at the outset, but when the individual who pays the power bill comes in your office under full steam, don't say you weren't warned.

This processor has wide support in the Linux community, primarily due to its tremendous floating point capability. It's primary limitation, at this point, is the lack of support for AGP and its following technologies 2x and 4x AGP.

## PowerPC

A consortium of manufactures including IBM, Motorola, and Apple Computers developed the PowerPC chip. It is a very versatile chip design and has many different flavors from the different vendors. It can be found in many applications from workstations to pagers and cell phones. As with the x86 chips, the most common form is the 32-bit version known as the 60x family, but there are other PowerPC family members like the 750, used in the Apple G3, which have 64 and 32-bit modes.

PowerPC is an extremely powerful and versatile processor. Certainly a market leader in several areas, particularly in embedded systems. PowerPC is without doubt the leading competitor to the x86 in the end user PC market. The problem is that it has not enjoyed a significant amount of market penetration overall. This is largely due to Apple, Motorola and IBM, who have tended to focus on the high end or other markets for this product. If you want a consumer priced machine, you are exclusively limited to Apple products that have their own limitations. Having said that, there is a good selection of hardware to support PowerPC systems.

However, there is only very limited support for PowerPC from the various Linux vendors. Essentially, you will be limited to the LinuxPPC Project which produces a fine product that is only slightly behind the general Linux community. The down side is that you are limited in your choices and if you have an unusual problem or need you will generally have to fix or develop it yourself, or choose a different chip.

## SPARC

SPARC stations are a Sun Microsystems product, a very powerful system with many excellent traits. Today there is a good Linux port to most of the major flavors of SPARC stations including UltraSPARCs. The heart of the product is the UltraSPARC processor which is a 64 bit process with outstanding computational and graphics performance, although limited support is presently available for the graphics subsystem. This weakness will likely be changed quickly and may well be addressed by the time you read this.

Like the Alpha kernel, the SPARC kernel is not as advanced, but the support in the SPARC community for Linux over Solaris is growing, and the gap is narrowing. To date, Red Hat is producing a SPARC specific distribution of Linux. This distribution is perhaps the closest approach to the X86 distribution widely available at the time of this writing.

# X86

The x86 is the home of Linux. The tremendous number of x86 based machines has meant that a large number of diverse machines have been in the hands of those with a technical bent of mind, one of whom was Linux's inventor Linus Torvalds. Nowadays, the average Linux operating system developer is working with a x86 based system. The quantity of x86 systems, and their diversity of hardware and peripherals, has been the driving force that has made the x86 Linux kernel the leading kernel in the Linux world.

Intel was the maker of the original chip (8086 – 8 bit 4.77 MHz) used in the IBM PC. The IBM PC evolved into the more advanced IBM PC-Advanced Technology or AT (80286). The PC-AT brought with it a 16-bit architecture and the now infamous ISA peripheral bus. The ISA system architecture was an open standard that many other hardware vendors used to develop new peripherals for the IBM. Over time, the improvement in hardware and the ever increasing demands of software, caused Intel to develop newer processors which gave birth to a whole line of other processors, 80186 (embedded systems primarily), 80286, 80386, 80486 and finally the Pentium family of processors.

The strength that has carried the Intel x86 family is its backward compatibility. Backward compatibility was both a technical and business decision that effectively made Intel the dominant leader in the CPU market. Backward compatibility is also the limiting factor in that family's development. The need to remain compatible with systems that were developed generations before, has become an extremely heavy burden for the x86 family to carry, essentially limiting the growth of the underlying technology in x86 based computers.

## Intel

The Intel line of processors has the best floating point performance of the two major x86 processor manufactures. That performance is generally inferior to that to the UltraSPARC, PowerPC, and far behind that of the Alpha. The memory model is more complex and the internal architecture (CISC) is a mess, and the performance suffers. That is generally not an issue to most software developers. It has been reported that Intel has benefited from the acquisition of Digital Equipment by Compaq, particularly in the area of floating-point processor design. It is possible that improved floating-point capability will appear in future versions of the popular Pentium line and it's successor.

That said, Intel in conjunction with Hewlett-Packard has been developing a new chip standard called IA-64. Intel is also developing the first chip under this standard, with the code named Merced. Intel promises Merced will be a technological revolution. We will have to wait and see.

The IA-64 chip is not expected to be on the market in the after the year 2000, and according to Intel, will not be making a significant impact in the processor market until 2002. It is said that Intel intends to stop production of IA-32 (x86) class chips by 2005, effectively ending the longest, most successful processor family in the short history of PCs.

## AMD

Advanced Micro Devices (AMD) is the principle competitor to Intel in the x86 market. AMD has produced several different binary compatible CPUs that are architecturally different from Intel. Qualitatively, AMD processors can out outperform Intel processors at the same system clock speed, but AMD processors fall short in the floating point arena.

Historically, AMD processors have delivered floating-point performance of 50-80% of the Intel processors. If your application involves large amounts of floating point operations, then the AMD is definitely a poor choice. That is, unless cost is an overriding factor. AMD has historically been much more cost effective than Intel; on the other hand, if money is not a factor, then Alphas would probably serve you better. One other limitation the AMD processors suffer from is they do not support Symmetric Multi-Processors (SMP). AMD's lack of support for SMP is a significant handicap on high performance systems like server, essentially limiting AMD chips to desktop workstations until the K-7 chip becomes available.

AMD has released a new processor (Athlon) that they hope will finally give them a chip to challenge Intel's dominance. Athlon has benefited by the acquisition of some of the of Compaq/Digital Alpha development team members who have left Digital (the chief engineer of AMD's Athlon, Dirk Meyer, is ex-Alpha) in the last several months. Athlon has substantially improved floating point performance (Athlon offers 3 out-of-order, fully parallel FPU pipelines), as well as incorporating SMP support, and combine with an updated 3DNow (AMD's answer to MMX) capability.

From the Linux side, Athlon will require some modifications to the compiler and to the libraries in order to take full advantage of the new technology. Just how long that takes really depends on AMD. At the time of writing, AMD had not published any technical information for developers to work with, nor are there any SMP boards available although single processor boards are. The motherboard issue is difficult to deal with, but it is likely that there will be a good assortment of boards available, and the floating-point capability might well be worth the wait. AMD is committed to the Athlon, and it's continued development. Hence, it may be a prudent hedge position at least until the Alpha's future is a little clearer.

# Single Processors vs Symmetric Multi-Processors (SMP)

We have discussed chip makers, the available chips, and something about how well Linux can be used on each chip, but we have not talked about the options for motherboards. In this section we will consider the two primary options in system architecture, the traditional single processor, and the concept of Symmetric Multi-Processor (SMP).

## *Individual*

This is the traditional format for a desktop PC. In modern computers, there are generally several other processors that are specialized to perform functions like sound generation or video processing and display, but the central processor is the core of the system. The sheer number of available machines of this type means that you will likely be working with this sort of system.

In a single processor system, there are a number of components. The primary components are the I/O subsystem (including serial ports, parallel ports, video and audio, memory system), the memory subsystem (the memory modules, refresh circuits, and cache), and the CPU. All of these subsystems are connected through a set of three buses, the **address bus**, which is used to select the address of memory or I/O device locations, the **data bus**, which is used to move information to or from the selected address location, and the **control bus**, which is a set of control lines that are used by all the devices in order to determine what exactly is going on.

There are several things to bear in mind here. There have been some reported decreases in performance with large amounts of RAM in systems with poorly designed or insufficient cache RAM. Older systems may have BIOS issues which might or might not cause problems. They will not be able to take full advantage of modern components like Ultra DMA and even PCI, but if you can work around that, even very old systems can make adequate terminals or even some types of servers, packet routers, or firewalls, so don't throw the old box just yet. There are some older AMD chips which require an operating system patch to work properly, as there is always the infamous faulty Pentium tables problem to be dealt with.

If you have the luxury of purchasing new systems, be careful of BIOS versions as they can strongly affect the system's performance. Be mindful of the quality of the motherboard and its component systems. In a distributed system, even small performance issues can substantially affect the final performance of the system. Research the version of Linux you prefer and then research the boards/machines you are considering. It is worth spending some time checking old news group postings to see if anyone has had any specific problems with the type of configuration you are considering. Unfortunately it is difficult to give specific advice or recommendations in these instances. Generally various distribution vendors provide a hardware compatibility list, but they tend to be overly conservative and often too general to be of any specific help. On the other hand, Linux supports most hardware even if it does not appear so at first. Linux does require some research on some components, but if you have it in your hands and it has been available for more than a few weeks, it is likely that someone else has worked with it and has solved most of your problems for you.

## Multiple Processors

The advantage of this concept is obvious – more processors to share the work hence more work gets done!

Over the years, there have been several designs for multiprocessor systems. The bus design is the simplest. Here, several processors are given access to each other, and shared system resources, by a single set of buses. The concept is generally simple to implement. You need to have some method of communicating to the other processors, to negotiate a method of staying out of each other's way, and a way to share information between processors and processes. This is the simplest design, but is also very limited because it becomes impractical to scale up to a large number of processors; the number of processors was originally limited to sixteen.

In the market today, the dominant method of implementing multiple processors is a Symmetric Multi-Processing (SMP) system. We will not go into a significant amount of detail on this architecture, but suffice it to say that there is a single processor that works as a kind of master processor. The slave processors are assigned work by the primary or master processor, and share resources with each other through a single set of buses. The most common configuration in the x86 world is a two-processor configuration – one primary and one secondary processor.

These systems have been dropping significantly in price over the last several years. In fact, the cost of an SMP machine in the x86 world is roughly one tenth that of an SMP Alpha. There is an excellent SMP kernel for Linux available that is stable and well supported. SMP machines have become much more common since Intel introduced the Celeron processor. This is primarily due to a convergence of circumstances that made it possible for people to build SMP Celeron based systems for a fraction of the cost of the Pentium II version. Due to this situation the SMP Linux kernel has been maturing very rapidly as more and more developers move to very fast SMP boxes, therefore, the Linux vendors are supporting it more and more. Red Hat 6.0, for example, will recognize an SMP system and install the appropriate kernel right out of the box.

On the development side, software will not generally automatically utilize the full resources of an SMP system. If your project uses shrink wrapped software, check with the vendor to ensure that the software supports SMP systems and what exact configurations are required. If you are developing the software in-house, be aware that you will have to take SMP development requirements into account during development.

The advantages of SMP are that it reduces the number of systems that you have to support as well as improving performance, and fewer components mean fewer parts to fail. Additionally, SMP can change the types of problems you can attack. (For instance, you can modify the granularity somewhat because SMP machines are more tightly coupled than networked machines, hence the communications latency is substantially lower than any other communication method.) Under appropriate circumstances, SMP can greatly improve the overall performance. Most commercial high end servers utilize SMP (usually with more than two processors), and that substantially improves the capacity of the system to service client requests. Furthermore, the tighter connection between the SMP processors means that they can exchange information much faster than two processors over a network. This means that you can attack finer mesh problems than would be reasonable in a single-processor distributed system. This advantage is limited in a two-processor system which is presently most common in the PC world, but Alpha presently supports larger SMP systems (16 processors per board with systems of up to 64 processors total). It should be noted that the popularity of Beowulf has caused many board manufactures to increase the number of processors that them put on some specialty boards, many with 4 and some with 16 are becoming available for Athlon, Celeron and Pentium III CPUs. Interestingly, much of this interest has come from the availability of the Celeron and its ability to operate as a SMP chip. Originally, Intel disabled this ability but the hardware gurus have found a way to enable it again, thus inexpensive SMP boards became available and many more developers were able to acquire them, hence a substantial growth in SMP world is beginning.

All in all, SMP can be an excellent alternative to single-processor systems depending on the needs of the project. Their greatest strength may not be improved performance but simply reducing the number of boxes you have to maintain. This fact should not be under-emphasized. The amount of space that a 1000 node system requires is impressive, the power consumption requirements are not trivial, and the heating and cooling needs of that many nodes should not be overlooked. Anything that can reduce the number of boxes is something to be considered.

# Networking Issues

So far in this chapter, we have said several times that communication is critical to the success of a distributed system. The principle points of concern include

- ❑ The length of time for a connection to be established.
- ❑ How quickly information can be transferred.
- ❑ The efficiency of data transfer.
- ❑ How much overhead is involved.
- ❑ The reliability of the transmission.

We will look at some of these issues, as well as some of the technologies that have been developed for general networking, and we will touch on some of the tools that have been developed specifically for Linux distributed systems.

# What Affects Efficiency

In context of distributed computing, **efficiency** is used in the broadest sense. Whether a particular network is efficient for a particular application, depends on the application involved.

For example, let us suppose you are trying to implement a distributed system across a wide area network (WAN), and suppose that this WAN spans one or more continents, utilizing various types of media. Such an application might coordinate retail purchasing systems, or it coordinates banking transactions, or maybe you are giving your unused cycles to the SETI project data processing. WANs have certain limitations on performance and reliability which must be taken into account. For instance, it is unlikely that the organization using the system will have ownership of the media. Therefore, it is almost impossible to guarantee a route or its security. This would indicate that certain security precautions, such as data encryption, will have to be taken, as well as measures to ensure that packets are delivered. Both of these will incur increased processing overhead, from packet handling as well as the packets themselves. These are all issues that affect data transfer efficiency, but are necessary in order to implement the project, and so reduced performance is something that has to be endured. In this sort of problem, the limiting factor is not how long it takes to create a connection, or really how long it takes to send a given, reasonable amount of information, but whether the information gets there in the first place and whether it arrives complete and unmodified along the way.

On the other hand, lets suppose that you are going to build a dedicated Linux cluster to do complex mathematical calculations. Communications issues will place restrictions on the type of problems that can be effectively handled with the cluster. These restrictions limit the **grain** (or **mesh**) of the problems attached. The grain of a problem is the measure of how closely connected a set of component processes are.

Applications can be **coarse** or **fine** grained. In other words, the grain essentially measures how often inter-process communications take place, and may also include the amount of information within those communications. For example, a system of complex nonlinear differential equations, which is common in chaos theory and weather prediction, would be a very *fine*-grained problem.

This is because individual results of equations, terms within an equation, will be needed for other calculations in other processes. Where as, a Monte Carlos simulation (a very powerful and commonly used method of simulating large numbers of events) following the path of billions of individual neutrons through a reactor, or ray-tracing calculations in a computer generated image application would be *coarse*-grained, because each calculation is essentially independent of the other calculations. In this problem, network efficiency essentially means minimizing overhead so that no process is waiting on the network to furnish it with information. Any unnecessary overhead will reduce the performance of the system and hence the network efficiency. In this case, over a reliable dedicated network, the same protocols on encryption and reliability that were essential to the WAN example become hindrance to performance because they are not needed.

A *fine*-grained problem is one where there is a large amount of interdependence in the calculations, hence a large amount of network traffic with only small amounts of information per packet. In this sort of problem, you will have to worry more about how long it takes to form a connection than how long it takes to send a 256 bit floating point number. In the coarse-grained example, we may be worried about both connection and transfer rate depending on the number of processes and the amount of data transferred per packet.

There is simply no getting around it. To maximize the performance you have to understand the nature of the problem you are trying to solve. With that information, you will should be able to derive a reasonable estimate of types of communication that will take place, that will assist you in deciding what communications parameters you should be optimizing for, and the quantity of the traffic that will occur, which will further refine your options.

# Specific Comparisons

In this section we will discuss some specific technologies and look at their various parameters that are of interest to us: connection time, overhead, transmission rate, and reliability.

## Connection Time

The time required to establish a connection is called network latency, communications latency, or simply **latency**. The simplest definition for network latency is:

> **The amount of time needed to send a single object.**

There is a large amount of detail hidden in this definition. It includes all of the mechanical issues involved in making the connection to the communications media, as well as establishing a connection over the media, and the corresponding hardware issues on the node with which you are trying to communicate. Furthermore, there is a lot of work to be done through installing and configuring software. However, the communications protocol will be established in software, which will package the application information, move the packages across the connection, and unpackage the information on the recipient.

The upshot is that when you are moving a large number of packets around, you need to minimize the amount of time it takes to make the call. Latency kills performance, but like gravity or the IRS, it is always there.

## Overhead

The term **overhead** is defined as:

> **The information, contained in each packet, required by the protocol to properly package, handle, and transfer the data.**

This is essentially the information that the protocol needs in order to get the data to the proper destination. The amount of overhead required depends on how the data is moved. It is clear that if you can create some direct connection between two boxes, perhaps over a bidirectional parallel (or serial) port protocol, then you don't have to worry about such things as addresses and the like. On the other hand, if you have to communicate over a LAN or WAN, you will have increasing amounts of routing information required insuring that the data gets to its destination.

You have to bear in mind what sort of problem you are working with. Keep track of the overhead; any increase in overhead decreases performance, so keep it as low as possible. For example, if you can build a tightly coupled cluster, then you can live without extremely stringent flow control and reliability requirements, you might even be able to run without a large amount of protocol overhead through device drivers. (Protocol overhead is the information added to the basic application packet in order to route and ensure delivery, the amount of overhead is dependent on what specific protocols are involved and what components are implemented within those protocols.) On the other hand, if you have to communicate over a LAN you will have to add protocol overhead in order to live nicely with the other nodes. Things get even worse with a WAN system, because you have no control over much of the media and a significantly greater probability of packet loss. In a WAN environment you will have to incur even more overhead in order for the system to operate reliably.

## Data Rate or Bandwidth

Data Transfer Rate or **bandwidth** is the parameter most people think of when they discuss network performance. Bandwidth is defined as:

> **The theoretical maximum data transfer rates in bits per second.**

However, it is only one of the parameters. We are familiar with terms like 10Base2 or 10BaseT, in connection with networking. Both of these forms of networking (they use different media – 10Base2 is Coax and 10BaseT is twisted pair) are Ethernet networks, and claim a data transfer rate of 10 Million bits per second. That sounds good, but it is not true. As I have said before, Ethernet generally starts to reduce its efficiency when the traffic reaches roughly 30-35% of the theoretical maximum, and much above that is the realistic ceiling or roughly 375,000 bytes per second. And what's more, the quality of the equipment will strongly affect the performance of the system. Some network components simply do not have the bandwidth, packet processing, or buffering capacity to reach even the operational performance with a given technology. You will have to research the network technology and the products to be sure that the network will perform as indicated.

## Reliability

**Reliability** encompasses both the specific communications that will take place as well as whether the hardware supporting the communication will continue to function, or how likely is the total network subsystem going to perform such a that the distributed system will function properly.

Whether a message will reach its intended destination depends on the reliability of the network. There are several dangers in the migration of packets across the network, such as the node buffers becoming full, or network topology suddenly changing due to some catastrophe like a crash. Packets are lost, at least occasionally, on all networks. The probability of a packet reaching its intended destination depends strongly on the type of network involved. A WAN will have more dangers than a highly reliable, dedicated LAN. In fact, estimates of packet loss, in the range of 1 in 100,000 packets to 1 in 100,000,000,000,000 have been quoted. The truth is, whether you lose one every few seconds or one in the life of the universe, if that lost packet is packet is critical then the system has failed. If your application requires that every packet make the trip as expected, then use protocols that ensure reliable delivery and accept the performance hit due to overhead.

### Hardware Reliability

All parts fail eventually. Your only real option is to be sure to purchase quality products and plan for the failure. If you have a mission critical application, there are hardware implementations that utilize multiple media channels which ensure that at least one packet gets through. These systems claim that a packet is completely lost "only once in the life of the universe" thanks to multiple parallel pieces of hardware. Of course, you would have to insure that that those conditions hold throughout the entire network, which is impossible on a WAN. You may have to use some form of transaction logging to be sure that you can have a fall back position in case a hardware failure takes place. You might also have to incur some extra overhead such as a network check to see if the destination is accessible prior to transmission, but this is still susceptible to catastrophic failure of a critical component along the way.

Essentially, reliability can not be ensured, but it can be enhanced by making sure that the components are of high quality, well designed, and manufactured. Your project should have plans for failure and implement protocols which mitigate for any loss of data. You can presently build extremely robust networks, which can handle tremendous amounts of information with a high degree of reliability.

# Other Factors

You have a significant number of decisions to make regarding all sorts of hardware. Many of those decisions will depend on the environment you are working in. We will discuss a couple of the major categories of organization later, but for now, lets ask the basic questions. Are you going to build a system for experimental purposes using old hardware, or are you going to build a purpose built system using new hardware. That question will have a significant impact on the direction of your project and how you will proceed.

The next question is about your level of control of the resources. You may have complete control over the nodes, which will allow you to make whatever decisions you feel are necessary to maximize the overall performance and reliability. Alternatively, you might also have a more complex situation, in which users will be using the systems you are reconfiguring, and hence you will have more restrictions. Still another situation might be that you have access and control of older systems that were not designed or configured for a distributed system and you will have to make do with the hardware you have. All of these situations will be discussed in turn.

## Corporate Culture

Two of the common scenarios of companies implementing a distributed system are described here:

### Organization A:

Over its history, the organization has acquired a large amount of equipment with which they are comfortable. Each member of the organization has had a significant amount of influence in the acquisition, configuration, and maintenance of their respective systems. The organization has operated reasonably happily with this situation for their entire history. However, for reasons of maintenance and the never ending upgrade cycle, the organization has decided to implement a distributed system in order to maximize the capacity of the existing system and extend its life.

### Organization B:

This organization has acquired their systems via a preferred vendor or through some other formal centralized procedure. All of the systems are essentially identical, meeting the lowest common denominator of performance. The users know nothing about their systems and don't want to. They are very suspicious of any changes that purport to help then, and will resist any changes made to their environment, regardless of who demands the changes or for what motive. The organization's management was sold on the idea of a distributed system as a panacea, and is really not sure what it will do for them, but they are very excited and have high expectations.

Realistically, no organization will fall completely into either of these categories; it is reasonable that most organizations will have attributes of both as well as some that are not described.

Each organization has it's own challenges, and they have aspects in common. The principle point is that both will rely on existing hardware. It is likely that management will want to limit any additional costs. Why spend good money on older systems, when the increased cost would mean that they could purchase new systems? Furthermore, these organizations have another point in common, no clear understanding of what a distributed system will bring them. This is very common, distributed systems are generally not within the realm of experience for most management teams, and many senior IT professionals because historically they were limited in application and tended to be rather expensive to build and operate. That has been changing dramatically with the advent of Microsoft's DCOM and Linux.

The consequences of these mindsets is that it will probably be difficult to acquire a budget sufficient to allow for the acquisition of completely new systems which are configured to support the project from the first day of their selection. More likely, there will be enough money to allow you to configure a limited number of older systems with some room for infrastructure improvements such as a dedicated network or more storage. This system will be a proof of concept that will provide the basis for future deployment of a company wide system depending on the ultimate goals of the project.

Consequently, the original plan, discussed earlier, should be reviewed in the light of the longer-term goals of the company. One question you have to constantly keep in mind is, does this or that decision move the project toward the ultimate goal? That sounds obvious, but all to often it is easy to become lost in the morass of daily operations, putting out fires and trying to make the users happy while keeping the system up and running that it is very, very easy to lose sight of the goal.

## Budgets and Limitations

If you find yourself in the happy situation where money is no object, congratulations! You might find this section of little help in the short run, however you might want to skim it just in case your fortunes change.

Given the corporate culture of your organization, essentially your only choices are how you spend what budget you have, and how can you make decisions that maximize the systems performance as well as move toward the ultimate goal.

Your first order of business should be a thorough survey of the existing systems and hardware, keeping track of such things as components (including make and model), as well as system resources (storage disks, memory, etc.) and their locations, both physically and logically. Once this survey is complete, it will be helpful in determining which Linux distribution vendor will be able to provide a simple solution. With a large population of extant hardware, it is possible that there will be some components that will not have Linux distribution support (for example Micro-channel) and other hardware for which there is little support. You will have to do some research to determine which distribution vendor will be able to assist you, this can be done through direct contact to the various vendors, many have good presales support via email, and all have at least some hardware compatibility information on their web sites. You can also post the list to an appropriate news group to ask if others have used that equipment and evaluate the responses. The Linux community is very responsive and generally you will receive constructive information in a timely manner.

Once the survey is complete, you should have a good feel of exactly where the systems weaknesses are, and where you will have to put your budget in order to mitigate against any problems you encounter. If you are very lucky, you will find that you are able to spend your entire budget on things that will improve performance. It is more likely that you will have to amend your plan to accommodate the replacement of some components, and note those that should be retired as soon as is financially possible.

## Users

This should be obvious, to the author has seen several instances where this tenant has not been heeded, much to the detriment of the project. If you have users on the systems in question, don't disturb them any more than you have to.Users tend to be very sensitive to changes in their environment even for the better, and will resist any change that they feel will adversely affect their work environment. They will also feel territorial about their machines being fiddled with, so keep that in mind.

If you have extant infrastructure, use that infrastructure as much as possible, even if you take some sort of performance hit. Better that than driving your users crazy while you rewire! If it comes down to replacing the hub or the network cards (assuming that the network cards can handle the performance) change the hub first and forget the card. If you find that the network cards can't support the performance, upgrade to the best and fastest cards you can afford and swap the cards at night or on the weekend. Don't do this in secret however, since that will generally cause suspicion and resentment. Finally, remember most CPU cycles go to waste, so unless you are running a bunch of x486 boxes, leave the CPU alone.

## Complete Control

In this situation, you have complete control over the system including design, configuration, and implementation of the distributed system. This is the best situation to be in, and also the rarest. The only caveat that you will probably have a higher level of expectation and interest from the individuals who are signing the checks, but that always has to be managed

The figure below is a decision tree that suggests how you might optimize your hardware budget. It is essentially a series of suggestions, and several of them have been discussed previously. It does bring in some topics that have not been discussed previously such as diskless, disked, and hybrid systems, as well as file servers (usually NFS) which will generally be needed as a central repository of applications and user files. Each of these topics and their reasons for consideration will be discussed shortly, but the figure is presented in order to help you decide which category your project might fall into, and hence to determine what material in this chapter might be of interest to you.

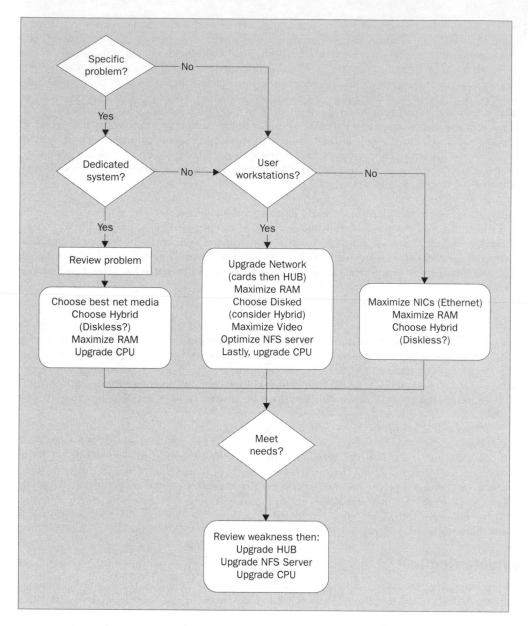

There are several possible options for purchasing hardware to augment the overall system. Costs range from essentially nothing to a potentially substantial investment, depending on the project and its aims. If you have an essentially unlimited budget, then just upgrade everything. If not, which is most of us, you should start at the top of the chart and work your way to the bottom. Distributed systems will operate even with limited resources, so it will generally serve you well if you try to build a basic system that will highlight weaknesses of the system in relation to your particular needs. Often a system has a single weakness, usually network infrastructure and sometimes limited node memory which, if addressed, will substantially improve the overall system performance.

Given time, a distributed system mission will tend to migrate toward a specific application. For example, you might have a distributed system that spends some of its time as a system for general use, and the rest of the time as a database server. As the database demands grow and the demand on the server increases, the systems might become a dedicated database. It is very unusual for a distributed system to be truly general purpose. However, such a situation might arise for system that is built around user workstations. It would generally be designed to support its users by providing improved workstation support, access to printers, and add greater access to system-wide resources, like storage.

# Node Configurations

Now, let's take a look at how you can configure the nodes within the distributed system. We will take a look at the three main ways to configure nodes: diskless, disked and a hybrid system. Essentially this determines where the operating system, swap space, and applications live. The decision you make here will have tremendous implications for what can and can not be done with the overall distributed system in the future, because it has the greatest impact on fundamental issues such as network traffic.

## Diskless Systems

A diskless system is exactly that, a node that does not have a hard drive or storage capacity. You might now be asking yourself why you would want to build such a system. What would you use it for? What would be the advantages and disadvantages of a diskless system?

### What is a Diskless System?

A diskless system is a box that contains a motherboard, a processor, memory, and some form of networking interface. Generally, this interface is a network card containing a PROM which contains a rudimentary boot application that will request assistance in order to boot over a network. The process begins when the NIC PROM code is executed. That PROM code contains bootp as well as tftp clients, which work in conjunction with a bootp and tftp server to provide the node with its kernel. The bootp client broadcasts the network card's hardware address to the bootp server. In Ethernet, each NIC (network interface card) contains a universally unique hardware address known as its **Ethernet address**. The bootp server then picks up the request and responds by checking its records to see if the Ethernet address is within its control. If so, it will then work with tftp to download the kernel to the system. There are other configuration issues that must occur with the NIS/NFS to set the environment, but generally the system is up and running.

### High Consistency or Concurrency

File **consistency** or **concurrency** is one of the greatest problems with all distributed systems, and indeed all multi-user/multi-instance operating systems.

File concurrency problems arise when a single file is opened (specifically for writing reading is less of a problem) by multiple applications, be they on a single node with a single user, or multiple nodes and multiple users. Generally speaking, multiple nodes access to a file over a network is the more difficult problem to handle. Various techniques have been developed over time to handle both situations, **file locking**, being the most common and widely used. File locking in is generally not as robust in networked file systems because of issues like race conditions between nodes. A race condition is the situation where multiple nodes are trying to gain access to the same resource and the outcome depends on who gets there first. Having said that, distributed systems in general and under Linux in particular are very hot topics of research and many technological improvements are becoming available to assist in the concurrency area.

## File Systems

In diskless systems, the file systems will reside on file servers. These file systems will generally be mounted using Network File System (NFS) in conjunction with the Network Information System (NIS). With integrated file locking on the server implemented by the application in necassary, multiple nodes should not be able to open for write at the same time. Because there is no local file system on which to make a working copy, there is no easy way to defeat file locking on the system, although network problems or problems with the file lock system could cause difficulties particularly under race conditions.

When a user logs into the system, the NIS system will check the user's login and password against files it received from the NIS server. If they are valid, the operating system will allow the login where NFS will provide the user's work directory

## System Maintenance

Diskless systems are easier to maintain because you substantially reduce the number of components that tend to fail. There are two kinds of hard drives: those that have crashed and those that will. Reducing the number of hard drives will reduce the number of system critical components that might fail, hence your potential problems. Furthermore, by centralizing the file systems to a single set of servers, the maintenance challenge is substantially reduced. One centralized location for file storage allows for substantially reduced difficulty in performing virtually all system maintenance tasks, from backups to server side hardware upgrades. Finally, the ease by which diskless systems can be maintained and kept consistent in tools and kernels among the nodes is the principle strength of diskless systems. It is relatively easy to keep a few, or even dozens, of machines consistent, but once that number increases to hundreds, consistency is much more difficult, and thousands are impossible.

## Lower Hardware Costs for Nodes

Although hard drives are cheaper than they have ever been, they are still a significant component cost, often approaching twenty per cent of the overall node cost. The cost increases dramatically if the quality of the drives is upgraded to a more capable type. For instance, high capacity SCSI-3 drives are generally twice that of comparable Ultra-DMA IDE (UIDE) drives, and the premium increases with increasing storage capacity.

## Focus Resources on Network and Servers

With centralization, it is possible to focus budget resources on acquiring the highest quality and most reliable components available. The fact that a totally diskless system allows this sort of option can not be understated. Today the amount of storage that is required in many applications, is vastly greater than it was only a couple of years ago. The cost of storage can become prohibitive in individual nodes, and this is compounded by the cost premium on high performance components. If all storage is concentrated in a single location, such as a server or set of servers, then it is may be possible to purchase higher quality components with multiple redundancy such as a RAID.

Perhaps the greatest advantage of centralized storage is that it makes comprehensive backups possible. On a 100BaseTx network, with a realistic capacity of 30 Mbps (one twentieth of SCSI-3), it would take 250 seconds to move 1 GB to a central tape drive. One hundred 10 GB machines would then require 250,000 seconds, that is about three days, to back up. Whereas a direct connection to a RAID farm with 1000 GB capacity would be 3.5 hrs.

### Higher Network Traffic

One of the downsides of diskless systems is that they generate significantly greater network traffic than the same number of independent nodes on a similar network.

From boot to shutdown, a diskless system essentially operates through the use of files stored on the file server, including swap space. We will look at diskless boot-up in more detail later, but when a diskless system is started, it sends out a request for a server to provide it a kernel. If the server responds, the client will receive all the information required to start up and run. It will also mount the server's file systems in order to operate and have access to applications and data. During operations, the client will engage in frequent operations on the file system, due to the needs of the user applications. If there is insufficient RAM on the node to run the user's application, then the system will have to resort to using swap space on the server. Swapping over the server will incur tremendous performance costs, because of the significant increase in network traffic generated by the swapping process.

### High Cost RAM versus Cheap HD Space

The high cost of RAM, when compared to the low cost of hard disk space, is also a significant disadvantage for diskless systems.

In order to minimize memory swapping over the network, it is important to install sufficient memory on each of the individual nodes. Just exactly how much memory this would be depends on the desired application which will be run on the distributed system. There would have to be enough RAM to allow the application to run without excessive swapping, preferably without any swapping at all. It is a good rule of thumb that if you have application X that is believed to generally require Y units of memory, then it would be best to have 2Y units of physical memory available. Unfortunately, it is at present cheaper to buy hard drive space than it is to purchase RAM. At the time of writing, 1 MB of RAM cost on average sixty fold more than 1 MB of hard disk space, and that is a significant difference. The only mitigating factor is that memory access is hundreds of thousands of times faster in RAM than hard disk access.

> For those of you who are interested, a 133 MHz memory module can be accessed in roughly one cycle, which is 133 million times per second or one access to $7.53 \times 10^{-10}$ second. Your average high performance Ultra Wide SCSI has an access latency on average of 9 ms and that is $9 \times 10^{-3}$ seconds to access an address. Given these numbers, RAM is 1,197,000 times faster than a disk. Even if it takes two cycles, since the Athlon is running 200 MHz memory the number still holds.

### Point of Failure Means System is Down

Diskless systems are susceptible to single point of failure (SPF) problems. To put it simply, if a server goes down the system goes down. Generally the failure order is Swap Server (highest traffic), then NFS, then NIS, and finally the network infrastructure through the hub. Fortunately, backup servers can generally handle single point of failure problems, a service that is fully supported by Linux.

### Ethernet Configuration of Hardware on the Client

The hardware configuration of a diskless client is actually easier than configuring a disked or hybrid client, in that you do not have to worry about configuring the operating system on the system's hard disk. In addition, in Beowulf clusters especially, the nodes will have no keyboard or video cards associated with them, either through hardware configuration or the use of a switching box (my personal favorite) – all configuration and modification of individual systems is done through the server/control nodes.

The only significant difficulty is that you have to know more about the network card than you normally would. For example, in Ethernet you would have to find out what the Ethernet hardware address of the NIC is for the `bootp` server. You would have to build or acquire a boot PROM that will work with your network card and Linux, then configure the system to boot from the boot PROM.

### Configuration of Kernel

This topic can easily get into configuration issues that are beyond the scope of this book, but there are certain issues that have to be addressed when creating a kernel for a diskless system. Essentially, the diskless kernel has to have all of the components it needs to operate on a network from the start. The kernel must include support for the specific network card the boot PROM is on, as well as `tftp` and TCP/IP and NFS client support – you can leave out local disk support to save space. Other than that, the kernel is the same as any other.

### Principle Handicaps of Diskless Systems

There is one substantial handicap that diskless systems suffer, one that limits their use in many applications. That handicap is the amount of network traffic they generate. Without a local hard disk all requests for information that is not in local memory will have to go out over the network. This eats bandwidth at a prodigious rate, and will clog a network very quickly.

The most common application of diskless clusters is in tightly coupled dedicated clusters that are intended to operate as a single entity. Each node is configured with every single byte of RAM that can be stuffed into the case, and has multiple network interfaces that support different communications pathways for inter-node communication, and node to server transactions, This level of specialization is useful for complex number crunching or certain data handling and manipulations, but is too specialized for this book and will not be discussed further.

## Disked Systems

In this sort of system, each node has a local storage facility of some kind. This is generally a traditional magnetic media hard drive, although static RAM drives and even dynamic RAM drives have been used. The drive will contain all of the material that the system requires to do a boot and to operate from that point.

There are cards available that use static RAM to act as a boot drive. They generally have sufficient space for a kernel and configuration files, perhaps 4 to 8 MB although larger ones are available. In diskless and hybrid systems, these cards are an alternative to NIC boot PROMs if you can afford them.

### Lower Network Traffic

Disked systems generally have lower network traffic because the only traffic they generate is associated with applications and not swap operations. There may be some significant traffic at times, due to a disk backup over the network. For this reason disked systems are preferred in high network traffic situations because their individual operations are not generally limited by network access. Depending on how the system is designed, snap shot information and data can be stored on the systems in order to safeguard against network failure and potential loss of data that might occur in the case of a system failure, while allowing some amount of autonomy in case of network failure. In this case, some sort of conflict resolution will have to be considered to alleviate the potential file consistency problems that might arise.

### Greater Speed of Disk Access

There is no question that a system with a local hard drive is going to enjoy far greater disk performance than an NFS mounted file system. At present, SCSI-3 can transfer 80 MB per second in comparison to 100BaseTX-switched which can transfer at most 12.5 megabytes per second. Gigabyte Ethernet might change the complexion on this, but for the present SCSI-3 still has the edge.

If a significant amount of swapping or other high intensity disk access is anticipated, either a local disk should be used, or a very high performance network. Alternatively, increasing the RAM might be a better solution to both. Swapping, whether it is over a net or locally, takes up a significant amount of valuable time.

### Local Disks are Limited

The flip side of the performance issue is the large amount of storage distributed over the system. Disk backup becomes an issue, and it essentially limits the storage potential of individual nodes. The limitation grows from the bandwidth limitation of the network, and the capacity of the system to move data to long term storage.

### Higher Resistance to Point Failure

With a local file system, if the network or server goes down, the system should be able to function on its own, perhaps by caching work for later integration into the system. Note that this is not as easy as it sounds, because of the file concurrency issue. Individual nodes may fail due to disk failures, but if properly engineered, this need not bring the entire system down.

### Concurrency Problems Due to Multiple Copies

With the potential for independent file access, file concurrency raises it ugly head. About the only alternative would be to store common files on a single server and use file locking to maintain concurrency. Concurrency is such an important issue there is a significant amount of research work being done on it.

### Higher Potential for Individual Node Failure

With an increased number of components, it is more likely that an individual component will fail. With an increasing number of hard drives, the likelihood that one will fail scales with the total number of drives in the system. If the chances are 1 in 1000 that a drive will fail on any given day, then if you have 1000 nodes, you can expect one failure per day. This is really not as outrageous as it sounds. Even estimating an average time to failure of 100,000 hours, and with most nodes in a distributed system operating seven days a week, this means each have a life expectancy of about ten years. However, not all drives will live that long, and with several hundred drives you will be changing them more often than you want to. While that drive is down, that node is down and all its data is at risk.

### Increased Maintenance of Individual Nodes

On average, hardware failures will be more frequent, therefore overall maintenance both responding to events and preventative maintenance will be more costly. Be prepared to touch individual nodes much more often. If you are operating a farm, which is a concentration of many nodes in a single location, this will not necessarily be an issue since they are all located close to each other. However, if you are working in a physically distributed location like a campus or across the country, this will definitely be a draw back.

## Hybrid System

If we could build a system that took the best from both diskless and disked systems, we can imagine a system that takes the best from both. The characteristics that we would like to preserve from both the diskless and the disked systems are:

❏ Concurrency – keep the files and file system concurrency issue under control.

❏ Low Network Traffic – minimize the network traffic necessary to operate.

❏ Centralized Mass Storage – keep all the file systems in one central location.

❏ Improved Reliability – minimize component number while maximizing their quality.

❏ Local Swap and File Cache – keep the high capacity access and data traffic local.

Essentially we can meet most of these requirements by building a system that has a local swap space drive, and perhaps a local scratch disk that can be configured on the fly to imitate the local cache of a user's working directory.

Such a hybrid system would be a diskless system with a local swap and scratch disk. The nodes would boot exactly the same way as a diskless system. However, only the swap space and a scratch partition would be initialized on the local hard drive. The user's home directory, or portions of it, might be copied to the local scratch disk, or perhaps just the working directory for a specific application. The scratch partition might well be written back to the permanent data store either on the fly, or when the user logs off. Concurrency problems might be minimized by utilizing a network-wide file locking system.

The hybrid solution meets all of the advantages while skirting many of the disadvantages of the previous systems. Since the local drives are small, the drives can be of better quality and achieve higher performance than would be the case in systems that would have to replicate the entire working directories of several different users. At the time of this writing a Seagate 4.5 GB Cheetah SCSI-3 high performance drive costs roughly the same as a commodity priced 20 GB generic UIDE drive. The Cheetah is capable of sustained data transfer rate four times that of the UIDE and with a much better mean time to failure. This price does not include the cost of the SCSI-3 interface, but those prices have been dropping, and many excellent quality motherboards are now including SCSI-3 either in place of or in addition to UIDE support. Further, unless the RAM and swap partitions are particularly large, smaller drives might be used, thus reducing the costs further. Local cache will substantially reduce the network traffic, because the swap will be local. Another advantage is that the bulk of the overall system storage can be placed in large centralized RAIDs attached to NFS file servers.

In the final analysis, a hybrid system with a small high performance hard drive is the best configuration for most applications.

### High Capacity Storage

The definition of **high capacity storage system** is continually changing. A decade ago the term high capacity storage would have meant a single drive the size of a washing machine with between 20-40 GB of storage. Today, it is common to see storage capacities of 264 GB and higher fit into a standard tower case. As a general rule, the concept of high capacity storage is generally a multi-drive system like a RAID. That storage can be built using RAID software within Linux, or by acquiring dedicated RAID systems that directly connect to a server system through a SCSI connection. RAIDs generally have multiple power supplies and swappable high performance hard drives with at least one, if not two, parity drives which allow the system to rebuild data lost resulting from a drive failure. In SCSI systems, it is possible to add a SCSI tape backup drive equipped with automatic tape exchange units that can create autonomous backups without the intervention of a system administrator. This sort of system often serves as the centralized file system, that is NFS, mounted to the clients.

### Server Support — General Duty Servers

This system will make use of the same support servers as the diskless systems. NFS, NIS and `bootp`.

### Domain Name Server DNS

Depending on your specific application the Domain Name Server may or may not be useful to you. It is a service where a single server answers queries from various clients who need to map a name of a system to an IP address of that system within a specific domain. DNS makes maintaining host name to IP files much easier, but comes at the cost of greater network traffic and delay. For that reason, and for the potential point of failure problem presented by having all mapping done in a single location, DNS is not used except where necessary. In the next chapter, we will discuss it more in connection with a particular useful feature of DNS, the round-robin mapping of IP address to the same server name.

# Example Configuration

So far we have discussed a large amount of distributed system theory and philosophy, in this section we will get into some specifics based on a proof of concept distributed system. This is where we will discuss the components that comprise the cluster used in the case studies that we will come to in the next chapter. For the project, fairly well known tools and utilities will be used. However, you might not have had the opportunity to install and configure those tools yourself; hence we take the time to discuss them. We will see the construction of a dedicated eight-node cluster, with a single server. Again, this system will be used for several projects that will be discussed in the next chapter, but for this chapter we will consider some of the issues that went into the design of the system and the decisions made regarding hardware and software used. Finally, we will walk through the configuration itself and see what issues arose during the configuration process, and how they were handled.

## *Acknowledgements*

At this point I would like to thank again the various vendors who either supplied equipment or discounts for this project. These include:

| | |
|---|---|
| Aopen | www.aopenuse.com |
| Apacer | www.apacer.com |
| Tyan | www.tyan.com |
| AMD | www.amd.com |
| Kingston | www.kingston.com |
| Seagate | www.seagate.com |
| Netgear | netgear.baynetworks.com |
| Belkin | www.belkin.com |
| Hewlett-Packard | www.hp.com |

# Linux — The Operating System of Choice

This should be self-explanatory at this point, but if you are leafing through this section, I will briefly cover it again. Operating systems are not created equal. If you have not heard by now, Windows 95 and NT Workstations are really single user systems, whereas Linux is a multi-user and multi-processing operating system. In my experience, Linux is faster and more powerful than its commercial competitors.

# Which Linux Version and Distribution

Just as operating systems are not created equal, so Linux distributions vary as well.

As far as I know, Linux and water are the only legal products that can be acquired from the public domain, repackaged by a particular vendor, and sold back to the public without any significant alteration from its original form. If this is a little exaggerated, after all other applications are available under the GNU license scheme, Linux is arguably the most successful. This is not to say that the distribution vendors do not produce valuable products, nor does it mean that they are not producing value added distributions of Linux. In fact, each of the vendors adds to the value of the basic Linux system in ways that are consistent with their target market segment. Red Hat, for example, developed an application called RPM that controls the installation of modules to a Linux system. This essentially replaces `tar` as a means of packaging complex files and file systems for distribution. RPM is an improvement that has actually been of sufficient value to greatly assist Red Hat in becoming the market leader in commercial Linux distributions.

What each vendor brings to its distribution is the vendor's particular perception of what the Linux community wants. More specifically, each vendor focuses on targeted portion of the Linux community and then tries to provide the distribution to meet there needs.

Which specific distribution you choose is dependent on your particular tastes and needs. Some of the distributions provide more tools and toys to play with; others are very conservative, and only distribute the most stable components, and still others include virtually everything that will compile under Linux. Whichever vendor you select, you should make an effort to get to know their customer support policy before you purchase. Some vendors are substantially more generous than others; you might also contact the vendor to see if a subscription option is available. If you are embarking on a specialized project, vendors may or may not be willing to provide technical assistance on problems other than the plain installation details. Linux distribution vendors are very competitive individuals, and they might very well like to have you talking up their assistance and your success using their product. Give it a try; you might be surprised.

### Red Hat 5.2

As you might have guessed, the distribution chosen for this project is Red Hat 5.2. The project was originally started with Red Hat 5.0, but network drivers for the Netgear NICs (TULIP) and some other issues required that the operating system be upgraded.

### Red Hat Extreme Linux

Red Hat has developed a product that is helpful in building a distributed system. It is a compilation of tools and reference materials that have been available on the net. This product includes Red Hat 5.0, MPI, PVM, and other tools, as well as documents and general information on what other projects are underway. Red Hat Extreme is an informative product and might be worth the few bucks it costs; hopefully, it will be maintained. Note that Red Hat Extreme does not come with any form of technical support; you are on your own with this one.

# Background

Originally this project consisted of a heterogeneous network of out dated systems including x386, x486, and Pentium systems. Originally these systems would include Sun SPARC stations, and perhaps a IBM RS6000 or two, all running Linux. This sort of system is excellent for experimentation, but the age of the equipment limited its usefulness as a research and development tool, let alone any useful work such as a web or database server. Over time, it became clear that in order for the system to be a reasonable example of what might be expected in the real world, newer systems would have to be acquired. The decision was made to acquire at least four systems and with at least two different processor vendors to show some sort of diversity in architecture. However, it was also decided that the x86 family would be the focus of the project, since that would reduce the configuration issue of individual nodes while ensuring the largest number of available machines.

# Research Phase and Decisions

With these restrictions in place, a period of research began. This research focused on the various vendors of the subsystem as well as providing information for the decision making process.

### Selection Factors

It can not be over emphasized that the type and quality of the components you select will strongly influence whether your project will be successful. During your selection process, carefully research the vendors of the principle products you are going to be using. These include the CPU, motherboard, memory modules, video cards (if any), mass storage devices and network cards. Contact the vendors directly and talk with their application engineers to see what level of experience they have with Linux and inquire about any suggestions or advice they might be able to give you.

Results from this sort of effort were principle reasons for the selection of the vendors used in this project. Several of the companies had applications engineers familiar with Linux and they provided valuable insight into their products compatible with Linux. For further information, check out the Linux news groups, people there generally are willing to share their experience and assist where they are able.

## CPU and Motherboards

Each of the prominent x86 vendors were considered; AMD and Intel were chosen because of significant market position. Intel is the market leader, and hence, it is likely that any distributed system will include at least one of Intel's chips. AMD is included because it is appearing more and more in home systems and Athlon is proving an effective competitor to Pentium III in higher performance systems. The other manufacturers were eliminated for no other reason than space. Alpha and SPARC were not included because of a lack of representative samples available to me for experimentation purposes.

The next question asked was which of the respective manufacture's lines of x86 chips should be used. Intel manufactures several chips that would have met the basic need of the project, adequately. It was decided to utilize the Celeron chip, which is the darling of the overclocking crowd. Due to price considerations, the Celeron 300A was chosen and a total of five were purchased, one for the server system and four for cluster nodes. The next decision was which version of Celeron: Slot 1 or PPGA? Luckily, a suggestion from AOpen solved the problem. AOpen was just releasing a new product (their MX3L) motherboard that uses a Celeron PPGA chip. AOpen was simply outstanding in their support of this project, providing timely technical and other assistance. That support is very important in this kind of project. Given this support, it was decided to obtain several AOpen MX3L systems and associated support hardware to be discussed later.

For AMD the choice was easier. The K6-2 series is the most abundant and affordable, with the fastest being the 400 MHz chip. A set of five K6-2 400 MHz chips were obtained, one would become a backup server and the other four were destined to be cluster nodes.

Again, customer support proved the deciding factor in choosing a motherboard vendor for the AMD chips. It was decided that the Tyan 1590s-100 would be an excellent choice for speed, reliability, and compatibility with the K6-2 400. Compatibility was confirmed by checking the AMD web site and consulting the motherboard compatibility list; the 1590 is listed as a compatible board if the BIOS is up to date. This was not a problem, and a set of four 1590s boards were obtained.

## Memory

Having selected the boards and chips, the next critical component chosen was memory. The quality of the memory components is often the limiting factor in whether a particular motherboard is actually capable of achieving maximum performance. To put it simply, if you buy a poor quality memory chip, then do not expect to get 100 MHz out of the motherboard, no matter what label is on the memory module.

The Tyan system is more sensitive to memory quality since it is a PC-100 motherboard, which means it can run memory at 100 MHz as opposed to the older standard of 66 MHz, which the Celeron/MX3L motherboard uses. This required a search for a high quality manufacturer and vendor. For cost considerations as well as compatibility, Kingston and Apacer (a division of the Acer/AOpen Corporation) were selected to provide DIMMs for the Tyan/AMD and AOpen/Celeron systems respectively. All the systems were configured with PC-100 unbuffered DIMMs as the cost difference was minimal between the PC-66 and PC-100 compared with the limitations that a PC-66 DIMM will have in a PC-100 (or 133) world.

## Network Components

Now we came to decide on the network infrastructure. As we have seen earlier on this chapter, communication is the backbone of a distributed system. Poor quality systems will be significantly degraded if the primary parameters of communications system – latency and bandwidth – do not match the needs of the application. On the other hand, if the required system's costs exceed the budget and you can accept the loss of performance, then you might be able to compromise and find a system that will be adequate. In this project, there is no specific application that would require a particular network infrastructure, and we had an extant Ethernet network, so Ethernet was chosen.

The existing network equipment is Bay Networks Netgear equipment and it is generally better to stay with a particular network equipment vendor to avoid conflicts or incompatibilities. Bay Networks was contacted to determine whether their products would meet the project needs. After lengthy consultation with their applications engineers, the following components were chosen and acquired for reasons of cost and flexibility:

❑   FA310TXC 10/100 PCI NIC (uses the TULIP driver in Linux)

❑   FS516 10/100MB Fast Ethernet Switch a 16 port hub.

The adoption of the FA310TXC was the impetus that prompted the upgrade to Red Hat 5.2 from 5.0, because the TULIP driver is better in the 5.2 package. As an alternative, a pure 100 MB Switch was considered, but the cost as well as the incompatibility with some of the older systems motivated the use of the 10/100 MB shared bandwidth FS516.

For those of you who are confused by this statement, the term *switched* has been compromised of the last few months by vendors who are misusing the term. Essentially a "switched hub" is a hub that provides the full bandwidth of the hub to each port rather than sharing the overall bandwidth among the various ports. Less expensive hubs have a fixed bandwidth, say 1 GB/sec, and that amount is divided among the various ports. Hence, with increasing port number the amount of bandwidth/port drops, and can drop bellow the purported 10/100 MB/sec per port. In more expensive hubs, the overall bandwidth is such that each port gets full access to defined bandwidth so a 100 MB/sec port will get 100 MB/sec. Other vendors have used the term *switched* to mean the hub can communicate with either a 10 or 100 MB/sec NIC. Honestly, this is very confusing; hopefully the industry will fix this problem one way or another.

For the AOpen system, it was decided to stay with AOpen components. An AOpen NIC was chosen, and a set of ALN-320 were acquired. (The ALN-320 is a PCI card that is a 10/100 MB/sec NIC and has a Linux driver, sold under the Acer brand name.) This card is very economical, and has the added advantage of having a bootrom socket that can be used for diskless systems. A set of diskless nodes was considered for the project, built around the AOpen systems, but the added technical burden of a building a diskless system was considered beyond the scope of the project.

## Video Subsystems

The project is centered on the construction of a dedicated system, with little or no projected high-end graphics work planned for the system. Therefore, a minimal graphics capability was required overall; this was particularly true for nodes themselves since they are intended as compute servers and will not have any individuals working at them. For this reason the most basic video cards would be adequate. Standard PCI and AGP S3 based video cards were acquired, AOpen/Celeron AGP Trio3D cards for the AOpen systems, and Generic PCI S3 Trio 64 cards for the Tyan/AMD systems.

It should also be noted that many PC systems will not boot without a video card in the machine, the boot strapping routine tests for the presence of the card prior to launching the operating system.

## Node Access and Control

Since PCs are generally designed to operate as desktop boxes, they generally do require some sort of interface to the outside world, otherwise they will not boot properly. This generally requires some sort of video as well as keyboard connection. This can be accomplished through either the acquisition of an inexpensive video card, video monitor, and keyboard for each system or by using a switch.

The small number of systems that will be incorporated into the cluster project allows for the use of a switching box (KVM). Belkin Corporation produces the best of these sorts of switches. Belkin was contacted and their engineers suggested the Belkin eight port OmniView Pro. The OmniView Pro has several advantages. First, Belkin produces models that work with several different machines, here PS/2 boxes, but Sun Workstations and other workstation versions are also available. Two features of the product are that it is daisy chainable with each box able to control eight different nodes and each node can be connected to other boxes with up to 1024 nodes. The boxes all coordinate with one another so that a single monitor and keyboard controls all 1024 nodes, of course this would require the acquisition of 128 of these boxes and associated cables, which will not be cheap. However, these switches make life a great deal easier. Without them you have to try to make network or terminal connections to the PCs and if they are behaving badly it is much more difficult to diagnose the problem without a direct I/O option. How do you get to the BIOS settings of a system without direct connection to a keyboard and video? Realistically, although these switches are expensive in general, it is really not that expensive since one of these components will support up to eight nodes. This will increase per node cost by roughly $55, at present market values.

If money is a key issue, you could acquire a keyboard and video card each, drop the mouse and just move a monitor around. Obviously there is the problem of space and generally it is not a good idea to connect a monitor to a hot machine so you will have to cycle them to check on them, but it is an option.

# Three Different Systems

There are two basic systems involved in this project: a server and several nodes, there are actually two types of nodes as well.

## Server — Code Name Alpha

In retrospect, it was probably a bad name choice, but it was meant in reference to the ALPHA leader of a pack.

This system is designed to function as the only node that will support a direct user. To support the user, as well as its other needs, this system is equipped with higher performance components. This system will function as the NIS and NFS server, as well as a CD-ROM drive available to the cluster.

### Motherboard

The motherboard chosen for the server is identical to that chosen for half of the nodes – the MX3L motherboard produced by Aopen, which is built around the Intel 82440LX chipset with no secondary (L2) cache. The board has one AGP slot, three PCI slots and a single. The maximum memory in DIMMs is 384 MB, which is the system's only drawback.

### CPU

As has been stated previously, the MX3L is a Celeron-based board.caused Intel to install a 128K fully integrated L2 cache, beginning with the Celeron 300A. Due to the excellent price point of the 300A, five of these chips were purchased. The price point of these chips is hard to beat.

### Cooling Fans and Cooling in General

Although Celerons run without producing too much heat, good quality fans are essential. Several Cool Master Socket 7 ball bearing fans were purchased, which were sufficient to supply the entire project. You cannot go wrong with good cooling; all the cases have an extra fan, even the low power AOpen cases described below.

### Video

The server will also function as a workstation. One potential project that might be tackled in the future is image processing or image generation through various software packages. Therefore, the video card used in the server was a Diamond Stealth 4000 3D AGP card with 4 MB of video memory from the S3 Trio3D. This is not to say that the AOpen video cards are not up to the task, but at the present time the S3 Trio3D chip sets are not fully supported by the X11 drivers and that limits their utility in this situation. By the time you read this the S3 Trio3D should be an X11 supported chip.

### NIC

The NIC used in the server is the AOpen ALN-320, using their production driver, which was acquired from their customer support web site. The driver still generates a significant amount of debugging information during shutdown; just ignore it – AOpen is just being careful about making sure information is available if there is a problem.

### CD-ROM

The CD-ROM is an Acer/AOpen 36x – MTRP. Installed as a master drive on IDE, the CD-ROM is bootable with the correct BIOS settings. It should be noted that there have been no problems with the IDE and SCSI interfaces living together. A Seagate drive was installed, for a period of time, to test whether there might be an issue. No conflict arose, and in addition, it was possible to switch boot drives from BIOS by switching between the SCSI as the boot and the C-drive as the boot drive

### Server SCSI Controller

In order to improve the disk performance of the server, SCSI was chosen as the hard drive interface. The author had excellent experiences with Adaptec SCSI adapters, and was able to acquire a 2940UW for a very reasonable price, so that was adopted. This particular card has somewhat of a checkered history with Linux, but both the Red Hat 5.0 and 5.2 installation/upgrade utilities recognized and properly handled the card. Therefore, in general, the author can highly recommend the card. The single drawback with the card is that it has three different interfaces only, two of which can be used at any given time. It has a 68 pin Ultra Wide (SCSI-3) internal ribbon cable connector, a 68 pin UW external connector, and a 50 pin Narrow (SCSI-1) connector. Any two of these can be used at the same time.

### Seagate Barracuda

The mass storage device chosen is a Seagate Barracuda. This is generally considered a high-performance server quality drive, second only to the Seagate Cheetah in performance. Due to several factors, including cost, a 4 GB drive was chosen. This will be consistent with the IDE drive sizes that will be used in some of the nodes.

## Nodes

There are two types of nodes in this project: four AMD K6-2 400 based machines and four Celeron based systems.

## Machines 1-4

These systems are essentially identical except that Machine 1 has a CD-ROM to facilitate software installation.

### CPU

The systems will be built around the American Micro Devices (AMD) K6-2 400 MHz chip. The K6-2 is an evolved form of the AMD K6 which is a direct competitor for the Intel Pentium MMX chip. The K6-2 has been augmented with both MMX and 3DNow technology that is AMD's answer to Intel's MMX technology. The K6 and the Pentium are binary and pin compatible with each other, the primary exception being that the AMD chips have operating voltages that are different for the core and I/O. This means that motherboards that support the Intel line may not support the AMD chip, this is a rarity these days, however. Further, the AMD chips generally put out more heat than do the Intel versions, so ventilation is much more of an issue with the AMD chips. The AMD chips do perform better overall than Intel chips at the same clock speed, although they're floating point performance generally lags behind the Intel chips.

### Motherboard

The Tyan 1590S PC-100(BIOS Rev 1.16) was selected for the AMD K6-2 400 MHz CPUs. This board is a highly recommended board for this chip, as long as the BIOS is 1.16(b) or later. The board does include a 1 MB L2 cache, with a VIA Apollo MVP3 100MHz AGP chipset. The larger L2 cache has its advantages, mainly in dealing with large amounts of RAM. There have been reports that increasing the memory available to a system without increasing the L2 cache, can actually decrease the systems performance. Therefore, increased L2 cache means fewer memory accesses and fewer cache invalidation processes, hence greater speed overall. This board supports 2x AGP, three PCI and three ISA and one shared PCI/ISA slot for a total of 8 slots.

### Video

Since these systems are simply compute nodes, there is generally no need to have any video systems. The problem is that you can't configure these systems that way. To keep the cost down, a set of inexpensive S3 Trio64V+/64 1MB cards were purchased.

### NIC

The in conjunction with the hub selected, a set of Netgear NIC (FA310TXC 10/100 PCI) were acquired. These NICs have an excellent reputation with the Linux community, once the driver was reasonably stable.

### CD-ROM

The primary CD-ROM drive for the entire system is the AOpen CD-ROM located on the Alpha server. However in order to facilitate maintenance an IDE CD-ROM drive was installed on one of the nodes, a Memorex 32X (CD-362E) which is an ATAPI drive, recognized by Red Hat 5.2 without any trouble.

### Seagate UIDE Drives

The boot drives used were Seagate St34310A 4 Gig Ultra DMA drives. The Seagate drives performance as outstanding, performing very well even in very warm cases. The performance and reliability of these drives was outstanding. On one experiment, a series of many small calculations was run, the author wanted to see just how long it would take for the cluster to perform the computations, the usage was very disk intensive with the drives being accessed almost constantly for nearly 48 hrs. Not one drive failed, even though the case temperatures exceeded acceptable limits for most of the period.

## Machines 5-8

These systems are not identically configured in hardware. Each of these machines has a hard drive that is much smaller than the AMD systems, and of differing sizes and manufacture. The partition tables for each drive was determined by the smallest drive (1 GB) and that was carried through each drive. Some space was wasted, but since these drives were not intended to store user data , this was seen as important. The more difficult issue is that the drives themselves were not identical in cache or latency.

### CPU

The Celeron chip was chosen for the AOpen Intel based systems, because of its low cost and versatility.

For those of you who are not fans of "overclocking" move to the next section

The Celeron has achieved a state of fame that is unprecedented. It runs very cool and if you put an oversized fan on it, you can achieve amazing results. In this project there was no overclocking attempted. First, overclocking is the adjustment of CPU voltages and frequencies to force the CPU to run a speeds greater than its stated speed. Overclocking is generally a hobbyist tool because it can cause all kinds of legal trouble for a corporation. Intel has become very testy about the whole concept, reportedly to protect the consumer from mislabeled machines. All fine and good, but they do reserve the right to claim that an organization that overclocks is violating their user license. Further, there is a real risk of damaging equipment if you either overclock too much, or you do it incorrectly. It is strongly suggested that you refrain from overclocking. If you do, keep in mind that if you have problems, they may be masked by the distributed system, that you might easily miss interpret problems caused by overclocking as drive problems or network problems, any number of things. If you decide to experiment with it, wait until you are certain that the distributed system is stable, and then try it with a single machine at a time. Good luck and keep a fire extinguisher handy.

### Motherboard

The choice of the motherboard was simple The AOpen systems came equipped with the MX3L board. This board is a Micro-ATX board, built around the Intel 82440LX. It has one AGP (2x), three PCI and one ISA slot. The board also has onboard sound and is jumper and battery free. All these feature and a small format make it ideal for this project.

### Video

The video system used on these nodes is an AOpen product called AOpen PG128 which uses the S3 Trio3D chipset. The card is an 66 MHz AGP card with 4 MB of RAM. At present there are no X11 drivers for the Trio3D, but the VGA driver works quite well.

### NIC

The network interface cards selected for the Celeron systems were Acer/AOpen ALN-320 10/100 MB PCI cards. Driver information is available from www.aopenusa.com.

### Bay Networks Netgear Hub

The Bay Networks FS516 10/100 Switch was chosen because of its excellent performance, reasonable cost, and because it will fit into the existing Netgear based topology. The latency was estimated as less than 80 microseconds, but the results were actually better than that on average.

# Configuration of the Nodes

The systems were grouped by the CPU manufacture, and RedHat 5.2 was installed on each systems drive.

## Installation of Linux on the Server

A copy of Red Hat 5.2 was obtained from a local vendor, and installed on a server; the BIOS was configured to allow CD-ROM booting and the installation scripts went from there.

### AOpen NIC

The AOpen NIC was different. Since the card's driver is not standard, and none of the standard drivers worked with the card, it was necessary to download the file from the AOpen web page (www.aopenusa.com) and then copy it to a floppy disk.

### Server Partition Table

The Seagate Barracuda was partitioned in the following way consistent with Red Hat recommendations:

| | | |
|---|---|---|
| / | 128 MB | growable |
| /usr | 500 | growable |
| /usr/src | 256 | growable |
| /usr/local | 256 | growable |
| /home | 128 | growable |
| /swap1 | 127 | fixed |
| /swap2 | 127 | fixed |

For an explanation of these partitions look up Appendix C or you r Installation guide.

### Video Card Settings

The video card is a Diamond 3D 4000 AGP (4 MB) card, with the S3 Virge chipset. The Xconfigurator application recommended the SVGA driver, at 32 bit with 1024x768, but that did not run correctly, giving a hashed screen. The SVGA with 24 bit/1024x768 worked fine so that was set as the default.

## Installation of Linux on Nodes

The installation process was the same for the nodes as the server – the BIOS was set to allow CD-ROM boot and the RedHat 5.2 install scripts took it from there. It was determined that the fastest way to install RedHat was to use the machine with the CD-ROM, hence RedHat installed, and configure the successive drives as slave IDE drives and install directly to the slave IDE drive. The only complication, and it is a very minor one, was keeping track of which drive was assigned which machine name and IP address.

In a real world situation with several dozen or hundreds of machines to configure where each machine had a boot image installed on its local drive, the best approach would probably be NFS mounted upgrades or the use of an inexpensive commercial gang copier, which is a device that can copy byte for byte information from one drive to several other drives at the same time

## Configuration of Client and Server

There are several key components of the system that must be configured on each of the nodes, and others that must be unique or specific to the server. These components are required to run a network in general and a distributed system specifically.

## Fixed IPs

As has been stated previously, each node in a network requires an IP address if it is to be placed on an Ethernet network. There are generally two ways to get an IP address; either the machine acquires one from a central source or it is permanently assigned one. If it acquires one, this is generally done through a tool like Dynamic Host Configuration Protocol (DHCP). When a machine boots, and if configured to do so, it will request an IP address from the DHCP server which will assign it one from a pool of IP addresses it controls. DHCP will then work with the Domain Name Server (DNS) to make sure that DNS know which IP address now goes with which machine name. In a fixed IP configuration an, IP address is assigned to a machine and does not change form boot to boot. Fixed IP is generally faster because it does not depend on the DHCP server for its address.

Since an IP must be unique world-wide, the ownership of them has been given out through a formal procedure. However, there is a range of IP addresses that have historically been associated with experimental systems that are intended to be isolated from the general internet; it is a class C range of 192.168.x.x. If this is not the case in your system, then you are going to have to purchase or borrow a set of IP addresses sufficient to support our networking needs.

The IP can be assigned in several different ways. The simplest is through the X Window System utilities provided for network configuration. This requires that the X is configured as well as the network card.

## Drive Partitions

The drive partitions for the two node types are different. For the Tyan based systems there were four drives of identical manufacture and size – Seagate 4 GB UIDE drives. The AOpen systems were different because originally those systems were intended to be diskless systems or hybrid systems, hence, at the onset, no native system disks were ordered. However, due to the interests of time and technical reasons that effort was postponed until a future date, which meant that hard drives would be required for those systems. This necessitated a difference in the partition tables for the different groups of nodes.

### Tyan/AMD

The partition table was more spacious on these systems as they had a main drive of 4 GB. One additional point is that since the /home directory was NFS mounted from the server, there was no need for one on these nodes.

| / | 128 MB | growable |
|---|---|---|
| /usr | 500 | growable |
| /usr/src | 256 | growable |
| /usr/local | 256 | growable |
| /tmp | 128 | growable |
| /swap1 | 127 | fixed |
| /swap2 | 127 | fixed |

Note that the /home partition has been exchanged for a /tmp partition.

### AOpen/Celeron

As has been stated before, the AOpen systems were restricted to 1 GB drives:

| / | 80 MB | growable |
|---|---|---|
| /usr | 384 | growable |
| /usr/src | 128 | growable |
| /usr/local | 128 | growable |
| /tmp | 64 | growable |
| /swap1 | 127 | fixed |
| /swap2 | 127 | fixed |

## Network Configuration

The network cards and configuration has been discussed in some detail previously. Here we will discuss the actual configuration of the systems.

### AOpen

AOpen systems were equipped with their own 10/100BaseTX cards, Acer ALN-320 whose Linux driver and source were available on the AOpen web site. The GNU zipped file was placed in its own directory /usr, unzipped and followed the directions. That is, the script trans was run and it compiled the driver, generating aln320.o file, which was then copied to /usr/src/linux/modules/aln320.o. Then it was necessary to modify /etc/conf.modules to include the line

```
alias eth0 aln320
```

This will force the loading of the aln320 driver module if it is included in the modules directory listed above, you can include an absolute path but it can become confusing. Once the driver was properly loading during reboot, the rest of the configuration is common to both systems.

### Netgear NIC

The Tyan systems were equipped with Netgear NICs running the TULIP driver from the Red Hat 5.2 distribution. The Red Hat installation software picked up the card and all that needed to be done was select the driver from the list. The driver names are not always based on the NIC card vendor but are more generally based on the chip maker that the NIC card vendor used. It will be helpful to visit the makers web site or email their technical support staff to determine which driver you will need..

## General Configuration

The actual configuration of the system for operation was generally done through the X Window System configuration utilities that run under root. This utility makes configuring the system substantially easier, so use it if you can. If you cannot, there are several excellent HOWTOs on the subject and there are a couple of good books on the overall configuration of networking. As an overview, you will be spending most of your time in `/etc` modifying files that tell the system who it is, what protocols it is going to be working with, and how it is going to be communicating and with whom.

It is beyond the scope of this section to go into complete detail about the configuration of an individual host and all of the options that are available. Indeed that would warrant an entire section of its own. However, a general overview of the files that were modified for this project will be discussed, as well as other files that might be of importance for your particular needs. Note that not all of these files will be used by all distributions of Linux. Some vendors use their own installation and configuration utilities and hence they have their own specific files and scripts. The files, utilities and scripts discussed here relate to Red Hat.

The principle files in question include: `/etc/hosts`, `/etc/hostname` ( or `/etc/HOSTNAME`), `/etc/sysconf/network`, `/etc/sysconf/network-scripts/ifcfg-eth0`.

❑    `/etc/hosts` – tells the node what other computers are called and includes its IP.

❑    `/etc/hostname` – tells the node its name.

❑    `/etc/sysconf/network` – configures the network and may include hostname as well as the domain name, gateway IP etc.

❑    `/etc/sysconf/network-scripts/ifcfg-eth0` – configures the Ethernet card for the system and it includes the netmask, network, IP and other constants.

Other files that may need to be modified include:

❑    `/etc/networks` – lists names and IP address of your own network and others you might want to get to easily.

❑    `/etc/host.conf` – used to resolve host names. If it looks like:

```
order hosts, bind
multi on
```

then you are fine, otherwise check your documentation.

❑    /etc/resolv.conf — used to resolve hostnames, includes the domain name and the IP of the name server. This can be set or left unmodified depending on whether you are going static IP. This means no DNS or domain name will be used. Note that this domain name is something like ABCCorp.com. In the next chapter we will discuss a different kind of domain name in conjunction with MPI so keep that in mind.

❑    /etc/services — identifies the existing network services and their corresponding port numbers;under some situations you will need to check this file to see if there is a free port but don't modify this file unless you have to.

It should be obvious that the network configuration utilities are extremely helpful in reducing the amount of difficulty and potential for error that you are likely to encounter.

### NIS Server

The Network Information System (NIS) provides a series of files located on the NIS server to any approved NIS client who requests them. This means that there has to be at least one NIS server and one NIS client to work. The necessary files are included with the Red Hat 5.2 installation and that includes the server and client. The Red Hat installation scripts allow the automatic installation of all the required files, just be sure to be alert to the installation and indicate that you want them installed.

On the server side, the configuration consists of installing the correct ypserver components and creating the database required by the server. Installation is done through the use of and RPM for Red Hat, or a tar file for other distributions. Alternatively, you can download it from:

ftp.kernel.org/pub/linux/utils/net/NIS/ypserv-1.x.x.tar.gz.

Again, the option for installing the ypserver components is included in the Red Hat installation scripts, you might have to look for it a little depending on the version of Red Hat you are using.

Assuming that you have installed the software, the configuration is relatively straight forward. In this project, there were really not enough nodes to warrant a slave server, hence there will only be a master NIS server, which makes the configuration somewhat easier.

First you have to choose a domain name (in our case RESEARCH). Now look for the line DOMAIN="", which in Red Hat distribution is found in /etc/rc.d/rc.sysinit, and modify it to reflect the new DOMAIN name. Alternatively, you could experiment using the function DOMAINNAME which will set the systems domain name for the duration of the systems session.

The next step is to ensure that portmapper is running. You can do this simply by using the following command as root:

```
# rcpinfo —u localhost ypserv
```

A reasonable response from the command would look something like:

```
program ##### version # ready and waiting
```

If you don't see a response like that then you have a problem with portmapper and you should investigate, starting with the HOWTOs and the man pages (portmapper(8)).

If `portmapper` is functioning properly, your next step is to build the NIS master server database by running the command:

```
# /usr/lib/yp/ypinit -m
```

You will be presented with some information telling you the files which have been placed into the database, and then asked for some specific information on the master and slave server names. Answer with the unqualified server names, not IP or fully qualified names. A `make process` should follow, and if all goes well a directory under `/var/yp/YourDomainName` should be created with all the appropriate files in the database. At this point you should be ready to go; either manually start `ypserv` or reboot.

Depending on your specific network configuration you might want to take a look at the `ypserv.conf` file located in `/etc`. This file modifies some of the behaviors of the NIS server, and depending on just how your systems are configured — for example, DNS. You might want to make some modifications there. It is a well-documented file, and if you are armed with the HOWTOs, you should be well prepared to make any necessary changes.

### NIS Client

The NIS client is generally easy to configure. As usual, you will need the `ypbind` software. This is a daemon that runs on the client and makes the connections to the servers. Remember, don't configure the client until after you have successfully configured the master and slave servers. To configure the client, some of the same actions apply as in the server. Starting with the domain name in `/etc/rc.d/rc.sysinit`:

```
DOMAIN="" to DOMAIN="RESEARCH"
```

Next, you have to tell the system to start `ypbind` on boot, this was done by placing `/sbin/ypbind` in the `/etc/rc.d/rc.local` script. Now that the client daemon is running on every reboot, I have to tell the daemon where to find the server. That is done in the `yp.conf` file located in `/etc`, `yp.conf` allows you to make decisions on how the client will search for the server. A broadcast or more tailored approach using IP and hostnames are available. For experimentation purposes, all three were configured and enabled, once it was established that at least one of the choices was working properly, each was disabled in turn, with each functioning properly.

Once all this is done, you should be able to reboot your client.

### NFS Server

The Network File System (NFS) provides a bridge between a system which wants to have access to a particular systems file system, and the system that is providing access to that file system. Like the NIS system discussed previously, this is a client-server system, however, unlike the NIS system, an NFS system can be both a client and a server of file systems depending on the configuration of the components. In this project, a little of both was done. First, the principle file system made available to all nodes was the `/home` directory on the server which functions as the development system and is the principle workstation of the project. The other file systems are the CD-ROM drives located on some of the nodes including the server as well as two of the slave nodes of the cluster. This was done to minimize maintenance hassles and trips up and down flights of stairs. Initially, the `/home` directory was shared for convenience' sake, but you will see later that several primary development tools like MPI and PVM actually require this sort of shared file system in order to operate.

To configure the NFS, the principal decisions that must be made are: which systems will act as servers and which as clients, followed by which file systems will be shared with which clients. Once that is done, it is a matter of configuring the correct files, and starting the right daemons.

In this installation the NFS server will be providing access to its /home as well as its /cdrom directories. To facilitate this, a copy of the NFS-Server-2.2beta37.rpm was installed and configured. Since there will be only one server on the cluster, the server package will not be installed to any other systems.

Once the NFS server package is installed, the next step is to check portmapper. You should have it up and running if you installed NIS; you can check if it is or not by typing:

```
# ps aux | grep -e portmap  # or potentially rpc.portmap
```

or

```
# rcpinfo -u localhost ypserv
```

If not, then you are going to have to investigate portmapper and figure out what the problem is. It should be living in /sbin or perhaps /usr/sbin depending on your distribution. From this point on, lets assume that portmap is up and running.

The next daemons that we will need to configure are mountd and nfsd. To do that we have to configure the /etc/exports file. You may find that you do not have such a file yet, so you have to create one. To accomplish the mapping of the directories, the following lines were added to /etc/exports:

```
/mnt/cdrom (ro)
/home (rw)
```

Where (ro) and (rw) specify read-only and read-write respectively. If you want to restrict the access to a specific node then you would place its name before the access permissions, by way of example: node11(rw). For more details on this, see the HOWTO listed in the chapter bibliography.

Next, you have to tell the daemons nfsd and mountd that the change has been made to /etc/exports. To do that, you can either use a commonly available script called exportfs which may or may not exist on your distribution; it is short so it is included here:

```
#!/bin/sh
killall -HUP /usr/sbin/rpc.mountd
killall -HUP /usr/sbin/rpc.nfsd
echo re-exported file systems
```

There are more complex versions of this script that have more functionality, but this one will do the job.

Now it is back to `rpcinfo -p` to see if the gang is all at the party, you should see something like:

```
Program vers proto port
100000 2 tcp 111 rcpbind
100000 2 udp 111 rcpbind
100005 1 udp 635 mountd
100005 2 udp 635 mountd
100005 1 tcp 635 mountd
100005 2 tcp 635 mountd
100003 2 udp 2049 nfs
100003 2 tcp 2049 nfs
100007 2 udp 616 ypbind
100007 2 tcp 618 ypbind
100004 2 udp 627 ypserv
100004 1 udp 627 ypserv
100004 2 tcp 630 ypserv
100004 1 tcp 630 ypserv
```

There is a lot going on here. You might be looking for specific member of the crew like `portmapper`, but their presence depends on just how things are configured in the distribution. The above result comes directly from Alpha and all of its children are happy and able to find their `/home` directory – and the `/cdrom`, if it exists. If you don't see this sort of result and get a warning about RPC or something to that effect, then `portmapper` is not properly configured, which sometimes happens if some service it depends on failed or it has a configuration problem itself. If this is the case, then you have to solve the `portmapper` problem before you can go on.

Well, that is essentially it, at least for the server. You will have to go and change your `rc` scripts to start `nfsd` and `mountd` at boot time.

## NFS Client

Now things are a little different on the client side. With Red Hat you don't have to worry about NFS being available. Unless you specified not to include it, you will find that it was installed automatically. Assuming your server is up and running, you should be able to mount the remote partitions using the `mount` command. On our experimental system, you would use the command:

```
# mount –o rsize=1024,wsize=1024 Alpha:/home /home
```

This should successfully provide access to the Alpha server's `/home` partition mounted on the local node as its `/home` partition. To undo this command you would use:

```
# umount /home
```

To make the mounting permanent you would have to modify `/etc/fstab` to include the mounting and you will have to make some decision on how you want to mount these partitions. The behavior of the system will vary depending on the choices you make; consult the man pages on `fstab` and the NFS HOWTO for further details, but I chose the following for the clients `/etc/fstab` parameters in mounting Alpha's `/home` and `/cdrom` directories:

```
/dev/sda1     /         ext2    defaults   1 1
/dev/sda7     /usr      ext2    defaults   1 2
/dev/sda8     /usr/local  ext2    defaults   1 2
/dev/sda9     /usr/src  ext2    defaults   1 2
/dev/sda5     swap      swap    defaults   0 0
/dev/sda6     swap      swap    defaults   0 0
/dev/fd0      /mnt/floppy ext2    noauto     0 0
Alpha:/home   /home     nfs     rsize=1024,wsize=1024,hard,intr 0 0
Alpha:/cdrom  /cdrom    nfs     rsize=1024,wsize=1024,hard,intr 0 0
```

All you have to do is reboot and the mounting will be done for you.

### Domain Name Server (DNS)

Now it is true that if you wanted to try and maintain a hosts list on each system you could do that, but it is really very difficult to do in larger networks. That is why DNS makes life so much easier, which is particularly true in heterogeneous networks.

Previously we discussed the decision to used fixed IP instead of DNS because the cluster was small and because the added network traffic and associated overhead would substantially increase the network latency that limits the granularity of the problems that can be handled by distributed or parallel systems. However, for some applications, it is a particularly powerful tool. For that reason, the installation and configuration of DNS will not be discussed here, but will be covered in greater detail in conjunction with the specific case studies in the next chapter.

# Summary

This chapter has been part lecture and part tutorial. The information section can be summed up rather quickly.

- ❑   Distributed systems allow you to maximize the value of existing systems.

- ❑   Communication is the heart and soul of a distributed system and you have to make sure to match your problems with the communications methods.

- ❑   Distributed systems are complex, requiring more technology than presently exists to fully implement, but they can still be substantially more reliable with better performance and usability than present technology affords.

- ❑   Distributed software is not as plentiful as traditional software.

- ❑   Distributed systems require you to keep in mind the type of problem you wish to solve and accommodate the limitations while you try and optimize their strengths.

- ❑   Distributed systems allow users to enjoy a level of flexibility and interoperability that can not be matched by any presently envisioned technology.

- ❑   Distributed systems offer the most transparent and reliable systems available if properly designed and supported.

- ❑   Distributed systems can not be outdone in the long run for performance and they allow you to solve problems that simply can not be touched by any other technology.

In this chapter we also reviewed some of the hardware choices that we would have to make, such as choosing the chips and motherboards and other features for our server and client machines.

Then we referred to some of the primary tools needed to build a distributed system, namely the Network Information System (NIS) and the Network File System (NFS), as well as their role in a transparent distributed system. NIS provides access control in a uniform manner to all nodes, and NFS provides common disk access to all the nodes. With NIS and NFS combined, a system can be built in which a user will have no direct knowledge of his or her file system locations, thus creating at least a primitive transparent environment.

Towards the end of the chapter we covered a large amount of territory, the intent of which was to give a detailed description of the decisions and options that were considered in designing and construction of the cluster used in this project. This chapter provided sufficient detail that if you were so disposed, you could build essentially the same cluster simply by following the same steps. Of course there may be issues that are of interest to your project, but were not discussed because they are either not particularly important to the general configuration of the project at this time (DNS for example), or they essentially have no place in the project in general (like Samba). If that is the case, you are referred to the appropriate reference materials such as HOWTOs, the NET, or the myriad of published material on a wide variety of Linux applications.

# Bibliography

Dietz, Hank, *Linux Parallel Processing HOWTO*, on most Linux distributions under `/etc/doc/HOWTO`.

Geist, Al; Beguelin, Adam; Dongarra, Jack; Jiang, Weicheng; Mancheck, Robert; Sunderam, Vaidy, *PVM: Parallel Virtual Machine A User's Guide and Tutorial*, MIT Press (Also available at ftp://netlib2.cs.utk.edu/pvm3/book/pvm-book.ps)

Gwennap, Linley, *Compaq, Intel Fight Digital Brain Drain*, Microprocessor Report, Vol. 12, Issue 14, Oct. 26, 1998, Cahners MicroDesign Resources

Kukuk, Thorsten, *NIS(YP)/NYS/NIS+ HOWTO*, v0.12, June 1998

Halsall, Fred, Data Communications, Computer Networks, and Open Systems, Addison-Wesley, 1993, ISBN 0-201-56506-4

Langfeldt, Nicolai, *NFS HOWTO*, v. 0.7, November 1997

Nemkin, Robert, *Diskless Systems HOWTO*, on most Linux distributes under `/etc/doc/HOWTO/mini`

Pacheco, Peter S., Kaufmann, Morgan, *Parallel Programming with MPI*, ISBN 1558603395

Shanley, Tom, *PowerPC System System Architecture*, Addison-Wesley, 1995, ISBN 0-201-40990-9

Shanley, Tom, *ISA System Architecture*, 3rd edition, Addison-Wesley, 1995, ISBN 0-201-40996-8

Shanley, Tom, *PCI System Architecture*, 3rd edition, Addison-Wesley, 1995, ISBN 0-201-40993-3

Shanley, Tom, *Pentium Processor System Architecture*, 2nd edition, Addison-Wesley, 1995, ISBN 0-201-40992-5

Stern, Hal, *Managing NFS and NIS*, O'Reilly, 1991, ISBN 0-937175-75-7

Stevens, Richard W., *Unix Network Programming*, 2nd edition, Prentice Hall, 1998 ISBN 0-13-081081-9

Tanenbaum, Andrew S., *Distributed Systems*, Prentice Hall, 1995 ISBN 0-13-219908-4

Tanenbaum, Andrew S., *Computer Networks*, Prentice Hall, 1988 ISBN 0-13-349945-6

# 13

# Implementing Distributed Systems

In the last chapter, we discussed the steps required to set up and configure a clustering system. In this chapter, we will build on what we have learned, and implement some distributed software.

## Introduction

At this point in time, you should have a fully functional distributed system up and running. This system should be built in such a way that an individual user enjoys transparency on his or her file location after logging on to any of the systems nodes, the NFS mounted home partition appearing without any evidence of the cluster topology or system configuration. If you have chosen not to implement such a system, then you will have more work to do. You will also not receive the full benefit of the subject matter of this chapter without a cluster to work with.

It must be noted that all of the items covered in this chapter are complex and powerful tools in their own right, quite independent of Linux. Therefore, it would be unreasonable to expect all aspects of each subject to be fully explained within a single chapter. As a result, the content in this chapter provides only that which is necessary to demonstrate what can be achieved through clustering without becoming a tutorial or road map of how a specific outcome might be acquired. Hence, there are details and procedures that simply will not be discussed in great detail, and others that will not be discussed at all, which might have significant bearing on the success of an individual implementation of one or more of these case studies. Many of the omitted topics included details like database design, construction and maintenance for both the Oracle and Sybase products, as well as certain aspects of the support software installation, which is both complex and difficult to convey in a concise format.

Now with all that out of the way, let's get started. This chapter is about making your cluster useful. The approach is to discuss several potential uses for your cluster and to explore some potential projects along the way.

# Distributed Application Development Tools

For distributed applications to be useful, they have to be created first. There are certain limitations on this statement that should be noted.

Linux is very good at "paralleling" some functionality. For instance, if you have a symmetric parallel processing (SMP) machine and you run an application that delegates a portion of it's operations to a separate process, then depending on system utilization and resources, the operating system may send that process to the second processor. This is largely automatic and is one activity of an SMP kernel. Having said that, load balancing and parallel processor support over a network are not simple technologies that Linux can automatically emulate. The software packages that you use to attack complex and difficult applications tend to be specialized tools to affect a parallel design. If the application is well written using supported tools, there is a smart cluster process queuing tool (GNU Queue) that can communicate with other processes and share them between processors that have available resources. This is a major step forward in the development of a truly transparent cluster with dynamic automatic resource allocation. There are substantial limitations on this tool, but one can hope that with time and the seemingly boundless resource and imagination of the Linux community, we will see enhancements to both the kernel and its support tools that will allow fully autonomous and transparent load balancing and process distribution within Linux clusters, both heterogeneous and homogeneous.

We will discuss in some detail two of the most prominent tools presently available for Linux, the Message Passing Interface (MPI) and the Parallel Virtual Machine (PVM), then we will discuss briefly some of the alternatives. These are alternatives that are either in existence, and some that are under development with the potential to make a significant impact on the parallel development front in the near future.

# Message Passing Interface (MPI)

MPI is essentially what it says, a method of passing information between processes either on the same machine or on different machines. It is a set of utilities that package, distribute, and control the flow of information and operation of processes running on all processors. Although heterogeneous versions of the tools have been created, generally it is expected that MPI will be running on a homogeneous system. MPI has been implemented as the principle process communications method on many commercial parallel processing machines, because each of the vendors of Massively Parallel Processor (MPP) systems were developing their own proprietary interfaces and APIs, thus limiting the potential growth of the technology. Roughly forty experts in parallel processing theory were assembled, to develop a common methodology that eventually became the early MPI protocol. There have been several versions of the protocol; MPI 2.0 is the most recent with MPI 3.0 on its way, at the time of writing. Because of wide industry support, there is some significant experience in the development community for the MPI protocol. Finally, MPI has been anointed as the 'official' replacement for PVM, which has been historically dominant, and will be discussed later in this chapter.

We will be discussing one of the multitudes of implementations of the MPI interface. One of the most common and mature, MPICH, is a widely supported and discussed implementation of the protocol. See: http://www-unix.mcs.anl.gov/mpi/MPICH/ for more details.

This is not to say that MPICH is perfect, or will fit all of your specific needs, but it is a reasonable place to start. Furthermore, it is generally easy to get, as it appears both at the previous site, but on several mirror sites and is included with several distributions including Red Hat Extreme, which has a prepackaged RPM version that is easy to install.

A thorough explanation and discussion of MPI itself is beyond the scope of this book. For detailed discussion of MPI and MPICH, please see the MPICH web site for further details, and to the bibliography at the end of the chapter for references that might assist you in your understanding of this and other tools discussed in this chapter. For other implementations of MPI, you will have to go to the web, since URLs become stale rather quickly.

## Underlying Concepts

Fundamentally, MPI is intended to implement a shared memory model of parallel computing by emulating shared memory systems on physically distributed memory systems. The shared memory model is the most common form of system architecture used by large parallel processor machines and follows the Many Instruction streams – Many Data streams (MIMD) set up which essentially means that there are several architecturally independent processors working on their own applications within their own memory.

So what does shared memory really mean? Well, it essentially means that each processor must have equal access to the general pool of memory that is available to all processors within the system. There are several architectural methods by which an integrated multiprocessor system can be constructed to meet the shared memory requirements. These architectures might involve the direct physical access of the processors (and processes) to the memory pool via a physical connection like an address or data bus, or it might well mean a virtual sharing by requesting the contents of a specific memory location from some black box interface. That black box then is instructed to perform whatever is required to find the memory location and return what ever is stored within that location, generally without changing any of the content.

The question is how can this be done for the cluster systems? With MPI generally, and MPICH specifically, the answer is that memory is shared through message passing and control operations. Essentially no direct connection exists between the various processors or processes except through the MPI interface. The developer is required to know what information is required, and when, and then to implement the communication through the use of MPI and its various tools. The developer is tasked with the bulk of the timing and processing efforts; the trade off for more effort and design/development challenges is greater flexibility.

## Advantages

MPI is an excellent solution for many problems from coarse to fine-grained problems. MPI also allows the reuse of existing algorithms originally developed for commercial parallel processing machines, which commonly use MPI as their principle inter-process (and inter-processor) communication tool. That point should not be taken lightly. There are millions of lines of code that have been developed for various tasks such as chemical structure modeling, nuclear reactor and weapons modeling, and other similar mathematical models that were written during the heyday of parallel processing machines. Much of this code has fallen into disuse after the demise of the vendors of large scale supercomputers and parallel computers. There are still vendors out there making supercomputers, but many organizations are now shy about making further purchases when they look at the million dollar machines that sit idle, due to lack of support from potentially defunct vendors. Clustered Linux machines allow them to at least make some use of these same tools, if they have to source code.

## *Disadvantages*

The principle disadvantage the MPI suffers from is the burden that it places on the developer. MPI is a relatively low-level method of achieving parallelism. The developer is expected to handle so much detail of operation that MPI has been compared to assembler in this respect. It is hoped that with time and growing development efforts that much of this detail will be encapsulated into libraries or classes that will ease the burden on the developer, but for now, the MPI developer is responsible for many of the application's most basic operations.

Furthermore, MPI has a strong dependence on homogeneous systems. Life is much simpler in such a system, and although there are attempts to develop implementation that are friendlier to heterogeneous networks, they do not have the same level of support or history as standard MPI implementations.

A less severe disadvantage is the dependence of MPICH on a common file structure, shared via NFS. Although NFS is rather reliable and a key component of the overall transparent cluster environment, it does create a potential weakness through the creation of a single-point-of-failure problem as well as a performance hit and added network loads. More seriously, depending on NFS brings about a significant increase in network security vulnerability. The network load and performance issue can be mitigated by the implementation of a parallel network that is dedicated to support the NFS as well as other system maintenance operations. This does increase the cost of the system, but network hardware is decreasing in cost daily.

## *Applications*

There are many applications that use MPI; they are all dedicated to a specific process or application that requires parallel processing. There are some libraries that support MPI and its operations in specific requirements such as complex computations involving the solution of a series of partial differential equations or the like. In reality, it is reasonable to expect that your application will require a basic rewrite using the MPI API to convert to parallel form any existing application. If you are designing from scratch, then you are really better off. MPI does show at least some similarity to classic client/server applications in the interaction of communications, using either synchronous or asynchronous communications.

It is reasonable to expect that a serious development effort might well be required to implement a parallel application. This holds true for any particular tool, MPI, PVM, CORBA etc. There were many motivations for converting single processor applications to parallel applications, but initially the cost of parallel processor systems made them scarce and hence the development process lagged behind single processor application development. This is beginning to change because of the increasing availability of SMP machines and now the phenomenal growth of Linux and clustering. In fact, the use of clusters was inevitable for many reasons, and the number of problems that would benefit from parallel processing (or simple clustering) has not decreased but increased, due to the needs of large web and e-commerce servers.

# Installation of MPICH

This section discusses the steps to follow in order to acquire, install, and configure the Message Passing Interface implementation called MPICH.

## Acquisition and Installation

Installation of MPICH is straightforward, although there are certain pitfalls that should be avoided. These are generally associated with permissions and potential problems with remote shell daemons on the individual cluster nodes. First things first, how to acquire MPICH. Again, URLs tend to change, but the most stable source so far has been available from: ftp://info.mcs.anl.gov/pub/mpi/MPICH-X.X.X.tar.gz.

Alternatively, if you purchase the Red Hat Extreme Linux CD there is an older version of MPICH (1.1.0) that is in the RPM format; the other option is to search the Red Hat site for the latest version that they supply. As the RPM installation is relatively painless and automatic, we will examine the installation of the source code version.

We will assume that you have already acquired the software and have it on your machine. There are many places you can begin the overall install process, the author suggests that you install to /usr/local/mpi but as this is a matter of personal preference; you may install to any location you have sufficient room for.

The first steps are to unzip and then untar the files using the standard command:

```
# tar xvzf mpich.tar.gz
```

This will produce a rather extensive directory tree directly under the directory you run the command on, in this case /usr/local/mpi. Once this is done, you have to configure the package as directed.

## Configuration

At this point, you have to move to the root directory of the created tree /usr/local/mpi/MPICH-X.X.X which will all the files needed to build the MPI utilities. First, however, let's define and export an environment variable that contains the path to the home directory of the package:

```
# MPICHHOME=/usr/local/mpi/mpich-X.X.X;export MPICHHOME
```

This will help when you come to use make later on. Also you might have fewer problems if you execute make under the environment shell sh rather than the default shell bash. This can be changed by editing the /etc/passwd file. Now, to eliminate a potential security hole, you will not be able to run any MPICH applications as root. You will have to move back and forth between root and a user account; it is a pain, but otherwise you will have to deal with a potentially serious security hole that has proven dangerous in the past. Once this is done, it is time to configure the package.

To configure MPICH you have to be in the MPICHHOME directory, defined above. In this case, configuring means setting up the various makefiles and other required support structures needed to compile and install the package properly. Once you're in that directory you will execute:

```
# ./configure {parameters depending on your system}
```

Now, if you are running a standard Linux distribution on a common x86 class machine, then you probably can get away without any parameters at all, the configuration utility is pretty good at figuring out what you have on your system and setting things up to run as needed. If you see any errors or warnings go flying by, you can store them by using:

```
# ./configure 2>&1 config.out
```

It is not suggested as the default operation because it is unlikely that you will have any problems with this utility, so why create a text file unless you need one. Bear this in mind; it generally works for all sorts of applications, as we will see shortly.

Once configured, you have to launch the `make` utility, which as you will have seen before will process the Makefiles. Again you can redirect the output to a text file if you see any errors:

```
# make >& make.out
```

Once `make` has completed, we can do a little check, but first we have to see if a file called `machines.XXX` (generally `machines.LINUX`) was created in the `$MPICHHOME/util/machines` directory. This file will contain the name of the system you are presently using, repeated about five times. This file must have at least five lines with a single, but not necessarily unique, node name on each line. This file lists the names of the machines that are accessible for remote processing. Note, you can perform some crude load balancing by putting the name(s) of more powerful systems in this file more than once. In general, you will have one entry for each node in a homogenous system.

## Sample Code and More Configuration

At this point, we can try to build and run a simple test program called `cpi` which lives under `$MPICHHOME/examples/basic`, which will have several files including source code and a makefile which will create several simple test applications by just running `make` at the prompt. Go ahead and run the makefile; which should go smoothly. The source code (shown below) calculates the value of $\pi$ using one to several processors then integrates the various computations and compares the value to a defined value, calculates the error and reports the overall results plus computation time. Within the example code, you will see how MPI is used, with some of the MPI API calls that control communication, data and process flow.

```c
#include "mpi.h"
#include <stdio.h>
#include <math.h>

double f(double a)
{
      return (4.0 / (1.0 + a*a));
}

void main(int argc,char *argv)
{
    int done = 0, n, myid, numprocs, i;
    double PI25DT = 3.141592653589793238462643;
    double mypi, pi, h, sum, x;
    double startwtime, endwtime;
    int namelen;
    char processor_name[MPI_MAX_PROCESSOR_NAME];

    MPI_Init(&argc,&argv);
    MPI_Comm_size(MPI_COMM_WORLD,&numprocs);
    MPI_Comm_rank(MPI_COMM_WORLD,&myid);
    MPI_Get_processor_name(processor_name,&namelen);
```

```
        fprintf(stderr,"Process %d on %s\n",myid, processor_name);
        n = 0;
        while (!done)
        {
           if (myid == 0)
           {
               if (n==0) n=100; else n=0;
               startwtime = MPI_Wtime();
           }
           MPI_Bcast(&n, 1, MPI_INT, 0, MPI_COMM_WORLD);
           if (n == 0)
               done = 1;
           else
           {
              h = 1.0 / (double) n;
              sum = 0.0;
              for (i = myid + 1; i <= n; i += numprocs)
              {
                  x = h * ((double)i - 0.5);
                  sum += f(x);
              }
              mypi = h * sum;
              MPI_Reduce(&mypi, &pi, 1, MPI_DOUBLE, MPI_SUM,0, MPI_COMM_WORLD);
              if (myid == 0)
              {
                  printf("pi is approximately %.16f, Error is %.16f\n", pi,
                                                    fabs(pi - PI25DT));
                  endwtime = MPI_Wtime();
                  printf("wall clock time = %f\n", endwtime-startwtime);
              }
          }
       }
       MPI_Finalize();
}
```

Once the make is complete, you should see a set of files like `cpi`, `fpi`, etc. To run them, you need a parallel executable loader. This application is called `mpirun` and lives in `$MPICHHOME/bin`. You will likely have to build a symbolic link to `mpirun` or modify your path to include the directory it is in, hence you can do one of these two things:

```
# ln -s $MPICH/bin/mpirun mpirun
```

```
$ PATH=$PATH:$MPICHHOME/bin; export $PATH
```

Remember that you can't run an MPI parallel application as root because of security considerations, you will have to be in a user account. If you must create a user account to do this, keep in mind that you will have to rebuild the NIS database so that all the nodes on the network will know who that user is. We can launch CPI from within the `$MPICHHOME/examples/basic` directory by:

```
$ mpirun -np {N} cpi
```

Where N is the number of processes.

In this case, you should start with one processor and work your way up; if it works for one processor it should work for all the processors. Recall that you must have at least five entries in the $MPICHHOME/util/machines/machines.LINUX file. Therefore you have five or more processors. Note that they do not all have to be unique or even be on different machines, which is helpful for development purposes. Moreover, you can actually exceed the number of processors requested without changing machines.LINUX, the parallel loader will then go down the machines.LINUX list assigning processes to each node until it either runs out of nodes or processes; if there are more processes than nodes, then it will start again at the beginning of the list. If this little test works then its time to move to a more complex set of tests, otherwise you have to take a step back to diagnose the problem.

Possible problems that might occur are related to permissions. You will need a file called .rhosts in the home directory of the user who is launching the application. In the case of the project at hand, that file is simple and looks like this:

```
Alpha       {user id}
Machine1    {user id}
Machine2    {user id}
Machine3    {user id}
Machine4    {user id}
Machine5    {user id}
Machine6    {user id}
Machine7    {user id}
Machine8    {user id}
```

The {user id} is not required on all systems, but is helpful for security reasons. This file should be saved as .rhosts file in the root directory of the appropriate user. The permissions on this file are critical, and the system requires group and all access be limited to read only, and this is done using the chmod command in the user's home directory: chmod 744 .rhosts.

Now, on the permissions front, there is one more to address and that is the permissions of the directories and files themselves. You should not change the permissions unless you have done all the previous steps and are still getting messages like permission denied then you might try changing permissions on all the MPI files and directories by typing chmod 777 -R /usr/local/mpi/MPICH-X.X.X, which as you know will allow access to anyone to do anything. As you can see, this is a drastic step and should not be necessary in general, but might be required on some systems and configurations. This should be maintained for testing purposes only. Once the testing is done, you can reduce access permissions to, say, 755, which will allow execution and read access, but not write access to all but root. The method for granting access to other users will be discussed later.

## Thorough Testing

MPICH ships with a reasonably thorough testing suite that will exercise almost all of the functionality of the tools. This process is long and involved, taking up to an hour to complete on a dedicated network with only four nodes. It is important that at least one of the nodes in the machines.LINUX file be other than the home node of MPICH. After all, you are trying to build a clustered system, and configuring and testing the MPICH package with only the local host in the machines.LINUX files is not really getting you anywhere in the long run. You will find the testing suite under $MPICHHOME/examples/test you fire it off by running:

```
$ make testing
```

Beware that these tests consume resources; this can be rectified in part by using the execution parameter:

```
$ make testing TESTARGS=-small
```

The problem here is that you will not get the best benefit from the suite. Finally, you should run the following after the test completes:

```
% make clean
```

This will clean up the leftovers and make sure the directory structure is as free from junk as possible. In the end, you might simply want delete the entire $MPICHHOME/examples/test directory, once you are certain that the testing is completed and successful.

## Other Issues

There are other issues that must be considered in the long run. Some systems do not support remote shells (rsh) and must use another tool. MPICH provides a solution called a secure server (ch_p4 and ch_nexus) which are servers that must be placed on each of the nodes listed in machines.LINUX. Their configuration is very machine-dependent and will not be discussed here, but they are discussed in detail in the documentation that accompanies MPICH. These tools provide another advantage as well; they improve performance and security. The performance is due to their being customized to MPI, and their use of a dedicated port on each node. Security is improved because you can configure them to allow selected user access on each node. However, with these utilities being tricky to configure, it is better to work with the general MPICH package until you are familiar with it and its capabilities and then look to optimize performance. (This of course assumes that you have been successful in installing the general package. If not, refer to the installation documentation for details on compiling and configuring the secure servers.)

One other potential issue concerns NFS automounting. Depending on how the configuration is done, the path to the various directory trees required for the system may be different on an automounted system than on a hard mounted system. The MPICH documentation discusses ways to alleviate this sort of issue Generally, it is a straight forward procedure and uses regular expressions to solve the problem. On the other hand, it is reasonable to expect that in a dedicated system, the shared file system be permanently mounted within each node. This is the basis of transparency, so it is reasonable to expect that there will be no 'on demand' automounting, but that the NFS file systems will be hard wired into the fstab file located in /etc.

Once you have successfully configured and tested the entire package, you can make it available to everyone. This is done by choosing a directory in a location that will be available to all for example /usr/local/mpi. Note the difference in name from the original installation directory which does not indicate the version number. This allows older packages to be maintained without changing paths. Enter the following commands:

```
# make install PREFIX=/usr/local/mpi/mpich-X.X.X
# /bin/rm -rf /usr/local/mpi
# ln -s /usr/local/mpi-X.X.X /usr/local/mpi
```

The first statement fires off the MPICH install script with a focus on installing the package generally. The second clears out any potential pre-existing directory called /usr/local/mpi and finally the third line creates symbolic link between /usr/local/mpi and /usr/local/mpi-X.X.X. Remember you will have to do this as root, and don't forget to change the permissions to 755, as stated previously. (You will have to insure that the users have the /usr/local/mpi in their PATH; it would be worth while to include /usr/local/mpi/bin, as well as updating the $MPICHHOME to the general directory.

If you have any trouble, refer to the documentation that accompanies the package, as well as a the original web site at: http://www-unix.mcs.anl.gov/mpi/mpich/. This site has documentation, some bug reports, and assistance, as well as sample applications that you can try out. However, it is unlikely that you will have any problems as long as you install the package as stated above and in the documentation.

# Parallel Virtual Machine (PVM)

The Parallel Virtual Machine or PVM has a history that is much more like that of Linux than that of MPI. PVM grew out of a project implemented by a single individual and has grown by mutual consensus and a non-centralized community contribution, rather than a formal organization producing proposals for review. It does have its own formalized underpinnings, but they came after the original implementation of the PVM tool. It is fundamentally an outgrowth of a need to utilize the resources of very diverse architectures, because it was difficult to acquire homogeneous systems and there were so many perfectly functional machines that were lying unused.

The ultimate goal of PVM was to create a virtual parallel shared memory system over many different systems by creating a virtual machine on each system that shares the same functionality as every other virtual machine on every other node within the system.

Most of PVM operates in the user domain, which means that a user can install all of the components and run a PVM application without the direct intervention of a system administrator with root privileges. This has several advantages, not the least of which is the ability of any user to implement PVM for testing and evaluation purposes.

## Underlying Concepts

Conceptually this is similar to what the Java Virtual Machine does. A separate application runs within each node, it handles all architecture and operating system specific requirements such that a virtual machine with a uniform and platform independent interface is presented to the user.

## Advantages

As well as presenting a consistent interface to the user, an advantage of using PVM is that it has the capability to dynamically add and subtract nodes from the system without adversely affecting operation. Because PVM is implemented at the user level, it is easy to install and configure and is able to be adjusted quickly to respond to node failures, i.e. it is more fault tolerant than MPI is.

PVM is well known, with substantial amounts of software developed for the PVM package. Like Linux, it is decentralized and therefore will still continue to be developed in the near future, though probably not with the same level of intensity that it might have once enjoyed. PVM has several advantages over MPI; it presently has better process control and this control is transparent and portable throughout the virtual system, a capability that simply does not exist in MPI versions 1 or 2 at present. Finally, there is substantial technical expertise associated with this technology in the parallel computing industry.

## Disadvantages

The principle disadvantage of PVM is that it is generally considered to be in decline, due to the ascendancy of MPI. PVM is considered to be an old technology; whether that is true or not is debatable, since it shares many of the same technological goals as Java and CORBA, which are far from antiquated. However its demise is not imminent.

## Applications

There is a significant number of applications that use PVM. Because MPI was designed for tightly integrated parallel machines, this means that it is well suited for fine-grained problems. PVM on the other hand, was intended to create a virtual machine spread over several potentially different systems via a local virtual machine interface located on each system. By its nature, this increases the grain size of the applications best suited to PVM. It has been stated that because of their design, MPI should be significantly faster than PVM in most if not all situations. This has not proven to be true; various studies of applications written in MPI and PVM show a very competitive performance for PVM. The essential question is which paradigm is more reasonable for your problem – message passing (MPI) or shared memory (PVM).

# Installation of PVM

This section will discuss the steps to acquire and install a representative implementation of PVM, then configure and use it.

## Acquisition and Installation

There is a somewhat reduced number of choices of PVM implementations in comparison of MPI. The package chosen was the one provided on the Red Hat Extreme Linux CD or the Red Hat web site. Red Hat generally supports and updates PVM on its PowerTools distribution that is mirrored on several sites. The principle source of software and information on PVM is found at www.netlib.org/pvm3/. Alternatively, you can directly download the package via anonymous ftp at ftp://netlib2.cs.utk.edu.

Once the package is acquired, you will be presented with either an RPM (from Red Hat) or a zipped `tar` file containing the source. In this case we will discuss both install procedures.

### Installation using RPM

The RPM process is very quick, first place the RPM into a user account `/home` directory. (You can use root if you wish, but you will likely run into permissions issues again.) Once that is done, you can install the package using the following command:

```
$ rpm -ivh pvm-X.X.X.rpm
```

The specific revision of PVM will vary with time. The package will install, and then configuration will proceed automatically for the appropriate architecture. Note that the RPM package is not a complete package, it essentially holds just what you would put on a node rather than a development station – you are left with going out and acquiring the `tar` file anyway. However, the RPM does make it very easy to install to the client nodes.

### Installation using the Source Code

The zipped `tar` file is installed in largely the same way as the MPI package in the previous discussion. This will install the package to a subdirectory `/home/pvm3`, assuming that you put the source code in the `/home` directory. Now at this point, you will have to define some environmental variables. How you do that depends on the shell you are using.

> *Linux uses the default `bash` (Bourne) shell which is different from the more common C Shell (`csh`) or even the old standard shell (`sh`). There is nothing wrong with using `bash`; however if you notice some strange behaviors that you cannot explain, it might prove worth while modifying `/etc/passwd` and then us either `csh` or `sh` to see if that helps.*

## Configuration

Once you have uncompressed and extracted the package, you will need to carry out one more configuration step, by concatenating some lines to your log in script, which is located within the PVM package tree under `/pvm3/lib` and is created when the users account is created. In the case of a `bash` shell it is called `bashrc.stub` and issues certain commands that set environment variables and other options to make the shell more PVM-compatible. You perform the concatenation of the existing `.bashrc` file with the stub file by typing this:

```
$ cat $PVM_ROOT/lib/bashrc.stub >> $HOME/.bashrc
```

At this point, you should have a file that looks similar to this `.bashrc` file:

```
# .bashrc

# User specific aliases and functions

# Source global definitions
if [ -f /etc/bashrc ]; then
  . /etc/bashrc
fi


#
# append this file to your .bashrc to set path according to machine
# type. you may wish to use this for your own programs (edit the last
# part to point to a different directory f.e. ~/bin/_$PVM_ARCH.
#
if [ -z $PVM_ROOT ]; then
  if [ -d ~/pvm3 ]; then
    export PVM_ROOT=~/pvm3
  else
    echo "Warning - PVM_ROOT not defined"
    echo "To use PVM, define PVM_ROOT and rerun your .bashrc"
  fi
fi

if [ -n $PVM_ROOT ]; then
  export PVM_ARCH=`$PVM_ROOT/lib/pvmgetarch`
  #
```

```
# uncomment one of the following lines if you want the PVM commands
# directory to be added to your shell path.
#
#    export PATH=$PATH:$PVM_ROOT/lib       # generic
#    export PATH=$PATH:$PVM_ROOT/lib/$PVM_ARCH # arch-specific
#
# uncomment the following line if you want the PVM executable directory
# to be added to your shell path.
#
#    export PATH=$PATH:$PVM_ROOT/bin/$PVM_ARCH
fi
```

## Compiling and More Configuration

Again, this file establishes the environment that the PVM package expects to exist. At this point, we need to execute a make at the top of the PVM tree. Change to your PVM root directory and type make, which will compile all of the required tools and applications required by PVM. After that, it is a matter of trying out some of the examples. To do that, directory and look for the PVM make utility call aimk. Check first to see if it exists by doing find:

$ **find . -name aimk -print**

If it does not exist, cd to the $PVM_ROOT/examples directory and create a symbolic link to the $PVM_ROOT/lib/aimk file.

Now, if you have multiple nodes to work with, you need to create a file that is equivalent to the machines.LINUX file that we looked at a few pages ago. This file, which can have any name, contains the very same information as the machines.LINUX file, so you can simply copy the data across. The file lists the names of each node that should be added to the overall virtual machine. Although conceptually similar to the machines.LINUX file, this file may contain parameters that control how PVM acts on a particular node. The specific parameters and their behavior are beyond the scope of this section; just remember that you can tweak the behavior of PVM by adding parameters to this file. For the time being, simply copy the machines.LINUX file to $PVM_ROOT/lib/pvmhosts.

## Testing

Once aimk is accessible from $PVM_ROOT/examples, we can begin to compile some of the examples. We will discuss only one of these; the hello application is divided into two pieces: hello.c and hello_other.c. These applications are compiled by executing the following command:

$ **aimk hello.c hello_other.c**

If all goes well, you should have an executable file created, but it will not be where you expect. The executable will be automatically moved to $PVM_ROOT/bin/LINUX. This way, PVM will be able to keep track of all the applications that are executable on the virtual machine; all executables must be stored here. (There is a way to change the default path to the executable storage directory, but there really is no reason to do that at this point. If you are interested, please refer to the documentation that is included in the package, as well as those discussed in the bibliography.) At this point, you should be ready to run PVM. Note that PVM is not just an API, but a virtual machine, with a virtual console. There is even an X Window System interface with a graphical representation of the virtual network, but setting this up would require a discussion on configuring X which is beyond the scope of this chapter.

Initially, you should try and start PVM alone, with no extra nodes. You do that by just typing pvm:

```
$ pvm
```

What happens here, depends on many variables, but if you are lucky you will see a stream of information that indicates that something is happening and eventually you will get a different shell prompt:

```
pvm >
```

At this point, you should have a functional PVM virtual system. You can be brave and try to add some of your other hosts by using the add {machine name} command:

```
pvm > add Machine5
```

If you are successful then you will see some information on that machine; if not, it will indicate a problem that is likely associated with your rsh configuration. That can be tested by a simple command:

```
$ rsh {Machine Name} ls
```

If all is well, then you should get back a listing of files from the directory you are in. Remember, if you are in a user account, the home directory should be NFS-mounted to all of the nodes. If not, you will have to manually copy the files over and install again on each machine. Now if you don't get a list, then you need to investigate your .rhosts file in the users home directory. And make sure you did an update to the NIS database after creating the user.

At any rate, we will assume that all is well, and that the nodes have been added properly. You can run the hello application on one or several nodes by executing the following:

```
$ pvm > spawn -> hello
```

Note that you don't have to include the hello_other program here. This should be kicked off by the master in this master-slave relationship. If this application is successful, you will get a message saying "hello from system XYZ". If not, then you have a problem; this would be unusual at this point, simply because most PVM installation problems will have been discovered by now. If you do have difficulties, the documentation is excellent and there is an outstanding book on PVM listed in the bibliography that is very good at trouble shooting the more subtle problems. It is also an excellent introduction to the PVM system, and how to develop applications with it.

# Remote Procedure Calls (RPC)

One of the underlying problems conceptually with MPI and PVM is that they fail the fundamental test of a true distributed system. They tend to focus on messaging and communication rather than on processes. Theoretically, a true distributed system would focus on the work, not how it was done or how information was exchanged. A purer method of attacking distributed systems technology is through the use of a **Remote Procedure Call**, which can be defined as an application or portion of application that can be invoked remotely by another system or application.

## Advantages

The concept is very elegant and can be very powerful. Many forms of RPC operations are in use in virtually every networked operating system in production today. They are essentially ubiquitous within the operating system and software development world. That means that the tools and utilities required to develop them are very mature, and that there is a very large body of developers who have significant experience using and developing RPC and RPC-based applications. This is particularly true in relation to MPI and PVM. There are simply many more individuals with extensive experience with RPC than with the other packages combined.

## Disadvantages

Although theoretically more elegant, RPC based applications can be difficult to implement. Furthermore, it is often the case that real world problems have processes that spend a significant amount of their time communicating with other processes. That means that message based protocols, although substantially less attractive from an aesthetic point of view, are often more efficient in solving real problems. Finally, there is significantly less experience in building more complex applications using RPCs in a distributed environment, though significant advances in that area have been made recently.

# Other Technologies

In this section we will review some alternatives to PVM, MPI and RPC. These technologies are but a few of all of the various efforts in this field, but they represent the areas that have a significant amount of market penetration, particularly CORBA.

## Distributed Computing Environment (DCE)

Distributed Computing Environment (DCE) is conceptually similar to PVM and is intended to be a vendor/hardware neutral implementation set of distributed computing technologies to form yet another industry standard. DCE is designed to provide increased security and functionality over preexisting technologies such as MPI and PVM, as well as greater support for web enabled applications and distributed objects.

DCE is a powerful solution to the heterogeneous environment problem that provides much of the functionality of PVM with increased security and functionality. It is not as widely received and supported as PVM, but as its popularity grows this will change. You can learn more about DCE, from their official site at http://www.opengroup.org/dce/. Support for Linux is provided exclusively by compiling the source; there are no precompiled binaries for Linux known to the author.

## CORBA

The Common Object Request Broker Architecture (CORBA) is one of newer entries into the distributed system support arena. At its core, CORBA is a consortium of companies (over 700) whose purpose was to create a common protocol that allows for architecture independent sharing of resources over a network. It essentially serves the same function as the Microsoft Distributed Component Object Model (DCOM) which is better known, but is actually a latecomer to the area.

Essentially, CORBA has the very ambitious goal of allowing intelligent components living on different machines on a potentially widely distributed network to find, assist and share resources with each other in a seamless and transparent manor. In this architecture, all of the applications and objects, interface with a generic or platform-independent middleware component called an ORB (Object Resource Broker) which interacts and supports each client and its respective objects and facilitates the sharing of information and objects throughout the system.

**417**

## DCOM on Linux

As strange as it may seem, there is a project to create a DCOM implementation on Linux. This is being ported by a company called Software AG (www.softwareag.com/) which has a deal with Microsoft to port DCOM support to various Unix platforms including Linux. The general idea is to make various Unix platforms work better with NT platforms, or visa versa, depending on you point of view. The reviews within the Linux community have not been that favorable, but it is likely that the product will improve and it does provide for a method to integrate Linux systems into existing NT environments while maintaining functionality. DCOM on Linux is discussed further in the next chapter.

## A Dynamic Area of Research

Distributed applications are quite simple one of, if not the most, dynamic and richest area of investigation in computer science research today. No mater how hard and fast you try to cover the amount of material that is being produced, let alone published, you will be very hard pressed to keep up. There are dozens of attempts to implement MPI available today, and many more total attempts to implement a protocol to facilitate a distributed system. As part of the research for this section, the author was able to find over two dozen operating systems that imply they are specifically designed to support distributed computing. With that kind of effort, it is actually dangerous to even cover this sort of material, because it becomes dated so quickly. One must simply forge ahead and hope for the best, always with a realization that the best distributed system paradigm or protocol has yet to be invented.

# Case Studies Involving Distributed Applications

From this point on, we will discuss specific case studies of applications that are prevalent in the business community, these applications are otherwise know as enterprise solutions to business problems. We will discuss how to create more reliable and powerful web servers using a cluster of identical Apache servers on Linux that will respond to any request in a transparent and consistent manner without respect to which of the servers process the request. We will also discuss two of the leading database solutions presently available in enterprise form on Linux: Sybase and Oracle. The specific focus for both is reliability and redundancy. How that is handled differs between the two applications.

# Supporting Applications

As with any complex project like this, there are several applications that support the overall operations of a project and others that form an integral part of a particular implementation of a case study. This section discusses an application that falls into this first category, DNS. We will not discuss the installation of DNS software because it is referred to in other chapters of this book and is not critical to the application at hand. It is briefly discussed to make the reader aware of its contribution to the project as a whole.

## Domain Name Server – DNS

DNS is a powerful and useful tool that we will use to great effect in the two main case studies, that of the clustered Apache server and the Sybase database server. DNS is a set of services that allow appropriately configured client computers to request IP address information pertaining to another system somewhere on the Internet.

Now you might ask why we are discussing DNS now, when we have already decided to use fixed IP addresses. Well, the answer is that fixed IP addresses with /etc/host files is reasonable and in fact the best solution for small clusters or even dedicated computational clusters (i.e. it reduces overhead when communicating with another server) but as the cluster grows, maintaining larger and larger /etc/hosts files becomes a definite challenge. At some point, it actually becomes a burden that is very difficult to sustain. Furthermore, as we will discuss later, there are things that can be done with DNS that simply cannot be done with strict /etc/hosts files. For that reason, it is strongly encouraged that you make yourself very familiar with DNS, its acquisition and configuration, as well as its administration.

The DNS package comes bundled with most if not all Linux distributions, and there are excellent references both within this book, and in the HOWTO documents that will allow you to configure DNS on your systems.

# Apache Web Server — Case Study

Apache is one of the most popular web server on the Internet. That popularity comes from many sources, a powerful implementation, diverse and growing software support, and it is free. The configuration and installation of Apache has been covered in Chapter 5, so will not be discussed in full here. The chapter goes into detail about `httpd.conf` file, where all the runtime information required by Apache is contained. Also virtual hosting is discussed which, just to remind you, is an arrangement where a single web server supports multiple web sites.

## Multiple Server Configuration

It is well known that the cost of high performance servers far exceeds the cost of a PC that is equipped with the same processor. The premium is due to several factors, including improved architecture, a greater storage capacity and system performance. As a consequence, many organizations wait to replace or augment their server capacity, often to the detriment of their site's performance.

What if there was a way to augment or even replace those expensive servers with a scalable and cheaper alternative. A cluster of Linux boxes running Apache could provide the answer. So, how do we improve the reliability and performance of the web server by the use of clustered Apache servers on Linux? It is not a panacea, but is close enough until a real solution comes along. So how is it going to be done?

We will use DNS servers and a series of Apache web servers. We will use DNS in such a way that each request is made to a different server, so that if an individual server is down when a request times out, it will be redirected to a different server which will hopefully be up and running. The solution described is not particularly new, but is an effective way to achieve the goal of a high reliability. What's more, there are modifications that can be made to this scheme that will improve it still further. However, we will explore the simplest case in this case study.

## Objectives

First, I must put some limitations on the problem in order to simplify it. It is very common to utilize proxy servers in the implementation of such a system. It is advisable to do so, and Apache supports this very well. However, due to the added level of complexity for what is essentially a network security issue, proxy servers are beyond the scope of this project and will not be included. Furthermore, though DHCP is a powerful tool in this configuration (i.e. rolling IP addresses can help to increase the random nature of the system), the same dynamics are at work, so that will not be discussed either. Finally, it is assumed that this is a single IP addressed site rather than a name-addressed virtual site. It should be noted however, that the same principles would be used in either case; the configuration would be somewhat more involved, essentially repeating the same process for each of the named domains.

> In light of later discussion, what is meant by a single IP addressed site is the Apache configuration will have a single IP address to listen to rather than several (or one with several named sites) to watch via HTTP 1.1. This has nothing to do with the DNS round robin mapping that will be discussed later.

Now that we know what will not be included, we need to specify what will be. In its simplest form, the solution we are pursuing will connect a cluster of Apache web servers to the Internet via some means. When a request is given for the domain, a DNS will have to resolve that request to a particular IP address owned by one of the various servers. Given all this, we need the following:

- ❑ Domain Name Server to resolve the domain name to one of the web servers.
- ❑ Apache Servers configured identically
- ❑ Means of insuring consistency of web server files (HTML source, scripts, etc.)

## Configuration

Now that we know what we want, how do we get there? The first requirement is relatively straightforward. We have already had some experience with DNS, from discussions earlier in this book. What we will introduce here, though, is enabling the DNS server to resolve various queries to different Apache servers, using a round-robin method of matching requests with server IP addresses. We will focus our attention on the modification required to the DNS to meet our needs.

The second and third requirements are interrelated and are more complex than the first requirement. We have already discussed the acquisition of the Apache server tools and how to install and configure them. It is reasonable to assume that the required systems have already been configured identically on each of the machines. With that in mind, we essentially have a farm of servers each with its own unique IP address and server name associated with it. The Apache servers on the other hand are all reporting the same server name, and their document and script retrieval directories are all pointing to the identical directories within their directory tree.

To achieve the consistency between servers we require, we will have to use some means of distributing required files from a staging server to each of the Apache servers in their appropriate directories. To do that, we can do several different things including using NFS to share all of the files between each server. This has its advantages, in that it is simple and straightforward with a guarantee that any change to the NFS server files will be reflected in each of the Apache servers at the same time. The disadvantage is that the NFS method is much slower than local drive access, and depending on the level of traffic, this can be a major disadvantage. Alternatively, we could use a well-established tool developed to solve just this sort of problem: **Remote File Distribution** (rdist). The rdist when combined with the cron utility will be able to assist us in this regard, we will use rdist to distribute the HTML source and cron to launch rdist at regular intervals.

The next question that we have to answer is where do we keep the staging directories? We have already decided that the Apache servers are best left doing their job, so let's conserve systems and place the staging directories on the DNS server in appropriate directories. These files and directories will be shared through rdist and NFS, as we shall see.

The `rdist` solution will work well for HTML source, but there are limitations here for CGI scripts because of potential file inconsistency issues with `rdist`. Because `rdist` does not perform its actions as atomic operations, there will be moments when there is a potential discrepancy between the servers. This might be tolerable in the HTML source, but it is not with respect to scripts. To solve that problem, we will use NFS only for the scripts. This is reasonable, since most of the traffic that a server will be supporting is the distribution of HTML source and its supporting files; scripts and script usage generally do not produce high traffic demands that will strain NFS.

> **There is some controversy about distributed file locking on NFS systems under Linux. It does exist, but is less robust for shell scripts, although there are solutions like `rlock` which do the job, but at the time of this writing it is a good idea to implement file locking within each script to overcome NFS ambiguities in this area.**

To meet the needs of the example, let us assume that the required file will live in their own partition with the structure shown below, we will be discussing how to share the contents of each of the subdirectories (`/cgi-bin` and `/htdocs`) separately in the coming sections.

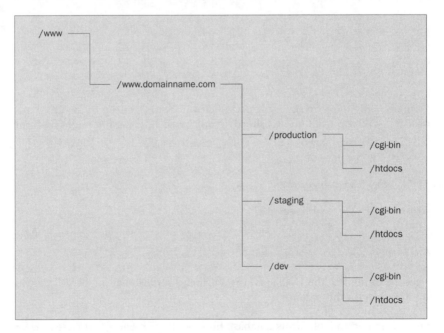

The three different stages of development are represented here, with completed work living in the production directories after they have been copied to the production servers. The production directories should be maintained as identical copies of what is running on the production servers. If there is enough work to be done, it is reasonable to place these directories on different machines, that is, have a development server configured exactly like the production server, then development and testing can be done on that machine. Once the development is complete, it is moved to the staging server which is a holding area and an area for final testing, once that process is complete, a process or script is run to promote the materials to the production servers through the process we will outline later. This directory structure should not be maintained on production servers, or the staging server for that mater, and should reside on the development boxes only.

## *DNS Configuration for Round-Robin*

At this point it is reasonable to assume that you have a fully configured DNS supporting a cluster of fully configured Apache servers all identically configured. What we will now discuss is how to configure these components to provide access to the various Apache servers through a round-robin method of mapping domain name calls to specific IP addresses of servers. In this way, with each request the browser will receive a different server and if one of the servers is down or otherwise engaged when the browser times out, the requests will be resubmitted to a different server.

The configuration of the DNS daemon is actually rather easy. DNS can internally support a round-robin scheme to assist load balancing since BIND 4.9, and there were patches that supported it prior to that. What we have to do is to tell the `named.conf` file what we intend to do; the exact process depends on how you have configured NFS so you might have to modify this process for your system.

We will assume that there are three files we will be considering, the first is `/etc/named.boot` which tells the `named` daemon what DNS servers exist (both forward and reverse) and their relative importance with respect to each other (primary or secondary). Here is a typical listing of the distribution file:

```
;
; a caching only nameserver config
;
directory               /var/named
cache                   named.ca
```

Assuming a domain name of `mycompany.com` which will be referenced by two files `Network.db` and `Network.rev` which we will discuss shortly, your `named.boot` file might look something like this:

```
;
; a caching only nameserver config
;
directory               /var/named
cache                   named.ca
primary     mycompany.com                Network.db
primary     168.168.192.in-addr.apra   Network.rev
```

Note that we are assuming that the DNS server is a primary server, that might will depend on your configuration but works for this example.

Now, we have told `named` to look for its database files in `/var/named` and to search for several files, including our two database files `Network.db` and `Network.rev` which will allow forward (name to IP) and reverse (IP to name) addressing. Those files must live under `/var/named`. Lets look at `Network.db` first, and assume two different web servers as well as a DNS server:

```
@   IN   SOA      mycompany.com. root.mycompany.com. (
                  1997022700 ; Serial
                  28800    ; Refresh
                  14400    ; Retry
                  3600000  ; Expire
                  86400 )  ; Minimum
```

```
        IN    NS         DNS.mycompany.com.
        IN    MX         mail.mycompany.com.

; A sections
localhost.mycompany.com. IN A  127.0.0.1
DNS  IN A  192.168.168.1
www1 IN A  192.168.168.101
www2 IN A  192.168.168.102
; CNAME section
ftp  IN CNAME    DNS
www  IN CNAME    www1
www  IN CNAME    www2
```

This file will provide for a mapping between the machine names DNS, www1, and www2 to the appropriate addresses. The second section, under CNAME, is what implements round-robin functionality in DNS.

The next file to be considered is the reverse mapping file we have named Network.rev:

```
@    IN    SOA        mycompany.com. root.mycompany.com. (
                      1997022700 ; Serial
                      28800    ; Refresh
                      14400    ; Retry
                      3600000  ; Expire
                      86400 )  ; Minimum
     IN    NS         DNS.mycompany.com.
     IN    MX         mail.mycompany.com.

localhost.mycompany.com. IN A 127.0.0.1
1    IN PTR    DNS
101  IN PTR    www1
102  IN PTR    www2
```

That is basically it. You might need to tweak here and there depending on your specific implementation of DNS. You will need to either restart the DNS server or reboot the server itself.

## Distribution Tools

As we said earlier, we will be using rdist and NFS to support the distribution of the various files required by the Apache servers. We will use cron to support rdist as well.

### rdist and cron

Configuring rdist has several steps. First, you have to create identical accounts on each of the web servers. That way you can log into each with the same user ID and password. Now, as we discussed in the section on MPI, you need to create a .rhosts file on each of the Apache servers within the user's home directory. This file will allow the remote shell (rsh) sessions to be run under that user ID. The .rhosts file will be very simple, it will contain a single line with the name of the server that will be responsible for the cron process. We have three machines involved, machines www1 and www2 are busy doing their jobs, so let's use the name server as the home base, hence the .rhosts file consists of this:

```
DNS.mycompany.com
```

At this point we have to create a file for the `rdist` utility. This file will define the machines that will participate, which user account will be used, what directories and files will be copied. A simple example `rdist_config` file is listed bellow:

```
# RDIST Configuration for Apache Server Cluster support
#

# Hosts
HOSTS = (userid@www1.mycompany.com userid@www2.mycompany.com)

#
# List of directories to be copied
FILES = (/www)

#
# List of directories to be excluded
EXCLUDE = (/www/cgi-bin/  /www/production/  /www/staging/  /www/dev/)

#
# Here are the instructions to do the work
${FILES} -> ${HOSTS}
install ;
except ${EXCLUDE }
```

This file lives on the machine that will be serving as the staging server, which we decided would be the DNS server `DNS.mycompany.com`, from the `/www` directory and its subdirectories. Now, we can put this file anywhere we want, but it is reasonable to put it under the `/home` directory of the account you are using to the web servers, that means you need to create the same account on the staging server system then put the `rdist_config` file in the `/home` directory. To run `rdist` from the command line on the staging server you can do the following:

> # **/usr/bin/rdist -p /usr/sbin/rdistd -oremove,quiet -f /home/userid/rdist_config**

This command is a little involved but it launches `rdist`, tells it where `rdistd` lives, orders it to remove all extraneous files from the target directories and to operate as quietly as possible. Finally it indicates where `rdist` can find the `rdist_config` file containing its instructions. For the `cron` operations, bundle this command into very simple script `rdist_script`:

```
#!/bin/sh
#(@) rdist_config script for starting rdist from cron

/usr/bin/rdist -p /usr/sbin/rdistd -oremove,quiet -f /home/userid/rdist_config
```

> **There are some potential conflict issues that might arise when you are moving large amounts of data around, hence it is reasonable to build a wrapper script around the `rdist` command given previously, one that does some sort of file locking and any other required house keeping.**

Now, we want this to run not only from command line, but as a `cron` process run on the staging server. Put the following entry in `/etc/crontab`:

```
0 * * * * userid /home/userid/rdist_script > /dev/null
```

This entry will cause `cron` to run the above script with all output going to the bit bucket. The script will be run once per hour; anything that you put under `DNS.mycompany.com:/www` will be pushed out to the `www2` server.

### NFS and CGI-BIN

That is all we have to do to distribute HTML text to the servers, but what about the scripts and other CGI material that we have left out? Well, we will be using NFS to host those files. We have already told `rdist` not to copy the files `/www/cgi-bin` over to the servers because that is exactly where we want to put them.

Red Hat supports NFS pretty much right out of the box if you set your systems up to support it. The first thing to do is put the directory into your `/usr/exports` file so the at the NFS server will know what to export. In our example, we will restrict the machines that can mount these directories to the two Apache servers we have called `www1` and `www2`. The export file will contain a line like this:

```
/www/cgi-bin  www1.mycompany.com(rw)  www2.mycompany.com(rw)
```

This line in the `/usr/exports` file will export the DNS server's `/www/cgi-bin` and allow read/write privileges to `www1` and `www2` but to no other machines. At this point you can either reboot or restart the NFS daemon by running `exportfs`. You are now ready to worry about the clients. They are configured by first adding the entry into their `/etc/fstab` files which will allow them to mount the servers `/www/cgi-bin` partition automatically on booting. Now add the following line:

```
dns.mycompany.com:/www/cgi-bin  /www/cgi-bin  nfs
```

Don't forget to create a mount point on each of the servers for the `/www/cgi-bin`, that is done simply by using the `mkdir` command on each of the servers to create an empty directory that NFS will use to connect to the mounted directory, or you can manually install the NFS partition to the directory by issuing the following command:

```
# mount -t nfs /dns.mycompany.com:/www/cgi-bin  /www/cgi-bin
```

At this point you should be ready to go. You have the servers configured, the DNS doing a crude but reasonably effective load balancing with the round-robin mapping, `rdist` is moving files from the staging server to the production server on a regular schedule, and NFS is providing access to your CGI scripts.

The figure below shows a diagram of the final system, with a brief explanation of what is going in each step.

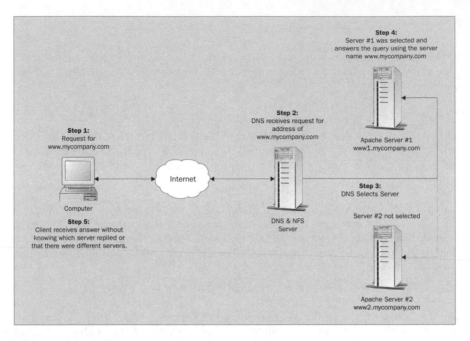

## Summary of the Apache Case Study

In this section we have discussed on possible solution to a requirement for increased reliability and performance using Linux, NFS, NIS, `fdist` and the Apache web server. In reality this system is rather primitive, it contains only minimal security safe guards and is not as refined as the various tools allow. One example is the lack of a proxy server or the use of SSL, both of these are well supported by Apache. The maturity and flexibility of the Apache system and its tools make Apache on Linux a more than adequate solution for the majority of enterprise solutions implemented today.

# Sybase Database Server — Case Study

Sybase is one of the top database engine providers and was one of the earliest adopters of the Linux platform. Sybase is available through several means, both free and a subscription format. The author would like to thank Kai Matsuda, Kelly Challenger, Wim ten Have, and Rene Quakkelaar at Sybase for their invaluable assistance and support.

## Acquisition and Installation

You have essentially two choices in acquiring Sybase. You can go to their site and download it, or you can contact them and purchase a CD with the Enterprise edition on it. Promotions and various other programs have a dramatic impact on the cost of the CD so you should be sharp and ask questions about promotions, if you decide to purchase. At the time of this writing Sybase allowed purchasers of Red Hat to register and download a copy of their production product through a link on the Red Hat page, but that may change in the future time. Your best bet is to go direct to the Sybase site at www.sybase.com, which not only provides access to the Sybase tools, but also contains a wealth of invaluable information.

> Originally when this chapter was first written, the only available product was 11.0.3.3 but at the end of editing 11.9.2 was released at $99 including written installation instructions. It requires kernel 2.2.5 and glibc 2.0.7-29 which would require yet another major upgrade of the kernel. The web page includes downloading instructions as well as RPM installation instructions that will assist the configuration process. The installation of 11.9.2 generally follows that of 11.0.3.3 only minor differences.

The installation is all done through RPMs. This has the advantage of being very easy, on the other hand it reduces your choices somewhat to Red Hat products and whatever directories they specify. You will have seen many examples of RPM installs, and for that reason the installation of Sybase will not be discussed in great detail. The version of Sybase that was used for this case study was 11.0.3.3 rev 2; the CD contains two files under the Sybase directory:

```
sybase-ase-11.0.3.3-2.i386.rpm
sybase-doc-11.0.3.3-2.i386.rpm
```

Install them in that order and you will find that Sybase has been installed under /opt/sybase. Now that the files have been unpacked and the appropriate directories created you need to configure the package. This is relatively painless and is done by running a script as root:

```
# /opt/sybase/install/sybinstall.sh
```

The script will run through a question about the license and then ask if you wish to create accounts which will be a sybase group and sybase user account to function as the DBA account.

> For the 11.0.3.3 release, if the script indicates that it has discovered the NIS is running on your system, stop the install script. DO NOT CONTINUE INSTALL. The install script might mess up permissions and ownership of the group and password file which, although not destructive, will give you a serious headache to fix.
>
> Instead create the **sybase** group and **sybase** user at the command prompt:
>
> ```
> # addgroup sybase
> # adduser sybase
> # passwd sybase
> ```
>
> Don't forget to run **/usr/lib/yp/ypinit -m** if you are on a NIS system, otherwise your account will not work and things will get confusing.

Next, you will be asked to run the configuration script as Sybase, so log out and log back in as the sybase account. The first time you log in you will be prompted to continue on with the Sybase configuration script that can be run at the command line as /opt/sybase/install/sybinit.

## Configuring the Database

At this point you should have all the files installed, and you are ready to run SYBINIT. This is a script that assists in the configuration of the various Sybase tools located on your system. You will need to know some details about SYBINIT, so read through this section before you start. Also, there is some excellent documentation in the Sybase manuals included in the documentation (in /opt/sybase/doc) as well as on the Sybase web site, so bear this in mind.

> **Before you start SYBINIT, you will need to know two things: what system to run the application on, and the port number.**

When you start SYBINIT, you will get this screen:

```
SYBINIT

1.  Release directory:  /opt/sybase

2.  Edit / View Interfaces File

3.  Configure a Server product
4.  Configure an Open Client/Server product



    .

    .
Ctrl-a Accept and Continue, Ctrl-x Exit Screen, ? Help.
 Enter the number of your choice and press return:
```

You select option number 3, Configure a Server Product and press *Return*, and you will be presented with another screen. Rather than displaying every screen, one after another – and there are a lot of them – the options for the project I carried out will be explained, which, I hope, you will be able to follow.

In the second screen, choose option 1, SQL Server, and then option 1 again, Configure a new SQL Server. In the next screen you can change the name of the database if you so wish, but I don't recommend you do so for this project. Just press *Return* again and you will get a screen entitled 'SQL Server Configuration'. You want option 1, Configure Server's Interfaces File Entry.

Now choose Add a new listener service. The next screen has four options, including a Delete option that you don't need. The first, Hostname/Address:, should have the server that is running the script already inserted. The second and third options, Port: and Alias:, are blank. Here, you have to specify the port number here by typing in after Port: (7100, for example) and pressing *Return*. You can leave the Alias: field empty if you want. You exit this screen by typing *Ctrl-A*.

The next screen is entitled 'Service Interfaces File Entry Screen'.; this does not need to be altered, so press *Ctrl-A* again and *y* to confirm. That completes the first stage of the configuration; the next screen confirms this:

```
            SQL SERVER CONFIGURATION

            1. CONFIGURE SERVER'S INTERFACES FILE ENTRY      Complete

            2. MASTER DEVICE CONFIGURATION                   Incomplete
            3. SYBSYSTEMPROCS DATABASE CONFIGURATION         Incomplete
            4. SET ERRORLOG LOCATION                         Incomplete
            5. CONFIGURE DEFAULT BACKUP SERVER               Incomplete

            6. CONFIGURE LANGUAGES                           Incomplete
            7. CONFIGURE CHARACTER SETS                      Incomplete
            8. CONFIGURE SORT ORDER                          Incomplete

            9. ACTIVATE AUDITING                             Incomplete

            Ctrl-a Accept and Continue, Ctrl-x Exit Screen, ? Help.

            Enter the number of your choice and press return:
```

Now move down the list to **Master Device Configuration**, which is essentially where the master database lives; this is where all of the information on all of the other databases on the system is stored. The size, configuration and performance of the master device have a profound impact on the performance and longevity of the master database and hence the overall system. Select option 2, and you will see the default values for the device itself and its size in megabytes.

You have to be as generous as possible with resources for the master database and therefore the master device. This device should be on its own drive, or in its own partition on a drive that it shares space on, this is the recommended configuration. However, for the purpose of this project, it will be put in to /opt/sybase. (If you created a partition on the drive, say /sybase, then it would be just /sybase.) Sybase recommends that new users accept the defaults wherever possible, and since this is a demonstration database, these will be acceptable. Sybase allows this configuration as a demonstration but issues a warning that /opt/sybase/master.dat is a regular file which is not recommended for a server device. Accept the defaults and continue.

The general configuration screen shown above will now have "**Complete**" next to option 2. Now move onto option 3: **SybSystemProcs Database Configuration**. Nothing needs to be changed here so press *Ctrl+A* and exit. The same goes with option 4: **Set ErrorLog Location**, though you might want to change this option at a later date.

At this point it is necessary to configure the default backup , option 5: **Configure Default Backup Server**. This is a tool that will feature quite prominently later in conjunction with clustered servers and Sybase. It is important not to change the settings here. The backup server expects to have the name SYB_BACKUP and will not behave if that is changed. So type *Ctrl-A* and move onto the option 6: **Configure Languages**. I used the default setting, us_english, but you might want to change this. I also accepted the default values for options 7 and 8.

Finally, you come to the last configuration option, **Activate Auditing**. Once again accept the default settings and continue. You must confirm the correctness of your configuration. After a repeat warning about the `/opt/sybase/master.dat` file, the system will proceed to build the database, which can take a while to complete. If the build is successful, this reassuring message is displayed:

```
Configuration completed successfully.
Press <return> to continue
```

## Configuring the Backup Server

The next step is to configure the backup server. To do that, you will be presented with another listing screen that you have to accept with *Ctrl-A* and then you will get a screen with the status of the two servers. Once you accept that, the original `SYBINIT` screen reappears.

Having completed step 1, now choose option 2: **Edit/View Interface File** in order to make room for the backup server. A new screen entitled 'Interfaces File Top Screen' appears which gives four options to choose from. You will want to **Add a new entry**. You will be asked to give the name of the new server which should be `SYB_BACKUP`. After confirming your choice, the next screen, entitled 'Server Interface File Entry Screen', displays three options. Choose option 3, **Add a new listener service**. An edit screen will appear , where, like before, you will have to supply an port number (and an alias if you so wish). Choose a different port number form the main server (7110 this time) and confirm you choice before proceeding.

After this, you will be asked to accept several screens as well being asked whether you wish to write the various tables to disk; answer yes to them all since that is exactly what you will want to do. Eventually you will arrive back at the main `SYBINIT` screen:

Now, it is time to configure the `SYB_BACKUP` server to run with the existing database `SYBASE` using the port specified for the backup (7110). Option 3 will take you to the configure screen, and since `SYBASE` is already configured, the only choice available is to configure the backup server. You will be asked to configure a new server or an existing one; your only option to configure a new server. After twice confirming that this is what you want, the configuration takes place. If all goes well, you will see the same message as before:

```
Configuration completed successfully.
Press <return> to continue.
```

## Configuring Server Products

Now you come onto the final part of the configuration process. Once again the main `SYSINIT` screen appears and you now choose the last option: **Configure an Open Client/Server product**. In the 'Configure Connectivity Products' page that follows, work your way through each the options, acknowledging each of the messages by hitting the *Return* key. Once finished, just press *Ctrl-A* until you exit `SYSINIT`.

Log out of the Sybase account and log back in. Once you are back in, you should be able to log into the Sybase database using the following command:

```
$ isql -Usa -P
```

If you are successful, you will see the (>) prompt  instead of the dollar sign ($), this is a sign that the Sybase server is up and running and the SQL interpreter is handling commands.

## *Testing*

At this point, you should be able to log into the server and get the > prompt. However, is the database server running? Well, you can check that with the following command to check processes:

```
$ ps aux|grep sybase
```

If all is well you will see several processes are up and running including the `dataserver` and `backupserver` processes. There will likely be several other processes running associated with `sybase`, the `isql` shell perhaps, and others. You can use the `isql` utility to check on system tables and parameters like the version using:

```
1> isql @@version
2> go
```

This should provide information like:

```
       SQL Server/11.0.3.3/P/Linux Intel/Linux 2.0.36 i586/1/OPT/Thu Sep 10 13:42:44
CEST 1998

(1 row affected)
```

Another test would be to see what was running:

```
1> sp_who
2> go
```

This gives the following results:

| spid | status   | loginame | hostname | blk | dbname | cmd             |
|------|----------|----------|----------|-----|--------|-----------------|
| 1    | running  | sa       | Alpha    | 0   | master | SELECT          |
| 2    | sleeping | NULL     |          | 0   | master | NETWORK HANDLER |
| 3    | sleeping | NULL     |          | 0   | master | DEADLOCK TUNE   |
| 4    | sleeping | NULL     |          | 0   | master | MIRROR HANDLER  |
| 5    | sleeping | NULL     |          | 0   | master | HOUSEKEEPER     |
| 6    | sleeping | NULL     |          | 0   | master | CHECKPOINT SLEEP |

```
(6 rows affected, return status = 0)
```

If these are the kind of responses you are getting, then you are good to go. The last thing you need to know is how to shut down the server; type `shutdown` at the prompt followed by > `go`:

```
1> shutdown
2> go
```

# Multiple Server Configuration

Within the Sybase package is a tool called the backup server which can be configured to move the contents of a database to or from a Sybase server. This means that backup server would take the place of `rdist` utility used in the Apache server discussed previously.

To have read and write access to multiple copies of a single database, you would need a means of communicating changes to both databases in a way that will maintain consistency between both the instances of the database. At present, there is no way to do this with Sybase. A new product is reported to be porting their replication server which will provide for this sort of functionality, but will not provide full clustering capability. This tool, called `Open Switch`, is released for only a limited number of platforms, but not Linux.

Given these limitations, why consider Sybase at all? Companies often have a significant investment in particular tools and would like to make as much use of that investment as possible. Furthermore, Sybase is particularly suited to the Linux operating system and its developers maintain great customer support for the Linux community. Finally, there are many real world applications for which Sybase is very suitable, limitations and all.

## A Case in Point

Consider MyCompany Inc. They maintain a large database of retailers that supply their products. This database is relatively static – updated just once a month. Due to historical reasons, the company uses Sybase and will continue to do so.

The company has maintained a vendor locator service whose operators used an application to query the location database free of charge. However, the cost of maintaining such a system has been growing over time, in parallel with that of the web, and the company has had to begin the process of moving the locator service to it corporate web site. The problem is how to make it work.

We can envision a setup similar to that of the Apache web server described previously. First, we will make use of the Apache system to operate as the web server, with the round-robin DNS set for the production server's resolution as well. The CGI scripts (for Perl) or servlets (for Java) will have to be designed to contend with the fact that no two queries are likely to be processed by the same machine, but that is not a significant hindrance, only a design issue, which is relatively common.

From this description, a set of read-only databases processing CGI requests from users would work quite well. Let us assume that two read-only database servers would be required, each with its own copy of the primary database and running independently of the other server. The servers will be sufficient to meet the needs of the project from the database server side. Let us also assume that two Apache servers will meet the need from the web side.

We will need to configure the DNS (`Network.db`) to round-robin both the web servers:

```
@    IN    SOA       mycompany.com. root.mycompany.com. (
                     1997022700 ; Serial
                     28800    ; Refresh
                     14400    ; Retry
                     3600000  ; Expire
                     86400 )  ; Minimum
     IN    NS DNS.mycompany.com.
     IN    MX mail.mycompany.com.

; A sections
localhost.mycompany.com. IN A  127.0.0.1
DNS      IN A      192.168.168.1
www1     IN A      192.168.168.101
www2     IN A      192.168.168.102
sybase1  IN A      192.168.168.103
sybase2  IN A      192.168.168.104
; CNAME section
ftp      IN CNAME  DNS
www      IN CNAME  www1
www      IN CNAME  www2
sybase   IN CNAME  sybase1
sybase   IN CNAME  sybase2
```

The reverse mapping (`Network.rev`) is configured as well:

```
@    IN    SOA       mycompany.com. root.mycompany.com. (
                     1997022700 ; Serial
                     28800    ; Refresh
                     14400    ; Retry
                     3600000  ; Expire
                     86400 )   ; Minimum
     IN    NS DNS.mycompany.com.
     IN    MX mail.mycompany.com.

localhost.mycompany.com. IN A 127.0.0.1
1     IN PTR      DNS
101   IN PTR      www1
102   IN PTR      www2
103   IN PTR      sybase1
104   IN PTR      sybase2
```

At this point, we can envision a system that would function much like that described in the diagram below. A specific query would be handled by different hardware depending on the access history of the individual servers. The process is not random but is deterministic, which depends on how, and in which order, the various servers were accessed.

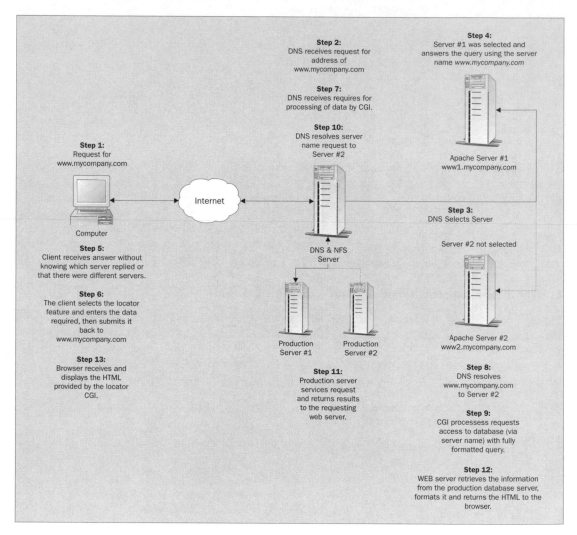

**Step 2:**
DNS receives request for address of www.mycompany.com

**Step 7:**
DNS receives requires for processing of data by CGI.

**Step 10:**
DNS resolves server name request to Server #2

**Step 4:**
Server #1 was selected and answers the query using the server name www.mycompany.com

Apache Server #1
www1.mycompany.com

**Step 1:**
Request for www.mycompany.com

Internet

Computer

DNS & NFS Server

**Step 3:**
DNS Selects Server

Server #2 not selected

**Step 5:**
Client receives answer without knowing which server replied or that there were different servers.

**Step 6:**
The client selects the locator feature and enters the data required, then submits it back to www.mycompany.com

**Step 13:**
Browser receives and displays the HTML provided by the locator CGI.

Production Server #1

Production Server #2

**Step 11:**
Production server services request and returns results to the requesting web server.

Apache Server #2
www2.mycompany.com

**Step 8:**
DNS resolves www.mycompany.com to Server #2

**Step 9:**
CGI processess requests access to database (via server name) with fully formatted query.

**Step 12:**
WEB server retrieves the information from the production database server, formats it and returns the HTML to the browser.

The databases themselves are populated via an automated script that would be built around the backup server operating the primary database, pushing copies of the backup onto the production servers which would then service requests. This might all be done with a relatively simple set of scripts running on each machine. The first script runs on the master server that contains the version of the location database. That database is created and maintained by means other than those described here (see the Sybase documentation for more details), but the data within the database is extracted using this script:

```
#!/bin/sh
rm -f /tmp/location.dmp
isql -U{userid} -P{password} -SASE_master<<FromHere
dump database test to "/tmp/location.dmp"
go
FromHere
```

The file created is then moved to each of the servers through FTP, NFS, etc., so that the loading scripts can operate on them. This transfer process may be automated or manual depending on the needs of the organization. For security reasons, some organizations do not like to have things like passwords embedded within their scripts and you might have observed the password reference in the previous script. The client scripts might look something like this:

```
isql -U{userid} -P{passwd} -S{servername}<<FromHere
load database test from "/tmp/location.dmp "
go
FromHere
```

The scripts can be launched as `cron` scripts; luckily Red Hat 5.2 and newer contains a simple way to configure `cron` scripts. One must simply write them, and place them under the appropriate `cron` script directory (/etc/cron):

❑   `cron.hourly`

❑   `cron.daily`

❑   `cron.weekly`

❑   `cron.monthly`

We could install the scripts under `cron.monthly` with no problems; the only difficulty is that the server might not have installed the extract by the time `cron` runs. If that becomes a problem, it would be worth while to make the script a little smarter and have it determine if the file was there, and if not, either exit or go to sleep for a period of time and recheck later.

One final point, the Sybase read-only servers need to be told not to perform a checkpoint on recovery. If it does, then it will not be able to properly load the next dump from the master server. This is modified under `isql` with the `sp_dboption` by selecting the no checkpoint on recovery option.

# Oracle

The Oracle database engine and its support utilities is one of the most complex installation and configuration processes for any application yet available for the Linux environment. Note on how to install and configure Oracle can be found in Chapter 7, so will not be discussed here. However we will discuss the way Oracle handles replication and what must be done to support this facility.

It should be noted that replication of any kind within the Oracle universe, is tightly connected with the design of each individual database. Therefore, it is difficult to describe just how to configure a replication environment without becoming bogged down in the minute details of specific database design. With that in mind, this discussion will essentially function as a starting point for further exploration and to highlight that the facilities to support a high level of replication under Oracle already exist in the Linux environment. For that reason, only limited discussion of the tools and their capabilities will be given here. We will discuss some of the key features and issues that will be important to you when implementing a real world solution.

> Oracle is product that requires a significant amount of knowledge to operate and utilize properly. If you are new to Oracle and do not have easy access to a qualified Oracle database administrator, preferably one with replication experience, then you are very likely to have significant difficulties with Oracle.

## Replication

Oracle provides a wealth of methods to support replication. First, replication is different from distribution. In replication, the data lives in different places to increase availability in case of difficulties, whereas distribution means that the data is available everywhere from a single source.

There are principally four different kinds of replication that can be used to meet different business needs. None of them will meet all needs, and some are overkill that will cost time and money that need not be spent on many applications. Each has its own complexity that will require a skilled database administrator (DBA) to assist in the configuration and effective utilization of the product.

First is the method of **read-only snapshots**, which is conceptually the same as the Sybase application discussed earlier. In the Sybase case, a `cron`-launched script grabbed the file created by the backup server to refresh the database on each of the slave servers. In Oracle, you configure the refresh process on each of the slave servers and they then refresh their snapshots from the master server itself, a procedure that is managed internally. This method is adequate for many different kinds of problems including the locator site we discussed in the Sybase section, as well as catalog site for a retailer, or even a status-reporting site for deliveries.

The second method is a variation of the read-only snapshots called **updatable snapshots**. In this process the snapshots are not fixed but can be updated by users directly. That data is then propagated back to the master server which handles updating the master database including conflict arbitration. Again, the timing of this process is handled by the slave servers and is internal to Oracle. An example of how this might be used is a low traffic ordering system or note taking system that allows the user to make changes or corrections in the data that is presented to them.

The third method is called **multi-master replication** which means that there are really no slave servers, each server is an equal partner in the overall process. Any modifications or changes to a particular database will be pushed to the other database in order to keep the whole set consistent across all the servers. The participating servers themselves control the timing of the updates. This solution is the most general of all available solutions in that it allows maximum scaling and query handling; it is also the most complex and resource intensive choice available. An example of a suitable problem is a high traffic ordering system in which multiple servers operate to service customer requests independently.

Finally, the forth option is called **procedural replication**. This is a means of applying procedural operation replicated across all the servers and tables that make up the overall system. As an example of its use, consider Bank A which purchases Bank B. Bank A will need to make system wide changes in both its own database, and that of Bank B, to harmonize its customer records. They will need to create procedures and replicate them via procedural replication, across all appropriate databases to make sure that all new check orders are printed with the correct information, and addresses to branches are correct in the phone book, etc.

With the exception of read-only snapshots, all of these replication methods require the installation and configuration of what are called **multi-master**, **symmetric**, or **advanced** replication components.

## Acquisition and Installation

The acquisition and installation of Oracle is referred to in Chapter 7 and so installation details will not be discussed here. However, Oracle was obtained for this project directly from Oracle Server Enterprise Edition Version 8.0.5.1.0, on CD. The Oracle 8 edition was selected because, at the time of this writing, it is the most stable and functional version of the Oracle family available on Linux, and is installed using its own proprietary installation script.

# Configuration

Again, the specifics of configuring Oracle will not be discussed in detail. However, some configuration issues are specific to distributed systems however, and will be discussed briefly.

Most of the Oracle configuration issues associated with distributed systems have to do with ensuring that sufficient resources have been allocated to meet the demands of the various processes, and indeed to allow those processes to run in the first place. The configuration modifications are not limited to the operations of the Oracle package itself, but include system-wide resources that can often require recompiling of the Linux kernel for optimal performance. Details of such modifications can be found in the Oracle installation and configuration documentation and will not be discussed further.

### System Parameters

You will have to check the settings of several system parameters to make sure that the minimum requirements are at least met for your system. The file you will be editing is the `initORCL.ora`, assuming that you used the default name of ORCL as the name of your database, which can be found in the `/oracle/admin/ORCL/pfile` directory. This contains the configuration values used by the Oracle instance at startup. You will need to confirm several operating parameters using the `SVRMGR` interface:

```
$ svrmgr
SVRMGR > connect internal
SVRMGR > spool /home/my_directory/parameters.txt
SVRMGR > show parameters;
SVRMGR > spool off
SVRMGR > quit
```

Review the entries in the parameter file and make changes as needed. I only had to make slight modification by adding or modifying the values shown below, but your installation may be different:

| Name | Default | Suggested Value |
|------|---------|-----------------|
| DISTRIBUTED_LOCK_TIMEOUT | 60 (s) | 60 (120 for slow net) |
| DISTRIBUTED_TRANSACTIONS | TRANSACTIONS/4 | NONE 0 |
| GLOBAL_NAME | FALSE | TRUE |
| JOB_QUEUE_INTERVAL | 60 (s) | faster than your fastest scheduled job. |
| JOB_QUEUE_PROCESSES | 0 | 5 |

| Name | Default | Suggested Value |
|------|---------|-----------------|
| OPEN_LINKS | 4 | 4+ |
| PARRALEL_MAX_SERVERS | 5 | 15 |
| PARRALEL_MIN_SERVERS | 0 | 5. |
| PARRALEL_SERVER_IDLE_TIME | 5 (min) | 5 |
| REPLICATION_DEPENDENCY_ TRACKING | TRUE | TRUE |
| RESOURCE_LIMIT | FALSE | FALSE |
| SHARED_POOL_SIZE | 3.5 (MB) | 64 (MB) |

In addition, I had to change the value of the **process number** in the
/app/oracle/admin/ORCL/pfile/initORCL.ora file and enabled **parallel servers**. You will
not be able to work with the standard database distributed with Oracle when you turn on the parallel
server capability, so don't be alarmed. This capability is built into the tables when they are created, and
cannot be added later.

### Rollback Segments and Redo Logs

While we are on the subject of what must be done during the creation of the database, remember that
replication will generate many times more traffic to and from the Redo Logs and Rollback Segments.
Make sure that you are generous with both, at least five each of 64 MB, that is five Redo Logs of 64 MB
and five Rollback Segments of 64 MB each, a total of 320 MB.

### Data Dictionary Objects

As with other things, replication is very demanding on the tables and indexes that are its foundation.
For that reason, it is important to create a separate table space for them. However this is not how the
default configuration will install Oracle; it will install these objects into the SYSTEM tables pace which
will quickly corrupt or at the very least become extremely fragmented so that many additional data files
will have to be added in order to keep it operational. This can be avoided if you do the following, when
you create the replicated databases:

❑   Create the previously mentioned table space for the replication data objects:

```
CREATE TABLESPACE repdata
DATAFILE '/u02/oradata/ORCL/repdata01.dbf' SIZE 500M
DEFAULT STORAGE (INITIAL 512K NEXT 1M PCTINCREASE 1);
```

❑   Now that you have the new table space created, you have to use it:

```
ALTER USER system DEFAULT TABLESPACE repdata;
```

❑ Now you have set up all that needs to be done, you need to run `catproc.sql` which will do some of the heavy lifting in creating the objects required to support the required transactions and queuing required for complex replication tasks in Oracle 8.

```
$ svrmgrl
SVRMGR> connect internal
SVRMGR> @catproc
```

Depending on your configuration and the database involved, this process will run for several minutes.

❑ Now it's time to run the replication catalog scripts `catrep.sql` and `catrepad.sql`.

```
$ svrmgrl
SVRMGR> connect internal
SVRMGR> @catrep
...
SVRMGR> @catrepad
...
```

❑ Note that if you are going to be using 15 or 20 tables, then the amount of SQL that will be added to your database is huge. You might want to consider making a change to the NEXT setting in the `sys.source$` table and the `sys.i_source$` index to accommodate:

```
ALTER TABLE sys.source$ STORAGE (NEXT 1M);
ALTER INDEX sys.i_source$ STORAGE (NEXT 1M);
```

That should at least give you a flavor of the process and the steps involved. It must be noted that much of this is dependent on the database you will be building. The parameters like size, table number and dependency can have a strong influence on performance that must be accommodated within the replication system parameters, so keep that it mind and plan accordingly.

## Accounts

In Oracle 7, life was vastly more complex. Fortunately, in Oracle 8 we have an easier time when it comes to accounts. We must create a **propagator** and **receiver** account that will process deferred operations. Once the previous section is complete you can do the following steps:

❑ Connect all the master databases with anonymous public links:

```
CREATE PUBLIC DATABASE LINK {dbserver.mycompany.com}
using {database alias}
```

❑ On each of the master databases you must create a replication administrator:

```
CREATE USER RepAdmin
IDENTIFIED BY replicator
DEFAULT TABLESPACE users TEMPORARY TABLESPACE temp;

EXECUTE dbms_repcat_admin.grant_admin_any_schema('RepAdmin');
```

❏   Now we need to create private links between the accounts on each of the master databases to each of the other master databases.

```
CREATE DATABASE LINK {dbserver.mycompany.com}
CONNECT TO RepAdmin IDENTIFIED BY replicator;
```

❏   Now we need to create the propagator and receiver accounts in each database, and then grant the privileges required to perform the replicated data manipulations:

```
CREATE USER ProPrep IDENTIFIED BY push
DEFAULT TABLESPACE users TEMPORARY TABLESPACE temp;

EXECUTE dbms_repcat_sys.register_propogator('ProPrep');
```

❏   The last step in this processes is to create private database links from the propagator account in each master database to each receiver account in the other master databases:

```
CREATE DATABASE LINK {dbserver.mycompany.com}
CONNECT TO ProPrep IDENTIFIED BY push;
```

Assuming that all went well, then you are ready to create replicated objects themselves. If you had any trouble, you might have to wipe what you have done and start again. You can create a spool file (spool /home/username/output.txt) that will record all of the messages generated by the various scripts, but the amount of garbage material is so great it is often difficult to separate the wheat from the chaff.

## Multi-Master Replication

The actual utilization of the Oracle replication tools is very firmly in the database administrator realm and is beyond the scope of this book. We will briefly describe some of its features and how they relate to the actual installation and configuration, but for a detailed design and implementation of a real world solution, you should consult a certified Oracle DBA with replication training and experience.

The design and implementation of applications that can both effectively utilize and continue to function while operating in a manner that is not detrimental to the performance of other resources is very challenging. Oracle's implementation of its replication functionality, while robust and powerful, is also complex. Each decision you make, from table design to replication groups, will have a profound impact on the performance and longevity of any Oracle implementation you build, regardless of the operating system it is running on. For that reason, the reader is referred to the outstanding references included in the bibliography whose authors have greater experience and space to describe this difficult subject in far greater detail than is possible here.

# Summary

In this chapter, we reviewed the principal development tools used in the distributed Linux world today: the Message Passing Interface (MPI) and the Parallel Virtual Machine (PVM). We explored how to acquire, install and configure each of these tools and looked at simple examples of their usage. We briefly discussed several of the support applications like NFS and remote hosting of operations, which are required for by the tools to achieve their objectives of providing a transparent environment that makes the cluster appear a single indivisible computer. Finally, we took a brief look at some of the rising stars of the parallel computational world: Distributed Computing Environment (DCE), and Common Object Request Broker Architecture (CORBA), just to make you aware of them.

Finally, we discussed the makings of a true enterprise solution using Linux. We discussed a highly scalable web server, capable of supporting multiple sites with a high degree of reliability and maintainability. These systems were designed around freely available applications such a Linux, Apache, NFS, NIS, `rdist`, and `cron` and provided the skeleton of a very serviceable system that would require only modest modification to provide truly world class performance in any environment.

We discussed the installation and configuration of the Sybase ASE 11.0.3.3 database package, its primary server and its backup server and how they might be used in a simple, web-enabled application that would meet a real world problem, and we did it by building on the previously discussed Apache configuration.

Finally, we discussed, in very peripheral terms, what would be involved in building a Oracle on Linux distributed system and the issues that are involved in building a robust distributed data delivery system around Linux and Oracle.

Although this chapter does not do justice to the immense power and versatility of the clustering capability possessed by Linux, it does provide a glimpse of its potential. It is that potential that has provided the impetus for dozens of institutions to develop Linux clusters for applications ranging from web servers to high performance number crunching systems.

# Bibliography

Albitz, Paul, *DNS and BIND* 3rd edition, Cricket Liu, O'Reilly, 1998, ISBN 1-56592-512-2

Dye, Charles, *Oracle Distributed Systems*, O'Reilly Press,1999, ISBN 1-56592-432-0

Geist, Al et al *PVM: Parallel Virtual Machine A User's Guide and Tutorial*, MIT Press, 1994, ISBN 0262571080
    available via ftp at: `netlib2.cs.utk.edu/pvm3/book/pvm-book.ps`

Hitchcock, Brian, *Sybase DBA Companion*, Prentice Hall,1997, ISBN 0-13-652389-7

Kabir, Mohammed J., *Apache Server Bible*, IBG Books, ISBN 0-7645-3218-9

Loney, Kevin, *Oracle 8 DBA Handbook*, Oracle Press, 1998, ISBN 0-07-882406-0

Orfali, Robert; Harkey, Dan; Edward, Jeri, *Instant CORBA*, Wiley Computer Publishing, 1997, ISBN 0-471-18333-4

Pacheco, Peter S., *Parallel Programming with MPI*, Morgan Kaufmann, 1997, ISBN 1-55860-339-5

# 14

# EntireX — DCOM on Linux

## Living With Bill

Readers who live outside the United Kingdom may not have seen a series of documentary television programs called "Living With The Enemy". The basic premise of this series is to take two groups of people with radically opposing views, put them together for a week and film what happens. You might imagine, naively, that this might lead to a sensible, well-informed debate where the participants are forced to overcome their own prejudices and learn to understand, if not necessarily adopt, their counterparts' views and that we're all fellow members of the human race underneath. Sadly, more often or not, both camps come out of the experience with their said prejudices firmly intact. Occasionally, the two parties come to blows. This is, of course, great television, so no-one really minds. All the same, you do feel like shouting "Hey! Be reasonable! Why can't we all live together?"

All of which is by way of introduction to this chapter, when I gingerly ask any of you tree-hugging, freeware-loading, penguin lovers out there if you'd like to spend a little while living with that nice Mr Gates. So if you'd like to come with me to Redmond...

# Yeah, but Why?

Let's start by looking at what we're going to try and do in this chapter. And whilst we're at it, we should seriously consider *why* we're going to do it. And when we're through with that, we'll take a good long look at *how* we're going to do it (that's the fun part, by the way).

This book is about using Linux as the basis for some serious, professional-grade systems. That is, systems that can support a wide variety of clients doing a wide variety of things. There are, of course, many ways of implementing these clients: Java, HTTP and whatever, most of which you can do satisfactorily without paying so much as a cent to Microsoft. However, there is one development community that, try as you might, you can't really ignore: the Visual Basic bunch. And much though the very word "Basic" is an anathema to hardcore Linux programmers, if you're considering offering a service that can be used by clients of all persuasions, you ignore Visual Basic at your peril; never forget that Basic was where Bill Gates started out.

It so happens that the best way to present new functionality to Visual Basic applications is to package it up in things called **COM objects**. These are also sometimes referred to as **ActiveX controls**, although they are, strictly speaking, slightly different things. However, for the purposes of this discussion, we can regard the two terms as pretty much interchangeable. COM stands for "Component Object Model", and it's basically Microsoft's interconnectivity methodology. If there's anything that truly lies at the heart of a modern Windows system, it's COM. What's more, COM is ready-built for distribution, and any client that can use COM can also use **DCOM**, or **Distributed COM** without any changes. So if you're looking to hook up any serious functionality-rich Linux system to Windows, you've basically got two options: either roll your own protocol on top of TCP/IP sockets (with all the maintenance headaches that that introduces), or use DCOM. This chapter is all about what happens if you choose the second route.

# The Shortest Introduction to COM and DCOM Ever

## Objects, Properties, Methods

When I was asked to write this chapter, I was told to provide a quick introduction to DCOM and then show how it works on Linux. My first thought was that I was being commissioned to write a book, but I presumed wrongly. A single, albeit important, chapter of about twenty pages was required of me. Shocked, I inquired whether I could assume a basic knowledge of important programming concepts like object orientated programming, and I was told that I couldn't! Again, I was told to write twenty good solid pages on DCOM from soup to nuts and I was left to get on with it.

I took a deep breath and closed my eyes. Now, I've always held the opinion that all programming concepts are fundamentally simple, but when it comes to COM and DCOM, we're probably talking about the programming equivalent of summarizing Einstein's General Theory of Relativity. They are highly complex topics that, if fully explained, could easily fill two hundred pages, so I should warn you at the onset that this introductory section is going to be *very* superficial indeed.

Let's kick off with a quick definition of object orientation. Basically, an **object** is a bit of program that you can order around the place. You give it instructions by invoking things called **methods** and by changing the values of things called **properties**. Each object belongs to a particular **class**, and each class only responds to a particular set of methods. Why is this a good programming model? Simply, it's because it represents the way we deal with the real world. Think about hiring a car. Often it turns out to be a model we have never driven before, and often it looks completely different from anything we have ever driven before. However, it generally responds to the same operations – start by turning the key in ignition, go around corners by turning steering wheel, change the speed, and so on. The crucial bit is that we don't need to know anything about what goes on under the hood. As far as we are concerned, it's a completely black box. Our only interface with it is the standard set of knobs and switches that the manufacturer supplies us with. (I dropped in a crucial word there: **interface**. Watch out for that one again in a few paragraphs' time.)

Let's complete the analogy. So far, we've got a **class** of hire cars, a set of **methods** on that class to carry out functions such as turning the key in the ignition and turning the steering wheel, and a specific instance of an **object** in that class. Let's now consider the rather obvious point that all hire cars aren't quite the same, and that any sensible hire company divides them up into categories of "compact", "family", "gas-guzzler" or whatever. All of these new classes **inherit** the basic characteristics of the class "hire car", and then add a few of their own on top. So one class can inherit from another. That's one of the key concepts of object orientation theory. There are one or two others, but they are of lesser importance to the DCOM discussion, so I won't go into them here. Interested readers are referred to the Wrox publication *Beginning ATL 3 COM Programming* for more information on COM fundamentals.

It only remains for me to mention the fact that there are basically two styles of inheritance: **hierarchical** and **multiple**. In hierarchical inheritance, every class derives from one other class, in a vast hierarchy that extends all the way from the most primitive, all-inclusive, class of all at the top, down to the most complex, specific series of classes at the bottom. In our case, the class at the top might be the class of anything that was capable of being hired out, whilst one of the classes at the bottom might be the class containing all instances of a particular model made in a particular year, of a given color.

In multiple inheritance, each class can inherit characteristics from a number of other classes. For example, an enterprising car hire firm might offer amphibious vehicles, which inherit characteristics from both car classes and boat classes. Both forms of inheritance are used in mainstream Windows programming, although, increasingly, multiple inheritance is coming to the fore, as it happens to be very convenient for COM. This brings me to the heart of the matter.

# COM

Imagine that you've been working late into the night, and you've just reached the point where you've finally admitted to yourself that you're getting nowhere, and you might as well turn in. You're just about to switch off the computer, when all of a sudden there is a strange buzzing noise and a bright light outside. You go out into the back yard, whereupon you notice a strange-looking person climbing out of what looks disconcertingly like a flying saucer. It raises a green tentacle in what appears to be a friendly salute.

You wave back, not really knowing what to do next. In this part of the world, you don't get that many aliens dropping in, and you aren't really sure of the etiquette. However, the alien soon puts you at ease by remarking to you that he seems to have landed in your garden, and asks if there is anything he can do. You express surprise that he speaks fluent English, and he replies that he speaks many tongues. At this point, your dog trots up and barks loudly at the intruder. Somewhat disconcertingly, the alien barks back. This continues for a good minute or so, until you manage to interrupt.

When you ask the alien if he talks dog as well, it expresses astonishment that you don't (and remarks, somewhat unnecessarily, that it's no surprise that your dog has such a low opinion of you). At this point, you look sharply at the dog, who slinks away sheepishly. Next, the cat trots up, and miaows loudly. However, the alien shakes its head, and explains that he doesn't speak cat. In fact, in his part of the universe, they tend to eat them, so he says that he'd better be going before temptation gets the better of him. You nod, the dog barks, the alien climbs back into the flying saucer and disappears.

Next morning, you relay the details of your encounter to your spouse, who looks at you strangely, before reminding you that you don't actually have a dog. Maybe you have been overdoing it lately.

Curiously enough, this is actually quite a neat illustration of the way that COM works.

COM objects are objects that **expose** a number of rigidly-defined **interfaces**. These interfaces consist of a set of methods and properties that a client can use to communicate with the object. So what's the difference between an interface and a class? None really, except that an interface can exist outside of its implementation, in the form of **IDL**, or **Interface Definition Language**. This is the crucial thing about COM − what the client is actually talking to is a language-independent interface definition, rather than the object itself. This means that you can truly separate the interface from the implementation, and when I say separate, I'm even thinking geographically separate. You can have your client on one machine (say one running Windows) and your objects on another one (say one running Linux)! Incidentally, did anyone spot where multiple inheritance comes in? Yes, I said that COM objects can implement a *number* of interfaces.

There are a number of standard interfaces defined in COM, all of which derive from the most primitive one of all, IUnknown. This interface (they all start with the letter I) contains just three methods: QueryInterface, AddRef and Release. At any one time, a client can hold references to one or more interface on the object. A reference is simply an object pointer, which the client can use to access the various methods and properties of the object. A client can get hold of a reference to another interface on the object by means of the QueryInterface method. It can release that reference by means of the Release method. When all the references to an object's interfaces have been released, the object is destroyed. If you want to increment the counter on an existing reference, you can use the AddRef method. QueryInterface automatically increments the reference counter of the interface returned. Notice that there isn't a ListInterface method; there's no way of finding out which interfaces a COM object exposes, except by trial and error, which is, I guess, why all the interfaces derive from IUnknown.

The alien who landed in your back yard started out as exposing ITalkEnglish. However, when your dog started barking, he was actually invoking the QueryInterface method for the interface ITalkDog. This was successful, unlike the cat's invocation of QueryInterface for ITalkCat. When the alien eventually decided to go, he was only able to go because both the dog and you had indicated to him that you had finished the conversation, thus releasing your references to, respectively, ITalkEnglish and ITalkDog.

Now consider this. A few nights later, a sort of hologram of the alien appears in your study. It explains that since it had made a bit of a mess of its last trip to Earth, it has been grounded, and is only able to appear by means of a long-distance projection. What it wants to know is what it should feed your dog on. Before you can ask it whether it feels that it would be sensible to raise the subject of canine alien abduction with your spouse, the hologram flickers and fades. Clearly, when you start distributing objects over long distances, you're at the mercy of the transport medium.

As I warned you earlier, this has been a very superficial introduction to COM and DCOM. If you're interested in reading more, there are plenty of excellent books available on the subject, mostly published by Wrox. As it happens, my favorite is *Professional DCOM Application Development* (ISBN 1861001312).

# Alien DCOM

## The Linux DCOM Environment

The Linux version of DCOM is developed and supported by Software AG, and is available for download from http://www.softwareag.com/entirex/download/free_download.htm. I'm not going to recommend particular versions of Linux for use with DCOM here; however, I would stress that you take note of the particular requirements specified in the installation instructions.

Installing EntireX DCOM on Linux is really quite easy. The instructions provided by Software AG are straightforward to follow; it's largely a matter of unpacking the single `tar` file, `EXX_v521.tar`, that constitutes the download and running the shell script `exxv521.bsh` (the documentation can be found at http://www.softwareag.com/entirex/download/dcomlinux/install.htm). There are just one or two points that may require a little clarification, and I'll deal with them in turn.

First of all, one of the first things that the installation process asks you to do is enter the full path of the file containing your EntireX license. Unfortunately, at the time of writing, licenses were not available for download, so I had to e-mail Software AG for one. With any luck, this will have been sorted out by the time this goes to press. At this point, you should also know that the suggested path (`$EXXDIR/$EXXVERS/erc/license.cert`) won't work, even if it exists, presumably because at this point, the environment variables `$EXXDIR` and `$EXXVERS` haven't been set up yet. Use the explicit path instead.

The second point is that you will be asked for your internet domain. If you're not actually running as a domain (if, for example, you're just trying this out with a stand-alone Linux machine and an NT workstation), you'll need to do some hand-editing once that install is over; I'll discuss this in a moment. One other thing is that early on, you will be asked for the details of the NT machine that will be handling authentication for you. This doesn't mean that you will be forced to use an NT machine as your authentication host, however, because later on you will be given the opportunity to select local authentication using the passthrough authentication daemon. If, incidentally, you select NT authentication, you'll have to install the passthrough authentication service on your NT machine; the instructions for doing this are straightforward. However, why do we need all this authentication stuff? It's because we're dealing with a *distributed* system. We can't just have any old client trying to invoke remote objects on our server.

Once you've completed the installation, you're ready to roll, unless – as I mentioned above – you're not running an internet domain. If this is the case, you'll have to manually edit the DCOM configuration file. This is located in `$EXXDIR/$EXXVERS/etc/dcomconfig`. The parameter that you'll need to change is `COOL_PAULA_DC_ADDRESS`.

Looking at the Software AG version of DCOM from a Windows perspective is a slightly weird experience. This is because all the usual features are there, but are ever so slightly different. For example, there's a `regsvr` utility on both versions. Instead of the Microsoft conventional `/u` switch to specify the unregistering option, you append `–u`, because that's the standard Unix syntax. There's even a registry, with keys that look pretty similar to Windows registry keys. For those of us who have grown to hate the Windows registry, I have to say that this is something of a disappointment, given the availability of real directory systems under Linux. I suppose it all boils down to how far you go with the porting process. The registry is accessed by means of a program called the Service Monitor, or `sermon`. Changes are made to the memory-resident version, so you should be careful to call `sermon commit` from time to time (or `sermon shut` on closedown) to ensure that any changes are made persistent, although `regsvr` does actually do this for you as well.

Authentication is achieved by means of a subsystem known as the **Private Authentication Layer**, or **Paula** for short. The Linux end of this is called `paulad`, the Paula daemon. The counterpart of this is an NT service known as `paulas.exe` that you will have to install on your Windows system. The Linux daemon runs if authentication is to be carried out there, and the Windows NT service runs if authentication is to be carried out there.

Here is the list of key executables that form the Linux DCOM runtime:

| | |
|---|---|
| `ntd` | NT daemon (a term wherein two worlds collide). This process handles access to DCOM shared resources such as the registry. |
| `ntwopper` | This command line process starts up daemons like `ntd` and `rpcss`. |
| `rpcss` | The Service Control manager (SCM), handles remote procedure calls. |
| `sermon` | This command line process controls the registry via the `ntd`. |
| `regsvr` | This is the command line proxy/stub library registration process, just like on Windows |
| `paulad` | This is the authentication daemon. |

There several others, such as `irotview`, which can be used for inspecting the Running Object Table (this can be safely ignored, as the ROT is a somewhat passé piece of technology) and `stgview`, which can be used for inspecting structured files (which is roughly equivalent to the Windows `dfview` utility).

# A Hybrid Example

The EntireX documentation details all the areas that are implemented in the Linux version of DCOM. For our example, I thought that it would be interesting to take a relatively simple application and explore what we have to do in order to turn it into a mixed operating system hybrid – with the Windows machine acting as the client and the Linux machine as the server, and vice versa. When I say Windows here, incidentally, I'm actually referring to Windows NT 4.0, Service Pack 4 (or greater) or Windows 2000. Unfortunately, we cannot get away without doing some serious programming here, but I'll try to make it possible to skip the sections of code without losing the flow of the discussion.

## Defining the Interface

Our DCOM example continues our extraterrestrial theme and revolves around an alien breeding program. Let's imagine that we have a number of aliens, represented by `Alien` objects, each with a single interface defined, `IAlien`. The properties in this interface represent the various attributes that parameterize each alien:

| Property | Type | Description |
|----------|------|-------------|
| Name | BSTR | Alien's name |
| Legs | Short | Number of legs |
| Tentacles | Short | Number of tentacles |

*Incidentally, a BSTR (pronounced "beaster") is a special type of string variable that's used for transferring strings between Visual C++ programs and Visual Basic.*

Obviously, for this example, I've kept things very simple here, but if you want to add your own properties such as color, number of eyes, antennae etc., go right ahead. The action all happens in the one method in the interface:

| Method | Parameters | Description |
|--------|------------|-------------|
| Mate | [in] IAlien* partner, [out,retval] IAlien** baby | Produce offspring. |

A word or two about some aspects of the syntax: `[in]` specifies an incoming parameter to the method, `[out]` specifies an outgoing one. The `retval` part means that the outgoing parameter will appear as a return value to a Visual Basic client. The method takes two alien parents as input and creates a third offspring alien, with a random combination of the two parents' characteristics. The access to each of the aliens is through the `IAlien` interface.

So how do we go about implementing this in a hybrid environment?

## The Joy of Visual Studio

The easiest place to start is on Windows. This is because the Visual Studio environment is heavily oriented towards developing COM objects. Without Visual Studio, we would have to code our interface definition language from scratch. With it, we can simply enter the methods and properties pretty much as specified above, and the IDL will be created for us. Under windows, we would have a choice of using C++, Visual Basic or Java as the language to develop our COM objects, but with EntireX, we're restricted to C++. We'll use Visual Studio 6.0, as – at the time of writing, at any rate – that's the latest and greatest version available.

We start off by creating a standard ATL executable server project, with the name `AlienServer`. I'd better explain a little what I mean by this. ATL stands for **Active Template Library**. As its name suggests, this is a library that supports the development of ActiveX controls, or COM objects. This takes more of the effort out of developing COM objects; unfortunately, at the time of writing, it isn't fully available under Linux, so there's more work involved – as we'll see later. The Windows versions of our COM objects will be held in an executable server; we won't be using them quite yet, as we're going to use Linux as our server first of all. I won't be explaining how to do all this in Visual Studio here, as this isn't principally a Windows programming manual. If you still want to look at the code, but don't want to go through the procedure of building the application, the source is available for download at www.wrox.com.

Having created our server, we need to add our `IAlien` interface, as specified above. This is what we end up with in our IDL file:

```
// AlienServer.idl : IDL source for AlienServer.dll
//

// This file will be processed by the MIDL tool to
// produce the type library (AlienServer.tlb) and marshalling code.

import "oaidl.idl";
import "ocidl.idl";

    [
        object,
        uuid(9A2CCDBD-EC2E-11D1-B161-004095D103A0),
        dual,
        helpstring("IAlien Interface"),
        pointer_default(unique)
    ]
    interface IAlien : IDispatch
    {
        [propget, id(1), helpstring("property Name")] HRESULT Name([out, retval]
                                                              BSTR *pVal);
        [propput, id(1), helpstring("property Name")] HRESULT Name([in]
                                                              BSTR newVal);
        [propget, id(2), helpstring("property Legs")] HRESULT Legs([out, retval]
                                                              short *pVal);
        [propput, id(2), helpstring("property Legs")] HRESULT Legs([in]
                                                              short newVal);
        [propget, id(3), helpstring("property Tentacles")]
```

```
                              HRESULT Tentacles([out, retval] short *pVal);
          [propput, id(3), helpstring("property Tentacles")]
                                      HRESULT Tentacles([in] short newVal);
          [id(4), helpstring("method Mate")]
                  HRESULT Mate([in] IAlien* partner, [out,retval] IAlien** baby);
     };
[
     uuid(9A2CCDB0-EC2E-11D1-B161-004095D103A0),
     version(1.0),
     helpstring("AlienServer 1.0 Type Library")
]
library ALIENSERVERLib
{
     importlib("stdole32.tlb");
     importlib("stdole2.tlb");

     [
          uuid(9A2CCDBE-EC2E-11D1-B161-004095D103A0),
          helpstring("Alien Class")
     ]
     coclass Alien
     {
          [default] interface IAlien;
     };
};
```

At this point, I hope you will appreciate why I chose to use the Visual Studio wizard. I would love to explain what all this means, but, once again, we don't really have the space.

Once we have created all of this, we can build it. As part of the build process, our COM object is registered for us. This means that a reference to it (well, actually quite a few references of various sorts) is placed in the Windows Registry, in a place that ensures that the COM runtime knows all about it. So when we try and create an instance of one of our objects, COM knows exactly what to do.

## Creating the Linux Server

On our Linux machine, we create a directory called AlienServer; it doesn't really matter where, provided that it has access to the DCOM environment. The first thing we do is transfer the IDL file that we created under Windows to it. Now the fun begins.

As I mentioned earlier, the most crucial difference between Linux DCOM and Windows DCOM, at the time of writing, is that *there is no direct support for ATL* under Linux. This is being addressed, and in fact in the very latest release, version 5.2.1, there is a first attempt at a Linux ATL implementation, including a rather neat code generator that converts your NT code directly. However, it still seems to be under development, so this should be approached with some caution.

Of course, COM existed before ATL was invented, so there's no reason why this should be a showstopper. It just means that we're going to have to do a bit more work, that's all. Let's take a look at what we're going to have to provide to build our Linux server.

First of all, we have to provide a main routine. Here's mine (which borrows heavily from the one supplied with the EntireX code samples):

```
#define INCL_OLE
#include <windows.h>
#include <objbase.h>
#include <initguid.h>
#include <stdio.h>
#include <coolmain.h>

#include "AlienServer.h"

#include "AlienServer_i.c"
#include "Alien.h"


//--------------------------------------------------------------------------
// Usage
//--------------------------------------------------------------------------

static void Usage(char * pszProgramName)
{
  printf("\n");
  printf(" This is the server portion of the Alien application.\n");
  printf(" \n");
  printf("Usage:  %s\n", pszProgramName);
  printf(" -r[egserver]              register server\n");
  printf(" -u[nregserver]            unregister server\n");
  printf(" -e[mbedding]              run the server interactively\n");
  printf(" -h[elp]                   this screen\n");
  printf("\n");
  exit(1);
}


//--------------------------------------------------------------------------
// main
//--------------------------------------------------------------------------

int CoolMain (int argc, char *argv[], char **endvp)
{
  HRESULT hr;
  DWORD   dwRegister;

  /* allow the user to override settings with command line switches */
  for (int i = 1; i < argc; i++)
  {
    if ((*argv[i] == '-') || (*argv[i] == '/'))
    {
      switch (tolower(*(argv[i]+1)))
      {
        case 'e':                 // -Embedding
          break;
        case 'r':                 // -RegServer
          return Install(0);
          break;
```

```
            case 'u':                    // -UnregServer
              return Uninstall(n_registryEntries-1);
              break;
            case 'h':
            case '?':
            default:
              Usage(argv[0]);
              return 0;
        }
      }
    }

  hr = CoInitializeEx (NULL, COINIT_MULTITHREADED);
  if (FAILED (hr))
  {
#if CE_GUNIX
    printf ("CoInitialize/CoInitializeEx() failed: Error %lx\n", hr);
#else
    wprintf (L"CoInitialize/CoInitializeEx() failed: Error %lx\n", hr);
#endif
    exit (1);
  }

// CoInitializeSecurity(0, -1, 0, 0, RPC_C_AUTHN_LEVEL_NONE,
RPC_C_IMP_LEVEL_ANONYMOUS, 0, 0, 0);
  CoInitializeSecurity(0, -1, 0, 0, RPC_C_AUTHN_LEVEL_CONNECT,
RPC_C_IMP_LEVEL_IMPERSONATE, 0, 0, 0);

  hr = CoRegisterClassObject (CLSID_Alien,
                              &g_ClassFactory,
                              CLSCTX_SERVER,
                              REGCLS_MULTIPLEUSE,
                              &dwRegister);
  if (FAILED (hr))
  {
#if CE_GUNIX
    printf ("CoRegisterClassObject() failed: Error %lx", hr);
#else
    wprintf (L"CoRegisterClassObject() failed: Error %lx", hr);
#endif
    exit (1);
  }

  WaitForSingleObject(g_heventDone, INFINITE);

  hr = CoRevokeClassObject (dwRegister);

  if (FAILED (hr))
  {
#if CE_GUNIX
    printf ("CoRevokeClassObject() failed: Error %lx", hr);
#else
    wprintf (L"CoRevokeClassObject() failed: Error %lx", hr);
#endif
```

```
      exit (1);
   }

   CoUninitialize();

   return 0;
}
```

You'll find this in `AlienServer.cpp`. Unless we're doing something special like registering, unregistering or getting usage information, all we do is initialize COM, initialize security, register the class factory object (a special class of object that creates the initial instances of COM objects) and then wait for something to happen. I've highlighted the few lines that are specific to this example; these are the one's that you'll need to change if you download the source from the Wrox web site in order to use it with your own server. Let's move on to look at this code behind this. This is what it looks like (again, borrowed from EntireX samples, and somewhat extended):

```
#define INCL_OLE
#include <windows.h>
#include "Alien.h"

//----------------------------------------------------------------------------
// Server locking/unlocking
//----------------------------------------------------------------------------

LONG        g_cLocks      = 0;

void SvcLock(void)
{
   InterlockedIncrement(&g_cLocks);
}

void SvcUnlock(void)
{
   if (InterlockedDecrement(&g_cLocks) == 0)
   {
     SetEvent(g_heventDone);
   }
}

//----------------------------------------------------------------------------
// Class Factory
//----------------------------------------------------------------------------

CClassFactory  g_ClassFactory;

//----------------------------------------------------------------------------
// CClassFactory::QueryInterface
//----------------------------------------------------------------------------

STDMETHODIMP CClassFactory::QueryInterface (REFIID riid, void **ppv)
{
    if (ppv == NULL)
    return E_INVALIDARG;
```

```
        if (riid == IID_IClassFactory || riid == IID_IUnknown)
        {
            *ppv = (IClassFactory *) this;
            AddRef();
            return S_OK;
        }

        *ppv = NULL;
        return E_NOINTERFACE;
}


//-----------------------------------------------------------------------------
// CClassFactory::AddRef
//-----------------------------------------------------------------------------

STDMETHODIMP_(ULONG) CClassFactory::AddRef (void)
{
    return 1;
}


//-----------------------------------------------------------------------------
// CClassFactory::Release
//-----------------------------------------------------------------------------

STDMETHODIMP_(ULONG) CClassFactory::Release (void)
{
    return 1;
}


//-----------------------------------------------------------------------------
// CClassFactory::CreateInstance
//-----------------------------------------------------------------------------

STDMETHODIMP CClassFactory::CreateInstance (LPUNKNOWN punkOuter, REFIID riid,
                                                void **ppv)
{
    *ppv = NULL;

    if (punkOuter != NULL)
    return CLASS_E_NOAGGREGATION;

    LPUNKNOWN punk = new CAlien;

    if (punk == NULL)
    return E_OUTOFMEMORY;

    HRESULT hResult = punk->QueryInterface(riid, ppv);
    punk->Release();
    return hResult;
}
```

```
//-------------------------------------------------------------------------
// CClassFactory::LockServer
//-------------------------------------------------------------------------

STDMETHODIMP CClassFactory::LockServer (BOOL fLock)
{
    if (fLock)
    SvcLock();
    else
    SvcUnlock();

    return S_OK;
}
```

Once again, you can use this code for pretty much any server, by just changing the lines I've highlighted. Incidentally, this is one of the things that is completely hidden from Windows COM programming by ATL. Indeed, many ATL programmers have forgotten about the existence of class factories! Now for the real meat of the server: the source and header file for the Alien object. The header file describes the IAlien interface, plus the IClassFactory interface:

```
#include <AlienServer.h>

#ifndef STR2UNI

#define STR2UNI(unistr, regstr) \
        mbstowcs (unistr, regstr, strlen (regstr)+1);

#define UNI2STR(regstr, unistr) \
        wcstombs (regstr, unistr, wcslen (unistr)+1);

#endif

#ifndef EXESVC
#   define EXESVC 1
#endif

const BOOL g_bIsDll     = ! EXESVC;

extern HANDLE g_heventDone;

extern void SvcLock(void);
extern void SvcUnlock(void);

extern const int n_registryEntries;

HRESULT Install(HINSTANCE hInstance);
HRESULT Uninstall(int iLastGoodEntry);

#ifdef __cplusplus
extern "C" {
#endif
```

```
//----------------------------------------------------------------------------
// Generic Class Factory
//----------------------------------------------------------------------------

class CClassFactory : public IClassFactory
{
private:
    LONG m_Ref;

public:

// IUnknown
    STDMETHOD(QueryInterface)(REFIID iid, void **ppv);
    STDMETHOD_(ULONG,AddRef)(void);
    STDMETHOD_(ULONG,Release)(void);

// IClassFactory
    STDMETHOD(CreateInstance)(LPUNKNOWN punkOuter, REFIID iid, void **ppv);
    STDMETHOD(LockServer)(BOOL fLock);
};

extern CClassFactory g_ClassFactory;

//----------------------------------------------------------------------------
// IAlien Interface
//----------------------------------------------------------------------------

class CAlien : public IAlien
{
private:
    LONG m_Ref;
    BSTR m_name;
    short m_legs;
    short m_tentacles;

public:
    CAlien()
    {
    m_Ref = 1;
    m_legs = 2;
    m_tentacles = 0;

    SvcLock();
    }

    ~CAlien()
    {
    SvcUnlock();
    }

// IUnknown
```

```
    STDMETHOD(QueryInterface)(REFIID iid, void **ppv);
    STDMETHOD_(ULONG,AddRef)(void);
    STDMETHOD_(ULONG,Release)(void);

// IAlien

    STDMETHOD(get_Name)(BSTR *pVal);
    STDMETHOD(put_Name)(BSTR newVal);
    STDMETHOD(get_Legs)(short *pVal);
    STDMETHOD(put_Legs)(short newVal);
    STDMETHOD(get_Tentacles)(short *pVal);
    STDMETHOD(put_Tentacles)(short newVal);
    STDMETHOD(Mate)(IAlien* partner, IAlien** baby);
};

#ifdef __cplusplus
}
#endif
```

Once again, I've highlighted the parts that you'll need to change for your own server. Let's turn to the corresponding source file now. We start off with some standard stuff to do the self-registration and unregistration (borrowed again from the EntireX code samples):

```
#define INCL_OLE
#include <windows.h>
#include <stdio.h>
#include <stdlib.h>
#include <string.h>
#include <time.h>
#include "Alien.h"

#if CE_GUNIX
#include <wchar.h>
#endif

static int verbose = 0;

//-------------------------------------------------------------------------
// Global Data
//-------------------------------------------------------------------------

HANDLE     g_heventDone = CreateEvent(0, TRUE, FALSE, 0);

//-------------------------------------------------------------------------
// Helper Functions
//-------------------------------------------------------------------------

#ifdef SAG_COM

wchar_t *_itow(int value, wchar_t *string, int radix)
{
  char buf[32];
```

```
  sprintf (buf, "%d", value);
  mbstowcs (string, buf, 18);

  return string;
}

#endif

//---------------------------------------------------------------------------
// Registry Info
//---------------------------------------------------------------------------

const char * const MODULE_FILE_NAME = (const char*)-1;
const char * const DEFAULT_VALUE   = 0;

#ifdef EXESVC
#define SERVER_TYPE "LocalServer32"
#else
#define SERVER_TYPE "InprocServer32"
#define THREADING_MODEL "Both"
#endif

struct REGISTRY_ENTRIES
{
  const char * pszSubKey;
  const char * pszValueName;
  const char * pszValue;
  BOOL         bDelete;
};

const REGISTRY_ENTRIES g_registryEntries[] = {
{ "Alien.Alien", DEFAULT_VALUE, "Alien Class", TRUE },
  { "Alien.Alien\\CurVer", DEFAULT_VALUE, "Alien.Alien.1", TRUE },
                        { "Alien.Alien.1", DEFAULT_VALUE, "Alien Class", TRUE },
  { "Alien.Alien.1\\CLSID", DEFAULT_VALUE,
                               "{9A2CCDBE-EC2E-11D1-B161-004095D103A0}", TRUE },
  { "AppID\\{9A2CCDB1-EC2E-11D1-B161-004095D103A0}",
                                      DEFAULT_VALUE, "AlienServer", TRUE },
  { "AppID\\AlienServer", "AppID", "{9A2CCDB1-EC2E-11D1-B161-004095D103A0}",
                                                                  TRUE },
  { "CLSID\\{9A2CCDBE-EC2E-11D1-B161-004095D103A0}",
                                      DEFAULT_VALUE, "Alien Object", TRUE },
  { "CLSID\\{9A2CCDBE-EC2E-11D1-B161-004095D103A0}",
                        "AppID", "9A2CCDB1-EC2E-11D1-B161-004095D103A0", TRUE },
  { "CLSID\\{9A2CCDBE-EC2E-11D1-B161-004095D103A0}\\" SERVER_TYPE,
                                      DEFAULT_VALUE, MODULE_FILE_NAME, TRUE },
  { "CLSID\\{9A2CCDBE-EC2E-11D1-B161-004095D103A0}\\ProgID",
                                      DEFAULT_VALUE, "Alien.Alien.1", TRUE },
  { "CLSID\\{9A2CCDBE-EC2E-11D1-B161-004095D103A0}\\VersionIndependentProgID",
                                      DEFAULT_VALUE, "Alien.Alien.1", TRUE },
};

const int n_registryEntries =
sizeof(g_registryEntries)/sizeof(*g_registryEntries);
```

```
//---------------------------------------------------------------------------
// Uninstall
//---------------------------------------------------------------------------

HRESULT Uninstall(int iLastGoodEntry)
{
  long result = 0;
  HRESULT hr = S_OK;

  for ( ; iLastGoodEntry >= 0; iLastGoodEntry--)
  {
    if (g_registryEntries[iLastGoodEntry].bDelete &&
        (result = RegDeleteKeyA(HKEY_CLASSES_ROOT,
                 g_registryEntries[iLastGoodEntry].pszSubKey)) != ERROR_SUCCESS)
      hr = MAKE_SCODE(SEVERITY_ERROR, FACILITY_WIN32, result);
  }
  return hr;
}
//---------------------------------------------------------------------------
// Install
//---------------------------------------------------------------------------
HRESULT Install(HINSTANCE hInstance)
{
  char szFileName[MAX_PATH];
  if (!GetModuleFileNameA(hInstance, szFileName, MAX_PATH))
    return E_FAIL;
  for (int i = 0; i < n_registryEntries; i++)
  {
    HKEY hkey;
    DWORD dw;
    long err = RegCreateKeyExA(HKEY_CLASSES_ROOT,
                               g_registryEntries[i].pszSubKey,
                               0, 0, REG_OPTION_NON_VOLATILE,
                               KEY_SET_VALUE, 0,
                               &hkey, &dw);
    if (err == ERROR_SUCCESS)
    {
      const char *pszValue = g_registryEntries[i].pszValue;
      if (pszValue == MODULE_FILE_NAME)
        pszValue = szFileName;
      err = RegSetValueExA(hkey, g_registryEntries[i].pszValueName,
                           0, REG_SZ, (const BYTE *)pszValue,
                           lstrlenA(pszValue) + 1);
      RegCloseKey(hkey);
    }

    if (err != ERROR_SUCCESS)
    {
      Uninstall(i);
      return MAKE_SCODE(SEVERITY_ERROR, FACILITY_WIN32, err);
    }
  }
  return S_OK;
}
```

By the way, those weird strings like 9A2CCDB1-EC2E-11D1-B161-004095D103A0 are GUIDs. You may recall seeing a load of them cluttering up the IDL file earlier. A GUID is a **Globally Unique Identifier**, which is pretty much guaranteed to be unique across all machines everywhere. COM uses a lot of these as the ultimate identifier for classes, interfaces and so on. By the way, the GUID for the object here should match the one that's been generated automatically by the Windows ATL wizard.

Next, we come to our implementation of IUnknown (remember that from our lightning tour of COM earlier?):

```
//-----------------------------------------------------------------------
// CAlien::QueryInterface
//-----------------------------------------------------------------------

STDMETHODIMP CAlien::QueryInterface (REFIID riid, void **ppv)
{
  if (ppv == NULL)
    return E_INVALIDARG;

  if (riid == IID_IAlien || riid == IID_IUnknown)
  {
    *ppv = (IAlien *) this;
    AddRef();
    return S_OK;
  }

  if (riid == IID_IDispatch)
  {
    *ppv = (IDispatch *) this;
    AddRef();
    return S_OK;
  }

  *ppv = NULL;
  return E_NOINTERFACE;
}

//-----------------------------------------------------------------------
// CAlien::AddRef
//-----------------------------------------------------------------------

STDMETHODIMP_(ULONG) CAlien::AddRef (void)
{
  return InterlockedIncrement(&m_Ref);
}

//-----------------------------------------------------------------------
// CAlien::Release
//-----------------------------------------------------------------------

STDMETHODIMP_(ULONG) CAlien::Release (void)
{
  LONG res = InterlockedDecrement(&m_Ref);
```

```
  if (res == 0)
    delete this;

  return res;
}
```

Finally, we come to the code for our IAlien interface:

```
//-----------------------------------------------------------------------
// CAlien::get_Name
//-----------------------------------------------------------------------

STDMETHODIMP CAlien::get_Name (BSTR *pVal)
{
  *pVal = ::SysAllocString (m_name);

  return S_OK;
}


//-----------------------------------------------------------------------
// CAlien::put_Name
//-----------------------------------------------------------------------

STDMETHODIMP CAlien::put_Name (BSTR newVal)
{
  m_name = ::SysAllocString (newVal);

  return S_OK;
}
//-----------------------------------------------------------------------
// CAlien::get_Legs
//-----------------------------------------------------------------------

STDMETHODIMP CAlien::get_Legs (short *pVal)
{
  *pVal = m_legs;
  return S_OK;
}


//-----------------------------------------------------------------------
// CAlien::put_Legs
//-----------------------------------------------------------------------

STDMETHODIMP CAlien::put_Legs (short newVal)
{
  m_legs = newVal;
  return S_OK;
}
//-----------------------------------------------------------------------
// CAlien::get_Tentacles
//-----------------------------------------------------------------------
```

```
STDMETHODIMP CAlien::get_Tentacles (short *pVal)
{
  *pVal = m_tentacles;

  return S_OK;
}

//---------------------------------------------------------------------------
// CAlien::put_Tentacles
//---------------------------------------------------------------------------

STDMETHODIMP CAlien::put_Tentacles (short newVal)
{
  m_tentacles = newVal;
  return S_OK;
}

//---------------------------------------------------------------------------
// CAlien::Mate
//---------------------------------------------------------------------------

STDMETHODIMP CAlien::Mate (IAlien* partner, IAlien** baby)
{
  IClassFactory *pFactory;
  HRESULT hResult = CoGetClassObject (CLSID_Alien, CLSCTX_ALL, NULL,
                                      IID_IClassFactory, (void **) &pFactory);

  if (FAILED (hResult))
    return hResult;

  hResult = pFactory->CreateInstance (NULL, IID_IAlien, (void **) baby);

  if (FAILED (hResult))
  {
    pFactory->Release();
    return hResult;
  }

  pFactory->Release();

  BSTR name;
  partner->get_Name(&name);

  short legs;
  partner->get_Legs(&legs);

  short tentacles;
  partner->get_Tentacles(&tentacles);

  name[0] = m_name[0];

  time_t now = time(NULL);
  srand(now);
```

```
    double random = rand();
    random /= RAND_MAX;

    double prop1 = legs * random;
    double prop2 = m_legs * (1 - random);

    legs = (int) (prop1 + prop2 + 0.5);

    random = rand();
    random /= RAND_MAX;

    prop1 = tentacles * random;
    prop2 = m_tentacles * (1 - random);

    tentacles = (int) (prop1 + prop2 + 0.5);

    (*baby)->put_Name (name);
    (*baby)->put_Legs (legs);
    (*baby)->put_Tentacles (tentacles);

    return S_OK;
}
```

As it happens, when I implemented the same interface under Windows, I only made one change, in the Mate method. I removed all the class factory stuff, and replaced it with this:

```
CComObject<CAlien>* pAlien;
CComObject<CAlien>::CreateInstance(&pAlien);

*baby = pAlien;
```

But then, that's the power of ATL for you. There's one last file that we need to produce, and that's our AlienServerps.def file, which specifies which functions need to be exported from the proxy/stub library. I won't go into details about this file here, but this is what it looks like:

```
LIBRARY        "AlienServerPS"


DESCRIPTION    'Proxy/Stub DLL'

EXPORTS
    DllGetClassObject        @1    PRIVATE
    DllCanUnloadNow          @2    PRIVATE
    GetProxyDllInfo          @3    PRIVATE
    DllRegisterServer        @4    PRIVATE
    DllUnregisterServer      @5    PRIVATE
```

OK, we've got all our source together, so what else do we need? We need a makefile. This is what it looks like:

```
#
# makefile: UNIX make makefile
#

include $(DCOMAKE)/makefile.incl

all: $(OBJDIR) $(BINDIR)/AlienServer $(LIBDIR)/libalienps.so register

register:
    @echo "Registering the Alien server ..."
    $(BINDIR)/AlienServer -regserver
    @echo "Registering the proxy-stub library ..."
    regsvr $(LIBDIR)/libalienps.so

unregister:
    @echo "Unregistering the Alien server ..."
    $(BINDIR)/AlienServer -unregserver
    @echo "Unregistering the proxy-stub library ..."
    regsvr $(LIBDIR)/libalienps.so -u

$(OBJDIR):
    mkdir -p $@

$(LIBDIR)/AlienServer.tlb AlienServer.h AlienServer_i.c AlienServer_p.c dlldata.c
: AlienServer.idl
    midl $(MIDL_FLAGS) $(MIDL_DEFINES) $(MIDL_INCLUDES) AlienServer.idl
    mv AlienServer.tlb $(LIBDIR)

OBJECTS = $(OBJDIR)/AlienServer.o $(OBJDIR)/Alien.o $(OBJDIR)/ClassFactory.o

$(OBJECTS) : $(@F:.o=.cpp) AlienServer.h
    $(CXX_COMPILER_NAME) -c -o $@ $(@F:.o=.cpp) $(CC_FLAGS) $(C_DEFINES) -DEXESVC
$(IDLINCS) $(C_INCLUDES)

$(BINDIR)/AlienServer : $(OBJECTS)
    $(CXX_COMPILER_NAME)  -o $@ \
            $(PROGRAM_LD_FLAGS) \
            $(OBJECTS) \
            $(PROGRAM_LINKLIBS)

AlienServerps_def.cxx : AlienServerps.def
    makedef -EDllMain $(C_DEFINES) $(C_INCLUDES) AlienServerps.def $@

$(OBJDIR)/AlienServerps_def.o : AlienServerps_def.cxx
    $(CXX_COMPILER_NAME)  -c -o $@ \
            AlienServerps_def.cxx $(CC_FLAGS) $(C_DEFINES) $(C_INCLUDES)

PS_OBJECTS = $(OBJDIR)/AlienServer_p.o $(OBJDIR)/AlienServer_i.o
$(OBJDIR)/dlldata.o
```

```
$(PS_OBJECTS) : $(@F:.o=.c) AlienServer.h
    $(C_COMPILER_NAME) -c -o $(@F) $(@F:.o=.c) $(C_FLAGS) $(C_DEFINES)
$(C_DEFINES_PROXY) $(C_INCLUDES)
    mv $(@F) $@

$(LIBDIR)/libalienps.so : $(LIBDIR)/AlienServer.tlb $(PS_OBJECTS)
$(OBJDIR)/AlienServerps_def.o
    $(CXX_COMPILER_NAME)  -o $@ \
            $(LIBRARY_LD_FLAGS) \
            $(PS_OBJECTS) \
            $(OBJDIR)/AlienServerps_def.o \
            $(LIBRARY_LINKLIBS)

clean:
    rm -f $(LIBDIR)/libalienps.so
    rm -f $(LIBDIR)/AlienServer.tlb
    rm -f AlienServer.h AlienServer_i.c AlienServer_p.c dlldata.c
    rm -f AlienServerps_def.cxx
    rm -rf $(BINDIR)/AlienServer $(OBJDIR)/*
```

This makefile creates both the `AlienServer` executable, which does not have the Windows `.exe` suffix, and the proxy/stub library which is called `libalienps.so`. If you take a close look at this, Windows COM fans will see all sorts of things that they'll recognize. For example, there's the MIDL compiler, which takes the IDL file as its input, and generates the type library, as well as all the usual header and interface definition files (`AlienServer.h`, `AlienServer_i.c`, `AlienServer_p.c` and `dlldata.c`). The one thing that will look a little unfamiliar is the `makedef` utility. This turns our `AlienServer.def` file into something that the Unix compiler can understand.

So, we can now build our Linux DCOM server, by means of the simple command:

```
$ make
```

Notice that it self-registers, because we've specified that as part of the `all` option in the makefile. Now, before we go back to Windows, let's quickly try this out under Linux, to make sure that it's working OK. We'll build a very quick client application with no user interface, just a command line for input:

```
#include "../AlienServer/AlienServer.h"
#include "../AlienServer/AlienServer_i.c"

main (int argc, char *argv[])
{
    CoInitializeEx(NULL, COINIT_MULTITHREADED);
    printf ("Run where? ");

    char reply[81];
    gets (reply);

    WCHAR server[81];
    mbstowcs (server, reply, 80);
    COSERVERINFO serverInfo;
```

```
memset (&serverInfo, 0, sizeof (COSERVERINFO));
serverInfo.pwszName = server;

MULTI_QI qi;
memset (&qi, 0, sizeof (MULTI_QI));
qi.pIID = &IID_IUnknown;

HRESULT hResult = CoCreateInstanceEx (CLSID_Alien, NULL,
                                      CLSCTX_LOCAL_SERVER |
                                      CLSCTX_REMOTE_SERVER,
                                      &serverInfo, 1, &qi);

if (FAILED (hResult))
{
printf ("Failed to create first instance, %x\n", hResult);
CoUninitialize();
exit (0);
}

IAlien *pAlien1;
qi.pItf->QueryInterface (IID_IAlien, (void **) &pAlien1);

memset (&serverInfo, 0, sizeof (COSERVERINFO));
serverInfo.pwszName = server;

memset (&qi, 0, sizeof (MULTI_QI));
qi.pIID = &IID_IUnknown;

hResult = CoCreateInstanceEx (CLSID_Alien, NULL,
                              CLSCTX_LOCAL_SERVER |
                              CLSCTX_REMOTE_SERVER,
                              &serverInfo, 1, &qi);

if (FAILED (hResult))
{
printf ("Failed to create second instance, %x\n", hResult);
CoUninitialize();
exit (0);
}

IAlien *pAlien2;
qi.pItf->QueryInterface (IID_IAlien, (void **) &pAlien2);

printf ("Alien 1: name? ");
gets (reply);

WCHAR wName[80];
mbstowcs (wName, reply, 80);
BSTR bstrName = ::SysAllocString (wName);

pAlien1->put_Name (bstrName);

::SysFreeString (bstrName);
```

```
    printf ("Alien 1: legs? ");
    gets (reply);
    pAlien1->put_Legs (atoi (reply));

    printf ("Alien 1: tentacles? ");
    gets (reply);
    pAlien1->put_Tentacles (atoi (reply));

    printf ("Alien 2: name? ");
    gets (reply);

    mbstowcs (wName, reply, 80);
    bstrName = ::SysAllocString (wName);

    pAlien2->put_Name (bstrName);

    ::SysFreeString (bstrName);

    printf ("Alien 2: legs? ");
    gets (reply);
    pAlien2->put_Legs (atoi (reply));

    printf ("Alien 2: tentacles? ");
    gets (reply);
    pAlien2->put_Tentacles (atoi (reply));

    IAlien *pAlien3;
    hResult = pAlien1->Mate (pAlien2, &pAlien3);

    if (FAILED (hResult))
    {
    printf ("Mating unsuccessful, %x\n", hResult);
    exit (0);
    }

    short legs;
    pAlien3->get_Legs (&legs);

    short tentacles;
    pAlien3->get_Tentacles (&tentacles);

    pAlien3->get_Name (&bstrName);
    char name[80];
    wcstombs (name, bstrName, 80);

    printf ("Mating successful, offspring (%s) has %d legs and %d tentacles\n",
                                          name, legs, tentacles);

    pAlien1->Release();
    pAlien2->Release();
    pAlien3->Release();
    CoUninitialize();
}
```

And if we try this out, we should see the two instances of the aliens being instantiated, followed by a successful mating:

```
Run where? noo-noo
Alien 1: name? Jack
Alien 1: legs? 12
Alien 1: tentacles? 90
Alien 2: name? Rose
Alien 2: legs? 100
Alien 2: tentacles? 200
Mating successful, offspring (Jose) has 32 legs and 126 tentacles
```

Now, let's try it out with a Windows client. As we saw earlier, as part of the Visual Studio development process, our dummy server has already registered itself under Windows, so all we need to do is go into the Windows DCOM configuration utility DCOMcnfg and set it up so that the Alien class is invoked on our Linux server. You'll find DCOMcnfg.exe in c:\winnt\system32 on an NT system.

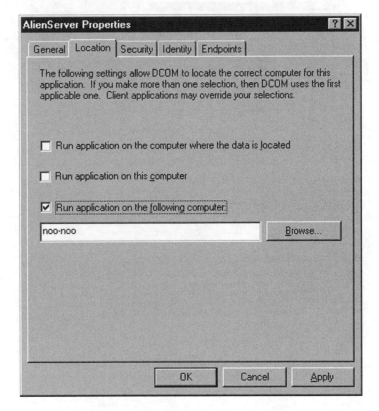

## Creating the Windows Client

Let's put together a simple Visual Basic client. Let's create a new project called `AlienClient` using Visual Basic 6.0. Next, we need to make sure that the project knows about out `Alien` objects, so we have to go into the Project/References dialog, and tick the box for `AlienServer`:

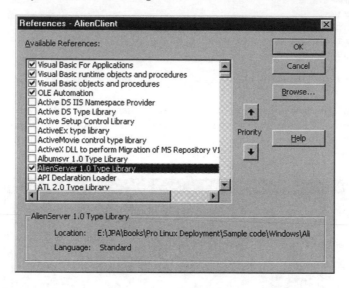

Here's the code:

```
Dim Alien1 As Alien
Dim Alien2 As Alien
Dim Baby As Alien

Private Sub Breed_Click()

    Alien1.Name = Name1.Text
    Alien2.Name = Name2.Text

    Alien1.Legs = Legs1.Text
    Alien2.Legs = Legs2.Text

    Alien1.Tentacles = Tent1.Text
    Alien2.Tentacles = Tent2.Text

    Set Baby = Alien1.Mate(Alien2)

    Name3.Text = Baby.Name
    Legs3.Text = Baby.Legs
    Tent3.Text = Baby.Tentacles

End Sub
Private Sub Form_Load()

    Set Alien1 = New Alien
    Set Alien2 = New Alien

End Sub
```

```
    Private Sub Form_Unload(Cancel As Integer)

        Set Alien1 = Nothing
        Set Alien2 = Nothing
        Set Baby = Nothing

    End Sub
```

And here's how it looks in practice:

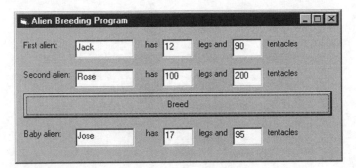

### Reversing the Roles

The next question is, of course, can we do the same in reverse? Can we have a Linux client talking to a Windows server? We can, of course, fill in the gaps in our dummy server on Windows with much the same code as we used under Linux, with the one exception referred to above, where we bypassed explicit reference to the class factory. And we already have a Linux client that is "network-ready" in the sense that it's already coded up to use CoCreateInstanceEx (because there's no DCOMcnfg yet available for Linux). All we need to do is specify that the object should be created on our Windows machine (laa-laa), rather than our Linux one (noo-noo):

```
    Run where? laa-laa
    Alien 1: name? Jack
    Alien 1: legs? 12
    Alien 1: tentacles? 90
    Alien 2: name? Rose
    Alien 2: legs? 100
    Alien 2: tentacles? 200
    Mating successful, offspring (Jose) has 41 legs and 134 tentacles
```

# Summary

I hope that this little example has demonstrated that DCOM on Linux isn't just a toy. There's absolutely no reason why COM should be restricted to Windows – it's just a protocol, after all. I hope you also spotted, without my drawing much attention to it, how easy it was to build a Visual Basic front-end application to make use of the underlying COM objects. If you are putting together an architecture that needs to support serious Windows-based clients, either using custom Visual Basic applications or (whispering quietly) Active Server Pages with VBScript, you should seriously consider using COM.

So, how do you feel about moving in with Bill now?

# 15

# Case Study: Migrating to Linux

## Overview

The Walton Centre is a small National Health Service Trust hospital based at Fazakerley in Liverpool, England, which specializes in neurology and neurosurgery.

**Infostat**, The Walton Centre Patient Administration System (PAS), provides users with a number of information recording and enquiry services including:

- ❑ Patients' medical records.
- ❑ Out-patient clinic scheduling and patient booking.
- ❑ In-patient waiting list and visit recording.
- ❑ Diagnosis and operation procedure accounting.
- ❑ Financial and contractual reports.

As such, Infostat is the most important information system at the hospital and is used by almost all the departments of the Centre. Careful consideration has to be given when porting any large database application from one system to another as it is an arduous task which requires a large share of IT resources, that is both personnel time and financial. When a system is as business critical to an organization as Infostat, then special care is necessary.

The Linux project at The Walton Centre was aimed at porting the existing PAS from HP-UX (A.09.00) running on an HP9000/H30 server, to Linux on an Intel-based server.

> Note that, although the case study covers a UNIX to Linux migration, many of the principles established in this chapter can be easily applied to any operating system migration, including Windows NT to Linux.

## Considerations for Moving Infostat to Linux

Over the years, Infostat had become increasingly functionally rich and tailored to The Walton Centre's needs. So taking in the initial cost of the PAS, there was a desire to retain the application for a long time in order to obtain the best return on the investment. Due to a site move, and the need for running Infostat on two sites, and in order to perform the required year 2000 compliance development, a second server would have to be purchased. The required expense for a second HP server, either to rent or buy outright, proved to be prohibitive.

The HP9000 server and the HP-UX (A.09.00) operating system were not year 2000 compliant and no maintenance support from HP for the system hardware would be forthcoming after December 1999. HP-UX support for this hardware stops at version 10, so an upgrade to this version was possible. As we would not be able to use features available with later operating systems, that solution did not look technically viable for future development. What's more, the yearly maintenance on the HP9000's was ten times higher than for the Intel-based Novell servers.

Taking all this into account, it was decided that the best viable option available would be to port the PAS onto two Intel-based servers running Linux, one live server for the users and a further server for system development. Thus the Linux Project at The Walton Centre began!

## Linux and x86 Based Systems

There are major financial gains to be made from moving to Intel-based servers. Not only are maintenance costs far less in the long run, the initial cost of a server and peripheral hardware (such as SCSI adapters, modems, CD-ROM drives etc) is also less due to the larger market. The choice of hardware is also that much greater. So how does Linux compare with the original HP System in the fast moving, diverse, hardware market Intel based machines provide? Generally very well! Although that is not to say you will not encounter any problems with devices on your system.

The biggest problem is probably video and SCSI adapters. In such a competitive market place, the manufacturers of these cards are continuously upgrading the performance and features of their hardware; these new cards are then incorporated into servers to improve their performance. There is a constant demand for new drivers to keep up with new technology, and although many of the larger companies are now producing drivers specifically for Linux, as they do with Microsoft systems, there are also many that leave this to the Linux community to develop (and in many cases, this takes a lot of time and effort, since the necessary technical specifications are not published).

In general, it is best to find out if hardware drivers for specific devices already exist before purchasing a server. This information can usually be obtained from Linux distributors' web sites, or www.linux.org. Another source of information may be the manufacturers of the device; try phoning them or paying a visit to their web site. The best place to find out which video cards are supported is the Linux X windows site www.Xfree86.org. Even with this information, having multiple SCSI adapters of the same make can cause problems. For example, two years ago, The Walton Centre purchased a Dell PowerEdge server for use with Linux. Checks were made to ensure new versions of Linux contained drivers for the SCSI adapters in this server before the machine was bought, but because this server had multiple Adaptec SCSI adapters that used the same Linux driver, only one was recognized by the system on boot up. Since the CD-ROM and hard disks used different adapters, this meant only one or the other, could be used. This made installation from a CD-ROM impossible. A Linux distributor pointed me to a newsgroup, which solved the problem rapidly. The solutions are usually there to be found, but until you find them, life can be frustrating.

If you prefer to perform as little configuration as possible, a better solution would be to purchase a server with Linux preinstalled. Most of the major manufacturers, such as Compaq and Dell and specialist Linux providers such as VA Linux and Penguin Computing in the USA and LinuxIT in the UK, are providing this service and it will take any risk of incompatible hardware out of the equation.

If research was put into device drivers before the purchase of the server, the only other likely hardware related problem would concern the system's memory.

## Early Linux Kernels May Not See All of the Memory

This was a common problem with many machines. The usual reason for this was that the BIOS sometimes had a limit on how much memory it told the operating system the computer contained. Versions of Linux from 2.2.x onwards no longer look at the BIOS for memory information so this problem should not occur anymore. However, if this problem is experienced, the usual solution is to add the following line to the image definition in the /etc/lilo.conf file (replace 128M with whatever is on your machine):

```
append="mem=128M"
```

This should now read something like this:

```
image=/boot/vmlinuz-2.0.36-0.7
label=linux
root=/dev/sda1
read-only
append="mem=128M"
```

## Performance of Intel Based Servers

Since moving to Linux on an Intel Pentium II 400 MHz based server, the Walton Centre has experienced an incredible increase in the speed of the application over the HP9000 dual RISC processor it used to run on, even though there are, on average, 25% more concurrent users. Quarterly financial reports that used to take seven hours to perform, locking that workstation for the best part of a day, now complete in about forty minutes!

The application itself has only expanded in that time and the Intel-based server has less memory, so these improvements can only be down to the processor, SCSI drives and Linux itself.

Reports from the database application on the Linux system are also executed faster than similar reports from the data warehouse, which is a SQL Server database running on Windows NT, with an even more powerful Intel platform.

# The Linux Project

Linux had been discovered by Neil Spencer-Jones, the then Head of IT at the hospital, who had downloaded the basic version of Slackware Version 3.0 from the Internet. He then installed this onto a spare 486DX2-66 PC which he had at home and instantly recognized the potential for its use at the hospital. Over the next few weeks Linux CD's were purchased and books borrowed revealing Linux as a true multi-user, multi-tasking UNIX like operating system that was more robust than Windows 95. Also, due to the number of enthusiasts developing Linux, it had better connectivity than any other LAN operating system. This was particularly important, as Infostat currently communicated with **Radstat**, the Walton Centre's Radiology system, and **Crescendo**, the hospital's patient care planning application, using TCP/IP sockets and FTP. In the near future, the purchasing of a new Radiology system would be required, as the application used at the time was not year 2000 compliant. Theatre and Pathology systems would also need to be purchased within the next few years as well, all requiring patient information to be passed from Infostat. A four-stage plan was now developed for the project:

**1.** Set up Linux on a networked PC at the Walton Centre, learn more about its commands and ensure it could communicate successfully with the other hospital systems. These included: Radstat running on HP-UX, Crescendo, and secretarial and finance systems running on Netware.

**2.** Port the **4thWrite** database engine and thoroughly test the Infostat application on Linux to ascertain whether it would be possible to effectively run the system on Linux using Intel based hardware.

**3.** Build an Intel processor based server. Install Linux and Infostat then, after testing the hardware and load levels, replace the existing HP based Infostat system with the new Linux based application for a final, crucial, user test.

**4.** Purchase a second Intel based server for the use of Infostat application development and year 2000 compliant coding as necessary.

The first two stages are of interest for this publication and now a detailed analysis of these stages will be discussed.

# Stage 1 — Networking Linux

At this stage we were still unsure whether Linux would be able to offer the reliability, handle the workload and provide all the TCP/IP connectivity facilities that would be necessary for the hospital's LAN. So, at this stage, it was important to test all these features out without investing too much time or resources. An Acer Acros Pentium 75 MHz, one of the fastest PCs we had at the time, was called into service; a network card installed, and Linux set up on the machine.

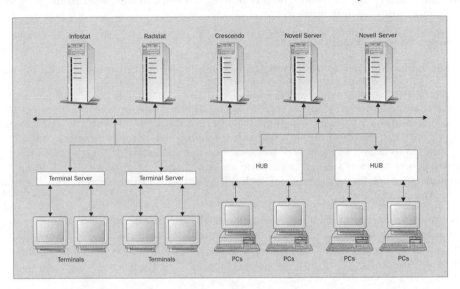

The simplified diagram above represents the basic layout of the LAN at the hospital at the beginning of the Linux project. There were in fact more terminal servers and network hubs on the LAN, with many other devices attached directly to the network, such as dedicated gateways and printers. The network itself was a thick ethernet backbone with thin ethernet and category 5 structured cabling to the PC's and RS232 serial cabling to the terminals.

## Network Configuration

The network configuration of a Linux server is usually done as part of the installation process. The information generally needed to complete this for a Class C network is:

- ❑ An IP address for the server.
- ❑ Host name.
- ❑ Sub net mask (usually 255.255.255.0 for Class C addresses).
- ❑ Network address (generally the IP address with the last part set to zero).
- ❑ Broadcast address (IP address with the last part set to 255).
- ❑ Default gateway (IP address of gateway used on your network).

This chapter also includes a section on manually configuring network cards, in the event the adapter used is unrecognized by the kernel.

Once the network has been configured and is working correctly, Linux needs to know what other devices on the network it can communicate with. If any of these devices are not a part of the network described by the network address, a route to these devices needs to be installed. This can be performed with the `route` command:

```
# route add -host 123.123.124.15
```

This will add a single device of the given IP address on a second network to the routing table, and allow communication with that device.

```
# route add -net 123.123.124.0
```

Will add an entire network to the routing table, enabling communication with all devices on that network.

It was essential that once a Linux server was set up, that users where able to connect to the server, either via a terminal, or from a PC using a terminal emulator. To do this the `/etc/hosts` file has to include the IP addresses of the terminal servers along with the IP addresses of the other network servers, or a Domain Name Service (DNS) could be used. The HP-UX system did not use DNS so to keep the two systems as similar as possible we edited the `/etc/hosts` file and enter the IP addresses as appropriate; an example of such a file is given in the `/etc/hosts` files and security, section in Appendix C.

After the appropriate additions have been made to the file, users should be able to connect from any of the devices described in the hosts table. But what about other TCP/IP services? Applications need to communicate with the other network devices, and other servers need to contact Linux in a number of ways.

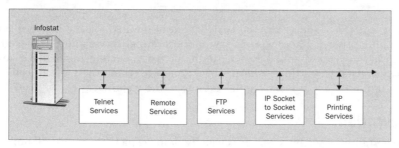

These services are used in logging onto, communicating with, and printing from Linux. Linux would have to provide all these facilities, and they would have to be rigorously tested to ensure reliability, if Linux was going to be the base for Infostat. As Infostat uses its own print spooler, the testing of the IP printing services could not be done until the second stage of the project.

We found that Linux had many security features that the HP-UX system did not, pertaining to superuser access to services. Most of our existing communication tasks required superuser access from other hospital information servers. This would have to change as `rsh` (Remote Shell) was being phased out on Linux for the more secure `ssh` (Secure Shell). Also, as administrators, we are used to being able to log on and make configuration changes with superuser rights to the Linux system from anywhere in the hospital. This is only possible from the console for Linux systems. To gain supervisor rights a login was created for general IT use with few rights, then the switch user (`su`) command was used as shown below:

```
$ su - root
Password: <appropriate password>
```

Even this is not secure, but as the network was not accessible to the outside world and, being a hospital, passes where needed to get access to any of the offices or wards, this would suffice. For information on secure shell (ssh), a secure method of remote access, and other Linux security issues and utilities read the book Maximum Linux Security (published by SAMS, ISBN 0672316706), or view the web page www.ecst.csuchico.edu/~jtmurphy.

Note: Depending on how much you wish to tie down the system, other important files regarding host access are /etc/ftphosts, /etc/hosts.allow, and /etc/hosts.deny. These are all described in more detail in Appendix C.

# Stage Two — Porting the Application

It was always known that this would be one of the most technically difficult phases of the project. Although no more cash was required at this stage, it would prove to be costly in personnel resources. Almost all the staff of the hospital's small Information Technology and Management Department was involved either in porting the application, or testing the hundreds of data entry screens and reports after Infostat had been transferred.

To port an application to a different system, the source code for that application is required for compilation on the new system. The Walton Centre had an ESCROW agreement with CHC and was entitled to the source code for Infostat when CHC were placed in the hands of the receivers. The hospital received two tapes in March 1996. As The Walton Centre had not opted for the NCC's verification service, the problem now was to find out what format the tapes were written in and what exactly was on them.

## Reading the Tapes

The first tape contained the Infostat application source code that was already in The Walton Centre's possession. These were the data entry screens and reports that are put together in the application itself.

Being in a standard format this tape was easily read using cpio (see the man pages for more details of this utility). Used for machine independent file transfers, cpio is a standard UNIX archiving utility.

However, the tape containing the C language source code for the 4thWrite database engine, the one necessary for year 2000 compliance coding, could not be read so easily. This was not a media problem with the tape itself, as the contents could be read raw using the HP-UX dd utility, which explained in detail in Appendix C in the section on *Reconfiguring Swap Space*. This utility can be used to convert a file, from one format to another, while copying the file, and is also available as a GNU utility for Linux.

Two external data recovery agencies were sent copies of the HP-UX dd output file and staff at NCC's ESCROW department, ex-CHC employees also assisted, but a solution to the problem could not be found. Hex dumps of the tapes suggested that they had been created on a DEC Alpha running OSF-1 and various Internet Newsgroups were contacted. Through this medium, a kind person in the United States offered to read the dd file on his DEC Alpha, but this also failed. Eric Taylor, The Walton Centre's UNIX Guru, was assigned the case. Eric discovered from the hex dumps that the files stored were clearly not streamed. He then tried for a few weeks to work out the data structure used as he was certain it was a file system of some kind, but without any indication what file system it was, this proved to be an impossible task. At this point what was needed was a bit of luck!

The file was transferred to a Linux machine to see if Linux had any utilities that would provide the extra information needed to read the file. This proved to be the luck that was needed, because when the Linux `file` command was performed on the output from the HP-UX dd file, as this checks a file's **magic-number**, which contains information on what utility or application created the file. It identified the dd file as a Little Endian New File System Dump. This supported the belief that the tape was produced on a DEC Alpha. Big Endian and Little Endian systems store integers differently and this is what had been causing the problems. The HP-UX server had dump and restore utilities but these could not work with the file, as the HP9000 is a Big Endian machine. Intel-based systems such as Linux on the other hand, are Little Endian. This is a common problem with such dumps and utilities such as `file` and `strings` can be useful in discovering if this is the case.

Now the format of the tape was known (i.e. the file created by dump utility of DAC Alpha file system) all that was needed was to convert it to the correct structure. A new version of BSD derived dump and restore source code was obtained and compiled on the Linux server. Feeling sure that this utility would solve the problem it was applied to the file using the commands:

| | |
|---|---|
| `cd /hdb1` | Change to an unused but mounted partition. |
| `restore -rf /hda1/datadump.dd` | Restore dump from file `/hda1/datadump.dd`. |

The restore utility needs a pristine file system to operate correctly; that is why an unused disk partition was used.

Dismay followed when this utility reported errors and could not process the dd file. What was wrong now? All the tools necessary to process the file were in place, so some part of the process was obviously feeding bad information. After a few days head-scratching, it was discovered that, by default, the HP-UX dd command was reading the tape in 2048 byte blocks but only writing the first 512 bytes to the output file, then throwing the rest away. Is it any wonder no one had got anywhere with the dd file!

Once this problem had been solved, the source code could be read using the HP server's DAT drive using dd with the appropriate output block size set, and then transferred to the Linux server using FTP, and processed using the Linux restore utility. This produced 80 MB of C language source code and configuration files. Now the real fun could begin!

## Setting up the System

At this point, we were still unsure just how far the Linux project could go. There was still a lot of work to do before a publicly funded organization like The Walton Centre could afford to spend enough to buy an Intel-based server with the equal power and size of the HP9000 that was currently being used for Infostat. Looking at the HP-UX based application it was decided that the basic database configuration and source files could be squeezed into 2 GB of disk space. Upgrading the Acer that was currently being used for Linux development with four 800 MB hard drives from the IT&M department's service stock failed whenever the hard disks on the second IDE controller was accessed. By now Linux had been installed on the home machines of many of the IT staff without a problem so it seemed unlikely that Linux itself was at fault.

The only PC's available at that time were some Compaq Presario 7106's. These were 486DX4-100 processor based machines that come in a slim line case and, as such, were not designed to be very expandable. With a bit of sticky tape and bubble wrap, four hard drives and 32 MB of ram were somehow crammed into the machine. Slackware Version 3.0 of Linux was installed on the Compaq using the latest stable production kernel (version 1.2.13 at that time). Development kernels with more features existed but it was decided that using these would introduce too many unknowns into the process leaving doubt as to where any fault actually lay.

The C source code was installed onto the new Linux development PC and examined. There was a directory called documentation, which of course was empty! Clearly the programmers believed in the old maxim "If it was difficult to write, it should be difficult to understand" So work on the source code would have to be done blind.

It was clear that, over a period of time, the source code had been compiled under different flavors of UNIX, including: SCO, DGUX, MIPS, HP, and SUN and there were compile flags for all these variations. So the source code was probably intended to be portable. There was also a `Makefile` to automate the compilation process. As Linux was running on an Intel processor based PC, it was decided to run `make` using the SCO UNIX flags, this also being an Intel processor based flavor of UNIX. Did this work? Not a hope! CHC had left the headers, libraries and utility sources all over the place. All intermingled together. This was a job for Eric and he took the source files home and spent the weekend sorting out which were headers, libraries and utilities; removing all duplicated files and putting them in sensible directories.

## The GNU Project C and C++ Compiler

Linux comes with `gcc` and `g++`, C and C++ compilers. They are essentially the same application except that `gcc` expects `.i` files are C and uses C style linking, whereas `g++` expects `.i` files to be C++ and assumes C++ style linking. Nowadays you can use `gcc` to compile C or C++ files, depending on the extension: `.c` for C and `.cc` for C++. Although it looks like the same command, in fact `gcc` is calling different programs for some processing, or the same program with different options in some places.

The general description of the command is the same for both and has the form:

```
gcc [ option | filename ]...
```

`gcc`/`g++` is a very powerful application that has a considerable number of options. Some of the more useful ones are listed below:

| | |
|---|---|
| `-ansi` | Force compilation to ANSI standard C/C++. |
| `-g` | Incorporate debugging information into code for `gdb` (the GNU Project debugger). |
| `-x c` | Explicitly state a language for the input files – do not use suffix to choose language. |
| `-c` | Compile and assemble the source, but do not link. |
| `-IdirPath` | Add `dirPath` to include paths. |

| | |
|---|---|
| `-LdirPath` | Add `dirPath` to library paths. |
| `-lfilename` | Use the library `filename` when linking code. |
| `-ofilename` | Output resultant object code to file `filename`. |
| `-DCPU=586` | Compile for an Intel Pentium processor. |
| `-m486` | Compile code optimized for an Intel x486 rather than x386. The code will still work on any Intel processor; by default `gcc` optimizes code for the x386 processor. |

Some examples follow:

To compile all the C sources in a directory and create a library file the following commands can be used:

```
gcc -ansi -g -x c -m486 -DCPU=586 -c -I../HEADER *.c
ar rc ../ARC/libMYLIB.a *.o
```

This example forces code to the ANSI C standard, compiled for an Intel Pentium and optimized for a x486. Specific optimization for Pentiums did not exist with this version of `gcc`. Debugging code is added using the `-g` option, and the header directory containing `.h` files is added to the standard header list. The code is not linked and remains as `.o` object files. Using the library archive utility `ar`; collect all the object files in the directory and store them in the file: `../ARC/libMYLIB.a`. The `rc` options specify replace files in an existing archive and create the archive if it doesn't already exist.

To link this library with all the utility and application sources in a different directory, use the commands:

```
for infile in `ls *.c`
do
    outfile=`basename $infile .c`
    gcc -ansi -x c -g -m486 -DCPU=586 -I../HEADER -L../ARC $infile -lMYLIB
        -o$outfile
done
```

Each iteration of the `for` loop puts the next C source filename into the variable `infile` for compilation. The first command in the loop uses the utility `basename` to strip the `.c` suffix off the filename to be compiled and then stores the result in the variable `outfile`. This will be used to store the executable file. The general options are similar to what we have seen before, but now the code is linked as well as compiled. Also the `../ARC` is also added to the standard library directory paths, and the `MYLIB` library is linked into the code. The `-l` option always adds the prefix `lib` to the filename and the suffix `.a`, so the actual library linked is `libMYLIB.a`

> **Note: Linkage options come after the source code filenames, it will not link correctly if they are placed before.**

Out of the thirty executables that comprised the application engine, only two would not compile at all. For some of the other situations, compiler warnings popped up as well, but these turned out to result from the source being compiled using a different compiler to that used for development; such issues would be dealt with later. On further investigation, the two executables that would not compile turned out to be utilities that were new, incomplete and unnecessary for the application, so they were disregarded.

## Starting the Database

Next the back end database needed to be started. This operation depended on a UNIX script that called three executables that read the configuration files for 4thWrite and set up the database accordingly; these configuration files were, or course, undocumented. The first executable set up and configured the shared memory segment that was utilized by various data caches used by the 4thWrite database engine. All these configuration files had been copied from the HP-UX Infostat system, so it came as a surprise when the system failed at this point. Under HP-UX the shared memory segment was defined to be 10 MB, and investigation showed that Linux only allowed for shared memory segments of 4 MB in length. According to the man pages for Linux-2.0.36 this is still the case, although this may well have changed for later versions of the kernel. The application did support multiple shared memory segments though. So, it was decided to use three 4 MB shared memory segments and the appropriate changes were made to both the shared memory configuration file and the setup file used to configure which cache uses which part of a given shared memory segment. The first executable would now run and the shared memory was now defined and configured. The following diagrams illustrate our situations, before and after:

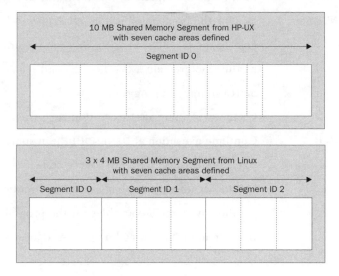

The second executable initialized the domain database and surprisingly failed when it tried to access the shared memory. On examination it was shown that this read the same configuration file as the previous utility. The GNU debugger (gdb) was used to see if that could throw any light onto the problem.

## *Using The GNU Project Debugger, gdb*

When a program crashes, it is not always immediately obvious where the problem occurred. Using a debugger can cut down the time it takes to find a problem considerably. Entering the program while it is executing performs this; setting a breakpoint in the program that will pause execution shortly before the error occurred. Then stepping through each line of the source code, or each library function called, and getting information on memory, stack and variables at that point.

The GNU debugger can be used from the command line or from the X Windows System. Since not all readers will have X installed, I will be describing the command line version. The gdb command takes the following syntax.

```
gdb [-d SourceDirectoryPath] [-cd DirectoryPath] Program
```

This is the most common form of this command. The -d option allows you to specify additional directories where source code is stored. To change the working directory the program will run in use the -cd option, otherwise the current directory will be the working directory.

Once gdb is started it will prompt you for a command, these commands can be found by pressing h for help but an explanation of the more common ones follows:

| | |
|---|---|
| break LINENUMBER | Set a breakpoint at line LINENUMBER in source code. |
| enable LINENUMBER | Enable the breakpoint at line LINENUMBER. |
| disable LINENUMBER | Disable the breakpoint at line LINENUMBER. |
| print EXPRESSION | Print value of EXPRESSION. This can include variable names. |
| set VAR EXPRESSION | Evaluate expression EXPRESSION and set VAR to equal it. |
| run | Start running the program. |
| continue | Continue running after execution is paused. |
| jump LINENUMBER | Continue execution at LINENUMBER in source code. |
| next | Execute next instruction in source code. |
| set args | Set the argument list at beginning of program. |
| set environment | Set the environment variables for the program to use. |
| until | Execute until the source line greater than the current is reached. |

This only describes some of the basic functions of gdb. For more information, the book *Using GDB: A Guide to the GNU Source-Level Debugger* by Richard M Stallman and Roland H Pesch is recommended.

Unfortunately gdb could not help with this problem, something was incorrect somewhere but the only anomaly that could be found was when the ipcs command was used to examine the shared memory segment. Using ipcs, with the -m option shows how shared memory has been set up from Linux's point of view. In the Infostat application, these memory segments had been given IDs of 0, 1, and 2. But ipcs was saying that Linux had their IDs as 0, 256, and 512. This was unexpected and at first was considered to be a quirk of Linux. Then it was realized, that as these numbers where powers of two, this was another Big Endian versus Little Endian problem. There is a byte swap involved in converting numbers from Big Endian to Little Endian, as described in the diagram below, which effectively means that all numbers are multiplied by 256.

Since it was known that the application could run on DEC Alphas which are Little Endian machines, then there had to be an option in the source code that could be set at compilation time to allow for Little Endian hardware. This was duly found, and now the Linux shared memory segment IDs matched the applications shared memory segment IDs. The back end of the application could now be started and all the database management utilities worked including SQL.

## Enabling the Front End Applications

Attention now turned to getting the front end of the application working. The data dictionary and user screens and reports where copied to the Linux server, with a small amount of data from the current live system and the application started. It was with a certain amount of joy and relief when the application's sign-on screen appeared and allowed users to log on. The patient data was being shown as expected in the various enquiry screens, but whenever a new record was added to the database the application promptly failed. What was more confusing was that data could be added without problem using the back end utilities. After some days of debugging the program it was found that some of the kernel function calls regarding the file system were returning invalid information. It was shown that the default data structures defined were invalid for the Linux ext2 file system, which had the same structure to HP-UX. But we were using the SCO compile option, which was different. There was already a compile option for HP-UX systems and the relevant C library source code for the application was modified to replicate the HP-UX flag with a Linux flag and the system recompiled. To our delight the front end now worked as expected.

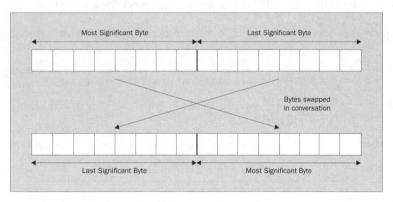

# Network Printing on Linux

Like many UNIX applications, the application The Walton Centre used it's own print spooler. I will not discuss this, as it will be irrelevant for other systems. Suffice to say when printing was tested the application failed. Examinations with the GNU debugger discovered that when the spooler initialized, it started various print tasks using `nice` and `nohup` background processes. This was regarded as poor programming, the problem being that the command parameters for `nice` that had been hard-coded into the source code were different for Linux. The code was modified and compiled and the print system was now up and running.

## Configuring the Linux Print Spooler

The application we were porting had its own TCP/IP print spooler, but Linux comes with extensive support for printing; IPX is supported along with TCP/IP. Configuration of printers is most easily performed using X windows utilities; the one described below is the Red Hat `printtool` utility and is taken from my home machine.

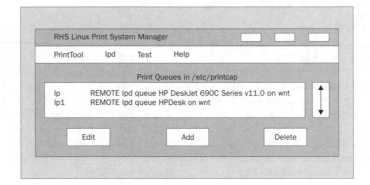

To edit an existing print queue, simply point to the necessary queue and double click the left mouse button or, alternatively, highlight the queue and select the edit button.

When a new queue is added to the system, a selection dialog is opened to select the printer type. These are:

| | |
|---|---|
| `Local printer` | The printer is attached directly to the server. |
| `Remote LPD Queue` | The printer attached to another server, or connected directly to the network. |
| `Samba printer` | The remote printer queue is accessed via the SMB protocol. |
| `Netware printer` | The remote printer queue is accessed using the NCP protocol. |

Servers do not usually have local printers attached so the configuration for this will not be given; However, most of what is necessary can be gained from the other specifications anyway.

## *Remote UNIX (LPD) Queue*

This is also used for IP printers connected directly to the network and printing to queues on UNIX or Windows NT servers.

> Note that Windows NT must have the Microsoft TCP/IP Printing service installed and running before IP printing can be achieved.

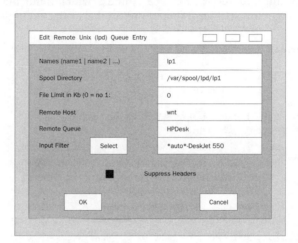

When adding a printer, default name and spool directory will be supplied. There will be no limit on the file size to print. Enter the name of the host you wish to print to, which can be found from the `/etc/hosts` file, and the queue name as defined on the remote host. Select an input filter for the printer from the given list and select OK. For printing to Windows NT queues, the share name can be given instead of the queue name.

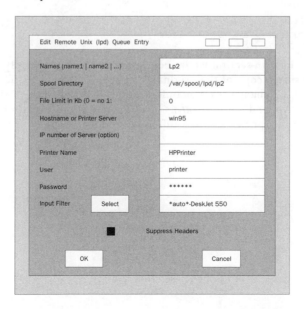

The configuration for both the Samba and NCP print queues are pretty much the same and are very similar to the setup for TCP/IP printing. Two new fields, User and Password are required. These should be different form those specified in the Linux account that was set up for the system. Using printtool to create a default account with very little access for the user of these printers is recommended, as the user name and password are passed unencrypted across the network.

Once configuration is complete the appropriate directories and configuration files will be created or updated. The spool directory is specified in the configuration. However, one other very important configuration file updated is /etc/printcap, which holds the capabilities of each printer defined. After setup this will look something similar to the example below:

```
$ more /etc/printcap
#
# This printcap is being created with printtool v.3.27
# Any changes made here manually will be lost if printtool
# is run later on.
# The presence of this header means that no printcap
# existed when printtool was run.
#
##PRINTTOOL3## REMOTE cdj550 300x300 letter {} DeskJet550 1 {}
lp:\
        :sd=/var/spool/lpd/lp:\
        :mx#0:\
        :sh:\
        :rm=wnt:\
        :rp=HP DeskJet 690C Series v11.0:\
        :if=/var/spool/lpd/lp/filter:
##PRINTTOOL3## REMOTE cdj550 300x300 letter {} DeskJet550 1 {}
lp1:\
        :sd=/var/spool/lpd/lp1:\
        :mx#0:\
        :sh:\
        :rm=wnt:\
        :rp=HPDesk:\
        :if=/var/spool/lpd/lp1/filter:
```

Each print queue has its own section where configurations are set. Simply editing this file will alter these settings. Make sure a copy of the original file is kept before any alterations are made as it is very easy to forget all the changes to the configuration. A list of some possible configurations is given in at the end of Appendix C – *Printer Capabilities*. More information on controlling printers on Linux is also given in Appendix C in a different section, called *Printers*.

# Summary

This chapter guided you through the complete process of porting the Walton Centre's Infostat Personal Administration System from the HP-UX to Linux operating systems and left out no details on some of the difficulties encountered. Our troubles were largely due to porting source code created by a Little Endian DEC Alpha system to a Big Endian Intel system. Once these problems were identified and modifications to the source code were made, then much of the hard work was done. Diagnosis used a combination of standard UNIX utilities and the GNU debugger. Solutions involved a lot of man-hours and brainpower, but the outcome was worth the effort.

None of the problems faced in this project were due to Linux. The operating system fared very well in this project, what with reduced software costs and highly improved system performance. This project illustrates that porting an entire application to Linux is very achievable, and though the example is a UNIX to Linux case study, come of the principles established in this chapter can be applied to any other similar project.

# Linux 101

If you're completely unfamiliar with the ways of Linux, this appendix will provide a quick "getting started" guide to help you log in, use a few basic commands, and give you a road map for the Linux file system. In the next appendix we will go on to look at some more complex commands, and at how simple commands can be linked together in a flexible way to perform quite intricate operations.

Linux is actually just another implementation in a set of UNIX (and UNIX-like) operating systems. Implementations of this type of operating system are defined by standards – initially the IEEE Std 1003.1 and related documents, and then the Command Applications Environment (CAE) specification first issued by the X/Open Company in September 1994. This specification is often colloquially referred to as *Spec 1170* because at one time it defined 1,170 interfaces. What makes Linux different is that its source code is freely available. If you ever come across a problem, the bottom line is that someone in your organization can, if they wish, have a look at the source code to see what's going on and how things should work.

As a UNIX variant, Linux is a very stable operating system, with a solid set of tools and utilities for developers and end users alike. Not only that, Linux shares UNIX's philosophy too.

## UNIX Philosophy

"Philosophy" may sound a rather grand word, but it's appropriate: UNIX has a very particular way of doing things, and understanding this will help you appreciate the elegant simplicity that makes it – and therefore Linux – such a powerful operating system. It's a way of doing things that's unique to the system, and it's fundamentally different from the Microsoft Windows way or the Macintosh way.

Originally, UNIX had no graphical user interface at all – there was just a Spartan command line – and yet there was beauty and elegance there that quickly endeared it to those who took the trouble to learn it. As an analogy, some of the greatest motion pictures of all time are in black and white, because there is more to movie making than color film. It would be a pity indeed if a new generation of movie-goers, weaned on color, failed to appreciate beauty in the old classics, and if the only way to get them to appreciate black and white movies was to colorize them.

Today, Linux is appearing before thousands of first-time users who expect to see nothing beyond the familiar, Windows-like graphical interface. They would perhaps conclude that Linux is nothing more than a 'cooler' version of Windows, just cheaper and more stable. But that would be a shame, because underneath all the pretty icons, windows and menus, the original UNIX qualities – great expressive power combined with simplicity and elegance – remain untarnished, waiting to be discovered and appreciated. If you learn how UNIX works, you will learn how to work with Linux.

# A Box of Simple, but Powerful, Tools

The UNIX approach to solving problems is firmly based on the principle of "divide and conquer". If you want a tool that searches a file to find all lines containing the word "Linux", enumerates those lines and then prints them out on paper, you won't find it. Instead, UNIX has one tool that searches files for all occurrences of a pattern, another that displays the contents of a file with line numbers, and yet another that sends a file to a printer.

Of course, these tools would be useless if UNIX didn't also give you a way of combining them to get what you want, and we'll see how it achieves that in the next appendix. For now, let's just reflect on the advantages this methodology brings. A program that has limited and tightly-defined requirements is usually small, efficient, and easier to debug and maintain. A more ambitious program, on the other hand, tends to be larger, more unwieldy, and less flexible. The UNIX philosophy says that you should avoid the temptation to write programs that attempt to solve more than one problem, and to concentrate instead on building small, modular tools that can be assembled in different ways to perform a wide variety of tasks.

# Users Know What They're Doing

UNIX assumes that users know what they are doing. For example, if you issue the following command:

```
$ rm *
```

UNIX will silently obey, and delete all your files. No confirmation, no warning. Usually, there's no way to get your files back.

Why is UNIX so... *unfriendly*? The UNIX philosophy says that users know what they're doing, so it's not good to second-guess them, or continually to ask them if they meant what they typed. UNIX tries not to get in your way or irritate you by asking questions; it just does what you tell it to do. Experienced users really appreciate a silent operating system that isn't forever trying to predict their actions.

Other operating systems assume their users are stupid, and condescendingly try to make things easy for them, no matter what their skill level really is. The user experience doesn't get richer as users get more sophisticated; it just gets more annoying. UNIX, on the other hand, assumes its users are intelligent. That can make it a bit forbidding for beginners at first, but as they get better, it never insults their intelligence. Nobody remains a novice forever.

# Multiprocessing, Multi-user

UNIX is a multiprocessing operating system. From the early days of its existence, it has been able to run several tasks at the same time. It has a scheduling algorithm that balances the multiple demands of different programs, and shares out the resources in a simple but effective way that favors interactive tasks while allowing CPU-intensive, long running programs to soak up spare CPU time when the interactive programs are not using it.

UNIX was also designed to be a multi-user operating system. Windows, on the other hand, started off as a single-user system, and is now struggling to reconcile some of its fundamental design aspects with the new multi-user demands it faces. There are many good critiques on the Internet of Windows' "single-user context", and the limitations that it imposes.

To support safe multi-user operation, UNIX users are given one of two fundamental levels of privilege: "administrator" (or more conventionally, "root" or "superuser") and "ordinary user". Ordinary users do not have certain privileges: some directories in the file system are off-limits to them, and they are denied the right to execute some commands. It is next to impossible for an ordinary user of a properly configured UNIX system to do damage to anything but his own files and directories.

> *This is one reason why UNIX and UNIX-like systems such as Linux are so stable – they protects themselves from their users. This is also why viruses rarely damage UNIX systems – unless the superuser runs them, viruses are not able to affect critical system files.*

# The Linux Way

Because Linux is an implementation of the standards that define UNIX, it shares the latter's philosophy. However, this discussion wouldn't be complete without a mention of "The Linux Way", since the processes by which Linux developed (and is developed for) differ from those of traditional UNIX in a few significant aspects.

## Open The Source

Source code is the lifeblood of Linux, and it needs to remain free for Linux to continue its breakneck pace of innovation and improvement. There is no danger of having any significant part of the system become proprietary at any point in the future, because the GNU General Public License, under which Linux is made available, forbids it.

## Maintain a Single Version

Almost as a corollary of being under the GPL, the actual Linux software remains undivided. Distributors may package different versions of applications with their CDs, but the pool from which they draw their software is the same. All contributions flow back to the same pool and are available to all. Although there are some differences between different Linux distributions, significant splintering of Linux is never likely to occur, because of the open source model. The reunification of UNIX under the Linux banner is already taking place.

## Release Early and Often

Linux would not have improved with such rapidity if it had developed under the jealous protection of a handful of hackers. On the contrary, Linux code-in-progress has been thrown open to the public with shameless abandon. Nothing elicits feedback faster or more effectively than the pounding of several thousand eager volunteers.

## Version Numbering

The status of Linux as a work-in-progress conflicts with its reputation as a stable product, doesn't it? That's why, early on, the developers adopted a numbering scheme that would explicitly distinguish stable versions from development versions. Odd-numbered versions, like the 2.3 kernel, are development versions and not recommended for production use. Even-numbered versions, like the 2.0 and 2.2 kernels, are stable. No new features are added to stable kernels; only bug fixes. Many other free software applications have taken their cue from the kernel and adopted a similar even-odd numbering scheme. It seems very likely that this will soon become standard industry practice.

## Rely on the Community For Support

The Internet has no precedent. It never sleeps, and it's the ideal 24/7 support organization. The Linux experience has shown that though there are no guarantees, it is possible to get decent support for software problems from other users at any time of the day or night, and that bug fixes are sometimes available within hours of bugs being detected.

## Compete Against Yourself

Though much is made of the Windows-Linux battle, most Linux contributors see themselves as simply wanting to improve what they already consider a great operating system. If Linux contented itself with competing against Windows, it would stagnate. That is not happening. Developers contribute code to Linux based on their ideas of where they think the OS should be going, and not necessarily based on what another OS has. That keeps the Linux momentum amazingly high.

## The Cathedral and the Bazaar

You can find another analysis of the development of Linux, and how its unconventional approach to software engineering has proved the skeptics (and more than a few software engineering textbooks) wrong, in Eric Raymond's *The Cathedral and the Bazaar*, at http://www.tuxedo.org/~esr/writings/cathedral-bazaar/cathedral-bazaar.html

# Getting to Know Linux

Understanding the philosophy of UNIX and Linux is interesting because it explains a great deal about why some things are the way they are, but it's no substitute for first-hand experience. Shortly, you'll see how to get logged in to a Linux machine; then we can look at some basic commands and start finding our way around the file system.

As we said before, Linux is a multi-user, multiprocessing operating system. Many people can use it at the same time, and each of these people may run many programs at the same time, subject to system limitations (such as available memory). Multi-user operations are supported by the allocation of **user identities** or **login names**, and assigning these is one of the jobs of the system administrator. Each user is given a unique login name and a password to prevent others from manipulating their personal files without permission.

Microsoft Windows NT (and, to some extent, Windows 9x) also supports more than one user identity, but it was rather an afterthought to the design. Linux has out-of-the-box support for networked users running shared applications both locally and on a remote server. It's fundamental to the way it works, because UNIX was built to support both multiprocessing and multiple users. Windows NT, on the other hand, needs additional software on the server and client machines to perform this task that Linux users take for granted.

## Understanding "X-Windows"

Contrary to the beliefs that some still hold, UNIX is not purely a command-line environment. Another myth, expounded by people slightly better informed, is that UNIX *does* have a graphical user interface – but it's a horrible-looking thing called "X-Windows". However, if you're sitting in front of a machine that's been set up using a modern Linux distribution, there's a good chance that when you start it up, it will eventually present you with a display that's not very different from what you'd see on a Windows or a Macintosh system.

A further myth, though, is at least *interestingly* wrong, because the explanation for it reveals some more about the minds of UNIX's authors. For starters, the name isn't "X-Windows"; it's the **X Window System**, or just **X** for short. Second, there is no way that X can look beautiful or ugly, because it doesn't define look-and-feel. X is *not* a GUI; it just provides the underlying support for one. The designers of X state this in classic style: "X provides mechanism, not policy".

Like most things in UNIX, the graphical interface is designed in a modular, layered fashion. The lower layer is X, which is designed to provide windowing capability alone. That simply means that X allows areas of the screen to be addressed, is capable of detecting and responding to mouse and keyboard activity, and can distinguish which area those events need to go to. The layer above X provides look-and-feel; such a layer is called a **window manager**, and it's possible to change window managers to obtain a totally different look-and-feel.

The mutual independence of pure windowing capability and look-and-feel is a great achievement of the X approach, allowing UNIX to don and shed various graphical personalities simply by changing the window manager. But that's not all that X can do – if it were, UNIX wouldn't have very much to boast about. The main feature of X is that it is *network-transparent*. This means that it is possible for a program to run on one computer, but to get its input and display its output on another computer's screen. UNIX was designed for networks from the start, and it shows in every aspect of its design. Using X, it is possible to run a computation-intensive simulation on a powerful server computer far away, and have the results displayed graphically on your desktop workstation.

"Wait a minute!" you exclaim, "That sounds a lot like client/server." You're dead right! X is a client/server windowing environment. And it was designed and developed more than 15 years ago! What's more, applications written for X 15 years ago work on it even today, a testament to the robustness of the X API. Remember that next time someone maligns "X-Windows".

# Logging In

But we're already getting ahead of ourselves. When you want to use a Linux system, the first thing you must do is log in. If your Linux installation is configured to boot into a graphical desktop environment such as KDE or GNOME, you'll see a screen that – to a greater or lesser extent – mimics the procedure for logging in to Windows NT. This is normally called an *xdm login*. If it starts up to a command line, on the other hand, Linux will simply offer a bland textual login prompt. Either way, you must enter your username, followed by your password, to be accepted into the system.

If you logged into a graphical environment, you might see something rather like the screenshot below, which is the GNOME GUI environment:

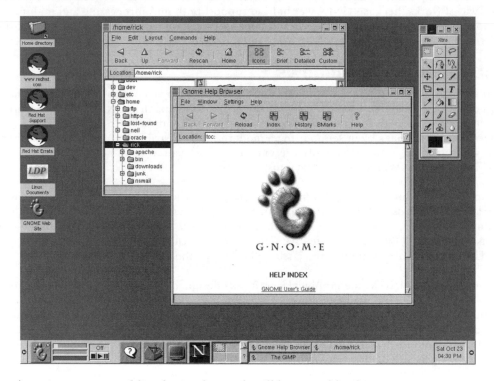

If you're using a command line login, the result will be more like this:

```
Welcome to Linux
login: jim
Password: <password-not-echoed>
Last login: Mon Oct 11 10:07:00 from console
You have new mail.
$
```

At this point, you have independently logged in to the Linux system, and everything is ready for you to start your work.

> If you have logged in as "root" (the administrative user) — perhaps because this is a Linux system you have just installed — your first job is to create an ordinary user, log out (most GUI environments will have an option on the menu; if it's a text mode prompt you can just type **exit**), then log back in as an ordinary user.
>
> Only *ever* log in as root when you need to do something that requires the special privileges root has — with such power comes responsibility. As an ordinary user, your scope for accidentally damaging your Linux installation is quite limited; as root you can do a lot of harm.

# The Shell

Most of the power of Linux lies at the command line, which is also the place where most Linux users normally use it. If you logged in using text mode, you are already at a command prompt. If you did a graphical login, you need to start a terminal session – there will often be a terminal icon to select, or a terminal option on the menu. A third option, should your system be so configured, is to switch from text mode to an X Window System session by typing `startx` at the command prompt, and then starting a terminal session as described above.

Depending on your version of Linux and how it is configured, this prompt may take many different forms. Since the prompt itself is configurable, you may find that yours is not quite the same as the one we've been using, but this has no impact on your ability to type commands. The two most common prompts are the dollar ($) or the angle (>), while the root login normally has a # prompt. In this book, we will generally use $ as a prompt, which means that any text shown after the $ is user input. Lines without a symbol are to be taken as computer output, and examples of privileged superuser commands will follow a # prompt.

*We'll explain how you can customize the prompt to your preference later in the appendix.*

The program giving you the prompt is just an ordinary program called a **shell** that's running on the computer, possibly alongside other shells for other users who might be logged in across a network. The main function of the shell program is to accept and perform commands; you type the name of a command, and the shell runs it for you. It bears a resemblance to (but is ultimately much more powerful than) the `command.com` program in DOS.

One thing that can sometimes be confusing to new Linux users is that not only can the shell on different machines have different prompts; it can be a different program altogether! This is because there is no fundamental difference between the shell program and other programs users can run, and it's not particularly difficult to change the program you use as a command prompt. Users like to control UNIX in different ways, and the number of widely available shell programs reflects this fact.

The original shell program was called the Bourne shell, after Steven Bourne who wrote it while working at Bell Laboratories. Later came the C shell, intended to be more like the C programming language, and written by Bill Joy while he was at the University of California. The shells in common use today are mostly based on ideas from the Korn shell, written by David Korn at AT&T Bell Laboratories. While superficially like the Bourne shell, Korn is more flexible and friendly to use. Linux users normally use **Bash** – the "*Bourne a*gain" *sh*ell – which differs from Korn mainly in that the source code for it is available. Bash is available on many different versions of UNIX, not just Linux.

> In the shell, as elsewhere, Linux is case sensitive. Most Linux commands' names are in lower case, and names using upper- or mixed-case don't refer to the same thing.

## Definitions

Before we can continue with our discussion of Linux shells, we need to define some of the terms we'll be using. As we explained earlier, it's important in UNIX to know exactly what you're doing, and to mean exactly what you say.

### Command

A **command** is a request from a user – that is, whatever the user types at the prompt. If the command is built into the shell, the shell may perform the action itself – this is similar to an internal command in DOS. The overwhelming majority of commands, though, are programs.

### Program

A **program** is an executable file. The shell will run the program whose name is given as the first word of a command. It finds the program to run by looking in the directories specified in an **environment variable** called PATH. We'll examine this subject later, in *Global And Customized Settings*.

> Beware: if you give a program the same name as a command, then either the program or the command will get masked by the duplicate name, and you will have trouble executing it. An example of this problem can be generated by naming a program "test", since there is actually a "test" command. To force execution of a command in the current directory, prefix it with ./, like this: ./test. This will always attempt to execute a local file called test.

### Process

When a program is running, it consists of code that is executing, and data that the program is working with. Together with some stack space and any open files, these form a **process**. Each time a program is run, there will be a distinct process. When a program is running twice or more, for one or more users, there will be two or more processes, each executing an image of the same program. This is similar to the way in which many Microsoft Windows applications are able to run at the same time.

### Arguments and Parameters

Commands often need **arguments** to specify their actions. Frequently, these will take the form of the names of files to act upon, and they're typed on the same line as the name of the command. For example, the echo command, like the DOS equivalent of the same name, simply outputs its arguments. All parameters are case sensitive:

```
$ echo Hello World
Hello World
```

Here, the echo command is given two arguments. The first is the word Hello, and the second is the word World. The echo command prints each of its arguments separated by a single space. The shell ignores spaces before the command and between arguments, so that even if we spread out the arguments, echo produces the same result:

```
$   echo       Hello          World
Hello World
```

To include spaces in an argument, they must be placed inside quotation marks. Single quotes or double quotes may be used, but they must be matched consistently. The shell treats all the characters between the quotes as a single argument, so the following command has two arguments:

```
$ echo "   Hello      World"    " again"
   Hello      World again
```

One thing that Linux (and UNIX) does in a subtly different way from the DOS command prompt, and which has important implications, is that wildcard characters are always expanded by the shell, *before* being passed to the command being invoked. This means that in Linux, the expansion of wildcards is always consistent and predictable, and you never have to code your program to allow for wildcards being passed. This makes for a much more sensible division of responsibility between the prompt and other programs, as you'll see shortly when we start to look at filenames.

### Options

**Options** are distinguished command arguments that are used to alter the actions of a command. Like arguments, they follow the command name, but they are usually preceded with a dash. This is a similar notation to DOS arguments, which are distinguished by a '/' instead.

The following example, using the ls command that lists the files in a directory, shows how options can affect the operation of a command:

```
$ ls
report.txt
$ ls -l
-rw-r--r--  1 neil     users        4553 Dec  8 10:52 report.txt                    ₁
```

### Combinations

In summary then, the user types a command into the shell program. The shell will run the program whose name is given at the start of the command, passing all arguments as parameters. The *program* can interpret one or more of the arguments as options, and the shell doesn't need to know how to do this.

**499**

Some programs allow options to be grouped together, so that:

```
$ program -a -b -c
```

is the same as:

```
$ program -abc
```

but you shouldn't rely on this behavior. However, it's *always* possible to run more than one command in sequence by separating them with semicolons. The shell looks for the semicolons and runs each command in turn. For example:

```
$ ls; ls -l; date
report.txt
-rw-r--r--   1 neil     users           4553 Dec  8 10:52 report.txt
Fri Dec  4 20:18:38 GMT 1999
```

Of course, your output will differ greatly, depending on the files in your current directory. For simplicity, we only had the one file.

# A User's View of Linux

Now that you've seen a little of how the shell works in Linux, we need to take a look at what we can do with it. As you'll soon see, one of the most important features of Linux is that it treats *almost everything* as a file. Files are a very natural way to model the source and destination of data – input appears to come from a file, output appears to go to a file, and even hardware devices appear as files in the file system. This approach involves some work in building a software layer to get every entity to *behave* like a file, but it pays off because once that's done, all the interfaces become simpler, more predictable, and more interoperable.

Another feature of Linux is that it makes no distinction between different *types* of file. A file can be an executable, a data file, a link library or binary code – it doesn't make any difference to Linux, which will treat it as a collection of bytes, regardless of its name. In DOS, a file must have the right type of extension for it to be considered an executable. In Windows, there is a list of 'registered file types' that relates file extensions to programs. In Linux, which is generally much more flexible about filenames (there are certainly no 8.3 restrictions!), names are for the benefit of users, not for the benefit of the operating system. If you wish to have an executable file called `wibble.splat`, or a PNG graphic file called `foobar.baz`, you can.

All Linux files are arranged in a *single* hierarchy, rather as a single hard disk is arranged in DOS or Windows. In Linux, there are no drive specifiers like `A:` or `C:` for you to worry about, and the user will often neither know nor care how the files are physically arranged across the one or more disks that actually store the data. Imagine all your DOS drives rolled into one universal disk space – this is how the Linux file system operates.

# The Layout of Files and Directories

The top level of a Linux file system consists of a single directory, referred to as the **root directory** or simply 'root' or 'slash', since the path to it is simply '/'. In the early days of UNIX, the root user or administrator would have a login that left them in the root directory. These days that's no longer the case, but the use of the name "root" for both the administrative user and top of the directory tree remains.

All manner of files and directories descend down and expand from the root directory. A very simple example is shown below:

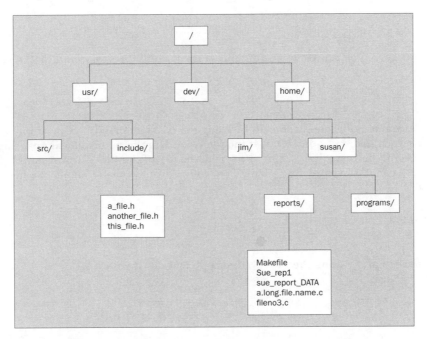

*We will come back to discuss the Linux Filesystem Hierarchy Standard (FHS), which defines the standard layout in rather more detail, a little later in this appendix.*

## Moving Around the Hierarchy

If you're using Linux from a graphical environment based on the X Window System, there are a multitude of file managers available that enable you to navigate around the directory hierarchy in much the same way as you would with Windows Explorer. However, moving around the tree and examining files from a shell is also very simple, especially if you're familiar with DOS – the only major difference is that the separator between the entities in a complete filename is the forward slash, /, rather than the DOS backslash, \.

When users first log into the system, they're placed in their **home directory**, which will normally be located beneath /home. For example, suppose you're in the directory called susan, shown above. The complete **pathname** of this directory is /home/susan, and it's the one that Susan starts in when she logs in. To change to the reports subdirectory, you use the cd (change directory) command:

```
$ cd reports
```

If you forget or lose track of where you are in the system hierarchy, you can use the pwd (print working directory) command to find out which directory you're in:

```
$ pwd
/home/susan/reports
```

As you've already seen, you can view the contents of the current directory with the ls command:

```
$ ls
Makefile    Sue_rep1    sue_report_DATA    a.long.file.name.c    fileno3.c
```

It's possible to examine the contents of a *file* by using the cat command, which simply outputs the contents to the screen (like type in DOS). If the file is too large to be displayed on a single page, however, it will scroll on regardless, losing the text at the top of the file. To prevent this from happening, there is another command called more, which displays the contents of a file one page at a time.

```
$ cat Makefile
This is the contents of the file Makefile!
```

You move up the hierarchy using the cd .. command, and down with cd <subdirectoryname>:

```
$ pwd
/usr/local
$ cd ..
$ pwd
/usr
```

> **You will likely be familiar with the '.' and '..' notations; these conventions originally appeared in UNIX, and were subsequently emulated by DOS and Windows.**

The parameter to the cd command can be either an absolute path from the root directory (one that starts with /), or a relative path in which the first character *isn't* a slash. For example, to change from the directory /usr/local to /usr/bin, both cd /usr/bin and cd ../bin will have the desired effect.

```
$ cd /usr/local
$ cd ../bin
$ pwd
/usr/bin
```

Most UNIX-based shells allow a shorthand notation for a user's home directory: ~username, often referred to as "tilde", "twiddle", or "home". Assuming that the directory /home/susan *is* actually Susan's home directory, we can move to it from anywhere in the directory tree with the command cd ~susan. Susan can also use an even shorter version – cd ~ – as a tilde on its own refers to the *current* user's home directory. Additionally, if you type cd without any arguments, you will also return the user to their home directory.

```
$ pwd
/usr/include
$ cd ~susan
$ pwd
/home/susan
```

## The Structure of a Typical Root Directory

The root directory structure is usually divided up into a series of functional areas, each relating to the purpose of its contents. There is a standard for this structure called the **Filesystem Hierarchy Standard** (it's actually applicable to all UNIX variants) that Linux distributions follow quite closely, though it would be nice if all the vendors would follow the standard exactly. We will describe the standard here, and although you should find your actual system is very close to it, you may find the odd minor difference.

| Directory Name | Purpose |
| --- | --- |
| / | The root directory has a variety of subdirectories. It occasionally contains some files that are used for starting up the system, most notably vmlinuz (the operating system kernel), though nowadays this is more usually stored in /boot. |
| /bin | Important system command files. |
| /boot | Files used at system startup time. Contains device drivers and loadable modules. |
| /dev | Devices. In Linux, all devices appear as files. |
| /etc | Important system configuration and control files, normally only accessible to the system administrator. |
| /home | Users' personal files are usually stored in this directory. On some older systems, /usr, /users or /u could be used. |
| /lib | System libraries and kernel modules. |
| /mnt | Temporarily mounted devices, such as floppy disks or CD-ROM drives, are usually mounted here or at levels beneath this directory. |
| /opt | Additional, optional software that has been installed. |

| Directory Name | Purpose |
| --- | --- |
| /proc | This directory is *not* mentioned in the Filesystem Hierarchy Standard, but it's so common on Linux distributions that it deserves a special mention. /proc provides a unification of the file system with the processes executing on the system. Inside this directory you will find a subdirectory for each process executing on the system (that is, each subdirectory is actually a number), plus a few special additions. Inside the numbered directories are files containing information about each executing process, so /proc/325/cmdline contains the command line for process 325. |
| /root | The home directory of the root user (superuser). |
| /sbin | Statically linked system binary files, essential to system operation. On older UNIX systems, these files are sometimes stored in /etc. |
| /tmp | A place for temporary, short-lived files. They are normally shared between all users, and may be deleted on reboot. |
| /usr | These are files required to support multi-user working, but they're not owned by users. User programs and compiler files are stored here. A network of computers may share a common /usr directory. |
| /var | Machine-specific variable files are stored here – things like printer configuration files, mail files, log files, and spool files. |

This 'division by purpose' allows the most critical and stable parts of the system to be separated neatly from the less important and more erratic files. Often, the directories /, /bin, /boot, /etc, /lib and /sbin will be put on a separate physical disk from the others. These are normally the only directories required to boot a Linux system, and rarely ever change. Keeping them apart from the other files is a sensible precaution against corruption.

The /dev directory mainly contains special files that perform the task of accessing physical devices. Normally, only the system administrator needs to use these, except for one special file: /dev/null. This is *always* an empty file that users can use as a data sink to throw away data.

The /usr hierarchy is quite a complex tree in its own right, so we'll briefly look at the principal directories found at the next level:

| Directory Name | Purpose |
| --- | --- |
| /usr/X11R6 | Files for release 6 of version 11 of the X Window System. |
| /usr/bin | User commands. |
| /usr/include | Header files for compiling programs. |
| /usr/lib | Libraries for compiling and running programs. |
| /usr/local | Local files applicable to all users. This is usually for files installed after the main installation. |
| /usr/src | Source code files. |

The /var hierarchy is quite important for discovering what's going on in a Linux system, so we'll look briefly at the principal directories found at the next level of /var as well. There are usually other directories under /var too, but these are the ones you're most likely to need to know about:

| Directory Name | Purpose |
| --- | --- |
| /var/lock | Lock files are normally created here. |
| /var/log | Log files, often in separate subdirectories. |
| /var/spool | Spool files, such as those for printing and mailing. |

# File and Directory Naming

The naming rules that exist for files and directories in Linux are actually very flexible. Because case is significant, freds_file is completely different from Freds_file. Because command names are files as well, case is significant there too: ls is a command, but LS will not be recognized.

Files and directories whose names *start* with . are considered 'hidden', and are not normally displayed. Unlike DOS, being 'hidden' isn't an attribute; it is purely a naming convention. The ls command and shell programs will ignore all hidden files by default, although it's always possible to force them to be shown.

> Invoking **ls -a** (that is, specifying the **-a** option) will show you all the hidden files and subdirectories in a given directory. You may be quite surprised to see just how many hidden files are lurking around!

There is a limit to the length that a filename can have, but since this will be at least 250 characters, it's unlikely ever to be a problem. Filenames may contain any character, including spaces, but the following characters have special meanings to the shell and are best avoided, along with non-printable characters and control codes.

```
*   .   <   [  ]  {  }  >  \  /  !  |  &  ;  (  )  <space>  <tab>
```

Rather like DOS, Linux uses wildcards to refer to groups of files. Remember however that unlike DOS, it's the *shell program* that's responsible for expanding the wildcards and passing the resulting filenames on to the program being run.

Suppose that we have a directory containing a number of files that we want to manipulate, such as the following:

```
$ ls
We.Like--longer.file.names--        file2      file4.txt      file1      file3
```

If we wish to delete the files whose names begin with 'file', we can use the rm command, like this:

```
$ rm file*
```

Just as it does in DOS, the asterisk stands for any sequence of characters. To delete only the files file1, file2 and file3, we can use a question mark to act as a single character wildcard, like so:

```
$ rm file?
```

As we suggested earlier, the difference between wildcards in DOS and Linux is that when the rm program is run, it is given a sequence of three arguments: file1, file2, and file3. The equivalent DOS command, del, is given a single argument – file? – and has to expand the wildcards itself. Under DOS, wildcards can only be used with programs that accept them – some simply don't cater for them. In Linux, the shell expands the wildcards, so the programs don't have to deal with them. The programs are made simpler, and wildcard expansion is totally consistent for all programs in Linux.

|  | Linux | DOS |
| --- | --- | --- |
| User types: | rm file? | del file? |
| Program sees: | rm file1 file2 file3 | del file? |

Because the shell automatically expands wildcards as filenames, we can use them with *any* command. Here's echo, for example:

```
$ echo file?
file1 file2 file3
```

Unlike the DOS asterisk, the Linux version can be followed by more characters or wildcards, making complex file specifications possible:

```
$ echo *.*
We.Like--longer.file.names--        file4.txt
```

> The file specification *.* matches those files containing a dot in their name, and *not* all files. To match all files, use * on its own. The special meaning of *.* in DOS is caused by its anachronistic 8.3 filename restriction, a problem Linux doesn't have.

If there are no files matching the pattern, Linux will pass the pattern to the command unchanged, just like DOS does. A command given *.xyz, where the current directory doesn't have any files with that extension, will be passed an argument *.xyz.

The shell also supports other filename wildcards (or **patterns**) – notably, the square brackets that are used to denote character classes. Thus, this pattern:

```
[...]
```

matches any one of the enclosed characters. Take the following example:

```
$ echo f*[31]
file1      file3
```

This matches all files that have a name starting with 'f', and ending in '3' or '1'.

A pair of characters separated by a minus sign denotes a range, and any character within that range is successfully matched. If a ! or a ^ follows the first bracket, then any character *not* enclosed in the brackets is matched. If you need to match a dash or an actual square bracket, then you must include it as the first or last character in the set.

# File Permissions

Because Linux is a multi-user system, files and directories are subject to very specific access controls that can be employed by the owners of data or programs in order to prevent other users from using them, viewing them, modifying them, or even being aware of their existence.

A single Linux user is considered at once to be distinct from other users, and to belong to one or more groups of users. In addition, there will always, as we mentioned earlier, be a special user – the system administrator – commonly referred to as the **superuser** or **root user**. This user has access to *all* files and areas in the system. Most Linux systems will also have several different 'pseudo-users' for different administrative purposes such as configuring devices, making backups, or shutting down the system in an orderly fashion.

In Linux, each file and directory:

❑   Has an owner

❑   Is associated with a group

❑   Has (at least) twelve flags associated with it

The twelve flags are arranged into four categories: three for managing permissions, and one for other, special purposes that are usually of interest only to the system administrator. This last category is not usually obvious in a directory listing. The system is actually rather simpler than the one employed by Windows NT, but in practice it's quite sufficient.

Before we look into file permissions more deeply, we need to know a little more about users on UNIX systems. Each user on a Linux system exists as a uniquely identifiable entity, and additionally belongs to one or more 'groups' of users. Defining multiple groups then provides us with a flexible way of sharing files between different users.

The three permission categories of a file control the access allowed to the **owner** (the person who creates the file), the **group**, and **others** (all other possible users). In each of these three categories, there are three permissions that may be given: 'read', 'write' and 'execute'. Each of these may be set to either true or false.

## Viewing and Understanding Permissions

As we have seen, files and directories are displayed with the ls command. This command takes many different options, but the most commonly used is -l, which gives a detailed listing rather than just a bunch of filenames.

In the listing that's output by the ls -l command, each file and directory name is preceded by information about its type and permissions. The categories are shown in the figure below:

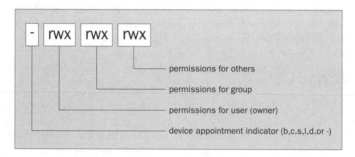

As you've probably already deduced, the file type indicator is a dash (-) for a normal file, or d for a directory; we will return to the other file types later. The position of each r, w or x character is fixed. If an r, w or x is present then a permission is granted; a dash indicates that no permission is granted. The meanings of the permissions are listed in the following table:

| Permission | Symbol | On a file | On a directory |
|---|---|---|---|
| Read | r | Allowed to read | Allowed to read the directory to show information about the files in it, but only if the filenames are known |
| Write | w | Allowed to write (and overwrite) | Allowed to create and delete files in the directory |
| Execute | x | Allowed to execute | Allowed to search the directory – that is, to discover what files are present |

For example, the result of running the command ls -l in the home directory of a user called Jim could be some output like this:

```
-rw-r-----   1 jim      softdev     2654 Jul 27  9:33 report_data
-rwxr-x---   1 jim      softdev    53456 Jul 21 13:36 run_report
```

After the permission flags, the next attribute is the number of **links** to the file – usually 1 for a file or 2 for a directory. (The reasons for a directory having two links are a little complex, and not generally important. Suffice to say that a directory notionally has two names in UNIX: the one you see when you view the directory containing it, and `..` – the way you refer to it from any directories it contains.) The subsequent items are the name of the owner, the name of the group, the size in bytes, the modification date and time, and bringing up the rear is the all-important filename itself.

*The nature and creation of links will be explained in a later section of this appendix.*

In the above listing, the file `report_data` is owned by `jim`, is in the group `softdev`, contains 2654 bytes, and was last written to at 0933 on July 27. The user `jim` can both read from and write to the file; members of the `softdev` group may read from (but not write to) the file, and no one else (apart from the superuser) can access it.

The second file, `run_report`, is an executable file, and Jim has granted the same permissions for it as for the data file, plus the additional permission that both he and members of the `softdev` group can execute it. Remember that Linux doesn't look for `.exe`, `.bat` or `.com` files to execute – it just looks for the name you specified and checks the permissions.

## Nuances of Permissions

You should take particular care with the permissions on directories. Even if you create a file in your directory with no write permissions for anyone but yourself, the file can still be deleted by other users *if you have granted them write permission on the directory*. For example, a file with these permissions:

```
-rw-r--r--   1 jim      softdev      2634 Jul 21 10:31 undeletable_file
```

could be deleted if it were within a directory with these permissions:

```
drwxrw-rw-   2 jim      softdev      1024 Jul 21 10:25 deletable_dir
```

If you try to access a file to which you don't have permission, access will be denied. For example, if the user `jim` belongs to the group `softdev`, and there's a file that's owned by `root` and has the following permissions, Jim won't be able to read it:

```
-rw----rwx   1 root     softdev      1024 Jan  1  9:50 foo1
```

Although this file has read, write and execute flags *on* for 'other' users, `jim` won't be able to read it because he belongs to the group `softdev`, and access will be denied based on the fact that `softdev` doesn't have read privileges.

## Special Permissions

The 'special' permissions we mentioned earlier have the unusual names **setuid**, **setgid** and **sticky**. The reason for their existence is that *all* processes running under Linux have an effective user and group to control access to files. Normally, when a user executes a program, the program has the same permissions as the user who ran it.

However, if a file has its setuid flag set, and it's an executable file (other than a shell script), then when it is executed it runs as though it was executed by the owner of the file. This is often useful for allowing users to access information in other files, without allowing them actually to read those files.

Returning to our earlier example, imagine that Jim would like to permit all the other users on the system to run a summary report that contains only some of the information in the report_data file. He *could* create a new report named summary_rep that produces the correct information and allows all users to execute it. The directory would then have the following three files:

```
-rw-r-----   1 jim       softdev      2654 Jul 27  9:33 report_data
-rwxr-x---   1 jim       softdev     53456 Jul 21 13:36 run_report
-rwxr-x--x   1 jim       softdev     24732 Jul 28 16:52 summary_rep
```

Unfortunately, if the program summary_rep is executed by a user called rob, who isn't a member of the softdev group, and the program tries to read data from the file report_data, it will fail because Rob hasn't got permission to read the file.

This difficulty can be overcome by adding the setuid permission to the executable file. The next listing displays the execute permission for the owner of summary_rep as s, to indicate that the program will run under setuid:

```
-rw-r-----   1 jim       softdev      2654 Jul 27  9:33 report_data
-rwxr-x---   1 jim       softdev     53456 Jul 21 13:36 run_report
-rwsr-x--x   1 jim       softdev     24732 Jul 28 16:55 summary_rep
```

When Rob runs the file summary_rep, it executes as though it has been run by Jim, and is able to read the file report_data successfully.

The setgid flag is the equivalent flag for groups, and is indicated by an s in the 'execute by group' position. These flags should be used with caution, since they reduce the security of the system considerably. If the file summary_rep allowed any other command to be executed, then Rob could potentially ask it to delete files owned by Jim, since the system allows the program to have the same permissions as Jim himself.

The last special flag is the sticky flag, whose presence is represented by a t in the 'execute by others' position of a file listing. It tells the operating system that the executable program with this flag set is to be held in memory if possible, even if it isn't running. This was once useful for small, frequently run programs, but is becoming less popular as Linux installations become faster and more advanced, and caching and swapping algorithms improve.

> *On some Linux distributions, the* sticky *flag may be used on a directory. It then has the special meaning that only the owner of a file may delete that file from the directory. This is sometimes used on temporary directories shared by many different users, such as* /tmp.

## Changing Permissions

Permissions (sometimes referred to as modes) are set and changed using the chmod (change mode) command, which has two forms. The simplest to use is the following, which adds or removes permissions:

```
$ chmod <who><add or remove><what> <filename>
```

*<who>* denotes which user's permissions are to be changed: u for user (the owner of the file), g for group, or o for others. To *<add or remove>* we simply use + or -, and *<what>* presents the new permission: r for read, w for write or x for execute. These may be combined, so given the following:

```
-r--r-----  1 jim      softdev      4536 Jul 21  9:33 report
```

we can add permission for the owner to write to it like this:

```
$ chmod u+w report
$ ls -l
-rw-r-----  1 jim      softdev      4536 Jul 21  9:33 report
```

To add permission for the user, group and others to execute the file, we could issue the following command:

```
$ chmod ogu+x report
$ ls -l
-rwxr-x--x  1 jim      softdev      4536 Jul 21  9:33 report
```

However, instead of using ogu in the last example, we could have used a, so the previous command could have been expressed as chmod a+x report.

The other way of using chmod is the so-called **absolute form**. This ignores the current state of the permission flags, and sets them using an octal value. To repeat the success of the above example, we need to set the user's rwx flags, the group's rx flags, and the others' x flag. As a bit pattern, this is 111101001, or 751 in octal. The command we require is therefore:

```
$ chmod 751 report
$ ls -l
-rwxr-x--x  1 jim      softdev      4536 Jul 21  9:33 report
```

As you can see, the absolute form can be quicker, but it can also be quite laborious to apply. A common octal series is 755 for programs, which represents the permissions -rwxr-xr-x.

The special setuid, setgid and sticky bits are set with the u+s, g+s and o+t options respectively, straight to the chmod command. They can also be specified using the absolute form, in which they form a fourth trio of bits that comes *before* the permission sets. The command chmod 5755 sets the setuid and sticky bits, as well as granting read, write and execute permissions to the owner, with read and execute permission going to both group and others.

Armed with this information, you can see the point of assigning users to groups. Suppose that we had two development groups on a system: one for a web server (called, say, webdev), and one for LDAP development (ldapdev). In this situation, we could make all the users working on the web project members of webdev, and give ownership of all common files to the webdev group. Similarly, the LDAP people would belong to the ldapdev group, and their common files would be owned by that group. Now, each group can share files that can be protected from other users. (Though in the friendly, cooperative Linux world, they would almost certainly grant read permissions to each other, so that they can easily share ideas and code techniques!)

Suppose that Gavin is a roving consultant, and bit of a whiz at both web servers and LDAP servers. He periodically helps out both groups, so he needs full access to both groups of files, and that's extremely easy to achieve: we make him a member of both the webdev and the ldapdev groups. Simple, but effective: a typical UNIX solution to a problem.

# Global and Customized Settings

UNIX recognizes that not all information can be put inside programs. Sometimes, programs need to read data whenever they start up, or they have some other 'per user' customizations. This is known as **configuration information**.

When Linux users want to alter the way things behave, they usually have two choices. First, they can modify the environment, by changing an **environment variable**. A popular item to customize is the command prompt, the format of which is held in an environment variable called PS1. Assuming you're using Bash, you can change your prompt simply by changing PS1 (note the capitals). This simply involves assigning it a string containing a selection of control codes; the most common of these are:

- ❑ \$ Use $ if the user is 'ordinary', or # if it's 'root' (the administrative user)
- ❑ \h The hostname
- ❑ \u The username
- ❑ \w The working directory

If we set PS1, the prompt changes, just like this:

```
$ PS1="\u@\h:\w$ "
jim@mynode:~$
```

For more complex customization, UNIX programs generally store configuration information in **resource files**. You can usually tell a resource file from its name – they tend to end in 'rc'. For example, the file called .bashrc maintains configuration information for Bash. Resource files are similar to the .ini files found in the Windows environment, with one major difference that's related to Windows' single-user context.

Windows' .ini files are purely local. UNIX programs, on the other hand, look for configuration information in *two* places, because they are designed to work in a multi-user context. There are global settings that affect all users, and there are settings specified in a user's home directory, where user-specific information is stored.

A good example of the latter is the **profile** of a user that's read when a user logs in. We met one aspect of a user's profile earlier in this appendix; the **path** is the set of directories that should be searched when the user tries to call a program by name. The system administrator can define a standard path for all users of the system and put it into the global file `profile` in the directory `/etc`. Individual users can also tailor their profiles to override or modify the global setting by defining the `PATH` variable to include their own set of directories. This configuration information is kept in their `/home` directory under the name `.bash_profile`.

A sample `/etc/profile` file for a system could define the `PATH` variable as follows:

```
export PATH=/bin:/usr/bin:/usr/local/bin:/usr/X11R6/bin
```

With this setting, when a user tries to execute a program called `xyz`, the system looks in the directories `/bin`, `/usr/bin`, `/usr/local/bin` and `/usr/X11R6/bin` (in that order), and executes the first file it finds with that name. Users can have their own path variables that either build on this, or are independent of it. Consider this `.bash_profile` file in the home directory of User A:

```
export PATH=.:$PATH
```

User A includes his current directory (that is, `.`) in his path, but he doesn't want to lose the directories in the global `PATH` variable, so he just appends the global path to his present directory. When User A types a command `xyz`, the system first searches the current directory, and then searches the rest of the path. Notice that unlike DOS, UNIX *doesn't* include the current directory in the search for commands by default. Indeed, it is considered a significant security risk for the root user to include `.` in the search path, because of the danger of someone putting a malevolent program there and 'tricking' the root user into executing it, thus allowing the program to run with administrator privileges. Many UNIX and Linux users avoid putting `.` in their own paths for the same reason.

In contrast, look at User B's `.bash_profile`:

```
export PATH=$PATH:.:/home/userb/utilbin
```

User B wants the global path to be searched first, *before* the current directory. She also wants to include her own directory of utility programs in the search path. Next consider User C:

```
export PATH=.:/home/usrc/bin:/usr/bin:/usr/local/bin
```

This user has decided to ignore the global path and define a path himself. The advantage of having global and local settings for every program is that certain changes can be made globally with ease. If a new program is being installed in `/usr/local/newprog/bin`, the system administrator only has to add this directory to the path in the `/etc/profile` file.

```
export PATH=/bin:/usr/bin:/usr/local/bin:/usr/X11R6/bin:/usr/local/newprog/bin
```

All users who include the global path in their customized paths will be able to run programs in this directory without specifying its full path. (This new setting will only take effect when they next log in.)

An exactly analogous treatment occurs in the case of Bash's configuration. The global settings are in /etc/bashrc, and User B's customized settings are in /home/userb/.bashrc. UNIX thus supports centralized administration as well as individual customization.

Another very common environment variable to set is EDITOR. This defines the editor that UNIX (and Linux) will use by default when no editor is explicitly specified. This is handy, because text editor users generally fall into two camps: those who love vi, the original visual editor, and those who hate it. By setting the EDITOR environment variable, you can customize your login to default to the text editor you prefer – and leave others to have different choices if they so wish.

# The Administrator's View of Linux

As you might expect, the administrator's view of files is rather more complex than the one presented to users. Usually, a Linux system will have its actual disk space split into more than one partition, perhaps over several physical disks. All this complexity is hidden from the user, and managed by the administrator.

## Devices

Before we can look at the file system from the point of view of the administrator, we need to understand a little more about **devices**, the special files that normally appear in the /dev directory. An important concept of Linux is that all hardware is accessed via the file system. There are two types of device files: 'character special' and 'block special'. Both types are created with the mknod command.

Block devices are normally used to access hardware that supports random access, so disks are usually block devices, and serial and parallel ports are character devices. There is a restriction that a block device must be read and written in a multiple of its own, 'natural' block size. This is commonly 1 kilobyte, but it may be larger or smaller. Since disks can be accessed in a serial fashion as well as by random access, it is usual for a disk to have both a block and a character device.

Most systems will have two filenames for some physical devices: a normal name and a name prefixed with 'r' for '**raw** device'. Thus, both /dev/mt1 and /dev/rmt1 may refer to a magnetic tape drive, but the second device will access the hardware without using the operating system's internal buffers.

The type of a special file is indicated in the 'directory' flag position of a long listing: b for a block device or c for a character device. A typical listing of part of the /dev directory might look like this:

```
crw--w--w-   1 root     root     21,  1 Jul 21        console
crw-------   1 root     root     21,  2 Jul 19        serial
brw-------   1 root     root      2,  1 Jul 21        dsk/0s0
brw-r--r--   1 root     root      2,  2 Jul 21        dsk/0s1
brw-r--r--   1 root     root      2,  5 Jul 21        dsk/1s0
brw-r--r--   1 root     root      2,  6 Jul 21        dsk/1s1
crw-------   1 root     root      7,  1 Jul 21        dsk/r0s0
crw-r--r--  .1 root     root      7,  2 Jul 21        dsk/r0s1
crw-r--r--   1 root     root      7,  5 Jul 21        dsk/r1s0
crw-r--r--   1 root     root      7,  6 Jul 21        dsk/r1s1
brw-r--r--   1 root     root      2, 14 Jul 21        floppy
crw-r--r--   1 root     root      7, 14 Jul 21        rfloppy
```

This shows two character devices (/dev/console and /dev/serial), four hard disk devices, (typically two physical disks, each with two partitions), and a floppy disk device. The entries for the hard and floppy disks include both block and character devices. The block device transfers data in groups of characters, while the character device is a 'raw' device that allows more direct access to the underlying data – it transfers data character-by-character. A character device can both produce and/or consume streams of characters. The main character devices are keyboards and printers.

*The two columns of numbers between the group owner (root) and the date are the major and minor device numbers, which the operating system uses to access the physical device. The first number – the **major device number** – is the type of device and interface. Devices that use the same device number also use the same device driver. The second, **minor device number** identifies the particular device being accessed. Terminals have minor numbers to identify them.*

# Other File Types

There are a couple more file types that we haven't encountered yet. We will take a look at **sockets** and **links** right now.

### Sockets

Sockets are used for inter-process communication, and are denoted by an s. Like the other devices, they are created with the mknod command. A socket is a named **data pipe**, the function of which is for a command or program to write data into it, and an unrelated program to read the data out again, on a first in first out (FIFO) basis. The difference between this and reading from a standard file is that the second program can start reading before the first program has finished writing.

*We'll look at the syntax of using data pipes in the next appendix.*

The named pipe acts as a buffer. The operating system will automatically suspend the data generator if it tries to write to a full pipe, and then resume it when space is available. Similarly, it will suspend the data reader when no data is available, and resume it when data becomes available. This allows two unrelated programs to pass data without them having to worry about synchronization.

### Links

A link file type is created with the ln command, and represented by an l. This allows two different names to refer to the same set of data. As you'll see later, names in the file system reference a structure called an **inode**, which then points at a set of data blocks. Where two or more names refer to the same file, the different directory entries refer to the same inode.

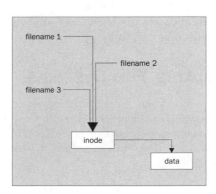

As we've already seen, the **link count** is shown after the permissions flags in the output from the ls -1 command. Each inode maintains a count of the number of names pointing at it, and if the count becomes zero (that is, there are no names referencing it), both the inode and the data it references are no longer in use and are marked as free.

There are two types of link, both of which are created with the ln command: hard links and soft links. Hard links are only allowed between two files in the same file system, while soft links (also known as symbolic links) are more flexible and allow links across different file systems. An example of creating a hard link is:

```
$ ln myfile linkfile
```

This would create a new file linkfile that is linked to the file myfile, resulting in two filenames pointing to the same file. The link and the original file are identical, and the extra link takes up only the space of an extra directory entry.

An example of a soft link would be:

```
$ ln -s myfile linkfile2
```

This actually creates a new file linkfile2, which is also a pointer to myfile. Soft links can be used across file systems, and if you use the ls -1 command, you will be able to see which file the link is pointing to.

It is also possible to link *directories* – the directory /usr/lib/news/spool, for example, may be a link to the directory /var/news/spool. This can be confusing, because cd .. may then not return you to the directory you expected; this behavior is shown below:

```
$ pwd
/usr/lib/news
$ cd spool
$ pwd
/var/news/spool
$ cd ..
$ pwd
/var/news
```

Generally, you use hard links where possible, because they use less disk space and are rather more elegant than soft links.

# Mounting File Systems

Once a disk partition has a file system, it needs to be **mounted** to make it appear as part of the standard tree structure. This allows all the files on a system to appear as part of a single hierarchy – much more elegant than the Windows drive letters! Suppose that a very small Linux installation on a single disk has exceeded the disk space available. The existing tree structure might be something like:

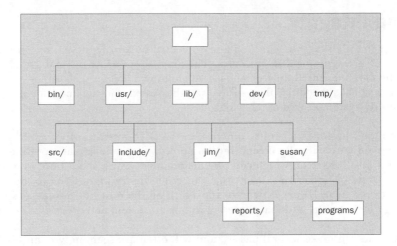

To expand the available space, a second disk was purchased and a file system created upon it. We now need to attach this second disk into the tree structure, which we do with the `mount` command. A sensible choice is to move the user files from `/usr/jim` and `/usr/susan` onto the new disk, since it is normally the user files that will grow, and we would like them separated from the system files anyway. We first create an empty directory to attach to; in this case we will use `/home`.

We then mount the new disk onto the `/home` directory with the command:

```
$ mount /dev/dsk/1s0 /home
```

Now we have all the free space on the new disk available in the directory `/home`, and we can copy the users' directories from `/usr` into their new location under `/home`. If `/home` wasn't an empty directory then mounting a file system on it will have the effect of hiding all the files. To ensure that the new file system is automatically mounted for future reboots of the system, you may need to edit a configuration file — normally `/etc/fstab` — though depending on your distribution of Linux, there may be some configuration tools to change this file for you. Note that the **mount point** — the place where we attached the new file system to the old directory tree — could have been at a lower level. Had we wanted to, we could have created a new subdirectory under `/usr/jim` and added the new file system there.

The most important option to the `mount` command is `-r`. This mounts the file system as 'read only', which can be useful when you want to check the contents of a file system without risking changing any important data, or when the file system doesn't allow writing (such as a file system on CD-ROM). Where different types of file system are used, the `-t` option allows the file system type to be given.

File systems are dismounted using the `umount` command (not unmount). Linux will prevent you from dismounting a file system if any process has a file on the file system that is currently open.

# Maintaining Integrity

The structure of the file system is checked and corrected by a program called fsck, in conjunction with a special 'dirty' flag in the disk structure. This flag is set during normal use of the file system, and can only be cleared (unset) on a clean system shutdown. When the system tries to mount a file system, it always checks the 'dirty' flag – if it's set, the system did not shut down cleanly, and the integrity of the file system should be checked.

The fsck command performs a similar function to the DOS scandisk or chkdsk commands. It is normally invoked automatically if required on boot, but may be run at any time if required. Apart from the root file system, which can't be dismounted, fsck should only be run on a dismounted file system – otherwise, user programs could be trying to write to the file system while fsck is trying to repair it. If you *do* need to run fsck on the root file system, ensure that Linux is running in single user mode, and that there is little or no system activity, before continuing.

The fsck program can make several passes, and will often ask seemingly complex questions before proceeding. Fortunately, this isn't a problem. If you want fsck to check a file system without changing anything, use fsck -n, which means, "Answer no to all questions." To repair a file system, run fsck -y, which means, "Answer yes to all questions." Very few experts know more about a file system than the authors of the fsck program. They did a good job, so trust in fsck's ability to do a good job for you. If you run fsck -y on a file system and fsck reports it has made changes, then you should run fsck -y again. Often, fsck will require two or even more invocations before a badly corrupted file system is properly repaired. If it was the partition containing the root directory that fsck was cleaning, the system should be rebooted once fsck has finished.

# Run Levels

In the same way that Windows NT has a safe mode, to allow restricted running of a system, Linux has an equivalent (though more flexible) capability. Unlike Windows, however, it is rarely necessary to run a Linux system in a restricted way because of booting problems – Linux is pretty good at sorting itself out, and at least getting to a command prompt. Linux's restricted running mode is usually used for system maintenance, such as temporarily disabling networking, or putting the system into single user mode so that major work can be done on the installation.

Linux calls this capability **run levels**, and it's a very flexible way of controlling what services are available to users of the system. The exact files used vary slightly between different Linux distributions, but there is often a GUI for configuring run levels that hides slight differences in particular installations.

Run levels are defined by the file /etc/inittab, which defines the default run level and the actions to be performed when the run level is changed. Normally, only three run levels are of interest, though the exact definition of each level is a matter of common use rather than a requirement.

❏ Run level 1 is single user mode. Most file systems are not mounted, only the root login is enabled, and all networking is turned off. This level is used for system administration work.

❏ Run level 2 is multi user mode. In this mode, file systems are mounted and ordinary users can log in, but all networking is disabled. Useful for maintaining any networking configuration, or for those times when you wish to disconnect a machine from the network.

❏ Run level 3 is the normal mode, when the system is fully networked and may be used by multiple users.

Since different distributions of Linux vary slightly in the exact files used, and normally provide a GUI tool for manipulating run levels, we won't delve deeper here except to say that /etc/rc.d and etc/init.d are usually the directories to look in if you want to get under the hood of Linux run levels.

## Shutting Down the System

Like Windows, Linux systems must be properly shut down – failing to do this can result in the loss of data not yet written to disk, or damage to the internal structure of the file system. Internally, Linux goes to a lot of trouble to ensure that file system integrity is maintained, but there are limits to what can be done while still benefiting from the significant performance advantages that buffering disk activity can bring.

Shutting down a Linux system is easy. On the command line, simply type shutdown -h now. That's generally all you need to know. If you just wanted to reboot, replace the -h option with -r. Often, Linux systems are configured to catch *Ctrl-Alt-Delete*, the Windows three-fingered salute, and take that as a reboot command too.

If you have managed to get lost (or otherwise stuck) in an X Window System session, and you can't get back to a command prompt, try *Ctrl-Alt-Backspace*. This should cause a controlled shutdown of X, and leave you back at a command prompt.

# File and Directory Manipulation Commands

To conclude this appendix, here is a list of the commands for manipulating files and directories we've met so far, together with some other similarly fundamental operations. To help you get a feel for how they work, we've also listed their closest DOS equivalents:

| Linux | DOS | Command Effect |
|---|---|---|
| basename <filename> | | Converts a full pathname to a local name. The command basename /tmp/jim gives the output jim. |
| cat <filename> | type | The command cat report will display the contents of the file report on the screen. The name is short for 'concatenate', since multiple files may be given. |

| Linux | DOS | Command Effect |
|-------|-----|----------------|
| cd \<path\> | cd | Changes directory to \<path\>. |
| chmod \<mode\> \<filename\> | attr | Changes mode (permissions). |
| cp \<srcfile\> \<destfile\> | copy | Copies one file to another. |
| diff \<file1\> \<file2\> | fc | Compares the contents of two files. The Linux version gives a lot more information than the DOS version. |
| df | dir | Disk free. Shows the free disk space. |
| du \<directory\> | dir | Disk used. Shows the disk space used. |
| ed \<filename\> | edlin | A simple (but powerful) line editor (ed, that is – no one could describe edlin as powerful!) |
| emacs \<filename\> | edit | A powerful file editor from the GNU project. Requires some effort to learn, but the rewards are considerable. |
| file \<filename\> | | Uses a data file and a heuristic algorithm to determine the type of file. The result isn't guaranteed to be correct, but it usually is. |
| find \<path\> \<expression\> | dir /s | Locates files matching a pattern in a directory tree. |
| grep \<pattern\> \<filenames\> | find | Search file(s) for a pattern. We'll have much more to say about grep in the next appendix. |
| head \<filename\> | | Shows the first few lines of a file. |
| ln \<oldfile\> \<newname\> | | Link. Makes another name refer to an existing file. See later in this appendix. A bit like Windows .lnk files, but without the overhead and ability to lose the target. |
| ls \<options\> \<pattern\> | dir | List the contents of a directory. The most useful options to this command are l (a long listing), t (chronologically sorted with the newest files first) and r (sorting alphabetically). |
| mkdir \<directory\> | mkdir | Make a directory. |
| more \<filename\> | more | Display a file page by page. |
| mv \<oldname\> \<newname\> | ren; move | Move (or rename) a file. Linux also permits directories to be renamed. |
| od \<options\> \<filename\> | | Octal dump. |

| Linux | DOS | Command Effect |
|---|---|---|
| pr <options> <filename> | | Print listing. Displays a formatted listing of the file on the screen, suitable for printing. |
| pwd | cd | Print the working directory. Displays the path to your current directory. |
| rm <filename> | del; deltree | Remove a file. The command rm -r mydir recursively removes the directory mydir, including all files and directories in it (and of course any files within those directories, and so on). |
| rmdir <directory> | rmdir | Remove an empty directory. |
| sort <filename> | sort | Sort the lines in a file and display the output on the screen. |
| tail <filename> | | Show the last few lines of a file. |
| touch <filename> | | Updates the modified time of a file, without changing its contents. This command also creates the file if it does not exist. |
| uniq <filename> | | Outputs the file to the screen, removing any repeated lines. |
| vi <filename> | edit | Visual edit. The standard full screen, console-based Linux editor. Powerful but very difficult to learn. |
| wc <filename> | | Count the words, characters and lines in a file. |

# Summary

In this appendix, we've taken a look at the philosophy of UNIX, tried out some basic Linux commands, and found our way around the Linux file system. We have talked about the directory hierarchy, file permissions, and many useful file system commands. You should now feel comfortable about traversing the UNIX system and completing file management tasks including directory and file manipulation.

We shall move on in the next appendix to examine a small selection of the vast array of useful commands that UNIX offers the user. By its end, you should have a real taste for the way UNIX operates, and the knowledge to strike out and find any further information you require.

# References

As you might expect, there is an astonishing quantity and variety of information available for UNIX and Linux users; all we'll do here is give you a couple of 'jump points' from which to begin looking. First, there's the FAQ maintained by regulars of the `comp.unix.questions` Usenet newsgroup, which is archived at ftp://rtfm.mit.edu/pub/usenet/comp.unix.questions

Second, a couple of reliable sources for information on Linux issues are the Linux Online Help Center at http://www.linux.org/help/index.html, and X.Org's resource page at http://www.x.org/resources.htm

# Linux Commands and Utilities

In this appendix, you'll see some more about using Linux to get work done – how to run programs, control programs, and manipulate their output. Linux has a large number of tools, each of which performs a specific task. These tools may be used collectively to perform useful work; it is very much a part of the UNIX culture that programs be reusable. Many jobs may be accomplished by reusing and adapting existing tools, rather than writing new programs. This chapter begins at the most basic level of Linux commands, and briefly details many of the most useful commands and utilities available to the user:

❑ Information commands

❑ Input and output within Linux

❑ Processes and job control

❑ Regular expressions

❑ Different editors available with Linux

## Information Commands

Given the wide range of commands available under Linux, it's just as well that help is at hand. Possibly the most useful and informative feature, for both novice and expert users, is the man command. Most Linux distributions provide the online manual pages as an optional package. Be sure to select them when you install, or add them later.

# man

The man command, short for 'manual', displays the Linux manual page for the command given as its argument. There is even a manual page for the man command itself:

```
$ man man
MAN(1)                                                              MAN(1)

NAME
        man - format and display the on-line manual pages
        manpath - determine user's search path for man pages

SYNOPSIS
        man [-acdfFhkKtwW] [-m system] [-p string] [-C config_file]
            [-M path] [-P pager] [-S section_list] [section] name ...

DESCRIPTION
        man formats and displays the on-line manual pages.  This
        version knows about the MANPATH and (MAN)PAGER environment
        variables, so you can have your own ...
```

Most manual 'pages' consist of a lot more information than will fit on one page; in these cases you will have to scroll through the information using the *Spacebar*. Nearly all pages follow the same format, splitting into several distinct sections describing the command's use and the options available.

The SYNOPSIS section describes the way the command is run, together with the proper syntax. Items in square brackets are optional, and program options are displayed after a leading '-' character. Ellipses (...) mean that the preceding item may be repeated. The manual is divided into a number of sections, and the section that a manual page comes from appears in its title line in parentheses. man(1) indicates that the man command was found in section 1. The sections are:

**1.** User commands

**2.** System calls

**3.** Library calls

**4.** Devices

**5.** File formats

**6.** Games

**7.** Miscellaneous information

**8.** System administration

There may be two entries in the manual for the same thing – for example, the program crontab has an entry in section 1, and the file format used by crontab has an entry in section 5. By default, man will print the first entry it finds, so to see the section 5 entry, the section argument must be given:

```
$ man 5 crontab
CRONTAB(5)                                                    CRONTAB(5)


NAME
crontab - tables for driving cron

DESCRIPTION
A crontab file contains instructions to the cron(8) daemon
of the general form: ''run this command at  this  time  on
this  date''.   Each  user has their own crontab, and com-
mands in any given crontab will be executed  as  the  user
who  owns  the  crontab.
```

The command apropos is an alternative name (or alias) for man -k, which is very useful if you are looking for all references to a command throughout the help files. It can only be used once the whatis database has been created. (The whatis database is a set of files containing short descriptions of system commands for keywords.) Some Linux systems arrange to create the database on installation; others require you to build it yourself. For details on how to create the whatis database, type man whatis. For further options, see man man.

# date

On Linux, as in DOS, the date command is used both to report and to set the date. However, only the superuser may set the date on Linux machines. Unlike DOS, the date command also reports and sets the *time*. The Linux time command has a different purpose: timing programs, as we shall see later.

```
$ date
Thu Oct 14 16:14:45 BST 1999
```

Here, you can see that the date command tells you both the time and the date. The format of the result can be altered in many ways.

To set the date and time, as superuser, use an argument of the form MMDDhhmmYY.ss where MM is the month, DD is the day of the month, hhmm is the time (using the 24-hour clock), YY is the year, and .ss are the seconds.

```
# date 05082020
# date
Thu Nov 11 20:20:01 GMT 1999
```

*Linux systems running on PCs usually have two versions of the date and time. One is the operating system's internal clock; the other is the PC's hardware (CMOS) clock. When Linux starts, it sets its internal clock from the value stored in the CMOS. The date command only affects the internal clock.*

*For a date change to 'stick' across a reboot, the CMOS clock must be updated with the internal date and time. This is often done in scripts run on shutdown, but the mechanism varies from system to system. If you find that your Linux forgets your date and time changes when you reboot, take a look at the manual page for hwclock, the program used to manipulate the hardware clock.*

# who

The who command provides information about users of the Linux system. It lists all the users logged in, when they logged in, and from where they logged in. The format of the output varies, but this is a typical response:

```
$ who
neil      tty1      Oct 25 19:06
neil      pts/0     Oct 25 19:54  (:0.0)
chris     pts/1     Oct 25 21:15  (alex)
unclbob   pts/2     Oct 25 20:03  (192.168.1.111)
```

This shows that Neil has logged in once from the system console (/dev/tty1), and once from a command window running under the X Window System (:0.0 denotes an X display). Chris has logged in across the network from a computer called alex, while Uncle Bob has also logged in from a terminal called 192.168.1.111.

There is a special option that can be given to who, used mainly by programs, to find out who the user is. This is the -m option, or 'who am i' command:

```
$ who am i
tilde!neil        pts/0     Oct 25 19:54  (:0.0)
```

A final option that might be of interest is who -u. This shows all of the users logged on, together with an indication of how long ago they executed a command (their idle time). This can tell you which users are the currently active users – who are doing something on the system.

# finger

The finger program gives information about a particular user. This information is gleaned from the system, and also from special files in the user's home directory. For example:

```
$ finger neil
Login: neil                       Name: Neil Matthew
Directory: /usr/neil              Shell: /bin/bash
On since Mon Oct 25 19:06 (BST) on tty1,  idle 0:12
On since Mon Oct 25 19:54 (BST) on ttyp0, idle 0:04
On since Mon Oct 25 19:54 (BST) on pts/0 from :0.0
New mail received Sat Oct 23 09:02 1999 (BST)
Unread since Sat Oct 23 08:46 1999 (BST)
Project:
Take over the world
Plan:
Finish this book
```

The information regarding projects and plans originates from files called .project and .plan in the user's home directory. These are created by some users to give others an idea about their work. A shorter form of finger output can be obtained by using the -s (short) option.

```
$ finger -s neil
Login      Name               Tty     Idle  Login Time   Where
neil       Neil Matthew       pts/1   12    Mon 19:06    192.168.1.111
```

`finger` can also be used to ask about users on remote machines, if you are connected to a network:

```
$ finger a.user@somehost.somecompany.co.uk
```

Some host computers run information services accessed by the `finger` command. For example, to find out if there is mail waiting on a mail gateway machine, you might be able to use `finger` in this way:

```
$ finger mycomputer@postoffice.service-provider.co.uk
There are 3 messages for mycomputer on postoffice
```

Other uses of the `.plan` file include using it to present a public encryption key for use in secure communications. However, after a notorious virus in the late 1980s, a lot of commercial sites disabled the `finger` command; so don't be surprised if you can't use it.

# Linux Building Blocks

Anyone who has examined the popular children's toy Lego understands the concept of the "building block". Almost every piece in a Lego set has two standard 'interfaces': a depression at one end, and a protrusion at the other. These are of standard dimensions, so that the protrusion of any piece is guaranteed to fit into the depression of any other. With a relatively small number of types of parts, it is possible to build a potentially infinite number of objects. You don't need to buy a toy plane, or boat, or house. You can build anything you want from a few standard pieces. The creativity that this freedom fosters has made Lego the popular toy that it is.

What gives Lego its unique appeal? It's not the actual pieces of plastic that are important. It's not the bright colors or the attractive shapes. *The special feature of Lego is its standard interface for interlocking.* UNIX has a Lego-like interface that lets you 'click' tools together to form more powerful ones. Such a combination of tools, each with its behavior modified through appropriate arguments, allows users to do almost anything they want.

The UNIX equivalent of depressions and protrusions that click together are called **standard input** (often called `stdin`) and **standard output** (`stdout`). Almost every tool or program is written to expect data from standard input, and to display its results to standard output. Normally, standard input means the keyboard, and standard output means the monitor. In the simplest case, a tool expects you to type in data, and will display its results on your monitor.

So far, all the commands in this appendix have been fairly simple. You type their name and arguments, and they respond with some output to the screen. By default, this is what happens with most commands, but just as it can be in DOS, the output may be redirected. To make the output from a command go to a file, you can use the redirection operator:

```
$ echo Hello Everyone > file1
```

**529**

The shell responds to the use of the output redirection operator, > (sometimes spoken as "onto"), by running the echo command with the arguments Hello and Everyone. Whatever the command outputs is written to file1. To examine the contents of your newly created file, use the cat command:

```
$ cat file1
Hello Everyone
```

In this way, we can capture the output of most Linux commands. To append output to the end of a file (rather than creating a new one), use >> instead of >:

```
$ echo Welcome to Linux >> file1
$ cat file1
Hello Everyone
Welcome to Linux
```

As well as standard output, which you can think of as stream 1, there is a second output stream called **standard error**. This is stream 2, often called stderr. Typically, commands write error messages to this stream. By default, both the standard output and standard error appear on the screen, but the latter can also be redirected by using 2> in the shell.

As there are two output streams, you can separate them by redirecting stderr to a separate file, like this:

```
$ rm file-that-does-not-exist
rm: file-that-does-not-exist: No such file or directory
$ rm file-that-does-not-exist 2> file2
$ cat file2
rm: file-that-does-not-exist: No such file or directory
```

A lot of Linux programs need input in order to function. Many will read their input directly from the user's terminal. For example, the sort command reads lines from the user and prints them out again in alphabetical order. To end the input, the user must type the end-of-file character, typically *Ctrl-D*. (The DOS equivalent is *Ctrl-Z*; in the output below it is represented as ^D.) Each line is terminated by pressing *Return*. Note that the shell is configured to recognize an end-of-file character; it does not itself form part of the input or of the file.

```
$ sort
the
cat
sat
on
the mat
^D
cat
on
sat
the
the mat
```

In this example, the `sort` program is reading from its **standard input**: stream 0, often called `stdin`. We can use the shell to redirect the standard input to come from a file by using < (sometimes spoken as "from"). Suppose that `file3` contains a list of names. We can see the list in alphabetical order by using the file as the input to `sort`:

```
$ cat file3
john
bill
fred
ian
john
$ sort < file3
bill
fred
ian
john
john
```

*In fact, since `sort` can take an argument, we could have just said `sort file3` and not used input redirection here. Note that `sort` does not actually sort the file given as an argument; it merely produces sorted output (in this example, the result of sorting the contents of `file3`), leaving the file unchanged. Where a command operates solely on its standard input and produces a result on its standard output, it is said to be a **filter**.*

Duplicates lines aren't removed by `sort`, but we can us the `uniq` program to remove repeated lines from sorted input. If we capture the output from the `sort` command into a temporary file, we can list the unique names:

```
$ sort < file3 > temporary-file
$ uniq < temporary-file
bill
fred
ian
john
```

However, there is a simpler way to achieve this result without having to create a temporary file. The technique to be used is called **piping**.

# Pipes

We can run the `sort` and `uniq` programs at the same time, and make the output of the `sort` command become the input of the `uniq` command. This is called a **pipeline**, and it's created by the shell using a | character, sometimes called a 'pipe'. In a pipeline, command data is passed from left to right – the standard output of the command on the left hand side is connected to the standard input of the one on the right hand side.

```
$ sort < file3 | uniq
bill
fred
ian
john
```

*Despite the fact that a pipe is operating here, any standard error output will still appear on the screen.*

Some people prefer not to mix input redirection and pipes, and instead start the pipeline off with the cat command:

```
$ cat file3 | sort | uniq
bill
fred
ian
john
```

Here, three programs are running at once, the output of one connected to the input of the next. This type of 'computer plumbing' is typical of how Linux utilities can be strung together to solve more complex problems.

A useful program called tee can be used to capture the data flowing in a pipeline. It is a simple program that copies its standard input to its standard output, but also writes it to a file.

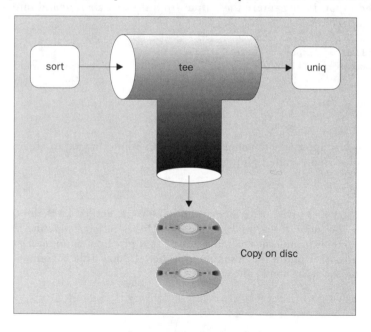

We can capture the sorted, non-unique names in a file called `allnames` with this pipeline:

```
$ cat file3 | sort | tee allnames | uniq
```

This use of `tee` can prove handy when you are trying to debug a complex pipeline of commands that don't quite perform as you expect.

When the shell performs input and output redirection, it opens the files it will use before running the command. This means that the following attempt to sort `file3` and save it directly over `file3` will not work as intended:

```
$ sort < file3 > file3
```

The file `file3` will be opened for writing by the shell, as it is going to contain redirected standard output. This has the effect of emptying the file before it can be read and sorted. Unfortunately, this error means that the file will effectively be deleted.

> In Linux pipelines, unlike DOS pipelines, there is *real* concurrency. In a DOS pipeline, a temporary file is used to store the complete output of one command before the next command is run. Of course, that doesn't mean we can't save the sorted, unique list of names in a file if we wish to do so.

Perhaps the most common use of piping is in the syntax | `more`, which DOS pinched from UNIX. If you add this extension to the end of any command that produces output covering many screens, the information will be displayed one screen at a time.

# Processes and Job Control

To this point, we have been running commands and waiting for programs to finish. However, as Linux is a multi-user, multiprocessing operating system, it's possible to run more than one program at a time, independently of one another. To demonstrate this, we will use a very simple command: `sleep`. This does nothing, and does it for as long as you like:

```
$ sleep 10
```

After ten seconds, the next command prompt will appear. The `sleep` program waits for the given number of seconds; then it terminates. It produces no output, but it can be useful for introducing delays, especially where timing is important.

We can run programs 'in the background' by using another special shell character, `&`, as the last character in the command, like this:

```
$ sleep 100 &
[1] 1797
```

Now we get a shell prompt again immediately, but the sleep program continues to run. The shell tells us that this command is job number 1 ([1]), and that its process identifier is 1797. Running a program in the background allows us to continue with other work, and although we'll illustrate the use of background processing with a simple program, it can be very useful for long, time consuming jobs such as database reports or compiling large software systems. When time is important, having to wait for your terminal to finish would be very inefficient. Of course, modern graphical interfaces like the X Window System and Microsoft Windows make multitasking like this a natural experience.

As we said in the previous appendix, every program that is currently running is known as a process. Each process has a unique identifier – usually a number between 1 and around 32000. Every time a new process starts, it is given the next process identifier in sequence, as long as that identifier isn't in use. At roughly 32000, the process identifiers 'wrap', and start again from 1.

# Job Control

We can see the processes currently being run by using the jobs command.

> *Whether job control is available to you at all, or takes the form described here, will depend on which shell you are using. The choice of Linux shell was mentioned in the last appendix, and the most common one, Bash, does support job control.*

```
$ jobs
[1]+  Running                 sleep 100 &
```

We can bring this job back into the foreground, so that we have to wait for it to finish, by using the fg command:

```
$ fg %1
sleep 100
```

The syntax %1 refers to job number 1. On this occasion, we could have just used %, which refers to the current job (although there can be more than one background job). The current job is the job marked with a + in the jobs listing. All others are marked with a dash.

Now that the sleep process is back in the foreground, we can terminate it with *Ctrl-C* (interrupt), or pause it with *Ctrl-Z* (suspend). For now, let us pause it:

```
^Z
[1]+  Stopped                 sleep 100
```

Now the `sleep` program *isn't* running, and it will stay that way until we resume it. We can allow it to continue executing in the background by using `bg`:

```
$ bg %
[1]+ sleep 100 &
```

> The **`sleep` program will run until it has slept for 100 seconds, not including the time we stopped it. Note that you can also restore a suspended process into the** *foreground*, **with the `fg` command.**

When a background process finishes, the shell notifies you of the fact, usually just before the next time it issues a prompt:

```
[1]+  Done                    sleep 100
$
```

If the process running in the background requires input. However, it will stop and issue a message informing the user of the suspension. You can only continue the process by bringing it to the foreground and typing the required input.

If the user logs out and there are still jobs running in the background, they will all be terminated by default. However, there is a way of preventing this: the `nohup` command (short for 'no hang-up'). Take the following:

```
$ nohup sleep 999 &
[1] 15282
```

This process will continue after you log out, but it won't be visible to you via the `jobs` command. This is because you have disconnected it from the terminal. If any errors occur during the execution of the process, they are logged into a file called `nohup.out`, located by default in the current directory. The output from the execution of a `nohup` process is also directed to this file, if not already redirected elsewhere.

You can use the `nohup` command to redirect output to another file and print any errors to standard output by using the > operator. For example:

```
$ nohup sleep 500 > sleepfile &
[1] 15835
```

This command is useful if you want to run lengthy operations, such as the `find` command, and you don't wish to hang around waiting for the result.

# nice

Programs running in the background share the available CPU time with programs running in the foreground. To maintain a good response time to user commands, background processes automatically run at a lower priority. This means that they get a smaller share of the available CPU time. You can explicitly request an even lower priority for particular processes by setting 'nice' values for them. Take this `weekly_report` program, for example:

```
$ nice weekly_report weekly_data &
```

This runs the `weekly_report` program (together with its data) in the background at a lower-than-usual priority. We may wish to do this if we know that it's a very CPU-intensive program, and we don't want to slow the computer down too much – it might affect other users.

*Every* running process has a *nice* value attached that controls how much CPU time it gets allocated – the range of values is -20 to 19. The higher the 'nice' value, the less time it gets to run. Only the superuser may use negative 'nice' values. The `ps` command, described below, can be used to find the priority of a process; to change the priority of a process while it is running you can use the `renice` command.

# ps

We can see more details about the processes currently running by using the `ps` (process status) command. For example:

```
$ ps
  PID TTY STAT  TIME COMMAND
 1783 p0  S     0:04 -bash
 1797 p0  S     0:00 sleep 10
 1798 p0  R     0:00 ps
```

Here we can see that there are three running processes. The `PID` column shows the process identifier, while the `TTY` column shows the terminal or window that started the process. The `STAT` column shows the status of the process, which can have one of many possible values, including:

| Status Code | Meaning |
| --- | --- |
| S | Sleeping. The process is currently suspended, waiting for a call to wake it up. |
| R | Running. Actually using the CPU at that instant. |
| T | Stopped. The process can be run, but is temporarily stopped. |
| D | Uninterruptible. The process is waiting for the disk. |
| SW | Sleeping (again). Waiting for a kernel function to complete. |

The `TIME` column shows how much CPU time has been used by each process, while the `COMMAND` column displays what the actual program and its arguments are.

The shell program is shown here as the '-bash' entry. The leading hyphen in '-bash' indicates that the shell is being used as a login shell – that is, it's running as the primary interface for a user.

In the above output, we can see that the shell is sleeping, waiting for the ps command to finish. The sleep command we are running in the background is also sleeping, because that is its function. The ps command is currently running, producing the output we can see.

There are many options that we can pass to the ps command, including:

| Option | Meaning |
| --- | --- |
| l | A long listing. |
| a | Show all the processes, even other users'. |
| u | User format, giving user name and start time. |
| x | Shows all processes without a controlling terminal. If you log out but leave a process running in the background via the nohup command, and then return later on, you no longer control that process. It can only be seen with the x option, as the process no longer has a controlling terminal. |

ps has a long and interesting history, and its use of options is a little arcane. It is recommended that the current options to ps should *not* be prefixed with a hyphen. This is because a future version of ps is intended to conform to the UNIX 98 standard; this version *will* use hyphens to indicate options, but these may differ from those used currently.

Use the manual pages on man ps to find out about some of the other options available; here's another extract from typical ps output:

```
$ ps aux
USER        PID  %CPU %MEM  SIZE   RSS TTY STAT  START   TIME COMMAND
at          151  0.0  0.2  1264   552  ?  S     19:05   0:00 /usr/sbin/atd
bin          76  0.0  0.2  1152   404  ?  S     19:05   0:00 /sbin/portmap
man        1063  0.0  0.5  2648  1016  ?  S     20:08   0:00 man ps
man        1069  0.0  0.2  1468   488  ?  S N   20:08   0:00 gzip -c7
neil        410  0.0  0.6  2232  1288  1  S     19:06   0:00 -bash
neil        805  0.0  0.4  1920   884  1  S     19:54   0:00 sh /usr/X11R6/bin/sta
neil        806  0.0  0.1  1108   360  1  S     19:54   0:00 tee /home/neil/.X.err
neil        815  0.0  0.4  2324   776  1  S     19:54   0:00 xinit /home/neil/.xin
neil        819  0.0  2.1  6496  4176  1  S     19:54   0:00 kwm
neil        841  0.1  2.9  8744  5724  1  S     19:54   0:01 kfm -d
neil        847  0.0  1.8  6452  3652  1  S     19:54   0:00 kbgndwm
neil        850  0.0  1.8  6104  3576  1  S     19:54   0:00 krootwm
neil        853  0.1  2.3  6736  4436  1  S     19:54   0:00 kpanel
neil        886  0.0  2.2  6696  4400  1  S     19:54   0:00 kvt -T ption Terminal
neil        887  0.0  0.7  2328  1400 p0  S     19:54   0:00 bash
neil        896  0.0  0.6  2268  1328  ?  S     19:54   0:00 bash
neil        938  0.2  2.4  6620  4664 p0  S     19:57   0:01 emacs
```

```
neil       939  0.1  2.9  8116  5780  p0  S    19:57   0:00 xemacs
neil       940  0.0  0.6  2236  1288  p1  S    19:57   0:00 /bin/bash -i
neil      1016  0.0  0.6  2244  1292  ?   S    20:03   0:00 -bash
root         1  0.1  0.1   368   196  ?   S    19:04   0:04 init
root         2  0.0  0.0     0     0  ?   SW   19:04   0:00 (kflushd)
root         3  0.0  0.0     0     0  ?   SW   19:04   0:00 (kupdate)
root         4  0.0  0.0     0     0  ?   SW   19:04   0:00 (kpiod)
root         5  0.0  0.0     0     0  ?   SW   19:04   0:00 (kswapd)
root         6  0.0  0.0     0     0  ?   SW   19:04   0:00 (md_thread)
root       171  0.0  0.3  1492   624  ?   S    19:05   0:00 /usr/sbin/lpd
root       190  0.0  0.6  2228  1172  ?   S    19:05   0:00 sendmail: accepting
connections on port 25
root       197  0.0  0.3  1704   692  ?   S    19:05   0:00 /usr/sbin/sshd
root       202  0.0  3.2  8292  6268  ?   S    19:05   0:01 /usr/sbin/httpd -f /e
root       208  0.0  0.3  1288   628  ?   S    19:05   0:00 /usr/sbin/cron
root       816  0.5  2.9 16224  5708  ?   S    19:54   0:04 /usr/X11R6/bin/X :0
```

The columns of output include:

| Column | Meaning |
|--------|---------|
| %CPU   | The amount of available CPU time being used |
| %MEM   | The amount of available memory being used |
| SIZE   | The total process size (code, data and stack) in kilobytes |
| RSS    | The resident set size – kilobytes of program in memory |
| USER   | The user name of the owner of the process |
| START  | The time or date the process was started |

Other possible columns (available with the l option) include:

| | |
|--------|---------|
| PRI    | Priority: the number of times per time slice that the process will get a chance to run |
| NI     | The 'nice' value. The higher this value, the less CPU time the process will be allocated |
| WCHAN  | The kernel function the process is waiting on |
| PPID   | The identifier of the parent process (the one that started this process) |

Even on a single-user Linux machine, there are often many processes running at once. Notable ones from the example output above are:

### The init Process

This is the 'init' process, essentially the Linux kernel itself:

```
root          1  0.1  0.1  368  196  ?  S   19:04   0:04 init
```

It is the first process started, and always has the process identifier 1. It is the ancestor of all other processes, and is responsible for maintaining the run level of the system, which we discussed in the previous appendix.

### The Kernel Processes

A number of processes provide housekeeping for the kernel, including writing any output buffers to disk:

```
root          2  0.0  0.0    0    0  ?  SW  19:04   0:00 (kflushd)
root          3  0.0  0.0    0    0  ?  SW  19:04   0:00 (kupdate)
root          4  0.0  0.0    0    0  ?  SW  19:04   0:00 (kpiod)
root          5  0.0  0.0    0    0  ?  SW  19:04   0:00 (kswapd)
root          6  0.0  0.0    0    0  ?  SW  19:04   0:00 (md_thread)
```

Because Linux routinely uses disk buffering, it's possible for a large amount of data to remain in memory. To protect against loss in a power failure, the kernel processes make sure that this data is regularly written out.

Notice that some processes are shown in parentheses. This indicates that the process has been 'swapped out' – that is, the program is no longer in memory, but has been written to the swap area. This is normally due to other processes needing the memory. When a swapped out process needs to run again, it will be swapped back in to memory and allowed to continue.

### The X Window Server

```
root        816  0.5  2.9 16224 5708  ?  S   19:54   0:04 /usr/X11R6/bin/X :0
```

This is the X Window server program. If you have installed the X Window System and are running a graphical environment such as GNOME or KDE, this process runs and has ultimate control of your screen, keyboard and mouse. All of the other graphical applications cooperate with the X server for their input and output.

### The Line Printer Daemon

This is the line printer daemon. (A **daemon** is a resource manager, which operates rather like an NT service. There are several daemons on the system, each assigned to a specific individual task, such as the mail.) This program controls the available printers, allowing printing to be performed in the background:

```
root        171  0.0  0.3  1492  624  ?  S   19:05   0:00 /usr/sbin/lpd
```

The daemon also controls print request queuing, to allow many users to share one or more printers.

### The cron Daemon

```
root        208  0.0  0.3  1288   628  ?  S    19:05   0:00 /usr/sbin/cron
```

This is the `cron` daemon, a system for running programs automatically at regular intervals. We will meet `cron` again later on in this appendix.

### The mail Daemon

```
root        190  0.0  0.6  2228  1172  ?  S    19:05   0:00 sendmail: accepting
connections on port 25
```

This is the `mail` daemon, responsible for ensuring that mail is delivered. There are many different versions, each with their own features. This one, for example, will check the mail queue every ten minutes and try to deliver outstanding mail messages.

# kill

We can control running or sleeping processes still further by sending them **signals**. These are software interrupts that cause processes to stop executing and perform one of a number of different actions. Common signals include:

| Signal Number | Signal Name | Signal Action |
|---|---|---|
| 1 | SIGHUP | Hang up. This is the signal received by a process when its standard input is finished. It is usually the result of a user logging out. |
| 2 | SIGINT | Interrupt. The signal sent when you type *Ctrl-C* (interrupt). The process then usually terminates, but it is able to catch the signal and either ignore it or perform some internal housekeeping (such as freeing resources and printing end messages) before finally exiting. |
| 3 | SIGQUIT | Quit. The signal that the shell sends to a process when you type *Ctrl-\* (quit). It is similar to SIGINT, in that it terminates the process, but it also dumps a **core file** for that program. (The core file is a file of output that is generated when a program terminates abnormally.) It may be caught in a similar way to SIGINT. |
| 9 | SIGKILL | Kill a process (can't be ignored). SIGKILL causes the process to exit immediately. It can't be caught. It should only be used as a last resort. |
| 15 | SIGTERM | Terminate. This is a request to terminate. It is sent to processes on system shutdown. It asks them to exit quietly. |
| 19 | SIGSTOP | This may be sent to a process to cause it to stop. It is equivalent to typing *Ctrl-Z* (suspend) to a foreground process. This can be signal number 18 on some systems. |

There are also other signals such as SEGV (11; segmentation violation), which is the signal issued when you try to access illegal memory. Details about the different signals will vary according to the system you are using. Use man kill to discover more details about your own system.

The kill command can send one of these signals to one or more processes. As arguments, it takes a signal to send and a list of process identifiers. The signal can be either a number or a name (the name is as listed above, but without the leading SIG). Take the following sequence of commands:

```
$ sleep 100 &
[1] 2956
$ kill -STOP %1
$ jobs
[1]+  Stopped                 sleep 100
$ bg %1
[1]+ sleep 100 &
```

Here, we have created a process and sent a signal to stop it running (remember that the process is referenced by using % beforehand, which stands for job number). By typing jobs, we can see that it is stopped.

# time

A program may be accurately timed with the shell's equivalent of a stopwatch: the time command. This is very different from the DOS program of the same name. Take a look at this imaginary example:

```
$ time backup
384.86 user 32.38 system 7:16.79 elapsed 95 %CPU
```

The output of the time command does vary between UNIX and Linux variants, so you might see something like:

```
real    7m16.790s
user    6m24.860s
sys     0m32.380s
```

However, the time command will usually reveal at least the following:

❑   user – The time spent executing the program itself.

❑   sys or system – The time spent by the system on behalf of the program. This will include time spent during input and output.

❑   real or elapsed – Total time.

Times are given in hours, minutes and seconds in the form hh:mm:ss.sss or hhmmss.sss, where hours and minutes may be omitted. In the above example, the backup program spent about 5% of its time writing to the backup device, and 95% of the CPU time compressing the data.

# Running Programs Automatically

To run a program automatically at a given time in the future, the at command can be used. After reading commands from the standard input (or from a specified file), at executes them at the specified time. For example:

```
$ at 1215
at> backup /usr
at> ^D
warning: commands will be executed using /bin/sh
job 1 at 1999-10-15 12:15
```

> The command "at 1215" *must* be on a separate line from "backup /usr".

At 12:15 p.m. (we are using the 24-hour clock), the system will run the backup program on the usr directory. To see the list of pending jobs, use atq or at -l. (The q stands for queue in this case.):

```
$ atq
1           1999-10-15 12:15 a
```

To remove a job from the queue, use the atrm command (or at -r) with the appropriate code:

```
$ atrm 1
$ atq
$
```

The implementation of the at command differs from system to system. Some only allow at jobs to be queued up to 24 hours in advance, while others lack the ability to show or remove queued jobs.

## cron

The cron utility provides users with the ability to schedule tasks for automatic execution at regular intervals. In fact, behind the scenes, cron is usually responsible for starting jobs in the at queue as well.

The cron daemon runs in the background all the time, waiting until a command is due to be executed. It gets its information from a special file called the crontab file. There is a separate crontab file for each user.

To see the list of commands scheduled, simply run crontab -l. This will print the list of commands that the user has scheduled. In the following example, the superuser examines three scheduled system maintenance commands:

```
# crontab -l
# Expire C News
59 0 * * * su news -c /usr/local/lib/news/bin/expire/doexpire
# Manage news files and report if needed
10 8 * * * su news -c /usr/local/lib/news/bin/maint/newsdaily
00 5,13,21 * * * su news -c /usr/local/lib/news/bin/maint/newswatch
```

To change the `cron` information, you must create a `crontab` file with the task information in it, and then run `crontab` on the file:

```
# crontab root.crontab
```

This replaces all existing entries with those in the file `root.crontab`. Therefore, to add to existing entries, we need to use `crontab -l` to list the tasks that are scheduled and edit the output of the file according to these tasks.

Entries in `crontab` files have a fixed format. Blank lines and those beginning with a # (comments) are ignored. Active lines in the `crontab` file consist of six fields:

- ❑ Minute (0-59)
- ❑ Hour (0-23)
- ❑ Day of month (1-31)
- ❑ Month (1-12)
- ❑ Day of week (0-7; 0 and 7 both mean Sunday)
- ❑ Command (Task to be run)

Each field (except the command) may be an asterisk, in which case it means 'every period'. An asterisk in the fifth field, for example, would mean 'every day'. Each field may contain a range in the form x-y, meaning all the values between x and y. It may also contain a list separated by commas. There can be more than one entry to run a given program; the one below runs the command `example` at 8:00, 8:30, 9:00, 9:30, 10:00 and 10:30 on weekdays in July:

```
00,30 8-10 * 7 1,2,3,4,5  example
```

Linux provides a further option that you can use with `crontab: -e`. This allows you to edit the contents of the `crontab` file and use the resulting output as the new `crontab` file. You can edit it using whichever editor you have specified in the `EDITOR` environment variable we saw in the previous appendix; we will look at some of the different types of editors very shortly.

# Regular Expressions

Many Linux programs behave in a similar manner – we have seen, for example, that utilities often treat options in a consistent fashion. Another common task that Linux utilities deal with in a unified way is searching, and the specification of search strings.

The editors `ed`, `vi` and `emacs` (which we'll see later), and the search program `grep`, all use wildcard search patterns for locating or selecting data – usually, lines in a file. They all use a common set of wildcards and conventions called **regular expressions**.

We have already seen wildcards in action in the selection of files. Shell wildcard expansion, however, is a little different from the editors' regular expressions. The rules are given below:

| Wildcard | Matches |
|----------|---------|
| ^ | The beginning of the line |
| $ | The end of the line |
| . | Any single character |
| [..] | One of the characters in a range |
| char | Any non-special character |
| \char | Any character, even if it's a special character |

Ranges may consist of a number of characters in square brackets, so [abc] matches either a, b or c. A range may contain a dash, in which case all characters between those on either side of the dash are included. For example, [A-Za-z] matches any alphabetic character of either upper or lower case. If the first character of the range is ^, it denotes an excluded range – [^abc] matches any character that *isn't* a, b or c.

A regular expression (or **pattern**) may be denoted as optional by following it with a question mark. For example, A[BCD]?Z matches AZ, ABZ, ACZ, ADZ, and nothing else.

A pattern may also be repeated zero or more times by following it with an asterisk. For example, A[BCD]*Z matches AZ, ACZ and ABDCCZ, along with any other combination of B, C or D in between A and Z.

Note that the asterisk wildcard is used very differently from the one used in shell filename expansion. It doesn't stand for any sequence of characters, but for the possibility of many occurrences of the preceding pattern. As a full stop matches any single character, the pattern A.*B matches all occurrences of strings starting with an A and ending with a B. Anything may appear between those two delimiters.

# grep

To extract lines that match a pattern from a file, we use regular expressions with the grep utility, which can be very useful for simple searches. By default, grep performs sub-string searches – that is, it looks for any lines that contain the specified pattern. The ^ and $ regular expression characters are known as **anchors**, and restrict the search's scope to the start or the end of the line respectively. Here we have an example list:

```
$ cat phonelist
W. Johnson and Sons Telephone List
Bob     123    Robert Johnson
John    567    John Frederick
Bill    665    William Stiles
Chris   222    Christopher Jones
Christine   333    Christine Hickman
Mary    456    Mary Johnson
```

We can use `grep` to implement a simple telephone directory search. The file `phonelist` contains names in short form, telephone extensions, and employees' full names. Of course, it *could* contain many more details, and if they were all on one line per employee, `grep` would become very useful indeed. As a simple example, let's find John's directory entry:

```
$ grep John phonelist
W. Johnson and Sons Telephone List
Bob    123    Robert Johnson
John   567    John Frederick
```

We have selected three lines from the phone list because the title line and the line for Bob also contain the match string, `John`. To restrict the search to start at the beginning of the line where the short form name is, we can use ^ to anchor the matches:

```
$ grep ^John phonelist
John   567    John Frederick
```

That's better. Now let's try Chris:

```
$ grep ^Chris phonelist
Chris     222    Christopher Jones
Christine 333    Christine Hickman
```

This isn't quite right. We need to match the whole of the short form name to distinguish Chris from Christine. To do that, we can match on the space or tab character that the `phonelist` file has between the short name and the telephone extension number:

```
$ grep '^Chris[<space><tab>]' phonelist
Chris     222    Christopher Jones
```

> **There has to be a space character and a tab character between the square brackets. This pattern has to be quoted to prevent the shell from passing two arguments to `grep`.**

There are two variants of the `grep` utility – `fgrep` and `egrep` – that can be used in slightly more specific circumstances. `fgrep` is optimized for searching for fixed strings without regular expressions in them. `egrep` contains support for extended regular expressions, which allow a number of expressions to be combined. With `egrep`, you can search for lines containing one of several patterns. Consult the `man` pages for further information on these two commands.

Options to `grep` include:

❑ `-n`    Print line numbers for matching lines

❑ `-v`    Print lines that don't match the pattern

The nearest DOS equivalent to `grep` is `find`, but it's nowhere near as versatile.

# Locating Files

It doesn't matter how careful you are or how well you manage your own data, there will always be moments when you can't find the file you want. To alleviate this problem, we have been given the find command.

## find

find is a command that searches for files, and can in turn run commands on the files that it finds. The parameters to find are a directory to search and a series of one or more operations. It searches the specified directory and all subdirectories in the tree below it. For each file that it finds, it runs the given commands, executing each one in turn until one of them returns false.

This sounds rather complicated, but in practice find is both easy to use and very useful. For example, suppose we have 'lost' a report file called invent_424. We know it was put somewhere in the /usr directory, but we just can't locate it. The command we need is:

```
$ find /usr -name invent_424 -print
```

This tells find to search all the directories below /usr (including /usr), and then for each file tested, if its name is invent_424, it prints out the full pathname of the file. The commands to run are -name and -print.

There are a large number of commands (operations) associated with the find command, including:

| Command | Purpose |
| --- | --- |
| -type | This specifies the type of file to be found – it requires an additional parameter that selects the file type. The usual options are f for normal files and d for directories. To find only directories, we can use find -type d. |
| -name | This selects the name of the file. Wildcards are accepted, but must be quoted so they are only expanded once a file has been found. To test for object files (files with the .o extension) we could use find -name "*.o". |
| -user | This is to search for a file having a particular owner. To find only files owned by the user Susan, we would use find -user susan. |
| -perm | This tests for a particular set of file permissions. These should be given in octal, so find -perm 755 will succeed for files that have rwxr-xr-x permissions. |
| -exec | This invokes a Linux command on the file that has been found. The full pathname of the current file can be referred to by using {} in place of the filename in the command. Further parameters may be given to the Linux command. -exec is terminated with the sequence \; to mark the end of the command parameters. To invoke ls -l in order to give a long listing of the current file, for example, we would use find -exec ls -l {} \; |

| Command | Purpose |
|---------|---------|
| -newer | This test succeeds if the file found has a more recent date and time than another file. This can be useful for finding files that need backing up. |
| -mtime | This test succeeds if the file found has a 'last modified' time that meets a specified criterion. For example, find -mtime 7 succeeds if the file has been modified exactly seven days ago. +7 would mean more than seven; -7 would mean less than seven. |
| -ctime | The same as mtime, but the file has had an attribute changed. |
| -atime | The same as mtime, but the file has been accessed. |

Now let's put all of these elements together. Suppose that we're porting some code to our Linux system. We create a new directory called porting, and install the original source code in a set of subdirectories within that directory. Before we start porting the code into the system, we create a file called TIMESTAMP in the porting directory. Then assume we make our changes to the source code.

When we have finished, we would like to discover which files we have changed, so that we may return them to the author of the code for reference. We don't want to return the object files, neither do we want to return the large number of files we didn't have to change. All we want is the new executable file and the modified source files. find is the ideal command to tidy up our porting directory. First we remove the object files by asking the command to delete all the object files in the directory:

```
$ find porting -name "*.o" -exec rm {} \;
```

This finds only those files with the extension .o, and then invokes the rm program with the full pathname of the file we want to remove.

Then, we use find to produce a list of modified files by finding files newer than our TIMESTAMP file, and save the list in a file called changed_files:

```
$ find porting -newer TIMESTAMP -print > changed_files
```

We can even arrange to use find to produce a list of files that need to be backed up, and then use this with a backup program, such as cpio:

```
$ find porting -ctime 7 -print | cpio -oBcv >/dev/rmt0
```

# Editors

There are a large number of good editors available on the Linux platform, ranging from a remarkably powerful line editor based on regular expressions, to complete graphical user environments. We shall now take a brief look at three of the most popular.

If they seem a little arcane, that's probably because they hail from a pre-GUI era, but be sure not to overlook them. If you find yourself trying to repair a broken system, a simple editor that does not require a GUI can be an immense help. Graphical environments such as GNOME and KDE usually ship with additional editors of their own (gedit and kedit respectively), and if you've ever used anything like Windows' venerable Notepad, you'll feel right at home with those.

## ed

The editor called ed is available on *all* Linux machines, and can reasonably be described as the lowest common denominator. Because it's a line editor – one that operates on a single line of text at a time, rather than a whole screen – it doesn't require any particular input devices. In some ways, it is like the DOS editor edlin. It's worth knowing how to use ed just in case you ever find yourself accessing a Linux machine from a dumb terminal without any screen facilities.

ed uses regular expressions and addresses much in the same way that grep does. The most useful functions are:

| | |
|---|---|
| p | Print (to the screen) |
| s | Substitute |
| i | Insert text, up to a line containing just a full stop |
| a | Append text, up to a line containing just a full stop |
| w | Write (save) file |
| r | Read (insert) file |
| e | Edit (another) file |
| m | Move lines |
| j | Join lines |
| t | Copy lines |
| g | Globally perform a command |
| RET | Next line |
| q | Quit |

Line addresses may include:

| | |
|---|---|
| . | The current line |
| +n | The line n lines after the current line |
| -n | The line n lines before the current line |
| $ | The last line |
| /.../ | Next line containing ... |
| ?...? | Previous line containing ... |

Using `ed`, we can edit the phone list from our earlier examples to change Mary Johnson to Mary Perkins as follows:

```
$ ed phonelist
194
```

`ed` tells us the size of the file we are editing or writing. Before we start editing, we can list the file by specifying all the lines from 1 to the end, and issuing the print command:

```
1,$p
 W. Johnson and Sons Telephone List
Bob    123   Robert Johnson
John   567   John Frederick
Bill   665   William Stiles
Chris  222   Christopher Jones
Christine   333   Christine Hickman
Mary   456   Mary Johnson
```

Now let's search for "Johnson". We can do this simply by specifying the match in the address part of the command we give to `ed`. We can repeat the search by specifying a blank match:

```
/Johnson/
Bob    123   Robert Johnson
//
Mary   456   Mary Johnson
```

Now we are at Mary's line, so change her name and print the result:

```
s//Perkins/p
Mary   456   Mary Perkins
```

We can print all the lines that contain the string "Johnson" by globally performing the `p` command on all the lines that match:

```
g/Johnson/p
 W. Johnson and Sons Telephone List
Bob    123   Robert Johnson
```

*Since the match string can be a regular expression (RE), this command gives one explanation for the name of the* `grep` *command, which performs a similar task:*

```
g/re/p
```

Having made our change, let's add a couple more employees. We will go to the end of the list and append some more lines. We end the additions with a line containing just a dot. This line does not get added to the file:

```
$
Mary   456   Mary Perkins
a
Richard   292   Richard Belvedere
Sue   761   Susan Wells
.
w
246
q
```

Although ed may appear quite cryptic, it can be used in shell scripts because it doesn't rely on any kind of display. There are also programs such as diff (find differences) and patch that produce ed scripts to transform one input file into another.

# vi

vi, or *visual* editor, is a screen-based editor common on most Linux systems. It's a little like the DOS edit program, but rather more idiosyncratic. It also has a lot in common with ed, in that it has a command mode that accepts ed-style commands and regular expressions. vi runs full-screen, and shows one page of the file at a time:

```
$ vi phonelist
 W. Johnson and Sons Telephone List
Bob    123   Robert Johnson
John    567   John Frederick
Bill    665   William Stiles
Chris   222   Christopher Jones
Christine   333   Christine Hickman
Mary    456   Mary Perkins
Richard   292   Richard Belvedere
Sue    761   Susan Wells
~
~
~
~
~
~
~
~
~
~
~
~
~
~
~
~
~
~
~
~
~
~
~
"phonelist"  9 lines, 246 chars
```

Lines on the screen that are not part of the file are shown as a tilde, ~. In this case, as the file is only nine lines long, the remainder of the screen is filled with these characters.

vi has two main screen modes: command mode and insertion mode. We start in command mode, which allows us to navigate and perform operations on text.

We can move around the file in command mode using cursor control keys. Functions are performed by pressing one of the following keys:

| | |
|---|---|
| *k* | Go up one line. |
| *j* | Go down one line. |
| *l* | Go right one character. |
| *h* | Go left one character. |
| *a* | Append to end of current line (enters insertion mode). |
| *x* | Delete the character under the cursor. |
| *dw* | Delete to the end of the current word. |
| *dd* | Delete line (into paste buffer). |
| *cw* | Change the current word (end with *Esc*). |
| *cc* | Change to end of the line (end with *Esc*). |
| *G* | Go to the last line. |
| *p* | Paste from the paste buffer. |
| *J* | Join the current line with the next line. |
| *r* | Replace the current character with the next one typed. |
| *u* | Undo/redo the last command. |
| *i* | Enter insertion mode. |
| *b* | Move back a word. |
| *w* | Move forward a word. |
| */* | Search for a regular expression. |
| *n* | Repeat search using the previous regular expression. |
| *Esc* | Exit insertion mode. |
| *:* | Enter the extended command mode. |

Many functions may be given an argument by typing a number before the function letter. For example, *3dd* deletes three lines, while *120G* goes to line number 120.

Text can be inserted into the file by pressing *i* for insert, typing the required text, and then pressing *Esc* to exit insertion mode.

Using a colon when you are in command mode allows you to enter extended commands. This enters extended command mode, and brings up a : prompt at the bottom of the screen. From this point, ed-style commands are available. The most useful of these is probably s for substitute, which works in the same way as it does in ed. The w command writes the file, and the q command quits vi. Adding an exclamation mark to a command makes it unconditional, so to quit without saving changes, use:

*Esc : q !*

It is as well to know how to exit vi even if you don't plan to use it, as it is often configured as the default editor for utilities that allow the user to edit files.

# emacs

The original emacs was an editor written by Richard Stallman for the PDP-10. There are now a number of versions available for UNIX machines, including Stallman's own GNU emacs and Xemacs, which is a graphical version for use with the X Window System.

emacs is a very capable full screen editor, supporting the display and editing of multiple files at once, sophisticated macros, and syntax-directed editing for a large number of file types, including C, Pascal and Lisp programs. It is extremely configurable, and is often the editor of choice for systems capable of supporting it.

Control key sequences play a large part in navigating emacs, and learning these can seem a little daunting. Fortunately, emacs comes with a tutorial for beginners and an extensive online manual.

To learn emacs, start by pressing *Ctrl-H*, followed by *t* for the tutorial. emacs has its entire manual available online – try *Ctrl-H* and then *i* for information. Alternatively, if your version of emacs has menus, select Help | Tutorial.

emacs allows you to edit more than one file at a time, and to view them in their own windows. Each file that you edit is read into a buffer, and you use the buffer commands to navigate between them. emacs also allows you to use its windows to view part of a buffer. It's possible to view two parts of the same buffer in two different windows. This can be confusing for beginners, but can be a real boon to experienced users.

Some of the more common emacs commands are listed below. The caret, ^, is used to indicate control characters:

| | |
|---|---|
| ^@ | Set a mark |
| ^A | Go to the beginning of the current line |
| ^D | Delete a character |
| ^E | Go to the end of the current line |
| ^H | Help |
| ^K | Delete to the end of the current line |
| ^V | Page down |
| ^W | Delete the text between mark and cursor |
| ^Y | Paste text that has been previously deleted |
| ^X^C | Quit emacs, optionally saving files |
| ^X^F | Find and load a specified file; if it doesn't exist, create a new file with the specified name |
| ^Xb | Switch buffer |
| ESC v | Page up |
| ESC < | Go to the start of the file |
| ESC > | Go to the end of the file |

# Summary

In this appendix, we have seen how Linux programs can be run and manipulated. We have met a large number of utilities that most Linux systems have installed as standard. We have also seen that the Linux environment is a flexible one, allowing small programs to be used together to solve complex problems. We examined the use of pipes, whereby you can feed the output of one command straight into the input of another, and finally, we looked at some of the different editors available.

Armed with the information in this appendix and its precursor, you should be able to find your way around a Linux machine. Perhaps more importantly, you should have a good idea of where and how to look for more information when you need it. All the best Linux applications – certainly, all the ones we cover in this book – are well maintained and well documented. Even if this has been your first introduction to Linux, you'll be able use the things you've learned here to get help with the other tools you meet in this book on the majority of occasions.

# C

# System Administration

In the previous appendix, we described many of the general Linux commands, such as `cd`, `ls` and `mount` which you will almost certainly use every time you log on to your Linux machine. In this appendix, more standard Linux commands and utilities will be described. These will be less frequently used than those commands already described, but are nevertheless just as important, especially from a system administrator's point of view. All the essential systems administration tasks will be discussed, as follows:

- ❏ Hard disk partitioning and modifying the file system table.

- ❏ Running scripts and environment variables.

- ❏ General housekeeping, such as:

    - ❏ Dealing with users.

    - ❏ Automating common administration tasks, such as monitoring the usage of system resources, printer usage and security issues.

    - ❏ Dealing with specific problems, including those of processes, memory, printing and network communications.

    - ❏ Archiving and compression

    - ❏ Backing up and restoring the system.

- ❏ General Linux configuration, including:

    - ❏ Adding user accounts

    - ❏ Starting processes at system boot-up, and running scripts immediately after boot-up and during server shutdown.

❑     Network configuration, which includes system security, configuring network cards, Internet services and routing.

❑   Configuring and compiling a new Linux kernel.

❑   Using the Red Hat Package Manager (RPM) to create application installation files.

❑   Other uses of RPM, such as installing, upgrading and removing packages, querying and verification of application RPMs.

❑   Using File Transfer Protocol (FTP) to automate application updates.

# Disk Partitioning

One of the first tasks to perform in a Linux installation is to create the necessary disk partitions to store the various parts of the operating system, application software and user data. This is usually carried out as part of the installation and different distributions of Linux will use different utilities to perform this – see the installation manual that comes with your distribution for details on the utility used. No matter what distribution is utilized, the system will need two mandatory partitions and a number of non-mandatory partitions to control disk space allocation. However, you might have to rearrange your file system should one partition fill up and you need to clear some space on it.

## Mandatory Partitions

The two partitions all Linux systems will need are:

❑   A root partition, where the system will install itself, and any other software not allocated to a non-mandatory partition. The root partition is mounted on / and all other partitions are mounted to a directory in or below /, except for the swap partition.

❑   A swap partition that is used by the system as virtual memory. Memory is paged to and from the swap partition when the physical memory on the machine gets full. Swap partitions are not mounted in the usual way as they can only be accessed by the system.

## Non-Mandatory Partitions

These partitions are used to physically divide up the total disk space to ensure important partitions, such as the `root` partition, do not become full. Non-mandatory system partitions which may be of use are:

❑   A partition where much of the software for Linux will resides – mounted on `/usr`.

❑   A partition used to store the users home directories – mounted on `/home`.

❑   Temporary storage partition – mounted on `/tmp`.

❑   Print spooling and log file partition where Linux writes its system logs – mounted on `/var`.

❑   A boot partition, advisable if you use Linux Loader (LILO) to boot the system – mounted on `/boot`.

## *Partition Sizes*

A rough guide to the disk space needed for the system partitions is useful at this point. After an initial installation these can be changed where necessary, depending on the type of system needed. It is always a good idea to leave some disk space free for later allocation if the need arises. In the suggestions for disk space allocations below, the partitions are identified using their mount points, i.e. /, /usr, /tmp etc,

❑   / (root) – If you are separating the disk space into the non-mandatory partitions described above, 100MB should be sufficient for the root partition. This will then contain only the executables and configuration files needed to boot the system. If you decide not to create any non-mandatory partitions, then the size of the / partition will have to increase to accommodate files that would have been saved on these partitions.

❑   swap – a quick way to gauge the swap partition size is to make it at least the same size as the physical RAM on your computer (a more suitable method will be discussed later). The largest usable swap partition is 127MB, and anything greater will not be used by the system. If more swap space than this is needed create more swap partitions as appropriate.

❑   /usr – try to be generous with this partition, as any utilities installed later will be installed here. 1GB should be enough for a full installation and give plenty of room for expansion later.

❑   /home – the home partition size will depend on the number of users that are expected to use the system, both now and in the future, and what type of work they will be doing.

❑   /tmp and /var – the temporary and log file partitions are only really necessary for large multi-user servers. If a large amount of logging and printer activity is expected it is essential these are separated to ensure the root partition does not needlessly fill up.

❑   /boot – the boot partition can be very useful for systems running LILO on older Intel-based systems. Some older systems could not recognize data stored beyond cylinder 1023 on any drive. Although this has been corrected for newer systems it will not do any harm to have a small 10MB partition defined at the start of a disk specifically for the LILO boot partition. For more information on LILO refer to your installation guide.

The type of partition will need to be specified and the two usual cases are Linux swap, for swap partitions, and Linux Native for the rest (more details of other partition types can be found in the installation guide). Before any partition can be used they have to be mounted to a blank directory created in the appropriate place on the root partition. If these partitions are created as part of the installation process, these directories will be created and the partitions mounted for you. When a partition is created after installation that needs to be mounted on boot-up, then details of that partition will have to be entered in the file system table (/etc/fstab) configuration file.

## Modifying /etc/fstab

Always make a backup copy of this file before modification in case of corruption; in fact this is true of any of the system configuration files mentioned in this appendix. This file is a simple text file and can be edited with any the text editors that come with Linux (such as vi, vim, emacs, joe, etc.). Each line of the file corresponds to information for a specified device and contains six fields. The fields are separated by white space and specify:

❏ The device to be mounted.

❏ Its mount point.

❏ File system used for the device.

❏ Mount options.

❏ A dump flag to show which file systems need to be dumped when using the dump command. A value of zero specifies that this file system will not be dumped.

❏ The pass number, used by the fsck (file system check) command to determine the order to check each file system on boot up. The root partition should always be the first partition checked by Linux and other partitions are usually the second to utilize parallel checking where the hardware supports this. A value of zero for this field indicates the file system does not need to be checked.

An example of /etc/fstab is shown below using the more command.

```
# more /etc/fstab
Device          Mount point     File system     Options     Dump    Pass
/dev/hdb1       /               ext2            defaults    1 1
/dev/hda1       /hda1           ext2            defaults    1 2
/dev/hda2       swap            swap            defaults    0 0
/dev/fd0        /mnt/floppy     ext2            noauto      0 0
/dev/cdrom      /mnt/cdrom      iso9660         noauto,ro   0 0
none            /proc           proc            defaults    0 0
```

See the man pages for mount and fstab for details of all the file systems and options available.

> **Note on removable media: CD-ROM's and floppy disks have to be mounted before use, unlike Microsoft operating systems which mount on booting. While mounted you cannot remove CDs, the system will disable the eject button until the CD-ROM is unmounted. Floppy disks, however, use a mechanical mechanism that Linux cannot control. NEVER remove a floppy disk before unmounting the file system as this will totally confuse Linux, especially if a different disk is inserted. Always unmount before removing a floppy disk.**

## Partition Limitations

There is a limitation of four primary partitions for each drive, which can cause problems, especially on machines with a hardware diagnostic partition installed. If the server has more than one disk, I would suggest storing the largest partitions (such as /usr and /home) on the first disk; swap, boot and root partitions can be created on other drives.

# Running Scripts and Environment Variables

All operating systems need a script processing capability and Linux has the added advantage of having a great range of shells it can run on. Some of the common ones are:

- ❑  sh – the original shell.
- ❑  bash – the GNU Bourne Again Shell, based on sh the original command interpreter.
- ❑  ksh – Korn shell with extensive programming support.
- ❑  zsh – enhanced Korn shell.
- ❑  tcsh – C Shell, features C programming style syntax.
- ❑  bsh – System V shell.
- ❑  ash – A lightweight shell, similar functionality to System V shell.

To change from one shell to another at the command line simply enter /bin/ShellName. Entering exit will return the system to the previous shell. For script programming the first line of every script should contain the statement:

```
#!/bin/Shell
```

Shell refers to the command shell required for the script to operate in. Basically this statement will open up the required shell for executing all the following commands in. In this appendix, we are only discussing standard shell programming and so we will specify either #!/bin/sh, or #!/bin/bash. When a script is executed in a shell it was not designed for, it will stop when it comes across an unknown command syntax and issues an error.

## Running a Script

Scripts can be written with any of the Linux text editors, the important thing to remember is that before they can be run, the scripts execute attribute has to be set. See Appendix B for details of the chmod command on how to do this. The script can then be executed by entering:

```
$ ./Scriptname
```

Where Scriptname is the file you called the script, or alternatively, if the script is written for a different shell to the current one, use:

```
$ /bin/Shell Scriptname
```

Where Shell is the shell to run the script in.

### Running a Script in the Background

To run a script, or another command, in the background, suffix the command with an &. This will allow you to continue working on the command line without having to wait for the script to complete, for example:

```
$ ./Scriptname &
```

# Variables

There are three type of variables used by Linux to store data, these are:

- ❑ Built-in – system variables that cannot be modified.
- ❑ Environment – variables that are part of the system but can be modified by the user. If modified, the changes will only effect the user who made them.
- ❑ User – variables defined by the user that can be modified without effecting system functionality.

Variables can be of any type, i.e. character string or number, and the type can change with use. Generally, the variables of interest to the system administrator when executing script programs are the built-in and environment variables, which are discussed in this section. For a complete guide to user variables and script programming see Beginning Linux Programming by Wrox Press [ISBN 1861002971].

## Common Environment Variables

Environment variables are user (or even process) specific. They include:

- ❑ PATH – this contains a colon-separated list of all the directories to search for executable files.
- ❑ HOME – this contains the home, or login, directory of the user.
- ❑ USER – this contains the user name used by Berkley Software Distribution (BSD) derived programs.
- ❑ LOGNAME – this contains the user name used by System V derived programs (the same as USER).
- ❑ PWD – this specifies the current working directory. The name of this variable comes from the pwd command, which stands for Print Working Directory. (It does *not* stand for "password".)
- ❑ SHELL – this specifies the default shell for user.
- ❑ TERM – this specifies the terminal type.

*Note*: *All these variables can be modified, but changing PWD will have the effect of changing the working directory, not the current directory.*

## Accessing, Modifiying and Assigning Variables

Variables are accessed by preceding the name with the $ character, which operated by expanding the variable into the command. Assignment is performed using the '=' operator. For example:

```
# PATH=$PATH:/home/geoff
```

```
# TERM=vt100
```

In the first example case the PATH variable is modified by appending : /home/geoff to the end of the current list. In the second example, the terminal type is assigned the value "vt100".

### Variables Used as Parameters to Scripts

Parameters passed to scripts are stored in numbered variables depending on the position passed. The first parameter is stored in 1, the second in 2, etc. These variables are then accessed like any other, $1, $2, $3, through to $9. When fewer parameters are passed to a script than expected, the later variables will contain blanks. If more parameters are passed than the maximum of 9, then they will be ignored as the script was not designed to cope with them.

The four built-in variables are #, ?, * and 0:

❑   # will contain the number of parameters passed to the script.

❑   ? will contain the return code of the last statement or script executed.

❑   * specifies all the arguments passed.

❑   0 (zero) will contain the command used to call the script. For example a script containing the line:

```
echo $#.$?.$*.$0,$1
```

will display the following, when executed passing the parameters 140 and 160:

```
2,0,140 160,./params.sh,140
```

Where:

❑   2 – is the number of parameters.

❑   0 – is the return code of the last statement (0 means successful).

❑   140 160 – is a single string containing all the parameters passed to the script.

❑   ./params.sh – is the command used to executed the shell.

❑   140 – is the first parameter.

Numbered variables are built-in and cannot be assigned values, although the shift command can change these values.

### The Shift Command

This command can be used to process numbered variables one at a time using a single variable. The effect it has is to shift each parameter along to the left, that is to say, the value of $2 is placed in $1 and the value of $3 is placed in $2, and so on. The syntax is very simple:

```
shift [Number]
```

Without the optional Number this will shift all the parameters along by 1. The example script below uses the command both with and without the number option:

```
#!/bin/sh
echo $1
shift
echo $1
shift 2
echo $1
```

The script first opens up a standard shell and display the first parameter, then it applies a shift before displaying the first parameter again, containing the value originally passed as the second parameter. It then applies two shifts this time and displays once again the first parameter, now containing the value of the fourth. The results of the shifts can be seen in the output below:

```
[root@ /root]# test.sh a b c d
a
b
d
```

Note that, unlike the DOS command of the same name, shift never replaces the $0 parameter.

# General Housekeeping

Although often seen as the tedious side of system administration, day-to-day housekeeping is the most important part of the administrator's role. It covers a wide range of tasks from resource management to disaster recovery and dealing with users.

# Commands Dealing with Users

An administrator will often need to find out more details of users while performing their duties, or to communicate with a user directly. The following commands all have some aspect of user administration involved:

❑ groups [User] – shows the groups a user belongs to.

❑ id [Name] – displays the username, group and their respective IDs of user Name.

❑ passwd [User] – changes password, or the password of the user given if you are the super-user.

❑ su [User] – switches to a different user ID, in this form it will run an interactive shell as the specified user. Handy for testing new accounts. Unless you are the super-user a password will be requested.

❑ talk [Person] – interactive conversation program. Two windows are opened allowing both users to simultaneously type messages to each other. The person is a username on the current server or user@host for remote hosts.

❑ users – displays user names of users currently logged in.

❑ w [User] – shows information of the command currently being used by the specified user, or everyone on the system if a user is not specified. The information includes details of when the user logged in, and how much of the processor that user has used since logging in.

❑ wall [Message] – usually used to send a message to all users logged in warning that the system will soon be unavailable. If Message is not supplied at the command line, input is taken from standard input. This allows for multiple line messages. Use *Ctrl D* to terminate the message.

❑ who – displays user names, terminal line and login times of users who are logged in.

❑ whoami– shows who you are; handy for users who are using su.

# Automating Administration Tasks

Many housekeeping tasks need to be performed on a daily basis, often more frequently. These include monitoring crucial system resources to pre-empt the possibility of any problems. The four most important resources are processor, memory, hard disks and printers. Linux provides commands to examine all of these resources; these can then be placed in a script to automate the process. Once a problem has been identified, then specific actions are necessary to correct any problems. These will be discussed later under the section: *Dealing with Specific Problems*

## Monitoring the System

If the system is running sluggishly, it could be for a number of reasons – all of which have their own commands to help determine a specific cause. First, though, a check has to be made to confirm which is the case and the easiest way to do this is with the vmstat command. This command gives information regarding processor, memory, block input and output, traps, and CPU activity.

```
# vmstat [-n] [delay] [count]
```

where:

❑ -n – this causes the header to be displayed only once rather than periodically, which is the default.

❑ delay – the number of seconds to pause before each update.

❑ count – the number of updates to be shown.

If the command vmstat -n 3 4 is entered, the output will look like this:

```
procs                     memory      swap          io     system          cpu
 r  b  w   swpd   free   buff cache   si   so    bi   bo   in    cs   us  sy   id
 0  0  0      0  31540   2116 13496    0    0     1    0  104    14    0   0   99
 0  0  0      0  31540   2116 13496    0    0     0    0  104    14    2   0   98
 0  0  0      0  31540   2116 13496    0    0     0    0  104    13    1   1   98
 0  0  0      0  31540   2116 13496    0    0     0    0  103    12    1   1   98
```

The output is split into 6 general areas:

**procs** or processes:

- ❏ r – The number of processes waiting for run-time.
- ❏ b – The number of sleeping processes that are not interruptible.
- ❏ w – The number of processes currently swapped out but otherwise able to run.

**memory**:

- ❏ swpd – Amount of virtual memory used (in kilobytes).
- ❏ free – Amount of memory available for use (in kilobytes).
- ❏ buff – Amount of memory used as buffers (in kilobytes).
- ❏ cache – Amount of memory left in the cache (in kilobytes).

**swap**:

- ❏ si – Amount of memory swapped in from disk (in kilobytes).
- ❏ so – Amount of memory swapped to disk (in kilobytes).

**io**:

- ❏ bi – Blocks sent to a block device in blocks per second.
- ❏ bo – Blocks read from a block device in blocks per second.

**system**:

- ❏ in – The number of interrupts per second, including the clock.
- ❏ cs – The number of context switches per second.

**cpu**:

- ❏ us – CPU cycles spent on performing user tasks, as a percentage of total processor time.
- ❏ sy – CPU cycles spent on system tasks, as a percentage of total processor time.
- ❏ id – CPU cycles not used; the amount the processor is idle, as a percentage of total processor time.

This one command provides much of the information necessary to analyse a system's performance and is usually the first command used when investigating a problem with the server.

### Possible Problems

The following table lists some of the problems you might encounter when using vmstat:

| | |
|---|---|
| Processor | If the processor has an unusually low idle percentage, there may well be a process that has run away with itself. The number of processes waiting for runtime is also a good indication of a problem — these are processes waiting to access the processor. |
| Memory | When the si field is high, this indicates that the system needs more memory to be able to perform effectively. |
| Input/Output | If the bi and bo fields are high this could mean that some process is hammering the hard disk. This will only be a problem if a process has run away with itself and doing something unexpected. This is usually a development problem caused most often during the testing of a new program. The bi field is the most relevant as this could indicate the process is rapidly filling up the hard disk partition. |

## Disk Usage

The vmstat utility will display how many blocks per second are being read in and out of block devices such as hard disks, but not how full they are. The best indicator of hard disk utilization is the disk free command df, which displays the amount of disk space available on a file system. This utility will display all file systems mounted; if partitions are mounted on remote systems, these can be excluded using the −x parameter.

```
$ df [-x FileSystemType]
```

And this is what you get:

```
Filesystem        1024-blocks  Used     Available  Capacity Mounted on
/dev/hdb1         1610919      886141   641519     58%      /
/dev/hda1         905261       6554     851938     1%       /hda1
```

This example is taken from my home system, and, as you can see, I have a very simple set up; usually Linux servers have more partitions than this, but it serves the purpose of showing the information displayed. Obviously when the capacity grows too large for a partition (usually around 90% depending on the daily use), some maintenance needs to be performed. This could involve removing temporary or old and unused files, trimming log files, or moving files and directories to another partition and creating links (using the ln command as described in Appendix B) to the relocated files at their original locations.

## Printers

Many applications use their own print spooler, which comes with command line utilities which provide information about the status of various printers, the print jobs that are being queued, and so on. Obviously, we can't go into details on each and every available spooler, but the standard spooler that comes with your Linux installation is described. It is invoked using the lpc command.

The easiest way to see if there are any problems with any printers on your network is to issue this command:

```
# lpc status
```

Depending on the setup, this will display the following:

```
lp:
        queuing is enabled
        printing is enabled
        2 entries in spool area
        no daemon present
lp0:
        queuing is enabled
        printing is enabled
        1 entry in spool area
        no daemon present
```

The number of entries in the spool area means that printer has that many jobs queued. If this number is unusually large, say 20, then there could be a problem with that printer and that is something that you should investigate further. All printers currently in use by the system should have queuing and printing enabled, as above; if not the printer should be stopped and restarted using lpc. See the man pages for lpc for further information on how to use this facility.

The topic of setting printing configurations is a highly complex one. For more information you should look up the installation and configuration instructions that come with your Linux distribution. For a full list of the Linux print spooler capabilities, see the section entitled 'Printer Capabilities' at the very end of this appendix.

## System Logs

System log files also require regular attention. These are stored in /var/log and are constantly updated with information regarding connection problems. The most important of these is the messages log which can have output like this:

```
Aug 18 11:46:30  PAM_pwdb[2422]: 1 authentication failure; geoff(uid=500) -> root
for su service
Aug 18 11:46:36  PAM_pwdb[2423]: (su) session opened for user root by
geoff(uid=0)Aug 18 12:00:51  innd[437]: s
...

Aug 18 12:01:01  PAM_pwdb[2936]: (su) session opened for user news by (uid=9)
Aug 18 12:01:01  PAM_pwdb[2936]: (su) session closed for user news
Aug 18 12:03:26  innfeed[463]: decwrl checkpoint seconds 5644 spooled 0 on_close 0
sleeping 0
Aug 18 12:03:26  innfeed[463]: uunet checkpoint seconds 5644 spooled 0 on_close 0
sleeping 0
Aug 18 12:05:51  innd[437]: ME time 303400 idle 303398(2) artwrite 0(0) artlink
0(0) hiswrite 0(0) hissync 0(2)
Aug 18 12:06:13  ftpd[2983]: FTP LOGIN FROM w98 [123.123.123.10], croot
Aug 18 12:07:41  ftpd[2983]: FTP session closed
Aug 18 12:10:51  innd[437]: ME time 300010 idle 300010(1) artwrite 0(0) artlink
0(0) hiswrite 0(0) hissync 0(1)
Aug 18 12:10:54  innd[437]: s
```

Each system will receive different messages depending on the services installed. Most of the messages will not be of any importance but I have highlighted two lines that could show security problems. The first shows that someone tried to switch user to root and failed to enter the password correctly. It even reports the user ID of the person making the attempt. The second displays an FTP session from another host where the user logged in as `croot`, which means that this user has supervisor rights on this system. Unless this is a usual occurrence, then further investigation will be necessary by looking at the contents of the `/var/log/xferlog`. This has the example output shown here:

```
Wed Aug 18 12:07:11 1999 1 w98 510 /bktest/housekeep b _ o r croot ftp 0 *
Wed Aug 18 12:07:37 1999 1 w98 3252 /tmp/housekeep.txt b _ o r croot ftp 0 *
```

From this it is possible to see the files transferred which could give an indication of who made the transfer by tracking it on the other system, if that system is a local server. The only way to get used to the messages produced in these log files is to frequently read them. Once some understanding is made of the messages; `grep` can be used to filter out what is appropriate and the task can be automated.

Other useful log files that require investigation are `secure`, `cron` and `maillog`. These logs give information on user and services connection, `cron` jobs executed and mail usage respectively.

## Automating General Housekeeping Tasks

Using a script all these tasks can be performed in one chunk. This is necessary, as regular checks need to be performed to ensure the system is running satisfactorily.

```
echo Please wait — reviewing system. . .
echo Printer status. . . >/tmp/housekeep.txt
lpc status >>/tmp/housekeep.txt
echo System check. . . >>/tmp/housekeep.txt
vmstat -n 3 4 >>/tmp/housekeep.txt
echo Disk usage. . . >>/tmp/housekeep.txt
df >>/tmp/housekeep.txt
echo Backup logs... >>/tmp/housekeep.txt
cd /backup/log
tail `ls -t | head -n 2` >>/tmp/housekeep.txt
echo Authentication failures... >>/tmp/housekeep.txt
grep authentication /var/log/messages | tail >>/tmp/housekeep.txt
more /tmp/housekeep.txt
```

The above example uses the general system utilities explained earlier and creates a temporary file called `housekeep.txt` that all standard output is redirected to. At the end of the script this file is viewed automatically using `more`. Notice the last two backup logs have been tailed and the last 10 authentication failures displayed. An example output from the above script is:

```
Printer status. . .
lp:
    queuing is enabled
    printing is enabled
    no entries
    no daemon present
lp0:
```

```
        queuing is enabled
        printing is enabled
        no entries
        no daemon present
System check. . .
   procs               memory    swap       io    system        cpu
   r b w  swpd  free  buff cache  si  so  bi  bo   in  cs  us sy  id
   0 0 0     0 25952  6980 14420   0   0   3   1  110  22   1  1  98
   0 0 0     0 25952  6980 14420   0   0   0   3  109  13   1  1  98
   0 0 0     0 25952  6980 14420   0   0   0   5  113  13   1  1  98
   0 0 0     0 25952  6980 14420   0   0   0   0  103  12   1  1  98
Disk usage...
Filesystem          1024-blocks   Used Available Capacity Mounted on
/dev/hdb1              1610919  886260    641400     58%   /
/dev/hda1               905261    6554    851938      1%   /hda1
Backup logs. . .
==> FI03081999.log <==
-rw-r--r-- root/root    2204580 1999-08-03 16:20 bktest/backup.log
-rwxr-xr-x root/root         56 1999-08-03 16:20 bktest/restore
-rwxr-xr-x root/root         17 1999-08-03 16:20 bktest/temp
drwxr-xr-x root/root          0 1999-08-03 16:20 bktest/lib/
-rw-r--r-- root/root         12 1999-08-03 13:34 bktest/lib/test1
-rw-r--r-- root/root         12 1999-08-03 13:34 bktest/lib/test2
drwxr-xr-x root/root          0 1999-08-03 14:03 bktest/lib/modules/
-rw-r--r-- root/root         12 1999-08-03 14:03 bktest/lib/modules/test3
-rw-r--r-- root/root         12 1999-08-03 14:03 bktest/lib/modules/test4
-rw-r--r-- root/root          0 1999-08-03 16:20 bktest/newfile

==> FI04081999.log <==
-rw-r--r-- root/root    2204580 1999-08-03 16:20 bktest/backup.log
-rwxr-xr-x root/root         56 1999-08-03 16:20 bktest/restore
-rwxr-xr-x root/root         17 1999-08-03 16:20 bktest/temp
drwxr-xr-x root/root          0 1999-08-03 16:20 bktest/lib/
-rw-r--r-- root/root         12 1999-08-03 13:34 bktest/lib/test1
-rw-r--r-- root/root         12 1999-08-03 13:34 bktest/lib/test2
drwxr-xr-x root/root          0 1999-08-03 14:03 bktest/lib/modules/
-rw-r--r-- root/root         12 1999-08-03 14:03 bktest/lib/modules/test3
-rw-r--r-- root/root         12 1999-08-03 14:03 bktest/lib/modules/test4
-rw-r--r-- root/root          0 1999-08-03 16:20 bktest/newfile
Authentication failures...
Aug  3 16:07:40  PAM_pwdb[445]: 1 authentication failure; geoff(uid=500) -> root
for su service
Aug  5 12:39:01  PAM_pwdb[768]: 1 authentication failure; geoff(uid=500) -> root
for su service
Aug  5 16:52:12  login[3106]: FAILED LOGIN 1 FROM w98 FOR geoffs, User not known
to the underlying authentication module
Aug  9 11:43:38  login[2559]: FAILED LOGIN 1 FROM w98 FOR geoffs, User not known
to the underlying authentication module
Aug  9 13:33:32  PAM_pwdb[5256]: 1 authentication failure; (uid=0) -> root for
login service
Aug  9 13:33:41  PAM_pwdb[5267]: 1 authentication failure; geoff(uid=500) -> root
for su service
```

```
Aug  9 14:36:55  login[434]: FAILED LOGIN 1 FROM w98 FOR geofff^H, User not known
to the underlying authentication module
Aug  9 21:45:07  PAM_pwdb[660]: 1 authentication failure; (uid=0) -> root for
login service
Aug 17 12:34:26  PAM_pwdb[2968]: 1 authentication failure; (uid=0) -> geoff for
FTP service
Aug 18 11:46:30  PAM_pwdb[2422]: 1 authentication failure; geoff(uid=500) -> root
for su service
```

The script takes about ten seconds to run and most of this is caused by the `delay` specified in the `vmstat` command. On a normal system there could be more than a dozen things to check; the size of various files, communications tasks, application logs etc. If the general housekeeping is done manually four times a day, there's a good chance that some of the dozen or so tasks will be missed. By automating the process, not only is the task quicker to perform, it is also more reliable.

# Dealing with Specific Problems

The last section explained a simple automated method of pre-empting general problems with the system, such as resource usage, printer and security problems. Once a problem has been identified then it needs to be investigated further to identify the cause of the problem before a solution can be attained.

## Processor and Processes

The most common problem in this area is low idle CPU, caused either by a single process that is hogging the processor time, or a high level of zombie processes, which are processes that are waiting to terminate but are unable to do so. Zombie processes are not uncommon on UNIX systems but should always be investigated, especially if there are a large amount of them all created by the same parent. This is usually a development problem – if the processes have been developed in house, contact the programmers to determine why this problem may be occurring. It is safe to kill off any process that is in the zombie state. Usually the first indication of a problem with the processor can be ascertained from the `vmstat` command, discussed earlier. An example of such a problem is shown below:

```
# vmstat -n 3 4       # poll resources 4 times for information 3 seconds apart
procs              memory      swap         io     system        cpu
 r b w  swpd  free  buff cache  si  so    bi   bo   in  cs  us sy id
 1 0 0     0 31936  1604 13884   0   0    37    3  182  39  17  4 79
 1 0 0     0 31940  1604 13884   0   0     0    0  107  14  99  1  0
 1 0 0     0 31940  1604 13884   0   0     0    0  103  13  99  1  0
 1 0 0     0 31940  1604 13884   0   0     0    5  114  14  99  1  0
```

In the example above it can be seen that there is a user task that is eating up all the processor time. It is obvious from the fact there is no idle CPU left that this is causing a problem. To identify which process is causing a problem the `top` command can be used to find out more information. The `top` utility displays the processes making the most use of the processor and is a more dynamic form of the `ps` command, which was discussed in Appendix B. It is very handy if some process is eating all the CPU time or memory. The syntax is:

```
$ top [delay]
```

Where delay is the time, in seconds, between successive updates of the display, the default being 5.

An example of the information displayed follows:

```
9:21pm  up 7 min,  2 users,   load average: 0.52, 0.21, 0.10
54 processes: 52 sleeping, 2 running, 0 zombie, 0 stopped
CPU states: 99.0% user,  1.1% system,  0.0% nice,  0.0% idle
Mem:   63132K av,  29080K used,  34052K free,  27248K shrd,   1540K buff
Swap:  16380K av,      0K used,  16380K free                 12356K cached

   PID USER     PRI  NI  SIZE  RSS SHARE STAT  LIB %CPU %MEM   TIME COMMAND
   693 root      17   0   216  216   176 R       0 97.4  0.3   0:38 infinite
   706 geoff      6   0   728  728   560 R       0  2.7  1.1   0:00 top
     1 root       0   0   388  388   328 S       0  0.0  0.6   0:03 init
     2 root       0   0     0    0     0 SW      0  0.0  0.0   0:00 kflushd
     3 root     -12 -12     0    0     0 SW<     0  0.0  0.0   0:00 kswapd
     4 root       0   0     0    0     0 SW      0  0.0  0.0   0:00 md_thread
     5 root       0   0     0    0     0 SW      0  0.0  0.0   0:00 md_thread
   440 news       0   0   752  752   592 S       0  0.0  1.1   0:00 innwatch
   665 news       0   0   276  276   232 S       0  0.0  0.4   0:00 sleep
   350 nobody     0   0  1164 1164  1068 S       0  0.0  1.8   0:00 httpd
    30 root       0   0   348  348   296 S       0  0.0  0.5   0:00 kerneld
   203 bin        0   0   332  332   264 S       0  0.0  0.5   0:00 portmap
   217 root       0   0   428  428   352 S       0  0.0  0.6   0:00 syslogd
   226 root       0   0   536  536   324 S       0  0.0  0.8   0:00 klogd
   237 daemon     0   0   404  404   328 S       0  0.0  0.6   0:00 atd
   248 root       0   0   472  472   392 S       0  0.0  0.7   0:00 crond
   260 root       0   0   400  400   332 S       0  0.0  0.6   0:00 inetd
```

The display is updated frequently and at the top is a summary showing how long the system has been running, the number of current users, number of processes running, the percentage of CPU used and memory data. In this example, there is no idle CPU because the infinite process is eating it all up. The list of processes is listed in order by CPU usage. From this list, the owner of the infinite process and the process ID can be obtained. The user can be contacted to confirm that a problem exists and that he is not just using a processor intensive application. On the other hand, the process can be killed off using the PID if it is known to be in a zombie state (i.e. the value for STAT will be Z). To order the list by memory usage press M (capital M) and press h for a list of key commands. Pressing q will quit the utility.

From this information it is obvious that the task infinite is the one causing the problem in this case. It can also be ascertained who owns the process and the process ID. After confirmation from the user that this program is not doing what it's supposed to, the task can be terminated using the kill command which is described in Appendix B.

### Long Term Processor Problems

If there are CPU usage problems every day over a long period of time, top can be used to indicate whether this is a general problem, or specific applications or utilities that are eating up the processor. It may well be that a particular user runs a program that produces a very large report or does a complex update on a database every morning. If this is the case it should be possible to schedule this task using cron, or the at command, to run at a time when the system is little utilized. If on the other hand, it is a general problem then the only solution is to upgrade the processor capabilities of the server.

## Memory

Unlike processor usage, memory usage problems are not usually tied to single tasks, although such possibilities should always be investigated. If *Shift M* is pressed while running `top`, the list of processes is reordered by memory usage. When a memory problem is associated with a particular task, it can be rescheduled to run at a time when it will not interfere with the majority of users, in the same way as with processes. However, the problem is more likely to be a general system problem. The first thing to check is that the swap space is large enough. The server utilizes this when all the physical memory has been used for paging memory to disk. The `free` command can be used to examine how much physical and virtual memory is available.

```
# free -bkm -s[delay] -t
```

The various options are given below.

❑    b – display memory in bytes.

❑    k – display memory in Kilobytes.

❑    m – display memory in Megabytes.

❑    s[delay] – delay between updates. Use *Ctrl C* to terminate.

❑    t – Show line containing totals

The output of the `free` command when used without parameters is shown below.

|                    | total  | used   | free   | shared | buffers | cached |
|--------------------|--------|--------|--------|--------|---------|--------|
| Mem:               | 63140  | 61592  | 1548   | 49628  | 5568    | 26300  |
| -/+ buffers/cache: |        | 29724  | 33416  |        |         |        |
| Swap:              | 129020 | 72     | 128948 |        |         |        |

From this output it can be seen that on my home machine I have a swap partition about twice the size of the physical memory. Almost all the swap memory is available for use, which shows that the partition is really too large for my domestic needs. So how much is enough? To calculate this it's best to set up a bogus large swap space first. Then connect twenty per cent more users than normal to the system and open up the corresponding number of the largest applications they are likely to be using. Check how much swap space is then being used and add fifty percent to that total. The minimum swap space considered should be about 16 MB, so if the figure calculated is below that, create a partition of 16 MB anyway. There is a minimum and maximum swap partition size for Linux, which is given by the formulae:

```
Mimimum = 10 * PAGE_SIZE / 1024
Maximum = (PAGE_SIZE - 10) * 8 * PAGE_SIZE / 1024
```

This gives an answer in blocks (which is why you divide the result by 1024); the number of bytes per block can be found from the `df` utility. The normal page size for Intel-based machines is 4 KB, but for other systems it may be possible to find the page size by using the command:

```
# cat /proc/cpuinfo
```

For a normal Intel based server the minimum and maximum size of a swap partition is 40 KB to just over 127 MB, although Linux can use more than one swap partition if more swap space is required.

## Reconfiguring Swap Space

If there is plenty of unused disk space then the easiest way to create swap space is to add a new partition using fdisk or Disk Druid, then changing its type to that of a swap partition. Perform mkswap on the partition and finally turn swapping on for the new partition and off on the old. Then use fdisk to remove the old partition. If a new swap partition is created instead, no alterations are necessary to start up and shut down configuration files. However, if you decide to create a swap file, which is a block of memory on the root partition that serves the same purpose as a swap partition, then the start-up and shutdown configuration files have to be modified.

### Creating a Swap File

The following example shows you how to create a swap file and explains the commands necessary in setting up swap space. A swap file will be created and then reconfigured as a swap area, before being switched on. Afterwards the 128 MB swap partition will be removed from use.

The first task is to create a swap file. Note cp cannot be used to do this as no 'holes' are allowed in the file, i.e. the swap file has to consist of a block of contiguous memory. The dd utility is used to achieve this. This command has not been covered in the previous appendices and so a description has been included here for your information.

> **The dd command is used to copy and convert a file. It has the following syntax:**
>
> ```
> dd [if=infile] [of=outfile] [ibs=bsize] [obs=bsize] [count=blocks]
> [conv=format]
> ```
>
> **The explanation of the parameters is given below.**
>
> **if** — input file instead of standard input.
> **of** — output file instead of standard output.
> **ibs** — number of bytes to read at a time.
> **obs** — number of bytes to write at a time.
> **count** — copy only the number of input blocks specified by **blocks**
> **conv** — conversion process, see man pages for the various options for **format**:
>
> **(Note that you can also use bs=bsize instead of specifying ibs=bsize and obs=bsize.)**

To create a file 16 MB in size, type this command.

```
# dd if=/dev/zero of=swapfile bs=1024 count=16384
16384+0 records in
16384+0 records out
```

This will create a file called swap file consisting of 16384 contiguous 1 KB blocks. The same result would be obtained by using the following command:

```
# dd if=/dev/zero of=swapfile bs=1M count=16
```

Where `1M` is shorthand for a megabyte (1024 x 1024 bytes). See the man page for `dd` for more details about other options.

Configure the new file as a swap file:

```
# mkswap swapfile 16384
Setting up swapspace, size = 16773120 bytes
```

Commit buffer cache to disk

```
# sync
```

Allow swapping to the new swap file

```
# swapon swapfile
```

Check memory to see swap space has been added.

```
# free
            total     used      free    shared   buffers    cached
Mem:        63140     61980      1160     46868      6500     26228
-/+ buffers/cache:    29252     33888
Swap:      145400        72    145328
```

Turn off the original 128 MB swap space.

```
# swapoff /dev/hda2
```

Check that space is now not available to the system.

```
# free
            total     used      free    shared   buffers    cached
Mem:        63140     61592      1548     46868      6512     25820
-/+ buffers/cache:    29260     33880
Swap:       16380         0     16380
```

The original partition can now be removed using `fdisk` or Disk Druid. The system start-up and shutdown files then need to be updated to take account of the new swap space. On Red Hat systems these are `/etc/rc.d/rc.sysinit` for `swapon` and `/etc/rc.d/init.d/halt` for `swapoff`. When the system is rebooted it will now automatically turn swapping off and on to the new swap file as appropriate. For users of other systems the commands:

```
# grep swapon `find /etc *`
# grep swapoff `find /etc *`
```

Will help find all the configuration files containing the commands `swapon` and `swapoff`.

## Printing

If there is a problem with a specific printer or queue the `lpc` command can be used with various options as a method of resolving these issues. The basic form of the command is:

```
lpc [command [printer...]]
```

Useful commands to use with `lpc` are:

- ❑ `disable` – turns specified queue off and disables printer.

- ❑ `enable` – enables spooling on the queues for the named printers.

- ❑ `restart` – attempts to start a new printer daemon. This is often useful when the daemon dies unexpectedly with jobs in the queue.

- ❑ `start` – enables printing and starts a new spooling service for the specified printers.

- ❑ `stop` – disables the spooling services after the current job completes.

- ❑ `down` – turns the specified printers off disabling printers.

- ❑ `up` – enables everything and starts a new printer daemon.

Sometimes a single job could be hanging a printer's queue and stopping other jobs from being output. To remove a job from the queue use the command:

```
lprm -PPrinter JobNumber
```

## Network Communications

It is very rare that network communications break down. This is usually due to a process that has hung an IP socket and is often shown by the state of that socket. This can be discovered using the `netstat` command, which displays network connections and interface statistics. The common form of the command is:

```
netstat [-venca] [-t] [-u] [-w] [--inet] [--ipx]
```

The options are:

- ❑ `v` – gives useful information on unknown family addresses.

- ❑ `e` – displays user ID.

- ❑ `n` – shows numerical addresses rather than hostnames.

- ❑ `c` – continuously displays table. Break with *Ctrl C*.

- ❑ `a` – displays all sockets including listening sockets. Listening sockets are not displayed by default.

❏ t – shows TCP sockets only.

❏ u – shows UDP sockets only.

❏ w – shows RAW data sockets only.

❏ inet – displays all inet sockets.

❏ ipx – displays IPX connections.

For example, the command netstat -t will display:

```
Active Internet connections (w/o servers)
Proto Recv-Q Send-Q Local Address       Foreign Address     State
tcp      0      0 .geof:ftp             w98:1027            ESTABLISHED
tcp      1      0 .geof:1029            .geof:ftp           TIME_WAIT
tcp      0      2 .geof:telnet          w98:nterm           ESTABLISHED
tcp      0      0 .geof:telnet          w98:listen          ESTABLISHED
```

In the above case the -t option was used to limit the display to sockets using the TCP protocol. Normally the state of these sockets should be closed, established, waiting or listening. If a socket is stuck on CLOSE_WAIT then for some reason the local side of the connection cannot be shut down. It is possibly a problem with the inetd daemon and this may have to be killed and restarted to cure this. Current tasks should not be affected as inetd starts other processes to establish connections.

The netstat command has many options that help to focus on the type of connection under investigation and display the routing table. See the man pages for further information on this command.

# Data Archiving and Compression

In this section, archiving and compression utilities will be discussed where directories and files are prepared for transportation to another system or for archiving. This is closely related to the following section which will discuss full system backup and restoration procedures. Most applications and kernel updates come archived and zipped, i.e. compressed. The most common utility for archiving is tar, which originally stood for 'tape archive', but it can output to any block device. The standard compression utilities are gzip (GNU compression utility) and bzip2 (block-sorting file compression). The latter uses a better compression algorithm than gzip but much of the software available for download is still in the gzip format.

### The tar Archiving Utility

There are two common forms of the tar command:

```
tar c[v] [-f Filename] FileList
```

Using tar with the -c option will create an archive, i.e. gather all the files and directories into a single file, maintaining any directory structures internally for later restoration. Another useful option is -v, which will display the files and directories written to the archive. FileList can be file names, directory names, a pattern or the wildcard * for all files and directories in and below the current directory. If a directory is archived all its subdirectories are included as well. The -f option allows you to specify a filename (or a device) to save the archive to; when this is not included the default is the standard archiving device (usually /dev/rmt0).

```
tar x[v] [-f Filename]
```

In this form tar will extract files and directories from an archive, it will automatically strip leading slashes from the names to allow recovery to the current directory – not the absolute path. In this case the input will be taken from the standard archiving device (usually /dev/rmt0), or the file/device specified using the -f option. There is one more important option, -z, which filters the archive through gzip facility which means that an archive can be extracted and decompressed in one step; this is a GNU tar option.

Other commands relating to archiving of data that can be useful are the following:

❑   cpio – copy input, output. Standard UNIX machine independent copy utility. This is explained in more detail in Chapter 15.

❑   dump – file system backup utility.

❑   restore – file system restore from a backup created by dump.

### Compression Utilities

The tar utility will collect all the files into one archive, maintaining the directory structure where necessary. However, these files will often still be large and hence unwieldy for transportation; that's where the gzip and bzip2 utilities come in. Both commands have similar options and all the choices described below apply equally to both utilities.

```
gzip  [-cdftv#] FileList
bzip2 [-cdftv#] FileList
```

Compress or expand (-d) the files in FileList. FileList can also be directories for gzip, but the individual files within the directory are compressed in this case. Files in FileList will be renamed with the suffix .gz for compression using gzip, .bz2 for bzip2. The suffixes will be removed after decompression with either utility. Below is an explanation of some of the options available. See the man pages for more details:

❑   c – instead of renaming the file, send output to standard output.

❑   d – decompress (expand) files.

❑   f – force overwriting of files if the destination already exists.

❑   t – check a compressed file's integrity.

❑   v – display the name and percentage reduction for each file compressed.

❑   # – compression type desired. This is a number ranging from 1-9 where 1 will give a fast execution, but least compression. 9 will execute the slowest but give the highest possible compression of the files.

Note that neither gzip or bzip2 will compress complete directories. Archive these using tar to a file first, then compress the file.

The commands gunzip and bunzip2 are synonymous to gzip -d and bzip2 -d respectively.

# System Backup and Restoration Using the tar Utility

Backup and restoration procedures are generally given little space in current Linux documentation, even though it is essential to be able to completely trash a system and put it back the way it was. I believe a good backup and restoration procedure should be the first requirement of all systems. I have used similar systems at the Walton Centre (see chapter 15 for details of the Linux project carried out there), and they have been tested and proven to work. It anyone else wishes to use the scripts and procedures for their systems, please remember to test them out thoroughly as all systems have their own foibles. Also take into account the fact that most applications that run continuously have their own backup methods and these should also be incorporated into the procedure.

## Backing up a Linux System

Once a backup procedure has been drawn up that is suitable for the system in question, all that is needed is a way of performing the tasks required. Below is the listing of a shell script that can be used to perform full, incremental and daily backups. It is called /backup/archive.scr:

```sh
#!/bin/sh
case $1 in
   'f')
# Full Backup
      outlogname=/backup/FO`date '+%d%m%Y'`.log
      inlogname=/backup/FI`date '+%d%m%Y'`.log
      echo Performing full backup on `date`, log name $outlogname
      echo Performing full backup on `date`. . . >$outlogname
      umount /mnt/cdrom
      if [ $# -eq 2 ]
      then
         if [ $2 != '--notouch' ]
         then
            touch /backup/last.backup
         else
            echo Using the notouch option >>$outlogname
         fi
      else
         touch /backup/last.backup
      fi
      tar cv / -f/dev/rmt0 >>$outlogname
      echo Backup completed at`date` >>$outlogname
      mount -t iso9660 /dev/cdrom /mnt/cdrom
      tar tv -f/dev/rmt0 >$inlogname;;
   'i')
# Incremental backup
      outlogname=/backup/IO`date '+%d%m%Y'`.log
      inlogname=/backup/II`date '+%d%m%Y'`.log
      echo Performing incremental backup on `date`, log name $outlogname
      echo Performing incremental backup on `date`. . . >$outlogname
      umount /mnt/cdrom
```

```
        tar cv `find / -newer /backup/last.backup
                                        -print` -f/dev/rmt0 >>$outlogname
        echo Backup completed at `date` >>$outlogname
        mount -t iso9660 /dev/cdrom /mnt/cdrom
        tar tv -f/dev/rmt0 >$inlogname;;
    'd')
# Daily backup
        outlogname=/backup/DO`date '+%d%m%Y'`.log
        inlogname=/backup/DI`date '+%d%m%Y'`.log
        echo Performing daily backup on `date`, log name $outlogname
        echo Performing daily backup on `date`. . . >$outlogname
        umount /mnt/cdrom
        tar cv `find / -newer /backup/last.backup -print`
                                              -f/dev/rmt0 >>$outlogname
        touch /backup/last.backup
        echo Backup completed at `date` >>$outlogname
        mount -t iso9660 /dev/cdrom /mnt/cdrom
        tar tv -f/dev/rmt0 >$inlogname;;
    *)
# Invalid option
        echo Invalid or no parameter entered for archive on `date`;;
esac
```

This script can be divided into four parts; the first three depend on the option given, whether to perform a full, incremental or daily backup. The final part is a catch-all, which reports an error when an incorrect parameter is passed.

### Script usage:

❑   `archive.scr f [--notouch]` will perform a full backup.

❑   `archive.scr i` is used to make an incremental backup.

❑   `archive.scr d` proceeds with a daily backup.

In all cases the script creates two log files, one containing a list of the files written out and the other a list of the files read back in. These should be the same unless there was a media error. The log file names have the format:

`BXDDMMYYYY.log`

Where:

❑   B is either F, I or D, identifying a full, incremental or daily backup log respectively.

❑   X is either O or I depending on whether it is a backup (out) log or a restore (in) log.

❑   DD the day backup was made.

❑   MM the month backup was made.

❑   YYYY the year backup was made.

❑   `.log` identifies the file as a log file.

The log file names are created using the date utility via command expansion.

> **Command expansion is used a lot in script processing and is performed using the `** **(open single quote — usually found directly below the *Esc* key) character to delimit commands, the standard output of these commands can then be used as parameters in other commands. The output of one command is expanded into the command line of another. For example the command:**
>
> echo The time is: `date +%H`:`date +%M`
>
> **This will use the date command twice to display the text:**
>
> The time is: 21:20

Then any devices mounted to the system which are unnecessary to backup, in this case the CD-ROM, are detached to save time and the space required for the backup. After archiving the system, the completion date and time is output to the out log file. Detached devices are remounted using the mount command. Finally the tape contents are read back into the in log file, again using tar, for comparison with the out log file.

## Full Backup

Selects the first case in the script and archives all files in and below the root directory using tar and the file listing is appended to the out log file. This will also backup any devices mounted onto a directory under root.

When the optional parameter --notouch is not given, the modified date and time attributes of the file /backup/last.backup are adjusted using touch to allow incremental and daily backups to know when the last full archive was performed, and therefore when they have to store data from. The reason for the --notouch option is allow full backups to be made out of the routine backup cycle. When the --notouch option is given this fact is appended to the out log file to inform the administrator that this is not a routine full backup.

## Incremental Backup

The case for incremental backups is very similar to the case for full backups. The differences being:

- ❑ Log files begin with I not F.
- ❑ The command

  find / -newer /backup/last.backup -print

  is used in the tar command using command expansion to find all the files in and below the root directory that are newer than when the file /backup/last.backup was last modified.

- ❑ The date and time attributes of the file /backup/last.backup are left unaltered so the next incremental backup will also archive all files modified since the last full backup.

## *Daily Backup*

This is very similar to the incremental backup option with the following minor differences:

❑ Log files begin with D not I.

❑ The date and time attributes of the file /backup/last.backup are updated to allow the next backup to archive only the files modified since the last backup.

Something to be noted is the order of the statements. The date and time attributes of the file /backup/last.backup are modified before the archive in the full backup, but afterwards in the daily backup. This is because the full backup usually takes a long time to run and files could be created, or modified, after the backup process has started. These files will be backed up during the next incremental or daily backup. If the attributes were changed before the archive on the daily backup – no data would be saved because the find command uses this file to determine which files are more recent. There is therefore a possibility that some files will be created during the backup process and therefore not archived when using a daily backup, but if the time slot is chosen well it should be unlikely that this will have much of a consequence. If the risk is too much for your system choose one of the other backup methods and this problem is overcome.

## *Automating the Backup Process with cron*

The cron program, which has already been described in Appendix B, can be used to run the above script to run at predetermined times. Here is an example of cron processes set up to run an incremental backup for each weekday, and full backups at the weekend.

```
# DO NOT EDIT THIS FILE — edit the master and reinstall.
# (/tmp/crontab.710 installed on Wed Aug  4 12:40:13 1999)
# (Cron version -- $Id: crontab.c,v 2.13 1994/01/17 03:20:37 vixie Exp $)
# Run an incremental backup each weekday at 11:00pm
00 23 * * 1-5 /backup/archive i
# Run a full backup every Saturday at 10:00pm
00 22 * * 6 /backup/archive f
# Run a full backup every Sunday without altering the time of the last backup
00 22 * * 7 /backup/archive f --notouch
```

From the above example it can be determined that:

❑ Monday to Friday, incremental backups are made of the system at 11:00pm.

❑ Saturday will see a full backup started at 10:00pm and the date/time attributes of the file /backup/last.backup will be modified for any following incremental backups to use.

❑ A full backup will also be made on Sunday at 10:00pm – this is just in case Saturday's tape fails to read back when performing a restore. The attributes of /backup/last.backup are left unchanged by setting the --notouch switch, so that any incremental includes Sunday's data changes as well. This is in case Sunday's tape has a media error when trying to restore the system.

Using two full backups a week, this system has a built in redundancy. If one of the full backup tapes fails when trying to restore the system the other can be used – another good reason for having the notouch option for the full backup. This is to tell the weekday incremental backups to archive from Saturday's backup and not Sunday's.

Using cron to perform backups enables better error reporting. For example, if the tape ran out before the backup was completed, an e-mail with the appropriate error would be received by the user (usually the root) that added the backup processes to the cron table. When the user logged on the following morning and read their e-mails he or she would be notified that the backup had failed and has the logs to determine why this is so. If the script was run from the console, these messages could easily be missed.

## Restoring a Single File from a Backup

Various methods have been discussed when backing up a system, but how are these files restored when necessary? The most common type of restore is when a user corrupts a single file and needs a working version reinstated on the system. The tar command can not only be used to archive data, but also to restore data to the system as well. An example of restoring a single file from magnetic tape is given below:

```
# tar -xvp home/geoff/doc.txt -f /dev/rmt0
```

Using tar with the -p switch will strip off leading slashes when storing files, which allows files to be recovered into a different place from where they were originally stored. In this case, two new directories are created below the current working directory, one called home, and then geoff. Then the file doc.txt is extracted into the geoff directory.

The -f option is only necessary in the previous example if there are multiple tape drives on the system, as tar will use the default tape drive, which is normally /dev/rmt0.

## Restoring an Entire Directory

Occasionally entire directories will need to be restored. For example, often systems administrators log how long a users account has been left untouched. For example, say an employee leaves a company, then after confirmation that the employee will not use the directory again, and after at least one monthly backup has been taken, the home directory of that user can be removed to free up disk space. If a new employee then takes over the role of the old employee and requires access to previous work carried out, it is easy to restore the entire home directory of the ex-employee. To allow this tar accepts wildcards for restoring multiple files and subdirectories. The previous example could be modified in this way to restore geoff's entire home directory.

```
# tar -xvp home/geoff/* -f /dev/rmt0
```

Again two new directories are created below the current directory, home and geoff. All files and subdirectories belonging to geoff will then be placed in the geoff directory.

## *Restoring a Complete System*

Documentation on a complete restore of a Linux system is thin on the ground. Who wants to trash their system to see if it can be restored again? Well this restore procedure has been tried and tested – I know I've used it twice! But it the last resort. A full system restore will only be required when a major hardware fault has occurred, such as a major catastrophe rendering the original system useless, a fire for instance. However, restoring a complete system is far more difficult than it may initially seem. A base Linux system needs to be installed first to provide the systems administrator with the tools required for recovery. Then a full backup needs to be restored on top of the base system, followed by incremental or daily archives as required. The problem here is that the base system being replaced is currently being used for the restore. If care is not taken the server will crash when files being used by the base system are overwritten.

## *Requirements of Full System Restore*

To perform the restoration of a complete Linux system the following items are needed:

❑   Boot and root floppy disks used in the initial installation of the Linux system. Some releases of Linux only require a single boot disk while others like Slackware require more – this should be known from the initial installation process. Nowadays, you can also boot straight from the CD-ROM.

❑   CD-ROM distribution of the Linux system you are using.

❑   A detailed printed description of the hard disk partitions on the system being restored.

The boot and root floppy disks and the CD-ROM are used to install a base system of Linux. Hard disk partitions will also need to be recreated in this process using the printed configuration to ensure exact duplication. Note networking, the X windows system, help files and other bulky components do not need to be installed, all that is required are basic disk and file utilities such as `fdisk` and `tar`. The minimal install should be enough.

Once a minimal system has been installed and the system rebooted so that it is now using the hard disk instead of the floppy boot disks then it is necessary to put the last full backup into the tape drive for the restore process. Below is a script that can be used to restore a complete Linux system if the backup process described previously was used. It is called `/backup/restore.scr`

```
#!/bin/sh
cd /
ls -R lib >lib.files
tar -xvp -f/dev/rmt0 -X lib.files
rm lib.files
/sbin/lilo
```

A description of this script now follows:

❑ After changing to the root directory, all the files in the /lib directory are listed and their filenames stored in the lib.files file.

❑ In the example above, tar is used to restore the system from magnetic tape, although any other backup medium can be used. The -X lib.files option is the only one not seen previously. This informs tar to exclude the files stored in the /lib directory from the process. This is necessary otherwise the system will hang when it tries to restore the system libraries because tar uses dynamically loaded library functions to operate. Notice that it will not stop other library files from being copied over, only the ones that it needs to run the basic system. So there is no need to worry if the restored system had the X windows system or other application libraries, these will still be recovered.

❑ The process no longer needs the lib.files file, so it is removed.

❑ Finally LILO must be reconfigured if Linux Loader is being used to boot the system to employ the restored configuration and kernel.

The server should be rebooted at this point and the system will be restored to the last full backup.

### Incremental System Restore

If the incremental backup method was used, then the previous evening's tape (if this was not a full backup) should be placed in the tape drive and the restore script executed again. After the process has completed the server should be rebooted and the system should be fully restored to the previous evening's state.

### Daily System Restore

This is the most time consuming restore operation. After the full backup has been restored, the same script is run on every tape used since the full backup. Then the server is rebooted to restore the system to the previous night's position.

# General Linux Configuration

Configuration of Linux can be a very technical task. To make life easier, the main Linux distributions come with helpful utilities which prompts the administrator for the information required and updates the necessary configuration files. Perhaps the most well-known of these facilities is Linuxconf, which comes with one of the most common commercial distribution currently available, Red Hat. This section will discuss how to configure systems with Linuxconf, but will mainly be concerned with using standard command line tools or directly editing system files. So if you don't use Red Hat products, you can skip the next section.

# Linuxconf

Linuxconf can be activated in a number of ways:

❑ From the command line, which is useful when automating processes and working with scripts.

❑ Entering Linuxconf at the command line can activate a Character-Cell API; this is the interface that will be described in this section.

❑ X Window based interface for a GUI giving similar configuration options as the Character-Cell API.

❑ Web-based for remote administration.

This screen gives an example of the opening menu for Linuxconf. Note that it is not too dissimilar to what you will be familiar with in Windows Explorer: the + on the left hand side of some options means that a submenu with further options for the selected category can be displayed. In this case the Config, User accounts and both Normal and Special accounts have been expanded and displayed. Selection of an option is as simple as using the cursor keys to highlight the option then pressing enter to expand the submenu or open configuration window.

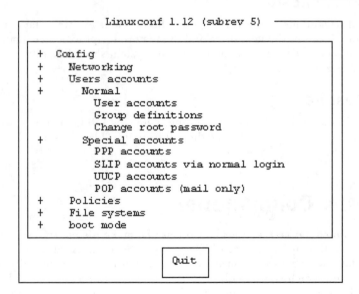

```
┌─────────────── Linuxconf 1.12 (subrev 5) ───────────────┐
│                                                         │
│  ┌──────────────────────────────────────────────────┐  │
│  │  +   Config                                        │  │
│  │  +      Networking                                 │  │
│  │  +      Users accounts                             │  │
│  │  +         Normal                                  │  │
│  │                 User accounts                      │  │
│  │                 Group definitions                  │  │
│  │                 Change root password               │  │
│  │  +         Special accounts                        │  │
│  │                 PPP accounts                       │  │
│  │                 SLIP accounts via normal login     │  │
│  │                 UUCP accounts                      │  │
│  │                 POP accounts (mail only)           │  │
│  │  +      Policies                                   │  │
│  │  +      File systems                               │  │
│  │  +      boot mode                                  │  │
│  └──────────────────────────────────────────────────┘  │
│                                                         │
│                      ┌─────────┐                        │
│                      │  Quit   │                        │
│                      └─────────┘                        │
│                                                         │
└─────────────────────────────────────────────────────────┘
```

For more detailed information of the possible configuration options available with Linuxconf see the section called 'Configuration Options Available with Linuxconf' at the end of this appendix, which lists every option available with version 1.12 r5.

# Adding Users

One of the most common tasks an administrator has to perform is to add new users onto the system. This will generally require a number of steps:

❑ Edit /etc/passwd. This file contains a line for every user on the system and takes the form of:

    Username:Password:User ID:Group ID:Comment:Home directory:Login
    command

Here is a description of each of the fields:

❑    Username – a unique log-in name for the new user.

❑    Password – deleted, or left blank to be set by the passwd command.

❑    User ID (UID) – unique number given to user for administrative and security purposes.

❑    Group ID (GID) – unique number identifying primary group associated with user.

❑    Comment – a general description field that is displayed when a user is fingered; often the name of the user.

❑    Home directory – the users home directory, where they are placed after log-in.

❑    Login command – the command that is executed when the user first logs in. This is usually a script that directs the user straight to the application required or a shell.

With each field being separated by a colon. It is easiest to copy an existing user of the same group and login command, deleting the password field and modifying the username, user ID, comment, and home directory appropriately.

> **Warning** — Before editing the **/etc/passwd** file it should be copied, with the user logged in as root until after the new login has been successfully tested. This is in case the file gets corrupted during the editing process; a super-user will still be able to copy the original file back into place — thus allowing logins.

An example of such an addition is given below:

    geoff::500:100:Geoff Sherlock:/home/geoff:/bin/bash

❑ Edit /etc/group. Each user should be attached to at least one group and this file is where these group associations are set up. Usually each system will have a number of local groups present. One for each major application in use on the system, another for development staff, etc. The format of the /etc/group file is as follows:

```
Group name:Password:Group ID:User list
```

Each field is described below:

❏      `Group name` – unique name for group.

❏      `Password` – usually left blank, but passwords can be assigned here if necessary.

❏      `Group ID` (GID) – unique number representing the group.

❏      `User list` – a comma-separated list of users associated with the group. It is not necessary to add a user here if this group is the users' primary group. Only supplementary member user names are required. Note that the GIDs are the same in both the `passwd` and `group` files, which means that `geoff` is a member of the users group.

Again the fields are colon separated and an example of such a definition is given below:

```
users::100:
```

❏ Create a home directory for the user. Each should have a home directory which will become the current directory after log-in. This could be a general directory for users of a specific application or an individual home directory where personal files are stored. For example Geoff's file could be created at `/home/geoff`.

❏ Skeleton configuration files need to be copied to this new directory. To do this the following commands are used: `cp /etc/skel/.* /home/geoff` and `cp /etc/skel/* /home/geoff`.

This will copy initial configuration files, which may need to be updated for the specific user.

❏ The ownership rights of the directory and files need to be modified with the commands, as in the following example where `geoff` is the user:

```
# chown -R geoff:users /home/geoff
# chmod 644 /home/geoff/.*
# chmod 644 /home/geoff/*
# chmod 700 /home/geoff
```

❏ Set the new users password:

```
# passwd UserName
```

This will ask you to enter the new password and then for it to be re-entered in case of a typing error.

### Adding User Accounts Using Linuxconf

The figure below shows how the same information is entered using Linuxconf. To get to this entry screen the menu options Config, User accounts then Normal are expanded and User accounts is then selected followed by the Add option. The Login name, Full name, group, Home directory and Command interpreter are the same as those entered in the appropriate places in the `/etc/passwd` file. If the group is unknown, the Linuxconf will then ask for more information.

The supplementary groups are those groups associated with the user contained in the /etc/group file. If group, Home directory or Command interpreter are left blank, the defaults are taken (usually users, /home/login_name and /bin/bash respectively) and leaving the User ID field empty will cause Linuxconf to generate a unique UID. Note that the account can be created without enabling anyone to use it; this is for an account set up prior to use. The account can later be enabled using the same screen by selecting to modify that user account.

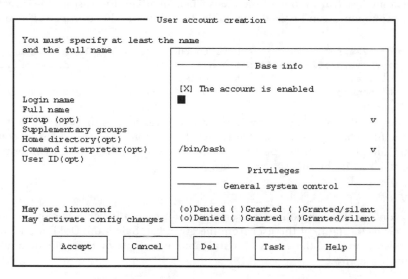

Linuxconf will automatically create the user's home directory, then copy the files in /etc/skel to that directory, then set the ownership and permissions accordingly. It will not make any personal modifications to the skeleton files for the user. When Accept is selected the administrator will be asked to enter a new password for the user.

Groups can be added by expanding the menu options Config, User accounts and Normal then selecting Group definitions followed by Add. Note that passwords cannot be entered on this screen; they can only be added by editing the /etc/group file. The GID is generated automatically but a different one can be forced.

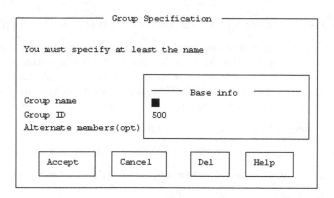

### Archiving User Accounts

When a user's account is no longer needed, it is inappropriate to remove their home directory straight away. The directory should be archived to a file then compressed using `gzip`. Then kept on the systems for at least two months to ensure that two permanent backups are kept of the user's data – you never know when it may be needed again. Two are needed for the sake of redundancy; there may be a media error on one of the tapes when an attempt to restore the directory is made. The following commands can be used to archive, then remove, the user `geoff`'s home directory:

```
# cd /somewheresafe          # Move to the dir. the archive will be stored.
# / tar cv /home/geoff -fgeoff.tar # Archive the directory into geoff.tar
# gzip geoff.tar             # Compress the directory
# rm -f -R /home/geoff       # Remove the original directory.
```

This will create the file `geoff.tar.gz` in the `/somewheresafe` directory. Use the user's login ID to name the file where possible, so that retrieval is obvious at a later date. To complete the task delete the line added in the `/etc/passwd` file for that user and remove any information pertaining to the user in the file `/etc/group`.

#### Using Linuxconf

To use Linuxconf for the task, follow the same procedure used for creating an account but instead of adding a new user, highlight the user from the given list. Select the Del button and you will be asked if you wish to archive the account's data, remove the data or leave the data in place. Select the option that is required.

# Starting Processes at Boot-up Using /etc/inittab

It is often useful to be able to start a System V compatible process at boot-up and this can be configured using the `init` daemon in the file `/etc/inittab`. Each process is described on a single line with colon-separated fields. The format of each line is:

```
ID:RunLevels:Action:Process
```

Where:

- ❑ `ID` – a unique sequence of four characters (or less) that describe the process.

- ❑ `RunLevels` – a list of system run levels for which the specified action should be taken. Run levels range from 0-6: 0 halt; 1 single user mode; 2 multi-user without NFS; 3 full multi-user; 4 is unused; 5 X11, and 6 reboot. For example `123` states the specified process will be started at run levels 1, 2 and 3. If, during operation, the run level is changed to a level the process should not be operating under, the process is terminated by the system.

- ❑ `Action` – the action to be taken, see the following list.

    - ❑ `respawn` – the process is restarted whenever it terminates.

    - ❑ `wait` – the process is started once and `init` will wait for its termination.

    - ❑ `once` – the process is started once.

- ❑ boot – the process will be started during system boot and run levels are ignored.

- ❑ bootwait – is the same as boot but init will wait for its termination.

- ❑ off – will specify that no process is performed.

- ❑ ondemand – executed when the specified run level is called.

- ❑ initdefault – specifies which run level should be entered after system boot.

- ❑ sysinit – process executed during system boot but before boot and bootwait processes.

- ❑ powerwait – executed when init receives the SIGPWR signal, which indicates something is wrong with the power, and then waits for the process to terminate.

- ❑ powerfail – same as powerwait but init does not wait for the process to complete.

- ❑ powerokwait – executed when init receives the SIGPWR signal, so long as the file /etc/powerstatus exists containing the word OK, indicating the power has come back up.

- ❑ ctrlaltdel – executed when init receives the SIGINT signal, indicating someone at the console has pressed the *Ctrl Alt Del* key sequence.

- ❑ kbrequest – executed when a special key combination signal is received. A line in inittab such as: alt keycode 103 = KeyboardSignal will cause a keyboard signal when *Alt+ArrowUp* is pressed.

- ❑ Process – specifies the process to be executed.

See the /etc/inittab file on your system for examples of how these processes are set up.

# Running Scripts at Boot-up and Shutdown

The previous section discussed a method of executing System V compatible processes at boot-up. Sometimes it is necessary to run scripts immediately after the system has booted and again on system shutdown. This can be done using the rc files /etc/rc.d/rc.sysinit and /etc/rc.d/init.d/halt on Red Hat systems; for other distributions see the installation manual for which files to use. This is useful for setting user defined environment variables and for multi-user applications that need to be started and terminated automatically for initialization and safe shutdown, such as databases.

They are simply script files and any Linux text editor can be used to edit these files, but make a backup before modifying any of them.

# Network Configuration

This section explains how to configure a Linux server to communicate with other networks and hosts, and how to let them talk to Linux. The most common reason why a networked device will not operate with Linux is that it has not been given the access. Access to a Linux server is configured through the host tables.

## *The /etc/hosts File and Security*

When configuring a Linux server it is important that you restrict access as much as possible for security reasons. Even if the server is not connected to the outside world it does not mean that another device on the network isn't! The host tables allow the administrator to tie the system down and to only allow other hosts and networks the access they require.

Linux contains a number of hosts files in the /etc directory that are accessed every time a user or device tries to connect to the server. The rules for access specified in these files determines whether access is granted, or refused, and what to do when access has been denied.

### */etc/hosts*

This file does not restrict other hosts from connecting to your server, but if the host is not mentioned in this file, the server will fail to respond to any connection requests and the connection will eventually time out. Only devices that need to use the services on this server should have their addresses stored in here. This usually includes other servers and remote IP printers on the LAN. It is essentially a lookup table that holds information about other devices on the LAN and is used to allow more meaningful names to be given to IP addresses, for example:

```
127.0.0.1       localhost   localhost.localdomain
123.123.123.1   alpha       # This server
123.123.123.99  beta        # Sales Novix server for Novell
123.123.123.3   gamma       # Admin Windows NT server
123.123.123.20  spider1     # Reception terminal server (8 ports)
123.123.123.21  spider2     # Accounts terminal server (16 ports)
123.123.123.50  prman1      # TCP/IP Printer 1 for management
123.123.123.51  prman2      # TCP/IP Printer 2 for management
...
```

The file contains fields separated by white space which give the IP addresses, the host name and its alias. Anything on a line after the # symbol is treated as a comment.

When using other commands, such as telnet or ftp, the host name can be used instead of the IP address for connection. The localhost is the loopback address for this server and is usually set up for during the installation of Linux. This can be very handy for testing services on the server without having to connect to another machine first. All the other devices are servers and printers the machine must be able to communicate with.

The only necessary field to include is the IP address to allow communication, but it is wise to use a short mnemonic name, even on a very small network, as this will result in fewer errors than entering a complete address; IP addresses are not designed to be easily remembered by people – that's why we use host names!

## *Restricting Access from Hosts*

Two very important files used for restricting access to services are /etc/hosts.allow and /etc/hosts.deny. The first allows specified clients to make use of the services on this system and the second denies access for services requested by specified clients. The general form of each line in the /etc/hosts.allow file is:

```
Daemons: Clients
```

Where `Daemons` is a list of service daemons the clients stated in the `Clients` list are allowed to use. Both lists are white space separated. The services that can be trapped are: `telnet`, `finger`, `ftp`, `exec`, `rsh`, `rlogin`, `tftp`, `talk`, `comsat` and any other services that have one-to-one mapping onto executable files.

There are a number of ways to filter these lists using patterns, wildcards and operators.

### Patterns

Patterns are used to match hosts names and IP addresses:

❑ `.pattern` — if a host name ends in the pattern it is said to be matching. For example: the pattern `.website.com` will match connections from `www.website.com` or `ftp.website.com`.

❑ `pattern.` – the host name matches if it begins with the pattern. For example: the pattern `www.website.`, will match connections from `www.website.com` but not `ftp.website.com`.

❑ `@pattern` – names beginning with @ are NIS (Network Information System) netgroup names. A host name is matched if it is a member of the specified netgroup, which are configured when setting up a NIS server.

❑ IP1/IP2 – expressions separated by a slash are interpreted as 'net/mask' pairs. E.g. 123.123.124.0/255.255.254.0 matches all the addresses in the range 123.123.124.0 – 123.123.125.255. This allows for super-netting where an organization has multiple, and consecutive class licenses. The net address and mask given in these expressions must be complete, i.e. 123.123.124/255.255.254 is not allowed.

### Wildcards

There are a number of explicit wildcards that can be used:

❑ `ALL` – will match everything.

❑ `LOCAL` – will match any host that does not contain a dot character, such as devices on the LAN.

❑ `UNKNOWN` – will match any user whose name is unknown or any host whose name or address is unknown. This wildcard should not be used as there are many reasons these names and addresses may not be known to the system, such as the name being unavailable due to name server problems, or the server does not know what type of network it is communicating with.

❑ `KNOWN` – will match any user whose name is known or any host whose name or address is known Again this should not be used.

❑ `PARANOID` – for any host whose name does not match the address. When `tcpd` is built with the `-DPARANOID` flag, which is the default mode, it drops the requests from these clients before accessing the access control tables. You would build without the `-DPARANOID` flag set if you want to process these connections further.

### Operators

There is only one operator, EXCEPT. The form it takes is usually the following:
list EXCEPT list. Everything in the first list is matched except those belonging to the second list.

The EXCEPT command can be used more than once, e.g. listA EXCEPT listB EXCEPT listC. Multiple EXCEPTs are processed in reverse order, so that everything in listB is matched except those that appear in listC, creating a temporary list that called, say, listD. Then everything in listA is matched except those that appear in listD.

## Examples of Network Service Filtering

Making use of the patterns, wildcards and operators in both the hosts.allow and hosts.deny, provide an easy catchall of hosts. An example of a hosts.allow file could be:

```
ALL EXCEPT in.ftpd: LOCAL EXCEPT 123.123.123.11
```

In this case all services except FTP are allowed to local hosts except the device with address 123.123.123.11. This device may allow for external logins and you do not want to give direct access to this server from that device.

If some FTP services are required to other hosts, these can be added to the file with the line:

```
in.ftpd: beta gamma
```

This will allow beta and gamma access to FTP services on the server. Note that the host names are resolved into IP addresses from the /etc/hosts file.

When a service and host combination is found to match in the /etc/hosts.allow file, the /etc/hosts.deny file will be ignored and the requested service provided. If a service and host combination is not found, the /etc/hosts.deny file is then used to determine whether the connection should be allowed.

### The Command Field and System Variables in Hosts Files

The command field follows the host field and can allow for further processing of a denied connection. This is usually used in conjunction with the spawn command, which will start a command after system variables have been expanded into the command line.

Some useful information can be gained about the client from system variables that can be passed to other commands using the spawn command. The spawn command will start a new shell to run the bracketed command or script in, expanding any variable stated into the command line. Below is a list of the system variables available for expansion:

- ❑   %a (%A) – The clients host address.
- ❑   %c – Client information: user@host, user@address, a host name, or an address, depending on how much information is available.
- ❑   %d – The daemon process name.

- ❑ %h (%H) – The clients host name, or address if this is not available.

- ❑ %n (%N) – The clients host name, or "unknown" or "paranoid".

- ❑ %p – The process ID of the daemon.

- ❑ %s – Server information: daemon@host, daemon@address, or a daemon name, depending on how much information is available.

- ❑ %u – The client user name, or "unknown".

- ❑ %% – Expands to a single % character.

The following example shows the filter that would be used to log all denied service connections, except finger, which uses the spawn command to finger the client and then passes the information to the mail command. This e-mails the user root with the information on the client. The spawned command is run in the background as specified by terminating the bracketed command with the ampersand character (&).

```
ALL EXCEPT in.fingerd: ALL : spawn (/usr/bin/finger -l @%h | /bin/mail -s
%d-%h root) &
```

It is recommended that the hosts.deny file should look something like this or contain only ALL: ALL to stop anyone accessing the system that shouldn't be. This can cause a lot of work for the administrator who will need to continually make additions to the /etc/hosts.allow file. However, making the hosts.deny file more complex would allow hackers a back door into the system.

It can be seen from the example above that a comprehensive security profile can easily be produced by combining the rules in /etc/hosts.allow and /etc/hosts.deny.

> **WARNING: The example used in the `hosts.deny` file is called a booby trap as information on the connecting user is processed further with `finger`. You should never booby trap the `finger` daemon itself as this could cause an infinite loop.**

### More Information

More information about the use of these files can be gained by reading the man pages on hosts_access and hosts_options.

## FTP Configuration

Another file that can be used to restrict access to the FTP service is /etc/ftphosts. In this case it works on a per-account basis rather than for particular hosts. The configuration is far simpler than for hosts files and consists of lines with the format:

```
AccessCommand UserName HostNames
```

Where `AccessCommand` is either `allow` or `deny`, for example:

```
allow me beta gamma
deny * *
```

This allows FTP access using the login me from devices `beta` and `gamma`, which are defined in the `/etc/hosts` file. Access is denied to the FTP services for all other users on all other systems, including itself!

This file needs to contain all the users that are allowed access. The wildcard can be used to allow or deny multiple users. To allow all users to connect via the loopback device, add the following command to the file before the final deny statement:

```
allow * 127.0.0.1
```

### /etc/ftpusers

This file is simply a list of all users that are not allowed to login via FTP. The super-user root is placed in here automatically during the installation of Linux for security reasons. If you do need to have root access via FTP, *do not remove root from this file*. It is better to create another user with supervisory rights for the task, and then a would-be hacker would have to guess both the login name and password:

```
root
bin
daemon
adm
lp
sync
shutdown
halt
mail
news
uucp
operator
games
nobody
```

If you do not wish to provide anonymous access, the user `ftp` can be added to this file.

### /etc/ftpaccess

This file is used to configure the operation of the FTP daemon. To illustrate, I will show you the default file set up from the installation on my home system, with most lines accompanied by a comment:

```
# Defines the class for the users
class all real,guest,anonymous *

# Specifies the e-mail address of the FTP archive
email root@localhost
```

```
# The number of login attempts allowed before the connection is closed
loginfails 5.

# Display message in the given file to user at login time.
readme  README*     login

# Display message in the given file to user on changing the working directory
readme  README*     cwd=*

# The contents of the file specified here are displayed when the user logs in.
message /welcome.msg            login

# The contents of the file specified here are displayed when user changes
# working directory.
message .message               cwd=*

# Enables or denies various utilities to the users specified
compress    yes    all
tar         yes    all
chmod       no     guest,anonymous
delete      no     guest,anonymous
overwrite   no     guest,anonymous
rename      no     guest,anonymous

# Log file transfers for users of the anonymous and real classes, both inbound
# and outbound; i.e. file transfers both to, and from the server.
log transfers anonymous,real inbound,outbound

# The file to check regularly if a shutdown is planned.
shutdown /etc/shutmsg

# Define the level and enforcement of password checking.
passwd-check rfc822 warn
```

Some of the lines in the above code are described more fully below:

❑ class all real,guest,anonymous *: the anonymous, guest and real classes all belong to the class all.

  ❑ anonymous refers to users that log in without a user ID or password.

  ❑ guest refers to users that have logged into guest accounts

  ❑ real refers to users that have accounts set up on the system.

  The wildcard is used instead of specific IP addresses as a catch-all. Specific addresses can be assigned here and given their own class.

❑ shutdown /etc/shutmsg: new connections are not allowed a short time before shutdown and current FTP connections are terminated a specified time before shutdown.

❏  passwd-check rfc822 warn: rfc822 checking is requested and as warn is used instead of enforce the user will be shown a message when the password is invalid, but still allowed to log on. If enforce is used instead the user is shown the message and then logged out. This line has the general form:

passwd-check <none | trivial | rfc822> [enforce | warn]

Where:

❏    none – means no password checking is performed.

❏    trivial – password must contain an @.

❏    rfc822 – password must be an rfc822 compliant address.

❏    enforce – will warn the user before logging him out.

❏    warn – will warn the user but will allow him to log in.

There are many more settings that can be made in this file and these are detailed in the man pages under ftpaccess; it is worth taking time to read this document.

### Granting Access with /etc/hosts.equiv

This file should *never* be used. It allows devices equivalent super-user access rights to your server – without even needing a password! Some hosts using old communication tasks may need to be inserted into this file; but if so this should only be done on a temporary basis until the tasks can be rewritten or a work around created.

> **WARNING: It is very dangerous to give any device equivalent rights.**

## Configuring Network Cards

Usually the network card is found and configured during the Linux installation. However, some older cards do not respond well to probing, or a second network adapter may be added at a later date; in either case, the network card will have to be installed and configured manually. To do this, the ifconfig command is used. This command takes parameters in a slightly different way to most Linux commands. Parameters should not start with a minus unless that feature needs to be turned off. The command can be used on its own to get details of the current adapter settings, for example:

```
# ifconfig
lo        Link encap:Local Loopback
          inet addr:127.0.0.1  Bcast:127.255.255.255  Mask:255.0.0.0
          UP BROADCAST LOOPBACK RUNNING  MTU:3584  Metric:1
          RX packets:118 errors:0 dropped:0 overruns:0 frame:0
          TX packets:118 errors:0 dropped:0 overruns:0 carrier:0
          collisions:0

eth0      Link encap:Ethernet  HWaddr 00:00:21:52:90:05
          inet addr:123.123.123.1  Bcast:123.123.123.255  Mask:255.255.255.0
          UP BROADCAST RUNNING MULTICAST  MTU:1500  Metric:1
          RX packets:666 errors:0 dropped:0 overruns:0 frame:0
          TX packets:1162 errors:0 dropped:0 overruns:0 carrier:0
          collisions:0
          Interrupt:5 Base address:0x340
```

The first card is really a dummy, it's the loopback device. The second contains the settings used by the physical network card installed on the server.

Here are the description of the fields:

❑   Link encap – displays the type of adapter used.

❑   Hwaddr – is the MAC address of this Ethernet card. This is ascertained from the card itself and each card is manufactured with a unique address.

❑   inet addr – shows the IP address, the address given to the server by the systems administrator.

❑   Bcast – displays the broadcast address, usually the Class A, B and C parts of the IP address with 255 on the end to take in all devices on the LAN. This could be different if sub-netting or super-netting is used.

❑   Mask – specifies the sub-net mask defined for this adapter.

❑   Interrupt – specifies the hardware interrupt used by this device.

❑   Base address – specifies the memory base address used by the network card.

The line beginning with UP BROADCAST means that all broadcast and multicast packets matching the broadcast address (in this case 123.123.123.0 – 123.123.123.255) are received by this card. RX packets and TX packets displays the number of packets received and transmitted respectively, with information on how the network is performing.

This is an example of using the ifconfig command to set up a network card:

```
# ifconfig eth0 123.123.123.1 netmask 255.255.255.0 \
> broadcast 123.123.123.255 irq 5 io_addr 0x340
```

This command would be used to configure the network card to be the same as in the previous example. Although this should be sufficient for most cards, there are many more options available with the ifconfig command and you might want to look at the man pages for a more detailed description.

The ifconfig command is also used to set up virtual hosts – see Chapter 5 for more details.

### Changing Network Settings using Linuxconf

You can use Linuxconf to change some settings on your network card. To get to this screen expand Config, Networking, Client tasks and then select Basic host information. Not everything can be set here, for instance, the broadcast address is calculated from the other information and may need to be set manually for your system. If you need to configure a secondary adaptor, simply scroll down to Adaptor 2.

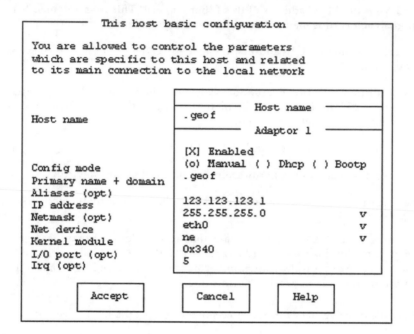

## Routing

When a number of networks are running on one site, or there are different networks over a number of sites, it may necessary to route your LAN's packets to the other networks and receive their packets on your local network. Usually a router is needed for this, but Linux also has to be configured to recognize a particular network or host. Routes can be added and viewed using the `route` command and in its most usual form appears like this:

```
route cmd type target_ip t_netmask gateway options
```

Where:

❑ cmd – usually add or del to add or delete a route.

❑ type – this is normally -net or -host depending on whether you are routing to a network or a specific host.

❑ target_ip – the IP address of the target network or host. If the keyword default is used instead of the IP address, all packets that do not have a specific address are transferred to this route.

❏ `t_netmask` – this applies only when using the `-net` option and gives the netmask of the target network. This is specified using the `netmask` keyword.

❏ `gateway` – the address of the router or the same address as the server if this server is to be used to route the packets. This is specified using the `gw` keyword.

❏ `options` – usually `dev eth#`, where `#` is the device number of the network card. It will use this device to route the packets.

In the following example, the network 124.124.124.0 is added, using this server (123.123.123.1) as the gateway and the network adaptor `eth1`:

```
# route add -net 124.124.124.0 netmask 255.255.255.0 gw 123.123.123.1 dev eth1
```

To delete to route we have just added use the command:

```
# route del 124.124.124.0
```

There is more of setting and using routes in Chapter 9.

### Changing Routing Settings using Linuxconf

Again Linuxconf provides a simple user interface for specifying routes to other networks for hosts. Expand Config, Networking, Client tasks, Routing and gateways and then select either Other routes to networks or Other routes to hosts. Next choose Add to get the data entry screen shown here. Select Accept to finish and the new route will be added.

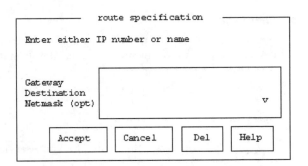

## Configuring Internet Services

Internet services daemons, such as `httpd` and `ftpd` use two configuration files: `/etc/services` and `/etc/inetd.conf` for configuration. The `/etc/services` file is used to provide a mapping between service names and their underlying service port and protocol. The file `/etc/inetd.conf` is needed to know what service process are run to deal with connections to a port.

### /etc/services

This file contains a single line for each service defined and each line has the format:

```
ServiceName Port/Protocol [AliasList]
```

where:

- ❏ ServiceName – the official service name, such as HTTP or FTP.
- ❏ Port – the port number for the required service.
- ❏ Protocol – the protocol used to deal with this service, such as TCP or UDP.
- ❏ AliasList – a white space separated list of other names to used for the service, such as httpd or ftpd.

> **Many port numbers are reserved for use and their use is controlled by the Internet Assigned Numbers Authority (IANA). This list is constantly changing and more information about reserved ports can be gained from ftp://ftp.isi.edu/in-notes/iana/assignments/port-numbers.**

The example below, taken from /etc/services, shows how the time service can be set up, giving its official name time, a TCP port of 37 and the alias timserver.

```
time     37/tcp        timserver
```

### /etc/inetd.conf

Like /etc/services, this file contains a single line for each server provided, each field in the line is separated by white space and has the format:

```
ServiceName SocketType Protocol wait|nowait User[.group] ServerProgram Args
```

where:

- ❏ ServiceName – the name of a valid service in the /etc/services file.
- ❏ SocketType – should be stream, dgram, raw, rdm or seqpacket depending on whether it is a stream, datagram, raw, reliably delivered message or sequenced packet socket.
- ❏ Protocol – a valid protocol, such as TCP or UDP.
- ❏ wait|nowait – should be nowait for all non-datagram sockets and wait if it is a single threaded datagram socket.
- ❏ User[.group] – the user (and group if specified) to run the server program under.
- ❏ ServerProgram – the complete path, and program name of the server to run.
- ❏ Args – are separated by white space and contain the normal arguments to pass to the server program.

An example entry in /etc/inetd.conf for an HTTP server such as Apache, running under the user root, would be:

```
httpd stream tcp nowait root /sbin/httpd httpd -f /etc/httpd/conf/httpd.conf
```

# Configuring and Compiling the Kernel

When Linux is first installed on a system; the distribution used usually sets up a generic kernel configured for a wide range of differing hardware. This includes SCSI adapters, CD-ROM drives and file systems. Even if this system works well there are a number of reasons you may wish to recompile the kernel:

- ❑ Initial installations are usually compiled to the weakest processor available in the architecture you installed; in the case of Intel processors this will be a 386 or a Pentium. To make use of new instructions available in later processors, and therefore operate faster, the kernel will have to be re-compiled.

- ❑ Some devices may not be recognized by the generic system (multiple SCSI adapters of the same manufacturer is a good example) and the kernel may need to be patched to identify these devices.

- ❑ Certain networking features may need to be purged for security considerations. The Network File System and the SMB protocol both have security implications, and if they are not required they are best left out of the kernel.

- ❑ A particular application that you wish to use may need a later release of the kernel than that which came with the distribution you installed.

- ❑ New functionality is constantly being added to the Linux OS – an upgrade will be necessary if you require those features.

- ❑ Reconfiguration of the kernel to only include those features and device drivers you require will produce a smaller kernel core that will compile much faster and boot faster too! Making the set up of the new system that much quicker and less frustrating.

The configuration and compilation of a Linux kernel is a three stage process:

- ❑ Upgrade the kernel. This is not required if the kernel only needs to be reconfigured.

- ❑ Prepare and configure the new kernel for compilation.

- ❑ Compile the new kernel.

## Upgrading the Kernel

There are a three ways to upgrade a kernel: using a complete new kernel source; using one or more patches from your existing version, and updating device drivers. The last two are performed using the `patch` command in pretty much the same way and will be discussed together later on. First, I would like to discuss the version numbers for Linux kernels as some knowledge of these are needed for any upgrade.

Linux kernels all follow the same version naming system:
`linux-version.release.patch.tar.gz`.

Patches to a kernel usually contain new device drivers and the odd bug fix. If you are having problems with your server the first thing to try is upgrading to the latest patch release. The chances are someone else will already have had the very same problem and the solution will already have been incorporated in the latest kernel.

# Installing a New Kernel Source

Kernel sources are constantly being posted at various Linux sites and because they are archived and compressed they take around 20-30 minutes to download – which can be considerably slower if you have a slow modem or if the network traffic is heavy. On the other hand, the distributor you use may have the version required in their latest CD-ROM disk set. If a completely new version of the kernel is required, rather than a patch on the same release, I would recommend the latter. Existing applications written for older versions of the kernel are not guaranteed to work correctly with the newer version of the Linux operating system – the latest versions of the applications can the be re-installed from the new disk set.

As an example let us assume that a kernel is being upgraded from, say, 2.2.6 to 2.2.13 and the complete source code for the new release has been downloaded as the file linux-2.2.13.tar.gz. This file contains pristine source files and should be kept in a safe place so the kernel can be re-installed if it is later patched and then it is decided to go back to the original. First move to the directory the source files are kept in, and then check if the linux subdirectory is a symbolic link to another directory:

```
# cd /usr/src
# ls -l linux
lrwxrwxrwx   1 root       root              12 Jul 19 22:54 linux -> linux-2.2.6
```

If the first character in the display of the long file listing is an l (as it is here), the directory is linked; it will be a d for a normal directory. You will next have to type either of these two commands to delete the link or move the old directory:

```
# rm -rf linux          # if it is a symbolic link to another directory.
# mv linux linux-2.2.6  # if it is a normal directory.
```

And then continue the installation with the following sequence:

```
# cp /SourceDirectoryPath/linux-2.2.13.tar.gz
# gunzip linux-2.2.13.tar.gz
# tar -xv -f linux-2.2.13.tar
# mv linux linux-2.2.13
# ln -s linux-2.2.13 linux
```

This will copy the compressed file to the correct location, uncompress and expand the archive, change the directory's name and create a symbolic link to the directory. If a copy of the original compressed file was used this file is no longer needed:

```
# rm linux-2.2.13.tar
```

# Patching an Existing Linux Kernel

It is usually much quicker and easier to download and apply patches to an existing kernel if only a minor upgrade is required.

One thing of great importance when patching a kernel is that ALL the patches between the existing version and the new release you require need to be incorporated in the correct order. If, for example, you wish to upgrade from version 2.2.11 to 2.2.13, two patches will be required and they will have to be added in the correct order for them to be applied properly. Taking the above case as an example the steps needed to apply the patches would consist of the following. First make a backup of the current linux directory in case of problems with the later release.

```
# cd /usr/src
# tar -cv -flinux-2.2.11.tar linux-2.2.11
```

After downloading the patches (from http://kernelnotes.org for example) copy and apply the patches to the current kernel, assuming that the subdirectory linux is a symbolic link to the subdirectory where the kernel source is stored, which will usually be the case. The patch utility by default takes input from standard input and so the output from gunzip is piped to patch. Option p0 specifies to leave the filenames intact.

```
# cp /SourceDirectoryPath/patch12-2.2.12.gz
# cp /SourceDirectoryPath/patch13-2.2.13.gz
# gunzip -cd patch12.gz | patch -p0
# gunzip -cd patch13.gz | patch -p0
```

Again assuming the linux directory is linked, remove the link then rename the old directory to the new version and create a new link. Finally remove any applied patches.

```
# rm -rf linux
# mv linux-2.2.11 linux-2.2.13
# ln -s linux-2.2.13 linux
# rm patch*.gz
```

Patches to device drivers are applied in the same way, although often they will come as a single patch from the first release they appeared in.

# Preparing and Configuring the Kernel

This section describes the actions necessary to prepare the kernel for compilation after a new kernel source has been installed. This involves removing traces of previous compilations and configuring what services and hardware are to be supported in the new kernel.

## *Preparing the Kernel*

When a kernel has been upgraded, as detailed above, there needs to be some preparation for successful configuration and compilation. This is a fixed process and as such I have listed below a useful script for the operation, `prepare_kernel.sh`:

```
#!/bin/sh
cd /usr/include
rm -rf asm linux scsi
ln -s /usr/src/linux/include/asm-i386 asm
ln -s /usr/src/linux/include/linux linux
ln -s /usr/src/linux/include/scsi scsi
cd /usr/src/linux
make mrproper
echo Now do a "'make config'" to configure the kernel and run the
echo "'compile_kernel.sh'" script to compile and set-up the new kernel.
```

This is a simple script that removes symbolic links to source headers and reinstates them for the new kernel sources. The command `make mrproper` is then used to remove any stale object files and dependencies.

## *Go Configure*

There are several configuration utilities for configuring the kernel, `make config`, `make menuconfig` and `make xconfig`. The first is a simple outdated line utility, whose use I do not recommend. The second is a character cell menu and windows system. The final one is for servers with the X windowing system up and running. They all do the same job but with slightly different views. For the purpose of this book I will be describing the `make menuconfig` utility, as much of what applies can be taken directly to the X system. (There is a fourth configuration: `make oldconfig` that uses the previous configuration as the basis of the new one and only prompts you to supply any new options.)

In the first diagram below the entire configuration options for kernel version 2.2.12 are displayed. All bar the last two options will open configuration windows by using the cursor keys to highlight the option, and then selecting that menu item by pressing the space bar when the `Select` button is highlighted.

The second diagram shows an example of one of these configuration screens, that of general setup. Again the required option is highlighted using the cursor keys and the desired configuration is cycled using the space bar. Much of the functionality of the kernel can be modularised. Modules are not directly compiled into the kernel but can be dynamically loaded by the system when they are required. Angled brackets show when an option can be modularised, a square bracket displays options which do not have this ability. M states that the option will be incorporated as a module, and the * means that it will be compiled directly into the kernel, and a space means that option will be excluded from the kernel. Some options when disabled will automatically disable later options, for example if the SCSI support option in diagram 2 is unselected, no other SCSI options will be available. In either diagram, press the ? key for a brief description of the option highlighted if you are unsure of what to do.

```
                              Main Menu
Arrow keys navigate the menu.  <Enter> selects submenus --->.  Highlighted letters are hotkeys.
Pressing <Y> includes, <N> excludes, <M> modularizes features.  Press <Esc><Esc> to exit, <?>
for Help.  Legend: [*] built-in  [ ] excluded  <M> module  < > module capable

    ┌────────────────────────────────────────────────────────────────────┐
    │                    Code maturity level options  --->                │
    │                    Processor type and features  --->                │
    │                    Loadable module support  --->                    │
    │                    General setup  --->                              │
    │                    Plug and Play support  --->                      │
    │                    Block devices  --->                              │
    │                    Networking options  --->                         │
    │                    SCSI support  --->                               │
    │                    Network device support  --->                     │
    │                    Amateur Radio support  --->                      │
    │                    IrDA subsystem support  --->                     │
    │                    ISDN subsystem  --->                             │
    │                    Old CD-ROM drivers (not SCSI, not IDE)  --->     │
    │                    Character devices  --->                          │
    │                    Filesystems  --->                                │
    │                    Sound  --->                                      │
    │                    Kernel hacking  --->                             │
    │                    ----                                             │
    │                    Load an Alternate Configuration File             │
    │                    Save Configuration to an Alternate File          │
    │                                                                      │
    │                                                                      │
    │                                                                      │
    │                                                                      │
    └────────────────────────────────────────────────────────────────────┘

                 <Select>      < Exit >     < Help >

                              General setup
Arrow keys navigate the menu.  <Enter> selects submenus --->.  Highlighted
letters are hotkeys.  Pressing <Y> includes, <N> excludes, <M> modularizes
features.  Press <Esc><Esc> to exit, <?> for Help.  Legend: [*] built-in  [ ]
excluded  <M> module  < > module capable

    ┌────────────────────────────────────────────────────────────────────┐
    │        [*] Networking support                                       │
    │        [*] PCI support                                              │
    │        (Any) PCI access mode                                        │
    │        [*]     PCI quirks (NEW)                                     │
    │        [ ]     PCI bridge optimization (experimental)               │
    │        [*]     Backward-compatible /proc/pci (NEW)                  │
    │        [ ] MCA support (NEW)                                        │
    │        [ ] SGI Visual Workstation support (NEW)                     │
    │        [*] System V IPC                                             │
    │        [ ] BSD Process Accounting (NEW)                             │
    │        [*] Sysctl support (NEW)                                     │
    │        <*> Kernel support for a.out binaries                        │
    │        <*> Kernel support for ELF binaries                          │
    │        <*> Kernel support for MISC binaries (NEW)                   │
    │        < > Kernel support for JAVA binaries (obsolete)              │
    │        < > Parallel port support (NEW)                              │
    │        [*] Advanced Power Management BIOS support                   │
    │        [ ]     Ignore USER SUSPEND                                  │
    │        [ ]     Enable PM at boot time                               │
    │        [ ]     Make CPU Idle calls when idle                        │
    │        [ ]     Enable console blanking using APM                    │
    │        [ ]     Power off on shutdown                                │
    │        [ ]     Ignore multiple suspend                              │
    │        [ ]     Ignore multiple suspend/resume cycles (NEW)          │
    │        v(+)                                                         │
    └────────────────────────────────────────────────────────────────────┘

                 <Select>      < Exit >     < Help >
```

A brief description of some of the main configuration options (from the first of the above diagrams) is given below, highlighting some of the decisions that will have to be made during the configuration.

- ❑ Code maturity level options – switch this off unless you want to use newly developed drivers and features. If left on, it will warn you in the menu that this portion of code is new or experimental.

- ❑ Processor type and features – allows you to set the characteristics of your processor

- ❑ Loadable module support – Linux contains many dynamically loadable modules, which is code that is not directly compiled into the kernel but can be called upon without any user interaction when needed. It is best to set all these options, as Linux becomes more modular with each issue of the kernel. There is very little overhead to be gained by not using modules.

- ❑ General setup – these options mainly relate to the motherboard. If you have a math co-processor installed (and every Intel processor from a 486DX onwards has one) then the kernel math emulation can be disabled. Another important option here is the processor. Select from the given list for the processor that most closely matches the processor used by your server to compile the kernel for that instruction set.

- ❑ Block devices – mass storage options are given here, select the relevant items and clear the others, except the chipset bug-fixes. It may not be obvious which chip-set is being used so leave these enabled.

- ❑ Networking options – in general, keep the defaults for IP unless there is a feature you require. At the end of the list are a number of supported protocols; these should be deselected if they are not to be used.

- ❑ SCSI support – if you are using SCSI devices select this option and any SCSI devices in the selection. Leave the rest as defaults. SCSI low-level drivers will open a new window allowing you to select any appropriate adaptors for your server. All the others should be deselected.

- ❑ Network device support – for the most part these can be kept as the defaults if your network is running OK. At the bottom is a list of network cards, select those that match your server and deselect the rest.

- ❑ CD-ROM drivers (not SCSI, not IDE) – if you're using a non-standard CD-ROM – no problem there should be a driver for your CD-ROM listed here. Again deselect the ones that do not match your device. If you have SCSI or IDE deselect this option altogether.

- ❑ File systems – Linux supports many file systems. Select the ones you require. Leave the Codepage and NLS ISO lists as modules, these may come in handy later if you have dealings with foreign countries.

- ❑ Character devices – keep the defaults appropriate for your system and deselect the rest.

- ❑ Load an Alternate Configuration File – prompts administrator for the configuration file to load.

- ❑ Save Configuration to an Alternate File – this will prompt you for a file name to save the configuration you have just set up. This option is most recommended once configuration is complete. This file will be needed if alternative configuration utilities are used.

When the configuration has been completed, select the Exit button and the utility will inquire if you wish to save the configuration, selecting No at this point will undo any changes made.

# Compiling the Kernel

As with the preparation section, the compilation of the kernel is a fixed process. A simple script compile_kernel.sh is given below to perform the necessary action.

```
#!/bin/sh
if [ $# -eq 1 ]
  cd /usr/src/linux
  make dep
  make clean
  make bzImage
  make modules
  rm -fR /lib/modules/old$1-3
  mv -f /lib/modules/old$1-2 /lib/modules/old$1-3
  mv -f /lib/modules/old$1-1 /lib/modules/old$1-2
  mv -f /lib/modules/$1 /lib/modules/old$1-1
  make modules_install
  mv -f /boot/oldvmlinuz2 /boot/oldvmlinuz3
  mv -f /boot/oldvmlinuz1 /boot/oldvmlinuz2
  mv -f /boot/vmlinuz-$1-0.7 /boot/oldvmlinuz1
  cp /usr/src/linux/arch/i386/boot/bzImage /boot/vmlinuz-$1-0.7
  sleep 10
  /sbin/lilo
  echo If the compilation was successful, reboot the server when disk
  echo activity stops. This process copies old versions of the kernel to
  echo the files:
  echo /boot/oldvmlinuz1
  echo /boot/oldvmlinuz2
  echo /boot/oldvmlinuz3
  echo In the case of incorrect configuration please run the script
  echo "'restore_kernel.sh'" to copy old versions back into place.
  echo Ensure "'/etc/lilo.conf'" contains the line
  echo image=/boot/vmlinuz-$1-0.7
  more /etc/lilo.conf
else
  echo Kernel version number in the form version.release.patch must be supplied.
fi
```

This script takes one argument ($1), the version number of the kernel, allowing the same script to be used for different kernels. The file name highlighted in bold is the file name (after parameter expansion) of the kernel used for my system, this will almost certainly be different on other systems. The name needed can be found from the /etc/lilo.conf file and the line to look for is described at the end of the script.

If a parameter is given it is assumed to be a valid kernel version number. If you want to add validation, check that the directory /lib/modules/$1 actually exists. When a parameter is given, it first places itself in the correct directory. A make dep followed by a make clean are then performed to set up all the dependencies needed for the compilation and remove any trace of previous configurations.

The compilation of the kernel itself is performed by the make zImage command. Finally the modules are compiled and placed in the correct position using the make modules and make modules_install commands. Notice that backup copies of old modules and kernels are kept just in case a restoration of a previous kernel is needed later. Only three previous copies along with the current version are kept so if you expect to be regularly reconfiguring the kernel, suitable changes can to be made to the script to ensure more copies.

Finally the Linux Loader is reconfigured for the new kernel, only do this if LILO is being used to boot the server. This is necessary and, if omitted, will probably cause the server to hang on boot-up. If this occurs, reconfigure LILO *only* from the disk sets that came with your distribution – there is no need for a full restore or re-installation.

Keep an eye out for any errors that occur during the compilation, this is more likely to be a problem with the script itself rather than the configuration of the kernel. If there is, check the file and directory names used in the script and ensure they match those on the system being used. Now reboot the server and check there are no errors on boot up. In the rare circumstances of an error ocurring, this could well be a configuration problem. Take a note where the error occurred and what it pertained to, and check the configuration at these points.

An alternative to using the above script would be to type: make dep | make bzImage | make install, which will just compile the kernel without making the additional housekeeping that the above script does.

# Restoring a Kernel

This is simply a matter of reversing the copies made of the kernel and modules during the compilation process. The script below will perform this adequately, and like the compile script, requires the kernel version number as a parameter. The script is called restore_kernel.sh:

```
#!/bin/sh
if [ $# -eq 1 ]
then
  rm -f /boot/vmlinuz-$1-0.7
  mv /boot/oldvmlinuz1 /boot/vmlinuz-$1-0.7
  mv /boot/oldvmlinuz2 /boot/oldvmlinuz1
  mv /boot/oldvmlinuz3 /boot/oldvmlinuz2
  rm -fR /lib/modules/$1
  mv /lib/modules/old$1-1 /lib/modules/$1
  mv /lib/modules/old$1-2 /lib/modules/old$1-1
  mv /lib/modules/old$1-3 /lib/modules/old$1-2
  sleep 10
  /sbin/lilo
  echo Restoration of kernel finished, please wait till disk activity has
  echo completed and reboot the server to restore previous kernel.
else
  echo Kernel version number in the form version.release.patch must be supplied.
fi
```

Again LILO is reconfigured with the command /sbin/lilo before the reboot.

# Updating Applications using RPM and FTP

This section describes how to use the Red Hat Package Manager (RPM) to update applications and utilities and includes a tutorial on creating your own application installation files. The source directories needed for this section have been archived and compressed and can be downloaded from the Wrox web site. The file should be copied to the root directory and uncompressed using the standard command:

```
# tar -xvfz conv_tar.gz
```

# Using Red Hat Package Manager (RPM)

Development of software is one thing; installing that software on another server is another. Fortunately Red Hat have developed a utility which can perform this automatically. The Red Hat Package Manager is freely available and is not tailored to the Red Hat distributions alone. If you are not currently using Red Hat Linux, RPM can be downloaded from ftp.redhat.com.

So why should we use RPM? If software is simply archived to a file and transferred to another system, then, more often than not, it will not be until after the installation has been completed that a vital part of the package will be found to be missing. RPM deals with this possibility by forcing a rebuild of the application while making the installation file, thus ensuring all the sources are present and in the correct place for recompilation. RPM also builds a database of software installed using the utility. This allows for extra features such as the uninstalling, upgrading, querying and verification of packages. Some examples of this will be shown at the end of this section, but first a .rpm file is needed to perform these tasks, and good examples of creating these are largely undocumented. In the following section I will concentrate on building a .rpm file that can then be used for the demonstrations of RPM's other features.

## Creating an Installation File

In the following tutorial I have created a command line utility, convertbase, which will convert numbers between different number bases. Although this could have been written as one C program, I have created a library and header file, as this is what is more likely to occur in a larger development project. The diagram below shows the directory tree of the application and the files each directory contains. This structure is similar to that used in the development of many applications and is therefore far more complex than need be.

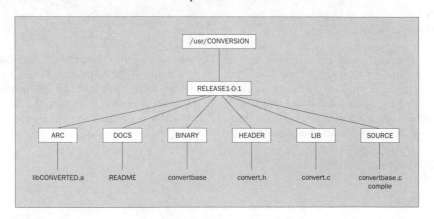

- ❑ ARC – the archive of all the library object files is held here.
- ❑ DOCS – finally any documentation to do with the package is stored in this directory.
- ❑ BINARY – is where all the package's executables, created by the compilation process, are stored.
- ❑ HEADER – Holds all of the header files needed by the C sources for compilation.
- ❑ LIB – Contains the library source used by the package.
- ❑ SOURCE – This directory contains the source of the application and any utilities used by the package. Also I have created a script (called compile) that will perform all the necessary compilation steps for the convertbase utility. This would normally be a makefile but for such a simple example that was unnecessary.

## Building the .rpm Installation File

When the package has been compiled, tested, and is ready to be installed on another system, the first thing that is required is to archive all the code and associated documentation into a single file. The commands that follow are where you begin after the sources have been uncompressed.

```
# cd /usr/CONVERSION
# tar cv RELEASE1-0-1 -f /usr/src/convertbase1-0-1.tar
```

This archive will later be incorporated in the .rpm installation program.

RPM needs files placed in a specific directory tree to perform the building of a package from pristine sources and for this a directory called CONVERSION was created under /usr/src. The location of this tree is found from the /etc/rpmrc configuration file, which contains developer specific configuration and must be present to build an application with RPM. Only a simple configuration is needed here and below is a listing of the /etc/rpmrc file:

```
require_vendor: 1
require_distribution: 1
vendor: jeeniSoft
distribution: UsefulUtils
packager: jeeniSoft Utilities

topdir: /usr/src/CONVERSION
tmppath: /usr/tmp
```

None of the first section of the file is really needed. Although any information placed here will be recorded with the installation file and can be displayed using RPM after installation of the package. Often web addresses are placed here so anyone interested in the product can get further information. The required fields are the two directory specifications; these are the directories that will be used during the build process. For more information regarding the environment of RPM all the fields can be viewed with the command:

```
# rpm --showrc
```

The necessary directory tree is then created under the CONVERSION directory and is outlined in the diagram below.

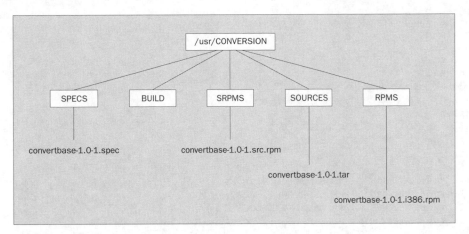

- ❑  SPECS – This is where the specification file that is used to control the build process is placed. This file is what will be created next in this section.
- ❑  BUILD – The directory the package is build in.
- ❑  SRPMS – After the build processes, the source .rpm is placed in this directory.
- ❑  SOURCES – The application source files that were archived earlier using tar, are now moved to this directory for the build process.
- ❑  RPMS/i386 – The .rpm file that is used for installation on other servers is created below this directory by the build process.

> **Note: RPM expects all these directories to exist — the build process cannot be performed without them.**

## The Specification File

RPM needs to know all the steps necessary to unpack the application tree and then compile the package prior to installation. To get this information it reads the spec file in the Specs directory and follows each step outlined in that file. The spec file used is listed below. It is called /usr/src/CONVERSION/SPECS/convertbase-1.0-1.spec.

```
Summary: Converts numbers between various specified bases.
Name: convertbase
Version: 1.0
Release: 1
Copyright: Sherlock Software
Group: Utilities/Text
Source: .geof:/usr/src/convertbase1-0-1.tar
%description
```

```
This utility provides a means of converting a number stored in one number
base; to another given number base.
%prep
%setup -n /usr/src/CONVERSION/BUILD/RELEASE1-0-1
%build
cd SOURCE
./compile
%install
mkdir /usr/CONVERSION
mv /usr/src/CONVERSION/BUILD/RELEASE1-0-1 /usr/
%files
%dir /usr/CONVERSION/RELEASE1-0-1
%dir /usr/CONVERSION/RELEASE1-0-1/ARC
%dir /usr/CONVERSION/RELEASE1-0-1/BINARY
%dir /usr/CONVERSION/RELEASE1-0-1/HEADER
%dir /usr/CONVERSION/RELEASE1-0-1/LIB
%dir /usr/CONVERSION/RELEASE1-0-1/SOURCE
%dir /usr/CONVERSION/RELEASE1-0-1/DOCS
%doc /usr/CONVERSION/RELEASE1-0-1/DOCS/README

/usr/CONVERSION/RELEASE1-0-1/ARC/libCONVERTLIB.a
/usr/CONVERSION/RELEASE1-0-1/BINARY/convertbase
/usr/CONVERSION/RELEASE1-0-1/HEADER/convert.h
/usr/CONVERSION/RELEASE1-0-1/LIB/convert.c
/usr/CONVERSION/RELEASE1-0-1/SOURCE/convertbase.c
/usr/CONVERSION/RELEASE1-0-1/SOURCE/compile
```

This configuration file consists of all the logical steps needed to unpack the utility sources and compile them; the package will be built in the Build directory. The file itself is split up into four sections:

**1.** The header – this contains information about the application or utility and usually includes:

❑ Summary: – a brief description of the package.

❑ Name: – the name of the package.

❑ Version: – the version of the package.

❑ Release: – which release of the package this is. The Name, Version and Release fields are combined to make the name of the .rpm files created by the build process in the following way:

Name-Version-Release.src.rpm and
Name-Version-Release.Architecture.rpm

❑ Copyright: – to whom the software belongs.

❑ Group: – high-level installation programs, such as Red Hat's glint, use this to specify where to place this particular program in its hierarchical structure. These groups are the folders shown in glint.

(The convertbase utility used will reside in Utilities->Text.)

❑    `Source:` – this is where a pristine copy of the source code is kept if the originals ever need to be recovered. This is usually a URL that the sources can be downloaded from; in this case it is my home machine. Note that the filename must match that of the filename you have on your own system. Do not download the source and change its name.

❑    `%description` – this is a macro rather than a header item, but should appear at the end of a header. This is a multiple line field that gives a comprehensive description of the package.

**2.**   Preparation – this section is used to get the sources ready to be built and usually requires the extraction of the source files. I have used the `%prep` and `%setup` macros to perform this and their actions are:

❑    Make the `Build` directory the current directory.

❑    Remove any previous sources in this directory.

❑    Extract the archived files in the `Sources` directory into the `Build` directory.

❑    Make `/usr/src/CONVERSION/Build/Release1-0-1` the current directory used in the build process by supplying option `-n` with the `%setup` macro.

**3.**   Build – this section performs all the required steps to build the application. First it makes the build directory specified with `%setup` the current directory; then it moves down to the `SOURCE` directory with the `cd` command; then executes the compile script used to create the executable files. The script used is found at:

`/usr/src/CONVERSION/BUILD/RELEASE1-0-1/SOURCE/compile`

```
cd ../LIB
# Compile all the library files as object files using the headers in ./HEADER
gcc -ansi -g -x c -c -I../HEADER *.c
# Collect all the object files together in one archive and move it to the
# ../ARC directory
ar rc ../ARC/libCONVERTLIB.a *.o
# Clear out object files as they are no longer needed.
rm --f *.o
cd ../SOURCE
# Compile all the source files linking them with the archive created
# previously, then move the executables to the ../BINARY directory.
for infile in `ls *.c`
do
        outfile=`basename $infile .c`
        gcc -ansi -x c -g -I../HEADER -L./ARC $infile -lCONVERTLIB -o$outfile
        mv $outfile ../BINARY
done
```

Notice how all the directory paths are relative to the current directory, this makes it possible to compile the package in different places on the system – so long as the directory tree structure remains intact.

**4.** Install – everything needed to install the application on the new system is placed in this section. In this case a new directory /usr/CONVERSION is created and the package built in the previous section moved to the new directory. Lastly all the files installed are listed. This is to tell RPM what files have been installed and is necessary to allow for uninstallation and querying of the package. If a directory name is given without the %dir macro, all the files within that directory and any subdirectories will be included as well as the specified directory. Notice that the document files have been specified with the %doc macro. Marking files in such a way helps to identify them in later queries on the package. All the directories, and documents, could have been listed on one line, but due to the length of the directory path they have been listed separately for legibility.

Once the specification file is written then all that needs to be done is to build the .rpm files. The following commands can be used to perform this after changing to the /usr/src/CONVERSION/SPECS directory:

```
# mv /usr/CONVERSION /usr/oldCONVERSION
# rpm -ba convertbase-1.0-1.spec
```

The build process copies files to /usr/CONVERSION and will fail if the directory already exists, so this directory is moved before building the package. This will build the package and create two new files:

❑ SRPMS/convertbase-1.0-1.src.rpm – the source RPM.

❑ RPMS/i386/convertbase-1.0-1.i386.rpm – the binary RPM. This is the one used for installation.

Once these files have been successfully created, the binary RPM can be copied to another machine for an installation check. This is necessary as the package may use configuration files on the machine that it was built on, configurations that will not be present on another system. Run-time problems such as these will only appear when the package is executed – since any configuration files will already exist on the current server, their absence will not be noticed until the package is moved.

## Installating the Package

For installation, the binary .rpm needs to be copied to the server and installed with the command:

```
# rpm -ivh convertbase-1.0-1.i386.rpm
```

As the vh options were used, RPM displays a progress bar represented by as growing line of # symbols. When this reaches the edge of the screen and the command prompt returns, the package is installed.

RPM knows when packages are already present on the server and will display the following error message if that is the case.

```
package convertbase-1.0-1 is already installed
error: convertbase-1.0-1.i386.rpm cannot be installed
```

This error can be overridden if necessary by using the --replacepkgs option.

Other errors that may occur on installation are conflicting files and unresolved dependencies. If a different package has already installed a file you wish to install, then this will cause a 'conflicting files' error. To override this, and force installation, use the --replacefiles option. RPM can be informed when a package depends on other utilities or applications by adding the relevant details to the specification file, for example:

```
Requires: python >= 1.3, perl
```

This will ensure that the system already has Python version 1.3 or higher and Perl already present before installation occurs. If they are not an unresolved dependency error will occur. This can be overridden with the --nodeps option, but it is unwise to do this as the package will not perform as it should. To get around problems such as these, simply install the necessary packages required.

## Uninstalling the Package

To remove the convertbase package from the system, simply use the command:

```
# rpm -e convertbase
```

Notice that only the utility name is needed — the name given in the specification file. This operation would fail and produce an error message if an installed package depends on the package being removed. This can be overcome by specifying the --nodeps option. The remaining package will not run correctly if this option is used, so care should be taken.

## Upgrading the Package

Upgrading a package involves removing any older versions of the package then installing the new one. This can be performed using a single command:

```
# rpm -Uvh convertbase-1.0-2.i386.rpm
```

The -U option can always be used for installation, as a previous version does not need to exist for installation to be successful.

As RPM uses its database when upgrading a package, it knows when configuration files may not be compatible. It will not overwrite these files first without making a backup copy and you will be informed of any saved files and their filenames, as upgrading commences. It is possible to replace a more recent version of a package with an older version using the --oldpackage option with the command. This may be a necessity if any serious bugs where found in the more recent version.

## Querying the Package

One of the advantages of keeping a database of all installed packages is that this database can then be used to present information about those packages. A simple query can be made using:

```
# rpm -q convertbase
```

This will just display the package name:

```
convertbase-1.0-1
```

Other more useful options, which can be added to the query are:

- ❏ -a – displays all currently installed packages.
- ❏ -f <file> – displays the package owning the given file.
- ❏ -p <name> – gives the same output as –q alone, but uses the full .rpm filename instead.
- ❏ -I – shows package information such as name, description, release etc.
- ❏ -l – lists the files that package owns.
- ❏ -s – displays the files a package owns that are marked as documents.
- ❏ -c – lists files marked as configuration files.
- ❏ -v – used in conjunction with options that display file lists, will present ls –l style info.

For example, the following command will display the following information about the convertbase utility:

```
# rpm -qil convertbase


Name        : convertbase          Distribution: UsefulUtils
Version     : 1.0                        Vendor: jeeniSoft
Release     : 1                      Build Date: Fri Aug 27 12:35:30 1999
Install date: Fri Aug 27 15:07:37 1999  Build Host: .geof
Group       : Utilities/Text        Source RPM: convertbase-1.0-1.src.rpm
Size        : 27851                    License: Sherlock Software
Packager    : jeeniSoft Utilities
Summary     : Converts numbers between various specified bases.
Description :
This utility provides a means of converting a number stored in one number
base; to another given number base.
/usr/CONVERSION/RELEASE1-0-1
/usr/CONVERSION/RELEASE1-0-1/ARC
/usr/CONVERSION/RELEASE1-0-1/ARC/libCONVERTLIB.A
/usr/CONVERSION/RELEASE1-0-1/BINARY
/usr/CONVERSION/RELEASE1-0-1/BINARY/convertbase
/usr/CONVERSION/RELEASE1-0-1/DOCS
/usr/CONVERSION/RELEASE1-0-1/DOCS/README
/usr/CONVERSION/RELEASE1-0-1/HEADER
/usr/CONVERSION/RELEASE1-0-1/HEADER/convert.h
/usr/CONVERSION/RELEASE1-0-1/LIB
/usr/CONVERSION/RELEASE1-0-1/LIB/convert.c
/usr/CONVERSION/RELEASE1-0-1/SOURCE
/usr/CONVERSION/RELEASE1-0-1/SOURCE/compile
/usr/CONVERSION/RELEASE1-0-1/SOURCE/convertbase.c
```

## *Verifying the Package*

This is another very useful feature of RPM. Perhaps a configuration file has been modified or a file accidentally removed since the installation of the package. This facility will track down any subsequent problems quickly; it compares the current installation with the original binary .rpm so that any differences can be noted. Among the attributes it checks are the size, the MD5 checksum, permissions, type, owner and group of the files and directories installed. If there are no discrepancies then nothing will be displayed. The command used for verification of a package is:

```
# rpm -V convertbase
```

Let's suppose the output is this:

```
S.5....T   /usr/CONVERSION/RELEASE1-0-1/SOURCE/convertbase.c
```

This means that the file convertbase.c has been modified in some way since the installation of the convertbase package. There are eight attributes stored with each file in the rpm database and any changes to these are displayed in the first eight characters of the output. These attributes are:

- ❏   5 – MD5 checksum.
- ❏   S – file size.
- ❏   L – symbolic link.
- ❏   T – file modification time.
- ❏   D – device.
- ❏   U – user.
- ❏   G – group.
- ❏   M – mode.

From the example above it can be seen that the file size no longer matches the original, the MD5 checksum no longer tallies, and the file modification time has changed. Many changes will not be problematic, especially if it is only a configuration file that has been updated. If it is decided that inconsistencies with the package have been introduced since installation, the package can be re-installed using the --replacepkgs option.

# Other Useful Specifications for RPM

In the previous section the specification file needed was only very simple. There are many other useful macros and fields that can be specified, some of which will be described here.

## Many Sources

If a number of different sources are collated together for the package, instead of just using the `Source:` field a number of fields can be specified:

```
Source0: firstsource.tar.gz
Source1: secondsource.tar.gz
Source2: thirdsource.tar.gz
...
```

These files would all reside in the SOURCES directory.

## Patch Files

If the sources need to be patched before the build process, all patches are placed in the SOURCES directory and identified in the header of the specification file with:

```
Patch0: firstpatch.patch
Patch1: secondpatch.patch
...
```

These patches can then be applied after preparation and setup of the sources with the macro:

```
%patch0 -p1
%patch1 -p1
...
```

## Icons

The package can be given an icon to represent it in graphical, high-level installation tools such as glint. The icon must be a GIF image and reside in the SOURCES directory.

```
Icon: IconFilename
```

## BuildRoot Directory

Sometimes it is required to use a different root directory than the BUILD directory for testing purposes prior to installation. This can be specified using:

```
BuildRoot: DirectoryName
```

This directory must exist prior to use; otherwise an error will occur when the attempt to unpack the sources to the build directory happens.

## Other Sources of Information on RPM

❑ *Maximum RPM:* by Ed Bailey. Is available for download or purchase at www.redhat.com.

❑ RPM documentation project at www.rpm.org.

❑ Man pages on Linux.

# Using FTP to Automate Application Updates

The previous section discussed a means of creating applications, or application updates, using RPM. In this section the FTP will be used to transfer these updates from one host to another to ensure the most current application is used across various hosts. An example of why this could be done would be a project currently undergoing the final stages of development on one host, while undergoing daily testing on another host. This allows the developers to continue their work on the first host without having to be concerned about interrupting the testers on the second host.

## Transferring the Files

In the script below, which will run on the host running the tests, .rpm files are transferred from the development host and bug reports are transferred back to the development host; then any application .rpm files are updated automatically. A thorough description of the script follows the listing. The file is called test_rpm.scr:

```
#!/bin/sh
# First get the updated application
ftp -n -i -g HostNameOrIPAddress <<FromHere
user Username Password
binary               # Transfers all files as binary files
cd /RemoteDirectoryPath
lcd /LocalDirectoryPath
glob                 # Switches globbing on to allow copying of multiple files
mget *.rpm
cd /RemoteDirectoryPath
lcd /LocalDirectoryPath
mput *.bugs
bye
FromHere
# Upgrade applications
rpm -ivh --replacepkgs *.rpm
```

This simple script performs a number of actions:

- ❑ Starts FTP. Note that it is necessary to turn off interactive prompting when copying multiple files with the -i option. FTP usually takes its input from the command line. The <<FromHere delimiter informs the Linux to redirect standard input to all the following lines in the script until the next FromHere is encountered.
- ❑ Logs in as the appropriate user with security rights to the necessary directories and files.
- ❑ Change to the necessary directories, both on the remote and local systems. Alternatively the full path names could be given in the mget and mput statements for the remote system.
- ❑ Switches globbing on, which allows multiple files to be copied using wildcards.
- ❑ First gets the updated .rpm files, storing them in a suitable place, then transfers the application's bug report files.
- ❑ Then, after changing directories again, sends the bug reports over to the development server.
- ❑ Exits FTP using the bye command.
- ❑ Reinstalls the updated application using RPM, overwriting any existing package.

This script can then be added to the cron table to allow automatic execution at a specified time, for more details of cron see the section 'Automating the Backup Process with cron' earlier in this Appendix.

> **Warning — For security reasons this script should be owned by and placed in a directory belonging to root, with read, write and execute permissions for that user only. This is because the script contains a username and password that other users should not be allowed to see.**

# Other Information

## Configuration Options Available with Linuxconf

```
+       Config
+                   Networking
+                           Client tasks
                                    Basic hoist information
                                    Name server specification (DNS)
+                                   Routing and gateways
                                            Defaults
                                            Other routes to networks
                                            Other routes to hosts
                                            Routes to alternate local nets
                                            The routed daemon
                                    Host name search path
                                    Network Information System (NIS)
                                    IPX interface setup
                                    PPP/SLIP/PLIP
+                           Server tasks
                                    Exported file systems (NFS)
                                    IP aliases for virtual hosts
+                                   UUCP (UNIX to UNIX copy)
                                            systems
                                            devices and modems
                                            scheduled tasks
+                           Misc
                                    Information about other hosts
                                    Information about other users
                                    Linuxconf network access
+                   Users accounts
+                           Normal
                                    User accounts
                                    Group definitions
                                    Change root password
```

+                    Special accounts
                          PPP accounts
                          SLIP accounts via normal login
                          UUCP accounts
                          POP accounts (mail only)
+               Policies
                          Password & account policies
                          Available user shells
                          Available PPP shells
                          Available SLIP shells
+          File systems
                    Access local drive
                    Access nfs volume
                    Configure swap files and partitions
                    Set quota defaults
                    Check some file permissions
+          Boot mode
+               Lilo
                          LILO defaults (Linux boot loader)
                          LILO Linux definitions
                          LILO other OS configurations
                          Default boot configuration
                          A new kernel
                          A kernel you have compiled
+               Mode
                          default boot mode
+     Control
+          Control panel
                    Activate configuration
                    Shutdown/Reboot
                    Control service activity
                    Configure superuser scheduled tasks
                    Archive configurations
                    Switch system profile
                    Control PPP/SLIP/PLIP links
+          Control files and systems
                    Configure all configuration files
                    Configure all commands and daemons
                    Configure file permissions and ownership
                    Configure Linuxconf modules
                    Configure system profiles
                    Override Linuxconf addons
                    Create Linuxconf addons
+          Logs
                    Boot messages
                    Linuxconf logs
          Date & time
          Features

# Printer Capabilities

| Name | Type | Default value | Description |
|------|------|---------------|-------------|
| af | str | NULL | name of accounting file |
| br | num | none | if lp is a tty, set the baud rate (ioctl(2) call) |
| cf | str | NULL | cifplot data filter |
| df | str | NULL | tex data filter (DVI format) |
| fc | num | 0 | if lp is a tty, clear flag bits (sgtty.h) |
| ff | str | `\f' | string to send for a form feed |
| fo | bool | false | print a form feed when device is opened |
| fs | num | 0 | like fc but set bits |
| gf | str | NULL | graph data filter (plot(3)) format |
| hl | bool | false | print the burst header page last |
| ic | bool | false | driver supports (non standard) ioctl to indent printout |
| if | str | NULL | name of text filter which does accounting |
| lf | str | /dev/console | error logging file name |
| lo | str | lock | name of lock file |
| lp | str | /dev/lp | device name to open for output |
| mx | num | 1000 | maximum file size (in BUFSIZ blocks), zero=unlimited |
| nd | str | NULL | next directory for list of queues (unimplemented) |
| nf | str | NULL | ditroff data filter (device independent troff) |
| of | str | NULL | name of output filtering program |
| pc | num | 200 | price per foot or page in hundredths of cents |
| pl | num | 66 | page length (in lines) |
| pw | num | 132 | page width (in characters) |
| px | num | 0 | page width (in pixels horizontal) |
| py | num | 0 | page length (in pixels vertical) |
| rf | str | NULL | filter for printing FORTRAN style text files |

| Name | Type | Default value | Description |
|------|------|---------------|-------------|
| rg | str | NULL | restricted group. Only members of group allowed access |
| rm | str | NULL | machine name for remote printer |
| rp | str | ''lp'' | remote printer name argument |
| rs | bool | false | restrict remote users to those with local accounts |
| rw | bool | false | open the printer device for reading and writing |
| sb | bool | false | short banner (one line only) |
| sc | bool | false | suppress multiple copies |
| sd | str | /var/spool/lpd | spool directory |
| sf | bool | false | suppress form feeds |
| sh | bool | false | suppress printing of burst page header |
| st | str | status | status file name |
| tf | str | NULL | troff data filter (cat phototypesetter) |
| tr | str | NULL | trailer string to print when queue empties |
| vf | str | NULL | raster image filter |

# D

# Support and Errata

One of the most irritating things about any computing book is when you find that bit of code you've just spent an hour typing simply doesn't work. You check it a hundred times to see if you've set it up correctly and then you notice the spelling mistake in the variable name on the book page. Of course, you can blame the authors for not taking enough care and testing the code, the editors for not doing their job properly, or the proofreaders for not being eagle-eyed enough, but this doesn't get around the fact that mistakes do happen.

We try hard to ensure no mistakes sneak out into the real world, but we can't promise that this book is 100% error free. What we can do is offer the next best thing by providing you with immediate support and feedback from experts who have worked on the book and try to ensure that future editions eliminate these gremlins. The following section will take you step by step through the process of posting errata to our web site to get that help. The sections that follow, therefore, are:

❑   Wrox Developers Membership

❑   Finding a list of existing errata on the web site

There is also a section covering how to e-mail a question for technical support. This comprises:

❑   What your e-mail should include

❑   What happens to your e-mail once it has been received by us

So that you only need view information relevant to yourself, we ask that you register as a Wrox Developer Member. This is a quick and easy process, that will save you time in the long run. If you are already a member, just update membership to include this book.

# Wrox Developer's Membership

To get your FREE Wrox Developer's Membership click on Membership in the navigation bar of our home site – `http://www.wrox.com`. This is shown in the following screenshot:

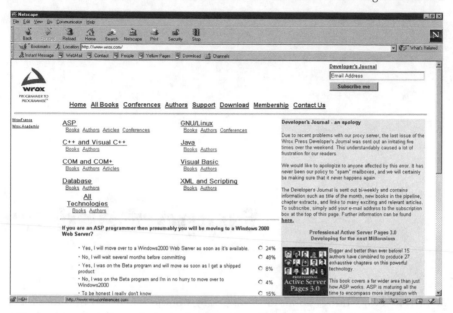

Then, on the next screen (not shown), click on New User. This will display a form. Fill in the details on the form and submit the details using the Register button at the bottom. Go back to the main Membership page, enter your details and select Logon. Before you can say 'The best read books come in Wrox Red' you will get the following screen:

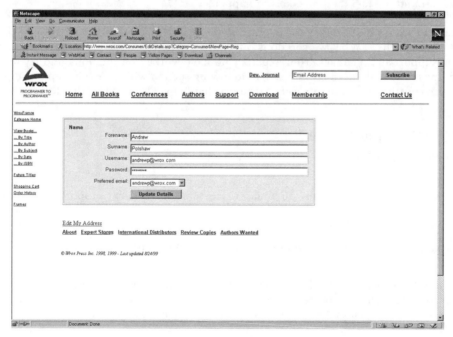

# Finding an Errata on the Web Site

Before you send in a query, you might be able to save time by finding the answer to your problem on our web site – `http:\\www.wrox.com`.

Each book we publish has its own page and its own errata sheet. You can get to any book's page by clicking on Support from the top navigation bar.

From this page you can locate any book's errata page on our site. Select your book from the pop-up menu and click on it.

Then click on Errata. This will take you to the errata page for the book. Select the criteria by which you want to view the errata, and click the Apply criteria... button. This will provide you with links to specific errata. For an initial search, you are advised to view the errata by page numbers. If you have looked for an error previously, then you may wish to limit your search using dates. We update these pages daily to ensure that you have the latest information on bugs and errors.

# E-mail Support

If you wish to directly query a problem in the book with an expert who knows the book in detail then e-mail support@wrox.com, with the title of the book and the last four numbers of the ISBN in the subject field of the e-mail. A typical email should include the following things:

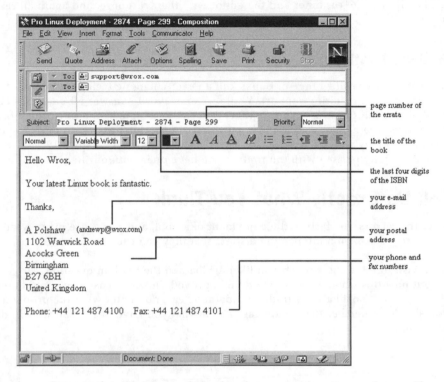

We won't send you junk mail. We need the details to save your time and ours. If we need to replace a disk or CD we'll be able to get it to you straight away. When you send an e-mail it will go through the following chain of support:

# Customer Support

Your message is delivered to one of our customer support staff who are the first people to read it. They have files on most frequently asked questions and will answer anything general immediately. They answer general questions about the book and the web site.

# Editorial

Deeper queries are forwarded to the technical editor responsible for that book. They have experience with the programming language or particular product and are able to answer detailed technical questions on the subject. Once an issue has been resolved, the editor can post the errata to the web site.

## The Authors

Finally, in the unlikely event that the editor can't answer your problem, s/he will forward the request to the author. We try to protect the author from any distractions from writing. However, we are quite happy to forward specific requests to them. All Wrox authors help with the support on their books. They'll mail the customer and the editor with their response, and again all readers should benefit.

## What We Can't Answer

Obviously with an ever-growing range of books and an ever-changing technology base, there is an increasing volume of data requiring support. While we endeavor to answer all questions about the book, we can't answer bugs in your own programs that you've adapted from our code. So, while you might have loved the help desk systems in our Linux book, don't expect too much sympathy if you cripple your company with a live adaptation you customized from Chapter 12. However, do tell us if you're especially pleased with the routine you developed with our help.

## How to Tell Us Exactly What You Think

We understand that errors can destroy the enjoyment of a book and can cause many wasted and frustrated hours, so we seek to minimize the distress that they can cause.

You might just wish to tell us how much you liked or loathed the book in question. Or you might have ideas about how this whole process could be improved, in which case you should e-mail feedback@wrox.com. You'll always find a sympathetic ear, no matter what the problem is. Above all you should remember that we do care about what you have to say and we will do our utmost to act upon it.

# Index

**wrox**

PROGRAMMER TO PROGRAMMER™

Wrox writes books for you. Any suggestions, or ideas about how you want information given in your ideal book will be studied by our team. Your comments are always valued at Wrox.

Free phone in USA 800-USE-WROX
Fax (312) 893 8001

UK Tel. (0121) 687 4100          Fax (0121) 687 4101

## Professional Linux Deployment - Registration Card

Name _____

Address _____

_____

_____

City_____ State/Region _____

Country_____ Postcode/Zip _____

E-mail _____

Occupation _____

How did you hear about this book? _____

☐ Book review (name) _____

☐ Advertisement (name) _____

☐ Recommendation _____

☐ Catalog _____

☐ Other _____

Where did you buy this book? _____

☐ Bookstore (name)_____ City _____

☐ Computer Store (name)_____

☐ Mail Order _____

☐ Other _____

What influenced you in the purchase of this book?

☐ Cover Design

☐ Contents

☐ Other (please specify) _____

How did you rate the overall contents of this book?

☐ Excellent        ☐ Good

☐ Average         ☐ Poor

_____

What did you find most useful about this book? _____

_____

What did you find least useful about this book? _____

_____

Please add any additional comments. _____

_____

What other subjects will you buy a computer book on soon? _____

_____

What is the best computer book you have used this year?

_____

*Note: This information will only be used to keep you updated about new Wrox Press titles and will not be used for any other purpose or passed to any other third party.*

2874                    *Check here if you DO NOT want to receive support for this book*  ☐   2874

**wrox**
PROGRAMMER TO PROGRAMMER™

**NB.** If you post the bounce back card below in the UK, please send it to:

Wrox Press Ltd., Arden House, 1102 Warwick Road,
Acocks Green, Birmingham B27 6BH. UK.

———— *Computer Book Publishers* ————

NO POSTAGE
NECESSARY
IF MAILED
IN THE
UNITED STATES

# BUSINESS REPLY MAIL
FIRST CLASS MAIL     PERMIT#64     CHICAGO, IL

POSTAGE WILL BE PAID BY ADDRESSEE

**WROX PRESS INC.,
29 S. LA SALLE ST.,
SUITE 520
CHICAGO IL 60603-USA**